# SOCIOLOGY 87/88

**Editor**

**Kurt Finsterbusch**

**University of Maryland, College Park**

Kurt Finsterbusch received his bachelor's degree in history from Princeton University in 1957, and his bachelor of divinity degree from Grace Theological Seminary in 1960. His Ph.D. in Sociology, from Columbia University, was conferred in 1969. He is the author of several books, including *Understanding Social Impacts* (Sage Publications, 1980), and *Social Research for Policy Decisions* (Wadsworth Publishing, 1980, with Annabelle Bender Motz). He is currently teaching at the University of Maryland, College Park, and in addition to serving as editor for *Annual Editions: Sociology,* is also co-editor for The Dushkin Publishing Group's *Taking Sides: Clashing Views on Controversial Social Issues.*

**Annual Editions**

*A Library of Information from the Public Press*

Cover illustration by Mike Eagle

**The Dushkin Publishing Group, Inc.**
**Sluice Dock, Guilford, Connecticut 06437**

# The Annual Editions Series

Annual Editions is a series of over forty volumes designed to provide the reader with convenient, low-cost access to a wide range of current, carefully selected articles from some of the most important magazines, newspapers, and journals published today. Annual Editions are updated on an annual basis through a continuous monitoring of over 200 periodical sources. All Annual Editions have a number of features designed to make them particularly useful, including topic guides, annotated tables of contents, unit overviews, and indexes. For the teacher using Annual Editions in the classroom, an Instructor's Resource Guide with test questions is available for each volume.

## PUBLISHED

Africa
Aging
American Government
American History, Pre-Civil War
American History, Post-Civil War
Anthropology
Biology
Business/Management
China
Comparative Politics
Computers in Education
Computers in Business
Computers in Society
Criminal Justice
Drugs, Society and Behavior
Early Childhood Education
Economics
Educating Exceptional Children
Education
Educational Psychology
Environment
Geography

Global Issues
Health
Human Development
Human Sexuality
Latin America
Macroeconomics
Marketing
Marriage and Family
Middle East and the Islamic World
Nutrition
Personal Growth and Behavior
Psychology
Social Problems
Sociology
Soviet Union and Eastern Europe
State and Local Government
Urban Society
Western Civilization, Pre-Reformation
Western Civilization, Post-Reformation
World Politics

## FUTURE VOLUMES

Abnormal Psychology
Death and Dying
Congress
Energy
Ethnic Studies
Foreign Policy
Judiciary
Law and Society
Parenting
Philosophy

Political Science
Presidency
Religion
South Asia
Third World
Twentieth-Century American History
Western Europe
Women's Studies
World History

Library of Congress Cataloging in Publication Data
Main entry under title: Annual editions: Sociology.
    1. Sociology—Periodicals.    2. United States—Social conditions—1960—Periodicals.
Title: Sociology.
HM1.A76        301'.05        72-76876
ISBN 0-87967-671-x

Sixteenth Edition

Manufactured by The Banta Company, Menasha, Wisconsin 54952

# Editors/ Advisory Board

# To The Reader

In publishing ANNUAL EDITIONS we recognize the enormous role played by the magazines, newspapers, and journals of the *public press* in providing current, first-rate educational information in a broad spectrum of interest areas. Within the articles, the best scientists, practitioners, researchers, and commentators draw issues into new perspective as accepted theories and viewpoints are called into account by new events, recent discoveries change old facts, and fresh debate breaks out over important controversies.

Many of the articles resulting from this enormous editorial effort are appropriate for students, researchers, and professionals seeking accurate, current material to help bridge the gap between principles and theories and the real world. These articles, however, become more useful for study when those of lasting value are carefully *collected, organized, indexed,* and *reproduced* in a *low-cost format,* which provides easy and permanent access when the material is needed. That is the role played by *Annual Editions.* Under the direction of each volume's *Editor,* who is an expert in the subject area, and with the guidance of an *Advisory Board,* we seek each year to provide in each ANNUAL EDITION a current, well-balanced, carefully selected collection of the best of the public press for your study and enjoyment. We think you'll find this volume useful, and we hope you'll take a moment to let us know what you think.

The 1980s have brought crises, changes, and challenges. Crime is running rampant. The public is demanding more police, more jails, and tougher sentences, but less government spending. The economy has experienced a major recession and the recovery has not eliminated high unemployment, trade deficits, budget deficits, and economic uncertainties. Government economic policies seem to create almost as many problems as they solve. Laborers, women, blacks, and many other groups complain of injustices and victimization. The use of toxic chemicals has been blamed for increases in cancer, sterility, and other diseases. Marriage and the family have been transformed, in part, by the women's movement, but new problems are surfacing. Schools, television, and corporations are commonly vilified. Add to this the problems of population and the threat of nuclear war and it is easy to despair.

The present generation may be the one to determine the course of history for the next two hundred years. Great changes are taking place and new solutions are being sought where old answers no longer work. The issues the current generation faces are complex and must be interpreted with a sophisticated framework. The sociological perspective provides such a framework. The articles that follow should help you develop the sociological perspective to determine how the issues of the day relate to the way society is structured. They will provide not only information, but also models of interpretation and analysis which will guide you as you form your own views.

*Annual Editions: Sociology 87/88* emphasizes social change, institutional crises, and prospects for the future. It provides an intellectual preparation for acting for the betterment of humanity in times of crucial changes. The sociological perspective is needed more than ever as humankind tries to find a way to peace and prosperity. The obstacles that lie in the path of these important goals seem to increase yearly. The goals of this edition are to communicate the excitement and importance of the study of the social world and provoke interest and enthusiasm among students for the study of sociology.

*Annual Editions* depends upon reader response to develop and change. You are encouraged to return the article rating form with your opinions about existing articles, selection of articles you think have sociological merit for subsequent issues, and advice on how the anthology can be made more useful as a teaching and learning tool.

Kurt Finsterbusch

*Editor*

# Contents

## Unit 1

## The Discipline

Two articles present several classic perspectives on the discipline of sociology and its impact on society.

## Unit 2

## Culture

Six selections consider the effect of American values, social conditions, and social mores on the individual in our human culture.

## Unit 3

## Socialization

Five articles examine the effects of social influences on childhood, personality, and human behavior with regard to the socialization of the individual.

The concepts in italics are developed in the article. For further expansion please refer to the Topic Guide, the Index, and the Glossary.

# Unit 4

## Groups and Roles in Transition

Eleven articles discuss some of the social roles and group relationships that are in transition in today's society. Topics include primary and secondary groups, reevaluating social choices, and the social impact of labeling.

The concepts in italics are developed in the article. For further expansion please refer to the Topic Guide, the Index, and the Glossary.

# Unit 5

# Social Institutions in Crisis

Eight articles examine several social institutions that are currently in crisis. Topics discussed include bureaucracies, special interest political groups, middle-class consumers, education, pro-life vs. pro-choice, and religion.

## Unit 6

# Stratification and Social Inequalities

Seven selections discuss the social stratification and inequalities that exist in today's society with regard to the rich, the poor and minorities.

---

The concepts in italics are developed in the article. For further expansion please refer to the Topic Guide, the Index, and the Glossary.

# Unit 7

# Social Change and the Future

Eight selections discuss the impact that technology, environmental degradation, and changing social values will have on society's future.

The concepts in italics are developed in the article. For further expansion please refer to the Topic Guide, the Index, and the Glossary.

# Topic Guide

This topic guide suggests how the selections in this book relate to the topics of traditional concern to sociology students and professionals. It is very useful in locating articles which relate to each other for reading and research. The guide is arranged alphabetically according to topic. Articles may, of course, treat topics that do not appear in the topic guide. In turn, entries in the topic guide do not necessarily constitute a comprehensive listing of all the contents of each selection.

| TOPIC AREA | TREATED AS AN ISSUE IN: | TOPIC AREA | TREATED AS AN ISSUE IN: |
|---|---|---|---|
| Abortion | 31. Between Pro-Life and Pro-Choice | Education | 12. Sexism in the Schoolroom of the '80s |
| Adolescence | 24. Growing Up Gay | | 30. Why Johnny Can't Think |
| Adults/Adulthood | 10. Erik Erikson's Eight Ages of Man | Family/Marriage | 9. Childhood Through the Ages |
| AIDS | 24. Growing Up Gay | | 14. The Secret of Strong Families |
| Automation | 29. Can America Compete? | | 15. The American Family in the Year 2000 |
| | 44. In Old Milwaukee | | 18. The Politics of Motherhood |
| | 45. Technology and the Changing World of Work | | 19. Working Women |
| | | | 20. Strategies of Corporate Women |
| Blacks | 36. What Does the Government Owe the Poor? | | 21. Great Expectations |
| | 37. A Nation Apart | | 22. Another Stereotype |
| | 38. For Men on the Streets | | 39. Mothers Raising Mothers |
| | 39. Mothers Raising Mothers | Future | 15. The American Family in the Year 2000 |
| Bureaucracy | 25. From Ouagadougou to Cape Canaveral | | 43. Living Dangerously |
| | | | 44. In Old Milwaukee |
| Business | 4. What Price Ethics? | | 45. Technology and the Changing World of Work |
| | 29. Can America Compete? | | 46. Apology to the Future |
| | 34. Corporate Welfare Out of Control | Generations | 7. The New Lost Generation |
| | 44. In Old Milwaukee | | 8. Brave New Wave of the '80s |
| Children/Childhood | 7. The New Lost Generation | | 14. The Secret of Strong Families |
| | 8. Brave New Wave of the '80s | | 22. Another Stereotype |
| | 9. Childhood Through the Ages | | 28. Middle-Class Squeeze |
| | 10. Erik Erikson's Eight Ages of Man | Groups | 11. Growing Up as a Fore |
| | 11. Growing Up as a Fore | | 17. Work: The Right to Right Livelihood |
| | 12. Sexism in the Schoolroom of the '80s | | 22. Another Stereotype |
| | 13. What Is TV Doing to America? | | 31. Between Pro-Life and Pro-Choice |
| | 14. The Secret of Strong Families | | 42. Promise of America |
| | 39. Mothers Raising Mothers | Handicapped | 23. Conquering a New American Frontier |
| Class | See Social Class | Homosexuality | 24. Growing Up Gay |
| Communications | 45. Technology and the Changing World of Work | Immigration | 42. Promise of America |
| | 47. Window of Opportunity | Life-Styles | 7. The New Lost Generation |
| Culture | 3. Why I Love America | | 8. Brave New Wave of the '80s |
| | 5. The Mountain People | | 19. Working Women |
| | 6. Social Time | | 21. Great Expectations |
| | 7. The New Lost Generation | | 28. Middle-Class Squeeze |
| | 8. Brave New Wave of the '80s | | 38. For Men on the Street |
| | 11. Growing Up as a Fore | | 39. Mothers Raising Mothers |
| Deinstitutionalization | 35. Abandoned Americans | | 45. Technology and the Changing World of Work |
| Demography | 40. People, People, People | | 47. Window of Opportunity |
| | 42. Promise of America | Media | 7. The New Lost Generation |
| Discrimination | 22. Another Stereotype | | 13. What Is TV Doing to America? |
| | 23. Conquering a New American Frontier | Personality | 10. Erik Erikson's Eight Ages of Man |
| | 24. Growing Up Gay | Politics | 7. The New Lost Generation |
| Ecology/Environment | 5. The Mountain People | | 25. From Ouagadougou to Cape Canaveral |
| | 11. Growing Up as a Fore | | 26. Lobbyists Go for It |
| | 16. Cities Won't Drive You Crazy | | 27. Populism and Individualism |
| | 43. Living Dangerously | | 33. Who Owns America? |
| | 46. Apology to the Future | Poor | See Poverty |
| Economy | 28. Middle-Class Squeeze | Population Growth | 40. People, People, People |
| | 29. Can America Compete? | | 42. Promise of America |
| | 33. Who Owns America? | | |
| | 45. Technology and the Changing World of Work | | |
| | 47. Window of Opportunity | | |

# The Discipline

To C. Wright Mills, the sociological imagination was the way by which ordinary people could understand what was happening to them. The need for such understanding is urgent at the present historical moment. Change has become so rapid that most people are bewildered and amazed by events of even a decade ago: the energy crisis transformed global economics; new technologies changed the workplace; and a complex, interdependent world threatened, and still threatens, to explode into frightening wars.

Most people today are associated with large, complex, and impersonal organizations, which sometimes take actions that disturb one's sense of justice. Universities herd students through large classes and seldom create truly joyful intellectual work. The medical system extorts stupendous fees from patients, making them feel like victims. The tobacco industry enthusiastically markets their highly addictive and harmful drug which endangers the health of hundreds of thousands of Americans every year. Corporations close factories in New England and open factories in Taiwan. American banks invest in the Japanese industries which are invading the American market. Is it surprising, then, that individuals often feel powerless against such indignities?

There lie ahead unprecedented opportunities to build a better world and improve the quality of life for many people. The study of sociology can help students figure out how society works and what they can do to change it by developing a sociological imagination and sociological perspective. The two articles in this section explain how the economic structures of society converge on people's lives in the context of history. C. Wright Mills says the sociological imagination enables individuals to understand how they are shaped by society which in turn is shaped by historical forces. Nevertheless the individual also ". . . contributes, however minutely, to the shaping of this society and to the course of its history. . . ." Peter L. Berger focuses more on the common occurrences of everyday life. He challenges the student to use the sociological perspective to "see" in daily events the sociological truths which most people miss.

## Looking Ahead: Challenge Questions

How can sociology contribute to one's understanding of the contemporary world?

In what ways can the sociological imagination become a significant factor in political policies?

Can sociology contribute to personal growth?

# THE SOCIOLOGICAL IMAGINATION

## The Promise

### C. WRIGHT MILLS

NOWADAYS men often feel that their private lives are a series of traps. They sense that within their everyday worlds, they cannot overcome their troubles, and in this feeling, they are often quite correct: What ordinary men are directly aware of and what they try to do are bounded by the private orbits in which they live; their visions and their powers are limited to the close-up scenes of job, family, neighborhood; in other milieux, they move vicariously and remain spectators. And the more aware they become, however vaguely, of ambitions and of threats which transcend their immediate locales, the more trapped they seem to feel.

Underlying this sense of being trapped are seemingly impersonal changes in the very structure of continent-wide societies. The facts of contemporary history are also facts about the success and the failure of individual men and women. When a society is industrialized, a peasant becomes a worker; a feudal lord is liquidated or becomes a businessman. When classes rise or fall, a man is employed or unemployed; when the rate of investment goes up or down, a man takes new heart or goes broke. When wars happen, an insurance salesman becomes a rocket launcher; a store clerk, a radar man; a wife lives alone; a child grows up without a father. Neither the life of an individual nor the history of a society can be understood without understanding both.

Yet men do not usually define the troubles they endure in terms of historical change and institutional contradiction. The well-being they enjoy, they do not usually impute to the big ups and downs of the societies in which they live. Seldom aware of the intricate connection between the patterns of their own lives and the course of world history, ordinary men do not usually know what this connection means for the kinds of men they are becoming and for the kinds of history-making in which they might take part. They do not possess the quality of mind essential to grasp the interplay of man and society, of biography and history, of self and world. They cannot cope with their personal troubles in such ways as to control the structural transformations that usually lie behind them.

Surely it is no wonder. In what period have so many men been so totally exposed at so fast a pace to such earthquakes of change? That Americans have not known such catastrophic changes as have the men and women of other societies is due to historical facts that are now quickly becoming 'merely history.' The history that now affects every man is world history. Within this scene and this period, in the course of a single generation, one sixth of mankind is transformed from all that is feudal and backward into all that is modern, advanced, and fearful. Political colonies are freed; new and less visible forms of imperialism installed. Revolutions occur; men feel the intimate grip of new kinds of authority. Totalitarian societies rise, and are smashed to bits—or succeed fabulously. After two centuries of ascendancy, capitalism is shown up as only one way to make society into an industrial apparatus. After two centuries of hope, even formal democracy is restricted to a quite small portion of mankind. Everywhere in the underdeveloped world, ancient ways of life are broken up and vague expectations become urgent demands. Everywhere in the overdeveloped world, the means of authority and of violence become total in scope and bureaucratic in form. Humanity itself now lies before us, the super-nation at either pole concentrating its most co-ordinated and massive efforts upon the preparation of World War Three.

The very shaping of history now outpaces the ability of men to orient themselves in accordance with cherished values. And which values? Even when they do not panic, men often sense that older ways of feeling and thinking have collapsed and that newer beginnings are ambiguous to the point of moral stasis. Is it any wonder that ordinary men feel they cannot cope with the larger worlds with which they are so suddenly confronted? That they cannot understand the meaning of their epoch for their own lives? That—in defense of selfhood—they become morally insensible, trying to remain altogether private men? Is it any wonder that they come to be possessed by a sense of the trap?

It is not only information that they need—in this Age of Fact, information often dominates their attention and overwhelms their capacities to assimilate it. It is not only the skills of reason that they need—although their struggles to acquire these often exhaust their limited moral energy.

What they need, and what they feel they need, is a quality of mind that will help them to use information and to develop reason in order to achieve lucid summations of what is going on in the world and of what may be happening within themselves. It is this quality, I am going to contend, that journalists and scholars, artists and publics, scientists and editors are coming to expect of what may be called the sociological imagination.

**1**

The sociological imagination enables its possessor to understand the larger historical scene in terms of its meaning for the inner life and the external career of a variety of individuals. It enables him to take into account how individuals, in the welter of their daily experience, often become falsely conscious of their social positions. Within that welter, the framework of modern society is sought, and within that framework the psychologies of a variety of men and women are formulated. By such means the personal uneasiness of individuals is focused upon explicit troubles and the indifference of publics is transformed into involvement with public issues.

The first fruit of this imagination—and the first lesson of the social science that embodies it—is the idea that the individual can understand his own experience and gauge his own fate only by locating himself within his period, that he can know his own chances in life only by becoming aware of those of all individuals in his circumstances. In many ways it is a terrible lesson; in many ways a magnificent one. We do not know the limits of man's capacities for supreme effort or willing degradation, for agony or glee, for pleasurable brutality or the sweetness of reason. But in our time we have come to know that the limits of 'human nature' are frighteningly broad. We have come to know that every individual lives, from one generation to the next, in some society; that he lives out a biography, and that he lives it out within some historical sequence. By the fact of his living he contributes, however minutely, to the shaping of this society and to the course of its history, even as he is made by society and by its historical push and shove.

The sociological imagination enables us to grasp history and biography and the relations between the two within society. That is its task and its promise. To recognize this task and this promise is the mark of the classic social analyst. It is characteristic of Herbert Spencer—turgid, polysyllabic, comprehensive; of E. A. Ross—graceful, muckraking, upright; of Auguste Comte and Emile Durkheim; of the intricate and subtle Karl Mannheim. It is the quality of all that is intellectually excellent in Karl Marx; it is the clue to Thorstein Veblen's brilliant and ironic insight, to Joseph Schumpeter's many-sided constructions of reality; it is the basis of the psychological sweep of W. E. H. Lecky no less than of the profundity and clarity of Max Weber. And it is the signal of what is best in contemporary studies of man and society.

No social study that does not come back to the problems of biography, of history and of their intersections within a society has completed its intellectual journey. Whatever the specific problems of the classic social analysts, however limited or however broad the features of social reality they have examined, those who have been imaginatively aware of the promise of their work have consistently asked three sorts of questions:

(1) What is the structure of this particular society as a whole? What are its essential components, and how are they related to one another? How does it differ from other varieties of social order? Within it, what is the meaning of any particular feature for its continuance and for its change?

(2) Where does this society stand in human history? What are the mechanics by which it is changing? What is its place within and its meaning for the development of humanity as a whole? How does any particular feature we are examining affect, and

how is it affected by, the historical period in which it moves? And this period—what are its essential features? How does it differ from other periods? What are its characteristic ways of history-making?

(3) What varieties of men and women now prevail in this society and in this period? And what varieties are coming to prevail? In what ways are they selected and formed, liberated and repressed, made sensitive and blunted? What kinds of 'human nature' are revealed in the conduct and character we observe in this society in this period? And what is the meaning for 'human nature' of each and every feature of the society we are examining?

Whether the point of interest is a great power state or a minor literary mood, a family, a prison, a creed—these are the kinds of questions the best social analysts have asked. They are the intellectual pivots of classic studies of man in society—and they are the questions inevitably raised by any mind possessing the sociological imagination. For that imagination is the capacity to shift from one perspective to another—from the political to the psychological; from examination of a single family to comparative assessment of the national budgets of the world; from the theological school to the military establishment; from considerations of an oil industry to studies of contemporary poetry. It is the capacity to range from the most impersonal and remote transformations to the most intimate features of the human self—and to see the relations between the two. Back of its use there is always the urge to know the social and historical meaning of the individual in the society and in the period in which he has his quality and his being.

That, in brief, is why it is by means of the sociological imagination that men now hope to grasp what is going on in the world, and to understand what is happening in themselves as minute points of the intersections of biography and history within society. In large part, contemporary man's self-conscious view of himself as at least an outsider, if not a permanent stranger, rests upon an absorbed realization of social relativity and of the transformative power of history. The sociological imagination is the most fruitful form of this self-consciousness. By its use men whose mentalities have swept only a series of limited orbits often come to feel as if suddenly awakened in a house with which they had only supposed themselves to be familiar. Correctly or incorrectly, they often come to feel that they can now provide themselves with adequate summations, cohesive assessments, comprehensive orientations. Older decisions that once appeared sound now seem to them products of a mind unaccountably dense. Their capacity for astonishment is made lively again. They acquire a new way of thinking, they experience a transvaluation of values: in a word, by their reflection and by their sensibility, they realize the cultural meaning of the social sciences.

**2**

Perhaps the most fruitful distinction with which the sociological imagination works is between 'the personal troubles of milieu' and 'the public issues of social structure.' This distinction is an essential tool of the sociological imagination and a feature of all classic work in social science.

*Troubles* occur within the character of the individual and within the range of his immediate relations with others; they have to do with his self and with those limited areas of social life of which he is directly and personally aware. Accordingly, the statement and the resolution of troubles properly lie within the individual as a biographical entity and within the scope of his immediate milieu—the social setting that is directly open to his personal experience and to some extent his willful activity. A trouble is a private matter: values cherished by an individual are felt by him to be threatened.

*Issues* have to do with matters that transcend these local environments of the individual and the range of his inner life. They have to do with the organization of many such milieux into the institutions of an historical society as a whole, with the ways in which various milieux overlap and interpenetrate to form the larger structure of social and historical life. An issue is a public matter: some value cherished by publics is felt to be threatened. Often there is a debate about what that value really is and about what it is that really threatens it. This debate is often without focus if only because it is the very nature of an issue, unlike even widespread trouble, that it cannot very well be defined in terms of the immediate and everyday environments of ordinary men. An issue, in fact, often involves a crisis in institutional arrangements, and often too it involves what Marxists call 'contradictions' or 'antagonisms.'

In these terms, consider unemployment. When, in a city of 100,000, only one man is unemployed, that is his personal trouble, and for its relief we properly look to the character of the man, his skills, and his immediate opportunities. But when in a nation of 50 million employees, 15 million men are unemployed, that is an issue, and we may not hope to find its solution within the range of opportunities open to any one individual. The very structure of opportunities has collapsed. Both the correct statement of the problem and the range of possible solutions require us to consider the economic and political institutions of the society, and not merely the personal situation and character of a scatter of individuals.

Consider war. The personal problem of war, when it occurs, may be how to survive it or how to die in it with honor; how to make money out of it; how to climb into the higher safety of the military apparatus; or how to contribute to the war's termination. In short, according to one's values, to find a set of milieux and within it to survive the war or make one's death in it meaningful. But the structural issues of war have to do with its causes; with what types of men it throws up into command; with its effects upon economic and political, family and religious institutions, with the unorganized irresponsibility of a world of nation-states.

Consider marriage. Inside a marriage a man and a woman may experience personal troubles, but when the divorce rate during the first four years of marriage is 250 out of every 1,000 attempts, this is an indication of a structural issue having to do with the institutions of marriage and the family and other institutions that bear upon them.

Or consider the metropolis—the horrible, beautiful, ugly, magnificent sprawl of the great city. For many upper-class people, the personal solution to 'the problem of the city' is to have an apartment with private garage under it in the heart of the city, and forty miles out, a house by Henry Hill, garden by Garrett Eckbo, on a hundred acres of private land. In these two controlled environments—with a small staff at each end and a private helicopter connection—most people could solve many of the problems of personal milieux caused by the facts of the city. But all this, however splendid, does not solve the public issues that the structural fact of the city poses. What should be done with this wonderful monstrosity? Break it all up into scattered units, combining residence and work? Refurbish it as it stands? Or, after evacuation, dynamite it and build new cities according to new plans in new places? What should those plans be? And who is to decide and to accomplish whatever choice is made? These are structural issues; to confront them and to solve them requires us to consider political and economic issues that affect innumerable milieux.

In so far as an economy is so arranged that slumps occur, the problem of unemployment becomes incapable of personal solution. In so far as war is inherent in the nation-state system and in the uneven industrialization of the world, the ordinary individual in his restricted milieu will be powerless—with or without psychiatric aid—to solve the troubles this system or lack of system imposes upon him. In so far as the family as an institution turns women into darling little slaves and men into their chief providers and unweaned dependents, the problem of a satisfactory marriage remains incapable of purely private solution. In so far as the overdeveloped megalopolis and the overdeveloped automobile are built-in features of the overdeveloped society, the issues of urban living will not be solved by personal ingenuity and private wealth.

What we experience in various and specific milieux, I have noted, is often caused by structural changes. Accordingly, to understand the changes of many personal milieux we are required to look beyond them. And the number and variety of such structural changes increase as the institutions within which we live become more embracing and more intricately connected with one another. To be aware of the idea of social structure and to use it with sensibility is to be capable of tracing such linkages among a great variety of milieux. To be able to do that is to possess the sociological imagination.

# Invitation to Sociology
# A Humanistic Perspective

## Peter L. Berger

. . . The sociologist, then, is someone concerned with understanding society in a disciplined way. The nature of this discipline is scientific. This means that what the sociologist finds and says about the social phenomena he studies occurs within a certain rather strictly defined frame of reference. One of the main characteristics of this scientific frame of reference is that operations are bound by certain rules of evidence. As a scientist, the sociologist tries to be objective, to control his personal preferences and prejudices, to perceive clearly rather than to judge normatively. This restraint, of course, does not embrace the totality of the sociologist's existence as a human being, but is limited to his operations *qua* sociologist. Nor does the sociologist claim that his frame of reference is the only one within which society can be looked at. For that matter, very few scientists in any field would claim today that one should look at the world only scientifically. The botanist looking at a daffodil has no reason to dispute the right of the poet to look at the same object in a very different manner. There are many ways of playing. The point is not that one denies other people's games but that one is clear about the rules of one's own. The game of the sociologist, then, uses scientific rules. As a result, the sociologist must be clear in his own mind as to the meaning of these rules. That is, he must concern himself with methodological questions. Methodology does not constitute his goal. The latter, let us recall once more, is the attempt to understand society. Methodology helps in reaching this goal. In order to understand society, or that segment of it that he is studying at the moment, the sociologist will use a variety of means. Among these are statistical techniques. Statistics can be very useful in answering certain sociological questions. But statistics does not constitute sociology. As a scientist, the sociologist will have to be concerned with the exact significance of the terms he is using. That is, he will have to be careful about terminology. This does not have to mean that he must invent a new language of his own, but it does mean that he cannot naively use the language of everyday discourse. Finally, the interest of the sociologist is primarily theoretical. That is, he is interested in understanding for its own sake. He may be aware of or even concerned with the practical applicability and consequences of his findings, but at that point he leaves the sociological frame of reference as such and moves into realms of values, beliefs and ideas that he shares with other men who are not sociologists. . . .

We would say then that the sociologist (that is, the one we would really like to invite to our game) is a person intensively, endlessly, shamelessly interested in the doings of men. His natural habitat is all the human gathering places of the world, wherever men come together. The sociologist may be interested in many other things. But his consuming interest remains in the world of men, their institutions, their history, their passions. And since he is interested in men, nothing that men do can be altogether tedious for him. He will naturally be interested in the events that engage men's ultimate beliefs, their moments of tragedy and grandeur and ecstasy. But he will also be fascinated by the commonplace, the everyday. He will know reverence, but this reverence will not prevent him from wanting to see and to understand. He may sometimes feel revulsion or contempt. But this also will not deter him from wanting to have his questions answered. The sociologist, in his quest for understanding, moves through the world of men without respect for the usual lines of demarcation. Nobility and degradation, power and obscurity, intelligence and folly—these are equally *interesting* to him, however unequal they may be in his personal values or tastes. Thus his questions may lead him to all possible levels of society, the best and the least known places, the most respected and the most despised. And, if he is a good sociologist, he will find himself in all these places because his own questions have so taken possession of him that he has little choice but to seek for answers.

It would be possible to say the same things in a lower key. We could say that the sociologist, but for the grace of his academic title, is the man who must listen to gossip despite himself, who is tempted to look through keyholes, to read other people's mail, to open closed cabinets. Before some otherwise unoccupied psychologist sets out now to construct an aptitude test for sociologists on the basis of sublimated voyeurism, let us quickly say that we are speaking merely by way of analogy. Perhaps some little boys consumed with curiosity to watch their maiden aunts in the bathroom later become inveterate sociologists. This is quite uninteresting. What interests us is the curiosity that grips any sociologist in front of a closed door behind which there are human voices. If he is a good sociologist, he will want to open that door, to understand these voices. Behind each closed door he will anticipate some new facet of human life not yet perceived and understood.

The sociologist will occupy himself with matters that others regard as too sacred or as too distasteful for dispassionate investigation. He will find rewarding the company of priests or of prostitutes, depending not on his personal preferences but on the questions he happens to be asking at the moment. He will also concern himself with matters that others may find much too boring. He will be interested in the human interaction that goes with warfare or with great intellectual discoveries, but also in the relations between people employed in a restaurant or between a group of little girls playing with their dolls. His main focus of attention is not the ultimate significance of what men do, but the action in itself, as another example of the infinite richness of human conduct. . . .

Any intellectual activity derives excitement from the moment it becomes a trail of discovery. In some fields of learning this is the discovery of worlds previously unthought and unthinkable. This is the excitement of the astronomer or of the nuclear physicist on the antipodal boundaries of the realities that man is capable of conceiving. But it can also be the excitement of bacteriology or geology. In a different way it can be the excitement of the linguist discovering new realms of human expression or of the anthropologist exploring human customs in faraway countries. In such discovery, when undertaken with passion, a widening of awareness, sometimes a veritable transformation of consciousness, occurs. The universe turns out to be much more wonder-full than one had ever dreamed. The excitement of sociology is usually of a different sort. Sometimes, it is true, the sociologist penetrates into worlds that had previously been quite unknown to him—for instance, the world of crime, or the world of some bizarre religious sect, or the world fashioned by the exclusive concerns of some group such as medical specialists or military leaders or advertising executives. However, much of the time the sociologist moves in sectors of experience that are familiar to him and to most people in his society. He investigates communities, institutions and activities that one can read about every day in the newspapers. Yet there is another excitement of discovery beckoning in his investigations. It is not the excitement of coming upon the totally unfamiliar, but rather the excitement of finding the familiar becoming transformed in its meaning. The fascination of sociology lies in the fact that its perspective makes us see in a new light the very world in which we have lived all our lives. This also constitutes a transformation of consciousness. Moreover, this transformation is more relevant existentially than that of many other intellectual disciplines, because it is more difficult to segregate in some special compartment of the mind. The astronomer does not live in the remote galaxies, and the nuclear physicist can, outside his laboratory, eat and laugh and marry and vote without thinking about the insides of the atom. The geologist looks at rocks only at appropriate times, and the linguist speaks English with his wife. The sociologist lives in society, on the job and off it. His own life, inevitably, is part of his subject matter. Men being what they are, sociologists too manage to segregate their professional insights from their everyday affairs. But it is a rather difficult feat to perform in good faith.

The sociologist moves in the common world of men, close to what most of them would call real. The categories he employs in his analyses are only refinements of the categories by which other men live—power, class, status, race, ethnicity. As a result, there is a deceptive simplicity and obviousness about some sociological investigations.

One reads them, nods at the familiar scene, remarks that one has heard all this before and don't people have better things to do than to waste their time on truisms—until one is suddenly brought up against an insight that radically questions everything one had previously assumed about this familiar scene. This is the point at which one begins to sense the excitement of sociology.

Let us take a specific example. Imagine a sociology class in a Southern college where almost all the students are white Southerners. Imagine a lecture on the subject of the racial system of the South. The lecturer is talking here of matters that have been familiar to his students from the time of their infancy. Indeed, it may be that they are much more familiar with the minutiae of this system than he is. They are quite bored as a result. It seems to them that he is only using more pretentious words to describe what they already know. Thus he may use the term "caste," one commonly used now by American sociologists to describe the Southern racial system. But in explaining the term he shifts to traditional Hindu society, to make it clearer. He then goes on to analyze the magical beliefs inherent in caste tabus, the social dynamics of commensalism and connubium, the economic interests concealed within the system, the way in which religious beliefs relate to the tabus, the effects of the caste system upon the industrial development of the society and vice versa—all in India. But suddenly India is not very far away at all. The lecture then goes back to its Southern theme. The familiar now seems not quite so familiar any more. Questions are raised that are new, perhaps raised angrily, but raised all the same. And at least some of the students have begun to understand that there are functions involved in this business of race that they have not read about in the newspapers (at least not those in their hometowns) and that their parents have not told them—partly, at least, because neither the newspapers nor the parents knew about them.

It can be said that the first wisdom of sociology is this—things are not what they seem. This too is a deceptively simple statement. It ceases to be simple after a while. Social reality turns out to have many layers of meaning. The discovery of each new layer changes the perception of the whole.

Anthropologists use the term "culture shock" to describe the impact of a totally new culture upon a newcomer. In an extreme instance such shock will be experienced by the Western explorer who is told, halfway through dinner, that he is eating the nice old lady he had been chatting with the previous day—a shock with predictable physiological if not moral consequences. Most explorers no longer encounter cannibalism in their travels today. However, the first encounters with polygamy or with puberty rites or even with the way some nations drive their automobiles can be quite a shock to an American visitor. With the shock may go not only disapproval or disgust but a sense of excitement that things can *really* be that different from what they are at home. To some extent, at least, this is the excitement of any first travel abroad. The experience of sociological discovery could be described as "culture shock" minus geographical displacement. In other words, the sociologist travels at home—with shocking results. He is unlikely to find that he is eating a nice old lady for dinner. But the discovery, for instance, that his own church has considerable money invested in the missile industry or that a few blocks from his home there are people who engage in cultic orgies may not be drastically different in emotional impact. Yet we would not want to imply that sociological discoveries are always or even usually outrageous to moral sentiment. Not at all. What they have in common with exploration in distant lands, however, is the sudden illumination of new and unsuspected facets of human existence in society. This is the excitement and, as we shall try to show later, the humanistic justification of sociology.

People who like to avoid shocking discoveries, who prefer to believe that society is just what they were taught in Sunday School, who like the safety of the rules and the maxims of what Alfred Schuetz has called the "world-taken-for-granted," should stay away from sociology. People who feel no temptation before closed doors, who have no curiosity about human beings, who are content to admire scenery without wondering about the people who live in those houses on the other side of that river, should probably also stay away from sociology. They will find it unpleasant or, at any rate, unrewarding. People who are interested in human beings only if they can change, convert or reform them should also be warned, for they will find sociology much less useful than they hoped. And people whose interest is mainly in their own conceptual constructions will do just as well to turn to the study of little white mice. Sociology will be satisfying, in the long run, only to those who can think of nothing more entrancing than to watch men and to understand things human. . . .

# Culture

- American Values (Articles 3-4)
- Contrasts to American Culture (Articles 5-6)
- Youth and Generational Cultures (Articles 7-8)

The ordinary, everyday objects of living and the daily routines of life provide a structure to social existence that is regularly punctuated by festivals and celebrations. Both the routine and special times are the "stuff" of culture, for culture is the sum total of all pieces of one's social inheritance. Culture includes language, tools, values, habits, literature, and art.

Because culture is often overlooked and taken for granted, it helps to pause and reflect upon shared beliefs and the relationships that form the foundations of group life. In a similar way, an examination of exotic and different cultures is valuable for recognizing how cultural assumptions affect all facets of life. A great deal can be learned by observing how other people treat their elderly or raise their young. Moreover, through such observations, individuals can recognize how misunderstandings begin and can appreciate the problems of maintaining cultural continuities in a rapidly changing environment. Through an awareness of culture people begin to "know" themselves, for culture lies at the heart of their personal and collective identities. Culture is one of the most powerful and important concepts in the discipline.

This section includes articles which look at culture from different perspectives and which portray cultural differences. Often it takes an outsider to see the peculiarities of a group. How do you think Americans look to outsiders? One visitor from England, Henry Fairlie, explains how unusual he thought Americans were because they say "Hi" to everyone. From this simple greeting Fairlie learned about American freedom and democracy. He also discusses other peculiarities of America and tells why he loves and adopted this country.

One of the important functions of culture is social control. Some beliefs, norms, and values prescribe what citizens should or should not do in various situations. Social life is much more pleasant if most people internalize these norms (provided they are humane) and have a desire to act in a socially acceptable manner. When commitment to basic ethical values becomes lax for many people, however, social trust erodes and social order must be maintained through more formal controls. Then the society is in trouble because formal controls are more clumsy than informal controls and do not generate positive motivation. Bernice Kanner argues that the level of commitment to ethical principles in business is dangerously low but there is also a new interest in ethics.

Specific cultures are shaped by the conditions of life. When those conditions change, the culture will also change over time. Colin Turnbull describes life with an African tribe that was moved off of its original land and was forced to live in a harsh environment. Literally all aspects of life changed for them, in a disturbingly sinister direction. The experience of this tribe leads Turnbull to question some of the individualistic tendencies of America. In the following selection, Robert Levine and Ellen Wolff compare Brazil and five other countries to the United States on attitudes toward time. Surprisingly, the Japanese outhustle Americans.

One facet of culture which is of perennial interest is the development of a new perspective and way of life by each new teenage generation. Obviously the continuity outweighs the diversity between generations, but the differences are fascinating to look at. The last two articles explore some of these differences. Leavitt describes the youth generation of the 1970s while Barnett examines the youth generation of the 1980s. The authors think their own generation is very unique, but that issue is debatable.

**Looking Ahead: Challenge Questions**

Why do individuals seldom question their cultural values?

What are the boundaries of a culture? How does one cross over boundaries?

What is the relationship between culture and identity?

What might a visitor from a primitive tribe describe as shocking and barbaric about American society?

# Why I Love America

## Henry Fairlie

I HAD REPORTED from some twenty-four countries before I set foot in America. I will never forget the first shock—even after having been in every country from the Sudan to South Africa—at realizing that I was in another place entirely, a New World. In the casbah of Algiers during the first referendum called by de Gaulle in 1959, when the women hurrying down the steep streets to vote for the first time pulled their yashmaks around their faces as they passed a man (which seemed to me only to make their dark eyes more fascinating), I was still in the Old World, however strange it was. But here in America it was all new.

I had been in the country about eight years, and was living in Houston, when a Texan friend asked me one evening: "Why do you like living in America? I don't mean why you find it interesting—why you want to write about it—but why you *like* living here so much." After only a moment's reflection, I replied, "It's the first time I've felt free." In the nine years that have passed since then, I have often reflected on that answer, and have found no reason to change it. What I mean by it is part of the story to be told here.

Other memories come to mind. One spring day, shortly after my arrival, I was walking down the long, broad street of a suburb, with its sweeping front lawns (all that space), its tall trees (all that sky), and its clumps of azaleas (all that color). The only other person on the street was a small boy on a tricycle. As I passed him, he said "Hi!"—just like that. No four-year-old boy had ever addressed me without an introduction before. Yet here was this one, with his cheerful "Hi!" Recovering from the culture shock, I tried to look down stonily at his flaxen head, but instead, involuntarily, I found myself saying in return: "Well—hi!" He pedaled off, apparently satisfied. He had begun my Americanization.

"Hi!" As I often say—for Americans do not realize it—the word is a democracy. (I come from a country where one can tell someone's class by how they say "Hallo!" or "Hello!" or "Hullo," or whether they say it at all.) But anyone can say "Hi!" Anyone does. Shortly after my encounter with the boy, I called on the then Suffragan Bishop of Washington. Did he greet me as the Archbishop of Canterbury would have done? No. He said, "Hi, Henry!" I put it down to an aberration, an excess of Episcopalian latitudinarianism. But what about my first meeting with Lyndon B. Johnson, the President of the United States, the Emperor of the Free World, before whom, like a Burgher of Calais, a halter round my neck, I would have sunk to my knees, pleading for a loan for my country? He held out the largest hand in Christendom, and said, "Hi, Henry!"

Small anecdotes? But I wish to suggest that it is there, in the small anecdotes, that the secret lies. America has—if one opens oneself to it—a bewitching power. From the very beginning the stranger feels its influence as a loosening. At first this can be disquieting. After all, one is not in an exotic land, where the differences are immediately striking, easy to see, so that one may be fascinated without really being touched by them. Yet from the beginning in America one feels this power, unsettling all that one had thought was familiar, fixed by the ages. To some—I have known them—it is alarming. For there do come moments when one realizes, more than in any other country not one's own, that here one may be being remade. If here history still invents itself, then here also, still, one may invent the future. But suppose that means that one may also invent oneself? Max Ascoli, the Italian Jew who fled from Fascism and founded and edited in America a remarkable magazine, *The Reporter*, once wrote: "It did not cause me any trouble to become an Italian, but my becoming an American is my own work." Every immigrant will know what he means; millions are still working on it in their own lives.

I remember also the time when I still resisted the very power of America to attract. After I had been here in

Washington, D.C., a little while, I noticed one day that all the Americans who had befriended me were preparing to participate in some ritual, and that I was not invited. It was the Fourth of July. I presumed that they were being tactful: How could they ask me to celebrate a British defeat? So I accepted an invitation from Patrick O'Donovan, then the Washington correspondent of *The Observer*. What could we do on the Fourth? We looked at the television listings, and were delighted to find that there was a midday rerun of the original *Scarlet Pimpernel*, with Leslie Howard as Sir Percy Blakeney. We may have been defeated by the Americans, but one Englishman, single-handedly, had outwitted Robespierre's police. So we sat with our elbows on the lunch table, watching Leslie Howard be English, brave, and debonair, and even when the table leaf gave way with a crash, it did not interrupt Sir Percy or our absorption.

Later in the afternoon, Patrick—who had been a strapping young Irish Guards officer during the Second World War, as handsome (as they say) as the devil—opened the screen door into his Georgetown garden, and peed. "It does one good," he proclaimed, "on the Fourth of July, to piss on American soil." But he let in an enormous bug—one of those gigantic bugs that make it all the more inexplicable why Americans like barbecuing on their patios in the fetid summer—which then banged from wall to wall, sometimes wheeling to dive-bomb us. "You shouldn't have pissed on America," I said to Patrick. "George III tried to piss on it, and look what happened to him." But Patrick was by now cowering behing the couch—all six-foot-four Irish Guards of him—shouting to his wife, " 'Mione, 'Mione, HELP!" She came downstairs, took one pitying look at her brave Britishers, got a can of Raid, and destroyed the American intruder. Patrick got up from behind the couch, drew himself up again to his full height, and said as if he were addressing his troops in the desert, "Henry, I cannot *bear* the tropics." By the time the fireworks began on the mall— "More shots to be heard round the world, I suppose," grumbled Patrick—we had the Dutch courage to ignore them. We had drunk our way—what else for exiles to do?—through the Fourth of July.

But as I stayed and felt America drawing me to it, I inevitably began to think of the others who have come. The curiosity about the country which first brought and kept me here scarcely entitles me to claim that I have shared the experience of most immigrants. I have no right to make it seem as if I came here traveling steerage, like the political refugees or those who simply had neither food nor hope in their native lands. But I will say this about the Statue of Liberty. It was an act of imagination, when the French proposed raising the money for it to celebrate the American Revolution, to choose such a site, and not Washington or Mount Vernon or Philadelphia, and to put on it that inscription, recalling not the English colonists who made the Revolution, but the millions upon millions of others who have come here since. They were drawn by the promise of this land; the land has performed for many

more of them than it has failed; and they in turn have helped remake the nation. And still they come.

The story of the immigration cannot be told bloodlessly. It cannot be drained of what Osbert Sitwell caught so well, in this hauntingly lovely passage from his *The Four Continents*, published in 1954: "New York, with all its faults, is yet the greatest and the most moving of modern cities . . . built by refugees to shelter and protect their dreams on alien soil. . . . For that is what it is, a metropolis of dreams realized and unrealized . . . dreams of every age and intensity. . . . So when in the small hours you open the window, and the cool of the darkness flows into the heated room, it is on a beautiful and improbable city of dreams that you look, some tragic, some naive, but many of them practicable and to be achieved in the future, near or distant, by the labors of these same dreamers when awake during the working day. Thus in the main the dreams will be fulfilled, and the hopes that prevail over fears are justified." How can one lose the sense that something quite miraculous has happened in the making of one nation from so many different peoples?

No other immigration into any other country has had anything like the same meaning for the rest of the world, for those who did not migrate, lifting the imagination of the world to horizons beyond even the expanse of this continent. The name of America still lends to countless millions its own dreams for them to dream themselves.

An English economist once said that it was America that had taught the world that it need not starve. Consider that. It cannot be denied. The achievements of American agriculture are one of the wonders of the modern world. Americans consume each year only a third of the wheat which American farmers produce; there is no other valley in the world which has been made, by irrigation, as fertile as the Central Valley of California. But it is not only such facts and figures that tell the wonder. One must look down the vastness of the Middle West, as the English poet Louis MacNeice did in 1940, "astonished by its elegance from the air. Elegance is the word for it—enormous plains of beautifully inlaid rectangles, the grain running different ways, walnut, satinwood or oatcake, the whole of it tortoiseshelled with copses and shadows of clouds. . . ." It is common for the American when he is in Europe to gasp at the hedgerows of England or the terraced vineyards of Italy, kept for centuries. But the gasp of the Englishman is no less when he gazes on a continent, immense in scale, still fabulous in its diversity, which not only is cultivated but has by its cultivation been given its own coherence; which unlike Europe has been made one. Who but the Americans would, so early, have made the Great Plains yield so much—those semi-arid lands which even they, at first, called "the Great American Desert"?

But let us return to small things. If America was to produce, it had also to invent. The English critic T. R. Fyvel once told a story of a friend, also English, who had "found himself for a fantastic weekend in a society of Texas millionaires who whizzed around in their private aircraft, dropping in on parties hundreds of miles away."

## 2. CULTURE: American Values

The friend found this unexpectedly refreshing. He was even more impressed when he saw the children of his host "buzzing around in special little pedal motor cars which were air conditioned." But one night his Texan millionaire host turned to him and said something like: "You know, Bob, I ask myself if our machine civilization isn't shot all to hell." The Englishman, horrified, burst out to his host: "Don't have those decadent thoughts! Don't have any thoughts! Leave them to us—while you stay just as you are!" I understand his response. There seems to be nothing, however fanciful, that the American, with his unflagging inventive genius, will not attempt.

MATTHEW ARNOLD was amazed at the warmth of American houses. "We are full of plans," he wrote to his daughter from Philadelphia in 1883, "for putting an American stove into the Cottage," when he got back to England. In 1912 Arnold Bennett was amazed that, whereas "the European telephone is a toy," in America it was regarded as an indispensable convenience for everyone. In 1942 Sir Philip Biggs was amazed by the supermarket, "where you grab what you want and wheel it to the cashier in steel perambulators made for the purpose," and leave "laden with a variety of food, beyond the range of English households even in peacetimes, from the A & P stores." (Twenty-three years later, on my very first morning in America, the wife of the English friend with whom I was staying took me, not to the Washington Monument, but to a supermarket—just to stare.) In 1963 T. H. White, who made a lecture tour in his old age, accompanied by the eighteen-year-old sister-in-law of Julie Andrews as "my secretary, but really as a protectress," was amazed at the change machine in the automat restaurant on a train: "In went a dollar bill which was inspected and out come [sic] four silver quarters. Why couldn't we put in bits of newspaper cut to the right size?" But he found more to wonder at: "In Long Island fishermen can buy *worms* from slot machines"; and again: "I also learned of *tab-opening cans*. You can open a beer can and, it is to be hoped, you will soon be able to open any can, without a tin opener." They were all responding to something I could not imagine America without.

How I have come to take it all for granted was brought home to me not long ago, when I was sitting in my house with a friend visiting from England. It was a quiet afternoon in early summer, the windows were open, I could hear the birds chirping in the garden. My friend suddenly exclaimed: "How can you bear to live in all this noise?" What noise? "All this noise in the house," he said. "Something is always switching itself off or on, humming or purring." He had destroyed my own peace, for I noticed it from then on. It is no wonder that America consumes so much energy. The electric gadgetry in an American home makes it its own Disney World. But to most Englishmen it is the physical evidence of a society that does not tire of innovation; which by its inventiveness still seems to keep the future open; and in whose inventiveness ordinary people find convenience.

THE INVENTIVENESS and gadgetry of the American reflects the spirit of a society which echoes the song: "It ain't necessarily so." If houses are insufferably cold, you invent a stove, and then you invent central heating; and if anyone writes in to say that the Romans had central heating, the important point is that the common man in Rome did not have it. Ben Franklin invented a prefabricated stove which could be produced for the common man; such a stove in Europe at the time would have been produced by craftsmen for the few. But then it has always been the American way as well, when faced with any injustice or harshness in this society, to say that "it ain't necessarily so," and to do something about it. If ever this spirit is allowed to languish, whether in the invention of things or the improvement of its society, America will have ceased to be what it means to the rest of the world.

When the cafeteria was first invented, the English responded to it with delight, from Clare Sheridan first being taken to one by Upton Sinclair in 1921, when she followed him as "he first took a metal tray from a column of trays," to S.P.B. Mais's description in 1933:

> You put your tray on a slide, help yourself as you rush along to orange juice, puffed rice, eggs, rolls, coffee, marmalade, or whatever it is you eat for breakfast, and when you reach the end of the counter a girl checks your loaded tray with lightning calculation, says "Thirty cents"—or whatever it is—and you take your tray and eat your breakfast at a table. The whole time spent in getting your food is thirty seconds.

The cafeteria has, of course, spread all over the world. But what these first encounters tell, above all, is of their convenience, and the fact that this convenience is liberating, as electrical gadgets (or Clarence Birdseye's invention, frozen foods) are liberating in the home. What they tell secondly is that these conveniences are not for a privileged few. Like the Franklin stove or the Ford Model T, these amenities were meant for all.

What I am trying to show is that, to other Englishmen besides myself, there is a meaning to the material progress of America which has traveled, and is still traveling, to the rest of the world, beyond the physical benefits which it bestows. It was a critic of fastidious taste and judgment, Cyril Connolly, who said in 1952:

> All American influence on Europe, however vulgar, brings with it an improvement in the standard of living and the dissipation of certain age-old desires. Should Europe oppose this influence? Europe, which has destroyed so many exotic civilizations, without even providing them with the democratic optimism which America brings with its films, its gadgets, and its *lingua franca*, the demotic language which obliterates all class distinctions.

BUT CONNOLLY left out the most significant American influence of all: the spread of the manners of a society which has always been more informal, less stiff, less bound by convention, than any other in the world; in which a person is accepted, as Thackeray said during one of his visits, for what he is. The impetus to informality in

America is, at least in part, the source of one of the most striking changes in our century: the change in the relationship between one individual human being and another, and so in their relationship to their society.

The informality is one characteristic which at first both jarred and drew me. By far the most infectious account of this characteristic of America was given by Dom Hubert van Zeller, an English monk who often preached retreats in both countries, and enjoyed America, but was still astonished at this scene:

> In a hall at Denver I had the privilege of being listened to by upwards of six hundred nuns, assembled from different communities, all of whom were eating ices off the ends of sticks. The distribution of the ices, effectively conducted by a member of the home team, took place during the earlier phase of my address, so from the elevated position which I occupied on the platform, I was able to lay bets with myself as to which religious order would finish first.

This is the public informality—often noticed in Congress, in the courts—but the training begins early, with the freedom given the American child.

The children, like the informality, can at first jar. But the true mark of American society is that its informality forms its own patterns and codes. Although the outsider cannot at first detect it, there is a rhythm of American life. This rhythm is a constant improvisation, a flexibility that will accommodate the wishes and whims of every member of the group. No one voice in the typical American family takes precedence over the rest. Someone is always leaving or coming back; someone is always asking if he or she can have the car; someone is always going to the refrigerator for a snack instead of a meal; someone is always arriving late at a meal or leaving it early. The rhythm of the American family is to be found in a system of communications by which the improvised activities of each of its members is made known to all so that they can be taken into account. What holds the home together is a pattern of wires and castings, as hidden from view as the inside of a transistor radio, along which a ceaseless flow of messages is carried, and accommodations made to them. Messages left on the refrigerator door can for days be the only visible form of communication between members of a family who otherwise succeed in never running into each other as they come and go.

This is one reason why Mom and Dad, Lois and Junior, are so noticeable as tourists, and look so uncomfortable. They are not used to doing things as a unit. One can notice this even in an ordinary restaurant in America, when a whole family has for once come out to have dinner together: one by one, each grows restless to get away, and the meal degenerates into a pitiless nagging of the one person (usually, the mother) who is actually having a good time, and so is holding up the rest. What has happened is that they are not using their transistors; since they are all together, the flow of messages has been interrupted; having to do the same thing, at the same time, their common life has lost its rhythm.

I NOTICED AT ONCE the general American aversion to sitting down to a meal, and the time spent, if you are a guest, sitting in an armchair, or a canvas chair on the porch, always with a low table within handy reach. What then happens was perfectly caught in 1952 by the English journalist Mervyn Jones:

> Darting in and out of the kitchen, your hostess keeps the table constantly loaded with sandwiches, plates of cheese, nice little things on crackers, bowls of fruit, nuts, olives, pretzels, rolls, cakes, cookies, and other refreshments. Gin, whisky, beer, and coffee are on tap without a moment's break. You are urged, in case there should be anything you lack, to help yourself from the two or three vast refrigerators. . . . People arrive in cars, sit down, stretch out their hands with the same air of unthinking habit as a horse reaching for a clump of grass, nibble for a while, get into their cars, and go—to be replaced, no matter what the hour, by other nibblers. All sense of time is lost. . . . You have, however, eaten twice as much as though you had sat round the table for three square meals.

The fact is that a wholly different manner of life was invented in America, contrasted with that of Europe (before it began to spread there from America): with more flexibility, more activity, more fragmentation, but still with its own patterns. American society is a kaleidoscope, in which the original pattern is always being rearranged. This is itself freeing, simply in day-to-day behavior, in the opportunities to meet other people, but also in deeper ways.

Though there are classes in America, there is no *class system*. When I answered, "The first time I've felt free," one thing I meant was that I was free of class. How could a class system be fastened onto a shifting kaleidoscope? If you imagine that you have discovered some symmetrical pattern in American society, you have only to change the angle at which you stand to it and the pattern changes. As Martin Green wrote in 1961, "America is not dominated by any single type, much less [a] class-limited one"; and he added, referring to Britain, "In these two ways, America stands for health, and we for sickness." This is strong, but it is just. Class—accent, vocabulary, dress, manners—not only confines the lower class in England, it also confines the upper class. It is much easier to mix here with people who are unlike oneself. To whom can this be more important than the immigrant making his way into the mainstream? Why the barriers remain so difficult for blacks to cross is too large a question to go into here; and the disappointing results so far of the Puerto Rican immigration (of which Nathan Glazer and Daniel Patrick Moynihan expected so much in *Beyond the Melting Pot*) also raise disconcerting questions which are beyond the scope of personal response. I will merely say that the sheer rise of the present colored—Asian, Latin American, Caribbean—immigration seems bound to present challenges which will make Americans again consider the virtues of assimilation.

## 2. CULTURE: American Values

OTHER LINES than those of class are also more easily crossed: those of sex, for example, and of age. When the English have come to America they have always written at length about American women. "And what luncheons," exclaimed Clare Sheridan, ". . . and apparently all for themselves. There is never a man. They even pay one another compliments. I wonder if they can be contented." (There has often been this ambivalence in the consistent praise of American women.) I too would comment when I first came here on the numbers of women lunching together in restaurants. But I soon came to believe that it is partly from her associations with other women that the American woman draws, not only a strength and subtlety of feeling for her own existence (a part of her superiority which almost every English visitor has acknowledged), but also her capacity for friendship with men. It is the American man's capacity for friendship with women which is in doubt, and I attribute it to the shallowness of his associations and lack of intimacy with his own sex. In a moment I will show why that last observation is not thrown in just to provoke a riot.

But first I must emphasize what it is in American women which, especially when they began to arrive in England in large numbers a century ago, took the English by storm. In 1907, Lady Dorothy Nevill calling her "bright and vivacious," said, "it is by the American girl we have been conquered." As early as 1864 Lord Bryce, who later married one, thought that American women had "so much more freedom in their manners; . . . the absence of primness was a very agreeable relief." To Rudyard Kipling in 1891, "the girls of America are above and beyond them all. . . . They have societies, and clubs . . . where all the guests are girls. . . ; they understand; they can take care of themselves; they are superbly independent." But the essential point was made by Jerome K. Jerome in 1904: "The American girl has succeeded in freeing European social intercourse from many of its hide-bound conventions. There is still work for her to do. But I have a faith in her."

The barrier of age is also crossed. My first editor in 1945 had lectured to a party of American students on the liner bringing them to observe postwar Europe. He exclaimed to me: "They are so different. They ask questions. They say what they think. They are not afraid to talk." Since I was twenty-one myself, and had never been afraid to talk, I thought he was a little gone in the head. There are few things more delightful than the way in which young Americans all over the country are willing to engage openly and freely in conversation and even friendship with someone perhaps more than twice their age. There is a democracy of manners in America which I would miss terribly if I ever left here.

I have been describing a society that is freeing. But there is no doubt it is also demanding. For if the immigrant feels here that he may invent himself, then is he not in that only being an American already? So much in the Old World is fixed for one: not only one's position but so much of one's life and even one's self. This is what weighs in the first part of Ascoli's remark: "It did not cause me any trouble to become an Italian." But even for an American born here, is it not his "own work" to become an American? This accounts for the one unease I still feel.

WITH THE CONTRAST I am about to draw, it is worth saying, I know many Americans who agree. It is much easier at first—and it is here that I am thinking of the men—to get to know an American. The welcoming "Hi!," the first names, the ready handshake, the quick generosity. You do not get through these first layers with an Englishman nearly as easily or as quickly. But once through them with an American, you come soon to a dead end, you are not admitted to the core or to any real intimacy. With the Englishman, whereas it is hard to get through the initial reserve, once through those outer layers, all resistance crumbles, and you find that you are sharing a level of extraordinary intimacy.

Julián Marías, the disciple of Ortega y Gasset, who spent much time here in the 1950s and 1960s, observed that although Americans get more mail than any other people in the world, they receive far fewer personal letters. An American friend of mine, Howard Higman, a professor of sociology, makes the point well. A letter from an American is like an itinerary, he says, a letter from an Englishman is like a diary. There is no questioning this, and I have often wondered what it is that Americans fear to expose, even whether they fear that there is nothing at the core to expose at all. But the answer, I believe, is simpler. If there has been so much freedom and informality in which to make oneself, if it really is one's "own work" to be an American, then one is bound to guard jealously a self which must often feel isolated and fragile, far more than in a society where so much of who one is has been determined for one. (For if one has been made by that society, it has made others like oneself, so what is there to fear?) This is the significance of the women's associations on which the English observers at once fixed their attention. The men's associations are far more likely to be centered on some activity—sports, watching football, hunting—anything to avoid having to talk about themselves and bare their souls. This is where one comes to a dead stop. These are the personal letters one misses. Almost all letters from American men are typed, even those from my friends, even those meant to be warmly personal. They might be dictated to a secretary, for the little they dare to say.

There is in all of this one reason why so many American attempts to describe the experience of being an American fall back on myth and metaphor, whereas almost all the English descriptions of what it seems to them to mean to be an American stick to the details and small encounters of everyday life. Americans take too much for granted the details of American life in which may often be found the meaning of the freedom and equality and opportunity which still draw people to it. We all know the wretched side of the life of the immigrants: the rough, menial, even dangerous work; the abysmally low wages; the abject conditions in which they lived, in the notorious dumbbell tenements of New York, for example, honeycombed with tiny rooms. And we know that those wretched conditions, whether in the large cities or in the acres of the Southwest baking under the sun, still exist. Yet there was and is another side. It was not all that long after the Italians began to arrive that, in their communities on the Upper East Side, there were shoulders of meat in the butcher's windows at twelve cents a pound; outside the macaroni shops, under improvised shelters, the macaroni was hung out to dry; along the curbs were the pushcarts with artichokes and asparagus, early melons and tomatoes; and a round of cheese cost twenty-four cents. And although only a third of the Italian immigrants had ever cast a vote in their native country, before the first generation had reached middle age they had politicians courting them; and Fiorello La Guardia was elected to Congress from East Harlem on his second attempt in 1916. As they shopped on their streets, where did their allegiance lie? To Genoa? We can still catch from that picture of their streets the smell of freedom.

As a young officer, George C. Marshall was surprised, when he inspected his troops on landing in France in 1917, at how many of them spoke broken English. But of their stake in America, in its industry, in its freedom, there could be little doubt; this was borne out by the astonishing lack of sedition in America throughout the war. I have tried from my own experience to explain some of the small but revealing reasons why America worked its influence so quickly and so deeply on them. It now seems to be working on some of the new immigrants. In my observation, the East Asians especially (and who would have predicted it?) are responding wholeheartedly to American life—their children are into the Little League almost as soon as they are out of the cradle—as they work their way, often by traditional routes such as running neighborhood stores, into the mainstream. This third wave of immigration is repeating, quite remarkably, many of the characteristics of the first two waves. America is still open, and it will be a tragedy if those who wish it to "think small," who will to keep America as a playground for those already here, have their way, and close America down.

I will give the last words to an American. Daniel Patrick Moynihan wrote in 1978: "... while the matter has not received much attention, the United States is quietly but rapidly resuming its role as a nation of first- and second-generation immigrants, almost the only one of its kind in the world, incomparably the largest, and for the first time in our history or any other, a nation drawn from the entire world. The Immigration Act of 1965 altered the shape of American immigration and increased its size.... Our immigrants in wholly unprecedented proportions come from Asia, South America, and the Caribbean. In fiscal year 1973 the ten top visa-issuing ports were Manila, Monterrey, Seoul, Tijuana, Santo Domingo, Mexico City, Naples, Guadalajara, Toronto, Kingston. I would expect Bombay to make this top ten list before long.... In short, by the end of the century, the United States will be a multi-ethnic nation the like of which even we have never imagined."

In this vision, America is still open. And America is about to be remade by its immigrants—again—as they become enthusiastic Americans. And what will the immigrants write home about? The gadgets, I beg, the gadgets.

# WHAT PRICE ETHICS?

## THE MORALITY OF THE EIGHTIES

*BERNICE KANNER*

IT'S A SPARKLING DAY, AND DAVE AND FRANK, two close friends, are on their routine golf outing. Today, however, Dave is morose and off his game. Frank presses him until Dave confides in his friend, who also happens to be a supplier to Dave's company. His son has been accepted at Cornell, but Dave can't afford the bill and aches with the thought of disappointing the boy. Frank considers the predicament, earnestly suggests a second mortgage, roguishly recommends robbing a bank, and then—eureka!—remembers that his company has set up a foundation to offer partial scholarships for the children of friends of the firm.

Many of the students at the University of Pennsylvania's Wharton School who watched this vignette—part of a video made for IBM—didn't see anything ethically compromising about the situation. Only a handful of 120 Pennsylvania State Troopers recognized the moral dilemma. And one young Sun Company employee confessed to being confused after seeing the entire video, with its various examples of people being drawn into compromising positions. "From watching his elders, this young man had assumed that the fruits of hard work—perks and payoffs—were a natural reward for ascending the corporate ladder," says Fred Bornhofen, director of security for Sun in Radnor, Pennsylvania.

The young man's assumption appears to be widely shared, for ethics in America seem to have dropped to one of the lowest points in history. A doctor is caught operating while under the influence of drugs; others are found practicing without licenses. Judges are caught accepting bribes and evading income tax. Municipal corruption in the Koch administration has toppled or stunted the careers of at least ten public officials and led to the suicide of Queens Borough President Donald Manes. The Justice Department's Bureau of Statistics reports a 53 percent increase in the prison population between 1980 and 1985. Students are found cheating on their SATs, and a couple of seniors at Brown are arrested for allegedly participating in a prostitution ring. A man plants rat poison in over-the-counter capsules to cash in on the anticipated stock surge of the drugmaker's competitor. E. F. Hutton admits to checking abuses; General Electric and General Dynamics are found guilty of wheeling and dealing with defense contracts. The Bank of Boston acknowledges that it facilitated money-laundering, A. H. Robins is accused of covering up the dangers of the Dalkon Shield, and NASA officials scurry to shift blame for the *Challenger* debacle. Eli Lilly fails to report the death of patients who took Oraflex, Texaco is caught trying unfair takeover practices, and Cartier is caught falsifying business records to help customers avoid sales tax. A military family pleads guilty to spying, and a New York rabbi is

# TODAY, MANY OF THE WORST LAPSES ARE AT MIDDLE-MANAGEMENT LEVELS AND AMONG YOUNG PEOPLE.

arrested in one of the largest fraud schemes ever uncovered in the history of the Customs Service. A 33-year-old investment banker rakes in $12.6 million from insider trading, and—just last week—the Securities and Exchange Commission implicates two other former Wall Street executives in the banker's ring. Five young men are charged with being part of another insider-trading ring. A president drummed out of office in 1974 tells a press luncheon what he thinks is the greatest lesson of Watergate: "Just destroy all the tapes." And everybody's talking about ethics, but nobody seems surprised by the lack of them.

In one sense, there's nothing surprising about it—moral lapses blot American history virtually from the start. There were the intrigues of Aaron Burr; the scandal-ridden Grant administration; Black Friday; the meat-packing scandals of the early 1900s; and Teapot Dome. There were the speakeasies and mobsters of the Prohibition era and the scandals of the Truman and Eisenhower administrations. And, of course, there were the overseas bribery scandals of the 1970s, as well as Agnew, Watergate, and brother Billy's finagling. William H. Vanderbilt seemed to say it all a century ago: "The public be damned."

But today's go-go ethics are in many ways new. For one thing, there's little doubt that idealism is in decline and cynicism on the rise. The climate has changed. The 1920s may have been hedonistic and the 1950s ethically lax, but even in those decades the country didn't seem as obsessed with riches as it does today. Part of the explanation may lie in *expectations*—many baby-boomers grew up when the American Dream was widely attainable and assume that they'll be able to go on leading comfortably affluent lives. What's more, the laissez-faire Reagan administration often gives the impression that it's looking the other way as the wheeling and dealing goes on around it (and sometimes within it).

Today, many of the lapses are at the middle-management levels and among young people—a stark contrast to the social activism of the late 1960s and early 1970s. "We're in a time when private interest is the solution to all problems and the sense of public purpose has faded away," says historian Arthur Schlesinger Jr.

Yet even while there's talk about the death of ethics, some people point to the seeds of a resurgence. The religious right is flourishing, as people fed up with moral lassitude and ambiguity seek definite answers—albeit sometimes simplistic ones. A new specialty—ethics consulting—has materialized, and ethicists are suddenly in demand as corporate advisers. Corporate codes of ethics seem as common—and sometimes as weighty—as annual reports, and ethics committees are being formed everywhere. The number of ethics courses in graduate schools has soared in the last decade.

OVERALL, THOUGH, THE MOOD AMONG ETHICS professionals is gloomy. "There have been periods before the New Deal when ethical breaches ran high, but in the last twenty years, all kinds of new forms of old crimes have been invented," says Joseph Bensman, a sociology professor at the City University of New York. "The opportunity to profit from crime today is almost unlimited. There are virtually no external controls, and there haven't been since the election of Nixon in 1968. The rule has been deregulation and the

appointment of foxes to watch the chicken coop, and disgraces that are treated with mere pats to the wrists. Students sense that businessmen do what they have to do to get ahead. This is different than it was 30 years ago. Today, nobody gives a damn."

*Commentary* editor Norman Podhoretz claims that the current ethics crisis—"selfishness as an absolute moral principle"—started "with the famous idealism of the 1960s. Young people told themselves that their generosity and outward concern reflected a special party of conscience, but it was really a veneer for the self-preoccupation and narcissism that is so much evident today. Young people were praised for opposing the Vietnam War, but you notice that so much of this so-called idealism disappeared when the real danger of being drafted did."

On the other end of the political spectrum, F. Forrester Church, minister of All Souls Unitarian Church in Manhattan, thinks the decline in ethics is evident in the bombing of Libya—"the ends justify the means"—and in Washington behavior. "David Stockman writes a book blowing the whistle on the Reagan administration and virtually all the reviews and chatter focus not on the moral flounderings of the administration but on whether Stockman was a rat for playing Brutus. If someone is in trouble, the discussion no longer centers on what he's done wrong, but on whether he can get out of it. What Nixon did wrong, it seems, is not to mastermind an entire system of deception but rather, simply, to get caught.

"We are living in a society of confused values, where people have lost a sense of confidence about right and wrong," Church adds. "When materialistic values become dominant, our heroes become superstars who value notoriety regardless of how they get it. People like John Hinckley and John DeLorean have been drawn like moths to the flame of notoriety. Even if they're immolated in the flame, they have their moment in the sun. There is a fascination with evil and abject behavior that is usually checked by society's strong condemnation of it. But that's not what is happening now."

What's happening is a rush for riches. David Ewing, head of a research project at Harvard Business School, finds that students "tend to get more involved in numbers and how to shift marketing share than in, say, the issue of duplicitous advertising. Everything has been so affluent lately that the temptation is for everyone to get on the bandwagon."

Professor Richard Eells of Columbia University's Graduate School of Business measures the decline in ethics by a different touchstone—that of the growing classification of information in the national interest. "The need to protect has overridden the need to take responsibility. Today, there are vast numbers of incompetent people who need protection, and thus far more classification, with the result of far less free exchange of information than ever before," he says. "This is a much more serious index of low ethics than insider trading."

Rabbi Seymour Siegel of the Jewish Theological Seminary thinks that people are "committing these infractions more obviously, and without shame. In times past, getting caught in a moral misdeed was an embarrassment. But now, because of the uncertainty about what is right and wrong and such influences as morning TV, where people confess to adultery, the scarlet letter doesn't have the scar it used to. If people are caught, their offenses are sloughed off as if they were not so bad anyway."

City Councilwoman Ruth Messinger argues that "greed has become accepted as a totally legitimate force, and people go into enterprises for what they can get out of them. There's whitewashing everywhere. Right after the Chernobyl incident, waves of experts announced that nothing like that could happen here. But then, lo and behold, someone discovers a reactor in Hanford, Washington, constructed dangerously like the Russian one. There's a generally lowered acceptance level too. Several people in [the Koch] administration were astounded that Lawrence Kieves [formerly the head of the City Office of Business Development] lost his job because he used his post to help a company [Enzo Biochem] in which he owned stock. They find his being fired excessive.

"I worry that people will take all the examples of unethical behavior as evidence that they should be unethical. 'See, I always knew everyone was doing it,' they'll say to themselves."

Many people worry about the effects of lowered ethical standards on the emerging generation. There's "a disillusionment and a timidity among young people to get involved," says the Reverend Joseph O'Hare, president of Fordham University.

Some of those symptoms are showing up in the interns of New York City's Urban Fellows program—a group that's under-going a sort of baptism by scandal. One intern told a *Time* reporter that she now believes that corruption is ubiquitous. Another fretted that believing in the public trust makes her sound ridiculously idealistic. Others chalked up the malfeasance to lowered expectations after Vietnam and Watergate. Another wondered why he didn't feel outrage.

There is no simple, tidy explanation for why things have gone awry. Rather, it seems that ethics have become a victim of changing times. "Ethics have always been an 'ought'—the goals of life we set, the ideals that we need," says Rabbi Balfour Brickner of Stephen Wise Free Synagogue. "But they're not really teachable. One has to absorb ethics through role models, and the traditional role models have failed us. Nuclear families have broken up, so the teaching of ethics has been squeezed out. The morally rectitudinous in high places have fallen down on the job. Role models have stopped role-modeling. And values are different today. We need new role models to do what presidents and fathers and mothers used to do—and what society by its own restricted nature did. If you traveled only 50 miles in your lifetime, you had a sense of community where moral values were laid down firmly. But in an anonymous urban environment, the burden of what you do when you know you won't get caught is heavy. It is what individuals do alone when no one is looking and when they know they won't get caught that makes the difference between a civilization and a jungle."

GARY EDWARDS, DIRECTOR OF THE WASHINGTON-based Ethics Resource Center, grew up in a contained universe. "My aunts, uncles, cousins were in the neighborhood. Our family—Mom stayed home while Dad worked—went to church regularly. And we used the *McGuffey Eclectic Reader*, the textbook that so consciously taught values and character. Now all those traditional ways of mediating values through the generations have weakened," he says.

Far from being contained, the universe of today's typical child has expanded—and splintered. Broken homes are common, and the influence of the church has declined. For the last twenty years, many schools have tried self-consciously not to teach values but to remain value-neutral. The trend toward mega-corporations in the business world has aggravated the problem. "All the mergers and acquisitions weaken the internal culture and organizational values," says Edwards. "People will know what the boss expects in a small firm but not in a massive one. And the current trend of management by objective seems to nurture ethical dilemmas. Workers are often set adrift without a moral compass."

Charles Ansell, a California psychologist, blames this lack of direction largely on the impersonal workplace. "I'd bet these moral psychopaths wouldn't be cruel to a pet and wouldn't cheat a person they saw face-to-face," he says. "The further we are from the product we make, the less responsible we feel for it. People who work with paper and money are less responsible. We don't owe paper or computers any allegiance."

Some think the problem begins at the top of the government. Robert Figlio, an associate professor at Wharton, thinks the "implied sanctioning of hypocrisy causes a disjunction between people's values and their behavior today. Our president has set this tone, appealing to the basic values of the American society—honesty, truthfulness, hard work—but his administration really just gives lip service to that. Almost 50 appointees have resigned because of allegations of gross misconduct."

New York *Times* columnist William Safire argues that if you're a crony of the president, almost any ethical lapse will be forgiven. He cites the secret recording of phone conversations by Charles Wick, head of the U.S. Information Agency, the nest-feathering by Michael Deaver, and the meeting with Qaddafi by Vatican envoy William Wilson.

Figlio complains that the double standard is apparent in the justice system. "Companies are not prosecuted for major wrongdoing; their wrists are simply slapped. Let a street criminal apologize and vow not to commit his crime again, and he would not get off so well."

Society deals more harshly with people who commit crimes against people than with those who commit crimes of manipulation. The public, however, generally considers such things as price-fixing and environmental pollution to be almost as bad as most kinds of violence, Figlio claims, citing a survey Wharton ran with the Census and the Bureau of Justice Statistics. But the survey also showed that high-income people tend to forgive such crimes as tax evasion and check forgery, while lower-income people are far tougher on such hidden-victim crimes. "Higher-income people consider drug smuggling a serious offense, but not the use of marijuana and cocaine. For them, the dealing is serious business, the possessing not," says Figlio. "People espouse a system that lowers the penal value of crimes they'd most likely be involved in—in short, rationalizing their behavior."

THOUGH, ACCORDING TO A 1983 GALLUP POLL, MOST Americans believe that at least half of the executives of big companies cheat on their taxes and pad their expense accounts, the poll found that business executives actually apply stricter standards to ethical issues than do average citizens.

In that Gallup poll, 95 percent of the executives surveyed called it wrong to "forget" $2,500 in interest income when filing one's tax return; only 75 percent of the general population felt the same way. The executives were also less inclined to condone wrongdoing under mitigating circumstances: Half those polled would dismiss an able employee who falsely claimed to have a college degree, while the public overwhelmingly would overlook the lie (affording, perhaps, some slight solace to Victor Botnick).

Older, less educated, and nonurban people tended to have stricter views on ethical issues than did younger, educated citizens from larger cities. Oddly, regular churchgoing made little difference, but just claiming a religious affiliation seemed to make for stricter ethical codes.

A 1983 American Management Association survey found that while most managers reported that their organizations were highly ethical, middle- and supervisory-level managers were twice as likely to say that this was not so. The middle managers were also much more likely to feel that they had to

# IN SIX YEARS, AN ETHICS CLASS AT HARVARD'S BUSINESS SCHOOL HAS GONE FROM 25 STUDENTS TO 160.

compromise their personal principles to conform to the organization's expectations.

Indeed, most unethical corporate behavior occurs among managers, supervisors, or project directors promoted on the basis of their results, says John R. Phillips, co-director of the Los Angeles-based Center for Law in the Public Interest. Un-realistically high performance goals may tempt managers to cheat in order to meet them. "Many mid-level employees ration-alize dishonest or illegal behavior by seeing themselves as loyal corporate soldiers. They fear being branded a troublemaker or fired if they fail to carry out orders." Cheating is an intrinsic part of the work environment in many organizations, he says.

Robert Jackall, an associate professor of sociology at Williams College, examined organizations to determine what shapes moral consciousness. He discovered the "bureaucratic ethic," a way of life at war with the Protestant ethic. The idea that hard work builds character carries less conviction than before, because our society has "little patience with those who make a habit of finishing out of the money. In the end, it is success that matters, that legitimates striving, and that makes work worthwhile," he wrote in the *Harvard Business Review*. He added that bureaucra-cies break apart older connections between the meaning of work and salvation and erode all standards of morality except their own.

"In this sense, bureaucracies may be thought of as vast sys-tems of organized irresponsibility," Jackall wrote. It's a pro-foundly ambiguous world, "because what matters . . . is not what a person is, but how closely his many personae mesh with the organizational ideal; not his willingness to stand by his ac-tions but his agility in avoiding blame; not what he believes or says, but how well he has mastered the ideologies that serve his corporation; not what he stands for, but whom he stands with in the labyrinths of his organization."

Clearly, corporations are aware of the potential price of un-ethical behavior. White-collar crime is estimated to cost business up to $200 billion annually, says Michael Hoffman, director of the Center for Business Ethics at Bentley College, in Waltham, Massachusetts. Fines and penalties run into the millions; result-ing government regulations, even now, cost business over $100 billion annually in compliance expenses; the damage to a firm's public image from a serious ethics violation has its own econom-ic ramification.

Though E.F. Hutton says it did not suffer any serious erosion of business following its guilty plea last year to 2,000 counts of mail and wire fraud, "we know that it is good business to be ethical," says Jay Partin, a senior vice-president at Hutton. That realization may have struck corporate America in part because of the success of Asian companies. "Some enterprises are be-having more and more morally, emulating the Japanese and be-ing, well, more Buddhist than Christian," says Robert G. Cox, chairman of the PA Executive Search Group. "The Peters and Waterman book [*In Search of Excellence*] has become the sym-bol of this ethics revolution the way Betty Friedan's book [*The Feminine Mystique*] became the flag of feminism."

S IGNS OF A NEW AWARENESS ABOUND. THE BUDGET doubled this year at the Ethics Resource Center, a nonprofit institution that was founded in 1977 in the aftermath of revelations about Watergate and about American companies making illegal political contributions to win overseas contracts. Publications with such titles as the *Journal of Business Ethics* and the

*Business and Professional Ethics Journal* have come out. And ethics courses have become a growth industry.

Students at the University of Washington in Seattle have studied corporate whistle-blowers and the sexual harassment of workers. Students of ethics at Yale have studied whether Citicorp evaded taxes in Europe by switching funds between countries—an issue raised and later dropped by the Securities and Exchange Commission. And classes at the Illinois Institute of Technology have considered the implications of the Manville Corporation's bankruptcy filing, which protected the company from asbestos-related lawsuits.

When Kenneth Goodpaster started teaching an ethics course at the Harvard Business School six years ago, 25 students chose the class; last year, 160 enrolled. His course covers personal dilemmas (such as when to blow the whistle), an organization's conscience (including the way minorities and employee health-and-safety measures are treated), and capitalism as an economic system (including such issues as doing business with countries that have troubled records on human rights).

Other classes use films to stimulate the ethical consciousness of students. In the golf scenario, for instance, the ethical dilemma becomes apparent when Frank, the supplier who came up with the scholarship, tells Dave he must cut back on the number of employees servicing Dave's account, and he asks Dave to look the other way. After all, that's one way Dave could thank Frank for the scholarship. "Couldn't you make it something easier, like another stroke on your handicap?" Dave implores.

In another vignette in the movie, a supplier to a man's company sends a bike to the man's home as a gift to his son. Should the man send it back? A consultant to a hotel chain gets a big discount on her home carpeting from a particular company, then finds that the yardage she bought for the hotel from that supplier is substandard. In a similar movie, produced by the Ethics Resource Center, a wife pleads with her husband to let her borrow an idea that had been presented to him in his capacity as project administrator for a large firm. "You're an entrepreneur, Bob," she argues. "If you're not giving [your employer] your heart and soul, you're still giving more than most people. You've got to look out for your own future. Can't you see that?"

All of the scenes are presented in benign, non-stressful circumstances, almost as if to lull the viewers into accepting the unethical. "And, generally, it works," says Wharton's Figlio. "The students have a problem figuring out what is proper and what's improper."

Hoffman's Center for Business Ethics surveyed the Fortune 1,000 in 1984 to gauge the extent to which ethics have become part of the business culture. "We concluded that there has been progress and more interest in ethics than ever before, but we're nowhere near home," says Hoffman. Almost 30 percent of the 1,000 companies responded to the questionnaire, and of that group, 80 percent claimed to be taking steps to institutionalize ethics. Ninety-three percent of them had adopted a written code of conduct. Today, 44 percent of the companies trying to institutionalize ethics have training programs for employees on dealing with ethical questions.

Still, Hoffman and other ethics experts are not optimistic about the effectiveness of these steps. "Companies feel that if they have a code, they've dispensed with the problem," says Hoffman. "This is very naïve. These codes need some policing

# A CORPORATE CODE OF ETHICS LACKS EFFECTIVENESS IF IT'S SIMPLY HANDED DOWN, SAYS ONE EXPERT.

mechanism to give them teeth, but only 18 percent of those making changes have an ethics committee, only 8 percent have ombudsmen to handle ethical complaints or adjudicate potential violations, and only three respondents have a judiciary board to listen to alleged violations and recommend solutions. And bills of rights for employees are virtually nonexistent."

What's more, about half of the companies with management-training programs in ethics focus exclusively on higher-level managers—not the lower-level managers, who often feel the most intense pressure to compromise their integrity. "A corporate code of ethics lacks overall effectiveness if it is simply handed down and run from on high, so to speak," says Hoffman. "A code stuck on a bulletin board in a workplace is meaningless gibberish.

"Frankly, we don't know if teaching ethics or institutionalizing it in corporations is working, but we do know it's really the only chance to realign our values ourselves," Hoffman adds. "The alternative is stricter government regulation. If America doesn't self-regulate, Uncle Sam will ultimately do it for us."

Hoffman is echoed by George Weissman, chairman of the executive committee of Philip Morris and chairman of Lincoln Center. "Lack of corporate responsibility often leads to impositions by the community of onerous legislation and restrictions, many of which would not have arisen if managements had not abused the power given to them in the first place," he claims. The antitrust movement in this country was a reaction to the abuses of monopolistic powers by oil and railroad barons at the turn of the century. The Environmental Protection Agency arose "because of horror stories, which we still read about daily. But America is a self-corrector," Weissman observes. "We go off course occasionally and in the next election throw the rascals out. We zigzag down the economic channels and somehow manage to find the center."

Weissman points out that there's nothing new about arguing over ethics. Two thousand years ago, Cicero posed a question about the conduct of an Alexandrian trader who'd arrived in Rhodes during a famine with a ship laden with corn. Should the trader tell merchants that other vessels were on their way—or say nothing, and let them bid up the price of his corn? Cicero declared that a businessman's responsibility to the community of starving people outweighed his responsibility to make a profit.

Some modern critics think that American business suffers from the problem that the Greek historian Polybius attributed to Carthage, where, he wrote, "nothing that results in profit is regarded as disgraceful." Most people, however, think the pendulum will swing back. "Inherent decency will reassert itself as people get fed up with public displays of immorality," says Rabbi Siegel.

THAT MAY ALREADY BE HAPPENING. DESPITE HIS friendship with the American government, deposed Philippine president Ferdinand Marcos is facing such widespread outrage over his alleged abuses that there's considerable question whether he'll be able to hold onto his fortune. Good samaritans like Robert Hayes, who heads the Coalition for the Homeless, are at last being recognized and honored for their work. Americans are examining the social policies of certain companies, and some people and institutions are trying to invest "ethically," taking company policies into consideration before buying stock. The Council on Economics Priorities found that the total funds that had been invested on the basis of ethical considerations amounted to $40 billion by 1984, $100 billion by 1985, and $220 billion by its May 1986 survey. And, after years of battling the authorities, Roy Cohn has been disbarred in New York State for ethics violations.

Some people suspect that the reaction to today's immorality will itself be exaggerated. "I expect we'll see censorship before we see a lessening of obscenity," predicts Siegel. "We've already seen the emergence of the extremist religious right as a reaction against the erosion of all moral standards and a narcissistic society not bound by commitment or obligation," adds O'Hare, Fordham's president.

What will it take to straighten things out? A grass-roots movement, says Hoffman. "People feel an impotence, but at the same time a moral outrage because they don't know what to do about it. The press wouldn't be publicizing the Bhopal tragedy if it didn't think the public was receiving that with some outrage. I think a lot more people were horrified that Nixon's been allowed to come back into the limelight than applauded it." But CUNY's Professor Bensman thinks it may take "a depression or something that produces a genuine epic of service before things get better."

Others think that time itself will change the mood. "We go through rhythms in our society where our sense of commitment to public purpose and private interest alternates," says Arthur Schlesinger Jr. "There will be a revulsion against all this crookedness and scramble for the fast buck as, after a time, people realize there's something more to life. We've had leaders like Roosevelt, F.D.R., and Kennedy, when people have gotten fed up with such selfishness, and another such period is on the horizon. We're just in another cycle of American history—perhaps the late autumn of this down cycle."

# The Mountain People

## Colin M. Turnbull

*Anthropologist Colin M. Turnbull, author of* The Forest People *and* The Lonely Africans, *went to study the Ik of Uganda, who he believed were still primarily hunters, in order to compare them with other hunting-and-gathering societies he had studied in totally different environments. He was surprised to discover that they were no longer hunters but primarily farmers, well on their way to starvation and something worse in a drought-stricken land.*

In what follows, there will be much to shock, and the reader will be tempted to say, "how primitive, how savage, how disgusting," and, above all, "how inhuman." The first judgments are typical of the kind of ethno- and egocentricism from which we can never quite escape. But "how inhuman" is of a different order and supposes that there are certain values inherent in humanity itself, from which the people described here seem to depart in a most drastic manner. In living the experience, however, and perhaps in reading it, one finds that it is oneself one is looking at and questioning; it is a voyage in quest of the basic human and a discovery of his potential for inhumanity, a potential that lies within us all.

Just before World War II the Ik tribe had been encouraged to settle in northern Uganda, in the mountainous northeast corner bordering on Kenya to the east and Sudan to the north.

Until then they had roamed in nomadic bands, as hunters and gatherers, through a vast region in all three countries. The Kidepo Valley below Mount Morungole was their major hunting territory. After they were confined to a part of their former area, Kidepo was made a national park and they were forbidden to hunt or gather there.

The concept of family in a nomadic society is a broad one; what really counts most in everyday life is community of residence, and those who live close to each other are likely to see each other as effectively related, whether there is any kinship bond or not. Full brothers, on the other hand, who live in different parts of the camp may have little concern for each other.

It is not possible, then, to think of the family as a simple, basic unit. A child is brought up to regard any adult living in the same camp as a parent, and age-mate as a brother or sister. The Ik had this essentially social attitude toward kinship, and it readily

lent itself to the rapid and disastrous changes that took place following the restriction of their movement and hunting activities. The family simply ceased to exist.

It is a mistake to think of small-scale societies as "primitive" or "simple." Hunters and gatherers, most of all, appear simple and straightforward in terms of their social organization, yet that is far from true. If we can learn about the nature of society from a study of small-scale societies, we can also learn about human relationships. The smaller the society, the less emphasis there is on the formal system and the more there is on interpersonal and intergroup relations. Security is seen in terms of these relationships, and so is survival. The result, which appears so deceptively simple, is that hunters frequently display those characteristics that we find so admirable in man: kindness, generosity, consideration, affection, honesty, hospitality, compassion, charity. For them, in their tiny, close-knit society, these are necessities for survival. In our society anyone possessing even half these qualities would find it hard to survive, yet we think these virtues are inherent in man. I took it for granted that the Ik would possess these same qualities. But they were as unfriendly, uncharitable, inhospitable and generally mean as any people can be. For those positive qualities we value so highly are no longer functional for them; even more than in our own society they spell ruin and disaster. It seems that, far from being basic human qualities, they are luxuries we can afford in times of plenty or are mere mechanisms for survival and security. Given the situation in which the Ik found

themselves, man has no time for such luxuries, and a much more basic man appears, using more basic survival tactics.

*Turnbull had to wait in Kaabong, a remote administration outpost, for permission from the Uganda government to continue to Pirre, the Ik water hole and police post. While there he began to learn the Ik language and became used to their constant demands for food and tobacco. An official in Kaabong gave him, as a "gift," 20 Ik workers to build a house and a road up to it. When they arrived at Pirre, however, wages for the workers were negotiated by wily Atum, "the senior of all the Ik on Morungole."*

The police seemed as glad to see me as I was to see them. They hungrily asked for news of Kaabong, as though it were the hub of the universe. They had a borehole and pump for water, to which they said I was welcome, since the water holes used by the Ik were not fit for drinking or even for washing. The police were not able to tell me much about the Ik, because every time they went to visit an Ik village, there was nobody there. Only in times of real hunger did they see much of the Ik, and then only enough to know that they were hungry.

The next morning I rose early, but even though it was barely daylight, by the time I had washed and dressed, the Ik were already outside. They were sitting silently, staring at the Land Rover. As impassive as they seemed, there was an air of expectancy, and I was reminded that these

were, after all, hunters, and the likelihood was that I was their morning's prey. So I left the Land Rover curtains closed and as silently as possible prepared a frugal breakfast.

Atum was waiting for me. He said that he had told all the Ik that Iciebam [friend of the Ik] had arrived to live with them and that I had given the workers a "holiday" so they could greet me. They were waiting in the villages. They were very hungry, he added, and many were dying. That was probably one of the few true statements he ever made, and I never even considered believing it.

There were seven villages in all. Village Number One was built on a steep slope, and even the houses tilted at a crazy angle. Atum rapped on the outer stockade with his cane and shouted a greeting, but there was no response. This was Giriko's village, he said, and he was one of my workers.

"But I thought you told them to go back to their villages," I said.

"Yes, but you gave them a holiday, so they are probably in their fields," answered Atum, looking me straight in the eye.

At Village Number Two there was indisputably someone inside, for I could hear loud singing. The singing stopped, a pair of hands gripped the stockade and a craggy head rose into view, giving me an undeniably welcoming smile. This was Lokelea. When I asked him what he had been singing about, he answered, "Because I'm hungry."

Village Number Three, the smallest of all, was empty. Village Number Four had only 8 huts, as

against the 12 or so in Lokelea's village and the 18 in Giriko's. The outer stockade was broken in one section, and we walked right in. We ducked through a low opening and entered a compound in which a woman was making pottery. She kept on at her work but gave us a cheery welcome and laughed her head off when I tried to speak in Icietot. She willingly showed me details of her work and did not seem unduly surprised at my interest. She said that everyone else had left for the fields except old Nangoli, who, on hearing her name mentioned, appeared at a hole in the stockade shutting off the next compound. Nangoli mumbled toothlessly at Losike, who told Atum to pour her some water.

As we climbed up to his own village, Number Five, Atum said that Losike never gave anything away. Later I remembered that gift of water to Nangoli. At the time I did not stop to think that in this country a gift of water could be a gift of life.

Atum's village had nearly 50 houses, each within its compound within the stout outer stockade. Atum did not invite me in.

A hundred yards away stood Village Number Six. Kauar, one of the workers, was sitting on a rocky slab just outside the village. He had a smile like Losike's, open and warm, and he said he had been waiting for me all morning. He offered us water and showed me his own small compound and that of his mother.

Coming up from Village Number Seven, at quite a respectable speed, was a blind man. This was Logwara, emaciated but alive and remarkably active. He had heard us and had come to greet me, he said, but he added the inevitable demand for tobacco in the same breath. We sat down in the open sunlight. For a brief moment I felt at peace.

After a short time Atum said we should start back and called over his shoulder to his village. A muffled sound came from within, and he said, "That's my wife, she is very sick—and hungry." I offered to go and see her, but he shook his head. Back at the Land Rover I gave Atum some food and some aspirin, not knowing what else to give him to help his wife.

I was awakened well before dawn by the lowing of cattle. I made an extra pot of tea and let Atum distribute it, and then we divided the workers into two teams. Kauar was to head the team building the house, and Lokelatom, Losike's husband, was to take charge of the road workers.

While the Ik were working, their heads kept turning as though they were expecting something to happen. Every now and again one would stand up and peer into the distance and then take off into the bush for an hour or so. On one such occasion, after the person had been gone two hours, the others started drifting off. By then I knew them better; I looked for a wisp of smoke and followed it to where the road team was cooking a goat. Smoke was a giveaway, though, so they economized on cooking and ate most food nearly raw. It is a curious hangover from what must once have been a moral code that Ik will offer food if surprised in the act of eating, though they now go to enormous pains not to be so surprised.

I was always up before dawn, but by the time I got up to the villages they were always deserted. One morning I followed the little *oror* [gulley] up from *oror a pirre'i* [Ravine of Pirre] while it was still quite dark, and I met Lomeja on his way down. He took me on my first illicit hunt in Kidepo. He told me that if he got anything he would share it with me and with anyone else who managed to join us but that he certainly would not take

anything back to his family. "Each one of them is out seeing what he can get for himself, and do you think they will bring any back for me?"

Lomeja was one of the very few Ik who seemed glad to volunteer information. Unlike many of the others, he did not get up and leave as I approached. Apart from him, I spent most of my time, those days, with Losike, the potter. She told me that Nangoli, the old lady in the adjoining compound, and her husband, Amuarkuar, were rather peculiar.

They helped each other get food and water, and they brought it back to their compound to eat together.

I still do not know how much real hunger there was at that time, for most of the younger people seemed fairly well fed, and the few skinny old people seemed healthy and active. But my laboriously extracted genealogies showed that there were quite a number of old people still alive and allegedly in these villages, though they were never to be seen. Then Atum's wife died.

Atum told me nothing about it but kept up his demands for food and medicine. After a while the beady-eyed Lomongin told me that Atum was selling the medicine I was giving him for his wife. I was not unduly surprised and merely remarked that

that was too bad for his wife. "Oh no," said Lomongin, "she has been dead for weeks."

It must have been then that I began to notice other things that I suppose I had chosen to ignore before. Only a very few of the Ik helped me with the language. Others would understand when it suited them and would pretend they did not understand when they did not want to listen. I began to be forced into a similar isolationist attitude myself, and although I cannot say I enjoyed it, it did make life much easier. I even began to enjoy, in a peculiar way, the company of the silent Ik. And the more I accepted it, the less often people got up and left as I approached. On one occasion I sat on the *di* [sitting place] by Atum's rain tree for three days with a group of Ik, and for three days not one word was exchanged.

The work teams were more lively, but only while working. Kauar always played and joked with the children when they came back from foraging. He used to volunteer to make the two-day walk into Kaabong and the even more tiring two-day climb back to get mail for me or to buy a few things for others. He always asked if he had made the trip more quickly than the last time.

Then one day Kauar went to Kaabong and did not come back. He was found on the last peak of the trail, cold and dead. Those who found him took the things he had been carrying and pushed his body into the bush. I still see his open, laughing face, see him giving precious tidbits to the children, comforting some child who was crying, and watching me read the letters he carried so lovingly for me. And I still think of him probably running up that viciously steep mountainside so he could break his time record and falling dead in his pathetic prime because he was starving.

Once I settled down into my new home, I was able to work more effectively. Having recovered at least some of my anthropological detachment, when I heard the telltale rustling of someone at my stockade, I merely threw a stone. If when out walking I stumbled during a difficult descent and the Ik shrieked with laughter, I no longer even noticed it.

Anyone falling down was good for a laugh, but I never saw anyone actually trip anyone else. The adults were content to let things happen and then enjoy them; it was probably conservation of energy. The children, however, sought their pleasures with vigor. The best game of all, at this time, was teasing poor little Adupa. She was not so little—in fact she should have been an adult, for she was nearly 13 years old—but Adupa was a little mad. Or you might say she was the only sane one, depending on your point of view. Adupa did not jump on other people's play houses, and she lavished enormous care on hers and would curl up inside it. That made it all the more jump-on-able. The other children beat her viciously.

Children are not allowed to sleep in the house after they are "put out," which is at about three years old, four at the latest. From then on they sleep in the open courtyard, taking what shelter they can against the stockade. They may ask for permission to sit in the doorway of their parents' house but may not lie down or sleep there. "The same thing applies to old people," said Atum, "if they can't build a house of their own and, of course, *if* their children let them stay in their compounds."

I saw a few old people, most of whom had taken over abandoned huts. For the first time I realized that there really was starvation and saw why I had never known it before: it was confined to the aged. Down in Giriko's village the old ritual priest, Lolim, confidentially told me that he was sheltering an old man who had been refused shelter by his son. But Lolim did not have enough food for himself, let alone his guest; could I . . . I liked old Lolim, so, not believing that Lolim had a visitor at all, I brought him a double ration that evening. There was a rustling in the back of the hut, and Lolim helped ancient Lomeraniang to the entrance. They shook with delight at the sight of the food.

When the two old men had finished eating, I left; I found a hungry-looking and disapproving little crowd clustered outside. They muttered to each other about wasting food. From then on I brought food daily, but in a very short time Lomeraniang was dead, and his son refused to come down from the village above to bury him. Lolim scratched a hole and covered the body with a pile of stones he carried himself, one by one.

Hunger was indeed more severe than I knew, and, after the old people, the children were the next to go. It was all quite impersonal—even to me, in most cases, since I had been immunized by the Ik themselves against sorrow on their behalf. But Adupa was an exception. Her madness was such that she did not know just how vicious humans could be. Even worse, she thought that parents were for loving, for giving as well as receiving. Her parents were not given to fantasies. When she came for shelter, they drove her out; and when she came because she was hungry, they laughed that Icien laugh, as if she had made them happy.

Adupa's reactions became slower and slower. When she managed to find food—fruit peels, skins, bits of bone, half-eaten berries—she held it in her hand and looked at it with wonder and delight. Her playmates caught on quickly; they put tidbits in her way and watched her simple drawn little face wrinkle in a smile. Then as she raised her hand to her mouth, they set on her with cries of excitement, fun and laughter, beating her savagely over the head. But that is

not how she died. I took to feeding her, which is probably the cruelest thing I could have done, a gross selfishness of my part to try to salve my own rapidly disappearing conscience. I had to protect her, physically, as I fed her. But the others would beat her anyway, and Adupa cried, not because of the pain in her body but because of the pain she felt at the great, vast, empty wasteland where love should have been.

It was *that* that killed her. She demanded that her parents love her. Finally they took her in, and Adupa was happy and stopped crying. She stopped crying forever because her parents went away and closed the door tight behind them, so tight that weak little Adupa could never have moved it.

The Ik seem to tell us that the family is not such a fundamental unit as we usually suppose, that it is not essential to social life. In the crisis of survival facing the Ik, the family was one of the first institutions to go, and the Ik as a society have survived.

The other quality of life that we hold to be necessary for survival—love—the Ik dismiss as idiotic and highly dangerous. But we need to see more of the Ik before their absolute lovelessness becomes truly apparent.

In this curious society there is one common value to which all Ik hold tenaciously. It is *ngag,* "food." That is the one standard by which they measure right and wrong, goodness and badness. The very word for "good" is defined in terms of food. "Goodness" is "the possession of food," or the "*individual* possession of food." If you try to discover their concept of a "good man," you get the truly Icien answer: one who has a full stomach.

We should not be surprised, then, when the mother throws her child out at three years old. At that age a series of *rites de passage* begins. In this environment a child has no chance of survival on his own until he is about 13, so children form age bands. The junior band consists of children between three and seven, the senior of eight- to twelve-year-olds. Within the band each child seeks another close to him in age for defense against the older children. These friendships are temporary, however, and inevitably there comes a time when each turns on the one that up to then had been the closest to him; that is the *rite de passage,* the destruction of that fragile bond called friendship. When this has happened three or four times, the child is ready for the world.

The weakest are soon thinned out, and the strongest survive to achieve leadership of the band. Such a leader is eventually driven out, turned against by his fellow band members. Then the process starts all over again; he joins the senior age band as its most junior member.

The final *rite de passage* is into adulthood, at the age of 12 or 13. By then the candidate has learned the wisdom of acting on his own, for his own good, while acknowledging that on occasion it is profitable to associate temporarily with others.

One year in four the Ik can count on a complete drought. About this time it began to be apparent that there were going to be two consecutive years of drought and famine. Men as well as women took to gathering what wild fruits and berries they could find, digging up roots, cutting grass that was going to seed, threshing and eating the seed.

Old Nangoli went to the other side of Kidepo, where food and water were more plentiful. But she had to leave her husband, Amuarkuar, behind. One day he appeared at my *odok* and asked for water. I gave him some and was going to get him food when Atum came storming over and argued with me about wasting water. In the midst of the dispute Amuarkuar quietly left. He wandered over to a rocky outcrop and lay down there to rest. Nearby was a small bundle of grass that evidently he had cut and had been dragging painfully to the ruins of his village to make a rough shelter. The grass was his supreme effort to keep a home going until Nangoli returned. When I went over to him, he looked up and smiled and said that my water tasted good. He lay back and went to sleep with a smile on his face. That is how Amuarkuar died, happily.

There are measures that can be taken for survival involving the classical institutions of gift and sacrifice. These are weapons, sharp and aggressive. The object is to build up a series of obligations so that in times of crisis you have a number of debts you can recall; with luck one of them may be repaid. To this end, in the circumstances of Ik life, considerable sacrifice would be justified, so you have the odd phenomenon of these otherwise singularly self-interested people going out of their way to "help" each other. Their help may very well be resented in the extreme, but is done in such a way that it cannot be refused, for it has already been given. Someone may hoe another's field in his absence or rebuild his stockade or join in the building of a house.

The danger in this system was that the debtor might not be around when collection was called for and, by the same token, neither might the creditor. The future was too uncertain for this to be anything but one additional survival measure, though some developed it to a fine technique.

There seemed to be increasingly little among the Ik that could by any stretch of the imagination be called social life, let alone social organization. The family does not hold itself together; economic interest is centered on as many stomachs as there are people; and cooperation is merely a device for furthering an interest that is consciously selfish. We often do the same thing in our so-called "altruistic" practices, but we tell ourselves it is for the good of others. The Ik have dispensed with the myth of altruism. Though they have no centralized leadership or means of physical coercion, they do hold together with remarkable tenacity.

In our world, where the family has also lost much of its value as a social unit and where religious belief no longer binds us into communities, we maintain order only through coercive power that is ready to uphold a rigid law and through an equally rigid penal system. The Ik, however, have learned to do without coercion, either

spiritual or physical. It seems that they have come to a recognition of what they accept as man's basic selfishness, of his natural determination to survive as an individual before all else. This they consider to be man's basic right, and they allow others to pursue that right without recrimination.

In large-scale societies such as our own, where members are individual beings rather than social beings, we rely on law for order. The absence of both a common law and a common belief would surely result in lack of any community of behavior; yet Ik society is not anarchical. One might well expect religion, then, to play a powerful role in Icien life, providing a source of unity.

The Ik, as may be expected, do not run true to form. When I arrived, there were still three ritual priests alive. From them and from the few other old people, I learned something of the Ik's belief and practice as they had been before their world was so terribly changed. There had been a powerful unity of belief in Didigwari—a sky god—and a body of ritual practice reinforcing secular behavior that was truly social.

Didigwari himself is too remote to be of much practical significance to the Ik. He created them and abandoned them and retreated into his domain somewhere in the sky. He never came down to earth, but the *abang* [ancestors] have all known life on earth; it is only against them that one can sin and only to them that one can turn for help, through the ritual priest.

While Morungole has no legends attached to it by the Ik, it nonetheless figures in their ideology and is in some ways regarded by them as sacred. I had noticed this by the almost reverential way in which they looked at it—none of the shrewd cunning and cold appraisal with which they regarded the rest of the world. When they talked about it, there was a different quality to their voices. They seemed incapable of talking about Morungole in any other way, which is probably why they talked about it so very seldom. Even that weasel Lomongin became gentle the only time he talked about it to me. He said, "If Atum and I were there, we would not argue. It is a good place." I asked if he meant that it was full of food. He said yes. "Then why do Ik never go there?" "They do go there." "But if hunting is good there, why not live there?" "We don't hunt there, we just go there." "Why?" "I told you, it is a good place." If I did not understand him, that was my fault; for once he was doing his best to communicate something to me. With others it was the same. All agreed that it was "a good place." One added, "That is the Place of God."

Lolim, the oldest and greatest of the ritual priests, was also the last. He was not much in demand any longer, but he was still held in awe, which means kept at a distance. Whenever he approached a *di,* people cleared a space for him, as far away from themselves as possible. The Ik rarely called on his services, for they had little to pay him with, and he had equally little to offer them. The main things they did try to get out of him were certain forms of medicine, both herbal and magical.

Lolim said that he had inherited his power from his father. His father had taught him well but could not give him the power to hear the *abang*—that had to come from the *abang* themselves. He had wanted his oldest son to inherit and had taught him everything he could. But his son, Longoli, was bad, and the *abang* refused to talk to him. They talked instead to his oldest daughter, bald Nangoli. But there soon came the time when all the Ik needed was food in their stomachs, and Lolim could not supply that. The time came when Lolim was too weak to go out and collect the medicines he needed. His children all refused to go except Nangoli, and then she was jailed for gathering in Kidepo Park.

Lolim became ill and had to be protected while eating the food I gave him. Then the children began openly ridiculing him and teasing him, dancing in front of him and kneeling down so that he would trip over them. His grandson used to creep up behind him and with a pair of hard sticks drum a lively tattoo on the old man's bald head.

I fed him whenever I could, but often he did not want more than a bite. Once I found him rolled up in his protective ball, crying. He had had nothing to eat for four days and no water for two. He had asked his children, who all told him not to come near them.

The next day I saw him leaving Atum's village, where his son Longoli lived. Longoli swore that he had been giving his father food and was looking after him. Lolim was not shuffling away; it was almost a run, the run of a drunken man, staggering from side to side. I called to him, but he made no reply, just a kind of long, continuous and horrible moan. He had been to Longoli to beg him to let him into his compound because he knew he was going to die in a few hours, Longoli calmly told me afterward. Obviously Longoli could not do a thing like that: a man of Lolim's importance would have called for an enormous funeral feast. So he refused. Lolim begged Longoli then to open up Nangoli's *asak* for him so that he could die in *her* compound. But Longoli drove him out, and he died alone.

Atum pulled some stones over the body where it had fallen into a kind of hollow. I saw that the body must have lain parallel with the *oror.* Atum answered without waiting for the question: "He was lying looking up at Mount Meraniang."

Insofar as ritual survived at all, it could hardly be said to be religious, for it did little or nothing to bind Icien society together. But the question still remained: Did this lack of social behavior and communal ritual or religious expression mean that there was no community of belief?

Belief may manifest itself, at either the individual or the communal level, in what we call morality, when we behave according to certain principles supported by our belief even when it seems against our personal interest. When we call ourselves moral, however, we tend to ignore that ultimately our morality benefits us even as individuals, insofar as we are social individuals and live in a society. In the absence of belief, law takes over and morality has little role. If there was such a thing as an Icien morality, I had not yet perceived it, though traces of a moral past remained. But it still remained a possibility, as did the existence of an unspoken, unmanifest belief that might yet reveal itself and provide a basis for the reintegration of society. I was somewhat encouraged in this hope by the unexpected flight of old Nangoli, widow of Amuarkuar.

When Nangoli returned and found her husband dead, she did an odd thing: she grieved. She tore down what was left of their home, uprooted the stockade, tore up whatever was growing in her little field. Then she fled with a few belongings.

Some weeks later I heard that she and her children had gone over to the Sudan and built a village there. This migration was so unusual that I decided to see whether this runaway village was different.

Lojieri led the way, and Atum came along. One long day's trek got us there. Lojieri pulled part of the brush fence aside, and we went in and wandered around. He and Atum looked inside all the huts, and Lojieri helped himself to tobacco from one and water from another. Surprises were coming thick and fast. That households should be left open and untended with such wealth inside . . . That there should have been such wealth, for as well as tobacco and jars of water there were baskets of food, and meat was drying on racks. There were half a dozen or so compounds, but they were separated from each other only by a short line of sticks and brush. It was a village, and these were homes, the first and last I was to see.

The dusk had already fallen, and Nangoli came in with her children and grandchildren. They had heard us and came in with warm welcomes. There was no hunger here, and in a very short time each kitchen hearth had a pot of food cooking. Then we sat around the central fire and talked until late, and it was another universe.

There was no talk of "how much better it is here than there"; talk revolved around what had happened on the hunt that day. Loron was lying on the ground in front of the fire as his mother made gentle fun of him. His wife, Kinimei, whom I had never seen even speak to him at Pirre, put a bowl of fresh-cooked berries and fruit in front of him. It was all like a nightmare rather than a fantasy, for it made the reality of Pirre seem all the more frightening.

The unpleasantness of returning was somewhat alleviated by Atum's suffering on the way up the stony trail. Several times he slipped, which made Lojieri and me laugh. It was a pleasure to move rapidly ahead and leave Atum gasping behind so that we could be sitting up on the *di* when he finally appeared and could laugh at his discomfort.

The days of drought wore on into weeks and months and, like everyone else, I became rather bored with sickness and death. I survived rather as did the young adults, by diligent attention to my own needs while ignoring those of others.

More and more it was only the young who could go far from the village as hunger became starvation. Famine relief had been initiated down at Kasile, and those fit enough to make the trip set off. When they came back, the contrast between them and the others was that between life and death. Villages were villages of the dead and dying, and there was little difference between the two. People crawled rather than walked. After a few feet some would lie down to rest, but they could not be sure of ever being able to sit up again, so they mostly stayed upright until they reached their destination. They were going nowhere, these semianimate bags of skin and bone; they just wanted to be with others, and they stopped whenever they met. Perhaps it was the most important demonstration of sociality I ever saw among the Ik. Once they met, they neither spoke nor did anything together.

Early one morning, before dawn, the village moved. In the midst of a hive of activity were the aged and crippled, soon to be abandoned, in danger of being trampled but seemingly unaware of it. Lolim's widow, Lo'ono, whom I had never seen before, also had been abandoned and had tried to make her way down the mountainside. But she was totally blind and had tripped and rolled to the bottom of the *oror a pirre'ï;* there she lay on her back, her legs and arms thrashing feebly, while a little crowd laughed.

At this time a colleague was with me. He kept the others away while I ran to get medicine and food and water, for Lo'ono was obviously near dead from hunger and thirst as well as from the fall. We treated her and fed her and asked her to come back with us. But she asked us to point her in the direction of her son's new village. I said I did not think she would get much of a welcome there, and she replied that she knew it but wanted to be near him when she died. So we gave her more food, put her stick in her hand and pointed her the right way. She suddenly cried. She was crying, she said, because we had reminded her that there had been a time when people had helped each other, when people had been kind and good. Still crying, she set off.

The Ik up to this point had been tolerant of my activities, but all this was too much. They said that what we were doing was wrong. Food and medicine were for the living, not the dead. I thought of Lo'ono. And I thought of other old people who had joined in the merriment when they had been teased or had a precious morsel of food taken from their mouths. They knew that it was silly of them to expect to go on living, and, having watched others, they knew that the spectacle really was quite funny. So they joined in the laughter. Perhaps if we had left Lo'ono, she would have died laughing. But we prolonged her misery for no more than a few brief days. Even worse, we reminded her of when things had been different, of days when children had cared for parents and parents for children. She was already dead, and we made her unhappy as well. At the time I was sure we were right, doing the only "human" thing. In a way we *were*—we were making life more comfortable for ourselves. But now I wonder if the Ik way was not right, if I too should not have laughed as Lo'ono flapped about, then left her to die.

Ngorok was a man at 12. Lomer, his older brother, at 15 was showing signs of strain; when he was carrying a load, his face took on a curious expression of pain that was no physical pain. Giriko, at 25 was 40, Atum at 40 was 65, and the very oldest, perhaps a bare 50, were centenarians. And I, at 40, was younger than any of them, for I still enjoyed life, which they had learned was not "adult" when they were 3. But they retained their will to survive and so offered grudging respect to those who had survived for long.

Even in the teasing of the old there was a glimmer of hope. It denoted a certain intimacy that did not exist between adjacent generations. This is quite common in small-scale societies. The very old and the very young look at each other as representing the future and the past. To the child, the aged represent a world that existed before their own birth and the unknown world to come.

And now that all the old are dead, what is left? Every Ik who is old today was thrown out at three and has survived, and in consequence has thrown his own children out and knows that they will not help him in his old age any more than he helped his parents. The system has turned one full cycle and is now self-perpetuating; it has eradicated what we know as "humanity" and has turned the world into a chilly void where man does not seem to care even for himself, but survives. Yet into this hideous world Nangoli and her family quietly returned because they could not bear to be alone.

For the moment abandoning the very old and the very young, the Ik as a whole must be searched for one last lingering trace of humanity. They appear to have disposed of virtually all the qualities that we normally think of as differentiating us from other primates, yet they survive without seeming to be greatly different from ourselves in terms of behavior.

Their behavior is more extreme, for we do not start throwing our children out until kindergarten. We have shifted responsibility from family to state, the Ik have shifted it to the individual.

It has been claimed that human beings are capable of love and, indeed, are dependent upon it for survival and sanity. The Ik offer us an opportunity for testing this cherished notion that love is essential to survival. If it is, the Ik should have it.

Love in human relationships implies mutuality, a willingness to sacrifice the self that springs from a consciousness of identity. This seems to bring us back to the Ik, for it implies that love is self-oriented, that even the supreme sacrifice of one's life is no more than selfishness, for the victim feels amply rewarded by the pleasure he feels in making the sacrifice. The Ik, however, do not value emotion above survival, and they are without love.

But I kept looking, for it was the one thing that could fill the void their survival tactics had created; and if love was not there in some form, it meant that for humanity love is not a necessity at all, but a luxury or an illusion. And if it was not among the Ik, it meant that mankind can lose it.

The only possibility for any discovery of love lay in the realm of interpersonal relationships. But they were, each one, simply alone, and seemingly content to be alone. It was this acceptance of individual isolation that made love almost impossible. Contact, when made, was usually for a specific practical purpose having to do with food and the filling of a stomach, a single stomach. Such contacts did not have anything like the permanence or duration required to develop a situation in which love was possible.

The isolation that made love impossible, however, was not completely proof against loneliness. I no longer noticed normal behavior, such as the way people ate, running as they gobbled, so as to have it all for themselves. But I did notice that when someone was making twine or straightening a spear shaft, the focus of attention for the spectators was not the person but the action. If they were caught watching by the one being watched and their eyes met, the reaction was a sharp retreat on both sides.

When the rains failed for the second year running, I knew that the Ik as a society were almost certainly finished and that the monster they had created in its place, that passionless, feelingless association of individuals, would spread like a fungus, contaminating all it touched. When I left, I too had been contaminated. I was not upset when I said good-bye to old Loiangorok. I told him I had left a sack of *posho* [ground corn meal] with the police for him, and I said I would send money for more when that ran out. He dragged himself slowly toward the *di* every day, and he always clutched a knife. When he got there, or as far as he could, he squatted down and whittled at some wood, thus proving that he was still alive and able to do things. The *posho* was enough to last him for months, but I felt no emotion when I estimated that he would last one month, even with the *posho* in the hands of the police. I underestimated his son, who within two days had persuaded the police that it would save a lot of bother if he looked after the *posho*. I heard later that Loiangorok died of starvation within two weeks.

So, I departed with a kind of forced gaiety, feeling that I should be glad to be gone but having forgotten how to be glad. I certainly was not thinking of returning within a year, but I did. The following spring I heard that rain had come at last and that the fields of the Ik had never looked so prosperous, nor the country so green and fertile. A few months away had refreshed me, and I wondered if my conclusions had not been excessively pessimistic. So, early that summer, I set off to be present for the first harvests in three years.

I was not surprised too much when two days after my arrival and installation at the police post I found Logwara, the blind man, lying on the roadside bleeding, while a hundred yards up other Ik were squabbling over the body of a hyena. Logwara had tried to get there ahead of the others to grab the meat and had been trampled on.

First I looked at the villages. The lush outer covering concealed an inner decay. All the villages were like this to some extent, except for Lokelea's. There the tomatoes and pumpkins were carefully pruned and cleaned, so that the fruits were larger and healthier. In what had been my own compound the shade trees had been cut down for firewood, and the lovely hanging nests of the weaver birds were gone.

The fields were even more desolate. Every field without exception had yielded in abundance, and it was a new sensation to have vision cut off by thick crops. But every crop was rotting from sheer neglect.

The Ik said that they had no need to bother guarding the fields. There was so much food they could never eat it all, so why not let the birds and baboons take some? The Ik had full bellies; they were good. The *di* at Atum's village was much the same as usual, people sitting or lying about. People were still stealing from each other's fields, and nobody thought of saving for the future.

It was obvious that nothing had really changed due to the sudden glut of food except that interpersonal relationships had deteriorated still further and that Icien individualism had heightened beyond what I thought even Ik to be capable of.

The Ik had faced a conscious choice between being humans and being parasites and had chosen the latter. When they saw their fields come alive, they were confronted with a problem. If they reaped the harvest, they would have to store grain for eating and planting, and every Ik knew that trying to store anything was a waste of time. Further, if they made their fields look too promising, the government would stop famine relief. So the Ik let their fields rot and continued to draw famine relief.

The Ik were not starving any longer; the old and infirm had all died the previous year, and the younger survivors were doing quite well. But the famine relief was administered in a way that was little short of criminal. As before, only the young and well were able to get down from Pirre to collect the relief; they were given relief for those who could not come and told to take it back. But they never did—they ate it themselves.

The facts are there, though those that can be read here form but a fraction of what one person was able to gather in under two years. There can be no mistaking the direction in which those facts point, and that is the most important thing of all, for it may affect the rest of mankind as it has affected the Ik. The Ik have "progressed," one might say, since the change that has come to them came with the advent of civilization to Africa. They have made of a world that was alive a world that is dead—a cold, dispassionate world that is without ugliness because it is without beauty, without hate because it is without love, and without any realization of truth even, because it simply is. And the symptoms of change in our own society indicate that we are heading in the same direction.

Those values we cherish so highly may indeed be basic to human society but not to humanity, and that means that the Ik show that society itself is not indispensable for man's survival and that man is capable of associating for purposes of survival without being social. The Ik have replaced human society with a mere survival system that does not take human emotion into account. As yet the system if imperfect, for although survival is assured, it is at a minimal level and there is still competition between individuals. With our intellectual sophistication and advanced technology we should be able to perfect the system and eliminate competition, guaranteeing survival for a given number of years for all, reducing the demands made upon us by a social system, abolishing desire and consequently that ever-present and vital gap between desire and achievement, treating us, in a word, as individuals with one basic individual right—the right to survive.

Such interaction as there is within this system is one of mutual exploitation. That is how it already is with the Ik. In our own world the mainstays of a society based on a truly social sense of mutuality are breaking down, indicating that perhaps society as we know it has outworn its usefulness and that by clinging to an outworn system we are bringing about our own destruction. Family, economy, government and religion, the basic categories of social activity and behavior, no longer create any sense of social unity involving a shared and mutual responsibility among all members of our society. At best they enable the individual to survive as an individual. It is the world of the individual, as is the world of the Ik.

The sorry state of society in the civilized world today is in large measure due to the fact that social change has not kept up with technological change. This mad, senseless, unthinking commitment to technological change that we call progress may be sufficient to exterminate the human race in a very short time even without the assistance of nuclear warfare. But since we have already become individualized and desocialized, we say that extermination will not come in our time, which shows about as much sense of family devotion as one might expect from the Ik.

Even supposing that we can avert nuclear holocaust or the almost universal famine that may be expected if population keeps expanding and pollution remains unchecked, what will be the cost if not the same already paid by the Ik? They too were driven by the need to survive, and they succeeded at the cost of their humanity. We are already beginning to pay the same price, but we not only still have the choice (though we may not have the will or courage to make it), we also have the intellectual and technological ability to avert an Icien end. Any change as radical as will be necessary is not likely to bring material benefits to the present generation, but only then will there be a future.

The Ik teach us that our much vaunted human values are not inherent in humanity at all but are associated only with a particular form of survival called society and that all, even society itself, are luxuries that can be dispensed with. That does not make them any less wonderful, and if man has any greatness, it is surely in his ability to maintain these values, even shortening an already pitifully short life rather than sacrifice his humanity. But that too involves choice, and the Ik teach us that man can lose the will to make it. That is the point at which there is an end to truth, to goodness and to beauty, an end to the struggle for their achievement, which gives life to the individual and strength and meaning to society. The Ik have relinquished all luxury in the name of individual survival, and they live on as a people without life, without passion, beyond humanity. We pursue those trivial, idiotic technological encumbrances, and all the time we are losing our potential for social rather than individual survival, for hating as well as loving, losing perhaps our last chance to enjoy life with all the passion that is our nature.

# Social Time: The Heartbeat of Culture

*TO UNDERSTAND A SOCIETY,
YOU MUST LEARN ITS SENSE OF TIME.*

**Robert Levine
with Ellen Wolff**

*Robert Levine is a professor of psychology at California State University at Fresno. Ellen Wolff is a freelance writer in Los Angeles.*

*"If a man does not keep pace with his companions, perhaps it is because he hears a different drummer."* This thought by Thoreau strikes a chord in so many people that it has become part of our language. We use the phrase "the beat of a different drummer" to explain any pace of life unlike our own. Such colorful vagueness reveals how informal our rules of time really are. The world over, children simply "pick up" their society's time concepts as they mature. No dictionary clearly defines the meaning of "early" or "late" for them or for strangers who stumble over the maddening incongruities between the time sense they bring with them and the one they face in a new land.

I learned this firsthand, a few years ago, and the resulting culture shock led me halfway around the world to find answers. It seemed clear that time "talks." But what is it telling us?

My journey started shortly after I accepted an appointment as visiting professor of psychology at the federal university in Niteroi, Brazil, a midsized city across the bay from Rio de Janeiro. As I left home for my first day of class, I asked someone the time. It was 9:05 a.m., which allowed me time to relax and look around the campus before my 10 o'clock lecture. After what I judged to be half an hour, I glanced at a clock I was passing. It said 10:20! In panic, I broke for the classroom, followed by gentle calls of "Hola, professor" and "Tudo bem, professor?" from unhurried students, many of whom, I later realized, were my own. I arrived breathless to find an empty room.

Frantically, I asked a passerby the time. "Nine forty-five" was the answer. No, that couldn't be. I asked someone else. "Nine fifty-five." Another said: "Exactly 9:43." The clock in a nearby office read 3:15. I had learned my first lesson about Brazilians: Their timepieces are consistently inaccurate. And nobody minds.

My class was scheduled from 10 until noon. Many students came late, some very late. Several arrived after 10:30. A few showed up closer to 11.

Two came after that. All of the latecomers wore the relaxed smiles that I came, later, to enjoy. Each one said hello, and although a few apologized briefly, none seemed terribly concerned about lateness. They assumed that I understood.

The idea of Brazilians arriving late was not a great shock. I had heard about "mãnha," the Portuguese equivalent of "mañana" in Spanish. This term, meaning "tomorrow" or "the morning," stereotypes the Brazilian who puts off the business of today until tomorrow. The real surprise came at noon that first day, when the end of class arrived.

Back home in California, I never need to look at a clock to know when the class hour is ending. The shuffling of books is accompanied by strained expressions that say plaintively, "I'm starving. . . . I've got to go to the bathroom. . . . I'm going to suffocate if you keep us one more second." (The pain usually becomes unbearable at two minutes to the hour in undergraduate

 From *Psychology Today*, March 1985, pp. 28-35. Copyright © 1985 American Psychological Association.

classes and five minutes before the close of graduate classes.)

When noon arrived in my first Brazilian class, only a few students left immediately. Others slowly drifted out during the next 15 minutes, and some continued asking me questions long after that. When several remaining students kicked off their shoes at 12:30, I went into my own "starving/bathroom/suffocation" routine.

I could not, in all honesty, attribute

*BRAZILIANS SAID THEY WOULD WAIT 33 MINUTES BEFORE CONSIDERING SOMEONE LATE. NORTH AMERICANS DREW THE LINE AT 19 MINUTES.*

their lingering to my superb teaching style. I had just spent two hours lecturing on statistics in halting Portuguese. Apparently, for many of my students, staying late was simply of no more importance than arriving late in the first place. As I observed this casual approach in infinite variations during the year, I learned that the "mãnha" stereotype oversimplified the real Anglo/Brazilian differences in conceptions of time. Research revealed a more complex picture.

With the assistance of colleagues Laurie West and Harry Reis, I compared the time sense of 91 male and female students in Niteroi with that of 107 similar students at California State University in Fresno. The universities are similar in academic quality and size, and the cities are both secondary metropolitan centers with populations of about 350,000.

We asked students about their perceptions of time in several situations, such as what they would consider late or early for a hypothetical lunch appointment with a friend. The average Brazilian student defined lateness for lunch as 33½ minutes after the scheduled time, compared to only 19 min-

utes for the Fresno students. But Brazilians also allowed an average of about 54 minutes before they'd consider someone early, while the Fresno students drew the line at 24.

Are Brazilians simply more flexible in their concepts of time and punctuality? And how does this relate to the stereotype of the apathetic, fatalistic and irresponsible Latin temperament? When we asked students to give typical reasons for lateness, the Brazilians were less likely to attribute it to a lack of caring than the North Americans were. Instead, they pointed to unforeseen circumstances that the person couldn't control. Because they seemed less inclined to feel personally responsible for being late, they also expressed less regret for their own lateness and blamed others less when they were late.

We found similar differences in how students from the two countries characterized people who were late for appointments. Unlike their North American counterparts, the Brazilian students believed that a person who is consistently late is probably more successful than one who is consistently on time. They seemed to accept the idea that someone of status is expected to arrive late. Lack of punctuality is a badge of success.

Even within our own country, of course, ideas of time and punctuality vary considerably from place to place. Different regions and even cities have their own distinct rhythms and rules. Seemingly simple words like "now," snapped out by an impatient New Yorker, and "later," said by a relaxed Californian, suggest a world of difference. Despite our familiarity with these homegrown differences in tempo, problems with time present a major stumbling block to Americans abroad. Peace Corps volunteers told researchers James Spradley of Macalester College and Mark Phillips of the University of Washington that their greatest difficulties with other people, after language problems, were the general pace of life and the punctuality of others. Formal "clock time" may be a standard on which the world agrees, but "social time," the heartbeat of society, is something else again.

How a country paces its social life is a mystery to most outsiders, one that we're just beginning to unravel. Twenty-six years ago, anthropologist Edward Hall noted in *The Silent Language* that informal patterns of time "are seldom, if ever, made explicit. They exist in the air around us. They are either familiar and comfortable, or unfamiliar and wrong." When we realize we are out of step, we often blame the people around us to make ourselves feel better.

Appreciating cultural differences in time sense becomes increasingly important as modern communications put more and more people in daily contact. If we are to avoid misreading issues that involve time perceptions, we need to understand better our own cultural biases and those of others.

When people of different cultures interact, the potential for misunderstanding exists on many levels. For example, members of Arab and Latin cultures usually stand much closer when they are speaking to people than we usually do in the United States, a fact we frequently misinterpret as aggression or disrespect. Similarly, we assign personality traits to groups with a pace of life that is markedly faster or slower than our own. We build ideas of national character, for example, around the traditional Swiss

*WESTERNERS LIKE OURSELVES DEFINE PUNCTUALITY USING PRECISE MEASURES OF TIME: 5 MINUTES, 15 MINUTES, AN HOUR.*

and German ability to "make the trains run on time." Westerners like ourselves define punctuality using precise measures of time: 5 minutes, 15 minutes, an hour. But according to Hall, in many Mediterranean Arab cultures there are only three sets of time: no time at all, now (which is of varying duration) and forever (too long). Because of this, Americans often find difficulty in getting Arabs to distinguish between waiting a long time and a very long time.

According to historian Will Durant,

*E*ACH
LANGUAGE
*HAS ITS OWN VOCABULARY
OF TIME, ONE THAT
DOES NOT ALWAYS SURVIVE
LITERAL TRANSLATION.*

"No man in a hurry is quite civilized." What do our time judgments say about our attitude toward life? How can a North American, coming from a land of digital precision, relate to a North African who may consider a clock "the devil's mill"?

Each language has a vocabulary of time that does not always survive translation. When we translated our questionnaires into Portuguese for my Brazilian students, we found that English distinctions of time were not readily articulated in their language. Several of our questions concerned how long the respondent would wait for someone to arrive, as compared with when they hoped for arrival or actually expected the person would come. In Portuguese, the verbs "to wait for," "to hope for" and "to expect" are all translated as "esperar." We had to add further words of expla-

nation to make the distinction clear to the Brazilian students.

To avoid these language problems, my Fresno colleague Kathy Bartlett and I decided to clock the pace of life in other countries by using as little language as possible. We looked directly at three basic indicators of time: the accuracy of a country's bank clocks, the speed at which pedestrians walked and the average time it took a postal clerk to sell us a single stamp. In six countries on three continents, we made observations in both the nation's largest urban area and a medium-sized city: Japan (Tokyo and Sendai), Taiwan (Taipei and Tainan), Indonesia (Jakarta and Solo), Italy (Rome and Florence), England (London and Bristol) and the United States (New York City and Rochester).

What we wanted to know was: Can we speak of a unitary concept called "pace of life"? What we've learned suggests that we can. There appears to be a very strong relationship (see chart on the next page) between the accuracy of clock time, walking speed and postal efficiency across the countries we studied.

We checked 15 clocks in each city, selecting them at random in downtown banks and comparing the time they showed with that reported by the local telephone company. In Japan, which leads the way in accuracy, the clocks averaged just over half a minute early or late. Indonesian clocks, the least accurate, were more than three minutes off the mark.

*L*OOKING
CAREFULLY AT
*DIFFERENT PACES OF LIFE
MAY HELP US DISTINGUISH
MORE ACCURATELY BETWEEN
SPEED AND PROGRESS.*

I will be interested to see how the digital-information age will affect our perceptions of time. In the United States today, we are reminded of the exact hour of the day more than ever, through little symphonies of beeps emanating from people's digital watches. As they become the norm, I fear our sense of precision may take an absurd twist. The other day, when I asked for the time, a student looked at his watch and replied, "Three twelve and eighteen seconds."

*" 'Will you walk a little faster?' said a whiting to a snail. 'There's a porpoise close behind us, and he's treading on my tail.' "*

So goes the rhyme from *Alice in Wonderland,* which also gave us that famous symbol of haste, the White Rabbit. He came to mind often as we measured the walking speeds in our experimental cities. We clocked how long it took pedestrians to walk 100 feet along a main downtown street during business hours on clear days. To eliminate the effects of socializing, we observed only people walking alone, timing at least 100 in each city. We found, once again, that the Japanese led the way, averaging just 20.7 seconds to cover the distance. The English nosed out the Americans for second place—21.6 to 22.5 seconds—and the Indonesians again trailed the pack, sauntering along at 27.2 seconds. As you might guess, speed was greater in the larger city of each nation than in its smaller one.

Our final measurement, the average time it took postal clerks to sell one stamp, turned out to be less straightforward than we expected. In each city, including those in the United States, we presented clerks with a note in the native language requesting

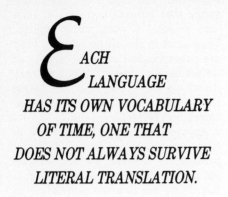

## The Pace of Life in Six Countries

| | Accuracy of Bank Clocks | Walking Speed | Post Office Speed |
|---|---|---|---|
| **Japan** | 1 | 1 | 1 |
| **United States** | 2 | 3 | 2 |
| **England** | 4 | 2 | 3 |
| **Italy** | 5 | 4 | 6 |
| **Taiwan** | 3 | 5 | 4 |
| **Indonesia** | 6 | 6 | 5 |

Numbers (1 is the top value) indicate the comparative rankings of each country for each indicator of time sense.

MICHAEL WITTE

a common-priced stamp—a 20-center in the United States, for example. They were also handed paper money, the equivalent of a $5 bill. In Indonesia, this procedure led to more than we bargained for.

At the large central post office in Jakarta, I asked for the line to buy stamps and was directed to a group of private vendors sitting outside. Each of them hustled for my business: "Hey, good stamps, mister!" "Best stamps here!" In the smaller city of Solo, I found a volleyball game in progress when I arrived at the main post office on Friday afternoon. Business hours, I was told, were over. When I finally did get there during business hours, the clerk was more interested in discussing relatives in America. Would I like to meet his uncle in Cincinnati? Which did I like better: California or the United States? Five people behind me in line waited patiently. Instead of complaining, they began paying attention to our conversation.

When it came to efficiency of service, however, the Indonesians were not the slowest, although they did place far behind the Japanese postal clerks, who averaged 25 seconds. That distinction went to the Italians, whose infamous postal service took 47 seconds on the average.

*"A man who wastes one hour of time has not discovered the meaning of life...."*

That was Charles Darwin's belief, and many share it, perhaps at the cost of their health. My colleagues and I have recently begun studying the relationship between pace of life and well-being. Other researchers have demonstrated that a chronic sense of urgency is a basic component of the Type A, coronary-prone personality. We expect that future research will demonstrate that pace of life is related to rate of heart disease, hypertension, ulcers, suicide, alcoholism, divorce and other indicators of general psychological and physical well-being.

As you envision tomorrow's international society, do you wonder who will set the pace? Americans eye Japan carefully, because the Japanese are obviously "ahead of us" in measurable ways. In both countries, speed is frequently confused with progress. Perhaps looking carefully at the different paces of life around the world will help us distinguish more accurately between the two qualities. Clues are everywhere but sometimes hard to distinguish. You have to listen carefully to hear the beat of even your own drummer.

# The New Lost Generation

## It's post-Sixties, pre-Eighties, and forever in between

## DAVID LEAVITT

DAVID LEAVITT's *first book*, Family Dancing, *is published by Knopf.*

On Saturday nights in 1971, when I was ten years old, I used to go folk dancing with my brother and sister in Tresidder Plaza at Stanford University. They were both undergraduates at Stanford, and my father taught there; I was what was known as a facbrat. I remember vividly those warm nights, the stone surface of the plaza illuminated like a skating rink and the little tinny record player blaring "Hava Nagila." As we approached I would start running. The air smelled of pot. Then we were there, and in the magic center a circle whirled madly in perfect step—the men long-haired, dirty, barefoot; the women wrapped in bolts of brightly patterned gypsy fabric, swathed in scarves, their hair held back by turquoise pins. Everyone reeked; deodorant, I suppose, was politically incorrect, like leg-shaving. Inevitably, in the course of the evening, someone would offer me a joint. I always refused. I only wanted to watch the dancers and learn the intricate patterned steps—the particular twining of ankles and arms, the systems for switching partners. The few times I actually joined in, I remember being shocked at the sudden intimacy I was thrown into with hand after hand, some bony and fragile, others heavy and lumbering and sweaty. Sometimes, in the more reckless dances, I would feel my feet quite literally lifted off the ground by their momentum.

Usually I did not dance, because usually I did not know the steps. Instead I would stand on the periphery, with a few other hesitant loners, behind one of the accomplished dancers, and I would falteringly, clumsily try to follow. Just as I was beginning to get it, the dance would end. The next week I would wait for the same dance to be played again, but it never was—at least not before 11:00, when I would hear a horn honking in the parking lot and see the glaring lights of my mother's car, come to fetch me home. "Did you have fun?" my mother would ask me as she opened the door. "Yes," I'd say, sliding in next to her. All that night the music drummed in my head. I knew the dancing went on and on after I had to go to bed, possibly all night, possibly until dawn, and as I fell asleep I tried to imagine what kinds of dances, what weirdly erotic configurations, those people would try in those late hours, the hours I had yet to witness, for I was just too young.

THE FIRST AND only time I ever saw a President, I was fourteen. The President was Gerald R. Ford, one year into his term, and he came to Stanford University to participate in a ceremony inaugurating the new law school. *Saturday Night Live* was in its first season that year, but I wouldn't get to see Chevy Chase's famous dunderhead imitations of the President until the series went into reruns. I had hardly heard of the show, which was on too late for me to watch. I remember thinking of President Ford as an only mildly evil character, at least in comparison with Nixon, whose hateful image on the kitchen television had more than once sent my mother into screaming fits so loud I had been convinced she was being murdered. "Conservative, but honest" was my father's estimation of Ford the man. My sister disagreed. She was a senior at Stanford and lived at Columbae House, a communal student residence devoted to radical thinking. I remember standing next to my sister that afternoon in a crowd of serious-looking young people holding signs and banners. In unison and with great dedication, they chanted: "The people—united—will never be defeated! The people—united—will never be defeated!" I listened. I loved the rhythm of the chant. At some point I joined in. A long time later than we'd been told, a helicopter came into view, hovered, and landed on the law school roof. It was like the arrival of a rock star at an outdoor concert. For a moment, even the demonstrators quieted and stood on tiptoe, straining to catch a glimpse of a real President. When he started to speak, the demonstrators increased the volume of their chant in an effort to drown him out. They were hundreds strong, but he was amplified.

It's hard to say, in retrospect, which meant less—the speech, or the protesters' endless declaration that the people, united, would never be defeated. But I was caught up in the spirit of the thing. When some of the demonstrators turned their eyes toward the SWAT men who stood armed on the roofs of the surrounding buildings and began to chant "Jump! Jump! Jump!," "I was thrilled. From the TV show I knew they were SWAT men. I didn't like their uniforms, or the fact that their guns were pointed at us. I joined in and shouted "Jump!" at the top of my lungs, until I felt a sharp tugging at my elbow. It was my sister. "Shut up," she said to me. "You don't have any idea what you're saying."

Ten years later my sister lives in San Francisco. After many different kinds of therapy, she has settled into marriage and a career as a social worker that almost fulfills her old ideals. She says she wants to have children but wonders if it would be selfish to bring new life into a world that is sure to end in the next twenty years. Gerald Ford, himself the most in-between of Presidents, has faded from public view, taking a backseat to his famous wife. Each week the *New York Post* carries news of another celebrity checking into the Betty Ford Center for treatment of "drug and alcohol dependency." My mother screams at Reagan on the television, but at a somewhat reduced volume in comparison with the Nixon days.

One evening during my freshman year at college, I was walking to the dining hall with my roommate, when I noticed a small group of students holding a sit-in on a square of carefully trimmed grass outside the president's office. There were only five of them. A sign explained that they were protesting President Carter's newly announced program for draft registration. They had a guitar and they were singing "We Shall Overcome." Although little frightened me at the age of eighteen more than the thought of getting drafted, I still felt an aversion toward the protestors. How ridiculous, I thought as I passed—a sit-in, in 1980, at Yale. "Throwbacks," I said to my roommate, unable to think of a word that carried more disdain. "Don't they realize their style is going to alienate people from their cause?" He nodded in agreement, and we continued on our way. My roommate wore small tortoiseshell glasses. My hair was short, and I was wearing a Brooks Brothers tweed jacket I had bought myself, but somehow it didn't occur to me that we were throwing back even further than they were. Then, as we approached the Freshman Commons, I heard the protestors begin to chant quietly: "The people—united—will never be defeated." For a moment I stopped, remembering that afternoon when Gerald Ford had visited Stanford. I knew that those demonstrators I had stood among, who had seemed so glorious to me, were themselves a mere shadow of Berkeley, or Kent State, or Harvard five years earlier. I had witnessed only the tail end of something that had once been great. It seemed easy to me, these days, for five Yale stu-

dents to chant, "The people, united, will never be defeated." What astonished me was that there had actually been a time when someone believed it.

MY GENERATION HAS always resisted definition. The younger siblings of the Sixties, we watched riots from a distance, sneaked peeks at the *Zap Comix* lying around our older siblings' bedrooms, grew our hair long, and in prepubescent droves campaigned door to door for McGovern. When I was ten I played the guitar and wanted to be like Joni Mitchell. A friend of my sister's, a fellow who must have fancied himself a Bill Graham in the making, arranged for me to sing my own compositions in a series of little concerts given in the communal dining hall of Columbae House. By the time I was old enough to take part in any real way, disillusion had set in, people had given up, cocaine was the drug of choice. Tail end. We have always been the tail end—of the Sixties, of the baby boom. We hit our stride in an age of burned-out, restless, ironic disillusion. With all our much-touted youthful energy

first generation whose members usually cannot remember their first plane trip. And the first in recent history that has never seen its friends missing in action or lost in combat or living and working in Canada.

It should have been perfect, the perfect time and place. As our parents always reminded us, we had so much they had not even been able to imagine as children. So little harm came to us. And yet, on those bright afternoons of my childhood, when I sat indoors, watching sunlight reflect off the face of *Speed Racer* on the television, I was already aware that rips were being made in the fabric of perfection. When my parents shouted at each other, their voices sounded like fabric ripping. My friends sat in the cafeteria of our middle school reading brightly colored books with titles like *The Kids' Book of Divorce*. On television the Brady Bunch and the Partridge Family continued on their merry ways. Sometimes I closed my eyes and tried to will myself through the television's scrim of glass and into their world. It was, in its own way, as appealing and as inaccessible as the world of the folk dancers, of my brother and sis-

---

## WE hit our stride in an age of burned-out, restless, ironic disillusion. With all our much-touted youthful energy boiling inside us, where were we supposed to go? What were we supposed to do?

---

boiling inside us, where were we supposed to go? What were we supposed to do?

Now the Rainbows and the Moon Units of the world (conceived at love-ins, "birthed" in birthing rooms) are hitting their teens. They are computer-literate. They own their own Apple Macintoshes. They watch MTV on VCRs. Those with an artistic inclination rent video cameras, make their own films, and proclaim that written language will soon degenerate until it serves only as a vehicle for nostalgia, eclipsed by the shot—videotape and its new alphabet of images.

My generation is somewhere in between. Born too late and too early, we are partially what came before us and partially what followed. But we can make certain claims. We are the first generation, for instance, that is younger than television. We knew the Vietnam War as something about as real as the *Mannix* episodes it seemed to interrupt so often. We learned stealth by figuring out how to get around our parents' efforts to ration the number of hours we watched each day. And we are the

ter, who went to college and were free of the big house with its burden of memories. But I knew that if I broke through the television, I wouldn't instantly emerge in that magical community of Sherman Oaks, with its homecoming dances, ice-cream floats, and wise maids. Instead I'd find circuits and wires, the complicated brainworks of the famous "tube."

In the real world, real parents were splitting up, moving out, questioning and in some cases rejecting the commandments to marry and have a family, commandments that had been the foundation of their parents' lives. In my family it was happening against our wishes. In a community where the divorce rate had reached a record high, and every family seemed to have at least one child in prison, or in a hospital, or dead of an overdose, my parents had never even separated. Still, there were sharp words, often, and a sense of desperate effort and hard, unrewarded labor through it all. We felt it in the politics of playing records, of who did the dishes, and who really cared around here, and who had slaved for whom for how long. Sometimes it seemed to me that we walked around the house opened up and bleeding, yet talking, laughing, smiling, like actors in a horror movie who, during a break in the shooting, simply forget to remove the prop knives from their backs or mop up the imitation blood. In this case the blood was real, though we pretended it wasn't.

I watched. During *Star Trek* my mother brought me dinner on a tray. Sometimes, after watching for hours and hours, I would have to get very close to the screen in order to focus, even though I knew it was bad for my eyes. Sometimes I'd see how close I could get, let the lenses of my eyes touch the hot lens of the television, soak in the pure light.

WHEN MY BROTHER and sister were my age, they had already seen much more of the world than I will probably ever see. They'd gone to India, Guatemala, Cuba, Hong Kong. They'd worked in prisons, and organized striking farm workers, and driven across the country half a dozen times each. They'd read Kerouac, Castaneda, *Zen and the Art of Motorcycle Maintenance*. And when, as a child, I'd ask them about their lives, they'd tell me about the movement. Movement. It seemed an appropriate word, since they moved all the time, driven by exploratory wanderlust into the vast American wilderness. I possess no similar desire whatsoever, and neither, I think, do most members of my generation. Rather than move, we burrow. We are interested in stability, neatness, entrenchment. We want to stay in one place and stay in one piece, establish careers, establish credit. We want good apartments, fulfilling jobs, nice boy/girl friends. We want American Express Gold Cards. Whereas my brother and sister, at the same age, if asked, would probably have said that their goals were to expand their minds, see the world, and encourage revolutionary change.

I've never thought of myself as naive; I've never imagined that I might lead a sheltered life. I am, after all, "sophisticated," have been to Europe, understand dirty jokes and the intricacies of sexually transmitted diseases. This is my milieu, the world I live in, and I have almost never stepped beyond its comfortable borders. A safety net surrounds my sophisticated life, and the question is, of course, how did it get there? Did I build it myself? Was it left for me? Sometimes I feel as if I live in a room with mirrored walls, imagining that the tiny space I occupy is in fact endless, and constitutes a real world. I remember when I first moved to New York, and I was looking for work, I dropped my résumé off with the manager of the Oscar Wilde Memorial Bookshop—a political gay bookstore—and he asked me to tell him about

my "movement experience." For a few seconds I just blanked out. I thought he was talking about dance.

LAST YEAR I went with three friends to see the film *Liquid Sky*, which was enjoying a cult following in lower Manhattan. The film portrays a culture of young people who live in lower Manhattan, dress in outlandish costumes, and spend most of their nights in wildly decorated clubs—a culture of young people very much like the young people in the theater that night watching the film. Margaret, the heroine, explains that she has moved beyond the suburban dream of having a husband, and also moved beyond the middle-urban dream of having an agent (and hence a career), and has now recognized the pointlessness of striving for anything. Her new dream lover is an alien creature that thrives on the chemicals released in the brain during orgasm and that will ultimately devour Margaret in the course of a final, quite literally cosmic climax. Perhaps the moment in the film that stuck most to my ribs is the one in which Margaret's ex-lover and ex-acting teacher, a man in his late forties, accuses her of dressing like a whore. She retaliates with a childish sneer that his jeans (throwbacks to his own heyday) are just as much a costume as her push-up bras and red leather skirts. Of her peers, she says something like, "At least we don't pretend we aren't wearing costumes."

*At least we don't pretend we aren't wearing costumes?* Well, yes, I guess they don't, I thought. For Margaret, to pretend one isn't wearing a costume is contemptible. She rejects the idea that the way one dresses might represent a claim made about the world today, or project an idea for the world tomorrow. Hell, there probably won't be a world tomorrow. Clothes have to do with what we aren't, not what we are. Screw art, let's dance.

And yet Margaret lets something slip when she makes this claim. She implicates herself by referring to her friends, her cronies, as "we." The "we" in *Liquid Sky* is disloyal, backstabbing, bitchy, and violent. But it is still a "we"; it is a group, defined by its belief in its own newness, its own green youthfulness; it is a generation. In performance spaces, bars that double as art galleries, clubs with names like 8 B.C. or Save the Robots, on the darkest and most dangerous streets of New York, a culture is being born out of the claim that there is no culture—that it's all mere dress-up, mere fakery, mere whooping-it-up-before-the-plague. This culture is downtown. It basks in the limelight of the present moment. It avoids tall buildings. Poverty is its kin, its company, and sometimes its reality, but it draws the curious rich like flies. Then real estate possibilities emerge out of nowhere: tenements turn

into town houses, yet another chic and colorful neighborhood for the new rich emerges. Sometimes I wonder whether my generation's lunatic fringe of trendsetters keeps moving into more and more dangerous parts because the gentrified keep pushing them out of the neighborhoods they've pioneered, or because they're attracted to the hopeless edge of the city, where the future means finding food and drugs to get you through tomorrow. That is about as far as you can get from long-term investments. And the irony is, of course, that where they have gone, the rich young future-mongers of the generation ahead have followed, attracted by the scent of potential development. Farther east, and farther down, their world keeps moving. It is sometimes decadent, destructive, dangerous. It is sometimes gloriously, extraordinarily fun.

I've seen that world. Good yuppie that I am, I've even dipped my toe in its freezing waters on select Saturday nights and Sunday mornings when an urge to dance came over me like an itch. When I was an undergraduate I was friends with a couple of women who became lovers and took to walking around the campus with dog collars around their necks connected by a link chain. And I remember going with them once to have tea at the home of one of their mothers—a big brownstone in the East Sixties, on the same block where Nixon used to live. They marched defiantly through the foyer, their very entrance a calculated affront, me following meekly, while the mother strove not to notice the white-blond tint of her daughter's hair, or the double nose ring (she had pierced the nostril herself, in the bathroom), and offered to take my jacket. "So how is school going, honey?" the mother said. In the course of tea she made a valiant effort to call her daughter "Max," as Max currently insisted. (Her real name was Elizabeth.) And a year later, in New York, I walked home from a party one night with an NYU student and her friend, a boy dressed like Boy George—eyeliner, dreadlocks, lipstick. And they were going to steal the boy's sister's food stamps so they could get something to eat. They said this matter-of-factly. And when I expressed amazement that the girl's affluent parents didn't send her enough money to buy food, she said equally matter-of-factly, "Oh, they send me plenty of money, but I use it all up on booze and drugs." Without a trace of self-consciousness she said it; but with more than a trace of self-pity.

It was Saturday night and we were going to a party. It was always Saturday night and we were always going to a party. Someone was stoned. Someone was drunk, lying snoring on the big sofa in the library. Someone was wearing Salada tea-bag fortunes as earrings. In their rooms, the boys

We have inserted into our minds the image of the mushroom cloud and the world in flames in order to justify a blind spot in us—an ability to conceive of any future at all.

were experimenting with eye makeup. In their rooms, the girls were experimenting with mushrooms. It was Saturday night and we were going to a dress party (everyone had to wear a dress), to a gender-transcendence party, to a party supporting the women's center, supporting the Marxist Literary Group, supporting the Coalition Against Apartheid. My friends were not active in these organizations; we expressed our support by giving the parties. For days beforehand we'd trade twelve-inch singles, mix them on our stereos, compete to produce the greatest dance tape ever, the one that would bring the dancers to the floor in an orgiastic heap.

The favorite songs that year, I think, were "Dancing with Myself," by Billy Idol, and "I Wanna Be Sedated," by the Ramones. But "Rock Lobster" seemed to turn up on every tape, as did "We Got the Beat" and "I Love a Man in a Uniform."

A photographer friend of mine used to come to all the parties that year, throw her camera out into the pulsating dark as arbitrarily as Richard Misrach, who was known for blindly aiming his camera out into the dark Hawaiian jungle. It became a kind of joke, Jennie's presence at every party. You could count on seeing yourself a few days later, stoned or drunk or vomiting, or making out with someone you didn't recognize on a sofa you couldn't remember. In the photographs bodies were frozen in the midst of flight, heads shook in beady haloes of light and sweat, clothes flew and were suspended, forever revealing small patches of white skin. There was

a quality of ecstasy. But when I see those pictures these days, I think *I was mad*.

I don't remember ever feeling as much joy as I did that year, when, on any Saturday night, on a crowded dance floor I'd hear my favorite song begin. It was as if my body itself had become an instrument, pulled and plucked and wrenched by the music, thrown beyond itself. This was no love-in of the Sixties, no drug-hazed ritual of communion. We were dancing with ourselves. Someone joked that each of us could have had on his own individual Walkman.

The mornings after such evenings always began around two in the afternoon. Exhausted and hung over, we would go back to the big rooms where the parties had taken place to confront the hundreds of empty beer cans and cigarette stubs, the little clots of lost sweaters stuffed into corners, forgotten, never to be retrieved. Sunlight streamed in. While the guests slept in late, and Jennie toiled in her darkroom, frenzied with creation, the partygivers took out their mops.

LIKE OUR OLDER brothers and sisters, my generation belongs to gyms. We find Nautilus equipment consoling. Nothing gets in your way when you're bench pressing, or swimming, or running, not even the interfering subconscious that tended to muck up all those Seventies efforts at psychological self-improvement. Muscles appear as a manifestation of pure will.

In contrast to our older brothers and sisters, however, the fact that we believe in health does not necessarily mean that we believe in the future. The same bright young person who strives for physical immortality also takes for granted the imminence of his destruction. At Brown University, students voted last October on a referendum to stock poison tablets in the school infirmary, so that in the event of a nuclear catastrophe, they could commit suicide rather than die of fallout. As if nuclear disaster, rather than being a distant threat, were a harsh reality, an immediacy, something to prepare for. I am reminded of Grace Paley's description of an eighteen-year-old in her story "Friends": "His friends have a book that says a person should, if properly nutritioned, live forever.... He also believes that the human race, its brains and good looks, will end in his time."

Brains and good looks. Last year I went dancing at Area for the first time, arguably the chicest dance club in New York. (A friend of mine who is more of an expert than I in these matters insists that the club called Save the Robots is chicer, since it is frequented by the people who work at Area and does not open until after Area has closed.) At this point Area was dressed in its nuclear holocaust garb. On our way in, we passed tableaux vivants of people in Karen Silkwood suits, peeling lurid green candy off sheets on a conveyor belt. Women danced inside fantastic, menacing pseudo-reactors. Signs reading DANGER— RADIOACTIVE MATERIAL glowed above the dance floor. Later, at a bar, I was introduced to an artist who had been asked to create a work of art in support of the nuclear freeze, and was thinking of carving a mushroom cloud out of a block of ice. It was hard for me to keep from wondering about the famed holocaust anxiety of my postnuclear generation. The world after the bomb, it seemed to me, had become a cliché, incorporated into our dialogue and our culture with an alarming thoughtlessness. Do most of us dream, like Eddie Albert as the President in the movie *Dream-*

*scape,* of a parched postholocaust landscape, peopled by weird halfhuman monsters and scarred children wailing, "It hurts! It hurts!"? I doubt it. I think we purport to worry about the world ending much more than we actually do.

Because the terror of knowing the world could end at any moment haunts them so vividly, older people seem to believe that it must be ten times worse for the young. The realization that nuclear disaster is not only possible, but possibly imminent, writes the noted essayist Lewis Thomas, "is bad enough for the people in my generation. We can put up with it, I suppose, since we must. We are moving along anyway....What I cannot imagine, what I cannot put up with... is what it would be like to be young. How do the young stand it? How can they keep their sanity?"

Well, I want to say, we do. Indeed, I think we are more sane and less hysterical about the issue of nuclear holocaust than are the generations ahead of us. We do not go crazy, because for us the thought of a world with no future—so terrifying to Dr. Thomas—is completely familiar; is taken for granted; is nothing new.

I have tried time and again to explain this to people who are older than I. I tell them that no matter how hard I try—and I have closed my eyes tightly, concentrated, tried to will my mind to do it—I simply cannot muster an image of myself fifty, or twenty, or even ten years in the future. I go blank. I have no idea where or what or even *if* I'll be. Whereas my parents, when they were young, assumed vast and lengthy futures for themselves, a series of houses, each larger than the one before, and finally the "golden years" of retirement, knitting by fires, bungalows in Florida. I think we have inserted into our minds the commercialized image of the mushroom cloud and the world in flames in order to justify a blind spot in us—an inability to think beyond the moment, or conceive of any future at all, which makes us immune to the true horror felt by older people. This blind spot has more to do with our attitude toward the nuclear family than with nuclear disaster—with the fact that our parents, as they now reach the golden years they once looked forward to, are finding themselves trapped in unhappy marriages or divorced, are too bitter to ever consider loving again, or are desperate to find a new mate with whom they can share those last happy years that they were promised, that they worked so hard for, that they were so unfairly cheated out of.

And we—well, we aren't going to make the same mistakes they did. Alone at least we're safe—from pain, from dependency, from sexually transmitted diseases. Those who belong to no one but themselves can never be abandoned.

IT IS 1983. I have just graduated from college and, like most of my friends, lead the sort of life that makes a good biographical note in the back of a literary magazine—"living and working in Manhattan." Most mornings, I have to get up at 7:30 A.M.—unnaturally early for someone like me, who finds it hard to fall asleep before 3:00. I don't eat breakfast, I shower in three minutes, timed. From inside my apartment, where it is warm, I head out into the cold, begin the long trek to the subway. My station is famous for its poor design. If I have a token, I must run down one staircase and up another to get to the train. Sometimes the train doors close on my nose. Other times I'm lucky, I squeeze in, find a space to stand. The train begins to move, and there are newspapers in my eyes, painted fingernails, noses, the smell of toothpaste and coffee everywhere around me. People are nodding, falling asleep on their feet. For six months now, this subway ride in the morning and afternoon has been the closest I have come physically to another human being.

I arrive at my office. For the length of the morning, I work, taking frequent breaks. I visit the cookie lady in publicity. I visit the water cooler. I gossip with friends on the phone, thinking about lunch.

I used to think there was something gloriously romantic about the nine-to-five life. I used to imagine there could be no greater thrill than being part of the crush riding the escalator down from the Pan Am Building into Grand Central at 5:00. The big station ceiling, with its map of stars, would unfold above you, the escalator would slip down under your feet—you, so small, so anonymous in all that hugeness and strangeness. Yet you'd know you were different. Light on your feet at rush hour, you'd dodge and cut through the throng, find your way fast to the shuttle. Like the north-or-south-going Zax in Doctor Seuss, you'd have one direction, and no choice but to move in it.

*Ha,* as the old woman who has worked forty years in accounting says to everyone. *Ha-ha.*

It's 5:30. Outside the sun has set. Inside other people are still typing, still frenzied. Everyone works harder than you, no matter how hard you work. Everyone makes more than you do, no matter how much you make. You slip out silently, guilty to be leaving only a half hour late, wondering why you're not as ambitious as they are, why you don't have it in you to make it.

But when you get outside, the wind is cold on your face, the streets are full of people herding toward the subway. You put on your Walkman. You think that tonight you might like to go dancing. Then the Pointer Sisters come on, and you realize that, like John Travolta tripping down the streets of Brooklyn in *Saturday Night Fever,* you already are.

A FEW YEARS after I stopped going, the Saturday night folk-dancing ritual at Stanford ceased. Lack of interest, I suppose. The women wrapped in gypsy fabric and the boys with dirty feet were getting cleaned up and prepping for their GMATs. Today they are baby-boomers. They are responsible, says a *People* magazine ad, for "the surge in microchips, chocolate chips, and a host of special services to help Boomers run their two-career households." They work, live, love in offices. They have "drive."

My generation, in the meantime, still trots outside their circle, eager to learn the steps. In every outward way we are perfect emulators. We go to work in corporations right out of college. We look good in suits. But we also have haircuts that are as acceptable at East Village early-hours clubs as they are at Morgan Stanley. And (of course) at least we don't pretend we're not wearing costumes.

There are advantages to growing up, as we did, on the cusp of two violently dislocated ages; advantages to becoming conscious just as one decade is burning out, and another is rising, phoenixlike, from the ashes of its dissolution—or disillusion. If the Sixties was an age of naive hope, then the Eighties is an age of ironic hopelessness—its perfect counterpart, its skeptical progeny. We are the children of that skepticism. We go through all the motions. But if we tried then to learn the steps from our brothers and sisters because we believed in what they were doing, we follow in their footsteps now for almost the opposite reason—to prove that we can sell out just as well as they can, and know it too.

I remember, as a child, listening to my mother talk about fashion. "Once you've seen stiletto heels come and go three times, you'll realize how little any of it means," she said. I don't think I knew yet what a stiletto heel was, but I understood already and perfectly how little any of it meant. It came to me very early, that ironic and distanced view on things, and it's stayed.

The voice of my generation is the voice of David Letterman, whose late-night humor—upbeat, deadpan, more than a little contemptuous—we imitate because, above all else, we are determined to make sure everyone knows that what we say might not be what we mean. Consider these words, from Brett Duval Fromson, in an op-ed piece for *The New York Times:* "Yuppies, if we do anything at all, respect those who deliver the goods. How else are we going to afford our Ferragamo pumps, Brooks Brothers suits, country houses, European cars, and California chardonnays?" The balance of the irony

is perfect—between self-mockery and straight-faced seriousness, between criticism and comfy self-approval. "If we do anything at all," Fromson writes, leaving open the possibility that we don't. Certainly, he acknowledges, during the recession we "didn't give much thought to those who wouldn't make it." And now I am thinking about a headline I read recently in *The Village Voice,* above one of a series of articles analyzing Reagan's victory last November. It read DON'T TRUST ANYONE UNDER THIRTY.

Mine is a generation perfectly willing to admit its contemptible qualities. But our self-contempt is self-congratulatory. The buzz in the background, every minute of our lives, is that detached, ironic voice telling us: At least you're not faking it, as they did, at least you're not pretending as they did. It's okay to be selfish as long as you're up-front about it. Go ahead. "Exercise your right to exercise." Other people are dying to defend other people's rights to speak, to vote, and to live, but at least you don't pretend you're not wearing a costume.

What is behind this bitterness, this skepticism? A need, I think, for settledness, for security, for home. Our parents imagined they could satisfy this urge by marrying and raising children; our older brothers and sisters through community and revolution. We have seen how far those alternatives go. We trust ourselves, and money. Period.

Fifteen years ago you weren't supposed to trust anyone over thirty. For people in my generation, the goal seems to be to get to thirty as fast as possible, and stay there. Starting out, we are eager, above all else, to be finished. If we are truly a generation without character, as is often claimed, it is because we have seen what has happened to generations with character. If we are without passion or affect, it is because we have decided that passion and affect are simply not worth the trouble. If we stand crouched in the shadows of a history in which we refuse to take part, it is because that's exactly where we've chosen to stand.

Characterlessness takes work. It is defiance and defense all at once.

DURING MY FRESHMAN year in college I remember going to see Mary Tyler Moore as a woman paralyzed from the neck down in *Whose Life Is It Anyway?* At intermission I ran into a friend from school who was practically in tears. "You don't know what it's like for me to see her like that," he said. "Mary's a metaphor for my youth. And looking at her on that stage, well, I can't help but feel that it's my youth lying paralyzed up there." Later, a woman I know told me in all earnestness, "When I'm in a difficult situation, a real bind, I honestly

think to myself, 'What would Mary have done?' I really do." I know people who significantly altered the shape of their lives so that they could stay up every weeknight for a 2:30 to 4:00 A.M. Mary tripleheader on Channel 4 in New York. Even John Sex, the East Village's reigning club maven, is famous for his early-morning rendition, at the Pyramid club, of the Mary theme.

Remember those words? "Who can take the world on with her smile? Who can take a nothing day and suddenly make it all seem worthwhile?" And of course, at the end of the opening credits, there is the famous epiphany, the throw of the hat. "You're gonna make it after all," sings Sonny Curtis, who faded quickly into obscurity, but whose dulcet voice will live forever in reruns, and in our hearts. She throws the red cap into the air; the frame freezes, leaving Mary's hat perpetually aloft, and Mary perpetually in the bloom of youthful anticipation. The great irony of that shot, underscoring the show's tender, melancholy tone, is that as the seasons wore on, and new images of a shorter-haired Mary were spliced into the opening credit sequence, it always remained the same. So that even in the last, saddest seasons, with Mary pushing forty and wanting a raise and still not married, we are still given a glimpse of Mary as she used to be, young Mary, full of youthful exuberance, and that image of Mary and her hat and her hope gently plays against the truth of what her life has given her. The fact is that Mary's life stinks. She is underpaid in a second-rate job at a third-rate television station. Her best friends, Rhoda and Phyllis, have both left her to fail in spin-offs in other cities, and she doesn't even have a boyfriend. That's Mary's life, and even the clever tactic of changing the last line of the theme song from "You're gonna make it after all" to "Look's like you've made it after all" fails to convince us that it's anything but rotten.

But Mary presses on, and the great epic film, which all the episodes of the Mary show comprise, ends as it began—with Mary not getting married. The camaraderie of the newsroom has provided her less with a bond of strength than with a buffer against sorrow. Mary and her friends share one another's loneliness, but they don't cure it. The station closes down, the lights go out, and still young Mary throws her hat.

I see Marys often these days; the other day I saw one going into a deli on Third Avenue in the Eighties, just after work. She's younger, a bit fatter, better paid, so she wears silk blouses with ruffles and bows. And because she lives in New York, she's a bit more desperate, the pain is a little closer to the surface. It's 9:00, and she's just gotten off from work. She buys herself dinner—chicken hot dogs, Diet

41

Coke, Häagen-Dazs—and heads home to the tiny apartment, with a bathtub in the kitchen, for which she pays far too much. And I can't help but think that, even as a child, when the goings-on in that Minneapolis newsroom were the high point of her week, she knew she was going to end up here. Remember the episodes where Mary and Lou quit in order to protest how little money they make? Mary is forced to borrow from Ted. Nothing upsets her more than the realization that, for the first time in her life, she's in debt. She never asked for more than a room to live in, after all, and someplace to go each day, and perhaps a little extra money for a new dress now and then.

Here in New York, all the prime-time shows of my childhood have found their way, like memories or dreams, to the darkest part of the night. First there's *Star Trek* and the familiar faces of the *Enterprise* crew. Tonight they are confronted with an android that has become human because it has felt the first pangs of love. Once again, no woman can win Kirk, because he's already married to the most beautiful woman of them all—his ship. At 1:00 *The Twilight Zone* comes on, another lost astronaut wanders a blank landscape, the world before or after man. At 1:30, only an hour before Mary begins, I watch the *Independent News*. I am, by this time, on the floor, and close to sleep. The newscaster's voice clucks amicably, telling us that Mary Tyler Moore has checked herself into the Betty Ford Center. She has bravely admitted to having a problem, and she is battling it.

I leap up. I stare at the screen. The image has already passed, the newscaster moved on to another story. And I think, how sad that Mary's life has come to this. And yet, how good that she is bravely admitting to having a problem, and battling it. And I wonder if Mary Tyler Moore sat and looked at herself in the mirror before she made the decision; sat and looked at herself in the mirror and asked herself, "What would Mary do?"

Mary would do the right thing. And that is a comfort to me, this dark night, as I drag myself from the living room floor and click the television into silence. We have learned a few things from Mary. We have learned, on a day-to-day basis, how to do the right thing. We have learned to be kind and patient with one another, to give comfort. We have learned how to be good and generous friends.

It is late. The apartment is close and quiet. Tonight I am alone, but this weekend I will be with my friends. Like the folks in Mary's newsroom or the crew of the *Enterprise* bridge, we are a gang. We go dancing, and afterward, to an all-night deli for babkas and French toast, our clothes permeated with the smell of cigarettes. We walk five abreast, arm-in-arm, so that other people must veer into the street to avoid hitting us. When we decide the time has come to head back uptown, we pile into a cab, sometimes five or six of us, and sit on each other's laps and legs, and feel happy that we have friends, because it means we can take cabs for less than the price of the subway. It is nearly dawn, and a few sour-looking prostitutes are still marching the sidewalks of the West Side Highway in the cold. In a moment when we're not looking a sun will appear, small and new and fiery, as if someone had thrown it into the air.

*The children of the flower children
may be rebelling against—guess what?
—the values of the 1960s.*

# Brave New Wave of the '80s

## Steve Barnett

*Steve Barnett is vice president of the Cultural Analysis Group at Planmetrics Inc., which has offices in Chicago, New York and San Francisco. Barnett, a Ph.D. in cultural anthropology, has taught at Princeton and Brown Universities and the Massachusetts Institute of Technology.*

In the background a rock band is playing "White Wedding," sung by Billy Idol. What viewers are watching on the TV screen is a wedding unlike any they've ever seen. A coffin is slowly nailed closed. The bride cuts her finger and screams hysterically. Explosions of unknown origin shake the church. The scene shifts to the happy couple's kitchen—appliances start blowing up.

Such bizarre, montage sequences are not unusual for MTV—Music Television—the two-year-old cable network created by Warner Amex, which claims a growing audience of 15½ million viewers around the country. MTV features rock bands playing nonstop music 24 hours a day and illustrated by "concept tapes"—film footage of people and scenes, often speeded up; fragments of action, flickering lights and displays of primary colors; imaginary worlds of space creatures (usually band members or actors). "The results are silly, pretentious, weird, and fun, like eavesdropping on playacting children in unselfconscious parody of adult behavior," wrote critic Helen Dudar in *The Wall Street Journal*.

Whether it's art or "the most exalted junk on the box" (as Dudar called it), MTV is saying something important to a new generation of American consumers. With its high-tech visual tricks (much like those used in TV commercials) and surreal fantasy worlds, the MTV format corresponds closely to what I call the "New-Wave mindset" of American youth. Although New-Wave teenagers now constitute less than half the

teenage population, recent studies by Planmetrics, a consulting firm that specializes in strategic planning, suggest that this segment is growing and may be in the vanguard of their generation's changing tastes.

The emergence of a significant teenage group with very different values and behavior from the young people of the late 1960s and 1970s has received relatively little attention so far. Just as the "flower children" were initially thought to be marginal to American society, but went on to reshape many consumption patterns in the U.S., these New-Wave youth of the 1980s will change the product and service market for young people in the coming decade.

Believing that many companies were not yet reacting to changing styles among young Americans, the Cultural Analysis Group at Planmetrics has been studying attitudes of young Americans since 1980. Our research methods are anthropological and linguistic, relying on careful observation (with their permission) of 120 teenagers interacting in small groups across the country. Our team of researchers, led by two anthropologists (myself and one other) and a psychologist, has observed them in their homes, at school, in video-game parlors and other hangouts for a week or two at a time. We have recorded and analyzed many of their conversations and interviewed them at length about their behavior and habits.

This qualitative data provided us with hypotheses to be tested in a telephone survey of 350 teenagers conducted by a nationwide polling organization using standard sampling methods. The questions we asked employed language that they use in their everyday lives. First, we took an inventory of their tastes: What clothes did they wear, what music did they like, who did they look up to. Then we probed their attitudes on a range of issues, with questions like: "Do you think conserving energy is important to ensure a prosperous future for the U.S.?" "Do you favor or oppose nuclear

From *Across the Board*, December 1983, pp. 5-12. Reprinted by permission of the author and The Conference Board.

Their rules—Below, a scene from Dungeons & Dragons. "In their retreat into fantasy worlds, the new generation is rejecting many of their parents' values from the 1960s."

Bart Bartholomew/Black Star

Their styles—A recent "Rockabilly-'50s" event in Los Angeles. "Many young people who share New-Wave attitudes dress in ways their parents find vaguely reminiscent of the 1950s."

energy?" "Do your parents understand your views on dating, school, jobs, and what matters to you in general?" "Do you try to explain your views to your parents when they disagree with you?" When we analyzed the results, we found that certain responses tended to go together in a statistically significant "cluster." We labeled this set of tastes, attitudes and other characteristics "New Wave." From both the qualitative analysis and the national survey, we found that in 1980 about 25 percent of American teenagers from ages 12 to 16 shared New-Wave characteristics. By this year, the figure had risen to 39 percent.

So-called New-Wave styles originated with punk-rock groups and teenage culture in England, and have spread to the U.S. In their extreme form they are associated with bizarre dress—multicolored hair, men with earrings and safety pins stuck in their skin—and drug taking.

But it would be a mistake to dismiss such styles simply as aberrations. Indeed, appearances are deceptive. Many young people who share New-Wave attitudes dress in less ostentatious ways which their parents would find vaguely reminiscent of the 1950s, including wearing pegged pants, charcoal gray and pink combinations, pedal pushers, bobby socks, and so on. There is even a "drugged preppy" look—combining preppy clothes and sustained drug taking.

New-Wave youth are deeply involved in creating an alternative identity through stylistic extremes. Moreover, when compared with previous generations, they are, even for their age, less political, much less con-

cerned with conservation and environmental issues, and very much protechnology. To a limited extent, their outlook corresponds to a general conservative swing in the United States. But it is important to remember that New-Wave youth are concerned with their own hermetically sealed world and do not easily adapt to current social rules and values.

As one articulate New-Wave representative put it: "We are searching for an identity outside of your society. Some things that we do may look outrageous, but it is the only way left to us to say we are not part of your crazy world. You won't let us in [he was referring to a lack of jobs], and so we can make another world outside yours that we can control." This overwhelming feeling of exclusion is at the heart of the New-Wave culture.

The easiest way to get an overall sense of how New-Wave teenagers think is to contrast their attitudes on several key issues with those of the previous generation of teenagers:

*Protechnology/Antitechnology.* Planmetrics developed a technology value scale for the national teenage survey and found that the respondents who identified themselves as New Wave consistently evaluated new technology positively, while "straight" respondents were more cautious about endorsing new technology (like robots, computerized homes, artificial environments).

Younger people have generally been ill-disposed to technology since the middle 1960s, when they asso-

## New-Wave Lyrics

*KNOW YOUR RIGHTS\**

*This is a public service announcement—with guitar*
*Know your rights—all three of them, I say*
*You have the right not to be killed*
*Murder is a crime*
*Unless it was done by a policeman or aristocrat*
*You have the right to food and money*
*Providing of course you don't mind a little*
    *humiliation,*
*Investigation and if you cross your fingers*
*Rehabilitation*
*Young offenders! Know your rights*
*You have the right to freeee speech*
*As long as your not dumb enough*
*To actually try it*

ciated it with an unpopular war and with unfeeling, hierarchical bureaucratic control. During the late 1960s, for example, students at the University of Rochester attacked and set fire to computers. In other schools students intentionally crumpled computer registration forms in defiance of the forms' instructions: "Do not bend, fold, spindle, or mutilate."

New-Wave youth, however, are genuinely fascinated by the technology behind computers and computer games, space exploration, robotics, electronic forms of music and communication, the creation of artificial environments through lighting and sound systems at concerts and dances. Increasingly, they see technology as a value-neutral conduit that can provide them with the sensory and emotional stimulation they seek.

Oddly enough, teenagers understand little of how technology actually works. For example, we found that very few can explain the basics of computers, even though most are adept at computer games. Most of the youngsters we studied did not even know how a simple light bulb works — or even that it has a filament (nowadays, most bulbs are frosted and the filament is not visible).

For many New-Wave youth, technology has become a magical part of their surroundings. They have no particular need to master its technical secrets, but neither do they understand the radical antitechnology stance of their parents. In California we observed this conversation between two teenagers after they were given printouts of their class schedules at the beginning of the semester:

"My mother told me that when she was in college,

they used to burn forms that came out of computers," one said.

"Why the hell would anyone do that? It [the printouts] makes things easier," the other student replied.

"Beats me. She gave me that old '60s line, but I don't know what she's talking about."

*Environmental Unconcerns.* Young people of the late 1960s and the 1970s were environmentally concerned, basically supporting all nature-preservation issues and strongly endorsing energy conservation. Now, many teenagers are becoming apathetic toward environmental issues. For example, they are turning away from traditional camping activities. (One small sign of the trend: To continue to attract families with teenagers, some campground owners have been forced to install electronic-game rooms at campsites.)

In a study of how Americans actually set their thermostats (versus what they *say* their thermostat setting is), Planmetrics found, in a study of homes with heating and air conditioning on the same system, that teenagers consistently and surreptitiously move the thermostat up in winter and down in summer, showing little concern for energy conservation. In addition, we surveyed teenagers on whether they would participate in political action around a specific environmental issue (for respondents near a coast, offshore exploratory drilling for oil; for inland respondents, exploratory drilling for oil on publicly owned parkland). The sample as a whole was significantly apathetic toward such issues. But of those identified as New Wave, only 5 percent said they would participate in environmental political action, versus 27 percent for the entire sample.

*Natural vs. Artificial.* Young people in the 1960s and '70s endorsed the notion of "small is beautiful," as a way of expressing a basic value of living in harmony with nature. The concept of harmony was a reaction against the dominance of a basic Western cultural value which tends to view nature as something to be subdued and controlled.

Throughout the '70s, teenagers preferred casual clothing made with natural fibers and downplayed makeup and hair dye. Now, many teenagers wear clothing made of heavily dyed artificial fabrics rather than natural yarns in low-key colors, and teenage girls typically become interested in makeup at age 12 or 13. New-wave youth ridicule "natural" or "health" food as tasting terrible, and identify it as the food that their parents prefer. Indeed, health food is to this generation of teenagers what spinach was to previous generations. As one teenager we observed said, "My parents want me to eat health food . . . ugh! I want food with artificial additives; that kind of food tastes good."

Actually measuring the concept of living in harmony with nature is elusive, since survey questions on such subjects contain too many implicit assumptions. Therefore, we relied on qualitative observations of teenagers in small groups. To stimulate discussions of

## 2. CULTURE: Youth and Generational Cultures

living in harmony with nature, we introduced the idea of small is beautiful and asked the young people what they felt about it. Typical was this exchange among a group of New-Wave young people in Boston:

First person: "You mean I got to grow things and look like a nature freak?"

Second person: "No, no, they're saying, 'Don't get too big so that you ruin the air and water.' "

Third person: "That's gone already—maybe it will produce mutations. Excellent! Sounds like our neighbor who tells me to lower my radio because it's not natural to play it loud. You can't get too big for me— imagine stereo speakers on every street corner."

First person: "Farmers are dumb; their kids can't wait to get off the farm and ditch that hick look."

Third person: "That small-is-beautiful stuff sounds like what my teachers say—maybe farmers believe it, but it can't work here."

*Political Apathy.* To measure political involvement, the Planmetrics teenage survey used a "political-efficacy scale," a modified version of similar scales used in the classic study by political scientist Donald Stokes and his colleagues in *American Voter* (University of Chicago Press). The survey asked such questions as "Would you vote if you could?" and "Would you express your opinion to your Congressperson on a political issue of importance to you?"

When we compared our results with similar data collected by various political scientists over the past 25 years, we found that today's teenagers felt significantly more alienated than previous generations. While feelings of political efficacy for just about all segments of the population have declined during that period, the New-Wave group's feelings were even more striking. Sixty-two percent of them felt that they have no political efficacy at all now—and will not have when they reach voting age either; another 26 percent perceived only a minimal effect on the political process. Clearly, New-Wave youth see themselves as outside the mainstream of the political process.

In their political attitudes, today's teenagers are more apathetic and cynical than were people their age in recent decades. They seem to be well aware of events during the Vietnam and Watergate eras, though they were mere children in those years. They see politicians as dishonest, but are not disposed to seek remedies through political action. In contrast, the previous generation often began active participation in causes and demonstrations from the age of 13 or 14.

This is not to say they are law-abiding, middle-of-the-road citizens who simply want to mind their own business. On the contrary, they appear to be indifferent to laws, and will often violate a rule if it suits them. Unlike young people in the 1960s who sought to

Their parents—Antiwar march in San Francisco (1967). The New Wave "is not disposed to seek remedies through political action."

change the rules, the new generation sees rules as obstacles to be gotten around, especially school rules regarding behavior in general and smoking and drug use in particular. Again, this attitude suggests that the new generation is withdrawing from the larger social arena into a smaller universe where they can create new values and where only these values have moral significance.

In our survey, we did not ask our young respondents how they felt about the prospects of a nuclear war; it's difficult to frame questions that don't sound trite or tendentious. However, in our field studies, we observed that many New-Wave youth seemed to view nuclear war with passivity, as almost inevitable. Indeed, a few talked about nuclear war and the atomic bomb as metaphors for creating an exciting undefined future; a few mentioned that the biological mutations that might ensue from such a war could bring changes for the better.

One sign of what is perhaps a chilling shift in attitudes was a recent advertisement for the movie, *A Boy and His Dog*, a tale about the survivors of a nuclear disaster, among them a talking dog. The ad, which ran in newspapers across the country, showed a mushroom cloud beaming like a happy face—an unthinkable image a generation ago.

*Substitute Worlds*. From our observations, we concluded that New-Wave youth have shorter attention spans than their peers, are bored more quickly, and find sustained involvement in anything difficult. In their daily lives, they often move from one imaginary world to another in rapid succession.

For example, teenagers play one computer game after another, and each time they drop another quarter into the machine they are lured into an imaginary world. A typical remark of our young subjects, while discussing the games, was: "Wow, look at that score. I am one ace space pilot; move over Buck Rogers, I'm taking over the galaxy." (This from a stoned 15-year-old in Santa Monica.) Identification with an imaginary alter ego is strong, even though the world created in most computer games is rudimentary and not especially compelling.

Therefore, it is not surprising that Dungeons & Dragons (and all its spin-offs) is an extremely important game for New-Wave youth. Unlike most other games, Dungeons & Dragons has few rules; the players not only dream up characters but create in their own heads virtually an entire medieval universe, complete with monsters, heroic knights, damsels in distress, sinister dukes and barons (though the plot basically involves a hunt for treasure and battles against creatures who are protecting it).

But New-Wave youth substitute activities in real life as quickly as they do in games. "Substitution" here means that each activity can be replaced by almost any other activity — even its opposite — with ease. Thus, doing schoolwork tends to be the same as not doing schoolwork, getting stoned on drugs is the same as being high on alcohol, and so on. Rather than sustain a connection with an environment they don't like, New-Wave youth are ceaselessly experimenting with alternate environments.

Why have teenage values shifted so drastically in the past few years? What accounts for the New Wave's feelings of exclusion? Identifying causes in social research is extremely difficult, but the Planmetrics research team believes that much of what we are seeing is a demographic reversal: In the 1960s, young people were a disproportionately large percentage of the population as a whole. Now, they are a relatively small portion of the total population. Unlike the 1960s rebels who felt the strength of their numbers and flexed their muscles in social action, the New Wave recognizes demographic realities and has withdrawn, at least at this stage of their lives, into a private, nonpolitical world.

That withdrawal, however, is itself a form of rebellion. For in their retreat into fantasy worlds, the new generation is, in effect, rejecting many of their parents values from the 1960s. In the Planmetrics national survey, we found that young people who identified themselves as New Wave consistently had younger parents

Their future?—The movie ad below may reflect a chilling shift in young people's attitudes toward nuclear war. The beaming mushroom cloud would have been "an unthinkable image a generation ago."

than other teenagers. The parents of New-Wave youth tend to come from the baby-boom generation. Thus, the idea of a generation gap broadly defines the New-Wave rebellion; the values of the 1960s, instead of becoming the guideposts for future generations of Americans (as some futurists have mistakenly predicted) have, instead, become the old-fashioned, to-be-rejected values of one's parents.

As a much smaller percentage of the population, the new cohort of Americans feels correspondingly isolated and powerless. After a decade of affirmative action, other groups—minorities, older people, the handicapped—have apparently won a greater degree of power and social acceptance. But more than previous generations, New-Wave youth tend to see action as futile in a world where so many other groups are demanding and getting attention. "No one listens to us," we often heard from them, "so let's just do what we have to do for ourselves." For New-Wave youth, the idea of powerlessness does not only lead to the negative emotion of frustration, but to the positive sense of being free to create alternate identities.

The specific feeling of powerlessness is magnified by a perception that good jobs may not be waiting for them. In the 1970s, members of the baby-boom generation were optimistic about job opportunities; it was only when they began to reach maturity in the economy that they realized they might have to settle for less

# The New-Wave Market

Just as the values of the '60s rebels did not persist and come to dominate America in the '80s, so the values of New-Wave youth will probably be significant for the remainder of this decade and then fade away or become fundamentally transformed in ways that cannot be anticipated now. New-Wave values, however, will be with us for some time, and companies would be well-advised to understand the implications of that for their products and marketing strategies.

A good example of the difficulties in communicating with New-Wave youth is the jeans and jean-jacket market. Traditional American companies assumed teenagers would reject highly styled jean jackets and jeans, as teenagers had done in the past. But New-Wave youth, who want to look different from their parents, favor highly styled clothes, and one company, Guess Inc., has taken advantage of this attitude. By creating assorted jean colors and using denim in a wider range of styles, Guess is beginning to penetrate the market. Highly styled clothes in general (especially from Japan, England, and Italy) are making significant gains in the New-Wave market.

Manufacturers of computer games misjudged the scope of teenage demand for expensive video-arcade and repetitious home-computer games. As a marketing executive of a major computer company said, "Arcades are growing cobwebs; we goofed by developing only six basic game types and using those to produce endless variations of games they already had." The movement away from arcades to home games enabled teenagers to put their money to other uses since parents typically paid for personal computers and games. Then, the home-game market slumped as teenagers didn't buy the next clone of a game they were already playing.

But the potential attraction of computer games for creating substitute worlds is still very real. New microchip capabilities will result in more realistic and flexible video presentations. We can expect a sales boom of second- and third-generation games that are visually compelling and that require players to move through open-ended, symbolically rich environments rather than simply scoring a "kill" over a rudimentarily sketched enemy.

Anticipating and meeting the needs of New-Wave consumers is not easy. The following are a few basic guidelines:
• Do not assume that young people today think and act like previous generations.
• New-Wave teenagers respond to products and services clearly directed at them (and not immediately suitable for other markets) as an indicator that they are taken seriously. Thus, the market is sharply segmented.
• Style is critical; a clear, identifiable style for a product (especially for movies, clothes, records, computer games, and food) is necessary.
• Advertise the concrete, immediate rewards of a product, not abstract values of health or environmental quality.
• Given an emphasis on substitute worlds, products can be expected to have a relatively short life cycle, and new-product planning should begin even though an existing product is doing well.
• Monitor carefully trends in Europe and Japan, which have been the source of several New-Wave styles.

New-Wave values have recently begun to spread to adult America. We are starting to see advertisements for automobiles and perfume in stark, overdone primary colors, with surrealist scenes and music, and with a close interweaving of fantasy and reality. A better understanding of the New Wave is important for all companies, not just those marketing directly to younger people.

—S.B.

in their careers than their parents—because of their numbers and a stagnating economy.

Now teenagers are acutely aware that good jobs are scarce and usually require intensive preparation. Many New-Wave youth seem to feel that they must become career-oriented very early—as young even as age 11—or they will have to abandon hope for getting a reasonably steady, well-paying, interesting job. Given the glamorous, inflated media images of some kinds of work (everyone wants to be *Star Wars* director George Lukas or members of a rock group like "The Police"), the group tends to look down on routine, blue-collar work. Or they perceive their job prospects as so bleak that they discount the future and concentrate obsessively on their friends and entertainment.

In the national survey, New-Wave youth were somewhat less likely than other teenagers to believe that they would be able to find a job acceptable to them. Just as significant was our finding that 72 percent of the entire teenage sample felt that the future would be bleaker than the present. In Los Angeles, a young person we observed at a music club said, "My dad keeps telling me how he's gonna get laid off, and how horrible things are, and how I should study all the time so I won't be in that fix. But I can't study that good. I'm gonna wind up just like him or worse probably."

# Socialization

- Childhood (Articles 9-10)
- Influences on Personality and Behavior (Articles 11-13)

Belonging is as essential to human survival as breathing. Recent studies confirm the threat to health and well-being caused by social isolation. Learning how to belong is one of the most fundamental lessons of socialization: the lifetime process of adapting to others and learning what is the expected behavior in particular situations. Through contact with others, one learns who he or she is and gains self-knowledge. Socialization may take place in many contexts. The most basic socialization begins in the family, but churches, schools, communities, media, and workplaces also play major roles in the process.

This section contains articles which deal with the conditions of childhood and both the negative and positive socialization of children. In the first article, Elin McCoy explains that parents were calloused and indifferent toward children hundreds of years ago. Before the eighteenth century, many children were punished severely for triffling offenses, many died in their first year, and many spent little time with their parents.

David Elkind's article, "Erik Erikson's Eight Ages of Man," about the stages of psychosocial development, has become a classic. A child learns to be an adult in stages. Erikson identifies five stages of childhood and explains what is learned in each stage. If these stages are navigated successfully the child develops a sense of trust, autonomy, initiative, industry, and identity by age eighteen. If problems are encountered in these stages, the child may develop feelings of mistrust, self-doubt, guilt, inferiority, and role confusion. The final three stages of development are young adulthood, middle age, and advanced middle age or old age. Growth in these stages produces intimacy, generativity, and integrity.

The last three articles in this section diagnose some of the major influences on personality development and behavior patterns. Richard Sorenson, an anthropologist, describes a New Guinea tribe with very permissive and successful child-rearing patterns that are very dissimilar to America's. The article compares the influences of peers, parents, and styles of interaction on personality formation in this foreign tribe with the child-rearing practices of American society.

The next article examines aspects of sex role socialization in grade schools. Myra and David Sadker focus on the differential treatment of boys and girls by their teachers. Boys participate more than girls because they are encouraged more by teachers who, according to the report, are unaware of their biases.

The final article discusses the effects of television as a major socializing agent in America. There is evidence that it increases violence and decreases traditional learning. On the other hand, there are claims that television brings families together, increases social awareness, teaches tolerance, provides company for lonely people, and entertains. The article reviews many other positive and negative effects of television and explores ways in which television will expand its role in American life in the future.

Socialization suggests learning and adaptation. It is a dynamic and ever changing process. In many ways, it is synonymous with living.

## Looking Ahead: Challenge Questions

How can the ways in which children are socialized in America be improved?

In what ways are people alone some of the time, as well as members of a group some of the time?

Why is socialization a lifetime process?

What are the principal factors that make people what they are?

# Childhood Through the Ages

## Elin McCoy

**Elin McCoy** is the author of "The Incredible Year-Round Playbook" (Random House)

A gentleman-in-waiting and the nurse of little Comte de Marle often amused themselves tossing the swaddled infant back and forth across the sill of an open window. One day one of them failed to catch him, and the infant landed on a stone step and died.

The surgeon of the newborn Louis XIII cut the "fiber" under his tongue a few days after he was born, believing that if it remained uncut, Louis would be unable to suck properly and would eventually stutter.

These aren't atypical examples of child rearing in the past. Recent historical research indicates that for most of the past 2,500 years, childhood was a brief, grim period in most people's lives, especially when judged against contemporary views of child rearing.

### A new field—family history.

Through a new field of historical research, known as family history, we now know that family life and childhood in the previous centuries were startlingly different from what most people, including historians, had imagined them to be. Scores of historians are currently probing such questions as: How were children treated in the past? What concept of childhood did people have in different centuries? How important were children to their parents? Is there such a thing as "instinctual" parental behavior? What do the prevailing child-rearing beliefs and practices of the past tell us about the political, social, and psychological ideals of society? And

what kind of adults resulted from such child-rearing practices?

"Family history is the most explosive field of history today," says Professor Lawrence Stone—director of Princeton University's Shelby Cullom Davis Center for Historical Studies—whose 1977 book, *The Family, Sex and Marriage in England 1500–1800*, came out in an abridged paperback last year. "In the 1930s only about 10 scholarly books and articles on the family and childhood in history were published each year, but, incredibly, between 1971 and 1976 over 900 important books and articles were published on that subject, just covering America, England, and France." Two scholarly journals devoted to the subject were also started in the 1970s.

Why, suddenly, have so many historians focused on the family? "A whole series of contemporary anxieties has contributed to this new interest," explains Professor Stone. "General anxiety about the state of the family and whether it's breaking down, concern about the rising divorce rate, anxieties about current permissiveness in raising children, and concern about what effects women's liberation will have on children, the family, and society. And underlying all of these anxieties are two questions: Are we really doing so badly? Was it better in the past?"

In addition, two other trends in historical research have focused attention on childhood and the family. The first is social historians' growing interest in the daily lives of ordinary people in history, which has meant a greater concern with children, parenting, marriage, disease, death, and aging. The second is historians' recent efforts to employ psychological concepts as

a research tool in order to understand human motivations and experiences in the past.

Although all family historians agree that child-rearing patterns influence what happens in history, they disagree about how much and in what precise ways the treatment of children shapes history. Some researchers in the field, like Lloyd deMause, founder of *The Journal of Psychohistory: A Quarterly Journal of Childhood and Psychohistory*, go so far as to say that, in deMause's words, "child-rearing practices have been *the* central force for change in history." Along with some other psychohistorians, deMause believes that "if you want to understand the causes of historical events like the growth of Nazism, you have to look at how the children who became Nazis as adults were treated as children." But many scholars have reservations about attributing the character of a society solely to the relations between parents and children, pointing out that these relations must be understood in the context of the society as a whole and that such factors as economics must also be taken into account.

### Surprising discoveries.

Family historians have recently exploded many long-standing myths about childhood and the nature of the family throughout history. It's now clear that the functions and structure of the family have changed continuously over the years and that a variety of family types coexisted in each historical period in different regions and classes. Scholars have found, surprisingly, that the prevailing family mode in America today (the small nuclear family of parents and children living apart from other relatives)—a structure that is under much attack—is not as new to our culture as they had previously thought. Even as long ago as thirteenth-century England, as many as half of all families consisted of only a mother and/or father and two to three children. In fact, the large, loving extended families we tend to picture, with eight to ten children and several generations of relatives living under the same roof, were more the exception than the rule, even in Colonial America.

According to Professor Tamara Hareven—founder and head of the first History of the Family program in the country, at Clark University in Worcester, Massachusetts, and founding editor of the *Journal of Family History*—one of the great surprises for today's historians was "finding out that in the past, the concept of childhood and children was not the same in all centuries, classes, and countries. While the middle classes were 'discovering' childhood and becoming interested in children," she explains, "the working classes still regarded children as small adults with the same responsibilities. And in the past, childhood as we know it lasted for a much shorter time." In medieval England, for example, children as young as seven were sent to live in other households as apprentices, and for peasant children, childhood was even briefer—they joined their parents to work in the fields as soon as they could.

Infants were regarded in medieval times as unimportant, unformed animals, in the sixteenth century as "exasperating parasites," and even as late as the seventeenth century they were not seen as individuals with their own identities. Children were considered interchangeable, and frequently were given the same name as an older sibling who had died. Small children were not even viewed as interesting; Montaigne, the French essayist, summed up the prevailing attitudes of a few hundred years ago when he dismissed infants as having "neither movement in the soul, nor recognizable form in the body by which they could render themselves lovable."

Scholars tell us that infants and small children were important only insofar as they could benefit their parents. Considered possessions with no individual rights, they were used to further adult aims, and they ended up as security for debts, as ways of increasing property holdings through arranged marriages, as political hostages, and even as slaves sold for profit.

**Infancy in the past.**

Throughout history, parents' treatment of infants and very small children has been characterized by psychological coldness and physical brutality that horrify most of us today. But this behavior becomes at least comprehensible when we realize some of the conditions of people's lives. The physical realities of life were oppressive. And there were severe parental limitations as well: in addition to being influenced by unscientific medical knowledge and religious views about the nature of man, most adults had to concentrate so much of their energy on mere survival that they had little time to care for or worry about infants and small children. Abusive and violent behavior was common among adults and, therefore, not looked on with disapproval when it appeared in the treatment of children.

In view of the following facts, consider what your experience as a parent and your child's experience as an infant would have been if you had lived prior to the eighteenth century.

***Your child probably wouldn't have been wanted.*** Lack of birth control meant that having children was not a choice. For poverty-stricken peasants, an infant meant another mouth to feed—and food was precious—as well as interference with the mother's role as a worker whose contribution was necessary to the family's ability to survive. In all classes, the high risk of maternal mortality made the birth of a child a traumatic event. Even in the relatively healthy conditions enjoyed by the inhabitants of Plymouth Colony, 20 percent of women died from causes related to childbirth (compared with under 1 percent today), and in seventeenth-century England and France, the rates were much higher. It's no wonder that most children were probably unwanted. In fact, Professor Stone suggests that the availability of birth control was probably one of the necessary conditions for the increase in affection for children that began in England and America in the eighteenth century.

***Your infant would have had a good chance of dying before his or her first birthday.*** In medieval England and seventeenth-century France, for example, between 20 and 50 percent of all infants died

## 9. Childhood Through the Ages

within the first year after birth. Complications of childbirth, prematurity, diseases such as smallpox and the plague, and generally unsanitary living conditions, as well as such customs as baptism in icy water in freezing churches, took a heavy toll among vulnerable newborns. America was healthier for infants—in Plymouth Colony, infant mortality was only 10 to 15 percent (which is still ten times higher than it is in America today). The likelihood that one's infants would die discouraged parents from investing much affection or interest in them and from regarding them as special, unique individuals until it appeared more certain that they might live to adulthood.

Illegitimate infants and infants of poverty-stricken parents (and parents who felt they already had enough children) were often the victims of infanticide through deliberate murder, abandonment, or neglect. In ancient Greece, for example, infants who seemed sickly or didn't have a perfect shape or cried too much or too little were "exposed," or abandoned to die, a decision that was made by the father shortly after birth. In mid-eighteenth-century England, so many babies—both legitimate and illegitimate—were abandoned to die in the streets of cities and towns that the first foundling home established in London received several thousand babies a year. In early America, infanticide seems to have affected only illegitimate children.

***If you were well-off, your baby probably would have been breast-fed by someone else.*** In spite of the fact that all medical advice since Roman times had stressed that babies breast-fed by their own mothers had a better chance of survival, for eighteen centuries any woman who could afford it sent her infant to a wet nurse.

Recuperation from a difficult childbirth prevented some women from breast-feeding, but many others thought it too demanding, especially since it was customary for infants to breast-feed for as long as two years. Also, many husbands would not allow their wives to breast-feed, partly because medical opinion held that women who were breast-feeding should not engage in sexual intercourse.

Underlying these reasons may have been parents' desire to distance themselves emotionally from their infants.

53

## 3. SOCIALIZATION: Childhood

In Renaissance Italy, middle-class infants were delivered to the *bália*, or wet nurse, immediately after baptism—two or three days after birth—and, if they survived, remained there for two years. Rarely did mothers visit their infants, and thus a baby was returned home at the end of that time to a stranger.

Although some wet nurses moved in with the family, most women left their babies at the wet nurse's home, where the child was often neglected and starved because wet nurses commonly took on too many babies in order to make more money. Frequently wet nurses ran out of milk, and infants had to be sent to a series of different nurses and thus were deprived even of a single surrogate mother.

The first groups of middle-class women to change this 1,800-year-old pattern on a large scale were the Puritans in the seventeenth century. Eventually, in the eighteenth century, there was a widespread cult of maternal breast-feeding in both America and England. Scholars have suggested that this shift may have contributed substantially to the shift in parental feelings for infants that began in the eighteenth century; certainly it reduced infant mortality.

*Your infant would have spent little time with you.* In the past, parents spent much less time with their children than even working parents do today and clearly did not feel the need to arrange supervision for them. Peasant women commonly left their infants and toddlers alone all day at home while they worked elsewhere. In one area of England during the thirteenth century, for example, half the infant deaths involved infants in cradles being burned while no one was home. Unsupervised toddlers frequently wandered off and drowned. In the middle and upper classes, parental neglect took the form of turning toddlers over to the servants to raise.

*Your infant would have been swaddled in tightly bound cloths from birth to as old as eight months.* Emotional distancing, economic necessity, and faulty medical knowledge are also evident in another common practice—swaddling. In England this practice continued up to the eighteenth century; in France, the nineteenth century; and in Russia, into the twentieth century. Kept in tightly bound bandages, swaddled infants were totally isolated from their surroundings for the first four months or so. After that, only their legs were bound. They couldn't turn their heads, suck their own thumbs for comfort, or crawl. Swaddling that was too tight occasionally caused suffocation. Although doctors advocated changing the infant two or three times a day, this apparently was uncommon, and even Louis XIII developed severe rashes because of his swaddling bands.

Medical reasons for the practice included the beliefs that if free, the infant might tear off his ears or scratch out his eyes, that swaddling was necessary to keep infants warm in cold, draughty cottages, houses, and castles, and that it ensured that the infant's pliable limbs would grow straight so he would be able to stand erect. Even when the swaddling bands were removed from their legs, children were not allowed to crawl "like an animal," but were forced to stand with the help

**Mother's helper:** The "roundabout" was a 19th-century gadget designed to keep baby out of mother's way. But it sacrificed a freedom of movement that today we know is crucial to a child's development.

of bizarre contraptions. Convenience was another reason for swaddling: it caused infants to sleep more and cry less, so they could be left for long periods of time while mothers worked. Also, swaddled infants were easier to carry and could even be hung on a peg on the wall out of the way.

*Your infant or child would probably have received harsh beatings regularly—from you or a servant—even for such "normal" behavior as crying or wanting to play.* For many centuries, discipline and teaching of the infant and young child concentrated on "breaking the child's will," which meant crushing all assertiveness and instilling complete obedience. This was accomplished through physical and psychological maltreatment that today we would consider "child abuse." Susanna Wesley, mother of John Wesley, the founder of the Methodist Church, records her treatment of her children: "When turned a year old, and some before, they were taught to fear the rod and cry softly." Louis XIII was whipped every morning, starting at the age of two, simply for being "obstinate," and was even whipped on the day of his coronation at the age of nine. The Puritans believed that "the newborn babe is full of the stains and pollutions of sin" and saw the first strivings of a one- and two-year-old to independence—which we now recognize as essential to a child's growing mastery of himself and understanding of the world—as a clear manifestation of that original sin. It was considered the duty of parents to use physical harshness and psychological terrorization—locking children in dark closets for an entire day or frightening them with tales of death and hellfire, for example—to wipe this sin out.

These child-rearing practices, as well as the difficult realities of life in the past, had important psychological effects on children's development. According to Professor Stone, the isolation, sensory deprivation, and lack of physical closeness that resulted from swaddling; the absence of a mother because of death in childbirth or the practice of wet-nursing; the common experience for small children of losing parents and siblings; and the suppression of self-assertion through whipping and other fear-producing techniques all resulted in an "adult world of emotional cripples."

**A change for the better.**

In the late seventeenth and eighteenth centuries, many of these child-rearing practices began to change among wealthy merchants and other groups in the upper middle classes of England and America. Some changes can be traced to the Puritans, who, even though they advocated harsh disciplinary measures, focused a new attention on children and the importance of their upbringing. By the late eighteenth century, among some groups, methods of contraception were available, swaddling had been abandoned, maternal breast-feeding had become the fashion, and "breaking the will" had given way to affection and a degree of permissiveness that seems extraordinary even by today's standards. In England the indulgent Lord Holland, for example, intent on gratifying his little son Charles's every whim, allowed him to jump and splash in the large bowl of cream intended for dessert at a grand dinner while the guests, a group of foreign ministers, looked on. Many adults feared the effect on society when these spoiled children reached maturity. And in fact, many of them did spend their lives in lifelong dissipation and often became followers of evangelical religions. While the Victorian era varied from harsh to permissive in the treatment of children, by the end of the nineteenth century the child-oriented family became a reality for all classes in Western society.

**What it all means for us.**

Were childhood and family life better in the past? The answer—obviously—is a resounding no. One is tempted to agree with Lloyd deMause that "the history of childhood is a nightmare from which we have only recently begun to awaken."

Nevertheless, Professor Hareven feels that there *were* some good aspects to childhood in the past, which we can learn from today. "Children were not so segregated from adults and responsibility," she points out. "The historical record shows children grew up in households that included servants, other workers employed by the family, lodgers, visiting relatives, and siblings of widely differing ages, as well as parents. They were exposed to a greater variety of adult roles than children usually are today and they interacted with a greater variety of people of all ages. They also knew more about their parents' work. And unlike today, children were working, contributing members of families and the society from an early age—as they are in contemporary China. Today's child-oriented family and the postponement of responsibility and work limit children's experience. The models are there in history for us to borrow and shape to today's ideals."

Historical research on childhood helps us view our own ideas about parenthood from a perspective in which it is clear that there are no absolutes. The new facts that are available to us show that assumptions behind child rearing change and that what we think of as parents' "instincts" actually depend on the beliefs and experiences of their society. The possessiveness and affection toward infants, which we take for granted, is a recent development. Even the "maternal instinct" to breast-feed one's own child was not instinctive for many women for over 1,800 years.

Family history also gives us an informative view of family structure. Those who are worried about the high divorce rate and the effect of parental separation on children, for example, should realize that in the past, approximately the same percentage of families were separated—only it was by the death of one of the parents instead of by divorce.

Although problems with child rearing will probably always be with us,

THE BETTMANN ARCHIVE

**"The Human Comedy":** That's the name of this 19th-century sketch—but the partially-swaddled child, left alone hanging on a wall, isn't finding anything in his situation to laugh about.

the very existence of family history means that we have come to the point where we are much more self-conscious about how we raise children, and, in turn, this may help us to be more thoughtful about the way we treat them. By examining childhood in the past, we become aware that our own attempts to do things differently—"nonsexist" child rearing, co-parenting, and different mixes of permissiveness and discipline—may have profound effects on society. If we can avoid the mistakes of the past, borrow what was good, and continue to examine our own aims and practices, the society our children make may be a better one than ours.

# Erik Erikson's Eight Ages Of Man
## One man in his time plays many psychosocial parts

# David Elkind

DAVID ELKIND *is professor of psychology and psychiatry at the University of Rochester.*

At a recent faculty reception I happened to join a small group in which a young mother was talking about her "identity crisis." She and her husband, she said, had decided not to have any more children and she was depressed at the thought of being past the child-bearing stage. It was as if, she continued, she had been robbed of some part of herself and now needed to find a new function to replace the old one.

When I remarked that her story sounded like a case history from a book by Erik Erikson, she replied, "Who's Erikson?" It is a reflection on the intellectual modesty and literary decorum of Erik H. Erikson, psychoanalyst and professor of developmental psychology at Harvard, that so few of the many people who today talk about the "identity crisis" know anthing of the man who pointed out its pervasiveness as a problem in contemporary society two decades ago.

Erikson has, however, contributed more to social science than his delineation of identity problems in modern man. His descriptions of the stages of the life cycle, for example, have advanced psychoanalytic theory to the point where it can now describe the development of the healthy personality on its own terms and not merely as the opposite of a sick one. Likewise, Erikson's emphasis upon the problems unique to adolescents and adults living in today's society has helped to rectify the one-sided emphasis on childhood as the beginning and end of personality development.

Finally, in his biographical studies, such as "Young Man Luther" and "Gandhi's Truth" (which has just won a National Book Award in philosophy and religion), Erikson emphasizes the inherent strengths of the human personality by showing how individuals can use their neurotic symptoms and conflicts for creative and constructive social purposes while healing themselves in the process.

It is important to emphasize that Erikson's contributions are genuine advances in psychoanalysis in the sense that Erikson accepts and builds upon many of the basic tenets of Freudian theory. In this regard, Erikson differs from Freud's early co-workers such as Jung and Adler who, when they broke with Freud, rejected his theories and substituted their own.

Likewise, Erikson also differs from the so-called neo-Freudians such as Horney, Kardiner and Sullivan who (mistakenly, as it turned out) assumed that Freudian theory had nothing to say about man's relation to reality and to his culture. While it is true that Freud emphasized, even mythologized, sexuality, he did so to counteract the rigid sexual taboos of his time, which, at that point in history, were frequently the cause of neuroses. In his later writings, however, Freud began to concern himself with the executive agency of the personality, namely the ego, which is also the repository of the individual's attitudes and concepts about himself and his world.

It is with the psychosocial development of the ego that Erikson's observations and theoretical constructions are primarily concerned. Erikson has thus been able to introduce innovations into psychoanalytic theory without either rejecting or ignoring Freud's monumental contribution.

The man who has accomplished this notable feat is a handsome Dane, whose white hair, mustache, resonant accent and gentle manner are reminiscent of actors like Jean Hersholt and Paul Muni. Although he is warm and outgoing with friends, Erikson is a rather shy man who is uncomfortable in the spotlight of public recognition. This trait, together with his ethical reservations about making public even disguised case material, may help to account for Erikson's reluctance to publish his observations and conceptions (his first book appeared in 1950, when he was 48).

In recent years this reluctance to publish has diminished and he has been appearing in print at an increasing pace. Since 1960 he has published three books, "Insight and Responsibility," "Identity: Youth and Crisis" and "Gandhi's Truth," as well as editing a fourth, "Youth: Change ·and Challenge." Despite the accolades and recognition these books have won for him, both in America and abroad, Erikson is still surprised at the popular interest they have generated and is a little troubled about the possibility of being misunderstood and misinterpreted. While he would prefer that his books spoke for themselves and that he was left out of the picture, he has had to accede to popular demand for more information about himself and his work.

The course of Erikson's professional career has been as diverse as it has been unconventional. He was born in Frankfurt, Germany, in 1902 of Danish parents. Not long after his birth his father died, and his mother later married the pediatrician who had cured her son of a childhood illness. Erikson's stepfather urged him to become a physician, but the boy declined and became an artist instead—an artist who did portraits of children. Erikson says of his post-adolescent years, "I was an artist then, which in Europe is a euphemism for a young man with some talent and nowhere to go." During this period he settled in Vienna and worked as a tutor in a family friendly with Freud's. He met Freud on informal occasions when the families went on outings together.

These encounters may have been the impetus to accept a teaching appointment at an American school in Vienna founded by Dorothy Burlingham and directed by Peter Blos (both now well known on the American psychiatric scene). During these years (the late nineteen-twenties) he also undertook and completed psychoanalytic training with Anna Freud and August Aichhorn. Even at the outset of his career, Erikson gave evidence of the breadth of his interests and activities by being trained and certified as a Montessori teacher. Not surprisingly, in view of that training, Erikson's first articles dealt with psychoanalysis and education.

It was while in Vienna that Erikson met and married Joan Mowat Serson, an American artist of Canadian descent. They came to America in 1933, when Erikson was invited to practice and teach in Boston. Erikson was, in fact, one of the first if not the first child-analyst in the Boston area. During the next two decades he held clinical and academic appointments at Harvard, Yale and Berkeley. In 1951 he joined a group of psychiatrists and psychologists who moved to Stockbridge, Mass., to start a new program at the Austen Riggs Center, a private residential treatment center for disturbed young people. Erikson remained at Riggs until 1961, when he was appointed professor of human development and lecturer on psychiatry at Harvard. Throughout his career he has always held two or three appointments simultaneously and has traveled extensively.

Perhaps because he had been an artist first, Erikson has never been a conventional psychoanalyst. When he was treating children, for example, he always insisted on visiting his young patients' homes and on having dinner with the families. Likewise in the nineteen-thirties, when anthropological investigation was described to him by his friends Scudder McKeel, Alfred Kroeber and Margaret Mead, he decided to do field work on an Indian reservation. "When I realized that Sioux is the name which we [in Europe] pronounced "See us" and which for us was *the* American Indian, I could not resist." Erikson thus antedated the anthropologists who swept over the Indian reservations in the post-Depression years. (So numerous were the field workers at that time that the stock joke was that an Indian family could be defined as a mother, a father, children and an anthropologist.)

Erikson did field work not only with the Oglala Sioux of Pine Ridge, S. D. (the tribe that slew Custer and was in turn slaughtered at the Battle of Wounded Knee), but also with the salmon-fishing Yurok of Northern California. His reports on these experiences revealed his special gift for sensing and entering into the world views and modes of thinking of cultures other than his own.

It was while he was working with the Indians that Erikson began to note syndromes which he could not explain within the confines of traditional psychoanalytic theory. Central to many an adult Indian's emotional problems seemed to be his sense of uprootedness and lack of continuity between his present life-style and that portrayed in tribal history. Not only did the Indian sense a break with the past, but he could not identify with a future requiring assimilation of the white culture's values. The problems faced by such men, Erikson recognized, had to do with the ego and with culture and only incidentally with sexual drives.

The impressions Erikson gained on the reservations were reinforced during World War II when he worked at a veterans' rehabilitation center at Mount Zion Hospital in San Francisco. Many of the soldiers he and his colleagues saw seemed not to fit the traditional "shell shock" or "malingerer" cases of World War I. Rather, it seemed to Erikson that many of these men had lost the sense of who and what they were. They were having trouble reconciling their activities, attitudes and feelings as soldiers with the activities, attitudes and feelings they had known before the war. Accordingly, while these men may well have had difficulties with repressed or conflicted drives, their main problem seemed to be, as Erikson came to speak of it at the time, "identity confusion."

It was almost a decade before Erikson set forth the implications of his clinical observations in "Childhood and Society." In that book, the summation and integration of 15 years of research, he made three major contributions to the study of the human ego. He posited (1) that, side by side with the stages of psychosexual development described by Freud (the oral, anal, phallic, genital, Oedipal and pubertal), were psychosocial stages of ego development, in which the individual had to establish new basic orientations to himself and his social world; (2) that personality development continued throughout the whole life cycle; and (3) that each stage had a positive *as well* as a negative component.

Much about these contributions—and about Erikson's way of thinking—can be understood by looking at his scheme of life stages. Erikson identifies eight stages in the human life cycle, in each of which a new dimension of "social interaction" becomes possible—that is, a new dimension in a person's interaction with himself, and with his social environment.

## TRUST vs. MISTRUST

The first stage corresponds to the oral stage in classical psychoanalytic theory and usually extends through the first year of life. In Erikson's view, the new dimension of social interaction that emerges during this period involves basic *trust* at the one extreme, and *mistrust* at the other. The degree to which the child comes to trust the world, other people and himself depends to a considerable extent upon the quality of the care that he receives. The infant whose needs are met when they arise, whose discomforts are quickly removed, who is cuddled, fondled, played with and talked to, develops a sense of the world as a safe place to be and of people as helpful and dependable. When, however, the care is inconsistent, inadequate and rejecting, it fosters a basic mistrust, an attitude of fear and suspicion on the part of the infant toward the world in general and people in particular that will carry through to later stages of development.

It should be said at this point that the problem of basic trust-versus-mistrust (as is true for all the later dimensions) is not resolved once and for all during the first year of life; it arises again at each successive stage of development. There is both hope and danger in this. The child who enters school with a sense of mistrust may come to trust a particular teacher who has taken the trouble to make herself trustworthy; with this second chance, he overcomes his early mistrust. On the other hand, the child who comes through infancy with a vital sense of trust can still have his sense of mistrust activated at a later stage if, say, his parents are divorced and separated under acrimonious circumstances.

This point was brought home to me in a very direct way by a 4-year-old patient I saw in a court clinic. He was being seen at the court clinic because his adoptive parents, who had had him for six months, now wanted to give him back to the agency. They claimed that he was cold and unloving, took things and could not be trusted. He was indeed a cold and apathetic boy, but with good reason. About a year after his illegitimate birth, he was taken away from his mother, who had a drinking problem, and was shunted back and forth among several foster homes. Initially he had tried to relate to the persons in the foster homes, but the relationships never had a chance to develop becuase he was moved at just the wrong times. In the end he gave up trying to reach out to others, because the inevitable separations hurt too much.

Like the burned child who dreads the flame, this emotionally burned child shunned the pain of emotional involvement. He had trusted his mother, but now he trusted no one. Only years of devoted care and patience could now undo the damage that had been done to this child's sense of trust.

## AUTONOMY vs. DOUBT

Stage Two spans the second and third years of life, the period which Freudian theory calls the anal stage. Erikson sees here the emergence of *autonomy*. This autonomy dimension builds upon the child's new motor and mental abilities. At this stage the child can not only walk but also climb, open and close, drop, push and pull, hold and let go. The child takes pride in these new accomplishments and wants to do everything himself, whether it be pulling the wrapper off a piece of candy, selecting the vitamin out of the bottle or flushing the toilet. If parents recognize the young child's need to do what he is capable of doing at his own pace and in his own time, then he develops a sense that he is able to control his muscles, his impulses, himself and, not insignificantly, his environment—the sense of autonomy.

When, however, his caretakers are impatient and do for him what he is capable of doing himself, they reinforce a sense of shame and doubt. To be sure, every parent has rushed a child at times and children are hardy enough to endure such lapses. It is only when caretaking is consistently overprotective and criticism of "accidents" (whether these be wetting, soiling, spilling or breaking things) is harsh and unthinking that the child develops an excessive sense of shame with respect to other people and an excessive sense of doubt about own abilities to control his world and himself.

If the child leaves this stage with less autonomy than shame or doubt, he will be handicapped in his attempts to achieve autonomy in adolescence and adulthood. Contrariwise, the child who moves through this stage with his sense of autonomy buoyantly outbalancing his feelings of shame and doubt is well prepared to be autonomous at later phases in the life cycle. Again, however, the balance of autonomy to shame and doubt set up during this period can be changed in either positive or negative directions by later events.

It might be well to note, in addition, that too much autonomy can be as harmful as too little. I have in mind a patient of 7 who had a heart condition. He had learned very quickly how terrified his parents were of any signs in him of cardiac difficulty. With the psychological acuity given to children, he soon ruled the household. The family could not go shopping, or for a drive, or on a holiday if he did not approve. On those rare occasions when the parents had had enough and defied him, he would get angry and his purple hue and gagging would frighten them into submission.

Actually, this boy was frightened of this power (as all children would be) and was really eager to give it up. When the parents and the boy came to realize this, and to recognize that a little shame and doubt were a healthy counterpoise to an inflated sense of autonomy, the three of them could once again assume their normal roles.

## INITIATIVE vs. GUILT

In this stage (the genital stage of classical psychoanalysis) the child, age 4 to 5, is pretty much master of his body and can ride a tricycle, run, cut and hit. He can thus initiate motor activities of various sorts on his own and no longer merely responds to or imitates the actions of other children. The same holds true for his language and fantasy activities. Accordingly, Erikson argues that the social dimension that appears at this stage has *initiative* at one of its poles and *guilt* at the other.

Whether the child will leave this stage with his sense of initiative far outbalancing his sense of guilt depends to a considerable extent upon how parents respond to his self-initiated activities. Children who are given much freedom and opportunity to initiate motor play such as running, bike riding, sliding, skating, tussling and wrestling have their sense of initiative reinforced. Initiative is also reinforced when parents answer their children's questions (intellectual initiative) and do not deride or inhibit fantasy or play activity. On the other hand, if the child is made to feel that his motor activity is bad, that his questions are a nuisance and that his play is silly and stupid, then he may develop a sense of guilt over self-initiated activities in general that will persist through later life stages.

## INDUSTRY vs. INFERIORITY

Stage Four is the age period from 6 to 11, the elementary school years (described by classical psychoanalysis as the *latency phase*). It is a time during which the child's love for the parent of the opposite sex and rivalry with the same sexed parent (elements in the so-called family romance) are quiescent. It is also a period during which the child becomes capable of deductive reasoning, and of playing and learning by rules. It is not until this period, for example, that children can really play marbles, checkers and other "take turn" games that require obedience to rules. Erikson argues that the psychosocial dimension that emerges during this period has a sense of *industry* at one extreme and a sense of *inferiority* at the other.

The term industry nicely captures a dominant theme of this period during which the concern with how things are made, how they work and what they do predominates. It is the Robinson Crusoe age in the sense that the enthusiasm and minute detail with which Crusoe describes his activities appeals to the child's own budding sense of industry. When children are encouraged in their efforts to make, do, or build practical things (whether it be to construct creepy crawlers, tree houses, or airplane models—or to cook, bake or sew), are allowed to finish their products, and are praised and rewarded for the results, then the sense of industry is enhanced. But parents who see their children's efforts at making and doing as "mischief," and as simply "making a mess," help to encourage in children a sense of inferiority.

During these elementary school years, however, the child's world includes more than the home. Now social institutions other than the family come to play a central role in the developmental crisis of the individual. (Here Erikson introduced still another advance in psychoanalytic theory, which heretofore concerned itself only with the effects of the parents' behavior upon the child's development.)

A child's school experiences affect his industry-inferiority balance. The child, for example, with an I.Q. of 80 to 90 has a particularly traumatic school experience, even when his sense of industry is rewarded and encouraged at home. He is "too bright" to be in special classes, but "too slow" to compete with children of average ability. Consequently he experiences constant failures in his academic efforts that reinforces a sense of inferiority.

On the other hand, the child who had his sense of industry derogated at home can have it revitalized at school through the offices of a sensitive and committed teacher. Whether the child develops a sense of industry or inferiority, therefore, no longer depends solely on the caretaking efforts of the parents but on the actions and offices of other adults as well.

## IDENTITY vs. ROLE CONFUSION

When the child moves into adolescence (Stage Five—roughly the ages 12-18), he encounters, according to traditional psychoanalytic theory, a reawakening of the family-romance problem of early childhood. His means of resolving the problem is to seek and find a romantic partner of his own generation. While Erikson does not deny this aspect of adolescence, he points out that there are other problems as well. The adolescent matures mentally as well as physiologically and, in addition to the new feelings, sensations and desires he experiences as a result of changes in his body, he develops a multitude of new ways of looking at and thinking about the world. Among other things, those in adolescence can now think about other people's thinking and wonder about what other people think of them. They can also conceive of ideal families, religions and societies which they then compare with the imperfect families, religions and societies of their own experience. Finally, adolescents become capable of constructing theories and philosophies designed to bring all the varied and conflicting aspects of society into a working, harmonious and peaceful whole. The adolescent, in a word, is an impatient idealist who believes that it is as easy to realize an ideal as it is to imagine it.

Erikson believes that the new interpersonal dimension which emerges during this period has to do with a sense of *ego identity* at the positive end and a sense of *role confusion* at the negative end. That is to say, given the adolescent's newfound integrative abilities, his task is to bring together all of the things he has learned about himself as a son, student, athlete, friend, Scout, newspaper boy, and so on, and integrate these different images of himself into a whole that makes sense and that shows continuity with the past while preparing for the future. To the extent that the young person succeeds in this endeavor, he arrives at a sense of psychosocial identity, a sense of who he is, where he has been and where he is going.

In contrast to the earlier stages, where parents play a more or less direct role in the determination of the result of the developmental crises, the influence of parents during this stage is much more indirect. If the young person reaches adolescence with, thanks to his parents, a vital sense of trust, autonomy, initiative and industry, then his chances of arriving at a meaningful sense of ego identity are much enhanced. The reverse, of course, holds true for the young person who enters adolescence with considerable mistrust, shame, doubt, guilt and inferiority. Preparation for a successful adolescence, and the attainment of an integrated psychosocial identity must, therefore, begin in the cradle.

Over and above what the individual brings with him from his childhood, the attainment of a sense of personal identity depends upon the social milieu in which he or she grows up. For example, in a society where women are to some extent second-class citizens, it may be harder for females to arrive at a sense of psychosocial identity. Likewise at times, such as the present, when rapid social and technological change breaks down many traditional values, it may be more difficult for young people to find continuity between what they learned and experienced as children and what they learn and experience as adolescents. At such times young people often seek causes that give their lives meaning and direction. The activism of the current generation of young people may well stem, in part at least, from this search.

When the young person cannot attain a sense of personal identity, either because of an unfortunate childhood or difficult social circumstances, he shows a certain amount of *role confusion*—a sense of not knowing what he is, where he belongs or whom he belongs to. Such confusion is a frequent symptom in delinquent young people. Promiscuous adolescent girls, for example, often seem to have a fragmented sense of ego identity. Some young people seek a "negative identity," an identity opposite to the one prescribed for them by their family and friends. Having an identity as a "delinquent," or as a "hippie," or even as an "acid head," may sometimes be preferable to having no identity at all.

In some cases young people do not seek a negative identity so much as they have it thrust upon them. I remember another court case in which the defendant was an attractive 16-year-old girl who had been found "tricking it" in a trailer located just outside the grounds of an Air Force base. From about the age of 12, her mother had encouraged her to dress seductively and to go out with boys. When she returned from dates, her sexually frustrated mother demanded a kiss-by-kiss, caress-by-caress description of the evening's activities. After the mother had vicariously satisfied her sexual needs, she proceeded to call her daughter a "whore" and a "dirty tramp."

As the girl told me, "Hell, I have the name, so I might as well play the role."

Failure to establish a clear sense of personal identity at adolescence does not guarantee perpetual failure. And the person who attains a working sense of ego identity in adolescence will of necessity encounter challenges and threats to that identity as he moves through life. Erikson, perhaps more than any other personality theorist, has emphasized that life is constant change and that confronting problems at one stage in life is not a guarantee against the reappearance of these problems at later stages, or against the finding of new solutions to them.

## INTIMACY vs. ISOLATION

Stage Six in the life cycle is young adulthood; roughly the period of courtship and early family life that extends from late adolescence till early middle age. For this stage, and the stages described hereafter, classical psychoanalysis has nothing new or major to say. For Erikson, however, the previous attainment of a sense of personal identity and the engagement in productive work that marks this period gives rise to a new interpersonal dimension of *intimacy* at the one extreme and *isolation* at the other.

When Erikson speaks of intimacy he means much more than love-making alone; he means the ability to share with and care about another person without fear of losing oneself in the process. In the case of intimacy, as in the case of identity, success or failure no longer depends directly upon the parents but only indirectly as they have contributed to the individual's success or failure at the earlier stages. Here, too, as in the case of identity, social conditions may help or hinder the establishment of a sense of intimacy. Likewise, intimacy need not involve sexuality; it includes the relationship between friends. Soldiers who have served together under the most dangerous circumstances often develop a sense of commitment to one another that exemplifies intimacy in its broadest sense. If a sense of intimacy is not established with friends or a marriage partner, the result, in Erikson's view, is a sense of isolation—of being alone without anyone to share with or care for.

## GENERATIVITY vs. SELF-ABSORPTION

This stage—middle age—brings with it what Erikson speaks of as either *generativity or self-absorption,* and stagnation. What Erikson means by generativity is that the person begins to be concerned with others beyond his immediate family, with future generations and the nature of the society and world in which those generations will live. Generativity does not reside only in parents; it can be found in any individual who actively concerns himself with the welfare of young people and with making the world a better place for them to live and to work.

Those who fail to establish a sense of generativity fall into a state of self-absorption in which their personal needs and comforts are of predominant concern. A fictional case of self-absorption is Dickens's Scrooge in "A Christmas Carol." In his one-sided concern with money and in his disregard for the interests and welfare of his young employee, Bob Cratchit, Scrooge exemplifies the self-absorbed, embittered (the two often go together) old man. Dickens also illustrated, however, what Erikson points out: namely, that unhappy solutions to life's crises are not irreversible. Scrooge, at the end of the tale, manifested both a sense of generativity and of intimacy which he had not experienced before.

## INTEGRITY vs. DESPAIR

Stage Eight in the Eriksonian scheme corresponds roughly to the period when the individual's major efforts are nearing completion and when there is time for reflection—and for the enjoyment of grandchildren, if any. The psychosocial dimension that comes into prominence now has *integrity* on one hand and *despair* on the other.

The sense of integrity arises from the individual's ability to look back on his life with satisfaction. At the other extreme is the individual who looks back upon his life as a series of missed opportunities and missed directions; now in the twilight years he realizes that it is too late to start again. For such a person the inevitable result is a sense of despair at what might have been.

These, then, are the major stages in the life cycle as described by Erikson. Their presentation, for one thing, frees the clinician to treat adult emotional problems as failures (in part at least) to solve genuinely adult personality crises and not, as heretofore, as mere residuals of infantile frustrations and conflicts. This view of personality growth, moreover, takes some of the onus off parents and takes account of the role which society and the person himself play in the formation of an individual personality. Finally, Erikson has offered hope for us all by demonstrating that each phase of growth has its strengths as well as its weaknesses and that failures at one stage of development can be rectified by successes at later stages.

The reason that these ideas, which sound so agreeable to "common sense," are in fact so revolutionary has a lot to do with the state of psychoanalysis in America. As formulated by Freud, psychoanalysis encompassed a theory of personality development, a method of studying the human mind and, finally, procedures for treating troubled and unhappy people. Freud viewed this system as a scientific one, open to revision as new facts and observations accumulated.

The system was, however, so vehemently attacked that Freud's followers were constantly in the position of having to defend Freud's views. Perhaps because of this situation, Freud's system became, in the hands of some of his followers and defenders, a dogma upon which all theoretical innovation, clinical observation and therapeutic practice had to be grounded. That this attitude persists is evidenced in the recent remark by a psychoanalyst that he believed psychotic patients could not be treated by psychoanalysis because "Freud said so." Such attitudes, in which Freud's authority rather than observation and data is the basis of deciding what is true and what is false, has contributed to the disrepute in which psychoanalysis is widely held today.

Erik Erikson has broken out of this scholasticism and has had the courage to say that Freud's discoveries and practices were the start and not the end of the study and treatment of the human personality. In addition to advocating the modifications of psychoanalytic theory outlined above, Erikson has also suggested modifications in therapeutic practice, particularly in the treatment of young patients. "Young people in severe trouble are not fit for the couch," he writes. "They want to face you, and they want you to face them, not a facsimile of a parent, or wearing the mask of a professional helper, but as a kind of over-all individual a young person can live with or despair of."

Erikson has had the boldness to remark on some of the negative effects that distorted notions of psychoanalysis have had on society at large. Psychoanalysis, he says, has contributed to a widespread fatalism—"even as we were trying to devise, with scientific determinism, a therapy for the few, we were led to promote an ethical disease among the many."

Perhaps Erikson's innovations in psychoanalytic theory are best exemplified in his psycho-historical writings, in which he combines psychoanalytic insight with a true historical imagination. After the publication of "Childhood and Society," Erikson undertook the application of his scheme of the human life cycle to the study of historical persons. He wrote a series of brilliant essays on men as varied as Maxim Gorky, George Bernard Shaw and Freud himself. These studies were not narrow case histories but rather reflected Erikson's remarkable grasp of Europe's social and political history, as well as of its literature. (His mastery of American folklore, history and literature is equally remarkable.)

While Erikson's major biographical studies were yet to come, these early essays already revealed his unique psycho-history method. For one thing, Erikson always chose men whose lives fascinated him in one way or another, perhaps because of some conscious or unconscious affinity with them. Erikson thus had a sense of community with his subjects which he adroitly used (he calls it *disciplined subjectivity)* to take his subject's point of view and to experience the world as that person might.

Secondly, Erikson chose to elaborate a particular crisis or episode in the individual's life which seemed to crystallize a life-theme that united the activities of his past and gave direction to his activities for the future. Then, much as an artist might, Erikson proceeded to fill in the background of the episode and add social and historical perspective. In a very real sense Erikson's biographical sketches are like paintings which direct the viewer's gaze from a focal point of attention to background and back again, so that one's appreciation of the focal area is enriched by having pursued the picture in its entirety.

This method was given its first major test in Erikson's study of "Young Man Luther." Originally, Erikson planned only a brief study of Luther, but "Luther proved too bulky a man to be merely a chapter in a book." Erikson's involvement with Luther dated from his youth, when, as a wandering artist, he happened to hear the Lord's Prayer in Luther's German. "Never knowingly having heard it, I had the experience, as seldom before or after, of a wholeness captured in a few simple words, of poetry fusing the esthetic and the moral; those who have suddenly 'heard' the Gettysburg Address will know what I mean."

Erikson's interest in Luther may have had other roots as well. In some ways, Luther's unhappiness with the papal intermediaries of Christianity resembled on a grand scale Erikson's own dissatisfaction with the intermediaries of Freud's system. In both cases some of the intermediaries had so distorted the original teachings that what was being preached in the name of the master came close to being the opposite of what he had himself proclaimed. While it is not possible to describe Erikson's treatment of Luther here, one can get some feeling for Erikson's brand of historical analysis from his sketch of Luther:

"Luther was a very troubled and a very gifted young man who had to create his own cause on which to focus his fidelity in the Roman Catholic world as it was then.... He first became a monk and tried to solve his scruples by being an exceptionally good monk. But even his superiors thought that he tried much too hard. He felt himself to be such a sinner that he began to lose faith in the charity of God and his superiors told him, 'Look, God doesn't hate you, you hate God or else you would trust Him to accept your prayers.' But I would like to make it clear that someone like Luther becomes a historical person only because he also has an acute understanding of historical actuality and knows how to 'speak to the condition' of his times. Only then do inner struggles become representative of those of a large number of vigorous and sincere young people—and begin to interest some troublemakers and hangers-on."

After Erikson's study of "Young Man Luther" (1958), he turned his attention to "middle-aged" Gandhi. As did Luther, Gandhi evoked for Erikson childhood memories. Gandhi led his first nonviolent protest in India in 1918 on behalf of some mill workers, and Erikson, then a young man of 16, had read glowing accounts of the event. Almost a half a century later Erikson was invited to Ahmedabad, an industrial city in western India, to give a seminar on the human life cycle. Erikson discovered that Ahmedabad was the city in which Gandhi had led the demonstration about which Erikson had read as a youth. Indeed, Erikson's host was none other than Ambalal Sarabahai, the benevolent industrialist who had been Gandhi's host—as well as antagonist—in the 1918 wage dispute. Throughout his stay in Ahmedabad, Erikson continued to encounter people and places that were related to Gandhi's initial experiments with nonviolent techniques.

The more Erikson learned about the event at Ahmedabad, the more intrigued he became with its pivotal importance in Gandhi's career. It seemed to be the historical moment upon which all the earlier events of Gandhi's life converged and from which diverged all of his later endeavors. So captured was Erikson by the event at Ahmedabad, that he returned the following year to research a book on Gandhi in which the event would serve as a fulcrum.

At least part of Erikson's interest in Gandhi may have stemmed from certain parallels in their lives. The 1918 event marked Gandhi's emergence as a national political leader. He was 48 at the time, and had become involved reluctantly, not so much out of a need for power or fame as out of a genuine conviction that something had to be done about the disintegration of Indian culture. Coincidentally, Erikson's book "Childhood and Society," appeared in 1950 when Erikson was 48, and it is that book which brought him national prominence in the mental health field. Like Gandhi, too, Erikson reluctantly did what he felt he had to do (namely, publish his observations and conclusions) for the benefit of his

Erikson in a seminar at his Stockbridge, Mass., home.

*"Young analysts are today proclaiming a 'new freedom' to see Freud in historical perspective, which reflects the Eriksonian view that one can recognize Freud's greatness without bowing to conceptual precedent."*

ailing profession and for the patients treated by its practitioners. So while Erikson's affinity with Luther seemed to derive from comparable professional identity crises, his affinity for Gandhi appears to derive from a parallel crisis of generativity. A passage from "Gandhi's Truth" (from a chapter wherein Erikson addresses himself directly to his subject) helps to convey Erikson's feeling for his subject.

"So far, I have followed you through the loneliness of your childhood and through the experiments and the scruples of your youth. I have affirmed my belief in your ceaseless endeavor to perfect yourself as a man who came to feel that he was the only one available to reverse India's fate. You experimented with what to you were debilitating temptations and you did gain vigor and agility from your victories over yourself. Your identity could be no less than that of universal man, although you had to become an Indian—and one close to the masses—first."

The following passage speaks to Erikson's belief in the general significance of Gandhi's efforts:

"We have seen in Gandhi's development the strong attraction of one of those more inclusive identities: that of an enlightened citizen of the British Empire. In proving himself willing neither to abandon vital ties to his native tradition nor to sacrifice lightly a Western education which eventually contributed to his ability to help defeat British hegemony—in

all of these seeming contradictions Gandhi showed himself on intimate terms with the actualities of his era. For in all parts of the world, the struggle now is for *the anticipatory development of more inclusive identities . . .* I submit then, that Gandhi, in his immense intuition for historical actuality and his capacity to assume leadership in 'truth in action,' may have created a ritualization through which men, equipped with both realism and strength, can face each other with mutual confidence."

There is now more and more teaching of Erikson's concepts in psychiatry, psychology, education and social work in America and in other parts of the world. His description of the stages of the life cycle are summarized in major textbooks in all of these fields and clinicians are increasingly looking at their cases in Eriksonian terms.

Research investigators have, however, found Erikson's formulations somewhat difficult to test. This is not surprising, inasmuch as Erikson's conceptions, like Freud's, take into account the infinite complexity of the human personality. Current research methodologies are, by and large, still not able to deal with these complexities at their own level, and distortions are inevitable when such concepts as "identity" come to be defined in terms of responses to a questionnaire.

Likewise, although Erikson's life-stages have an intuitive "rightness" about them, not everyone agrees with his formulations. Douvan and Adelson in their book, "The Adolescent Experience," argue that while his identity theory may hold true for boys, it doesn't for girls. This argument is based on findings which suggest that girls postpone identity consolidation until after marriage (and intimacy) have been established. Such postponement occurs, says Douvan and Adelson, because a woman's identity is partially defined by the identity of the man whom she marries. This view does not really contradict Erikson's, since he recognizes that later events, such as marriage, can help to resolve both current and past developmental crises. For the woman, but not for the man, the problems of identity and intimacy may be solved concurrently.

Objections to Erikson's formulations have come from other directions as well. Robert W. White, Erikson's good friend and colleague at Harvard, has a long standing (and warm-hearted) debate with Erikson over his life-stages. White believes that his own theory of "competence motivation," a theory which has received wide recognition, can account for the phenomena of ego development much more economically than can Erikson's stages. Erikson has, however, little interest in debating the validity of the stages he has described. As an artist he recognizes that there are many different ways to view one and the same phenomenon and that a perspective that is congenial to one person will be repugnant to another. He offers his stage-wise description of the life cycle for those who find such perspectives congenial and not as a world view that everyone should adopt.

It is this lack of dogmatism and sensitivity to the diversity and complexity of the human personality which help to account for the growing recognition of Erikson's contribution within as well as without the helping professions. Indeed, his psycho-historical investigations have originated a whole new field of study which has caught the interest of historians and political scientists alike. (It has also intrigued his wife, Joan, who has published pieces on Eleanor Roosevelt and who has a book on Saint Francis in press.) A recent issue of Daedalus, the journal for the American Academy of Arts and Sciences, was entirely devoted to psycho-historical and psycho-political investigations of creative leaders by authors from diverse disciplines who have been stimulated by Erikson's work.

Now in his 68th year, Erikson maintains the pattern of multiple activities and appointments which has characterized his entire career. He spends the fall in Cambridge, Mass., where he teaches a large course on "the human life cycle" for Harvard seniors. The spring semester is spent at his home in Stockbridge, Mass., where he participates in case conferences and staff seminars at the Austen Riggs Center. His summers are spent on Cape Cod. Although Erikson's major commitment these days is to his psycho-historical investigation, he is embarking on a study of preschool children's play constructions in different settings and countries, a follow-up of some research he conducted with preadolescents more than a quarter-century ago. He is also planning to review other early observations in the light of contemporary change. In his approach to his work, Erikson appears neither drawn nor driven, but rather to be following an inner schedule as natural as the life cycle itself.

Although Erikson, during his decade of college teaching, has not seen any patients or taught at psychoanalytic institutes, he maintains his dedication to psychoanalysis and views his psycho-historical investigations as an applied branch of that discipline. While some older analysts continue to ignore Erikson's work, there is increasing evidence (including a recent poll of psychiatrists and psychoanalysts) that he is having a rejuvenating influence upon a discipline which many regard as dead or dying. Young analysts are today proclaiming a "new freedom" to see Freud in historical perspective—which reflects the Eriksonian view that one can recognize Freud's greatness without bowing to conceptual precedent.

Accordingly, the reports of the demise of psychoanalysis may have been somewhat premature. In the work of Erik Erikson, at any rate, psychoanalysis lives and continues to beget life.

# Freud's "Ages of Man"

Erik Erikson's definition of the "eight ages of man" is a work of synthesis and insight by a psychoanalytically trained and worldly mind. Sigmund Freud's description of human phases stems from his epic psychological discoveries and centers almost exclusively on the early years of life. A brief summary of the phases posited by Freud:

*Oral stage*—roughly the first year of life, the period during which the mouth region provides the greatest sensual satisfaction. Some derivative behavioral traits which may be seen at this time are *incorporativeness* (first six months of life) and *aggressiveness* (second six months of life).

*Anal stage*—roughly the second and third years of life. During this period the site of greatest sensual pleasure shifts to the anal and urethral areas. Derivative behavioral traits are *retentiveness* and *expulsiveness*.

*Phallic stage*—roughly the third and fourth years of life. The site of greatest sensual pleasure during this stage is the genital region. Behavior traits derived from this period include *intrusiveness* (male) and *receptiveness* (female).

*Oedipal stage*—roughly the fourth and fifth years of life. At this stage the young person takes the parent of the opposite sex as the object or provider of sensual satisfaction and regards the same-sexed parent as a rival. (The "family romance.") Behavior traits originating in this period are *seductiveness* and *competitiveness*.

*Latency stage*—roughly the years from age 6 to 11. The child resolves the Oedipus conflict by identifying with the parent of the opposite sex and by so doing satisfies sensual needs vicariously. Behavior traits developed during this period include *conscience* (or the internalization of parental moral and ethical demands).

*Puberty stage*—roughly 11 to 14. During this period there is an integration and subordination of oral, anal and phallic sensuality to an overriding and unitary genital *sexuality*. The genital sexuality of puberty has another young person of the opposite sex as its object, and discharge (at least for boys) as its aim. Derivative behavior traits (associated with the control and regulation of genital sexuality) are *intellectualization* and *estheticism*.

—D.E.

# Growing up as a Fore

## E. Richard Sorenson

*Dr. Sorenson, director of the Smithsonian's National Anthropological Film Center, wrote* The Edge of the Forest *on his Fore studies.*

*Exploring, two youngsters walk confidently past men's house in hamlet. Smaller women's house is at right.*

Untouched by the outside world, they had lived for thousands of years in isolated mountains and valleys deep in the interior of Papua New Guinea. They had no cloth, no metal, no money, no idea that their homeland was an island—or that what surrounded it was salt water. Yet the Fore (for'ay) people had developed remarkable and sophisticated approaches to human relations, and their child-rearing practices gave their young unusual freedom to explore. Successful as hunter-gatherers and as subsistence gardeners, they also had great adaptability, which brought rapid accommodation with the outside world after their lands were opened up.

It was alone that I first visited the Fore in 1963—a day's walk from a recently built airstrip. I stayed six months. Perplexed and fascinated, I returned six times in the next ten years, eventually spending a year and a half living with them in their hamlets.

Theirs was a way of life different from anything I had seen or heard about before. There were no chiefs, patriarchs, priests, medicine men or the like. A striking personal freedom was enjoyed even by the very young, who could move about at will and be where or with whom they liked. Infants rarely cried, and they played confidently with knives, axes, and fire. Conflict between old and young did not arise; there was no "generation gap."

Older children enjoyed deferring to the interests and desires of the younger, and sibling rivalry was virtually undetectable. A responsive sixth sense seemed to attune the Fore hamlet mates to each other's interests and needs. They did not have to directly ask, inveigle, bargain or speak out for what they needed or wanted. Subtle, even fleeting expressions of interest, desire, and discomfort were quickly read and helpfully acted on by one's associates. This spontaneous urge to share food, affection, work, trust, tools and pleasure was the social cement that held the Fore hamlets together. It was a pleasant way of life, for one could always be with those with whom one got along well.

Ranging and planting, sharing and living, the Fore diverged and expanded through high virgin lands in a pioneer region. They hunted out their gardens, tilled them while they lasted, then hunted again. Moving ever away from lands peopled and used they had a self-contained life with its own special ways.

The underlying ecological conditions were like those that must have encompassed the world before agriculture set its imprint so broadly. Abutting the Fore was virtually unlimited virgin land, and they had food plants they could introduce into it. Like hunter-gatherers they sought their sources of sustenance first in one locale and then another, across an extended range, following opportunities provided by a providential nature. But like agriculturalists they concentrated their effort and attention more narrowly on selected sites of production, on their gardens. They were both seekers and producers. A pioneer people in a pioneer land, they ranged freely into a vast territory, but they planted to live.

Cooperative groups formed hamlets and gardened together. When the fertility of a garden declined, they abandoned it. Grass sprung up to cover these abandoned sites of earlier cultivation, and, as the Fore moved on to other parts of the forest, they left uninhabited grasslands to mark their passage.

The traditional hamlets were small, with a rather fluid system of social relations. A single large men's house provided shelter for 10 to 20 men and boys and their visiting friends. The several smaller women's houses each normally sheltered two married women, their unmarried daughters and their sons up to about six years of age. Formal kinship bonds were less important than friendship was. Fraternal "gangs" of youths formed the hamlets; their "clubhouses" were the men's houses.

*Learning to be a toddler, a Fore baby takes its first experimental steps. No one urges him on.*

During the day the gardens became the center of life. Hamlets were virtually deserted as friends, relatives and children went to one or more garden plots to mingle their social, economic and erotic pursuits in a pleasant and emotionally filled Gestalt of garden life. The boys and unmarried youths preferred to explore and hunt in the outlying lands, but they also passed through and tarried in the gardens.

Daily activities were not scheduled. No one made demands, and the land was bountiful. Not surprisingly the line between work and play was never clear. The transmission of the Fore behavioral pattern to the young began in early infancy during a period of unceasing human physical contact. The effect of being constantly "in touch" with hamlet mates and their daily life seemed to start a process which proceeded by degrees: close rapport, involvement in regular activity, ability to handle seemingly dangerous implements safely, and responsible freedom to pursue individual interests at will without danger.

While very young, infants remained in almost continuous bodily contact with their mother, her house

mates or her gardening associates. At first, mothers' laps were the center of activity, and infants occupied themselves there by nursing, sleeping and playing with their own bodies or those of their caretakers. They were not put aside for the sake of other activities, as when food was being prepared or heavy loads were being carried. Remaining in close, uninterrupted physical contact with those around them, their basic needs such as rest, nourishment, stimulation and security were continuously satisfied without obstacle.

By being physically in touch from their earliest days, Fore youngsters learned to communicate needs, desires and feelings through a body language of touch and response that developed before speech. This opened the door to a much closer rapport with those around them than otherwise would have been possible, and led ultimately to the Fore brand of social cement and the sixth sense that bound groups together through spontaneous, responsive sharing.

As the infant's awareness increased, his interests broadened to the things his mother and other caretakers did and to the objects and materials they used. Then these youngsters began crawling out to explore things that attracted their attention. By the time they were toddling, their interests continually took them on short sorties to nearby objects and persons. As soon as they could walk well, the excursions extended to the entire hamlet and its gardens, and then beyond with other children. Developing without interference or supervision, this personal exploratory learning quest freely touched on whatever was around, even axes, knives, machetes, fire, and the like. When I first went to the Fore, I was aghast.

Eventually I discovered that this capability emerged naturally from Fore infant-handling practices in their milieu of close human physical

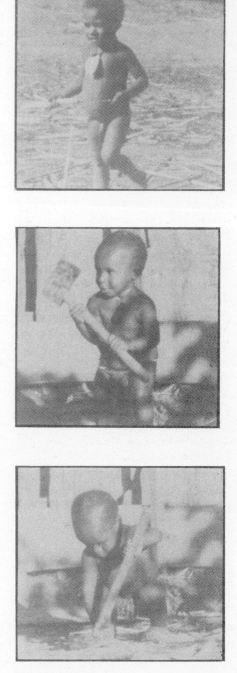

*In infancy, Fore children begin experimental play with knives and other lethal objects. Sorenson never saw a child warned away or injured by them.*

proximity and tactile interaction. Because touch and bodily contact lend themselves naturally to satisfying the basic needs of young children, an early kind of communicative experience fostered cooperative interaction between infants and their caretakers, also kinesthetic contact with the activities at hand. This made it easy for them to learn the appropriate handling of the tools of life.

The early pattern of exploratory activity included frequent return to one of the "mothers." Serving as home base, the bastion of security, a woman might occasionally give the youngster a nod of encouragement, if he glanced in her direction with un-

certainty. Yet rarely did the women attempt to control or direct, nor did they participate in the child's quests or jaunts.

As a result Fore children did not have to adjust to rule and schedule in order to find their place in life. They could pursue their interests and whims wherever they might lead and still be part of a richly responsive world of human touch which constantly provided sustenance, comfort, diversion and security.

Learning proceeded during the course of pursuing interests and exploring. Constantly "in touch" with people who were busy with daily activities, the Fore young quickly

learned the skills of life from example. Muscle tone, movement and mood were components of this learning process; formal lessons and commands were not. Kinesthetic skills developed so quickly that infants were able to casually handle knives and similar objects before they could walk.

Even after several visits I continued to be surprised that the unsupervised Fore toddlers did not recklessly thrust themselves into unappreciated dangers, the way our own children tend to do. But then, why should they? From their earliest days, they enjoyed a benevolent sanctuary from which the world could be confidently

*Babies have free access to the breast and later, like this toddler being helped to kernels of corn by an older girl, can help themselves to whatever food is around—indulged by children and grown-ups.*

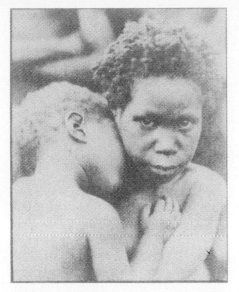

*Close, constant body contact, as between this baby and older girl, creates security in Fore children.*

viewed, tested and appreciated. This sanctuary remained ever available, but did not demand, restrain or impose. One could go and come at will.

In close harmony with their source of life, the Fore young were able confidently, not furtively, to extend their inquiry. They could widen their understanding as they chose. There was no need to play tricks or deceive in order to pursue life.

Emerging from this early childhood was a freely ranging young child rather in tune with his older and younger hamlet mates, disinclined to act out impulsively, and with a capable appreciation of the properties of potentially dangerous objects. Such children could be permitted to move out on their own, unsupervised and unrestricted. They were safe.

Such a pattern could persist indefinitely, re-creating itself in each new generation. However, hidden within the receptive character it produced was an Achilles heel; it also permitted adoption of new practices, including child-handling practices, which did *not* act to perpetuate the pattern. In only one generation after Western contact, the cycle of Fore life was broken.

Attuned as they were to individual pursuit of economic and social good, it did not take the Fore long to recognize the value of the new materials,

practices and ideas that began to flow in. Indeed, change began almost immediately with efforts to obtain steel axes, salt, medicine and cloth. The Fore were quick to shed indigenous practices in favor of Western example. They rapidly altered their ways to adapt to Western law, government, religion, materials and trade.

Sometimes change was so rapid that many people seemed to be afflicted by a kind of cultural shock. An anomie, even cultural amnesia, seemed to pervade some hamlets for a time. There were individuals who appeared temporarily to have lost memory of recent past events. Some Fore even forgot what type and style of traditional garments they had worn only a few years earlier, or that they had used stone axes and had eaten their dead close relatives.

Remarkably open-minded, the Fore so readily accepted reformulation of identity and practice that suggestion or example by the new government officers, missionaries and scientists could alter tribal affiliation, place names, conduct and hamlet style. When the first Australian patrol officer began to map the region in 1957, an error in communication led him to refer to these people as the "Fore." Actually they had had no name for themselves and the word, Fore, was their name for a quite different group, the Awa, who spoke another language and lived in another valley. They did not correct the patrol officer but adopted his usage. They all now refer to themselves as the Fore. Regional and even personal names changed just as readily.

More than anything else, it was the completion of a steep, rough, always muddy Jeep road into the Fore lands that undermined the traditional life. Almost overnight their isolated region was opened. Hamlets began to move down from their ridgetop sites in order to be nearer the road, consolidating with others.

The power of the road is hard to overestimate. It was a great artery where only restricted capillaries had existed before. And down this artery came a flood of new goods, new ideas

*On the way to hunt birds, cuscus (a marsupial) or rats, Fore boys stride through a sweet-potato garden.*

and new people. This new road, often impassable even with four-wheel-drive vehicles, was perhaps the single most dramatic stroke wrought by the government. It was to the Fore an opening to a new world. As they began to use the road, they started to shed traditions evolved in the protective insularity of their mountain fastness, to adopt in their stead an emerging market culture.

## THE COMING OF THE COFFEE ECONOMY

"Walkabout," nonexistent as an institution before contact, quickly became an accepted way of life. Fore boys began to roam hundreds of miles from their homeland in the quest for new experience, trade goods, jobs and money. Like the classic practice of the Australian aborigine, this "walkabout" took one away from his home for periods of varying length. But unlike the Australian practice, it usually took the boys to jobs and schools rather than to a solitary life in traditional lands. Obviously it sprang from the earlier pattern of individual freedom to pursue personal interests and opportunity wherever it might lead. It was a new expression of the old Fore exploratory pattern.

Some boys did not roam far, whereas others found ways to go to distant cities. The roaming boys often sought places where they might be welcomed as visitors, workers or students for a while. Mission stations and schools, plantation work camps, and the servants' quarters of the European population became way-stations in the lives of the modernizing Fore boys.

Some took jobs on coffee plantations. Impressed by the care and attention lavished on coffee by European planters and by the money they saw paid to coffee growers, these young Fore workers returned home with coffee beans to plant.

Coffee grew well on the Fore hillsides, and in the mid-1960s, when the first sizable crop matured, Fore who previously had felt lucky to earn a few dollars found themselves able to earn a few hundred dollars. A rush to coffee ensued, and when the new gardens became productive a few years later, the Fore income from coffee jumped to a quarter of a million dollars a year. The coffee revolution was established.

At first the coffee was carried on the backs of its growers (sometimes for several days) over steep, rough mountain trails to a place where it could be sold to a buyer with a jeep. However, as more and more coffee was produced, the villagers began to turn with efforts to planning and constructing roads in association with neighboring villages. The newly built roads, in turn, stimulated further economic development and the opening of new trade stores throughout the region.

Following European example, the segregated collective men's and women's houses were abandoned. Family houses were adopted. This changed the social and territorial arena for all the young children, who hitherto had been accustomed to living equally with many members of their hamlet. It gave them a narrower place to belong, and it made them more distinctly someone's children. Uncomfortable in the family houses, boys who had grown up in a freer territory began to gather in "boys' houses," away from the adult men who were now beginning to live in family houses with their wives. Mothers began to wear blouses, altering the early freer access to the breast. Episodes of infant and child frustration, not seen in traditional Fore hamlets, began to take place along with repeated incidents of anger, withdrawal, aggressiveness and stinginess.

So Western technology worked its magic on the Fore, its powerful materials and practices quickly shattering their isolated autonomy and lifestyle. It took only a few years from the time Western intruders built their first grass-thatched patrol station before the Fore way of life they found was gone.

Fortunately, enough of the Fore traditional ways were systematically documented on film to reveal how unique a flower of human creation they were. Like nothing else, film made it possible to see the behavioral patterns of this way of life. The visual record, once made, captured data which was unnoticed and unanticipated at the time of filming and which was simply impossible to study without such records. Difficult-to-spot subtle patterns and fleeting nuances of manner, mood and human relations emerged by use of repeated reexamination of related incidents, sometimes by slow motion and stopped frame. Eventually the characteristic behavioral patterns of Fore life became clear, and an important aspect of human adaptive creation was revealed.

The Fore way of life was only one of the many natural experiments in living that have come into being through thousands of years of independent development in the world. The Fore way is now gone; those which remain are threatened. Under the impact of modern technology and commerce, the entire world is now rapidly becoming one system. By the year 2000 all the independent natural experiments that have come into being during the world's history will be merging into a single world system.

One of the great tragedies of our modern time may be that most of these independent experiments in living are disappearing before we can discover the implication of their special expressions of human possibility. Ironically, the same technology responsible for the worldwide cultural convergence has also provided the means by which we may capture detailed visual records of the yet remaining independent cultures. The question is whether we will be able to seize this never-to-be repeated opportunity. Soon it will be too late. Yet, obviously, increasing our understanding of the behavioral repertoire of humankind would strengthen our ability to improve life in the world.

# Sexism in the Schoolroom of the '80s

*THINGS HAVEN'T CHANGED.*
*BOYS STILL GET MORE ATTENTION, ENCOURAGEMENT*
*AND AIRTIME THAN GIRLS DO.*

*MYRA AND DAVID SADKER*

*Myra and David Sadker are professors of education at American University, Washington, D.C.*

I f a boy calls out in class, he gets teacher attention, especially intellectual attention. If a girl calls out in class, she is told to raise her hand before speaking. Teachers praise boys more than girls, give boys more academic help and are more likely to accept boys' comments during classroom discussions. These are only a few examples of how teachers favor boys. Through this advantage boys increase their chances for better education and possibly higher pay and quicker promotions. Although many believe that classroom sexism disappeared in the early '70s, it hasn't.

Education is not a spectator sport. Numerous researchers, most recently John Goodlad, former dean of education at the University of California at Los Angeles and author of *A Place Called School*, have shown that when students participate in classroom discussion they hold more positive attitudes toward school, and that positive attitudes enhance learning. It is no co-

incidence that girls are more passive in the classroom and score lower than boys on SAT's.

Most teachers claim that girls participate and are called on in class as often as boys. But a three-year study we recently completed found that this is not true; vocally, boys clearly dominate the classroom. When we showed teachers and administrators a film of a classroom discussion and asked who was talking more, the teachers overwhelmingly said the girls were. But in reality, the boys in the film were out-talking the girls at a ratio of three to one. Even educators who are active in feminist issues were unable to spot the sex bias until they counted and coded who was talking and who was just watching. Stereotypes of garrulous and gossipy women are so strong that teachers fail to see this communications gender gap even when it is right before their eyes.

Field researchers in our study observed students in more than a hundred fourth-, sixth- and eighth-grade

classes in four states and the District of Columbia. The teachers and students were male and female, black and white, from urban, suburban and rural communities. Half of the classrooms covered language arts and English—subjects in which girls traditionally have excelled; the other half covered math and science—traditionally male domains.

We found that at all grade levels, in all communities and in all subject areas, boys dominated classroom communication. They participated in more interactions than girls did and their participation became greater as the year went on.

Our research contradicted the traditional assumption that girls dominate classroom discussion in reading while boys are dominant in math. We found that whether the subject was language arts and English or math and science, boys got more than their fair share of teacher attention.

Some critics claim that if teachers talk more to male students, it is simply because boys are more assertive in grabbing their attention—a classic case of the squeaky wheel getting the educational oil. In fact, our research shows that boys are more assertive in the classroom. While girls sit patiently with their hands raised, boys literally grab teacher attention. They are eight times more likely than girls to call out answers. However, male assertiveness is not the whole answer.

Teachers behave differently, depending on whether boys or girls call out answers during discussions. When boys call out comments without raising their hands, teachers accept their answers. However, when girls call out, teachers reprimand this "inappropriate" behavior with messages such as, "In this class we don't shout out answers, we raise our hands." The message is subtle but powerful: Boys should be academically assertive and grab teacher attention; girls should act like ladies and keep quiet.

Teachers in our study revealed an interaction pattern that we called a "mind sex." After calling on a student, they tended to keep calling on students of the same sex. While this pattern applied to both sexes, it was far more pronounced among boys and allowed them more than their fair share of airtime.

It may be that when teachers call on someone, they continue thinking of that sex. Another explanation may be found in the seating patterns of elementary, secondary and even postsecondary classrooms. In approximately half of the classrooms in our study, male and female students sat in separate parts of the room. Sometimes the teacher created this segregation, but more often, the students segregated themselves. A teacher's tendency to interact with same-sex students may be a simple matter of where each sex sits. For example, a teacher calls on a female student, looks around the same area and then continues questioning the students around this girl, all of whom are female. When the teacher refocuses to a section of the classroom where boys are seated, boys receive the series of questions. And because boys are more assertive, the teacher may interact with their section longer.

Girls are often shortchanged in quality as well as in quantity of teacher attention. In 1975 psychologists Lisa Serbin and K. Daniel O'Leary, then at

*WHILE GIRLS SIT PATIENTLY WITH THEIR HANDS RAISED, BOYS LITERALLY GRAB TEACHER ATTENTION.*

the State University of New York at Stony Brook, studied classroom interaction at the preschool level and found that teachers gave boys more attention, praised them more often and were at least twice as likely to have extended conversations with them. Serbin and O'Leary also found that teachers were twice as likely to give male students detailed instructions on how to do things for themselves. With female students, teachers were more likely to do it for them instead. The result was that boys learned to become independent, girls learned to become dependent.

Instructors at the other end of the educational spectrum also exhibit this same "let me do it for you" behavior toward female students. Constantina Safilios-Rothschild, a sociologist with the Population Council in New York, studied sex desegregation at the Coast Guard Academy and found that the instructors were giving detailed instructions on how to accomplish tasks to male students, but were doing the jobs and operating the equipment for the female students.

Years of experience have shown that the best way to learn something is to do it yourself; classroom chivalry is not only misplaced, it is detrimental. It is also important to give students specific and direct feedback about the quality of their work and answers. During classroom discussion, teachers in our study reacted to boys' answers with dynamic, precise and effective responses, while they often gave girls bland and diffuse reactions.

Teachers' reactions were classified in four categories: praise ("Good answer"); criticism ("That answer is wrong"); help and remediation ("Try again—but check your long division"); or acceptance without any evaluation or assistance ("OK" "Uh-huh").

Despite caricatures of school as a harsh and punitive place, fewer than 5 percent of the teachers' reactions were criticisms, even of the mildest sort. But praise didn't happen often either; it made up slightly more than 10 percent of teachers' reactions. More than 50 percent of teachers' responses fell into the "OK" category.

Teachers distributed these four reactions differently among boys than among girls. Here are some of the typical patterns.

Teacher: "What's the capital of Maryland? Joel?"

Joel: "Baltimore."

Teacher: "What's the largest city in Maryland, Joel?"

Joel: "Baltimore."

Teacher: "That's good. But Baltimore isn't the capital. The capital is also the location of the U.S. Naval Academy. Joel, do you want to try again?"

Joel: "Annapolis."

Teacher: "Excellent. Anne, what's the capital of Maine?"

Anne: "Portland."

Teacher: "Judy, do you want to try?"

Judy: "Augusta."

Teacher: "OK."

In this snapshot of a classroom discussion, Joel was told when his answer was wrong (criticism); was helped to discover the correct answer (remediation); and was praised when he offered the correct response. When Anne was wrong, the teacher, rather than staying with her, moved to Judy, who received only simple acceptance for her correct answer. Joel received the more specific teacher reaction and benefited from a longer, more precise and intense educational interaction.

Too often, girls remain in the dark about the quality of their answers. Teachers rarely tell them if their answers are excellent, need to be improved or are just plain wrong. Unfortunately, acceptance, the imprecise response packing the least educational punch, gets the most equitable sex distribution in classrooms. Active students receiving precise feedback are more likely to achieve academically. And they are more likely to be boys. Consider the following:

☐ Although girls start school ahead

of boys in reading and basic computation, by the time they graduate from high school, boys have higher SAT scores in both areas.

☐ By high school, some girls become less committed to careers, although their grades and achievement-test scores may be as good as boys'. Many girls' interests turn to marriage or stereotypically female jobs. Part of the reason may be that some women feel that men disapprove of their using their intelligence.

☐ Girls are less likely to take math and science courses and to participate in special or gifted programs in these subjects, even if they have a talent for them. They are also more likely to believe that they are incapable of pursuing math and science in college and to avoid the subjects.

☐ Girls are more likely to attribute failure to internal factors, such as ability, rather than to external factors, such as luck.

The sexist communication game is played at work, as well as at school. As reported in numerous studies it goes like this:

☐ Men speak more often and frequently interrupt women.

☐ Listeners recall more from male speakers than from female speakers, even when both use a similar speaking style and cover identical content.

☐ Women participate less actively in conversation. They do more smiling and gazing; they are more often the passive bystanders in professional and social conversations among peers.

☐ Women often transform declarative statements into tentative comments. This is accomplished by using qualifiers ("kind of " or "I guess") and by adding tag questions ("This is a good movie, isn't it?"). These tentative patterns weaken impact and signal a lack of power and influence.

Sexist treatment in the classroom encourages formation of patterns such as these, which give men more dominance and power than women in the working world. But there is a light at the end of the educational tunnel. Classroom biases are not etched in stone, and training can eliminate these patterns. Sixty teachers in our study received four days of training to establish equity in classroom interactions. These trained teachers succeeded in eliminating classroom bias. Although our training focused on equality, it improved overall teaching effectiveness as well. Classes taught by these trained teachers had a higher level of intellectual discussion and contained more effective and precise teacher responses for all students.

There is an urgent need to remove sexism from the classroom and give women the same educational encouragement and support that men receive. When women are treated equally in the classroom, they will be more likely to achieve equality in the workplace.

# What Is TV Doing To America?

**In its 43 years, television has been praised as a miracle and damned as a distorter of reality. Now, new evidence is emerging about the medium and how it affects the people who watch it.**

Soon after 28-year-old David Radnis watched the movie "The Deer Hunter" on TV in his Chicago-area home, he was dead—one of at least 29 viewers in the U.S. who shot themselves imitating the show's Russian-roulette scene.

When Hoang Bao Trinh fled from Vietnam to Silver Spring, Md., he spent months baby-sitting his grandchildren in front of the TV set. Soon the whole family was speaking English, much of it learned by imitating speech heard on the televised programs.

Such cases reflect TV's increasingly pervasive influence on America, both for good and bad. In a country where television has become a major—and in some cases primary—force determining how people work, relax and behave, the consequences are staggering. Recent studies show that the lives of Americans, from their selection of food to their choice of political leaders, are deeply affected by TV, and that influence is growing.

In an age when millions of inexperienced young people are growing up in front of the tube without close guidance of elders, many Americans worry that the nation could be ruined by a generation that gets its moral values from "Flamingo Road," its cultural standards from "Laverne & Shirley" and its sense of family relationships from "Dallas."

Most broadcasters, with support from some researchers, maintain that TV is unfairly blamed for merely conveying what the public demands and argue that the medium's power is exaggerated. They contend that most people treat television simply as one of many sources of information, and that most homes have basically been unaltered since the first modern home-TV set was marketed in 1939.

Others in the industry are worried that what author and actor Steve Allen calls the "amoral force" of TV and other popular media is helping to weaken old values. "It's horrendous," says Allen. "That our nation, our society, our culture is in some state of moral and ethical collapse is absolutely undeniable. In about 50 years, you could create what we already have a good percentage of—people who think it's perfectly OK to grab what they want, to do what they want, and the only bad thing is getting caught."

## Linking the Tube and Violence

A report released in May by the National Institute of Mental Health says that "violence on television does lead to aggressive behavior by children and teenagers who watch the programs." In one five-year study of 732 children, "several kinds of aggression—conflicts with parents, fighting and delinquency—were all positively correlated with the total amount of television viewing." Defenders of TV have long held that there is no clear link between viewing and violence.

The findings covered a wide range of topics. In one survey, more than half the parents thought their children learned more about sex from TV than from any other source except the parents themselves. TV also was cited for fostering bad habits by glamorizing highly advertised junk foods and frequent use of alcohol.

The federally sponsored study noted that almost all Americans watch TV, many for hours each day. Some of the most avid watchers are the very young and very old, women and minorities. Heavy viewers are usually less educated.

"Television can no longer be considered as a casual part of daily life, as an electronic toy," the report stated. "Research findings have long since destroyed the illusion that television is merely innocuous entertainment."

TV is also partly blamed for a sharp slide in traditional learning. Since television became nearly universal in the early 1960s, average scores for high-school students taking the Scholastic Aptitude Test, the broadest measure of academic ability, have plunged from 478 to 424 on the verbal exam and from 502 to 466 in mathematics.

A panel of educators appointed to study the decline noted that by age 16 most children have spent 10,000 to 15,000 hours watching television—more time than they have spent in school. The panel's conclusion: "Is television a cause of the SAT-score decline? Yes, we think it is. . . . Television has become surrogate parent, substitute teacher."

As TV's children graduated in the 1960s and '70s, an Adult Performance Level test found that "20 percent of the American population was functionally incompetent, that is, could not perform the basic kinds of reading, writing or computing tasks—such as calculating the change on a small purchase, addressing an envelope, reading a want ad or filling out a job application." The result, says Paul Copperman, president of the Institute of Reading Development in San Francisco, is that "society may be compelled to support an increasing percentage of dysfunctional or only marginally functional citizens."

## TV Has Brought Americans Together

Even the severest critics admit that television has achieved unprecedented results in making the public aware of a huge variety of developments—from war in Lebanon and the Falkland Islands to the plight of migrant workers.

Veteran broadcaster Eric Sevareid argues that television has had an enormously positive influence on America in three main areas: It has brought families together more, it has counteracted the country's tendency toward fragmentation, and it has stayed independent of government.

Says Sevareid: "On balance, TV is better for us than bad for us. When Gutenberg printed the Bible, people thought that invention would put bad ideas in people's heads. They thought the typewriter would destroy the muse, that movies would destroy legitimate theater, that radio would destroy newspapers and that TV would destroy everything. But it doesn't happen that way."

A main virtue of TV, according to scholars, is that the medium is a powerful force for freedom—a far better source of information and motivation than the party apparatus that used to dominate politics in many sections of the country.

Television's broadening of perspectives also is credited with boosting worthwhile causes and diminishing the ethnic, religious and geographic prejudices that have plagued American history. Cited as a key example are the "freedom marches" that caught the attention of TV viewers in the early 1960s. Laws were then passed guaranteeing civil rights that blacks had sought for more than a century.

Many educators add that television has given Americans a wealth of experience and knowledge that isn't being measured by today's school tests. The National Education Association, the nation's biggest teachers' organization, has called for cultivation of "electronic literacy" and has distributed guides to help teachers solidify what students learn from programs like "Holocaust" and "Shogun."

Millions of young Americans have been led through the alphabet and rudiments of algebra by the educational series "Sesame Street" and "Electric Company" of the Children's Television Workshop. One study suggested that children who watch a lot of TV in their early years tend to read more widely later on than children who were lighter viewers when they were young.

The medium also provides an invaluable window on the world for invalids and the elderly. Steve Allen recalls a series of visits he made to hospitals where Vietnam veterans were being treated: "What was helping to pull them through the day was television. The television set does provide company for lonely people, a voice in the house."

Broadcasters point out that, no matter what sociologists think, the public likes what it is getting on television. The A.C. Nielsen Company, an audience-measuring firm, announced that, despite a decline in network viewing, America's 80 million television households averaged a record level of 6 hours and 44 minutes a day in front of the tube in 1981—up 9 minutes from 1980. That's three times the average rate of increase during the 1970s.

Observes one network executive: "It's all there, good and bad. All you have to do is change the dial."

### How the Brain Reacts to TV

Until recently, there was little research on how the human brain absorbs information from TV. Many scholars long have been convinced that viewers retain less from television than from reading, but evidence was scarce.

Now, a research project by Jacob Jacoby, a Purdue University psychologist, has found that more than 90 percent of 2,700 people tested misunderstood even such simple fare as commercials or the detective series "Barnaby Jones." Only minutes after watching, the typical viewer missed 23 to 36 percent of the questions about what he or she had seen.

One explanation is that TV's compelling pictures stimulate primarily the right half of the brain, which specializes in

emotional responses, rather than the left hemisphere, where thinking and analysis are performed. By connecting viewers to instruments that measure brain waves, researcher Herbert Krugman found periods of right-brain activity outnumbering left-brain activity by a ratio of 2 to 1.

Another difficulty is the rapid linear movement of TV images, which gives viewers little chance to pause and reflect on what they have seen. Scientists say this torrent of images also has a numbing effect, as measured electronically by the high proportion of alpha brain waves, normally associated with daydreaming or falling asleep.

The result is shortened attention spans—a phenomenon increasingly lamented by teachers trying to hold the interest of students accustomed to TV. To measure attention spans, psychophysiologist Thomas Mulholland of the Edith Nourse Rogers Memorial Veterans Hospital in Bedford, Mass., attached 40 young viewers to an instrument that shut off the TV set whenever the children's brains produced mainly alpha waves. Although the children were told to concentrate, only a few could keep the set on for more than 30 seconds.

Other researchers have found unrealistic career expectations among young people who watch a lot of TV. According to "Television and Behavior," the new federal report: "Heavy viewers want high-status jobs but do not intend to spend many years in school. For girls, there is even more potential for conflict between aspirations and plans; the girls who are heavy viewers usually want to get married, have children and stay at home to take care of them, but at the same time they plan to remain in school and have exciting careers."

Frustration of these expectations, according to social scientists, can spill over into communities, helping to fuel destructive outbursts, ranging from disruption of schools to ghetto riots. Once civil disturbances are telecast, they may spread through imitation, as they did from Washington, D.C., to dozens of other cities in 1968.

Fictional shows can have a similar effect. An airplane bomb threat on "Doomsday Flight" was followed by a rash of similar occurrences across the nation.

### "Facts" Are Not Always as They Seem

Another concern is the growing number of Americans who rank television as their main source of news and information—more than two thirds, according to the Roper Poll.

Some complain that "facts" on TV are not always what they seem. A new form of program, the "docudrama," is cited as a potential source of confusion. Mixing established facts and conjecture, a docudrama often is accepted as totally accurate. One such program, "King," was criticized by associates of the Rev. Martin Luther King, Jr., for allegedly misrepresenting

## Who Watches TV the Most?
*Weekly TV Usage*

| | |
|---|---|
| Older women (ages 55 and over) | 36 hr., 33 min. |
| Older men | 33 hr., 15 min. |
| Younger women (ages 18-55) | 31 hr., 49 min. |
| Younger men | 28 hr., 3 min. |
| Teenagers | 22 hr., 59 min. |
| Children (ages 2-11) | 25 hr., 10 min. |

*USN&WR—Basic data: A. C. Nielsen Company*

the personality of the late civil-rights leader.

In his objections to video coverage of budget cutting and poverty, President Reagan joined a long list of politicians who charge that their efforts have been distorted by TV's need for dramatic pictures, rather than factual analysis. The late Chicago Mayor Richard Daley complained that "protesters" against various causes often would show up outside his office door, unknown to him inside, wanting not to present their grievances to him but to get coverage by TV crews whom they had notified in advance.

Television also is blamed for making viewers impatient by distorting their notions of what to expect from life. "TV teaches that all problems can be resolved quickly—within 30 minutes on a sitcom, 30 seconds in a commercial," says Neil Postman, a communications professor at New York University. When that doesn't happen in real life, he adds, "many people become frustrated or depressed."

Author Ben Stein, a speech writer during the Nixon administration, says the fictional creations of TV have tended to make Americans contemptuous and suspicious of their leaders. In his book, *The View From Sunset Boulevard: America as Brought to You by the People Who Make Television,* Stein notes that most "heavies" in TV shows are conservative authority figures such as high-ranking officials and business executives. And a recent study by the Media Institute in Washington, D.C., concludes that two thirds of business leaders in entertainment series are portrayed as foolish, greedy or immoral, and half their actions as illegal.

## Helping to Reshape Democracy

Scholars have grown increasingly troubled by some of the effects of TV on democratic government.

More than two decades ago, Richard Nixon's sweat during a televised debate with John F. Kennedy weighed heavily against the Republican candidate for President, and apparently became a factor in his defeat. Since then, other TV debates during political campaigns also have been judged as much for cosmetics as for content, and are regarded as having contributed to winning or losing.

Even in the midst of ballot counting, TV's effects are far-reaching. In 1980, networks declared Ronald Reagan the projected winner soon after polls in Eastern states closed but before balloting ended in the West. Experts say some prospective voters never went to the polls in the West, believing their choices would make no difference.

A lesser-known issue that worries many political scientists is the frequent satirizing of public officials by entertainers such as Johnny Carson and Mark Russell.

According to some scholars, widely viewed TV skits poking fun at former President Jerry Ford's occasional clumsiness may have contributed to his defeat in 1976 by popularizing the notion that Ford was too awkward to lead the nation. Subsequent Presidents—Jimmy Carter and

Ronald Reagan—also have been the objects of ridicule on TV—not a laughing matter if, as some believe, the satire prejudices a candidate's chance for election. Humorous commentary on politics in this country dates back to colonial times, but the immediacy and pervasiveness of television have given such satire added potency. "Now, one or two comics can start nationwide waves of derision that are almost impossible to overcome," says Robert Orben, a humor consultant to many politicians.

## Worries About Morality

Concern also is growing about the sexual content of programs flooding cable systems and videocassette machines now installed in more than one third of American homes.

Until recently, X-rated shows made up a heavy majority of the sales of prerecorded videotapes for exhibition on home sets. Among the three-dozen pay-cable networks, at least three—the *Playboy* channel, Eros and Private Screenings—include explicit sexual material. Depending on which channel they select, viewers can find everything from partial nudity to simulated intercourse.

Mainstream-movie channels, such as Home Box Office and Showtime Entertainment, also owe some of their success to occasional airings of unedited theatrical films intended for adults only. Such films often contain obscene language, gore and degrees of undress that would never make it past the in-house censors of conventional TV.

All this has prompted a backlash by communities trying to limit what can be brought into homes via cable. In Manhattan, officials have tried to deny use of the "public access" channel to amateur producers who air programs with footage of people who were persuaded to undress or even engage in sex acts in front of the camera.

Peggy Charren, president of Action for Children's Television, urged Congress to head off a wave of local censorship by requiring cable systems to offer free lock boxes—devices that keep children from watching certain channels.

Others have suggested antiobscenity statutes similar to the rules governing over-the-air television. Many constitutional experts believe, however, that cable will continue to be protected by the First Amendment in the same manner as theatrical movies, books and magazines—especially in light of a recent U.S. district-court ruling that Utah's ban on "indecent" cable programs was unconstitutionally vague.

Some scholars also are concerned about another aspect of moral values that may have been distorted by TV. Lois DeBakey, communications professor and head of a nationwide literacy movement, lists the television industry among "profit-hungry pleasure peddlers" who have created a national tendency to exalt entertainment above crucial needs such as health and education. Noting that highly televised sports stars are paid an average of $250,000 a year and teachers only $20,000, DeBakey asks: "Do we honestly

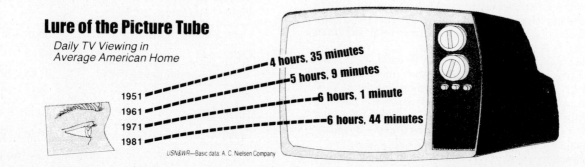

### Lure of the Picture Tube

*Daily TV Viewing in Average American Home*

1951 — 4 hours, 35 minutes
1961 — 5 hours, 9 minutes
1971 — 6 hours, 1 minute
1981 — 6 hours, 44 minutes

*USN&WR—Basic data: A. C. Nielsen Company*

expect to motivate young people to take school seriously when the highest monetary and social rewards are reserved for occupations in which education is often unnecessary?"

## Bigger Role for Special Interests?

Many business and political leaders are troubled by recent developments in video communications, including a movement toward deregulation of TV.

In conventional broadcasting, stations have always been licensed by the Federal Communications Commission to use a scarce public commodity, the airwaves. As a result, they are bound by laws and policies that strictly limit obscenity and prohibit any company from owning more than seven stations, as well as by the fairness and equal-time doctrines requiring free time for opposing views and candidates when controversial opinions are aired.

None of those rules applies, however, to the new outlets of cable, videocassettes and pay TV. Moreover, a drive is under way, backed by the Reagan administration, to repeal those rules for all broadcasters and leave ownership and program content up to what FCC Chairman Mark S. Fowler calls the new "competitive pressures of the marketplace." Fowler's proposals have drawn fire from critics, who call the deregulation movement an invitation for companies and organizations with the most money to control what people see on TV.

Already, various ideological groups are rushing to buy their way onto the tube. By raising as much as 70 million dollars a year from viewers and using the money to purchase air time, conservative evangelists such as Jerry Falwell and Pat Robertson have virtually drowned out the broadcasting voices of the major denominations. Falwell's TV operation launched the Moral Majority, cornerstone of a religious right wing that was active in the conservative shift of the last elections. A Falwell ally, Texas-based TV preacher James Robison, has aired two hour-long specials—"Wake Up, America" and "Attack on the Family"—in more than 50 cities. This spring, producer Norman Lear's liberal group, "People for the American Way," countered with "I Love Liberty," a 3-million-dollar extravaganza.

Local stations have taken the lead in what they call "issue-oriented advertising," commercials espousing political views. Participation so far has mostly been by big firms, such as Mobil Oil, attacking what they regard as excessive government regulation.

Backers of "message programing" maintain that rules of fairness and equal time are no longer needed because the many cable channels, independent stations and networks using relay satellites offer affordable soapboxes to almost anybody.

Opponents, however, say that is wishful thinking, because reaching a large portion of the national audience is too expensive except for a few rich organizations and individuals.

## Do Viewers Respond Too Quickly?

Fresh criticism is being leveled at the potential for abuse in two-way cable systems spreading across the country. These systems allow viewers with home computers or push-button consoles to communicate with central computers in requesting data, ordering merchandise, conducting banking transactions and responding to opinion polls.

Because computers can build dossiers from viewers' responses, civil libertarians fear violations of privacy by businesses or government agencies.

"Two-way systems are hitched to computers that scan each household every 6 seconds, recording all manner of information," explains Les Brown, editor of *Channels of Communication* magazine. "They know what we watch, what we buy through television, how we vote in public-opinion polls."

More than 90,000 homes now have two-way systems, and rapid expansion into a fully "wired society" is expected eventually. Already, there are TV alarm systems tied to police stations and customers' homes that can turn on TV sets and record when people enter or leave a home. Although these processes are now aimed solely at detecting intruders, the possibility of other uses is alarming to some observers.

Brown says he discovered one unsettling ramification of the cable age when he was discussing the issue of privacy in two-way-cable systems during an interview on the Cable News Network. Suddenly, the interviewer called for an instant plebiscite on Brown's concern, and an undetermined number of noontime viewers on the Columbus, Ohio, QUBE system pushed response buttons on their sets.

Eighty-five percent rejected Brown's suggestion that there was anything to worry about.

Knowing that daytime audiences are frequently dominated by preschoolers who may not understand what they are doing but who are capable of pushing the response button, Brown comments: "What's frightening to contemplate is that such polls are routinely conducted on every kind of important national issue, and their results cited as public opinion.

"You will never hear a cable newscaster say, 'QUBE took a poll today, and here's what some 4-year-olds think about the sale of AWACS to Saudi Arabia.' But some poor congressman may think he hears the voice of his constituents" in those results.

Despite the uncertainties, there is widespread hope that the new video age will benefit from the industry's past mistakes and triumphs and do the country far more good than harm.

As Benjamin Barber, a Rutgers University professor of political science, observes: "It is difficult to imagine the Kennedy generation, the '60s, Watergate, the Woodstock generation or even the Moral Majority in the absence of national television."

Now, he adds, those concepts "belong to history, for we stand—prepared or not—on the threshold of a new television age that promises to revolutionize our habits as viewers, as consumers and ultimately as citizens."

*JAMES MANN*

# Groups and Roles in Transition

- Primary Groups (Articles 14-15)
- Secondary Groups (Articles 16-17)
- The Job/Marriage/Family Difficult Choice (Articles 18-21)
- Relabeling Movements (Articles 22-24)

Primary groups are small, intimate, spontaneous, and personal. In contrast, secondary groups are large, formal, and impersonal. Often primary groups are formed within a factory, school, or business. Primary groups are the main source for developing an individual's values and self-identity. The family, couples, gangs, cliques, teams, and small tribes or rural villages are examples of primary groups. Secondary groups include most of the organizations and bureaucracies in a modern society, and carry out most of its instrumental functions.

Urbanization, geographic mobility, centralization, bureaucratization, and other aspects of modernization have had an impact on the nature of groups, the quality of the relationships between people, and individuals' feelings of belonging. Some of the issues explored in this section include the place of tradition in family life, the failure of neighbors and neighborhoods in metropolitan areas to provide primary group support, the alienation that blue collar and white collar workers are experiencing in the workplace, and the unfair assignment of traditional sex roles on females and males.

The first selection concerns the family—the basic primary group—and its contribution to the socialization process. Alex Haley presents an autobiographical sketch of an extremely strong family. He explains that families can be strengthened but it requires work and commitment. The second selection by Andrew Cherlin and Frank F. Furstenberg presents and interprets trends in family patterns. After reviewing statistics on divorce, unmarried couples, working wives, single parent families, and other family patterns, they conclude that "the traditional family will no longer predominate." They expect family patterns of the future to accommodate frequent divorce and remarriages.

The next two articles emphasize the shift from primary to secondary groups in modern society. A century ago most neighborhoods or communities and most work settings shared more characteristics of primary groups than secondary groups.

The city, typical of a secondary group, is berated for producing pathologies and social problems. It is viewed as impersonal at best and dangerous at worst. Creekmore calls this view a myth. His argument is based on literature that density is good for people. According to his report, cities are more beneficial than rural areas for improving an individual's physical and mental health. They are not bad environments generally, but rather complex ones which require complex adaptations. Nevertheless they stimulate activity, increase social ties, and generally produce higher quality lives.

Theodore Roszak explores the workplace as a secondary group. He blasts the modern American workplace for its emptiness and meaninglessness. His father, a skilled carpenter, longed to make quality houses or fine furniture. Instead he was forced to slap-dash houses together for builders who were after a "fast buck." Roszak believes this portrait of his father symbolizes the reality of modern work. Even when workers are paid well, they are often exploited and dehumanized.

The next four articles explore the changing roles of women from a number of viewpoints. Public opinion polls show that the majority of women want to combine marriage, career, and children but there is mounting evidence that this ambition is very difficult to attain. The articles by Deborah Fallows, Shirley Wilkins and Thomas A.W. Miller, Barbara Ehrenreich, and Pete Hamill show that women are, or should be, questioning the desirability of motherhood, careers, corporate life, and marriage. Women are divided on these issues, and men and businesses are doing very little to make the problem easier.

The last three articles consider three groups which are seeking to engineer a public redefinition of their role in society and improve the way other people see them. Arnold Arluke and Jack Levin contend that when the elderly are defined as childlike and treated accordingly, they are more likely to exhibit childlike behavior. They explore what the elderly are doing to change their image. Alan A. Reich describes the improving situation of the 36 million disabled. The last article examines the changing situation of homosexuals. All three groups are seeking to be accepted by the rest of society.

## Looking Ahead: Challenge Questions

What has been lost and what has been gained in the process of modernization?

What kind of community do most people want?

How can work and life in general be made meaningful?

In what ways are social relationships between men and women changing?

# Alex Haley: The Secret of Strong Families

## Alex Haley

I was only four years old, and so nobody told me the mysterious look I sometimes saw my Mama and Dad exchange in our little church on Sunday mornings had anything to do with that word "love." During those long-ago Sunday mornings, I'd be seated in the front pew beside my Grandma, and my Mama would be up alongside the choir at the piano. She'd be playing some opening bars, but without looking down at her fingers on the keys because she'd be gazing straight across the piano's top at my Dad who would be standing waiting to sing. His head would be turned just enough to look straight back at Mama, and as I watched, their looks would seem to fuse.

Every time they shared that particular look, it seemed to me so strong that somebody could just reach out and touch it. It also seemed clear they didn't care that the whole congregation was seated right before them, watching. I wasn't entirely sure if I should feel embarrassed about how they were acting up there. They *were* so close to our preacher seated in his pulpit in his big wing-backed, brown leather-covered chair.

And then Mama would strike a certain chord, and Dad would quickly turn his head and, smiling out at our congregation, start singing his baritone solo. I know one thing today, over fifty years later: That image of my Mama and Dad gazing across the top of the piano at each other remains for me synonymous with a man and a woman truly *loving* one another.

I have another image I carry from that time when I was growing up in my little hometown of Henning, Tennessee. I remember watching a strange thing that went on at our dining room table when Grandpa would say the prayer before

we'd eat our meals. In our 1930s Bible Belt South, neither our family nor, I guess, any others—black or white, that considered themselves decent—would ever think of eating any meal which hadn't first been prayed over by the head of the house. In our family that was Grandpa, although he would sometimes delegate to Dad with a quick glance or a nod.

But the thing that the little boy who was me found so bemusing was that always when nearing the end of the prayer, Grandpa would say, "And, please, O Lord, bless the hands that prepared this meal." I just couldn't help squinching open one eye and peeping across the tablecloth at Grandma's hands, so as not to miss if the Lord might decide to bless them *right then!* But always Grandma just sat as if she were carved, her graying head bowed over her wrinkled hands. On one of those loosely-clasped fingers was her worn gold wedding band about which she liked to say, "Ain't never been off since Will stuck it there."

I'd wonder how Grandma must feel when she'd be out in the kitchen using those hands to cook with, knowing that the Lord was soon going to be asked to bless them. And I hoped that if He would, that He'd also bless mine, so I'd know how something as powerful as that would feel. Anyhow, when any food blessing prayer ended, we'd eat and I'd feel once again there within our home a second variety of that word "love," which somehow this time seemed to me even more solemn and sacred.

During some portion of each summer, my Dad would catch a train and ride off up North to a Cornell University that was in an Ithaca, N.Y., to study some more toward obtaining what he'd often proudly tell people would eventually be his "master's

degree." I didn't understand what such a degree was. Neither did most of the people in the town. Finally our church's good sister, Miss Scrap Green, figured it out for herself and made it her business to tell everybody that the real meaning was "'Fesser Haley's just takin' all the educatin' that any one man's head can stand." Her explanation kind of settled that matter for most of our Henning people.

Anyhow, during those periods when Dad was gone off up North to do his studying, another memorable thing would happen. With Dad not there to help him, Grandpa generally got home much later than usual from his Will E. Palmer Lumber Company. Sometimes when he got home he'd say to Grandma that there was someone he needed to see before it got dark. I'd be hanging around practically under their feet, and always they'd frustrate me by acting as if I were nowhere in sight. But then Grandpa would give Grandma, or Mama, an exaggerated questioning look. If they nodded back, it meant that I'd acted pretty fair that day. Then Grandpa, with still not a glance at me, would just thrust down his right hand extending stiffly its big index finger. I'd jump like a watch spring to clutch it tightly within my fist. And we'd leave the house with Grandpa striding and me struttin'. I would be so happy and proud.

Grandpa was real black and he walked tall and erect. As we progressed, I'd sometimes look down at our feet and count silently to myself how it was taking three of my short, quick steps to keep up with his long, slow one. I remember that each step he took sent one of his pants cuffs jerking backward over one of his dully-shined, black hightop shoes, then just as that foot would set down, the other foot would have swung forward over the usually dusty footpath.

And somehow after we'd gone a pretty good distance with me steadily holding onto Grandpa's forefinger, I'd begin having a feeling that kind of resembled my Mama's and Dad's fusion of gazes. It would feel like something was flowing from deeply within my Grandpa and through his finger into my fist and on down within me. And an image would start up in my head, that Grandpa was our family's tall, strong tree. My Dad, Grandma and Mama each were stout limbs on it, while obviously I was still just a twig. But at least I knew that every day I was eating all that I could hold, trying my best to grow as strong and as big as I could.

Finally, let me share one further incident from my boyhood there in Henning. It remains for me *so* indelible, principally because at intervals ever since I've continued to realize with new insights and new gratitude how hard my family, a loving, protective Southern black family, tried to rear me in a positive manner. It wasn't easy in that time, amid the intense racial prejudices of the 1930s, which were at their most overt, of course, in the South. Anyway, I was still four and my forthcoming fifth birthday had me very excited. I was very anxious to get older, although that situation had been helped because I had a baby brother named George. Since his arrival I had seized every opportunity to observe to whomever I could that I had become a *"big* brother," which somewhat elevated my status.

But during the days immediately preceding my birthday, my frustration had steadily mounted because I somehow simply *knew* I'd soon be receiving some sort of *big* birthday present. I especially sensed this from my elders who had begun acting as if they were unaware that I even existed. I did my very best discreet searching within the house, both upstairs and down, and found absolutely nothing, whereupon I launched into my very best wheedling efforts for even any little hint, but that didn't get me anything more than my poor elders' blank, deadpan expression.

Awakening and bursting from the bed and snatching on my clothes, I fairly flew downstairs before breakfast on that August 11th morning. I met four impassive adults who then began walking solemnly out onto the back porch, clearly meaning that I should, as I did, follow, falling in behind Grandma, who was carrying baby George. Our little procession had crossed the backyard when I noticed Grandpa's Model-A Ford truck was parked by the cowbarn instead of its usual spot inside the garage, whose door now bore a shiny big new iron lock.

My Dad unlocked and swung wide open the garage door. Astonished, I saw a maybe foot-thick tree slice leaning up against a wall. It stood wider than I was tall, and had maybe twelve to fifteen round, white markers stuck on here and there, each bearing some small handprinting. I stood staring at it, wondering what on earth some tree slice could have to do with my birthday, when my Dad began pointing and explaining how each year a tree acquired one more of the clearly visible "annual growth rings," and this tree's many rings meant it had been cut down after growing for nearly 200 years. Then Dad told me how each one of those round, white markers represented how big and how old that tree was when whatever was printed on each marker happened.

Pointing out a marker that was positioned deep within the tree slice, Dad said that one represented—and it was the first time I ever heard the words—"the Emancipation Proclamation that freed the slaves." It was still confusing, even though I'd heard Grandma speak a whole lot about "slaves." She had often told me that her parents, then their parents, and plenty more before them, too, living away back in time, had been slaves working on plantations for white people who had owned them. What confused me was that I just couldn't understand how any person could go around *owning* other people.

Another marker represented the founding year of Lane College, in Jackson, Tennessee, where I'd heard countless times that Mama and Dad first met when he'd asked to walk her back to her dormitory after a choir practice. Another familiar Lane College story was that when Dad and Mama got married, Grandpa, sparing no expenses, had phoned the Lane College president and paid for the college choir to ride in a bus to Henning where they sang at the wedding.

Yet another marker showed how big and how old that tree was in the birth-year of my famous rooster-fighter great-grandpa. Although he was a slave, he was known and respected wherever he went as "Chicken George," and Grandma loved to tell stories about him. Some markers were for people of whom I'd never heard, like a Harriet Tubman, a Frederick Douglass and a Sojourner Truth, for instance. Dad told me they were important persons I'd be needing to learn a lot more about. And there were other birth-year markers representing Grandpa, Grandma, Dad and Mama—and even *me*. And I remember how strange I felt, looking at the marker of when I'd entered the world, because it was placed at just five years of those growth rings, practically right beneath the tree's bark!

Looking back on that August morning, I can see my parents' and grandparents' reasons for giving me that singularly imaginative gift for a fifth birthday. For one, they wanted me to have a useful perspective on history, and they also wanted to start broadening my vistas. Concurrent with those aims, their intention was to start—that early—shielding me the best they could against the racial harshnesses I'd inevitably meet. Young black persons suffered most when they were not girded in advance with some knowledge of their ethnic past coupled with pride in being black—or "colored," as was the ethnic term used at that time. My Dad later told me that often when I slept, the four of them would sit and discuss such concerns for hours, and that after Mama presented the tree slice idea, the actual thick cross-section of a California redwood was obtained by Grandpa through his lumberyard connection, but just barely in time for my birthday.

For me, I know that a tree slice, a symbol of a family's concern and love, certainly did implant my boyhood concept of history as a drama of people, some gone, others living, and of events as real as any in the present but which had actually happened during the past. And I know that my tree slice gift had the further effect of getting me to read all the books that I could as my desire grew to find somebody else worthy of yet another marker's placement, preferably away down within the tree slice. Most of my suggestions (such as Cinderella!) didn't qualify, but now and then something would, and my pride swelled. Before I reached age six, no one visiting us escaped my using my cut-down teacher's pointer in explaining all about trees' annual growth rings, then what each of my eventually fifty or more markers represented. As I sit here remembering this, I've no question that my fifth birthday's tree slice set into motion a whole long interrelated chain of events which turned me into a writer who prefers historical subjects.

Certainly it is this habit of looking at things with a historical perspective that makes me realize that in today's advanced society too many of us are losing our once-strong family ties, such as those I had as a boy in Henning. The symptomatic sounds of our loss are already familiar. Two pervasive examples are the common expressions, "I'm trying to find myself," or, "I need my own space." Whether these popular statements are made in a tone conveying matter-of-factness or sophisticated élan, to me the bottom-line translation is rootlessness. And also, a word that bothers me is "relationship," popularly applied across the whole range of human unions. To me it seems to avoid stating solid commitment, a fact reflected in today's unprecedented divorce rate. (Pray forgive my flashback to the most moving words I think I ever heard my Grandma utter. One evening during her last years, with Grandpa long dead, she sat quietly listening to several of us family members discuss new sexual mores, then abruptly she offered, "Ain't never knowed no man but Will." Thinking about it, I later wept at its simple majesty.)

Today I believe that we must pursue ways to rebuild our families, which may have eroded during the swiftly changing past years. We must recapture the values that interacting, interdependent, loving families once had. And I also believe that there *are* specific ways families can indeed strengthen themselves. For instance, while I'm a fourth-generation Methodist, I believe that any family will benefit by adopting the weekly tradition known as "Family Night" which is widely practiced by Mormons. Family members set aside an hour one night every week to get reacquainted with each other and to work and pray together and exchange candid views. Mormon bookstores usually carry a booklet, called *Family Time,* which is filled with concrete suggestions on how to spend that hour together. A characteristic gathering might see the family talking about traditions and how they were started or parents telling youngsters about their own childhood experiences. Group discussion of a recent movie or television show can richly fill an evening hour together as well. Finally, Family Nights end with a prayer of thanks for the gathering.

Another good way to strengthen a family is to research its history. This is best accomplished when youthful family members query elders and pursue the nigh-mystical interrelations of the past and the present. For some reason, grandparents and other aged folk will tell their own children far less than they will reveal to their grandchildren. Attics of old family homes should be searched. Precious treasures are probably lying in wait. (Imagine me the morning I blew dust off what turned out to be my ex-slave great-grandfather Tom Murray's ledger of his charge account as a free blacksmith.) Don't overlook any packets of letters. My most cherished old letter was Grandpa's written proposal to Grandma, herewith literally: "Dear Cynthia: We have been keeping company for two years. I feel it is now time we should discuss the contract of marriage. Yours sincerely, Will E. Palmer." Later, Grandma confessed to me that upon receipt of that letter, she, in her words, "went tearing out all through the house, hollerin' to my Mama and sisters, 'I got him! I got him!'"

Finally, nothing strengthens a family more than a planned reunion. Something almost mystical happens when numerous and widely-dispersed family groups converge somewhere en masse—and are suddenly a *clan.*

For all the thrills that happen during a reunion, I believe the most emotional moment of all is when the professional photographer starts arranging for the formal full-family portrait. Classically, all front-row steps are reserved for those of the eldest generation. Would you like to test your capacity for tearfulness? Then you just stand quietly watching as some two young members each gently takes an arm and starts carefully guiding an elder whose vision wavers now, whose footsteps falter, to a front seat.

Next, your clan's newest members are set into those elders' laps. Likely your tears will freshen, looking at sagging, aged ones clutching the lively, plump babies—and you realize that probably you will never again witness that particular pair occupying that seat of honor in that graphic generational contrast.

When at last the camera clicks, the resulting photograph will capture, at least for a moment, your clan, which is unique on this earth. With that experience and that photograph as evidence of the generational ties, every family involved can scarcely miss feeling a wellspring of new strength.

# The American Family in the Year 2000

**Andrew Cherlin
and Frank F. Furstenberg, Jr.**

Andrew Cherlin is associate professor of sociology at The Johns Hopkins University, Baltimore, Maryland 21218. The author of *Marriage, Divorce, Remarriage* (Harvard University Press, 1981), he has published many articles on trends in American family life.

Frank F. Furstenberg, Jr., is a sociology professor at the University of Pennsylvania, 3718 Locust Walk-CR, Philadelphia, Pennsylvania 91104.

"Diversity" is the word for the future of the American family. There will be more divorces, single-parent families, and mixed families from remarriages, but the ideal of marrying and having children is still very much a part of the American experience.

• At current rates, half of all American marriages begun in the early 1980s will end in divorce.

• The number of unmarried couples living together has more than tripled since 1970.

• One out of four children is not living with both parents.

The list could go on and on. Teenage pregnancies: up. Adolescent suicides: up. The birthrate: down. Over the past decade, popular and scholarly commentators have cited a seemingly endless wave of grim statistics about the shape of the American family. The trends have caused a number of concerned Americans to wonder if the family, as we know it, will survive the twentieth century.

And yet, other observers ask us to consider more positive developments:

• Seventy-eight percent of all adults in a recent national survey said they get "a great deal" of satisfaction from their family lives; only 3% said "a little" or "none."

• Two-thirds of the married adults in the same survey said they were "very happy" with their marriages; only 3% said "not too happy."

• In another recent survey of parents of children in their middle years, 88% said that if they had to do it over, they would choose to have children again.

• The vast majority of the children (71%) characterized their family life as "close and intimate."

Family ties are still important and strong, the optimists argue, and the predictions of the demise of the family are greatly exaggerated.

Neither the dire pessimists who believe that the family is falling apart nor the unbridled optimists who claim that the family has never been in better shape provide an accurate picture of family life in the near future. But these trends indicate that what we have come to view as the "traditional" family will no longer predominate.

## Diverse Family Forms

In the future, we should expect to see a growing amount of diversity in family forms, with fewer Americans spending most of their life in a simple "nuclear" family consisting of husband, wife, and children. By the year 2000, three kinds of families will dominate the personal lives of most Americans: families of first marriages, single-parent families, and families of remarriages.

In first-marriage families, both spouses will be in a first marriage, frequently begun after living alone for a time or following a period of cohabitation. Most of these couples

From *The Futurist*, June 1983. THE FUTURIST, published by the World Future Society, 4916 St. Elmo Avenue, Washington, D.C. 20014.

**81**

will have one, two, or, less frequently, three children.

A sizable minority, however, will remain childless. Demographer Charles F. Westoff predicts that about one-fourth of all women currently in their childbearing years will never bear children, a greater number of childless women than at any time in U.S. history.

One other important shift: in a large majority of these families, both the husband and the wife will be employed outside the home. In 1940, only about one out of seven married women worked outside the home; today the proportion is one out of two. We expect this proportion to continue to rise, although not as fast as it did in the past decade or two.

## Single-Parent Families

The second major type of family can be formed in two ways. Most are formed by a marital separation, and the rest by births to unmarried women. About half of all marriages will end in divorce at current rates, and we doubt that the rates will fall substantially in the near future.

When the couple is childless, the formerly married partners are likely to set up independent households and resume life as singles. The high rate of divorce is one of the reasons why more men and women are living in single-person households than ever before.

But three-fifths of all divorces involve couples with children living at home. In at least nine out of ten cases, the wife retains custody of the children after a separation.

Although joint custody has received a lot of attention in the press and in legal circles, national data show that it is still uncommon. Moreover, it is likely to remain the exception rather than the rule because most ex-spouses can't get along well enough to manage raising their children together. In fact, a national survey of children aged 11 to 16 conducted by one of the authors demonstrated that fathers have little contact with their children after a divorce. About half of the children whose parents had divorced hadn't seen their father in the last year; only one out of six had managed to see their father an average of once a week. If the current rate of divorce persists, about half of all

children will spend some time in a single-parent family before they reach 18.

Much has been written about the psychological effects on children of living with one parent, but the literature has not yet proven that any lasting negative effects occur. One effect, however, does occur with regularity: women who head single-parent families typically experience a sharp decline in their income relative to before their divorce. Husbands usually do not experience a decline. Many divorced women have difficulty reentering the job market after a long absence; others find that their low-paying clerical or service-worker jobs aren't adequate to support a family.

Of course, absent fathers are supposed to make child-support payments, but only a minority do. In a 1979 U.S. Bureau of the Census survey, 43% of all divorced and separated women with children present reported receiving child-support payments during the previous year, and the average annual payment was about $1,900. Thus, the most detrimental effect for children living in a single-parent family is not the lack of a male presence but the lack of a male income.

## Families of Remarriages

The experience of living as a single parent is temporary for many divorced women, especially in the middle class. Three out of four divorced people remarry, and about half of these marriages occur within three years of the divorce.

Remarriage does much to solve the economic problems that many single-parent families face because it typically adds a male income. Remarriage also relieves a single parent of the multiple burdens of running and supporting a household by herself.

But remarriage also frequently involves blending together two families into one, a difficult process that is complicated by the absence of clear-cut ground rules for how to accomplish the merger. Families formed by remarriages can become quite complex, with children from either spouse's previous marriage or from the new marriage and with numerous sets of grandparents,

stepgrandparents, and other kin and quasi-kin.

The divorce rate for remarriages is modestly higher than for first marriages, but many couples and their children adjust successfully to their remarriage and, when asked, consider their new marriage to be a big improvement over their previous one.

## The Life Course: A Scenario for the Next Two Decades

Because of the recent sharp changes in marriage and family life, the life course of children and young adults today is likely to be far different from what a person growing up earlier in this century experienced. It will not be uncommon, for instance, for children born in the 1980s to follow this sequence of living arrangements: live with both parents for several years, live with their mothers after their parents divorce, live with their mothers and stepfathers, live alone for a time when in their early twenties, live with someone of the opposite sex without marrying, get married, get divorced, live alone again, get remarried, and end up living alone once more following the death of their spouses.

Not everyone will have a family history this complex, but it is likely that a substantial minority of the population will. And many more will have family histories only slightly less complex.

Overall, we estimate that about half of the young children alive today will spend some time in a single-parent family before they reach 18; about nine out of ten will eventually marry; about one out of two will marry and then divorce; and about one out of three will marry, divorce, and then remarry. In contrast, only about one out of six women born in the period 1910 to 1914 married and divorced and only about one in eight married, divorced, and remarried.

Without doubt, Americans today are living in a much larger number of family settings during their lives than was the case a few generations ago.

The life-course changes have been even greater for women than for men because of the far greater likelihood of employment during the childbearing years for middle-class women today compared with their mothers and grandmothers. Moreover, the increase in life expectancy has increased the difference between men's and women's family lives. Women now tend to outlive men by a wide margin, a development that is new in this century. Consequently, many more women face a long period of living without a spouse at the end of their lives, either as a widow or as a divorced person who never remarried.

Long-lived men, in contrast, often find that their position in the marriage market is excellent, and they are much more likely to remain married (or remarried) until they die.

**Convergence and Divergence**

The family lives of Americans vary according to such factors as class, ethnicity, religion, and region. But recent evidence suggests a convergence among these groups in many features of family life. The clearest example is in childbearing, where the differences between Catholics and non-Catholics or between Southerners and Northerners are much smaller than they were 20 years ago. We expect this process of convergence to continue, although it will fall far short of eliminating all social class and subcultural differences.

The experiences of blacks and whites also have converged in many respects, such as in fertility and in patterns of premarital sexual behavior, over the past few decades. But with respect to marriage, blacks and whites have diverged markedly since about 1960.

Black families in the United States always have had strong ties to a large network of extended kin. But in addition, blacks, like whites, relied on a relatively stable bond between husbands and wives. But over the past several decades—and especially since 1960—the proportion of black families maintained by a woman has increased sharply; currently, the proportion exceeds four in ten. In addition, more young black women are having children out of wedlock; in the late 1970s, about two out of three black women who gave birth to a first child were unmarried.

These trends mean that we must qualify our previously stated con-clusion that marriage will remain central to family life. This conclusion holds for Americans in general. For many low-income blacks, however, marriage is likely to be less important than the continuing ties to a larger network of kin.

Marriage is simply less attractive to a young black woman from a low-income family because of the poor prospects many young black men have for steady employment and because of the availability of alternative sources of support from public-assistance payments and kin. Even though most black women eventually marry, their marriages have a very high probability of ending in separation or divorce. Moreover, they have a lower likelihood of re-marrying.

Black single-parent families sometimes have been criticized as being "disorganized" or even "pathological." What the critics fail to note is that black single mothers usually are embedded in stable, functioning kin networks. These networks tend to center around female kin—mothers, grandmothers, aunts—but brothers, fathers, and other male kin also may be active. The members of these networks share and exchange goods and services, thus helping to share the burdens of poverty. The lower-class black extended family, then, is characterized by strong ties among a network of kin but fragile ties between husband and wife. The negative aspects of this family system have been exaggerated greatly; yet it need not be romanticized, either. It can be difficult and risky for individuals to leave the network in order to try to make it on their own; thus, it may be hard for individuals to raise themselves out of poverty until the whole network is raised.

**The Disintegrating Family?**

By now, predictions of the demise of the family are familiar to everyone. Yet the family is a resilient institution that still retains more strength than its harshest critics maintain. There is, for example, no evidence of a large-scale rejection of marriage among Americans. To be sure, many young adults are living together outside of marriage, but the evidence we have about cohabitation suggests that it is not a life-long alternative to marriage; rather, it appears to be either another stage in the process of courtship and marriage or a transition between first and second marriages.

The so-called "alternative lifestyles" that received so much attention in the late 1960s, such as communes and lifelong singlehood, are still very uncommon when we look at the nation as a whole.

Young adults today do marry at a somewhat older age, on average, than their parents did. But the average age at marriage today is very similar to what it was throughout the period from 1890 to 1940.

To be sure, many of these marriages will end in divorce, but three out of four people who divorce eventually remarry. Americans still seem to desire the intimacy and security that a marital relationship provides.

Much of the alarm about the family comes from reactions to the sheer speed at which the institution changed in the last two decades. Between the early 1960s and the mid-1970s, the divorce rate doubled, the marriage rate plunged, the birthrate dropped from a twentieth-century high to an all-time low, premarital sex became accepted, and married women poured into the labor force. But since the mid-1970s, the pace of change has slowed. The divorce rate has risen modestly and the birthrate even has increased a bit. We may have entered a period in which American families can adjust to the sharp changes that occurred in the 1960s and early 1970s. We think that, by and large, accommodations will be made as expectations change and institutions are redesigned to take account of changing family practices.

Despite the recent difficulties, family ties remain a central part of American life. Many of the changes in family life in the 1960s and 1970s were simply a continuation of long-term trends that have been with us for generations.

The birthrate has been declining since the 1820s, the divorce rate has been climbing since at least the Civil War, and over the last half century a growing number of married women have taken paying jobs. Employment outside the home has been gradually eroding the patriarchal system of values that was a part of our early history, replacing it with a more egalitarian set of values.

The only exception occurred during the late 1940s and the 1950s. After World War II, Americans raised during the austerity of depression and war entered adulthood at a time of sustained prosperity. The sudden turnabout in their fortunes led them to marry earlier and have more children than any generation before or since in this century. Because many of us were either parents or children in the baby-boom years following the war, we tend to think that the 1950s typify the way twentieth-century families used to be. But the patterns of marriage and childbearing in the 1950s were an aberration resulting from special historical circumstances; the patterns of the 1960s and 1970s better fit the long-term trends. Barring unforeseen major disruptions, small families, working wives, and impermanent marital ties are likely to remain with us indefinitely.

A range of possible developments could throw our forecasts off the mark. We do not know, for example, how the economy will behave over the next 20 years, or how the family will be affected by technological innovations still at the conception stage. But, we do not envision any dramatic changes in family life resulting solely from technological innovations in the next two decades.

Having sketched our view of the most probable future, we will consider three of the most important implications of the kind of future we see.

## Growing Up in Changing Families

Children growing up in the past two decades have faced a maelstrom of social change. As we have pointed out, family life is likely to become even more complex, diverse, unpredictable, and uncertain in the next two decades.

Even children who grow up in stable family environments will probably have to get along with a lot less care from parents (mothers in particular) than children received early in this century. Ever since the 1950s, there has been a marked and continuous increase in the proportion of working mothers whose pre-school children are cared for outside the home, rising from 31% in 1958 to 62% in 1977. The upward trend is likely to continue until it becomes standard practice for very young children to receive care either in someone else's home or in a group setting. There has been a distinct drop in the care of children by relatives, as fewer aunts, grandmothers, or adult children are available to supplement the care provided by parents. Increasingly, the government at all levels will be pressured to provide more support for out-of-home daycare.

How are children responding to the shifting circumstances of family life today? Are we raising a generation of young people who, by virtue of their own family experiences, lack the desire and skill to raise the next generation? As we indicated earlier, existing evidence has not demonstrated that marital disruption creates lasting personality damage or instills a distinctly different set of values about family life.

Similarly, a recent review on children of working mothers conducted by the National Research Council of the National Academy of Sciences concludes:

> If there is only one message that emerges from this study, it is that parental employment in and of itself—mothers' employment or fathers' or both parents'—is not necessarily good or bad for children.

The fact that both parents work *per se* does not adversely affect the well-being of children.

Currently, most fathers whose wives are employed do little childcare. Today, most working mothers have two jobs: they work for pay and then come home to do most of the childcare and housework. Pressure from a growing number of harried working wives could prod fathers to watch less television and change more diapers. But this change in fathers' roles is proceeding much more slowly than the recent spate of articles about the "new father" would lead one to expect. The strain that working while raising a family places on working couples, and especially on working mothers, will likely make childcare and a more equitable sharing of housework prominent issues in the 1980s and 1990s.

## Family Obligations

Many of the one out of three Americans who, we estimate, will enter a second marriage will do so after having children in a first marriage. Others may enter into a first marriage with a partner who has a family from a previous marriage. It is not clear in these families what obligations remain after divorce or are created after remarriage. For one thing, no clear set of norms exists specifying how people in remarriages are supposed to act toward each other. Stepfathers don't know how much to discipline their stepchildren; second wives don't know what they're supposed to say when they meet their husbands' first wives; stepchildren don't know what to call their absent father's new wife.

The ambiguity about family relations after divorce and remarriage also extends to economic support. There are no clear-cut guidelines to tell adults how to balance the claims of children from previous marriages versus children from their current marriages. Suppose a divorced man who has been making regular payments to support his two small children from a previous marriage marries a woman with children from her previous marriage. Suppose her husband isn't paying any child support. Suppose further that the remarried couple have a child of their own. Which children should have first claim on the husband's income? Legally, he is obligated to pay child support to his ex-wife, but in practice he is likely to feel that his primary obligation is to his stepchildren, whose father isn't helping, and to his own children from his remarriage.

Our guess, supported by some preliminary evidence from national studies, is that remarriage will tend to further reduce the amount of child support that a man pays, particularly if the man's new family includes children from his new wife's previous marriage or from the current marriage. What appears to be occurring in many cases is a form of "childswapping," with men exchanging an old set of children from a prior marriage for a new set from their new wife's prior marriage and from the remarriage.

Sociologist Lenore J. Weitzman provides a related example in her book *The Marriage Contract.* Suppose, she writes, a 58-year-old corporate vice president with two grown children divorces his wife to marry his young secretary. He agrees to adopt the secretary's two young children. If he dies of a heart attack the following year:

> In most states, a third to half of his estate would go to his new wife, with the remainder divided among the four children (two from his last marriage, and his new wife's two children). His first wife will receive nothing—neither survivors' insurance nor a survivors' pension nor a share of the estate—and both she and his natural children are likely to feel that they have been treated unjustly.

Since the rate of mid-life divorce has been increasing nearly as rapidly as that of divorce at younger ages, this type of financial problem will become increasingly common. It would seem likely that there will be substantial pressure for changes in family law and in income security systems to provide more to the ex-wife and natural children in such circumstances.

## Intergenerational Relations

A similar lack of clarity about who should support whom may affect an increasing number of elderly persons. Let us consider the case of an elderly man who long ago divorced his first wife and, as is fairly typical, retained only sporadic contact with his children. If his health deteriorates in old age and he needs help, will his children provide it? In many cases, the relationship would seem so distant that the children would not be willing to provide major assistance. To be sure, in most instances the elderly man would have remarried, possibly acquiring stepchildren, and it may be these stepchildren who feel the responsibility to provide assistance. Possibly the two sets of children may be called upon to cooperate in lending support, even when they have had little or no contact while growing up. Currently, there are no clear guidelines for assigning kinship responsibilities in this new type of extended family.

Even without considering divorce, the issue of support to the elderly is likely to bring problems that are new and widespread. As is well known, the low fertility in the United States, which we think will continue to be low, means that the population is becoming older. The difficulties that this change in age structure poses for the Social Security system are so well known that we need not discuss them here. Let us merely note that any substantial weakening of the Social Security system would put the elderly at a great disadvantage with regard to their families, for older Americans increasingly rely on Social Security and other pensions and insurance plans to provide support. A collapse of Social Security would result in a large decrease in the standard of living among older Americans and a return to the situation prevailing a few decades ago in which the elderly were disproportionately poor.

The relations between older people and their children and grandchildren are typically close, intimate, and warm. Most people live apart from their children, but they generally live close by one or more of them. Both generations prefer the autonomy that the increased affluence of the older generation has recently made possible. Older people see family members quite often, and they report that family members are their major source of support. A survey by Louis Harris of older Americans revealed that more than half of those with children had seen them in the past day, and close to half had seen a grandchild. We expect close family ties between the elderly and their kin to continue to be widespread. If, however, the economic autonomy of the elderly is weakened, say, by a drop in Social Security, the kind of friendly equality that now characterizes intergenerational relations could be threatened.

One additional comment about the elderly: Almost everyone is aware that the declining birthrate means that the elderly will have fewer children in the future on whom they can rely for support. But although this is true in the long run, it will not be true in the next few decades. In fact, beginning soon, the elderly will have more children, on average, than they do today. The reason is the postwar baby boom of the late 1940s and 1950s. As the parents of these large families begin to reach retirement age near the end of this century, more children will be available to help their elderly parents. Once the next generation—the baby-boom children—begins to reach retirement age after about 2010, the long-term trend toward fewer available children will sharply reassert itself.

Were we to be transported suddenly to the year 2000, the families we would see would look very recognizable. There would be few unfamiliar forms—not many communes or group marriages, and probably not a large proportion of lifelong singles. Instead, families by and large would continue to center around the bonds between husbands and wives and between parents and children. One could say the same about today's families relative to the 1960s: the forms are not new. What is quite different, comparing the 1960s with the 1980s, or the 1980s with a hypothetical 2000, is the distribution of these forms.

In the early 1960s, there were far fewer single-parent families and families formed by remarriages after divorce than is the case today; and in the year 2000 there are likely to be far more single-parent families and families of remarriage than we see now. Moreover, in the early 1960s both spouses were employed in a much smaller percentage of two-parent families; in the year 2000, the percentage with two earners will be greater still. Cohabitation before marriage existed in the 1960s, but it was a frowned-upon, bohemian style of life. Today, it has become widely accepted; it will likely become more common in the future. Yet we have argued that cohabitation is less an alternative to marriage than a precursor to marriage, though we expect to see a modest rise in the number of people who never marry.

# Cities Won't Drive You Crazy

*NOT IF YOU LEARN THE TRICK: MAKE STRESS A STIMULUS RATHER THAN A THREAT.*

## C. R. CREEKMORE

*C. R. Creekmore is a freelance writer who lives in Amherst, Massachusetts.*

Trapped in one of those Olympian traffic jams on the Garden State Parkway in New Jersey, I waited to pay my toll for the Newark exit. Horns, insults and exhaust fumes had settled in a noisy, dark-tempered cloud. As I finally reached the end of the exact-change line, I faced a sudden dilemma. There was the automatic toll collector, side-by-side with a human toll taker standing in his little booth. I stared into the impersonal mouth of the collection machine, then at the person, and chose him. The man looked shocked. He regarded the quarter I thrust at him as if it were a bug. "Grow up!" he screamed at me with a sense of indignation that I assumed was generated by a life dedicated to the parkway system. "Grow up and use the machine!"

To me, the incident has always summed up the essence of what cities are: hotbeds of small embarrassments, dehumanizing confrontations, monetary setbacks, angry people and festering acts of God.

Many Americans agree with this stereotype and believe firmly that the dirty, crowded, dangerous city must gradually destroy an urbanite's psyche. This belief has a corollary: Rural life, haven of natural purity, wholesome values and the spirit of self-reliance, is the wellspring of physical and mental health.

A large body of research, conducted in the past 15 years by a diverse group of social scientists, challenges these heartfelt prejudices. These studies conclude that metropolitan living is more than OK. In many ways, researchers have found, city pavements outshine the sticks as healthy places to live and work.

Jonathan Freedman, chairperson of the psychology department at the University of Toronto, is an authority on how cities affect those who live in them. On the physical side, he believes that life expectancy is higher for people in urban areas and infant mortality rates are lower. The potentially unhealthy aspects of city life, such as pollution, stress and crime, are more than offset by better medical care, better water supplies and sewage systems and better systems for handling emergencies of all kinds.

What about mental illness? Surely the fabled rat race must eventually sap mental endurance and lead to breakdowns. Not according to mental-

*I N MANY WAYS, CITY PAVEMENTS OUTSHINE THE STICKS AS HEALTHY PLACES FOR PEOPLE TO LIVE AND WORK.*

health statistics. In a now classic study of the subject, *Mental Health in the Metropolis: The Midtown Manhattan Study,* sociologist Leo Srole and five colleagues compared mental-health statistics in Manhattan with those in small towns. They concluded that small towns have a slightly higher rate of mental illness.

This doesn't mean that cities are easy to live in. Manhattan psychiatrist Herbert E. Walker and C. Ray Smith, a writer on urban planning, point out in an article that certain environmental stress comes with the urban territory: automobile traffic, air pollution, high noise levels, lack of privacy and such architectural faults as poor lighting, tight spaces and inadequate seating.

With all this to contend with, why don't cities drive more people around the bend? One answer is that we learn to cope with the multiple problems. "It's not a bad environment, just a very complex one," says Gerda McCahan, chairperson of the department of psychology at Furman University in Atlanta, who once worked as a clinical psychologist in New York City. "An effect of living in the big city is that with time people learn to insulate themselves in a psychological sense. They learn not to allow a lot of stimuli to impinge on their consciousness. They sift out things that do not concern them."

Another answer is that mental illness goes deeper than environmental stress. "Severe mental illness is not caused by the kinds of environmental stimuli char-

From *Psychology Today,* January 1985, pp. 46-50, 52-53.

*U*NPLEASANT
CITY STIMULI
MIGHT AFFECT YOUR MOOD
TEMPORARILY, BUT THEY
ARE UNLIKELY TO CAUSE
REAL MENTAL ILLNESS.

acteristic of a city—loud noises, noxious odors, density of population and high levels of activity, for instance," Freedman explains. "Rather, it is caused by complex human and social problems such as genetic defects, interpersonal relationships and the stresses of dealing with one's needs. And these problems are carried wherever you go. City stimuli might affect your mood temporarily, but they are unlikely to cause real mental illness."

Crowding is perhaps the most studied problem of city living. As urbanites do battle with blitzing cabdrivers, crammed subway cars, the frustrations of traffic and deadly competition for parking spaces, they have one big thing going for them. As McCahan suggests, their saving grace is superior adaptability.

Take some of the ways city folk deal with common crowding situations. They live on many levels, so the entire population is not constantly milling together on the ground. They have complex social rules (walk on the right; stop at red lights; wait in line for services) for pedestrian traffic. Cities now install bicycle, horse and foot paths that connect parks and open space and make movement safer and more pleasant. Freeways are built to travel to and from downtown faster. And planners use a variety of methods (rotaries, coordinated traffic lights, one-way roads) to improve traffic flow in the most crowded areas.

Other improvements are on the way. "One feature now becoming standard on urban expressways is noise barriers," says Dorn McGrath Jr., a professor of urban and regional planning at George Washington University. "That's because research carried on

over the last 15 years has determined that highway noise is not only annoying to nearby residents, but can be psychologically and physiologically harmful."

This type of human adaptability is one reason Freedman is skeptical about the relevance of experiments that test the effect of crowding on rats and other animals—research that typically shows heightened levels of aggression, competitiveness, infant neglect and early death. Freedman feels that these findings can't be usefully applied to human crowding conditions. "Humans are much more adaptable creatures than other animals," he explains. Additionally, "the level of density you are talking about with laboratory animals is extraordinary, a level that would never appear in the real world."

Other researchers are less certain about the harmlessness of crowding to humans. For example, psychologists Janice Zeedyk-Ryan and Gene F. Smith report that crowding took its toll when 16 undergraduates volunteered to stay in a 12-foot-by-18-foot civil-defense shelter for 18 hours. Compared to a group of six students who occupied the same shelter in a second test, the densely packed students became markedly more hostile and anxious as the hours passed.

In another experiment, psychologists Yakov M. Epstein, Robert L. Woolfolk and Paul M. Lehrer created an environment that approximated the close conditions found in rush-hour mass-transit systems. They then compared the students' reactions under these conditions to what happened when they were put with the same number of strangers in a normal-sized room. The researchers found that the crowded students had higher blood pressure, reported that they felt unfriendlier and less in control and were rated by the strangers (who were actually working with the experimenters as observers) as tenser and more uncomfortable and annoyed than the uncrowded students.

Studies such as these suggest that crowding cramps the style of city dwellers and produces stress. Freedman has another interpretation. "Density intensifies people's reactions to events around them," he explains. "If you get people who are feeling aggressive for other reasons—who have been

angered at home or work, for instance—and you put them under high-density conditions, they are likely to be more aggressive. On the other hand, if the same people are feeling good and cooperative, density will also intensify that."

Freedman uses loud music as an analogy. If people like the music being played, turning it up usually enhances the experience. If they don't, increased volume makes the experience even more unpleasant.

Thus, when crowding occurs in situations normally considered negative, such as commuting to work or waiting in line for service in a bank or store, it intensifies those negative feelings. But place the same crowds in an amusement park, at a cocktail party or in a basketball arena, and crowding enhances the fun.

One recent study indicates that under the right conditions, population density can actually improve relations in a neighborhood. Sociologists Lois M. Verbrugge and Ralph B. Taylor explained how this worked in a study they did in Baltimore. As population density increases, some environmental resources diminish and people start to compete for limited space, ease of movement, services and other resources.

The ultimate result of this competition, however, is that people adapt. They add services, make adjustments in how they live and increase social interaction to make up for scarce resources. Think of the Guardian Angels, patrolling neighborhoods to augment police services. Or consider those neighborhood characters who direct people to vacant parking spaces and act as traffic cops for alternate-side-of-the-street parking changes. In

*U*NDER THE
RIGHT CONDITIONS,
POPULATION DENSITY
CAN ACTUALLY IMPROVE
RELATIONS IN
A NEIGHBORHOOD.

adaptive ways of this kind, neighbors get together.

"Local social resources actually increase," Verbrugge and Taylor point out. "High density provides opportunities for informal contact and assistance because people are more accessible. . . . It is very possible that increasing density enhances social ties."

Crowding aside, it seems obvious that other stimuli peculiar to cities can

*CROWDING INTENSIFIES PEOPLE'S REACTIONS— BOTH GOOD AND BAD— TO EVENTS HAPPENING AROUND THEM.*

be harmful to many people. In their article on urban stress, Walker and Smith list anxiety, depression, back pain, ulcers and heart attacks as diseases that can be traced to the high level of environmental stress in the city. "But for those people equipped to handle it," McCahan argues, "the city is the absolute optimum habitat." And, she adds, people can find their share of stress in the country as well. The boredom, lack of variety and low level of stimulation can be just as stressful as city living for those not accustomed to it.

Cities can also provide ties that help inhabitants handle stress better than their country cousins do. Home economist David Imig of the University of Missouri investigated the impact of life stress on 37 rural and 64 urban families with similar economic and educational backgrounds. He discovered that when the families suffered unemployment, money problems, relocation, illness and divorce, the city people suffered considerably less disruption in family relationships than did the rural families.

The difference seems to lie in the support systems that influence people's perception of stress. Urban families, Imig says, usually have closer

CARL MYDANS/BLACK STAR

*Telegraph Hill in San Francisco: a strong sense of neighborhood identity.*

connections to their social environment. They operate within a wide-ranging network of secondary relationships that may not involve close kinship or friendship, but which do offer informal support and exchange of services. You take my kid to dance class; I take yours to the ball game.

By contrast, rural families usually limit their support networks to a few close primary ties. This means that urban families have more outlets to diffuse stress. "Rural families don't have the large support system that urban families do," Imig believes. "They don't have anyone to turn to, to fall back on, when stress concentrates on their few close ties."

Another popular urban myth was depicted humorously in the movie *Terms of Endearment.* In one scene,

an Iowa banker chastises a rude and insensitive cashier by noting, "You must be from New York."

Many studies contradict this stereotype of the cold, impersonal city. We have already seen that dense population can improve social ties, and that the city support network often works better than that in the country. In a study reported in *Psychology Today* (April 1981), environmental psychologist Karen Franck and two colleagues at the City University of New York found that although good friends come slowly in the city, friendships there eventually seem to become more intimate and more highly valued than those in nonurban settings. City friendships also tend to be more varied, broadening people's perspectives and opportunities.

*IN THE CITY, A NETWORK OF SECONDARY RELATIONSHIPS OFFERS INFORMAL SUPPORT AND EXCHANGE OF SERVICES. YOU TAKE MY KID TO DANCE CLASS; I TAKE YOURS TO THE BALL GAME.*

"You have access to people at your own level in intellectual pursuits, sports, artistic interests—any area that you select," McCahan explains. "And you can seek out people at or above your own level who stimulate your growth."

Another measure of an area's elusive sense of warmth and personality is whether its inhabitants help one another in times of need. Do people help less in cities than in the country? The jury is still out on that one.

"A majority of studies find more help in rural areas," says Erwin Staub, a professor of psychology at the University of Massachusetts who has studied helping behavior extensively. "But some find no difference. And a minority even find more help in urban areas.

"The more confusing a situation, the more complex the stimuli, the more people's attention tends to be distracted," Staub says. "So the complexity of a city situation might distract people from helping." But, he points out, some areas also feature helping networks that can spur onlookers to come to the aid of victims.

People living in an urban neighborhood with a strong sense of identity—a Little Italy, a Chinatown or a rehabilitated neighborhood, for example—see emergency situations as their responsibility. After all, it's their turf. Cities also have concentrations of people with special helping skills such as CPR expertise, civil-defense training or medical backgrounds, and these people help in emergencies because they are conditioned to do so.

One of the most important mechanisms for triggering a person's helping response, Staub proposes, is a "prosocial orientation," previous experience being helpful. Since cities are the regional centers for charitable causes, social campaigns and reform efforts, many people learn to be helpers.

Thus, the whole process of solving city problems is part of a healthy cycle of activity. "If you want to look for problems that need addressing," says urban planner McGrath, "cities are the places where they tend to accumulate." Among the problems that he lists are "the awesome fabric of despair and difficulty" that covers our ghettos; bad traffic flow with its accompanying pollution and psychological frustration; noise; pollution of the environment; and frightening rises in already frightening urban crime rates.

"As one consequence, there are people drawn to deal with these problems. The whole process acts to revitalize a city," McGrath continues. "And the very problems that accumulate also serve to get meaning and satisfaction into the lives of the people who live there by giving them causes."

McGrath's viewpoint is another indication that the key to living in a city is adaptability. Stress is in the eye and mind of the beholder. An urbanite must be able to take apparently unpleasant stimuli and use them to his or her advantage.

Can people learn this psychological backflip? Yes, according to Walker and Smith, who tell in their article how to manipulate city stress. "Urban stress should be seen as a stimulus," they say. And to relieve pressure, they advise exercising regularly in enjoyable, varied places, attending a wide range of entertainments, living in a pleasant, well-lighted space, being assertive when a situation demands it and adopting a positive attitude about the city and its complexity.

"To flourish in the city, you must have a good sense of self-esteem and be able to tolerate competition," McCahan adds. "You must be able to pit yourself against the best and, win or lose, learn something positive about yourself. And you must be relatively assertive. If you are a shy person, the city can eat you up."

The city can also do you in if you are saddled with competitive handicaps; if you are financially, socially, physically or mentally restricted from competing. But for those geared to compete, city life can be a horn of plenty. "I always think of living in the city as a potential growth center for human beings," McCahan says. "One reason is that cities attract the best of everything."

There are good jobs. The city offers the opportunity, according to McCahan, of "seeking your own milieu" and level of competence, whatever your calling. You can see good plays and artsy movies. Professional and collegiate sports abound. You can go to street fairs and ethnic festivals in the park. Take your pick of music, art galleries and cultural exhibits. Or you can spend your days wandering among various periods of architecture, testing Lewis Mumford's observation that "In the city, time becomes visible."

And, of course, you can always take advantage of a city's most notable amenity—going out for Chinese food at 3 a.m.

All of this activity is what makes a city go: a great, roiling, collective energy. "It is as if, far down in the rocky bowels ... some vast, secret turbine were generating an extra source of power, capable of being shared by all the inhabitants of the city," wrote author Brendan Gill about New York's psychic energy. "It is a power that gives them the means of meeting the city on its own fierce terms of constant stress. And it is profoundly the case that your true (urbanite) rejoices in stress; the crowds, the dirt, the stench, the noise. Instead of depressing him, they urge him onto an unexpected 'high,' a state of euphoria in which the loftiest of ambitions seems readily attainable."

# Work: The Right to Right Livelihood

## Theodore Roszak

. . . In my family, with its almost proverbial American immigrant background, nobody ever entertained the notion that there might be cultural styles of work, that our livelihood, like the food we eat, should be a material we shape and flavor to our taste. Nobody could have afforded to see things that way. My grandparents arrived from Eastern Europe with one fixed star in their universe: their willingness to work, without raising questions, without making trouble. Work was their one chance to prove themselves and to make good as Americans. They stepped off the boat straight into the mines and shops and factories of Wilkes Barre, West Wheeling, Akron, Chicago, grateful and glad for any employment they could find.

Eventually, by dint of steady toil and fanatical thrift, they raised themselves into the lower margins of that sprawling social conurbation called the American middle class. From first to last, work was the center and substance of their lives; it was their validation as useful citizens. Even more, the work ethic, as they honored it in their every waking moment, was the bedrock of their security and their self-respect. When all else failed or collapsed—as it did for them in the Great Depression—or whenever injustice or discrimination touched them, they could always fall back upon their willingness to work unstintingly and at anything until they dropped.

Yet it was a strange, contradictory pride they took in their work. I remember vividly how my father would rehearse the family litany whenever he had been bruised by insult or injustice. "I had to sweat for every nickel I ever earned . . . I never got something for nothing . . . nobody in this family ever asked for any handouts. . . ." It was pride mixed darkly with bitterness, because, for all he might say for himself as a hard worker, my father, like his father before him, never took satisfaction in the work he was hired to do. He loathed and cursed all his jobs. He was a gifted cabinetmaker, but—with the exception of a few failed business efforts of his own—he spent his entire working life as an underpaid carpenter, with never a good word for any job he held. He despised his bosses and the work they assigned him, which always had to be done on the quick and cheap, making no use of his best skills. Worst of all, he came to despise himself

as one of the hundred million American nobodies who were stuck on the bottom rungs of the social ladder with no way up.

"Working poor" is the quaint social category we now have for families like mine, the sort of people who only get a little ahead of their debts by putting in ten or twenty hours a week of overtime. "OT" was like manna from heaven in our household; my father would announce its arrival like a portent of better days. But then he wound up working harder than ever, and it always showed. He would drag home dog-tired and short-tempered at night, leave bleary-eyed and unshaven the next morning, grumble as he ate warmed-over meals at how much less he was bringing home in his pay check than he deserved. And there was always the lament: The work wasn't worthy of him. It was slapdash and stupid and shoddy, none of it done with care or craftsmanship.

Hard work killed my father young—at forty-six. He died of heart failure and (I believe) of demoralization, with not enough money in the bank for a good funeral. My mother had to use up his life insurance to bury him.

My father was pugnaciously proud of being "hard-working." But his constant advice to me was, "Never work with your hands. Go to college. Become a professional man. If you work with your hands, you're not worth shit in this world." His pride, like that of all the working poor I have ever met, was the best face he could put upon his sense of helpless victimization. He had every right to the self-respect he claimed; he was the possessor of a noble and useful skill. He was a builder, a man who could make houses and fine furniture. He knew the true use of his tools. I have worked with executive paper shufflers and "decision makers" who will not contribute anything to the world as valuable as a single good table or chair my father made. In another age he would have been highly honored for his craft. But his pride could no longer be based on that, because he knew he was somebody's misused employee, the hireling of people who valued him only as a means to a fast dollar. So his self-esteem was infected with anger and envy; when he boasted of being "hard-working," he was making a slender virtue of a hated necessity. At last, his pride was an expression of belligerent and powerless resentment.

Whenever I hear politicians and labor leaders talk about "putting people to work," I wonder if they realize, as I suspect a great many working people do, what a pathetically minimal ideal that has become. What does "full employment" mean to men like my father whose daily work is an insult and a torment? Is it enough any longer for the economic index to measure how many people have jobs, without asking whether they take pride in the jobs they have? I wonder, when do we begin talking about the quality of employment, as well as its quantity? Another way of asking, when do we stop treating people like statistics and start treating them like persons?

There is one more thing I remember about my father's work life—something that always puzzled me in my youth. Every year my father got two meager weeks of paid vacation. When it came around, he swore he was going to lie out in the back yard and rot. And he would do just that . . . for perhaps the first two or three days he was off work. He would sit under a tree with some beer and a radio and do very nearly nothing. But soon enough, he would be banging away in some part of the house, remodeling a room; or he would be out in the garage, building a piece of furniture; or he would be clambering about under the floor boards, repairing the foundation. He would finish those long hours of work as tired and grimy as he ever came home from his job. But now he wasn't morose, he didn't complain. He would be talking about how well the job was going, or making sketches and puzzling out better ways to design the project.

One summer he used up his entire vacation working ten and twelve hours a day to help an incompetent neighbor put up a new porch. He finally took over the job, redesigned the porch, and pretty well did it all himself. All he got in payment was a bottle of whiskey. When my mother asked him why he was going to the trouble, he answered, "Because I can't sit out there and watch him do a half-assed job. It drives me nuts."

## The True Dimensions of Alienation

If there was ever an example of alienation in the classic Marxist sense of the word, my father was it. He was the quintessential proletarian: totally vulnerable both economically and psychologically. He never even found his way into an effective labor union to defend his interests. He was a man with nothing to sell for his livelihood but his labor; and at last even that was not enough. He had to surrender his self-respect as well. In that act of resignation, there is more than personal pathos. A noble tradition of craftsmanship is poisoned to death by such self-contempt, and the meaning of honest work is hideously distorted for all of us.

Yet, over the years, I have come to see, in large part through my own work experience at a variety of jobs, unskilled, white collar, and professional, that the problem of dehumanized labor barely begins with my father's example. His experience is really only the base line from which the further reaches of alienation may be measured. From the personalist viewpoint we adopt here, the hard core of the problem is not to be found among those who are, like my father, miserable and embittered, but among those who are exploited and acquiescent, alienated and yet complacent. It is only when we begin to appreciate how effectively people can be persuaded to will their own alienation from the work they do that we grasp the true dimensions of the problem.

One need not reach beyond a conventional left-wing analysis to recognize that a worker whose discontent is softened by a pay raise and shorter hours is still an exploited worker. Similarly, if working conditions are redesigned to make life on the job more relaxed and diverting (for example, the office is air-conditioned and carpeted, music is piped in, the day is strategically punctuated with coffee breaks in the handsome company lounge), we may still see this as alienated employment, even if those who work in this mellowed environment are unexceptionally cheerful. How so? Because their work still does not belong to them; it is still not an act of their own choosing done to their own standard. Instead, they remain dependent on the favor of employers and bosses; they are still powerless to determine the use to which their work is put; they own neither the means nor the fruits of their labor. They are still working as productive instruments at the disposal of forces they do not control and may not even understand.

In the years before I became a teacher and writer, I worked in factories that were unutterably dismal and hazardous. I worked in a chrome-plating plant where I was forever over shoes in muck and constantly breathing the fumes of boiling acid. I worked in a boiler factory where I was expected to sacrifice my eardrums to a hot and heavy riveting job that paid the dead minimum wage. The boss had to yell at the nearly deaf worker I was replacing (Dummy George, everyone called him) to tell him he was off the job. When I asked for a raise to do the work, I was fired. The plain wretchedness of work like this is obvious to all concerned; nobody needs to be persuaded that it is exploitive and humiliating.

But I have also worked at white-collar jobs—for both private and public organizations—where every effort was made to provide amenities. At one insurance company, the personnel department never let a week pass without announcing a busy agenda of activities and amusements: picnics and theater parties, baseball outings and amateur talent shows, tours and charter flights. There were company programs for everything: savings, mutual fund investments, discount purchasing, medical and dental care, retirement. Every pregnant typist was treated to a lunchtime baby shower by the firm; births, deaths, engagements, retirements were noted in the weekly bulletin, along with the company's generous contribution to the occasion. The corridors were carpeted; lunches in the well-upholstered cafeteria were kept cheap and nutritious; on one's birthday, everybody in one's department got a cupcake with a lighted candle on top.

There were people I worked with in that office who loved the company. They joined in on all the fun, subscribed to all the programs. It was the joy and mainstay of their lives. They *cared* whether "our" company caught up with Prudential or Mutual of Omaha in gross sales. From my work in the claims department, I could tell that the company sold some of the most dishonest health and accident insurance on the market. It also refused employment to Jews and blacks. But that, of course, was supposed to be none of *my* business. Nor were the totally reactionary politics which determined the company's influence in the city. There was no union; it was universally understood that there was no need for a union. And while the personnel office was always available to hear complaints or suggestions, there was no grievance procedure, no right of appeal upon dismissal. Without surrendering a fraction of its capitalist prerogatives, the company had found the secret of winning the hearts and minds of its employees.

Perhaps white-collar labor has always been the most coddled sector of the work force, but my guess is that, in the next generation, we will see ever more intensive efforts at morale-boosting of this sort in all areas of the economy. The literature documenting boredom, resentment, recalcitrance on the job grows by the year. Absenteeism, high turnover, industrial sabotage are prominently recognized as major obstacles to discipline and productivity. In response, "job enrichment" and "job restructuring" have become high priorities on the industrial agenda; academic study centers have been set up by government and the corporations to research the subjects, and imaginative experiments have been launched. No doubt there are tedious and dirty jobs which are very nearly intractable to any form of "enrichment": mining, waste collection, assembly-line and construction work, clerk-typing. But even here there are possibilities for blunting the edge of discontent: flextime scheduling, profit sharing, job sharing, work-gang assignments, more breaks, greater variety of job assignments. Recent contracts in the auto industry have stressed sabbatical leaves, paid time off, and more union participation in decision making, especially with respect to working conditions, quite as much as higher wages and overtime rates.[1]

If we can take Japan as an example, there is room for a good deal of enrichment and amelioration within industrial capitalism. There, a suave paternalism has managed to co-opt most of the services of the Western welfare state and has thereby done much to capture the loyalty and enthusiasm of workers. It may well be that the next phase of advanced capitalist expansion will, ironically enough, hark back to Robert Owen's enlightened experiments at New Lanark in Scotland, which proved at the very beginning of the Industrial Revolution that a major investment in employee morale more than paid for itself in productivity. Owen was prophetically right, but, in the early nineteenth century, the compulsions of primitive accumulation blinded his fellow capitalists to his insight—with the result that capitalism came to be indelibly marked in the eyes of radical critics by physical degradation and brutality.

But that was never the essence of capitalist employment, as Marx, in his best analytical passages, recognized. The fundamental act of alienation during the Industrial Revolution was the subordination of work to money, so that work—any work and all work—came to be an abstract commodity valued only as a means of earning the wages that purchased subsistence and (perhaps) some leisured enjoyment. "Alienation," as Marx put it, "shows itself not merely in the result, but also in the process of production, within productive activity itself. . . . The work is *external* to the worker, . . . it is not part of his nature, . . . consequently, he does not fulfill himself in his work but denies himself. . . ."[2]

At their most perceptive, both Marx and Engels noted that alienation in this deeper sense may be characteristic, not simply of capitalism, but of any high industrial system—especially one that serves the needs of a major economic power. But, convinced as they were (and, of course, Lenin and Stalin after them) that the medicine of revolution would somehow cure all the ills of society, they did not press the point or give it full theoretical scope. It was left to their despised radical opposition, the anarchists, to warn that such big systems, sunk as they are in a competitive nationalist ethos and the eternal arms race, are bound to overwhelm the human scale of life and so to subordinate work-as-personal-fulfillment to work-as-productivity. The sheer physical burden of work may then be ameliorated; but in its place, both in privatized and in collectivized economies, we discover that our work life has been infiltrated by clever strategies invented by planners and managers to seduce our allegiance and manipulate our energy for the greater glory of the system.

We may even progress then toward forms of workers' control and industrial democracy, but always with the understanding that our participation is constrained by certain abstract imperatives: efficiency, the rate of growth, the balance of world power, etc. "Participation" (by workers, consumers, investors, planners) has become a vogue word and prominent policy objective in many Western European governments; there, it is understood to be a major means of oiling away the discontent that inhibits planning on the scale of the Common Market. It may even be a sincere intention; but we should remember that every Nazi concentration camp was based on "participation," using inmates to police inmates in return for special favors.

### Responsibility and Vocation

I want to argue that none of the enrichments and inducements mentioned here, not even the ingenious methods the Chinese have developed for collectivizing the altruism of the work force, goes to the root of alienation. I do not mean to say these reforms make no difference; they obviously render life on the job more pleasant and secure than it was in the worst days of wage slavery. But they do not make the *right kind* of difference. They may be necessary changes in many respects, but they are not sufficient. They alter the atmosphere and incentives of work, but they do not in themselves redeem work by any acceptable personalist standard, because they do not place the whole and unique person at the center of economic life. . . .

*Responsibility*—there we have the missing factor in both capitalist job enrichment and collectivist work morale, the crucial distinction that separates mere employment from true vocation. To have a vocation is to work with responsibility—not in any merely legal sense, nor in the sense of fearing that one will be pointed out as a slacker by one's workmates and reported to the party—but in the sense that our work is ourselves; we are at one with it because it grows from all that we have chosen to become in this life. It is our personal emblem and pledge of honor before the world. We *care* about our vocation, because if it is misused or proves inadequate, all that gives our life distinction and meaning is called into question.

It is a stubborn fact of human experience: Except in the most technical legal sense, I cannot hold myself responsible for work that is personally meaningless, let alone for work I despise. Meaningless work, despicable work, is work I blame on others; I treat it as a mere necessity, an imposed duty, I may even feel ashamed that I waste my life at such work. So I say to myself (and secretly to the world), "I am only doing this because I need the money, or I need the grade, or I need the credit, or reputation, or publicity. I am doing something my boss wants to have done, or the system needs to have done. I did not invent this job; I do not believe in it; I do not endorse it. If I had *my* way, I would be doing something else. So don't hold me responsible for its waste, its shoddiness, its criminality."

In this way, I seek to distance myself from the job. And that, essentially, is what alienation is: the withdrawal of self from action, the retreat of the person from the performance. Work then becomes a foreign object in one's life which is, at most, a means to an end, but no proper part of one's real identity. Alienation is not—as left-wing radicalism customarily contends—an estrangement merely from the means and fruits of production. It is also estrangement from the activity itself which allows us to deny our responsibility for what we do. And this is what surely follows when work has no *craft* to it: no challenge, no taste, no personal style. Work of that kind is a zero, a hole in the middle of one's life. . . .

Responsibility, as I intend the word here, is double-edged. It means being responsible *to* and being responsible *for*. If we have a vocation, we are responsible *to* our work that it should be well done; we are responsible *for*

our work that it should be well used. We want it to be intrinsically excellent by the highest standards of our craft or profession; we also want it to be of good and honorable service in the world. In our vocation, we wish to see *the good* achieved in both its senses: the well crafted and the ethically right. Only one force will provide this double-edged sense of responsibility—and that is love: the love we bear toward the work we do. . . .

The Buddha, in his wisdom, made "right livelihood" (another word, I think, for vocation) one of the steps to enlightenment. If we do not pitch our discussion that high, we have failed to give work its true dimension, and we will settle for far too little—perhaps for no more than a living wage. Responsible work is an embodiment of love, and love is the only discipline that will serve in shaping the personality, the only discipline that makes the mind whole and constant for a lifetime of effort. There hovers about a true vocation that paradox of all significant self-knowledge—our capacity to find ourselves by losing ourselves. We lose ourselves in our love of the task before us, and, in that moment, we learn an identity that lives both within and beyond us.

What else should the highest yoga be, after all, but the work we turn to each day?

### "Take This Job and Shove It"

Each day I move through a world at work, an ocean of human activity as pervasively and as unobtrusively there as the ocean of air that surrounds me. I breathe in the labor of people around me; I live by it, yet I take it for granted like some free resource. People work, I work. That is what we are here to do; it is how we pass the time.

But our work is more than a pastime. It is our life. It takes up years of the portion we have been allotted on this Earth to work out our salvation. And not many of us work at a true vocation . . . sometimes I think very nearly none. Some, like my father, grind their substance away at hard and dirty work for too little pay and appreciation. Most are toiling at jobs whose worst burden is deadly and impersonal routine: typing, filing, checking groceries, selling across a counter, filling out forms, processing papers.

I have done such jobs myself. I still do them. A deal of what I do as a teacher in a colossal state college system is stale paper work and routine committee assignments that have nothing to do with education or scholarship, little enough to do with simple intelligence. Did any of us really have to read Studs Terkel's report *Working* to know what the daily deadly toll of alienated labor is? "I feel like a machine," "I feel like a robot," Terkel's interviewees complain. As I sit down to the task of revising this chapter, the record at the top of the American charts is Johnny Paycheck singing "Take This Job and Shove It." When we do not hear that lamentation from the people around us, it is only because we are not listening to what they say behind the heroic good humor that is the shield of their self-respect. Only look, and you can see their stifled person-hood written in their faces; you can see it in the distraction that carries their thoughts to imaginary pleasures and leads to slip-ups and mistakes each day on the job; it is there in their surliness and bad temper. I have seen it in myself whenever I have felt the vital hours of my life being turned to dust by work that did not use the best I have to offer, whenever I have had to carry out the orders of employers who had no interest in the bright and extraordinary powers I could feel within me yearning to be hard-worked for all they were worth.

All of us have a gift, a calling of our own whose exercise is high delight, even if we must sweat and suffer to meet its demands. That calling reaches out to find a real and useful place in the world, a task that is not waste or pretense. If only that life-giving impulse might be liberated and made the whole energy of our daily work, if only we were given the chance to be *in* our work with the full force of our personality, mind and body, heart and soul . . . what a power would be released into the world! A force more richly transformative than all the might of industrial technology.

But *they*—the company, the system—rarely have any use for that calling. Our bosses do not even look for it in themselves. It makes no difference to the profit and loss; it does not show up (so the experts believe) in the economic indicators. So they sweep it out of sight and continue to work us as personnel, not persons. That is very nearly the prerequisite for being a successful boss in this warped economy: to blind oneself to the person-hood of one's workers, to insist that business is business. That is treatment fewer workers will now accept; and the trend is by no means limited to middle-class, college-educated workers. In a recent statistical study, Daniel Yankelovich concludes that, in growing numbers through the seventies, "noncollege youth . . . take up the quest of their college peers for a new definition of success in which the emphasis is on self-fulfillment and quality of life, as well as on money and security."[3] Thus, the Department of Labor reports that, even in a tight job market, twice as many people quit their jobs in disgust as did a decade ago; the number has gone from 200,000 per year to 400,000 and continues to rise.

Yet somehow we carry on. I am always astonished at how resourcefully most people find ways to stick at their jobs without becoming bitter or corrupt. . . .

But there are so many others I meet who miraculously manage to stay human on the job. They invent little strategies of self-encouragement and compensation to get them through the day. They decorate their work space with trinkets and placards of their own choosing. They smuggle a transistor radio into the shop to play "their" kind of music, though most of what they hear is idiotic commercials and payola disk jockeys. They divide the day's work into so many little contests and competitions that will pace them along. They secretly challenge themselves to absurdly high standards of

neatness and precision to put some sport in the work. They organize games with workmates, they gossip, they flirt, they kid around, they kibbitz with the customers, they exchange jokes and novelties. Perhaps most of all, they gripe. Mutual griping always helps. It relieves the conscience to let someone know that *you* know this is a bitch of a job. That is a way to remind yourself and the world that you are bigger and smarter and better than this dumb job. And if you had *your* way . . .

When I worked as a teller for the Bank of America, I kept my head busy all day long repeating Greek declensions and memorizing poems. It kept my brain alive—and also made me a miserably bad teller. But even my mistakes were a secret gratification—a tiny way of obstructing B of A's smooth flow of high financial banditry. I imagine strategies like these have sustained people through all the most suffocating kinds of toil since the factory bells pealed in the first dawn of industrialism. They are symptoms of our vocational instinct fighting to survive: little sparks and flashes of our thwarted personhood. The pathos of the matter is that no private strategy of this kind will ever turn an empty or fraudulent job into a vocation—nor, for that matter, will any social reform. And far too many of us are entrammeled by just such work, struggling to avoid the embarrassment of acknowledging our entrapment. A phony job is a phony job; a wicked job is a wicked job. These are not matters of morale or social organization; not even revolutionary workers' control can change them. They are objective moral facts attached to certain forms of employment that have become the only jobs many industrial societies seem able to offer millions of workers.

Work that produces unnecessary consumer junk or weapons of war is wrong and wasteful. Work that is built upon false needs or unbecoming appetites is wrong and wasteful. Work that deceives or manipulates, that exploits or degrades is wrong and wasteful. Work that wounds the environment or makes the world ugly is wrong and wasteful. There is no way to redeem such work by enriching it or restructuring it, by socializing it or nationalizing it, by making it "small" or decentralized or democratic. It is a sow's ear that will yield no silk purses.

Here we have an absolute criterion that must enter any discussion of work. *Is the job honest and useful? Is it a real contribution to human need?* These are questions that can only be answered by a worker's own strong sense of responsibility. That is why the struggle for right livelihood is as important as the struggle for industrial democracy. For it does not matter how democratically controlled our work life is: If a job is inherently worthless, it cannot be a vocation. So, if we encourage people to search for responsible work—for work they can love as an image of their personal destiny—then we must not expect them to continue doing what is stupid or ugly. We must not expect them to go on working for the military-industrial complex or for Madison Avenue, to continue producing "people's bombs" or printing party propaganda. One cannot build a vocation on a lie.

The hard truth is that the world we live in, the high industrial world we presume to hold up as the standard of "development," is immensely committed to proliferating work that is wrong and wasteful. It does this in the name of growth, or the national security, or the standard of living; but at the bottom it all comes down to creating jobs that are unworthy of our best energies:

*Huckstering jobs*—inventing, advertising, selling expensive trash to gullible customers

*Busywork jobs*—sorting, recording, filing, computerizing, endless amounts of data, office memos, statistical figments

*Mandarin-administrative jobs*—co-ordinating, overseeing, supervising clerical battalions and bureaucratic hierarchies, many of which—especially in government operations—exist merely to spin their own wheels

*Financial sleight-of-hand jobs*—juggling cash and credit, sniffing out tax loopholes and quick speculative windfalls in real estate, arbitrage, stocks and bonds

*Compensatory amusements jobs*—marketing the vicarious glamour and escapist pleasures whose one use is to relieve the tedium and frustration of workaday life: spectator sports, mass media distractions, superstar entertainments, package tours, the pricey toys and accoutrements of "creative leisure"

*Cop jobs*—providing security against the theft and violence of society's have-nots, policing the streets, hassling the riffraff through the courts, guarding the prisons, snooping into credit ratings, school records, personnel evaluations

*Welfare processing jobs*—picking up the economy's casualties, keeping them on the public assistance treadmill, holding the social discontent below the boiling point

And at the dizzy top of the heap, we have the billion-dollar boondoggling—the cartel building, multinational maneuvering, military-industrial back scratching—which is the corrupted soul of our corporate economy. The list could go on indefinitely, a spreading network of waste and corruption that touches very nearly everybody's work life. How many of us could not finally be tied into it in at least some peripheral way—like it or not, know it or not? My own profession of university teaching has fattened enormously over the past generation by educating (or training) the personnel who have become the executive functionaries and white-collar rank and file in this flourishing surplus economy.

Many who are utterly dependent upon this dense congestion of socially useless getting and spending may never see the full context of the work they do. That is the peculiar moral dodge made available by our social complexity. It allows us to work in the blind at little, seemingly innocent fractions of big, dishonorable projects. The full extent of culpability may be nearly impossible to delineate; there are so many degrees and shadings. But the ethical issue is nevertheless there at the heart of our economy, and it must be addressed by any honest discussion of work. There is work that is good and useful; and there is work that is not. Work that is not good and useful is work that wastes the lives of people and the resources of the Earth—and industrial society generates a scandalous amount of that kind of work. Perhaps it is what our society does most. In our search for a true vocation, here is indeed a Himalayan obstacle. For it may mean there is a prodigious amount of work we are involved in which no healthy sense of responsibility should permit us to do at all. . . .

### Notes

The books I have drawn upon in preparing this chapter include the following: Folkert Wilken, *The Liberation of Work* (London: Routledge & Kegan Paul, 1969), and David Jenkins, *Job Power* (Garden City, N.Y.: Doubleday, 1973), which survey experiments in workers' control in America and Europe. Laile Bartlett, *New Work/New Life* (New York: Harper & Row, 1976), reports on new forms of self-management in the United States and offers a helpful resource kit of "networks" dealing in work reform. Fred Blum, *Work and Community* (London: Routledge & Kegan Paul, 1968), is a study of the Scott-Bader Commonwealth, one of the long-standing British experiments in industrial democracy. Clare Huchet Bishop, *All Things Common* (New York: Harper & Row, 1950), deals with the postwar French communities of work, especially Boimondau. David and Elena French, *Working Communally* (New York: Russell Sage Foundation, 1975), is a perceptive critique of contemporary collectives and communes, especially with respect to their need to create viable, communal workplaces. I have also found the following helpful: Ivan Illich, *Tools for Conviviality* (New York: Harper & Row, 1973); Studs Terkel, *Working* (New York: Pantheon, 1974); Stanley Aronowitz, *False Promises: The Shaping of the American Working-class Consciousness* (New York: McGraw-Hill, 1973), the last for its shrewd criticism of organized labor's failure to take industrial democracy as a serious social goal. Louis Davis et al., eds., *The Quality of Working Life* (New York: Free Press, 1974), is a good introductory collection of papers dealing with contemporary reforms of work.

1. Among the major centers of job-enrichment research are the Center for the Quality of Working Life at the Institute for Industrial Relations, University of California at Los Angeles, the Quality of Work Program at the University of Michigan, and the Work in America Institute in New York City. The Tavistock Institute of Human Relations in London has also issued a large body of literature dealing with the reform of working life. The Ford Foundation has financed a deal of job-enrichment programs. See its *Newsletter* for September 1, 1975.

2. Marx, from the *Economic and Philosophical Manuscripts,* in Karl Marx, *Early Writings,* trans. and ed. T. B. Bottomore (New York: McGraw-Hill, 1964), pp. 124–25.

3. Daniel Yankelovich, *The New Morality: A Profile of American Youth in the Seventies* (New York: McGraw-Hill, 1974), p. 29.

# the *Politics* of *Motherhood*

## Deborah Fallows

*Deborah Fallows is the mother of two sons. This article is adapted from her book,* A Mother's Work, *published by Houghton Mifflin.*

**B**etty Friedan launched the contemporary women's movement in 1963 by depicting the home as a domestic penal institution for women. In *The Feminine Mystique* she wrote that housewives "baked their own bread, sewed their own and their children's clothes, kept their new washing machines and dryers running all day. They changed the sheets on the beds twice a week instead of once, took the rug-hooking class in adult education. Their only dream was to be perfect wives and mothers; their highest ambition to have five children and a beautiful house; their only fight to get and keep their husbands."

Over the past 20 years, the women's movement has carefully proclaimed its intention to give women the "opportunity to choose" their own lives—as professionals, as wage earners, or as housewives. But in feminists' eyes, the real challenges lay outside the home—in the workplace. A career offered all the answers: Dependent on your spouse? Get an income, become self-sufficient. No power to back up your opinion? Money talks. Bored and lonely? Get out of the house and in with interesting people. Everyone taking you for granted? Find recognition with an official-sounding job.

One thing was missing from this strategy, however, and that was a concern for how it would affect the children. Leaders of the women's movement have never quite said that jobs should come before family. Those from the mainstream of the movement have taken care to point out that many of their guiding lights are young mothers. Still, their battles for political and economic equality have inevitably led them to prize achievement on the job above all else. Understanding as they might be of women who choose not to work, feminists tend to see such a choice as a step backwards for the cause. By questioning women's place in society, the women's movement threw motherhood into the political arena.

In the late 1970s, conservative forces coalesced to challenge feminism. The right offered women a clear, complete explanation of the wife's place at home. It is "good" to be there (it is traditional, Christian); the wife has a responsibility to be there (to husband and to children); she enjoys security in her position (her right to support by her husband); she should find all of her satisfaction there (from raising her children); it is important that she be there (to her family, she is irreplaceable).

While some leaders of the so-called "pro-family" forces concede that women may have to work for economic reasons, this doesn't shake the right's faith in an "ideal" division of labor and authority in the family. In the "ideal family"—a concept referred to routinely in pro-family literature—the husband is the breadwinner and decisionmaker. Next to him is his wife, a helpmate but not an equal.

Neither the women's movement nor the pro-family movement offers an adequate, or even honest prescription for mothers. The right preaches complacence and subservience. It

From *The Washington Monthly*, June 1985, pp. 40-49. Adapted from A MOTHER'S WORK, © 1985 Deborah Fallow. Reprinted by permission of Houghton Mifflin.

discourages women from seeking challenges in the world beyond the home, thereby reducing the spiritual resources that could enrich mothers' years with their children. Many conservatives have also succumbed to the familiar temptation of the comfortable to forget about or condemn those on whom fortune has not smiled.

The women's movement, with which I sympathize much more than I do with the right, defines success in terms of professional achievement, thereby implicitly downgrading the idea that parents should care for their children themselves. In coming to grips with the realities of motherhood, women will have to see through the symbolism and rhetoric of both sides of this debate.

## *Right-wing sweetheart*

Phyllis Schlafly, leader of the anti-ERA movement and founder of the conservative Eagle Forum, reigns as first lady of the pro-family movement. What Schlafly would have for all other women is her version of a perfect life—that is, a life much like her own.

From what I'd read about Schlafly in *Ms.* magazine and elsewhere, I expected her to be a harpy, or at least an excessively brisk woman. Instead, she is attractive and professional-looking—calm as an executive, warm as my best friend's mother. She ushered me into her Capitol Hill office, like a hostess having me in for coffee. "Hello, Debbie. Sorry to keep you waiting. Tell me about your book. Have you got a copy of *Sweetheart*?"

I have read her biography, *Sweetheart of the Silent Majority*, and many issues of her monthly newsletter, the *Phyllis Schlafly Report*, although neither publication is easy to locate. The proprietor of one women's bookstore I called told me she didn't know whether Schlafly had written anything, adding, "and we certainly wouldn't carry it if she did."

From talking with her, I soon knew many things about Schlafly's personal life: for example, she worked her way through college toiling in a munitions factory and taught her six children to read. She wrote and published her own numerous books, lives in financial security with her wealthy husband, and has waged several unsuccessful campaigns to hold political office. Her husband is much older than she is, and she employed a governess for her children for at least one summer.

In between the lines of her conversation lurk the prerequisites to the "perfect" life she has led: education, money, a healthy family, and a supportive husband.

But life doesn't work for most women the way Schlafly thinks it should. Half the women getting married today can expect to be divorced; by 1990, one child out of four under ten years old—almost nine million children—will have lived with a single parent at some point in his life. Over one-fourth of the women who are legally entitled to child support payments do not receive them. In hard economic times, husbands will lose jobs, and women can still expect to earn about 60 percent of what men earn. We know these things to be facts. And we can pretty well guess that during the days when divorce was rare and when women kept their own counsel, similar discontent and trouble existed—only secretly.

But Schlafly ignores statistics like these, and turns a judgmental ear to the stories of troubled women. She complacently advises wives to stay home, resting assured that "since God ordained that women have babies, our laws properly and realistically establish that men must provide financial support for their wives and children."

Connaught Marshner, director of the Family Policy Division of the Free Congress and Education Foundation, is a generation younger than Schlafly but, like her, a mother and a major power in the conservative movement. Marshner, like many conservative young women raising families, speaks with more realism than Schlafly does.

Marshner is an attractive, kind-looking woman in her mid-thirties, with dark, shoulder-length hair pinned back from her face. She has a company phone in her car so she can conduct business on her long commutes from Washington to Virginia, where she lives with her husband, who is a college professor, and her two elementary school-age sons. On her desk sits a photo of one of her sons bathing her infant daughter, who, she tells me at a difficult moment in our talk, has died from heart disease. Unlike Schlafly, Marshner has seen life's rougher side.

Like Schlafly, however, Marshner lives something of a contradiction. She agrees with the right's version of the "ideal" family, in which the mother stays home with the children. But, she says, "ideal" comes with two large qualifications: *if* a family can afford for the mother to stay home, and *if* she can be fulfilled at home. For Marshner and many younger conservative women, the fact of working mothers is just that—a fact. It is not a goal or an opportunity or a promising development. According to Marshner, women work because they are called upon to work, either for economic reasons or for community needs. Women, being "other-oriented" by nature, as Marshner describes them, are responding to a call from others to work, rather than to inner drives.

A mother who works or who is divorced or single, according to Marshner, can still raise a "traditional" family. The idea of "tradition" rests much less on the structure of the family or the detailed division of family labor than on a sense of mission about moral standards. The family must live by "a system of moral norms which, once well-defined, are taken to be without exception."

*C*onservatives may love their kids,
but their view of children is remote, studied, and
at odds with the reality of daily life.

In some general sense, it's hard to quibble with Marshner's morality. It sounds like an effort to raise honest, generous children—something all of us, conservative or liberal, strive to do. But Marshner's definitions of "traditional" morality are more specific than this and include prominently her staunch belief that, when push may come to shove, the father is the figure of authority in the family. "The husband is the head of the household," she says. "He *should* have responsibility for making final decisions. That *should* be the case."

Somewhere between Schlafly and Marshner the conservative pendulum rests. Much of the right still ignores the basic truth about women at home: that they are in a state of financial dependency. This is not necessarily evil—it is the situation in my household, by my husband's and my own choice—but it requires something more than Schlafly's pacifying assertions that little ladies should not trouble their pretty heads with thoughts about money.

Every woman needs to make sure she can take care of herself, and the children, if circumstances should change—and to this need the conservatives seem blind. Women owe it to themselves and their children to make financial provisions for such unforeseen but common occurrences as divorce or illness or death. Women should also at least be thinking of contingency plans for intolerable situations at home, such as infidelity or physical abuse.

For their self-protection, women need some form of insurance. It may be education, which would equip them to earn a living, even if they prefer not to while the children are young; it may be extra money, from an insurance policy or pension; it may also be a network of extended family or friends, who can help absorb the shock.

This need not imply what Schlafly suggests—that women who make such preparations are spurning their families. She characterizes the provoking call of the feminists as: "Come, leave your home, husband, and children and join all those unhappy females in a new sisterhood of togetherness." But wise precautions do not imply any less love, trust, or confidence in a marriage or fami-

ly situation. Behind every statistic of divorce, widowhood, or poverty, is the story of a woman whose life did not turn out the way she planned.

The right ignores not only these provisions for the unexpected but also plans for the inevitable. The responsibility of caring for children, consuming as it may be, has limits even while it is going on—and someday it will be over. What are women to do then?

Schlafly implies that such concerns stem from women with attitude problems— "whether you wake up in the morning with a chip on your shoulder or whether you have a positive mental attitude." Once you stop moping around the house and letting yourself get big ideas about meeting challenges in the outside world, then your troubles will disappear. "If you think diapers and dishes are a never-ending repetitive routine," says Schlafly, "just remember that most of the jobs outside the home are just as repetitious, tiresome, and boring." She writes that "if you complain about servitude to a husband, servitude to a boss will be more intolerable. Everyone in the world has a boss of some kind. It is easier for most women to achieve a harmonious working relationship with a husband than with a foreman, supervisor, or office manager."

Rita Kramer, author of *In Defense of the Family*, suggests that some feminists "attempt to substitute one form of tyranny [childrearing] with another [working at a job]." She argues that a mother's "natural desire to be with her baby may give way to the social pressure to 'be somebody' in a society that is increasingly telling women that what counts is achievement, however trivial, outside the home, just so it is outside the home and apart from childrearing."

Social pressures certainly do play a large part in many women's decisions to work, but Kramer underestimates the depth of feeling and the scope of the ambivalence that many women have about their desire to broaden themselves beyond motherhood.

With no grasp of how tearing an issue this is for many women, the right blithely offers an array of milquetoast alternatives for ways of keeping yourself busy outside the home. Schlafly proposes that women try volunteer work: "welfare, hospital, educational, cultural, civic, and political. All these avenues provide opportunities for women to perform useful services to the community—and in so doing to become happier, more interesting, and more fulfilled."

Volunteerism certainly meets a basic human need. It can be deeply satisfying to help others when they cannot help themselves. Attending community service club meetings, participating in museum benefits, doing library work—all have their place. The shortcoming of the conservatives is not their recognition of the merits of volunteerism; it is their simplistic notion that it can and should be enough for all women. Not everyone can find a life of fulfillment in volunteer work, just as not everyone can find fulfillment in a boardroom, a courtroom, a university, or at home.

To hear the right's hymns of praise to the family, one might guess that the welfare of children is the first and last item on their list of concerns. The reason that mothers and fathers must take their assigned places in the family hierarchy is that the children will thereby benefit.

But the details of the right's position—for example, pro-family opposition to day care (see sidebar, p.45)—reveal a seeming lack of interest in children and their needs. The right presents an abstract, peculiar sense of what children are like. I can't claim that conservatives don't love their children as much as anyone else does. But their view of children is remote, studied, and at odds with the realities of daily life.

Once again, Phyllis Schlafly is a remarkable example. As she tells it, she was able to write books while her children played contentedly at her feet. "I was able to compose and write with children right around me," she explains, adding, "My husband can't do that."

Having spent the last three years in such an effort myself, with my children ranging from as young as one year old to as old as seven during that time, I know the difficulties of writing with children around. I can do it only when my children are away—taking naps, at school, at friends' houses. Surely Schlafly has forgotten: could her children really have colored or built with blocks around her feet for sustained periods without interrupting with questions, requests for glasses of water, trips to the bathroom, or fights? Perhaps she closed her study door and the children knew not to enter. Some mothers boast that this is their secret to working at home and "caring" for their children at the same time. The technique might work for a ten-year-old, but it certainly won't—and shouldn't—for a child of three.

Schlafly's reminiscences of children greatly resemble those of Marabel Morgan's. In her book, *The Total Woman*, Morgan recommends, among other things, that women lift the spirits of their tired breadwinners by greeting hubby at the front door clad only in saran wrap. She counsels mothers to "draw out the venom inside a person" as a tactic for dealing with a recalcitrant child. "When a close friend spanked his three-year-old for hitting the baby, he did it in a loving way," Morgan writes. "Afterward the child hugged him and said, 'Thank you for saying no, Daddy!'"

As any parent knows, this scene is make-believe. Bearing and raising a child is far more complex and far less programmable than Morgan or Schlafly would have us think. Moreover, there isn't much room for bad luck in the pro-family world. What if a child is born ill or impaired in some way? Does it mean you have failed if you have nothing to show off to your friends and neighbors? What if you raise a plumber or a short-order cook instead of a lawyer or a business executive? What if you raise a liberal instead of a conservative? Just as you can't control the sex of your child, the skills she is born with, or the beauty he inherits, you can affect but not determine your child's future, his personality, her "success." You can do your best while raising your child, but you can't claim or bear complete responsibility for the life your child leads.

Yet this is the burden Schlafly seems to put on mothers who spend all their energy raising children. She implies that a perfect life with a perfect mother will automatically produce a perfect child. "A mother can see the results of her own handiwork in the good citizen she has produced and trained," Schlafly writes. She congratulates mothers on successes they aren't responsible for—and implicitly charges them with failures they can't control.

# Ms.-*ing the point*

While conservatives have in recent years reasserted a vision of the ideal homemaker, the women's movement has continued to look with a suspicious eye at women who stay at home. Feminist leaders are quick to deny this accusation, arguing that the press is to blame for unfairly depicting their position as being hostile to homemakers.

"Infuriating," says Letty Cottin Pogrebin, a founder and editor of *Ms.* magazine. "It's not a club with membership cards on behalf of women's interests," Pogrebin tells me one afternoon in the New York offices of *Ms.* Liberal women's groups include strong contingents of women at home; many of their leaders are mothers themselves. Feminists have pushed for legislative reform that directly assists homemakers. "Her issues are our issues," says Pogrebin, citing child care, healthcare, drug addiction, divorce reform, domestic violence, displaced homemakers, and comparable worth.

To its credit, the women's movement has made great progress for women in general, including mothers at home. To understand Pogrebin's pride

# Who'll Mind the Children?

In the political battle over motherhood, day care is a central point of contention, but one largely obscured by the passion of ideology. In feminists' eyes, day care is indispensable to the formula for women's equality. Conservatives see it as a threat to the foundation of the family.

The debate focuses on day care—meaning the organized care for large groups of children—more often than other forms of child care, in part because large centers are where government is involved and where innovations and regulations can most easily be applied. Large facilities are also the most economical and efficient way for caring for children.

Often the area of disagreement extends even to what "day care" is. Some people who "don't believe in day care" really mean that they wouldn't consign their children to large, impersonal facilities, yet they happily send them to family homes or nursery schools. Meanwhile, some people who say that "day care is fine for children" are thinking about several hours a day in a family home.

The most familiar conservative criticism of day care is that it amounts to a near-totalitarian separation of child from parent and should in no way be encouraged. For example, when the House of Representatives Select Committee on Children, Youth, and Families recently recommended more federal support of day care, four Republican committee members dissented, arguing that government-sponsored day care is unacceptable as a matter of first principles. "Let's look for a moment at the real subject of our discussion—children," the congressmen said. "When we talk about the comparative costs of care for infants, toddlers, and pre-school children, we ought never to forget that we are talking about children who will be taken from their mothers and cared for primarily by strangers from the first months of their lives." Of primary concern, they added, is the question, "how does day care affect our children?" This is certainly a good question, but it will not be answered with confidence

anytime soon. In the meantime, 2 million children are in day care centers, and 6.5 million under the age of 13 go without any supervision at home.

Often, conservative opponents of day care say they recognize that some mothers have to work and even sound broad-minded about it. The Rev. Jerry Falwell has said, "My pastoral advice is, if the wife must work, the husband should make the extra effort to compensate in any way possible for her absence . . . .The husband is as much responsible for rearing the children as the wife."

Yet the logical progression seems to come to a halt at this point. If Falwell really believed that mothers must sometimes work, would it not follow that someone else must look after their children? If day care is therefore necessary, shouldn't the right join in supporting improvements in the institutions where these children will spend so many hours? Apparently not, if that means further expansion of federal power. Rochelle Beck of the Children's Defense Fund points out that Falwell's Moral Majority is part of the network of " 'pro-family' interest groups [whose]...effective lobbying and fundraising efforts go to oppose federal funds for child-care services."

The conservative spokesmen do not explicitly block improvements in day care, but they oppose all the steps—especially further regulation and subsidy—that would make improvement possible. They support the kind of laissez-faire child care system we have today, whereby some combination of luck or money is the only answer to finding good care.

For example, Paul Weyrich, president of the far right Coalition for America, has said: "If a mother has to work, she should see to it her children are cared for by another family or by other family members. It is detrimental when so many kids are left in day care operations with strangers. . . .A child learns to hide the things he's worried about from some day care attendant."

Does Weyrich know what it is like to "try to see to it" that a friend or relative can handle

in these accomplishments, it helps to examine some specific examples.

In insurance and pensions, women's groups have worked to reform rates, terms, and conditions that discriminate on the basis of gender. For instance, women often pay more than men for

the same health insurance coverage. Pregnancy and childbirth are often excluded from coverage or qualify only for very inadequate coverage. Women who take time off to raise children don't fit the rules and provisions of retirement systems.

In the area of Social Security, feminist groups

all the day care? He is right about the drawbacks of large day-care centers but is content to push the problem away, since this fits conveniently with his overall political views.

Phyllis Schlafly, leader of the anti-ERA movement, touched on day care in her 1977 book, *The Power of the Positive Woman*. Her arguments still stand as a fair reflection of the "pro-family" attitude: "The energies and dedication of the Positive Woman are needed as never before to fend off the attacks on the moral, the social and economic integrity of the family. Take, for example, the tremendous drive to set up child-care centers—taxpayer-financed, government-managed, 'universally' available for 'all socioeconomic groups' regardless of means. This adds up to an attempt to make it public policy to remove babies from the family unit and place them in an institutional environment."

Obviously the government should not "substitute" for parents; but there are certain families in which parents cannot or will not care adequately for their children. To what extent will those parents' sins be visited upon their children? By defining those parents as morally unworthy—which in some cases they may be—the conservatives have successfully excluded the innocent *children* of those families from the universe of those deserving public help. This leads easily to a dismissal of subsidized day care as a national need.

As is so often the case in political life, the inflexibilities and excesses of one extreme are fully matched by the other. Leaders of the women's movement, who have done so much to remove barriers to women's occupational success, naturally view day care in a special light. Unless children can be left safely and happily in someone else's care, how will women continue to advance in the workplace?

The feminists don't delude themselves with dreams about fathers quitting work to tend the children while their wives move up. Day care has to be the answer.

According to the women's movement, the only people who object to day care are those who feel threatened by the idea of women succeeding in the workplace. Feminists may be willing to entertain private comments about the defects of certain facilities or certain approaches, as long as everyone understands that they all believe in day care as an institution. But when criticism is conducted in public,

where the gains made by the women's movement still seem so fragile, it's inevitably seen as a hostile act. For feminists it is but a short step from criticizing day care to suggesting that there are fundamental conflicts between parenthood and career.

Bettye Caldwell, president of the National Association for the Education of Young Children, reflects this doctrinaire attitude, denouncing even the most troubling reports about day care. No doubt Caldwell, who represents those who work in centers, is sincerely concerned about the conditions that make large group day care difficult for many children. But she reserves her public fury for something else—the *reports* about bad conditions, which she says give day care a bad name.

Caldwell was particularly outraged by a 1983 article by Dominique Browning published in *Texas Monthly* magazine. Browning described day-care centers in and around Houston:

"Workers are paid the minimum wage, and many of them take a job in a center only long enough to make money for a special purpose; then they quit....All day long, 11 to 15 babies from about eight weeks to 12 months old lie in their cribs or sit in their pens and scream for attention, stare at the ceiling, gurgle quietly, or sleep....The sitters cannot play with any child for very long because, as one of them explained, the child would get used to the attention and scream whenever he didn't get it."

In her remarks to the 1983 Junior League Parenting Conference in Washington, D.C., Caldwell said that in all her travels, she had never seen any day-care center like that. Caldwell has written that "the media need to highlight more of the positive aspects of quality child care if the public interest is to be served."

Bettye Caldwell may never have seen day-care centers like those Browning described, but I have, and I did not have to look very hard. Liberals in general have found it hard to confess the limitations of their social programs, even though such warts and imperfections are inevitable in even the best-run organizations. For this reluctance they have paid a steep political price. There is a lot of very bad day care out there, and the institution of outside-the-home child care must be strong enough to withstand scrutiny or it will not improve and flourish. —*D.F.*

such as the Women's Equity Action League (WEAL) advocate improving the fairness and adequacy of provisions for *all* women. In 1982, WEAL points out, the average man received $430 per month in benefits; the average woman, $308. Retired female workers averaged $335 per month

compared to $438 for retired male workers. These inequities arise, the feminists say, from historically low wages for working women and an undervalued estimation of homemakers' contributions to a family's income. To correct the situation, WEAL has supported a system of "earnings shar-

*The tensions between the women's movement
and nonworking mothers stems from politics,
but the hostility is deeply personal.*

ing." Under earnings sharing, a husband and wife would, for Social Security purposes, each be credited with half the family's total earnings during the marriage, whether both of them were working or not, plus individual earnings gained before or after the marriage. Later, each would receive pensions based on his or her own personal account. For the homemaker, earnings sharing could also provide disability benefits and survivor protection through the Social Security system, even though she may never have worked for pay.

But none of this addresses the question of spirit and tone. The deepest tensions between the women's movement and nonworking mothers are based on the attitudes the mothers perceive in the movement. Although its origin is in politics, the hostility is also personal.

Working mothers often feel that nonworking mothers are trying to drown them in guilt. They perceive homemakers sneering at them for being irresponsible toward home and family. On the other hand, nonworking mothers assume that working mothers look down on them, making them feel like weak sisters who just can't keep up. The withering comments are familiar to every at-home mother: "What's an educated young woman like you doing at home?" Or: "I'd go out of my mind if I stayed at home all day."

There is, of course, no inherent incompatibility between women reaching out for equality and women staying at home. But, as any woman under the age of 40 knows, there is an imposed incompatibility. The women's movement has not yet had the time or made the effort to understand and explore what life at home can be like for women today. Feminists may officially say that "choice" is at the top of their agenda for women, but there are too many hints suggesting that this talk comes fairly cheap. Throughout my years at home and well before that, I have gotten the message from the feminists that there is only one "right" choice that a progressive woman and young mother can make. Why did I feel that? Because of signals like these:

• Gloria Steinem is promoting her latest book, *Outrageous Acts and Everyday Rebellions* on a radio talk show in mid-1984. During a phone-in session, a caller asks, "What do you *really* think

of women who stay home?" The host of the show, a droll, forthright character named Joel E. Spivak, points out that on every show with a prominent feminist, at least one caller asks some version of this question. Steinem's answer, of course, is that the feminist movement created the choice for women to lead their lives as they want to. She even says that staying home is just as valid and reputable a choice as working. And yet, only minutes earlier, perhaps forgetting that housewives are listening, she has referred to the "narrow and stifled" lives of women at home.

• I am speaking with a spokeswoman for the National Women's Political Caucus about Social Security and insurance as well as about my children and my book. On the way out, she asks me, in a sister-to-sister tone, "Well, when *are* you going to go back to work?"

• A full-time mother writes to *Ms.*, complaining, "I get the feeling you look down on me, condescend to me because I'm not working." *Ms.* replies with a straight face, "We were surprised to hear this. We have tried to present topics of interest to women at home—childbirth, pregnancy, housework, daily lives, etc. We all have children ourselves and know what it's been like to face the decisions."

To prove its bona fides, *Ms.* sends writer Jane Lazarre to spend a morning with Jane Broderick, author of the challenging letter. Lazarre describes a meeting at the crossroads of feminism that takes place in a Long Island kitchen. A full-time mother of eight, Broderick lays out her positions on feminist issues: birth control, child-rearing, housework. Lazarre professes a closeness to Broderick, but the closest the writer comes to finding a key to Broderick's spirit is to focus on two things: her strong Catholicism, which has a lot to do with becoming a mother of eight children but very little to do with feminism, and Broderick's explanation that she sometimes finds it necessary "to hide. And I do just that. I really have to sit very still. Just be alone with myself. And become whole again."

All mothers can recognize that sitting very still is Broderick's gimmick for maintaining sanity. But they also understand that it reveals little about her method of sustaining herself as a

*O*ne of the reasons to push ahead
with the feminist campaign for fairer pay
is that it would permit fathers to take a
few years off to care for the children.

---

mother to eight children. Lazarre, and *Ms.*, are content with the superficial view and do not search for any real insights into full-time motherhood.

To be fair, an occasional insight slips into the feminist literature. For example, in a diary of a day with her small children, published in *Ms.*, Phyllis Rosser describes motherhood minute-by-minute:

"9:50. Stopped to feed the cat because she was making so much noise."

"10:28. Sat down again. Sam asked me to watch her turn somersaults."

"5:10. Took Sam to the toy store to buy birthday present for Tim while the boys stayed home with Bill."

Her days are not that interesting to read about, but the insights she gleans from examining her own diary are. They offer an important message to full-time mothers of small children:

"I was beginning to understand why raising children was so much harder than working in an office. I was allowing my children to dominate my life with trivia, and that left no time to do the things I wanted to do with them, like painting and hiking. It also kept me from having any blocks of time for projects of my own."

Betty Friedan has come closest to taking the scorn out of the word "housewife," much of which she introduced in the first place with *The Feminine Mystique*. In her sequel, *The Second Stage*, Friedan writes:

"We must at least admit and begin openly to discuss feminist denial of the importance of family, of women's own need to give and get love. . . . It would seem to me that in the second stage we should move for some very simple aids that make it possible for mothers (or fathers) who want to stay home and take care of their own children to do so, with some economic compensation that might make the difference."

The women's movement has addressed many issues of concern to women at home. But the heart of the matter—how women can lead rich and independent lives at home—is left hanging. Feminists offer women in the workplace a great sense of having asked the difficult questions about life: whether to work, what to expect on the job, what professional goals to set. The women's movement has not done the same for women at home. Feminists have not asked the questions that matter: Why stay at home? How can I find satisfaction there? How does life at home fit with important things in my family's life or the fabric of a larger community?

## Diapering is man's work

What, then, am I recommending? For people who are troubled by the blind spots and omissions in the standard political formulas, is there a better alternative? I think there is. It is possible at least to outline a political approach to children and parenthood that would emphasize the things that make a difference in children's lives.

The first principle is that parents should strive to care for their children themselves. It will not always be possible, and many children will get along fine in any case. Still, other conditions being equal, children are more likely to thrive when they spend most of their day with a parent rather than a hired caretaker. One of our political goals, therefore, should be to create the circumstances that allow more parents to care for their young children themselves.

Simply stating that as a goal would be important in itself. "Parenthood" is supposed to be one of our bedrock societal values, but it really isn't. I have heard many more speeches about inflation, taxes, the deficit, nuclear war, and the Sandinistas than about parenthood. Recognizing the potential political power of a rational approach to parenthood could lead to many practical steps: for example, encouraging businesses to change their policies on maternity leave, paternity leave, part-time work, and job-sharing.

The second principle is an insistence that the balance between parenthood and career be worked out by both parents. In part this is a practical economic problem. Because most women earn less money than most men, when it comes time to decide which spouse stays home, the choice is obvious. How can the family afford to lose its main breadwinner? One of the reasons to push ahead with the feminist campaign for fairer pay is that it would make it more feasible for fathers to take a few years off to care for the children.

Unfortunately, this issue transcends economics. Too many men view the parenthood/career balance as their wives' problem, of no concern to them. For the sake of the children, and the mothers, *and* the fathers, we need to remind men, day after day until it takes, that it is their concern, too. They are as responsible as their wives for finding a way to reconcile their professional ambitions with the welfare of their children.

Third, we must recognize that if spouses—for the time being, mainly mothers—are to stay out of the work force for a while, they need certain practical protections. Here, many of the steps toward reform already have been proposed by the feminists. Pension reform and enforcement of child-support orders will allow parents to care for their children without becoming too vulnerable to fate.

Fourth, we must have day care—more of it, and more of high quality. Day care has become a permanent feature of American life. Millions of children will spend billions of hours in these institutions. Those hours can be relatively pro-

ductive, or they can be actively damaging, depending on how the day care centers are run. If we are serious about improving day care, we must raise the regulatory standards imposed on the centers and put more money into their operation. Increased federal spending is unlikely at a time when government programs of all kinds are being cut back. But if the care of our children is important, we should find ways to improve day care that do not add to the federal deficit— perhaps by enlisting businesses to subsidize day care, or by using our talents more creatively in volunteer efforts.

Finally, we should insist on a principle missing from all the political manifestos about women and families I have seen. Women who stay home with their children should feel just as great an obligation to use their intellect and energy wisely as any young doctor or teacher of either sex. The women's movement and the pro-family forces seem to agree that a woman who ends up at home with the children ("by choice" according to the feminists, "by natural order" according to the right) has stepped off of life's main road. She's spending these years "at home," and there's not much more to say about her. But the exhortations feminists direct at careerists—to bring out the best in themselves, to be responsible, independent, and strong—should also be issued as challenges to women at home.

# Working Women: How It's Working Out

## Shirley Wilkins and Thomas A.W. Miller

Lynn and John are in their early thirties, married, and both lawyers. They are about to have their first child—and their first big marital problem.

How are they to raise their child? Which of these talented individuals will be called upon to make the greater professional sacrifice? Whose career will be at least temporarily, if not permanently, derailed in order to have a family?

The couple does have some options. Lynn is eligible for several months of maternity leave, but she worries that she will be taken off the interesting and important cases. John can take a more limited amount of paternity leave, but, frankly, it would be frowned upon. They certainly have the combined income to be able to afford a full-time nanny, but they are not anxious to entrust their child's early education to a professional—no matter how sensitive and intelligent that person may be. Day-care centers are available, but there the problem of paying an outsider to do their child-rearing is compounded by an environment that, however well managed, is in no sense a home.

In brief, Lynn and John do not want to be absentee parents—and yet both of them derive enormous personal satisfaction from their work.

This couple's problem is by no means an isolated one. Writ large, it exemplifies a growing challenge for a rapidly increasing number of American women and men: how to combine careers and families when both

spouses work. Time is of the essence—and for working couples, their time is particularly pressed. How can all of the things that people want for themselves—children, a happy marriage, a job—be fit into a twenty-four hour day?

The 1985 Virginia Slims American Women's Opinion Poll, conducted by the Roper Organization, has monitored and tracked Americans' opinions on social, familial, and personal issues since 1970. The fifth in a series of polls sponsored by Virginia Slims, this one is based on a representative nationwide sample of 3,000 adult women and 1,000 adult men. The results of this year's survey suggest that changing attitudes toward women's role in society, toward marriage, and toward the essential components of a full and satisfying personal life portend major social changes in the future. The traditional organization of family life, and the very nature of work itself, may never be the same.

### Once A Bread Baker, Now A Bread Winner

If one word could sum up the vast progress made by women in the past fifteen years, it would be "choice." The freedom to choose a fulfilling individual lifestyle—and, simultaneously, tolerance of others' choices—has been the essential force underlying the social transformations of this period.

And a key element in this ongoing social evolution has been, and undoubtedly will continue to be, women's

## 4. GROUPS AND ROLES IN TRANSITION: The Job/Marriage/Family Difficult Choice

move into the workplace. Over the past fifteen years, the percentage of women employed full time has doubled; combined with part-time workers, this brings the total percentage of working women to more than half (52 percent) of the adult female population.

It is not simply out of economic necessity, moreover, that this fast-rising number of women choose to work. When asked whether they would continue to work even if financially secure, an identical proportion of employed women and employed men (66 percent) reply that they would. Perhaps more to the point, for the first time ever a majority of women (51 percent) would prefer to have a job rather than stay at home and take care of a family, if that were their only choice. In 1970, six out of ten women chose home over the workplace.

In the opinion of a growing majority of women, the most personally satisfying and interesting life is one that combines marriage, a career, and children (see table 1). Particularly among younger women and better-educated ones, this preference for a full professional *and* family life is pronounced (see table 2). This result leads to two conclusions. First, as younger women mature, they may be more likely to stay in the workforce even as they attempt to raise a family. Second, as more women enroll in colleges and universities, so too will they tend to seek the best of both these worlds. It appears that the desire for a "working marriage"—in which career, marriage, and a family all contribute to a woman's personal satisfaction—is bound to spread in the future.

### Table 1

**Question:** Now let me ask you a somewhat different question. Considering the possibilities for combining or not combining marriage, children, and a career, and assuming you had a choice, which *one* of these possibilities do you think would offer *you* the most satisfying and interesting life? (Card shown respondent)

| | Women 1974 | Women 1985 |
|---|---|---|
| Combining marriage, career, and children | 52% | 63% |
| Marrying, having children, but not having career | 38 | 26 |
| Having career and marrying, but not having children | 4 | 4 |
| Having career, but not marrying or having children | 2 | 3 |
| Marrying, but not having children or career | 1 | 1 |
| Don't know | 3 | 2 |

**Source:** Surveys by the Roper Organization for Virginia Slims, latest that of March 1985.

This move of women into a traditionally male domain—the workplace—has enormous social consequences. In the first place, it is clearly linked to women's improving status in our society—and to women's increasing self-confidence as their own, ardent advocates. According to three-quarters of women and men, women's roles in society will continue to change, and larger majorities today (69 percent of women, 67 percent of

### Table 2

PREFERENCES FOR MARRIAGE, CHILDREN, AND CAREER BY DEMOGRAPHIC GROUPS, 1985

| | Combining marriage, career, and children | Marrying, having children, but not having career | Having career and marrying, but not having children | Having career, but not marrying or having children | Marrying, but not having children or career |
|---|---|---|---|---|---|
| All women | 63% | 26% | 4% | 3% | 1% |
| White | 63 | 26 | 5 | 3 | 1 |
| Black | 63 | 25 | 3 | 7 | 1 |
| 18-29 years | 70 | 19 | 6 | 3 | 1 |
| 30-39 years | 66 | 21 | 6 | 5 | 1 |
| 40-49 years | 66 | 22 | 4 | 5 | 1 |
| 50 years and over | 54 | 37 | 3 | 2 | * |
| Non-high school graduate | 53 | 37 | 3 | 4 | 1 |
| High school graduate | 63 | 28 | 3 | 3 | * |
| College graduate | 70 | 17 | 7 | 4 | 1 |

**Note:** * = less than .5%.
**Source:** Survey by the Roper Organization for Virginia Slims, March 1985.

men) than in 1980 think those roles *should* continue to change.

What is more, overwhelming majorities favor efforts to improve the status of women, and for the first time ever, more women than men support such efforts (see table 3). This is indeed a dramatic shift in opinion from fifteen years ago, when a slight plurality of women *opposed* efforts to improve their status. What accounts for such a massive swing? Back in 1970, many women were undoubtedly apprehensive about the implications of a change in their status. They were fearful of the unknown and were much more comfortable with the status quo. Men, not being the object of such efforts, either could afford to be more objective or were reluctant to appear too self-interested. Now, however, women have observed what has happened to many other women as a result of these efforts and have, apparently, decided that the result is good.

In step with women's changing roles, furthermore,

### Table 3

EFFORTS TO STRENGTHEN WOMEN'S STATUS

**Question:** Do you favor or oppose most of the efforts to strengthen and change women's status in society today?

| | Women Favor | Women Oppose | Men Favor | Men Oppose |
|---|---|---|---|---|
| 1970 | 40% | 42% | 44% | 39% |
| 1972 | 48 | 36 | 49 | 36 |
| 1974 | 57 | 25 | 63 | 19 |
| 1980 | 64 | 24 | 64 | 23 |
| 1985 | 73 | 17 | 69 | 17 |

**Source:** Surveys by the Roper Organization for Virginia Slims, latest that of March 1985.

has come greater respect for women as individuals, which helps to explain why growing majorities favor efforts to improve women's status. Today, 60 percent of women and 61 percent of men believe that women are more respected now than they were ten years ago. This, too, represents quite a change from the attitudes of 1970, when only 38 percent of women and 40 percent of men thought that women were more respected compared to ten years previously. And, once again, the young and college-educated are among the most optimistic women.

Despite such growing respect for women, however, working women have encountered difficulties in the professional world. Sexual discrimination does persist, and the consensus of both women and men is that, all things considered, there are more advantages in being a man in today's world. Yet it is heartening that majorities of working women say they stand an equal chance with men in three vital areas concerning their jobs: salary, responsibility, and promotion possibilities. The major barrier that remains, according to a plurality of these women (45 percent), is being promoted to a top management position (see table 4).

---

### Table 4
EQUAL OPPORTUNITY ON THE JOB, 1985

**Question:** Do you feel you stand an equal chance with the men you work with in the following areas?

|  | Working women say they have: | | | Men say working women have: | | |
|---|---|---|---|---|---|---|
|  | Equal chance | Not equal | Don't know | Equal chance | Not equal | Don't know |
| Salary | 57% | 33% | 10% | 48% | 46% | 6% |
| Responsibility | 73 | 18 | 9 | 61 | 33 | 6 |
| Promotion | 53 | 35 | 12 | 45 | 49 | 7 |
| Becoming an executive | 38 | 45 | 17 | 37 | 54 | 9 |

**Source:** Survey by the Roper Organization for Virginia Slims, March 1985.

---

Nevertheless, women with actual work experience think that things are generally better now than they were five years ago. But men do not agree. Men are *less* inclined today than they were in 1980 to think that women have equal chances in the workplace. Thus, those who are allegedly discriminated against believe that the situation is improving; those who are supposed to be doing the discriminating think it is getting worse. What explains this fascinating contradiction?

It would seem that men's attitudes toward this problem have been influenced, at least to some extent, by the increasing amount of information on sexual discrimination in general. That is, men have become more aware that there is a problem, and this is influencing their opinions about possible unfairness in the workplace. Men are now more sensitive, and perhaps even more defensive, about equal professional opportunities, even though the attitudes of working women suggest that real progress is being made.

Of course, it would be premature to declare the battle for equal economic opportunity, for completely nondiscriminatory treatment at work, over. Certain issues, such as the complex and emotional one of comparable worth, are still on the public agenda. Yet, women *have* come far in seeking and obtaining meaningful jobs for themselves. They *are* moving into occupations once considered the sole preserves of men, as Sally Ride's space flight in 1983 and Geraldine Ferraro's vice presidential nomination in 1984 symbolize. There *is* a widespread feeling today that a talented and capable woman can succeed in whatever profession she chooses.

More and more, women's professional potential is obstructed not by discrimination *in* the workplace but rather by obligations *outside* it. Women may increasingly enjoy equal opportunities at work, but, compared to men, they have relatively little time to capitalize on those opportunities. The major challenges for the future—challenges created by women's very success in moving into the workplace over the past fifteen years—concern the organization of *domestic* life. The problem is to find a new balance between work and home for both women and men—and, further down the road, perhaps to alter the structure of work in order to have a fuller and more satisfying family life.

### Marriages of Mutual Responsibility

Marriage these days is enjoying something of a comeback, despite all the attention typically paid to the divorce rate in this country. Although fewer men and women today are married and living with their spouses than in 1980—in part, it must be said, because the baby boom generation is still in its marrying years and tends to marry later—other signs indicate that attitudes about marriage may be changing.

Nine out of ten women and men say, for instance, that marriage is their preferred lifestyle. Substantially fewer people today than in 1970 believe that marriage as an institution is weaker now than ten years ago.

The fact is that marriage and the nuclear family have always been, and will long continue to be, the core of American society. True, large majorities say that people can be happy without being married. And they also think that a happy marriage does not require children. Yet, there has been virtually no increase since 1972 in the number of Americans who have or plan to have no children, and the extremely high proportion (90 percent) saying that marriage is their preferred lifestyle has remained remarkably constant. Instead, these attitudes toward the role of marriage and children in personal happiness demonstrate Americans' growing tolerance of alternative lifestyles—of those minorities who choose to remain single or childless.

Yet by far the most significant change in Americans' views of marriage concerns the *kind* of marriage that people want. Today, majorities of men and women desire a marriage of shared responsibility—one in which both spouses work and divide housekeeping and child-

## 4. GROUPS AND ROLES IN TRANSITION: The Job/Marriage/Family Difficult Choice

rearing equally. Merely a decade ago, a majority of women and a plurality of men opted for a traditional marriage, in which he was the financial provider and she ran the house and took care of the children (see table 5).

Once again, enthusiasm for this new type of marriage is most pronounced among younger women and men, which suggests that it will increasingly become the norm. But more indicative of the challenges ahead, and the problems obstructing such shared-responsibility marriages, is that women have more eagerly embraced this concept than men.

The main reason for this divergence in attitudes of women and men is that, while women have moved quickly into the "male" domain of the workplace, men have been much slower to help out with "female" tasks in the home. For instance, 30 percent of married women who are employed full time assert they do nearly all of the household chores, and another 44 percent claim they do a lot but their husbands help out some. Merely 24 percent say these tasks are evenly divided between the spouses. Men with working wives tend to be more charitable toward themselves—28 percent claim that the chores are evenly divided—but even so, the imbalance is evident.

Another factor that helps to explain men's relative reluctance about the shared-responsibility marriage is that they, much more than women, derive a greater sense of their personal identity from their work. For many men, their careers are the key element defining their place in society and even their concept of self-worth. Women, however, have long relied on other sources—particularly, perhaps, their children—to establish their sense of identity, precisely because customarily they have spent so much time with kids in the home. One indication of this major difference between the sexes can be found in attitudes toward work. A majority of employed men (56 percent) consider their work

to be a career, while a majority of employed women (58 percent) say their work is "just a job."

Yet what exactly do these figures mean? Is work just a stopgap measure or a kind of pastime for many women? This is hardly the appropriate conclusion, given that a majority of women consider work to be an essential ingredient of a full and satisfying life, that two-thirds of employed women would continue to work even if financially secure, that more employed women than employed men derive a great deal of personal satisfaction from their work, and that a majority of *all* women would choose a job instead of staying home. Instead, the proper conclusion would appear to be that women place a different *degree* of importance on their work—that, in the grand scheme of life, work may be somewhat less important than it is to many men.

### Working Toward A More Balanced Future

It may sound rather radical to suggest that the very nature of work may change as a result of these evolving attitudes, but that may be the case—someday. If so, what will be most obviously affected?

First, a larger number of employed women will probably consider their work to be a career rather than "just a job." Already the opinions of college-educated women on this issue are identical to the beliefs of college-educated men: more than six in ten say they are pursuing a career, not working a job. The very meaning of a career, however, could well be transformed. Career paths in most professions were established when men overwhelmingly dominated them. That is no longer the case. Some better mechanism will have to be found to accommodate these career-minded women—and their aspirations for a happy family life as well.

Second, working couples will face more difficult decisions about whose career should take priority. Right now, large majorities of women and men think a wom-

---

### Table 5

**Question:** In today's society, there are different lifestyles, and some that are acceptable today that weren't in the past. Regardless of what you may have done or plan to do with your life, and thinking just of what would give *you personally* the most satisfying and interesting life, which one of these different ways of life do you think would be the best as a way of life? (Card shown respondent)

| | 1974 | | 1985 | | | | | |
|---|---|---|---|---|---|---|---|---|
| | Total women | Total men | Total women | 18-29 years | 30-39 years | 40-49 years | 50 years and over | Total men |
| Marriage where husband and wife share responsibilities more—both work, share housekeeping and child responsibilities | 46% | 44% | 57% | 69% | 65% | 58% | 42% | 50% |
| Traditional marriage with husband assuming responsibility for providing for family and wife running house and taking care of children | 50 | 48 | 37 | 24 | 30 | 34 | 52 | 43 |
| Living with someone of opposite sex, but not marrying | 3 | 3 | 2 | 3 | 1 | 2 | 1 | 3 |
| Remaining single and living alone | 1 | 1 | 2 | 1 | 1 | 4 | 2 | 3 |
| Remaining single and living with others of the same sex | — | — | — | — | — | | — | 1 |
| Living in large family of people with similar interests in which some are married and some are not | 1 | 1 | 1 | 1 | 1 | — | 1 | 1 |

**Source:** Surveys by the Roper Organization for Virginia Slims, latest that of March 1985.

an should quit her job if her husband is offered a very good one elsewhere; at the same time, majorities also believe that a wife should turn down a very good job offer in another city so that her husband can continue his present career. In part this can be explained by the probability that the man has a higher salary and hence is the main source of income for the family. It may simply reflect the public's acceptance of economic reality. But as the earnings of both spouses draw closer together, issues concerning career advancement will become more complex—and Americans' attitudes toward them more ambivalent.

There may also be greater pressure from such two-income families for employers to allow more flexibility in work schedules. Staggering the hours that the parents are at work or shortening the work week could help alleviate some of the problems associated with day care. Or shared jobs, half-time jobs, and other forms of part-time work may take on even greater significance in the future, allowing at least one parent to spend more time with the family.

In the same vein, the provision of day-care services by employers—and perhaps better policies on maternity and paternity leave—may eventually come to be seen as more valuable employee benefits. Employers who provide these kinds of options will be better placed to attract talented individuals from two-income households.

These general attitudes also indicate that the trend toward smaller families is firmly established and will, in all likelihood, continue. It is one thing to hold down a job while attempting to care for two children, quite another if the parents have to look after five.

And even the nature of relationships between women and men undergo some fundamental changes. Hackneyed as the cliché may be, there is power in the purse—psychological as well as economic. Among other things, men's habit of paying for things may fade, in part out of deference to the more independent status of women and in part, perhaps, out of necessity. Plus, they will undoubtedly have to help out a lot more around the home, or the couple will have to learn to tolerate a less clean, orderly environment. But offsetting this, men may get to know their children a little bit better, because they spend more time with them. In fact, children who are raised more equally by both parents may well turn out to be different in many respects from previous generations.

These are just some of the adjustments, it seems, that Americans will be making in coming years. In many respects, this will be a period of consolidation, of sorting out how best to cope with the changing responsibilities of women and men. As Walt Whitman once wrote to Ralph Waldo Emerson: "Women in these States approach the day of that organic equality with men, without which, I see, men cannot have organic equality among themselves." The poet was simply a century and a half before his time.

# What feminism has learned at the office.

# STRATEGIES OF CORPORATE WOMEN

## BARBARA EHRENREICH

Barbara Ehrenreich is the author of *The Hearts of Men* (Anchor).

SOME of us are old enough to recall when the stereotype of a "liberated woman" was a disheveled radical, notoriously braless, and usually hoarse from denouncing the twin evils of capitalism and patriarchy. Today the stereotype is more likely to be a tidy executive who carries an attaché case and is skilled in discussing market shares and leveraged buy-outs. In fact, thanks in no small part to the anger of the earlier, radical feminists, women have gained a real toehold in the corporate world: about 30 percent of managerial employees are women, as are 40 percent of the current MBA graduates. We have come a long way, as the expression goes, though clearly not in the same direction we set out on.

The influx of women into the corporate world has generated its own small industry of advice and inspiration. Magazines like *Savvy* and *Working Woman* offer tips on everything from sex to software, plus the occasional instructive tale about a woman who rises effortlessly from managing a boutique to being the CEO of a multinational corporation. Scores of books published since the mid-1970s have told the aspiring managerial woman what to wear, how to flatter superiors, and when necessary, fire subordinates. Even old-fashioned radicals like myself, for whom "CD" still means civil disobedience rather than an

eight percent interest rate, can expect to receive a volume of second-class mail inviting them to join their corporate sisters at a "networking brunch" or to share the privileges available to the female frequent flier.

BUT FOR all the attention lavished on them, all the six-figure promotion possibilities and tiny perks once known only to the men in gray flannel, there is a malaise in the world of the corporate woman. The continuing boom in the advice industry is in itself an indication of some kind of trouble. To take an example from a related field, there would not be a book published almost weekly on how to run a corporation along newly discovered oriental principles if American business knew how to hold its own against the international competition. Similarly, if women were confident about their role in the corporate world, I do not think they would pay to be told how to comport themselves in such minute detail. ("Enter the bar with a briefcase or some files. . . . Hold your head high, with a pleasant expression on your face. . . . After you have ordered your drink, shuffle through a paper or two, to further establish yourself [as a businesswoman]," advises *Letitia Baldridge's Complete Guide*.)

Nor, if women were not still nervous newcomers, would there be a market

for so much overtly conflicting advice: how to be more impersonal and masculine (*The Right Moves*) or more nurturing and intuitive (*Feminine Leadership*); how to assemble the standard skirted suited uniform (de rigueur until approximately 1982) or move beyond it for the softness and individuality of a dress; how to conquer stress or how to transform it into drive; how to repress the least hint of sexuality, or alternatively, how to "focus the increase in energy that derives from sexual excitement so that you are more productive on the job" (*Corporate Romance*). When we find so much contradictory advice, we must assume that much of it is not working.

There is a more direct sign of trouble. A small but significant number of women are deciding not to have it all after all, and are dropping out of the corporate world to apply their management skills to kitchen decor and baby care. Not surprisingly, these retro women have been providing a feast for a certain "I told you so" style of journalism; hardly a month goes by without a story about another couple that decided to make do on his $75,000 a year while she joins the other mommies in the playground. But the trend is real. The editors of the big business-oriented women's magazines are worried about it. So is Liz Roman Gallese, the former *Wall St. Journal* reporter who interviewed the alumnae of Harvard Business School, class of '75, to write *Women Like Us*.

The women Gallese interviewed are not, for the most part, actual dropouts, but they are not doing as well as might have been expected for the first cohort of women to wield the talismanic Harvard MBA. Certainly they are not doing as well as their male contemporaries, and the gap widens with every year since graduation. Nor do they seem to be a very happy or likable group. Suzanne, the most successful of them, is contemptuous of women who have family obligations. Phoebe, who is perhaps the brightest, has an almost pathological impulse to dominate others. Maureen does not seem to like her infant daughter. Of the 82 women surveyed, 35 had been in therapy since graduation; four had been married to violently abusive men; three had suffered from anorexia or bulimia; and two had become Christian fundamentalists. Perhaps not surprisingly, given the high incidence of personal misery, two-fifths of the group were "ambivalent or frankly not ambitious for their careers."

WHAT IS happening to our corporate women? The obvious antifeminist answer, that biology is incompatible with business success, is not borne out by Gallese's study. Women with children were no less likely to be ambitious and do well than more mobile, single women (although in 1982, when the interviews were carried out, very few of the women had husbands or children). But the obvious feminist answer—that women are being discouraged or driven out by sexism—does gain considerable support from *Women Like Us*. Many of the women from the class of '75 report having been snubbed, insulted, or passed over for promotions by their male co-workers. Under these circumstances, even the most determined feminist would begin to suffer from what Dr. Herbert J. Freudenberger and Gail North call "business burnout." For non-feminists—or, more precisely, post-feminists—like Gallese and her informants, sexism must be all the more wounding for being so invisible and nameless. What you cannot name, except as apparently random incidents of "discrimination," you cannot hope to do much about.

Gallese suggests another problem, potentially far harder to eradicate than any form of discrimination. There may

be a poor fit between the impersonal, bureaucratic culture of the corporation and what is, whether as a result of hormones or history, the female personality. The exception that seems to prove the rule is Suzanne, who is the most successful of the alumnae and who is also a monster of detachment from her fellow human beings. In contrast, Gallese observes that men who rise to the top are often thoroughly dull and "ordinary"—as men go—but perhaps ideally suited to a work world in which interpersonal attachments are shallow and all attention must focus on the famed bottom line.

To judge from the advice books, however, the corporate culture is not as impersonal, in a stern Weberian sense, as we have been led to believe. For example, *The Right Moves*, which is a good representative of the "how to be more like the boys" genre of books for corporate women, tells us to "eliminate the notion that the people with whom you work are your friends"—sound advice for anyone who aspires to the bureaucratic personality. But it also insists that it is necessary to cultivate the "illusion of friendship," lest co-workers find you "aloof and arrogant." You must, in other words, dissemble in order to effect the kind of personality—artificially warm but never actually friendly—that suits the corporate culture.

Now, in a task-oriented, meritocratic organization—or, let us just say, a thoroughly capitalist organization dedicated to the maximization of profit—it should not be necessary to cultivate "illusions" of any kind. It should be enough just to get the job done. But as *The Right Moves* explains, and the stories in *Women Like Us* illustrate, it is never enough just to get the job done; if it were, far more women would no doubt be at the top. You have to impress people, win them over, and in general project an aura of success far more potent than any actual accomplishment. The problem may not be that women lack the capacity for businesslike detachment, but that, as women, they can never entirely fit into the boyish, glad-handed corporate culture so well described three decades ago in *The Lonely Crowd*.

THERE MAY also be a deeper, more existential, reason for the corporate woman's malaise. It is impossible to sample the advice literature without beginning to wonder what, after all, is the point of all this striving. Why not be

content to stop at $40,000 or $50,000 a year, some stock options, and an IRA? Perhaps the most striking thing about the literature for and about the corporate woman is how little it has to say about the purposes, other than personal advancement, of the corporate "game." Not one among the Harvard graduates or the anonymous women quoted in the advice books ever voices a transcendent commitment to, say, producing a better widget. And if that is too much to expect from postindustrial corporate America, we might at least hope for some lofty organizational goals—to make X Corp. the biggest damn conglomerate in the Western world, or some such. But no one seems to have a vast and guiding vision of the corporate life, much less a Gilderesque belief in the moral purposefulness of capitalism itself. Instead, we find successful corporate women asking, "Why am I doing what I'm doing? What's the point here?" or confiding bleakly that "something's missing."

In fact, from the occasional glimpses we get, the actual content of an executive's daily labors can be shockingly trivial. Consider Phoebe's moment of glory at Harvard Business School. The class had been confronted with a real-life corporate problem to solve. Recognizing the difficulty of getting catsup out of a bottle, should Smucker and Co. start selling catsup out of a wide-mouthed container suitable for inserting a spoon into? No, said Phoebe, taking the floor for a lengthy disquisition, because people like the challenge of pounding catsup out of the bottle; a more accessible catsup would never sell. Now, I am not surprised that this was the right answer, but I am surprised that it was greeted with such apparent awe and amazement by a professor and a roomful of smart young students. Maybe for a corporate man the catsup problem is a daunting intellectual challenge. But a woman must ask herself: Is *this* what we left the kitchen for?

Many years ago, when America was more innocent but everything else was pretty much the same, Paul Goodman wrote, "There is nearly 'full employment' . . . but there get to be fewer jobs that are necessary or unquestionably useful; that require energy and draw on some of one's best capacities; and that can be done keeping one's honor and dignity." Goodman, a utopian socialist, had unusually strict criteria for what counted as useful enough to be a "man's work," but he spoke for a generation of men who were beginning to question, in less radical ways, the corporate work world described by William H. Whyte, David Riesman, Alan Harrington, and others. Most of the alienated white-collar men of the 1950s withdrew into drink or early coronaries, but a few turned to Zen or jazz, and thousands of their sons and daughters eventually joined with Goodman to help create the anticorporate and, indeed, anti-careerist counterculture of the 1960s. It was the counterculture, as much as anything else, that nourished the feminist movement of the late 1960s and early 1970s, which is where our story began.

In the early years, feminism was torn between radical and assimilationist tendencies. In fact, our first sense of division was between the "bourgeois" feminists who wanted to scale the occupational hierarchy created by men, and the radical feminists who wanted to level it. Assimilation won out, as it probably must among any economically disadvantaged group. Networks replaced consciousness-raising groups; Michael Korda became a more valuable guide to action than Shulamith Firestone. The old radical, anarchistic vision was replaced by the vague hope (well articulated in *Feminine Leadership*) that, in the process of assimilating, women would somehow "humanize" the cold and ruthless world of men. Today, of course, there are still radical feminists, but the only capitalist institution they seem bent on destroying is the local adult bookstore.

As feminism loses its critical edge, it becomes, ironically, less capable of interpreting the experience of its pioneer assimilationists, the new corporate women. Contemporary mainstream feminism can understand their malaise insofar as it is caused by sexist obstacles, but has no way of addressing the sad emptiness of "success" itself. Even the well-worn term "alienation," as applied to human labor, rings no bells among the corporate feminists I have talked to recently, although most thought it an arresting notion. So we are in more or less the same epistemological situation Betty Friedan found herself in describing the misery—and, yes, alienation—of middle-class housewives in the early 1960s; better words would be forthcoming, but she had to refer to "the problem without a name."

Men are just as likely as women to grasp the ultimate pointlessness of the corporate game and the foolishness of many of the players, but only women have a socially acceptable way out. They can go back to the split-level homes and well-appointed nurseries where Friedan first found them. (That is assuming, of course, they can find a well-heeled husband, and they haven't used up all their child-bearing years in the pursuit of a more masculine model of success.) In fact, this may well be a more personally satisfying option than a work life spent contemplating, say, the fluid dynamics of catsup. As Paul Goodman explained, with as much insight as insensitivity, girls didn't have to worry about "growing up absurd" because they had intrinsically meaningful work cut out for them—motherhood and homemaking.

There is no doubt, from the interviews in *Women Like Us* as well as my own anecdotal sources, that some successful women are indeed using babies as a polite excuse for abandoning the rat race. This is too bad from many perspectives, and certainly for the children who will become the sole focus of their mothers' displaced ambitions. The dropouts themselves would do well to take a look at *The Corporate Couple*, which advises executive wives on the classic problems such as: how to adjust to the annual relocation, how to overcome one's jealousy of a husband's svelte and single female co-workers, and how to help a husband survive his own inevitable existential crisis.

Someday, I believe, a brilliantly successful corporate woman will suddenly look down at her desk littered with spread sheets and interoffice memos and exclaim, "Is this really worth my time?" At the very same moment a housewife, casting her eyes around a kitchen befouled by toddlers, will ask herself the identical question. As the corporate woman flees out through the corporate atrium, she will run headlong into a housewife, fleeing into it. The two will talk. And in no time at all they will reunite those two distinctly American strands of radicalism—the utopianism of Goodman and the feminism of Friedan. They may also, if they talk long enough, invent some sweet new notion like equal pay for . . . meaningful work.

---

*Women Like Us* by Liz Roman Gallese (Morrow, 252 pp., $15.95)

*The Right Moves: Succeeding in a Man's World Without a Harvard MBA* by Charlene Mitchell and Thomas Burdick (Macmillan, 242 pp., $18.95)

*Feminine Leadership: Or How to Succeed in Business Without Being One of the Boys* by Marilyn Loden (Times Books, 306 pp., $16.95)

*Women's Burnout: How to Spot It, How to Reverse It, and How to Prevent It* by Dr. Herbert J. Freudenberger and Gail North (Doubleday, 244 pp., $14.95)

*Corporate Romance: How to Avoid It, Live Through It, or Make It Work for You* by Leslie Aldridge Westoff (Times Books, 246 pp., $16.95)

*The Corporate Couple: Living the Corporate Game* by Peggy J. Berry (Franklin Watts, 296 pp., $16.95)

*Letitia Baldrige's Complete Guide to Executive Manners* (Rawson Associates, 519 pp., $22.95)

# GREAT EXPECTATIONS

## THE AMERICAN IMPERATIVE FOR PERFECTION
## MEETS A NEW GENERATION

### PETE HAMILL

*Pete Hamill is a journalist, novelist, and screenwriter. He is currently at work on a novel, to be published by Random House.*

he subject is men and what they want. If there is a calculated echo here of Freud's famous remark about women, I must also offer a large caution: the subject of men, like the subject of women, is not simple. Only fools or philosophers would presume to generalize about so many millions of individual lives. Human beings insist on having this one terrible fault: they will not fit neatly on charts or graphs. There seems no room for the myriad complexities of our lives: our triumphs, sorrows, brutalities, terrors. There is also no way to diagram hope.

So these are notes from a man who knows himself and some other men. Nothing more. At 50, I'm not yet old and no longer young. I'm part of a generation that was born in a major economic depression, came to consciousness during a world war, and arrived at young manhood in the 1950s.

Nobody is a typical case of anything (or we would cease writing novels and leave the human heart to the sociologists), but in some ways what happened to me also happened to many other men my age. We grew up before television conquered the American consciousness, before millions of the young began to think that lives could be as easily altered as the switching of a channel. The newspapers, radio, magazines all offered essentially the same message: work hard and steadily, master a craft or a trade, marry a good woman and have healthy children, and you will lead a long, serene life.

The world was more complicated than that. The 1960s arrived, with their storms and interruptions, their assassinations and riots, and their distant ugly war. Television jumbled its images and ours. Lives were ruined by drugs. People donned and doffed lifestyles as if they were clothes.

Marriages failed. Millions of them. Mine too. And at a point toward the end of that ferocious decade, I found myself alone with two daughters to raise. I bought a house. I worked impossible hours. I struggled to be a good parent, retired from the drinking life, made awful mistakes, had some triumphs, made more mistakes, was humbled, saddened, enervated, and was made infinitely more human. This is not the place to tell that story; it belongs more properly to my daughters. But we went the distance. I tried my best. I love them more than anyone else on this earth and they love me. I would not have lived the past 15 years in any other way.

I say all of this not to evoke sympathy. Others have struggled harder than I did and had much more difficult obstacles to overcome. But I do feel that I have a few meager credentials to discuss the subject at hand. I'm not the sort of person who looks at himself and sees the universe. But I've also talked to a lot of men my own age and younger who have tried to live in tough times. Some want nothing beyond what they have; they are content, it seems, reasonably happy. I know many who want more; the American imperative drives them beyond every hill, across every river, urging them to collect, acquire, multiply; the cars pile up, the homes and possessions and wives, and they remain all appetite, living in some permanent and unreachable future. But more and more these days, particularly in my wanderings among the young, I encounter those men who, as the brainless slogan puts it, Want It All.

This vague notion isn't always the same for men and women, of course. For some women, the "it" seems to mean the opportunity to have children *and* a career. The men I've spoken to offer a broader compound: a successful career, a traditional marriage based on romantic love, wonderful children, modern independence of action and spirit. Not for them lives of existential dread, nausea, or absurdity. Not for these brave voyagers the tedium of the daily rounds, the comical variety of our couplings, or what John Updike once described as "the peculiar crazy, sleepless staleness of our great domestic crises."

These are children of the Reagan era, almost wholly formed by television, free of the draft and the anxieties of dying in some foreign field (a chore reserved now for volunteers), becalmed by the genius of a President whose style, ideas, and oratory descend directly from Beverly Hills in the 1940s. Listen to them and you know they believe in happy endings. Their world is a kind of watercolor, devoid of shadows, certainly free of skepticism and doubt, existing without history.

"I want a wife who's understanding and supportive," a young stockbroker told me last summer. "I want her to have a career, if that makes her happy, but if she wants to stay home and have babies, that's okay too. She's got to be great in bed. She's got to be beautiful. She's got to have a sense of humor. She's got to be faithful." He laughed. "In other words, I believe in the American Dream, man."

Needless to say, this appalling young man was still single. But the formula he described for the Perfect Wife (admittedly led on by me) was repeated in a number of other casual researches. Young men, some of them married, spoke with almost schematic serenity about the adult lives they wanted or had embarked upon. Some had mastered the rhetorical buzzwords of what they perceived to be the feminist movement. Others insisted that the women they knew didn't care about being liberated; they wanted someone to take care of them. (To be fair, I talked to *these* young men on the sidewalk outside a movie house where we had all watched "Rambo" together; their language sounded as if it had just come off a Nautilus machine, and the women with them just giggled.) A few sounded as if they knew that a life with another human being was not going to be a stroll in the park, but they too said that with some luck, they could Have It All.

In a way, of course, this desire—virtually unique to the United States—could be traced to the Women's Movement itself. One of the major topics of what could be called the postliberation debate is the subject of Having It All. At the heart of the discussion is the imposing figure of Supermom. She has been discussed, delineated, condemned, applauded in millions of printed words. She is a stock character on talk shows. She is presented in various guises in the lies of advertising. She's always essentially the same person: in her thirties, well educated, almost always white, heroically juggling career, husband, children, and

self-respect in the forging of a happy fulfilling life. Some women are actually managing this extraordinary feat. But other reports from the field describe casualties and mutinies, the wounds inflicted by anger, guilt, and exhaustion.

"I tried," a 42-year-old woman friend told me last year. An investment banker, she married at 35, had two children before she was 38. "I tried like hell to put everything together, and I just couldn't manage it. Not because I'm weak; I think I'm a strong person. But there simply aren't enough hours in the day to be all the people I tried to be. The economy was booming, I was making good money. But so was my husband. I felt I was being a lousy mother. I was distracted at work. Something had to give. Sure, I could have asked my husband to quit his job and stay home but I don't think he could have done it. So *I* quit *my* job. I can't say I'm happier. But I'm healthier. I'm less exhausted. I love the children." She laughed in the telling and shook her head. "Of course, I also know that I tried to do something and failed. I'll have to live with that."

Other women I know have had to face the same dilemma; a few are writers and have been able to continue writing, usually at a slower pace, but writers and entertainers are an infinitesimally small elite. I don't know any who have been able to Have It All (which is not to say that such people don't exist). But when I hear men talking about attempting the same thing, I am reminded of a French novelist's maxim for living a life: "Optimism of the will, pessimism of the intelligence." And wonder if these young men truly understand the task before them, the life of struggle that their optimism will guarantee.

Consider the simple attempt to braid together two careers. Although the great majority of American mothers work (half of all married women with children under one, and a majority of those with children under 18), the usual arrangement is familiar and depressing. He has the career; she has a job.

Careers in America are essentially the province of the middle class and those who want to rise above that class. But there are certain extremely difficult problems involved in the attempt to forge two simultaneously growing careers. Most young middle-class families cannot live in the central cities; those centers are either in decay, seething with anger, violence, and crime, or they are too expensive for people in the early stages of careers. Certainly, in my town of New York the only people who can afford Manhattan apartments are in-

side stock traders, Eurotrash, and drug dealers. Unable to pay the skyrocketing rents or the tuitions at private schools, unwilling to hire people to ride shotgun with the children so they can play in public parks, these middle-class families must move to the suburbs.

Most American suburbs are at least an hour from the central city. Since the goals of most American corporate careers involve the acquisition of power, this means that a career-minded couple must emulate their superiors. A recent survey published in *The Wall Street Journal* showed that American senior executives work a total—on average—of 56 hours a week. That's more than 10 hours a day. Add two hours of commuting and you are talking about a 12-hour day, eight in the morning to eight at night.

If a two-career couple have children, they might see the kids for an hour in the morning and an hour in the evening, with weekends free (presuming their careers don't require extensive traveling). They will see them at that time in the morning when the mind is coiling for the challenges of the day; they will see them in the evening after a day packed with the stress, tension, collisions, conflicts, compromises, and evasions of normal existence in American corporate life. Such human beings do not arrive home in any state to enjoy or be enjoyed by children. It is doubtful if they can enjoy each other.

If this were a sensible world, of course, there would be a vast system of day-care facilities in the richest country on earth, so that small children could be brought to a safe, interesting place near where parents work. Such a system doesn't exist here (it does in France and a few other Western nations) and in the Reagan years will not be brought into existence. So a 1980s couple with two careers are forced to pay someone to care for the children.

And the man who Wants It All will soon learn that a marriage with two children, say, and two careers will not be a simple matter. Those men who have applied a patina of liberation rhetoric to themselves will be swiftly tested. Someone will have to give up the career. And though some one million American men now head single-parent families, and a small number are staying home while their wives work, the institution of the househusband will probably not be established in the age of Rambo. Most women who want to preserve the marriage will probably have to abandon the career.

Such a sad and terrible choice will

not guarantee that pacific dream house envisioned by so many of the Reagan-era young; if anything, it will guarantee the opposite. They have yet to learn (as my generation did) that romantic love always promises more than it can deliver, and that there is no way to prepare for this bittersweet truth when it is learned with its usual arctic clarity. Some feel cheated. All are disappointed. A few are crushed.

Men react to this realization in various ways. Some are so warped, sexually and emotionally (often after a sudden, startling epiphany), that they tumble into the black hole of depression. Others become grievance collectors, hoarding slights and affronts as if they were ammunition, firing them across the fault lines of the marriage. Some revert to type, abandoning responsibility, as Huck Finn says, "to light out for the Territory." Others actually grow up.

That, of course, is the most difficult task of all. There is much talk now about fathering, of developing a "new" kind of father, sensitive to his children, willing to listen, firm when necessary, guide, protector, imparter of wisdom. There have always been such fathers and there will be in the future, but I doubt if they will come about through the establishment of courses at the local community college. Such fathers can only exist in an atmosphere that includes time for those children.

"Growing up," for most American men, is actually a process, sometimes glacially slow, of escaping the self to recognize the other, and consequently dealing in a new way with time. All men I know speak with extraordinary warmth of the years of youth, when days lasted forever, when summers were plump with irresponsible joys and time could be squandered on the self. Maturity is another matter (I think it begins when you stop talking about the gifts you receive and mention only the gifts you've given). And giving time to children is the most difficult problem of all.

I've met men and women in the past few years who talk as if having children might be only a minor distraction for a few years, an intense period of nurturing after which a "normal" life can be resumed, interrupted careers reassembled, the equations of American happiness reasserted. But those of us who have raised children know that they are not, and can never be, a two- or three-year aside; they are a 20-year (at least) obligation. Young men who think that it would be "nice" to have children don't seem to realize often enough that when that obligation is completed, when the

children have gone off at last as relatively autonomous human beings, they will no longer be young. As for those men who decide in their fifties, usually in second or third marriages, that they will become fathers again, they must know that when *their* new children are in college, they'll most likely be dead.

I realize that the tone of these notes is not cheerful, or even mildly optimistic. But I would be a faker to describe a state of impending utopian perfection that common sense tells us is unlikely ever to come into existence and the desire for which might lead to a litter of human casualties. Having It All is a desire for perfection, and in many ways the notion of the perfect is the enemy of all human beings. (Consider only the millions who have been slaughtered in this century as a consequence of the lust for social, economic, or religious perfection.) There are no perfect marriages, perfect children, perfect careers, perfect living arrangements for a very simple reason: there are no perfect human beings. Mr. and Mrs. Right do not exist. You need not accept the doctrine of original sin to recognize that every human being is flawed. The goofy young man in search of a perfect woman is as foolish as the female reader of romantic novels seeking her yuppie Heathcliff. The desire for certain forms of perfection also leads to bizarre distortions of common humanity. I would not like to attempt to explain the billions spent in the United States on makeup, cosmetic surgery, or health clubs to men and women trudging across the plains of Ethiopia, or through the jungles of Cambodia, or dwelling in the hard highlands of Mexico.

It's unfashionable in the Reagan years to mention such things, of course. The ethos of the times urges us to tend our private gardens. But anyone who spends much time in the real world knows that such a willed isolation from the real almost always leads to disaster. Young Americans—men and women—are being fed images that make Having It All seem desirable and possible; the rhetoric of optimism is extremely seductive and politically quite powerful. Those images also sell a lot of goods. But they fly in the face of reality. Conservatives act as if the traditional American family exists; we know that only 12 percent of American families are built on the old structure of husband-as-breadwinner, wife-as-homemaker. Conservatives also speak as if the 1950s notion of the nuclear family in the house with the white picket fence (where the family practices, God help us, "togetherness") has

made an amazing comeback; the statistics indicate that 50 percent of all American marriages will still end in divorce. There is a sunny impression that a booming stock market, the fall in oil prices, the growth of a service economy have created a time of abundance and prosperity for all; but a recent issue of *Newsweek* reminds us that to maintain the middle-class lifestyle of 20 years ago, husbands and wives must both work. While spoiled young men talk to me about Having It All, there are an estimated 50,000 homeless people in the streets of New York City and almost one million people—more than 700,000 of them women and children without men in their families—on welfare.

The traditional family, so beloved of the American right wing, is as dead as the big bands. And Having It All, from the point of view of the young men I've met in the past few years, is really a renewed vision of that traditional family. Its surface is hipper, more civilized, more "sensitive." But it's a fantasy construct. The right has blamed feminism, in some cases, for the dissolution of that traditional family. But there were many more important factors. Money killed that family and wars killed it and the automobile killed it and welfare killed it and television killed it and education killed it and the romantic love industry killed it. Americans moved all over their country, seeking the Great Good Place; they left behind parents (who in most societies help with child care). They adopted the rhythms of television seasons, where a show that lasted seven years was a great hit and then dissipated into boredom and disappearance. Men looked at the minefield of human relationships and deserted. The young are now encouraged to ignore all that.

Can men Have It All? I don't think so. They can certainly lead more human lives, they can be better fathers and husbands, but not if they enter marriages as if they were accepting parts in movies. A marriage is a compact. And if mature human beings enter that compact, they must understand with great clarity that they will have to surrender certain freedoms. Once a child is born, neither mother nor father is free. Ever. And to create a home life in which men truly share the task of parenting, men will have to surrender some of their positions on the fast track.

Such surrenders go against some of the most deeply felt assumptions of the American vision. When American men speak about being free, they mean, in practice, being free of responsibility. Being a true father (as compared to those amazing men numbering now in the millions who become biological fathers and then hurry on to the next womb) is *all* responsibility. But for generations, cowboys have climbed on horses to ride into the sunset; heroes are lone men facing overwhelming odds. The tedium of family life, its excruciating dailiness, the tensions created by the illusion of perfection, the infinite number of crises and improvisations it requires: these are not the concern of our heroes. Imagine, for example, Rambo helping his daughters with biology homework. Or Dirty Harry helping carry a science project to his child's high school.

The surrender of some career goals also denies the training given to all American boys. From childhood, they are told they can be anything in this country: center fielder for the Yankees, the head of the Chrysler Corporation, President of the United States. They are trained to compete. On the playing field. In class. At their first jobs. Increasingly, they are competing in many of these arenas with women, and greeting the challenge with various degrees of acceptance, anger, trauma (those fragile male egos!), and resignation. Women have fought hard and intelligently for the right to such competition, and as a father

of daughters I have a special interest in the breaking down of all remaining barriers to what is, after all, a constitutional right.

But there remain extremely powerful cultural forces at play in the country that will not be easily altered. The images of success for men do not include changing diapers, nursing a child through illness or heartbreak, dropping off children at the company day-care center; would Lee Iacocca do such things? It would be a good thing if those images were swiftly altered—if the education and training of young American boys could be broadened, made more humane and less competitive. I wish that the relentless pressure in this country to be famous or powerful would ease up, so that more of us—men and women—could lead more civilized lives. I wish Americans were made to feel that being a good plumber is at least as important for a man or a woman (and for the country) as being a rock singer, a novelist, a politician, or heavyweight champion of the world.

For now, men and women will probably continue to muddle through. Families can be more democratic without losing the necessary parental authority, but they will never be little utopias. The government might be persuaded (after Reagan is gone) to build that day-care system, encourage paren-

tal leave for both parents, ask industry to give workers of both sexes shorter work-weeks while they're raising small children. But government will not be able to make human beings understand themselves and each other.

In the past 15 years, there has been much real change—particularly in increased male consciousness of women and their hopes, ambitions, and desires. Men probably would not be asking the questions about Having It All if women hadn't raised them first. For some men and for some women, new arrangements have been made, and more of the young will try to make them too. The operative word is "some." Neither legislation nor manifestos will change all men or all women. But I know this, as a man who raised children, changed diapers, was intricately involved in the nitty-gritty of the process: the struggle is worth it.

Nothing is more difficult. Nothing is more rewarding.

But that process requires clarity, sacrifice, humor, responsibility, a recognition of one's own flaws. It is made easier with patience and common sense. It is infinitely better if shared with another adult. But for those who truly make the effort, the notion of Having It All will soon sound like some adolescent slogan, and they will be involved in something of greater, more enduring value.

# Another Stereotype: Old Age As A Second Childhood

**Arnold Arluke Ph.D.**
**and Jack Levin Ph.D.**

*Dr. Jack Levin is a professor of sociology at Northeastern University in Boston and is the co-author of* Ageism: Prejudice and Discrimination Against the Elderly. *Dr. Arnold Arluke is Associate Professor of Sociology, also at Northeastern University, and is co-author of the forthcoming book,* Division of Labor As Marketplace: Rehabilitation Medicine, 1890-1980.

Stereotypes are more than privately held "pictures in our heads." They are more often culturally shared and institutionalized negative images which are used to justify unequal treatment, or discrimination, directed against minority groups, ranging from perpetrating, petty indignities in everyday life to slavery and genocide.

One common and particularly damaging stereotype, "infantilization," reduces minority group members to the status of children, ranging from infants to adolescents, who lack moral, intellectual, or physical maturity. According to this image, they are typically depicted as "irresponsible," "impulsive," "fun-loving," and "immature." In sum, they are seen as dependent on the "more mature" dominant group for guidance to accomplish the tasks to which they are assigned or even to survive.

The antebellum South provides an appropriate example. The "Little Black Sambo" image was extensively

I made a flower today

From *Aging*, August 1984, pp. 7-11. U.S. Department of Health, Education & Welfare.

117

applied to sell the ideology of a "white man's burden," whereby slaves would actually perish if denied the paternalistic "protection" of their masters who administered corporal punishment and withheld rewards to assure that tasks were accomplished. To this day, the epithet "boy" remains as a vestige of the infantilization of the slave (Blassingame, 1972). In the same manner, women before the liberation movement of the 1960's were often called "baby," "girl," "honey," and "sweety." Their fashions were made to reflect the fashions of children, frequently imitating the clothing worn by infants or teenagers of a previous generation (Lurie, 1982).

Similarly, many stereotypes currently portray old age as a time of second childhood. This dim view of the elderly suggests that they are losing, or have lost, the very things a growing child gains. It implies a backward movement to earlier developmental stages, with no recognition of the lifetime of experience that unquestionably separates the elderly from children (Gresham, 1973).

The image of old people as childlike has been with us for a long time. Tuckman and Lorge (1953) asked graduate students in psychology to indicate their agreement or disagreement with a number of statements about old people. Despite the fact that the students were well acquainted with psychology and enrolled in a course involving the aging process, there was a high level of agreement that old people are unproductive, have to go to bed early, need a nap every day, are in the "happiest" period of their lives, cannot manage their own affairs, and are in their second childhood.

More recent research indicates that stereotyping continues to be an integral part of public images of the aged, and that one of the major stereotypes still perpetuates the second childhood image. McTavish (1971) found considerable acceptance for an image of old people that is distinctly reminiscent of the view of toddlers during the stage known as "the terrible two's." Many of his subjects felt that old people are likely to be annoying, obstinate, and unreasonable. In 1975, the National Council on the Aging reported the results of a survey of 4,254 adult Americans (Harris, 1975). Old people were generally thought of as useless and inactive by participants in the survey. They viewed the elderly as spending most of their time watching television or "doing nothing," in the true spirit of directionless adolescence.

**Viewing the Old as Childlike**

The ubiquitousness of the "second childhood" stereotype becomes apparent when we examine its common forms.

First, old people are given the personality and moods of children. It is common, for example, in prescription drug ads to describe senility in terms normally associated with children. An ad for a tranquilizer "for the agitated geriatric" shows an elderly man angrily waving his fist. "TANTRUMS" is printed large across the page. Other tranquilizer ads use terms such as "nuisance," "disruptive," and "obstreperous" to describe the actions of elders. Even in a recent children's book, which was written to acquaint children with old age, the elderly woman who is explaining to a young girl what it is like to be old describes herself as sometimes "cranky," a word usually reserved for children. Television shows and movies characterize the personality of older people as childlike whether it is "Mother Jef-

He's out of diapers for the second time in his life.

ferson's" cantankerousness, the silliness of Johnny Carson's "Aunt Blabby," or the impulsiveness and recklessness of Ruth Gordon in the film, *Harold and Maude*.

Second, old people are given the dress and appearance of children. On the cover of one birthday card is a blackboard with "You're only young once!" chalked on it along with various doodles. Inside, an overweight, unshaven elderly man smoking a cigar is wearing a summer camp tee shirt, shorts, sneakers and cap and is playing with a yo-yo and a baseball bat. Above his grinning face the card says "Happy Birthday Playboy." In addition to its other connotations, the card suggests that when you get old, you are at liberty to play like a child again. One of the worst examples of attributing childlike qualities to the elderly is the appearance of an older man—dressed in pajamas and a birthday hat and blowing a noisemaker— in an advertisement for a "geriatric highchair." On the chair's tray is a birthday cake.

Third, old people are given the physical problems of children. One ad for catheters, which appears in a geriatric nursing journal, shows the forearms and hands of a baby as its model instead of an elder. A prescription drug ad for a stool-softener features a smiling bifocaled older woman. The text reads: "Minnie moved her bowels today. The day started right for Minnie. That young doctor feller gave her a stool softener to take last night. And it worked!. . .Minnie figures she's got the smartest doctor in town." It is not too farfetched to imagine that Minnie's smile not only expresses her physical relief but also her pride at being told she moved her bowels.

Fourth, old people are given parties in the spirit of children's parties. In a suburban smalltown newspaper, a recent article reported that the patients at a local nursing home "held their very own Christmas party." The article went on to indicate that patients "planned the party, made the invitations, decorated the cookies

made by the chef, and took part in the entertainment, which included a group singing of Christmas Carols." The article thanked a local drugstore for supplying "Santa's gifts." The intentions were admirable, but the message rang loud and clear: Old people are like big children.

Posters in a popular chain of fast-food restaurants urge customers to "Have a Senior Birthday Party." For the "birthday kid" who is "young at heart," the fast food chain offers to provide the cake, hats, and party favors. Also consider a telephone company ad for custom phones which can be given as gifts to "celebrate any occasion." One such occasion is "Gertrude's" retirement party, complete with colorful ribbons and balloons. In honor of her retirement, Gertrude is shown receiving her own Snoopy phone from her co-workers. A similar ad shows an elder receiving a Mickey Mouse phone at a party.

Fifth, old people are encouraged to pursue the activities of children. In an article called "The Fun Life for Young and Old," a major city newspaper provided "a guide to August activities for senior citizens and children." Pictures were shown of a puppet show and a magic act. Even the "Kiddies' Menu" of a popular Massachusetts ice cream parlor portrays an older man walking hand-in-hand with a young boy. As clearly stated on the face of the menu, "for all kids under 10 and over 65," the bill of fare consists of a "hot doggie," "kiddie burger," and "peanut butter and jelly samwhich."

Advice books for the elderly often treat them as children by advising them to reduce the work-related activities associated with adulthood (Arluke, et al., 1984). Programs in nursing homes and hospitals intended to make life more interesting for elderly patients also become infantilizing at times (Levin at al., 1983). One handbook of activities and recreational programs for nursing homes recommends discussing such topics as "growing things," "boys," "sunshine," "stones," and "favorite story."

Disruptive!

# Kiddies' Menu

**For all kids under 10 and over 65
offers the following Bill of Fare**

HOT DOGGY .99
KIDDIE BURGER .99
PEANUT BUTTER &
JELLY SAMWHICH .75

**all of the above served with Steak Fries**

Sixth, old people are given the playthings of children. A department store ad in *TV Guide* shows an elderly man riding a child's three wheeler. The caption reads: "Wish they had Hot Cycles when I was a kid. . .Yep, kids sure are lucky today. Hey, maybe when no one's around. . ."

A prescription drug used to treat symptoms associated with organic brain syndrome, claims in an ad that it "Usually leaves the disturbed elderly patient in the nursing home more alert, more responsive." In the ad, the photograph of an elderly woman shows her smiling limply and holding a large red and white checked cloth flower. Above her is the caption: "I made a flower today." A similar arts-and-crafts portrayal of the aged appears in an ad for a drug used to improve circulation. Three elders who are "deficient in peripheral circulation" but "proficient in the 'home'" are shown hard at work making ceramics—which is evidently considered to be a higher level activity in the nursing home. A major newspaper recently ran an article entitled "Latest Trends from Toyland," in which the reporter suggests that dolls can be a "companion to the elderly as they are to children."

## Implications

"Infantilization" justifies the paternalistic treatment of minority group members with the consequence that they may be "kept in their place" as dependent inferiors. Forms of discrimination supported by infantilization include slavery, forcing women to stay at home and various forms of institutionalization.

Casting old people as children has detrimental effects on old and young alike. The "second childhood" stereotype tends to make young people feel distant from their elders. Having just graduated from childhood, what adolescent wants to endure it again by associating with the old? The stereotype may well also encourage gerontophobia, the neurotic fear of old age. How many adults want to be thought of one day as a six-year-old who isn't toilet trained?

For old people, the second-childhood stereotype creates a self-fulfilling prophecy. Many elderly people come to accept the second-childhood stereotype and play the role with enthusiasm. But is that because they fail to see any alternative? Our society has traditionally offered certain rewards to those elderly citizens who are willing to "stay in their place." Riding on a special bus for senior citizens, or dancing with other seniors to the tune of Yankee Doodle, may isolate elderly people. But it may be preferable to watching re-runs of "Marcus Welby."

Acting like children has three negative consequences for old people. First, such behavior lowers their social status because their individual responsibility has been diminished, while their dependency has increased. Secondly, the perception of infantile behavior in the elderly may allow certain things to be done to them that would otherwise not be considered: the prescription of psychoactive medications, institutionalization, and declaration of legal incompetency. Thirdly, infantilization robs the "gray power" movement of adults who might otherwise work for political change and social betterment.

Not all old people buy the second-childhood stereotype. A large number of elderly Americans are thoroughly offended by infantilization and seek to avoid the consequences of the stereotype. For many, this means making efforts to "pass" for middle-age by dying hair, lying about their age, and using youth-oriented cosmetics. A positive form of avoidance is reengagement, whereby old people seek to become either re-employed or remarried after the loss of a job or spouse.

On the damaging side, an unknown number of cases of apparent senility may actually represent a refusal to accept the second-childhood syndrome. Rather than comply, some elders may retreat into a more comfortable, more secure psychological state which ironically has the appearance of infantile behavior. So, for example, we might see lack of sexual interest, giddiness, forgetfulness, inability to maintain a stable relationship, and lack of control over bodily functions.

## A Warning

In contemporary America, stereotyped images of the elderly may one day include less emphasis on infantilization and more emphasis on dehumanization. There is a tendency to view some aged people as mere "vegetables" —totally beyond the age of productivity and usefulness. They are viewed as no longer alive in the sense that we understand what it means to be human and therefore not worthy of the medical and social services available to those who are younger—such as expensive dialysis or lengthy rehabilitation for fractures, stroke, and other problems.

Another aspect of this dehumanization of the elderly may be "to color them all gray" and see them as a group that presents a threat. In periods of economic retrenchment, a large and growing elderly population may to an increasing extent be regarded as a major threat to the economic well-being of younger Americans. Those Americans who feel especially frustrated may look for a justification to reduce the power of their older competitors. Substantial reductions in social security and health benefit payments might be a first step.

Stereotypical or dehumanizing views of the elderly (or any age group) damage the social fabric of our nation even though they may not be held by all Americans. Much is being done currently to counter these views through education and advocacy in the public and private sectors. As the examples in this article illustrate, however, much remains to be done.

Blanche's bowel is "irritable"...again

## REFERENCES

Arluke, A., Levin, J., and Suchwalko, J. "Sexuality and Romance in Advice Books for the Elderly." *Gerontologist.* In press, 1984.

Blassingame, J. *The Slave Community.* New York: Oxford University Press, 1972.

Gresham, M. "The Infantilization of the Elderly." *Nursing Forum* 15, 1976, pp. 196-209.

Harris, L., and Associates. *The Myth and Reality of Aging in America.* New York: National Council on Aging, 1975.

Helmreich, W. *The Things They Say Behind Your Back.* New York: Doubleday, 1982.

Levin, J., and Arluke, A. "Our Elderly's Fate?" *New York Times,* September 29, 1983, p. A31.

Levin, J. Arluke, A., and Cheren, C. "The Challenge of Ageism." *American Health Care Association Journal* 9, March 1983, pp. 47-50.

Lurie, A. *The Language of Clothing.* New York: Random House, 1982.

McTavish, D. "Perceptions of Old People: A Review of Research Methodologies and Findings." *Gerontologist* 11 (4, Part 2), 1971, pp. 90-101.

Tuckman, J. and Lorge, I. "Attitudes Toward Old People." *Journal of Social Psychology* 37, 1953, pp. 249-260.

# Conquering a New American Frontier: Changing Attitudes Toward the Disabled

*"A slow and quiet revolution has enabled increasing numbers of disabled people to move from the stagnation of dependency into the mainstream of living."*

### Alan A. Reich

*Mr. Reich, president of the National Organization on Disability, Washington, D.C., uses a wheelchair as a result of a spinal cord injury in 1962.*

TODAY, there are signs of new attitudes toward the nation's 36,000,000 citizens with physical or mental disabilities. Although negative perceptions, stereotyping, and misconceptions still prevail about individuals with disabilities such as blindness, deafness, paralysis, mental illness, or mental retardation, our traditional, complacent acceptance of the segregation of disabled persons is starting to change.

While Americans with disabilities are a long way from participating fully in the mainstream of life, more of them are moving from the fringes of society, and wider public acceptance of their capabilities and potential is evolving. With growing recognition of disabled persons as voters, consumers, employees, and tax-paying citizens, we have begun the last great inclusion in American life, the inclusion of people with disabilities—16% of the population.

Indications that this new American frontier is being taken seriously are sprouting up in a variety of places, including our political life. The presidential nominating conventions of our two major political parties were addressed by disabled persons last summer. Twenty-two-year-old Edward Kennedy, Jr., who lost a leg to cancer, became the first disability rights advocate on the podium of a nominating convention when he addressed the Democratic conclave in San Francisco. Craig McFarlane, an Olympic skier who is blind, was the first blind person to speak to a nominating convention at the Republican gathering in Dallas. Both political parties included disability planks in their platforms. The Democrats, for the first time, addressed disability issues in the civil rights section of their platform and the Republicans addressed disability questions in the individual rights section of their platform. At the Democratic convention, speakers with disabilities also addressed meetings of the Women's Caucus, the Black Caucus, and the Hispanic Caucus.

The first nationwide registration drive targeted at voters with disabilities was initiated recently. Grassroots efforts by local organizations to register more disabled voters are continuing. In Kansas City, Mo., a women's club registered 450 disabled people in six weeks. In Union County, Pa., 741 disabled individuals were enrolled as voters in one day. In Buffalo, N.Y., 4,500 disabled citizens registered in one month. Simultaneously, higher priority is being given in many communities to eliminating or reducing physical and architectural barriers which limit the participation of disabled people at registration and polling places. More readers for blind voters and more interpreters for deaf voters in voting booths are also becoming available, and simplified absentee ballot forms are being devised to facilitate voting by handicapped citizens.

Growing attention to potential strength of disabled persons as voters is also reflected in the legislative branch of our Federal government. Congressional committees are hearing more about the rights of handicapped Americans as more disabled persons testify and as disability issues, formerly seen as social issues in America, take on dimensions of a civil rights movement. Sen. Robert Dole (R.-Kans.), one of a dozen disabled persons in the Congress, recently observed that, "over the past three years, disabled people have become an increasingly powerful political force."

Developing changes in other sectors of American life are gradually expanding both the participation and acceptance of disabled individuals. In education, for example, integrated classrooms of non-disabled and disabled students are on the rise in our public schools. More young people today are learning about disability and growing up with disabled friends. Integrated recreational facilities and activities are increasing. In sports, the presence of competing disabled athletes in the same Los Angeles Coliseum and on the same track as non-disabled athletes during the 1984 Summer Olympic Games was another progressive step, and millions of television viewers witnessed the capabilities of disabled persons in the wheelchair races on the final day of the Games.

In churches, the traditional mentality of "taking care of" people with disabilities, long reflected in churches and their congregations, is slowly diminishing. Rev. Harold Wilke, who was born without arms and is a minister in the United Church of Christ, says the churches today are "somewhere between" the mentality of caring for disabled people and serving "with" disabled people. Because the "taking care of" mentality has been so ingrained, Rev. Wilke adds, it is difficult for churches to move from "for" to "with."

## Opportunities in the media

Disabled individuals are conquering new employment frontiers in television, motion pictures, and theatre, thanks to such groups as the Media Office of the California Governor's Committee for Employment of the Handicapped. The number of disabled performers in the entertainment media—on the screen, on the stage, and behind the scenes—has grown in the last three years. The entertainment industry today is less concerned about an individual's impairment and more about his or her talent. Just as importantly, the manner in which the entertainment media portrays disability has become more realistic. Network television programs such as "Alice," "Hill Street Blues," "Facts of Life," "Different Strokes," and "Simon and Simon" have been nominated for awards in this regard. More television programs, including newscasts, also are being close-captioned for people who are hearing-impaired. However, the major frustration of the Media Office of the California Governor's Committee, according to Tari Susan Hartman, who heads the office, is the lack of success in getting people with disabilities into television commercials, with the exception of current Levi Strauss ads.

"People with disabilities are consumers of products, but the general public doesn't see them that way—as users of soap, toothpaste, and deodorant," Hartman says. Executives of a number of major corporations say they understand this, she adds, "but when it comes down to setting company policies disabled people are not considered." Product advertisers and manufacturers point out, however, that the problem lies in the American public's negative image of disabled people, and they are reluctant to be associated with negative images in their advertising. (Recently, three major merchandising companies in Canada utilized disabled models in their merchandise catalogs and retail advertising, with successful results).

Traditionally, American society, by and large, has ignored its disabled citizens or viewed them as objects of pity, as welfare and dependent cases, as people who deserved charitable assistance, as individuals incapable of holding jobs, as people to be feared because they might be different, and/or as inferior people who had little to offer society. Disabled persons have been perceived as a hidden minority—out of sight, out of mind—and non-disabled people often have referred to them in

hushed, whispered voices. Many Americans are not comfortable around sick or elderly handicapped people, probably because they have never been around them very much, or simply because of lack of knowledge about disability.

The images of disabled people projected to society in the past would often consist of the pathetic poster child or the courageous superhero. We have all seen motion pictures portraying disabled people as, on the one hand, extremely brave, or, alternatively, emotionally unstable and desperately searching for love and acceptance. Real-life portrayals of everyday situations have been rare.

There has been little recognition that disabled people have the same rights as all other American citizens, little recognition that people with disabilities also want to be independent, respected citizens who want to be treated as ordinary people like everybody else. Above all, public perceptions rarely have taken into account the potential capabilities of disabled people to participate in American life, if given the chance, and to contribute to our society. Independence and self-sufficiency, not dependence, and expanded opportunities so they can participate more fully in and contribute their talents and skills to society are the new goals of disabled Americans. Edward Kennedy, Jr., summed it up when he told the Democratic National Convention:

. . . 36,000,000 disabled people deserve the same fundamental human rights as every other American. We have a lot to contribute to America if only America will give us a chance to make that contribution. Remember, we are people first and disabled second. We want to be participants in life, not spectators on the sidelines.

While some important and some spotty progress toward fuller participation has been made, as I have indicated earlier, the majority of disabled people remain on the fringes. Far-reaching and important laws have been passed, pushing back frontiers and opening doors, like the Architectural Barriers Act of 1968, the Rehabilitation Act of 1973, and the Education of All Handicapped Children Act of 1975. Still, laws can only do so much; they can be enforced, but along with policy changes must come attitudinal changes and acceptance. "Rights and attitudes interrelate, and even though laws exist to protect the rights of disabled people, the problem is still attitudes," notes Evan Kemp, director of the Disability Rights Center in Washington.

A number of private, nonprofit organizations and governmental bodies have contributed to the growth of fragmented progress on America's unfinished agenda.

The legislative, educational, and information efforts of private organizations such as the Disability Rights Education and Defense Fund and the American Coalition of Citizens with Disabilities have made advances. Many other private organizations which were established years ago to serve the nation's disabled people have, in the last 10 years, changed their philosophy of viewing disabled persons as charity cases. The education and job-training programs conducted for disabled people by the Easter Seal program and others to expand employment opportunities have brought progress. Independent living centers, which provide assistance to physically disabled people in locating employment, housing, and other resources, are flourishing across the country and illustrating that disabled people can lead independent lives. In governmental organizations, the work of the President's Committee on Employment of the Handicapped has helped increase acceptance of disabled people seeking jobs.

Moreover, new economic forces and the changing nature of our society portend attitudinal changes toward disabled people. Vice Pres. George Bush, in a recent speech on the technological explosion taking place in America, stated that

New technological advances will be completely altering the character of the workplace and making the full participation of the handicapped easier and easier. We have only to expand our consciousness to be prepared to accept this expansive new world. The only real stumbling block is prejudice.

## Facing the facts

As mortified as Americans are today by the memory of racial segregation and discrimination, we will, I hope, be mortified by the end of this decade by the memory of our complacent acceptance of the segregation of disabled citizens. Since society perpetuated the exclusion of disabled people through attitudes, prejudice, architectural barriers, segregated schools, etc., can society "unperpetuate" it, if I may turn a phrase? The answer most certainly is yes; changes are beginning and more will follow if several things are done.

First, the American people, when they are aware of the facts, will understand better the importance of the problem, its seriousness, and how close it is to them and their families. With straightforward information in hand, the American public usually acts wisely. Here are some of the facts I am talking about:

● If we were not born with a disability, it could happen to any one of us today. At some point in life, disability touches almost every American.

● Disability knows no ethnic, religious,

racial, economic, sexual, educational, political, geographic, or age distinctions.

● The 36,000,000 Americans today who have disabilities are of all ages—10,000,000 children, 15,000,000 men and women in their prime working years, and 11,000,000 senior citizens. The are also all colors.

● At least an equal number of family members who live with disabled persons on a daily basis also are directly affected. The "disability family" thus comprises fully a third of our population.

● The number of Americans with disabilities is increasing for several reasons. Our population is aging, and older people tend to have chronic disabilities. Close to 46% of all Americans over age 65 suffer from functional impairments, compared to 18% of the general population, and this age group is expected to increase from 23,000,000 to 32,000,000 by the year 2000. Middle-aged Americans are becoming severely disabled at an alarming rate because of drug and alcohol abuse and accidents. Americans of any age are an accident away from becoming disabled; more babies are being born with developmental disabilities because of increased abuse of alcohol, other drugs, and tobacco by pregnant women; the number of premature children born in America is increasing; and the medical management of chronic disease and disability has improved, prolonging life. Thus, as our population ages and medical technology advances, more and more people are joining the ranks of the disabled every day.

The American people also should have a few of the appalling economic facts about disability—the costs to American society for the care and support of disabled people. One dollar in every 12 that the Federal government spent in 1980 was a direct payment to a disabled person or for funding of a disability program. The majority of this Federal budget allocation goes to support programs that foster the dependency of disabled people.

Sixty-two percent of the disabled population who are able and willing to work are unemployed, compared to 10% of the general population. There are an estimated 15,000,000 disabled people of working age and approximately 10,000,000 of them do not have jobs, though most of them could work and want to do so.

In my view, the numbing human facts of disability in America and the staggering economic costs confirm the price we continue to pay for our failure to achieve a higher degree of participation in American life by disabled citizens. As far back as 1954, Pres. Dwight D. Eisenhower sounded an alarm when he said, "We are spending three times as much in public assistance care for nonproductive disabled people as it would cost to make them self-sufficient and taxpaying members of their community."

In addition to providing the American people with facts about disability, it is important for non-disabled and disabled Americans to talk to each other and get to know each other better, if attitudes and perceptions and understanding are going to improve. This happens best in the process of their working, playing, worshipping, and going about life's activities together.

Although daily experiences differ because of the varied nature of disabilities, there are commonalities. Most people with disabilities are concerned with what the majority of people take for granted. They want to travel and move about, to enter and leave a building, to attend school, to play a role in their communities. They want to go shopping, attend church, go to concerts or sports events or libraries or movie houses or visit friends like everybody else.

## Barriers

Activities such as these are part of a routine day or week for most people. They don't require a second thought. For a person with a disability, these "routine" activities can be a major undertaking or even a frustration. Much of the frustration is the result of historic and contemporary barriers limiting or preventing them from participating—architectural barriers, attitudinal barriers, educational barriers, occupational barriers, and legal barriers.

For example, just finding a place to live can be very frustrating if you happen to use a wheelchair. Washing dishes or cooking is a difficult task from a sitting position, especially in kitchens designed for people who stand while performing such tasks. Moreover, even before ever getting to the kitchen, a wheelchair user must first get through doorways which may be narrower than the wheelchair.

Understanding and enjoying movies and television are impossible for millions who have hearing or visual impairments. Going to sports events, concerts, restaurants, etc. is simply impossible or extremely difficult to manage for many unless such places have barrier-free access. Just crossing a street can be a challenge. A flight of beautiful steps leading into a church or a concert hall may look impressive, but is nothing less than a hindrance to people who are in wheelchairs, on crutches, using walkers, or have difficulty walking.

Crossing a street also can be a dangerous venture for a person who is blind, and identifying male and female public restrooms can be a difficult task.

Mary Jane Owen, a writer and editor for the President's Committee on Employment of the Handicapped, finds that "disability doesn't just blend in. For me,

having a disability means everything I do will take much longer." A typical day for Owen, who is blind, involves many extras—such as putting her toothpaste directly in her mouth instead of on her toothbrush, organizing clothing in an exact order or position, folding one dollar bills differently from fives in order to differentiate, spending extra money eating in restaurants due to the frustrations of grocery shopping, and using readers and cassette tapes on the job.

Jim Flemming, a visually-impaired executive in the Federal government, also approaches the question of what concerns disabled people from the perspective of everyday living:

We simply want to have ordinary lives. We want to be treated as ordinary, voting, taxpaying citizens, not welfare cases or people to be pitied. And we want others to recognize that we, too, enjoy going to concerts or ball games or church, and we have to go shopping for groceries like everybody else.

Flemming, now in his early 40's, began losing his sight in high school. His lifestyle, he says, has slowed down and he has become much more methodical. He uses a walking cane and his days include a lot of trial and error. He took a month to work out a system for finding his house after getting off the bus each evening. After trying several methods which ended with him on someone else's doorstep, he finally realized that there was a big tree directly across from his front door, a tree that he could make out well enough to use as a landmark. He points out that,

Since the onset of my disability, I must place limitations on others as well as myself. It's tough working with people who don't have a lot of boundaries because you pay a price to impose these limitations. You lose immediate recognition. That is, because you can't accept every task offered to you, fellow workers or superiors will think you're not as willing to work or that you're not pulling your weight. Then, when promotion time comes around you're not considered.

Both Flemming and Mary Jane Owen have found that people treat them differently now than before they had a disability. Friends avoid them because, as Owen put it, "they find it difficult to accept my imperfection—to accept my blindness as being a part of *me*." Flemming explains that

when I lost my sight, I also lost some friends. But I've gained many and better friends. It's been a slow process, partially because I am much more selective about who I want to be with. Having a disability is a gross inconvenience, but you can certainly still have valued friends, a good work experience and a good family and home life. It takes a lot of work—but it does for anyone! The inconvenience or hardship simply forces you to make choices regarding values, lifestyle and friends that you might otherwise put off.

Mary Jane adds another note: "Being blind has its positive aspects, too. I find some of the most exciting people I know are disabled; they are people who have acknowledged their disability. Disabled people who have dealt with human frailty and discovered how precious human existence is often have a special zest and enthusiasm for life."

Jim Flemming and Mary Jane Owen are right. One can learn much from people with disabilities. As one who entered the world of disability in an instant 22 years ago, I had hardly known a person with a disability. (I do recall a schoolmate with a hearing aid.) I was totally unaware of the existence of the half-billion disabled people in the world, including 36,000,000 Americans, let alone their problems, hopes, and aspirations. Starting out on my career with my education and military service behind me, and with a wife and four children under six years of age, I hadn't planned on a life in a wheelchair. Family and friends rallied round, but others, like myself before I broke my neck, were cautious in their approach and often averted their attention. The attitudinal barriers were real, I found.

What has struck me most, however, is how much more profound and deep-rooted are these barriers in countries other than the U.S. While we have a long way to go, America is far ahead of other nations in accepting disabled persons. Visiting Latin America, Western Europe, and Eastern Europe, including the Soviet Union, as a disabled person, one gains a special appreciation of the meaning of opportunity in America and of the freedom to succeed or fail. Disability is no fun anywhere, but, if one is to be disabled, America is the place to be.

From its inception in January, 1982, the National Organization on Disability (NOD) recognized that the most meaningful place to address societal barriers to greater participation of disabled people, the place to reduce prejudice and discriminatory practices, and the place to pursue opportunities for constructive change is the local community. This is where disabled and non-disabled people live, work, and interact on the most basic level of social interchange.

If the major components of a community—business, education, religious, cultural, social, political, civic, disabled, and non-disabled citizens together—could form working partnerships based on shared values, needs, and concerns, then grassroots progress on a voluntary basis is possible. That was and is the unique strategy and approach of NOD. It is based on

the proposition that, over the previous 20 years, legislative and administrative actions have contributed toward positive progress, but that local level actions are needed now to push back frontiers even further and in an enduring way.

## Progress

Since our founding, almost 1,800 communities in all 50 states have joined our partnership network. Local citizens—both non-disabled and disabled—are working together and in cooperation with NOD to widen opportunities in everyday living for the benefit of the whole community. Results are encouraging.

● In Palm Beach County, Fla., landmark legislation has recently been passed requiring that all first-floor doorways in new homes, townhouses, condominiums, and hotels must be 32 inches wide to accommodate wheelchairs (usually 27 inches wide).

● In Northampton, Mass., the community partnership group of NOD has brought to near-completion a three-year project to make the downtown area totally accessible, and polling places have been revamped after Smith College interns found that most of them were inaccessible.

● In McAlester, Okla., our local partners published a directory of services available to disabled citizens, along with tips for improving access in the city. Local cable television and radio promoted the directory, and voluntary actions were taken that have now eliminated barriers and opened new opportunities.

● In San Antonio, Tex., our community partners have established JOB-LEAD, a clearinghouse for disabled job seekers which matches job-ready handicapped persons with employers. Within its first 30 days of operation, JOB-LEAD placed 17 people in permanent jobs. Bergen County, N.J., has set up a similar job bank.

● In Suffolk County, N.Y., our local partnership group, working with gasoline and trade associations and the county government, instituted the Handicapped Gasoline Program, in which 163 gas stations participated. Mobility-impaired drivers can now pull their cars up to full-service pumps and are charged only the self-service price. Before this, disabled drivers, who can't pump their own gas at self-service tanks, could not obtain the less expensive prices. Suffolk County also has launched a Parking Education Program to educate the public about the importance of designated parking for drivers with mobility impairments.

● In Coeur d'Alene, Idaho, our community partner, the Mayor's Committee

on Employment of the Handicapped, recently completed an impressive number of hearing assistance projects, including the placement of audio loops (sound-amplification wiring which circles the top of a room) in a local school; the placement of hearing aid-compatible devices on all pay telephones; the installation of amplifier pay phones at the local hospital, shopping center, and hotel-convention center; and audio loop demonstration at several recreation facilities including the playhouse, bingo hall, square dance center, and county fair.

In addition, more group homes for mentally retarded individuals are being developed in communities, and their success is diminishing concerns about property values in neighborhoods. However, a serious concern remains over the plight of the homeless mentally ill. They are being released by psychiatric institutions into communities often ill-prepared to receive them. An expansion of community programs is required as a national imperative.

Some American cities have recently installed beeping street-crossing signals for people who are blind. An uninterrupted beep means it is safe to cross, interrupted beeps mean one should cross with caution, and no beep means it is unsafe.

So, there is action out there at the grassroots in American communities, and many of the actions are replicable by thousands of communities. Much of the impetus for this activity began when the United Nations proclaimed 1981 as the International Year of Disabled Persons (IYDP). That spawned the National Organization on Disability the following year. With a board of directors composed of both non-disabled and disabled persons, we established the private, nonprofit organization to continue the momentum of the IYDP.

Shortly after we began operations, the UN recognized that the problems of the world's half-billion disabled persons called for long-term attention and action, and the General Assembly unanimously proclaimed 1983-92 as the Decade of Disabled Persons. Congress and the President subsequently issued proclamations supporting the Decade and its goals of developing fuller participation of disabled people in American life and public acceptance of disabled people.

The Decade of Disabled Persons represents a fresh focus. Our basic values move us in the direction of its goals. As a people living in a diverse democratic society, we cherish the principle of living independent lives, and what has always counted most with us is the potential of each individual. Pursuit of that supreme value in American society is gradually producing many changes around the country. A slow and

## 4. GROUPS AND ROLES IN TRANSITION: Relabeling Movements

quiet revolution has enabled increasing numbers of disabled people to move from the stagnation of dependency into the mainstream of living. Attitudes are slowly beginning to shift into an expanding awareness that all people can play a role in the life of their communities. More individuals and groups are recognizing that America should not be handicapping itself by excluding capable people. We are learning what Lincoln knew: "The dogmas of the quiet past are inadequate to the stormy present . . . we must think anew and act anew." Improving public attitudes and broadening the participation of people with disabilities in all aspects of American life will make ours a better society for all.

# Growing Up Gay

## For young homosexuals and their parents, it is still a desperately lonely and tortured experience

ames haunt them, names scrawled in hate and fear. Queer, fairy, faggot, dyke. They know they are different. They do not always understand why. They are often terrified that their parents or friends will find out before they are ready to tell them. They think they are alone with their secret. These things have not changed. Growing up gay can still be a long and often tortured journey toward self-acceptance. But in 1986, more than a decade and a half after the gay community in New York launched the gay-rights movement from a bar called Stonewall, it is easier.

**Despite more than a decade and a half of gay liberation, acceptance for many remains difficult.**

Experts no longer define homosexuality itself as a form of mental illness. There are, in some cities, places to turn to for advice. There is an organized gay community. Doctors, clergymen and politicians are openly and proudly gay. But there is a new specter more deadly than insult or social isolation. AIDS, the epidemic that is striking so many gay men, is providing a new excuse for bigotry and has added extra weight to the burden of being young and gay.

While it is hard to be different at any age, it is especially hard to be different in adolescence, when conformity is celebrated and even minor eccentricities can mean ostracism. Yet it is often during those difficult years that gay men and lesbians first discover they are fundamentally different from their friends. "It's terrifying," says the Rev. Walter Lee-Szymanski, a gay Episcopal priest in Rochester, N.Y., who counsels gay kids. "In high school, kids call each other all sorts of names, but nothing is more mortifying than to be called a faggot."

Adolescence *can* be a brutal and confusing time. A few homosexual experiences do not mean a lifetime of homosexuality, experts say. "Adolescents get turned on by

everything," says Wayne Pawlowski, a clinical social worker who deals with gay youths in Washington, D.C. "They can have what is identified as a homosexual experience and it won't mean a lot." Adds Dr. Emery S. Hetrick, a gay psychiatrist and clinical assistant professor of psychiatry at New York University Medical School: "You're not going to make a homosexual of an adolescent who plays around." Parents may remember having some of these feelings themselves and, for that reason, are likely to respond to a child's announcement that he's gay with the question: "Are you sure?" Counseling can help families sort out their feelings about the issue, experts say, and add the important thing is not to panic. Many psychiatrists view sexual orientation as a range of feelings with most people falling somewhere in between strongly homosexual or heterosexual. The widely held belief is that, sooner or later, one sexual orientation dominates; it is not clear how or why this happens.

For those who are sure they are gay, the social pressures can be intense. Because the rewards of being "normal" are so great, many young gays keep their feelings hidden from families and friends. Eric, a college freshman in Boston, has known for years that he is attracted to men. But it is a closely held secret and the cost has been high. "It creates a total façade," he says. "I don't act like me." His fear is that by coming out he will trade his inner pain for something worse: a hostile world.

Eric's situation is not so different from that of gays in earlier generations. As recently as 40 years ago, homosexuality was the greatest of taboos. "To be accused of being gay was to be guilty," says 68-year-old Harold Call, executive director of the Mattachine Society, an early gay organization. Don Baker, now a 38-year-old gay activist in Dallas, remembers his horror some 20 years ago when, after years of feeling "different," he finally had the courage to look up homosexuality in the dictionary. "I realized I was a sick person, that I was a sinner," said Baker, who grew up in a fundamentalist church. The growth of gay activism—which many say began when gays fought police who tried to close a gay bar, New York's Stonewall Inn, in 1969—has helped, but there is a legacy of prejudice.

In many communities, it can be risky to seek such usual sources of help as school counselors or doctors. Too often, experts say, these professionals simply advise young people to "go straight," or they tell parents before the young person feels ready to do so on his own. Although there are gay congregations in several denominations, many clergymen—another source of counseling—still take the view that homosexuality is a sin and should be discouraged. Kevin Cranston, a 28-year-old Harvard Divinity School student, told a church counselor he was gay when he was 17. "He

said, 'Have you ever had sex?' I said, 'No.' 'Well, then how do you know?' he asked me. I knew. It was crystal clear. I was attracted to men. In fact, I was attracted to him. But he wanted to leave it an open question."

Such reactions can leave young gays feeling alienated and lonely. They may have trouble establishing ordinary friendships. "Kids dealing with gay feelings go through adolescence in a skewed way," says Pawlowski. Heterosexual teen-agers learn how to date and establish relationships. "Gay kids don't learn any of that," Pawlowski says. "What they learn is how to hide what they are really feeling." Girls are generally even more isolated than boys, says Joyce Hunter, a lesbian activist and social worker in New York. They have fewer resources for meeting other young lesbians than young gay men have for meeting each other. Gay women, says lesbian author Rita Mae Brown, are "an invisible segment of American society."

In recent years more services for gay youths have become available. Last year New York's Institute for the Protection of Lesbian and Gay Youth Inc. made headlines around the country with one of its most controversial programs, the Harvey Milk School, a high school for gay kids that is named after the San Francisco city supervisor and gay activist who was murdered in 1978. It was set up to help young gays and lesbians who could not adjust to public schools. Support groups have been formed in other cities. In northern Massachusetts, for example, members of Gay and Lesbian Liberated Youth of the North Shore meet weekly. John Dixon, a social worker and adult counselor for the group, says peer support "limits the isolation these kids feel."

But there is still no easy way to face parents with the words "I'm gay." Parents' reactions often follow a pattern. The initial shock or horror has been intensified by AIDS, experts say. "Parents who love their kids are terrified that this sexual orientation will lead to trouble," says Dr. Marshall Forstein, associate director of outpatient psychiatry for Cambridge Hospital at Harvard Medical School and the medical director of the Gay and Lesbian Counseling Service of Boston. Shame and grief follow, says Paulette Goodman of Washington, D.C., local president of a national group called Parents and Friends of Lesbians and Gays. Parents often "go into the closet" by denying the child's homosexuality, says Goodman, who found out that her daughter was gay five years ago. Parents mourn for lost dreams of weddings and grandchildren. Guilt is next. Mothers often ask, "What did I do wrong?" says Hetrick. "These strong feelings of guilt occur because the parents take too much responsibility for the outcome of their children."

There are new resources available for parents as well. In addition to groups such as Goodman's, there are a number of books (below) that discuss the questions parents are most likely to ask. Chief among these is: what causes homosexuality? That very basic issue is still controversial among psychiatrists. In 1973, after intense debate, the American Psychiatric Association declared that homosexuality was not in itself a mental illness. But experts are still divided on whether sexual orientation is determined by upbringing or nature. The traditional theory, that it is the result of a domineering mother and an indifferent or absent father, is now largely discounted.

# Trying to Cope: A Reading List for Parents and Gays

The heightened awareness of homosexuality in recent years has led to a growing number of books and pamphlets designed to help young gays and their parents. Some of the better ones:

**Now That You Know: What Every Parent Should Know About Homosexuality** by Betty Fairchild and Nancy Hayward (*Harcourt Brace Jovanovich. $6.95*). A primer for parents by the mother of a lesbian and the mother of a gay man. It describes, in moving but not bathetic fashion, the authors' own experiences as well as the stories of other parents and children. The book is particu-

larly illuminating—and reassuring—in advising parents that early homosexual experiences do not necessarily mean their child is gay: "Almost all boys engage in masturbation, and most in mutual sex play."

**Loving Someone Gay** by Don Clark (*New American Library. $4.50*). The author, a gay psychologist, gives advice—some of it relentlessly upbeat—on relationships among gay children, parents and friends. A divorced father of two, he has a special understanding of the pain that can be involved when a gay comes out.

**Society and the Healthy Homo-**

**sexual** by George Weinberg (*St. Martin's Press. $5.95*). A dispassionate general discussion by a well-known therapist. The book includes intriguing historical details: as recently as the 1960s, for example, psychiatrists in Britain tried to "cure" male homosexuals by administering an emetic that caused vomiting as the patient was shown pictures of nude men. The author coined the term "homophobia."

**Coming Out to Your Parents** (Parents FLAG, Box 24565, Los Angeles, Calif. 90024 or P.O. Box 15711, Philadelphia, Pa. 19103. One copy available free to those who send a

long, self-addressed stamped envelope; additional copies are 25 cents each). Published by a major parents' group, this 15-page booklet deals with important issues involved in coming out. It discusses the various stages that parents commonly go through—shock, denial and guilt—and gives suggestions for handling the situation.

**Twenty Questions About Homosexuality** (National Gay Task Force, 80 Fifth Avenue, Suite 1601, New York, N.Y. 10011. $2). This pamphlet answers such basic questions as "Is homosexuality a matter of choice?" in clear terms.

No one has yet been able to prove absolutely that there is a biological cause, either.

Some gay psychiatrists think too much attention is paid to causes. "What's really important is that one looks at the outcome, whether one can develop what might be called a normal, healthy human relationship," says Forstein. Many experts do seem to agree that sexual orientation, once established, cannot be changed. "No one has documented that a homosexual orientation is any more changeable than a heterosexual orientation," says Forstein.

One thing that can be changed, in the shadow of AIDS, is sexual practice. Initially, according to some experts, young gays often seem relatively unconcerned about the disease. "When you're a young adolescent, you feel that nothing is going to do you in," says Hetrick. Psychiatrists and counselors are stepping up "safe sex" lectures.

There is evidence that the spread of AIDS has led to a new sense of responsibility among the young. Stephen Morin, a psychologist and clinical professor of medicine at the University of California at San Francisco, has spent two years studying gay men's reactions to AIDS and has found that younger gays are more likely to protect themselves than older men, who may be more entrenched in their sexual habits.

The spread of AIDS has also made it more difficult for many young gays to come out. Antonio, 15, attends high school in a working-class section of Boston. Although he is the acting president of a gay youth group in Boston, he worries that his friends at school will find out that he is gay. "If they ever found out, I think I'd be killed in the halls," he says. "Kids here seem to have gotten the word that if you touch someone who is gay, you'll get AIDS."

The extensive publicity about AIDS has, at the same time, raised the general consciousness of homosexuality. In the long run, the resulting public knowledge may help to overcome some prejudices. It will probably never be easy to grow up gay. But with new information and resources, the painful process of family reconciliation is no longer so lonely. It is a process that never really ends. Even those parents who accept their gay offspring often believe that perhaps this is just a "phase"—despite all the evidence that it is not. Concedes Goodman: "There's always a little bit of hope."

BARBARA KANTROWITZ *with* NIKKI FINKE GREENBERG *in Washington*, PETER MCKILLOP *in New York*, MARK STARR *in Boston*, BARBARA BURGOWER *in Houston and bureau reports*

# Social Institutions in Crisis

- The Political Sphere (Articles 25-27)
- The Economic Sphere (Articles 28-29)
- The Social Sphere (Articles 30-32)

Social institutions are the building blocks of social structure. They represent the ways in which the important tasks of society are accomplished. The regulation of reproduction, socialization of children, production and distribution of economic goods, law enforcement and social control, and organization of religion and other value systems are examples of social tasks performed by social institutions.

Social institutions are not rigid arrangements; they reflect changing social conditions. Institutions generally change slowly. At the present time, however, many of the social institutions in the United States are in a state of crisis and are undergoing rapid change. The political system is ineffective; it does not generate great leaders. Public consensus seems to be the less government intervention the better. American foreign policy sometimes appears to be guided more by fear than by reason. The United States economy is on shaky ground. The management of American businesses has been blamed for the decline in productivity. Medical care in some cases is uncaring. Institutional crisis is found everywhere. Even the family as an institution is under attack. Critics of the system complain that social institutions are not meeting the needs of society. Whether this is because institutions are changing too rapidly or too slowly will continue to be debated. However, in order to appreciate how social institutions endure, it is necessary to understand the development and process of such changes.

Americans have much to be proud of in the political sphere from human rights and civil liberties to democratic processes and the rule of law. Nevertheless, the polity also has its warts, as the first three selections point out. Charles Peters focuses on a major flaw of bureaucracies that bad news is screened out as information is passed up to the top. The next article describes the special interest lobbyists who are butchering the common good in Washington. Robert Bellah calls attention to the shortcom-

ings of the populist practice of Americans joining associations to press narrow demands on government.

The economic sphere is in more trouble than the political sphere. The two articles included in this section clearly describe some of the major problems. The first describes how the middle-class dream of a house, a car, and children's college education is fading somewhat since costs are rising faster than incomes. While the previous article shows that there is a real national economic problem, Stephen S. Cohen and John Zysman analyze the causes behind it in the next article. They blame, primarily, international competition and technological changes. Their main point is that today is a time of major economic transition.

The social sphere is also very dynamic. Three major areas of interest and change are religion, education, and abortion. Walter Karp discusses the failure of schools today to teach students to think. Instead, he insists, they train students to be passive and they stifle creativity. Victoria A. Sackett examines the public opinion on one of the most divisive issues of the day—abortion. Rather than finding two opposing camps, she discovers an ambivalent public which is troubled by abortion but at the same time is concerned with freedom to choose. Finally, Paul Bock surveys the current trends among religious groups.

## Looking Ahead: Challenge Questions

Why is it important to preserve some continuity in institutions?

Can institutions outlive their usefulness?

Why are institutions so difficult to change? Cite examples where changes are instituted from the top, down, and others where they are instituted from the bottom, up. Do you see a similar pattern of development for these changes?

# Unit 5

# FROM
# OUAGADOUGOU *TO*
# *CAPE CANAVERAL:*
## WHY THE BAD NEWS DOESN'T TRAVEL UP

## Charles Peters

*Charles Peters is editor-in-chief of* The Washington Monthly.

Everyone is asking why the top NASA officials who decided to launch the fatal Challenger flight had not been told of the concerns of people down below, like Allan McDonald and the other worried engineers at Morton Thiokol.

In the first issue of *The Washington Monthly*, Russell Baker and I wrote, "In any reasonably large government organization, there exists an elaborate system of information cutoffs, comparable to that by which city water systems shut off large water-main breaks, closing down, first small feeder pipes, then larger and larger valves. The object is to prevent information, particularly of an unpleasant character, from rising to the top of the agency, where it may produce results unpleasant to the lower ranks.

"Thus, the executive at or near the top lives in constant danger of not knowing, until he reads it on Page One some morning, that his department is hip-deep in disaster."

This seemed to us to be a serious problem for government, not only because the people at the top didn't know but because the same system of cut-offs operated to keep Congress, the press, and the public in the dark. (Often it also would operate to keep in the dark people within the organization but outside the immediate chain of command—this happened with the astronauts, who were not told about the concern with the O-rings.)

I first became aware of this during the sixties, when I worked at the Peace Corps. Repeatedly I would find that a problem that was well-known by people at lower and middle levels of the organization, whose responsibility it was, would be unknown at the top of the chain of command or by anyone outside.

The most serious problems of the Peace Corps had their origins in Sargent Shriver's desire to get the organization moving. He did not want it to become mired in feasibility studies, he wanted to get volunteers overseas and into action fast. To fulfill his wishes, corners were cut. Training was usually inadequate in language, culture, and technical skills. Volunteers were selected who were not suited to their assignments. For example, the country then known as Tanganyika asked for surveyors, and we sent them people whose only connection with surveying had been holding the rod and chain while the surveyor sighted through his gizmo. Worse, volunteers were sent to places where no job at all awaited them. These fictitious assignments were motivated sometimes by the host official's desire to please the brother-in-law of the president of the United States and sometimes by the official's ignorance of what was going on at the lower levels of his own bureaucracy.

But subordinates would not tell Shriver about the problems. There were two reasons for this. One was fear. They knew that he wanted action, not excuses, and they suspected that their careers would suffer if he heard too many of the latter. The other reason was that they felt it was their job to solve problems, not burden the boss with them. They and Shriver shared the view expressed by Deke Slayton, the former astronaut, when he was asked about the failure of middle-level managers to tell top NASA officials about the problems they were encountering:

"You depend on managers to make a decision based on the information they have. If they had to transmit all the fine detail to the top people, it wouldn't get launched but once every ten years."

The point is not without merit. It is easy for large organizations to fall into "once every ten years" habits. Leaders who want to avoid that danger learn to set goals and communicate a sense of urgency about meeting them. But what many of them never learn is that once you set those goals you have to guard against the tendency of those down below to spare you not only "all the fine detail" but essential facts about significant problems.

For instance, when Jimmy Carter gave the Pentagon the goal of rescuing the Iranian hostages, he relied on the chain of command to tell him if there were any problems. So he did not find out until after the disaster at Desert One that the Delta Commandos thought the Marine pilots assigned to fly the helicopters were incompetent.

In NASA's case chances have been taken with the shuttle from the beginning—the insulating thermal tiles had not gone through a reentry test before the first shuttle crew risked their lives to try them out—but in recent years the pressure to cut corners has increased markedly. Competition with the European Ariane rocket and the Reagan administration's desire to see agencies like NASA run as if they were private businesses have led to a speedup in the launch schedule, with a goal of 14 this year and 24 by 1988.

"The game NASA is playing is the maximum tonnage per year at the minimum costs possible," says Paul Cloutier, a professor of space physics. "Some high officials don't want to hear about problems," reports *Newsweek*, "especially if fixing them will cost money."

Under pressures like these, the NASA launch team watched Columbia, after seven delays, fall about a month behind schedule and then saw Challenger delayed, first by bad weather, then by damaged door handles, and then by bad weather again. Little wonder that Lawrence Mulloy, when he heard the warnings from the Thiokol engineers, burst out: "My God, Thiokol, when do you want me to launch? Next April?"

Mulloy may be one of the villains of this story, but it is important to realize that you need Lawrence Mulloys to get things done. It is also important to realize that, if you have a Lawrence Mulloy, you must protect yourself against what he might fail to do or what he might do wrong in his enthusiastic rush to get the job done.

And you can't just ask him if he has any doubts. If he's a gung-ho type, he's going to suppress the negatives. When Jimmy Carter asked General David Jones to check out the Iran rescue

plan, Jones said to Colonel Beckwith: "Charlie, tell me what you really think about the mission. Be straight with me."

"Sir, we're going to do it!" Beckwith replied. "We want to do it, and we're ready."

John Kennedy received similar confident reports from the chain of command about the readiness of the CIA's Cuban Brigade to charge ashore at the Bay of Pigs and overthrow Fidel Castro. And Sargent Shriver had every reason to believe that the Peace Corps was getting off to a fabulous start, based on what his chain of command was telling him.

With Shriver, as with NASA's senior officials, the conviction that everything was A-OK was fortified by skillful public relations. Bill Moyers was only one of the geniuses involved in this side of the Peace Corps. At NASA, Julian Scheer began a tradition of inspired PR that endured until Challenger. These were men who could sell air conditioning in Murmansk. The trouble is they also sold their bosses the same air conditioning. Every organization has a tendency to believe its own PR—NASA's walls are lined with glamorizing posters and photographs of the shuttle and other space machines—and usually the top man is the most thoroughly seduced because, after all, it reflects the most glory on him.

Favorable publicity and how to get it is therefore the dominant subject of Washington staff meetings. The minutes of the Nuclear Regulatory Commission show that when the reactor was about to melt down at Three Mile Island, the commissioners were worried less about what to do to fix the reactor than they were about what they were going to say to the press.

One of the hottest rumors around Washington is that the White House had put pressure on NASA to launch so that the president could point with pride to the teacher in space during his State of the Union speech. The White House denies this story, and my sources tell me the denial is true. But NASA had—and this is fact, not rumor—put pressure on *itself* by asking the president to mention Christa McAuliffe. In a memorandum dated January 8, NASA proposed that the president say:

"Tonight while I am speaking to you, a young elementary school teacher from Concord, New Hampshire, is taking us all on the ultimate field trip as she orbits the earth as the first citizen passenger on the space shuttle. Christa McAuliffe's journey is a prelude to the journeys of other Americans living and working together in a permanently manned space station in the mid-1990s. Mrs. McAuliffe's week in space is just one of the achievements in space we have planned for the coming year."

The flight was scheduled for January 23. It was postponed and postponed again. Now it was January 28, the morning of the day the speech was to be delivered, the last chance for the launch

When NASA's George Hardy told Thiokol engineers that he was appalled by their verbal recommendation that the launch be postponed and asked Thiokol to reconsider and make another recommendation, he was telling them, "Don't tell me," or "Don't tell me officially so that I won't have to pass bad news along to my bosses."

to take place in time to have it mentioned by the president. NASA officials must have feared they were about to lose a PR opportunity of stunning magnitude, an opportunity to impress not only the media and the public but the agency's two most important constituencies, the White House and the Congress. Wouldn't you feel pressure to get that launch off this morning so that the president could talk about it tonight?

NASA's sensitivity to the media in regard to the launch schedule was nothing short of unreal. Here is what Richard G. Smith, the director of the Kennedy Space Center, had to say about it after the disaster:

"Every time there was a delay, the press would say, 'Look, there's another delay....here's a bunch of idiots who can't even handle a launch schedule.' You think that doesn't have an impact? If you think it doesn't, you're stupid."

I do not recall seeing a single story like those Smith describes. Perhaps there were a few. The point, however, is to realize how large even a little bit of press criticism loomed in NASA's thinking.

Sargent Shriver liked good press as much as, if not more than, the next man. But he also had an instinct that the ultimate bad press would come if the world found out about your disaster before you had a chance to do something to prevent it. He and an assistant named William Haddad decided to make sure that Shriver got the bad news first. Who was going to find it out for them? Me.

It was July 1961. They decided to call me an evaluator and send me out to our domestic training programs and later overseas to find out what was really going on. My first stop was the University of California at Berkeley where our Ghana project was being trained. Fortunately, except for grossly inadequate language instruction, this program was excellent. But soon I began finding serious deficiencies in other training programs and in our projects abroad.

Shriver was not always delighted by these reports. Indeed, at one point I heard I was going to be fired. I liked my job, and I knew that the reports that I and the other evaluators who had joined me were writing were true. I didn't want to be fired. What could I do?

I knew he was planning to visit our projects in Africa. So I prepared a memorandum that contrasted what the chain of command was saying with what I and my associates were reporting. Shriver left for Africa. I heard nothing for several weeks. Then came a cable from Somalia: "Tell Peters his reports are right." I knew then that, however much Shriver wanted to hear the good news and get good publicity, he could take the bad news. The fact that he could take the bad news meant that the Peace Corps began to face its problems and do something about them before they became a scandal.

NASA did the opposite. A 1983 reorganization shifted the responsiblity for monitoring flight safety from the chief engineer in Washington to the field. This may sound good. "We're not going to micromanage," said James M. Beggs, then the NASA administrator. But the catch is that if you decentralize, you must maintain the flow of information from the field to the top so that the organization's leader will know what those decentralized managers are doing. What NASA's reorganization did, according to safety engineers who talked to Mark Tapscott of *The Washington Times*, was to close off "an independent channel with authority to make things happen at the top."

I suspect what happened is that the top NASA administrators, who were pushing employees down below to dramatically increase the number of launches, either consciously or unconsciously did not want to be confronted with the dangers they were thereby risking.

This is what distinguishes the bad leaders from the good. The good leader, realizing that there is a natural human tendency to avoid bad news, traps himself into having to face it. He encourages whistleblowers instead of firing them. He visits the field himself and talks to the privates and lieutenants as well as the generals to find out the real problems. He can use others to do this for him, as Shriver used me, or as Franklin Roosevelt used his wife Eleanor and Harry Hopkins, and as they in turn used Lorena Hickock* to find out what the New Deal was really accomplishing. But he must have some independent knowledge of what's going on down below in order to have a feel for whether the chain of command is giving him the straight dope.

What most often happens, of course, is that the boss, if he goes to the field at all, talks only to the colonels and generals. Sometimes he doesn't want to know what the privates know. He may be hoping that the lid can be kept on whatever problems are developing, at least until his watch is over, so that he won't be blamed when they finally surface. Or he may have a very good idea that bad things are being done and simply wants to retain "deniability," meaning that the deed cannot be traced to him. The story of Watergate is filled with "Don't tell me" and "I don't want to know."

When NASA's George Hardy told Thiokol engineers that he was appalled by their verbal recommendation that the launch be postponed and asked Thiokol to reconsider and make another recommendation, Thiokol, which Hardy well knew was worried about losing its shuttle contract, was in effect being told, "Don't tell me" or "Don't tell me officially so I won't have to pass bad news along and my bosses will have deniability."

In addition to the leader himself, others must be concerned with making him face the bad news. This includes subordinates. Their having the courage to speak out about what is wrong is crucial, and people like Bruce Cook of NASA and Allan McDonald of Thiokol deserve great credit for having done so. But it is a fact that none of the subordinates who knew the danger to the shuttle took the next step and resigned in protest so that the public could find out what was going on in time to prevent disaster. The almost univer-

sal tendency to place one's own career above one's moral responsibility to take a stand on matters like these has to be one of the most depressing facts about bureaucratic culture today.

Even when the issue was simply providing facts for an internal NASA investigation after the disaster, here is the state of mind Bruce Cook describes in a recent article in *The Washington Post*:

"Another [NASA employee] told me to step away from his doorway while he searched for a document in his filing cabinet so that no one would see me in his office and suspect that he'd been the one I'd gotten it from."

It may be illuminating to note here that at the Peace Corps I found my most candid informants were the volunteers. They had no career stake in the organization—they were in for just two years—and thus had no reason to fear the results of their candor. Doesn't this suggest that we might be better off with more short-term employees in the government, people who are planning to leave anyway and thus have no hesitation to blow the whistle when necessary?

Certainly the process of getting bad news from the bottom to the top can be helped by institutionalizing it, as it was in the case of the Peace Corps Evaluation Division, and by hiring to perform it employees who have demonstrated courage and independence as well as the ability to elicit the truth and report it clearly.

Two other institutions that can help this process are the Congress and the White House. But the staff they have to perform this function is tiny. The White House depends on the OMB to tell it what the executive branch is doing. Before the Challenger exploded, the OMB had four examiners to cover science and space. The Senate subcommmittee on Space, Science and Technology had a staff of three. Needless to say, they had not heard about the O-rings.

Another problem is lack of experience. Too few congressmen and too few of their staff have enough experience serving in the executive branch to have a sense of the right question to ask. OMB examiners usually come aboard straight from graduate school, totally innocent of practical experience in government.

The press shares this innocence. Only a handful of journalists have worked in the bureaucracy. Like the members of Congress, they treat policy formulation as the ultimate reality: Congress passed this bill today; the president signed that bill. That's what the TV reporters on the Capitol steps and the White House lawn tell us about. But suppose the legislation in question concerns coal mine safety. Nobody is going to know what it all adds up to until some members of Congress and some members of the press go down into the coal mine to find out if conditions actually are safer or if only more crazy regulations have been added.

---

*See Political Booknotes, May 1981, page 58. Other articles concerned with the issues raised here: "The Shriver Prescription: How Government Can Find Out What It's Doing," November 1972; "How Carter Can Find Out What the Government Is Doing," January 1977; "Blind Ambition in the White House," March 1977; "The Prince and His Courtiers," March 1971; "Why the White House Press Didn't Get the Watergate Story," July/August 1973. The latter two are included in the fourth edition of* Inside the System *(Holt Rinehart), the foreword of which, by Richard Rovere, describes evaluation in the Peace Corps. More about Peace Corps evaluation can be found in* A Moment in History, *by Brent Ashabranner (Doubleday) and* The Bold Experiment, *by Gerard Rice (Notre Dame).* Blowing the Whistle *(Praeger) is a collection of* Washington Monthly *articles dealing with employees who speak up. Also see* The Culture of Bureaucracy, *(Holt Rinehart) and* How Washington Really Works *(Addison-Wesley).*

Unfortunately, neither the congressmen nor the press display much enthusiasm for visits to the mines. Yet this is what I found to be the key to getting the real story about the Peace Corps. I had to go to Ouagadougou and talk to the volunteers at their sites before I could really know what the Peace Corps was doing and what its problems were. I wasn't going to find out by asking the public affairs office.

But that's where most reporters go and sit all day—outside Larry Speakes's office or its equivalent throughout the government.

Because the reporters don't know any better, they don't press the Congress to do any better. What journalists could do is make the public aware of how little attention Congress devotes to what is called "oversight," i.e., finding out what the programs it has authorized are actually doing. If the press would publicize the nonperformance of this function, it is at least possible that the public would begin to reward the congressmen who perform it consistently and punish those who ignore it by not reelecting them.

But the press will never do this until it gets itself out of Larry Speakes's office. Woodward and Bernstein didn't get the Watergate story by talking to Ron Ziegler, or, for that matter, by using other reportorial techniques favored by the media elite, like questioning Richard Nixon at a press conference or interviewing other administration luminaries at fancy restaurants. They had to find lower-level sources like Hugh Sloan, just as the reporters who finally got the NASA story had to find the Richard Cooks and Allan McDonalds.

Eileen Shanahan, a former reporter for *The New York Times* and a former assistant secretary of HEW, recently wrote "of the many times I tried, during my tenure in the Department of Health, Education and Welfare, to interest distinguished reporters from distinguished publications in the effort the department was making to find out whether its billion-dollar programs actually were reaching the intended beneficiaries and doing any good. Their eyes glazed over."

I have had a similar experience with reporters during my 25 years in Washington. For most of that time they have seemed to think they knew everything about bureaucracy because they had read a Kafka novel and stood in line at the post office. In their ignorance, they adopted a kind of wise-guy, world-weary fatalism that said nothing could be done about bureaucratic problems. They had little or no sense about how to approach organizations with an anthropologist's feel for the interaction of atttitudes, values, and institutional pressures.

There are a couple of reasons, however, to hope that the performance of the press will improve. The coverage of business news has become increasingly sophisticated about the way institutional pressures affect executive and corporate behavior, mainly because the comparison of our economy with Japan's made the importance of cultural factors so obvious. And on defense issues, visits to the field are increasingly common as reporters attempt to find out whether this or that weapon works.

But these are mere beachheads. They need to be radically expanded to include the coverage of all the institutions that affect our lives, especially government. This may seem unlikely, but if the press studies the Challenger case, I do not see how it can avoid perceiving the critical role bureaucratic pressure played in bringing about the disaster. What the press must then realize is that similar pressures vitally influence almost everything this government does, and that we will never understand why government fails until we understand those pressures and how human beings in public office react to them.

# Lobbyists Go for It

**A breed of powerful and sophisticated persuaders is jousting with Congress over issues vital to America.**

They don't have to sweat out elections or answer to the folks back home but, in the end, they sometimes have more to say about what happens to the pocketbooks of Americans than many legislators.

"They" are Washington's big-time lobbyists. More talented, more aggressive and better financed than ever, this army of subtle and not-so-subtle persuaders is putting its stamp on everything from the battle over tax reform to decisions on billions in foreign aid.

The cast of characters in this high-stakes game includes powerful corporate executives, high-priced lawyers and activist volunteers—all vying for the attention and allegiance of Washington's official decision makers.

Among their ranks are some of the most prestigious names in Washington: Former members of Congress, White House aides and cabinet secretaries and millionaire "superlobbyists" such as Robert Keith Gray. They represent small businesses and major corporations, farmers, workers, the elderly—even foreign governments.

Their formidable tactics include endless streams of facts and figures, sophisticated communications networks and bank accounts brimming with campaign cash for legislative allies. If all else fails, there's always the crash program to bring grass-roots pressure to bear on a wavering lawmaker.

Says Nancy Drabble, director of Congress Watch: "Lobbyists not only influence the legislative process but sometimes they control it. They can make things happen on Capitol Hill."

## The Battle Royal

If there were any doubt about lobbyists' ability to muster power and influence in a hurry, the fight over tax reform puts it to rest. In recent days—

• Union members flooded congressional offices with preprinted postcards and buttonholed lawmakers to object to proposed taxation of employer-paid fringe benefits.

• The insurance industry stepped up a 5-million-dollar publicity campaign, airing television ads in 62 cities, urging voters to protect President Reagan's plan to tax cash values of life-insurance policies.

• State and local officials and employe groups confronted lawmakers at home and in Washington to argue against abolishing deductions for state and local taxes. California alone sent nearly 40 people to Capitol Hill to lobby against the plan.

• Professional lobbyists, anxious to protect tax breaks for their clients, swarmed hearings of the tax-writing Ways and Means Committee. Said one harried lawmaker: "We need a private elevator and a secret entrance to avoid the lobbyists."

The pressure applied on the tax-reform issue has not been all one way. From the moment the President unveiled his plan May 28, the White House began enlisting support from its coalition of business and "profamily" groups to generate support for the proposal. By the first week in June, close to 1,000 business and group leaders had been briefed by White House tax experts.

While many in the big-business community are leery about the President's plan, the National Federation of Independent Business is urging its 500,000 members to get behind the President.

But the tax battle is just beginning. Predicts Clark Clifford, a former Defense Secretary and presidential adviser: "With all the interest groups at work, before it's over lobbyists will have a substantial impact on tax reform." Adds Senator David Pryor (D-Ark.): "Tax reform will be a lobbyist's bonanza."

## Age of Opportunity

Advocates for special interests have plied their trade in the nation's capital since the founding of the Republic. But only in recent years has lobbying mushroomed into one of Washington's leading growth industries.

Today, there are 7,200 registered domestic lobbyists—more than twice as many as in 1976. Thousands more never bother to report because of vague clauses in federal disclosure laws. The real total exceeds 15,000, authorities estimate.

No one knows, for sure, just how much lobbyists spend trying to influence Congress and the bureaucracy. Estimates range to well over a billion dollars a year, dwarfing the 42 million dollars in spending reported by registered lobbyists in 1984.

In the first quarter of this year, spending of more than $400,000 was reported by such diverse groups as the National Committee to Preserve Social Security and Medicare, a direct-mail lobbying group; Common Cause, a self-styled public-interest lobby, and Gun Owners of America.

But lobbyists do more than spend money. They earn plenty of it, too. A high-powered firm will command an annual retainer of $250,000 or more. Hourly fees range up to $400 an hour. As extra incentive, some contracts include "success bonuses"—$7,000 for getting a bill introduced, $10,000 for getting it through a committee, $25,000 for passage on the House or Senate floor.

"Lobbying is a healthy and growing business. All you have to do is look at K Street to see the monuments to that fact," observes Ray Denison, chief lobbyist for the AFL-CIO, referring to a prestigious downtown corridor of glass-and-marble office buildings that house Washington lobbyists.

While lobbyists seldom get Congress to enact laws tailored exactly to their specifications, their influence in shaping legislation is substantial.

During the 1970s, liberal "public interest" lobbies rang up a string of successes on Capitol Hill on environmental, safety and consumer measures. More recently, lobbyists representing business groups have held sway, blocking prolabor legislation, blunting regulatory thrusts and gaining tax breaks for corporate America.

Reagan's 1981 tax cuts were considered a big victory for business lobbies, as was the financial industry's 1983 success in persuading Congress to repeal a law requiring tax withholding for interest and dividends.

Rated by lawmakers as among the most influential interest groups today are milk producers, who for years have fended off attempts to cut dairy-price supports; the tobacco industry, which has kept its price supports intact despite government concerns over the health hazards of smoking; home builders and realtors, who have made mortgage-interest deductions untouchable in tax-reform drives during the past decade, and American Jewish groups, which have lobbied hard for U.S. aid and diplomatic support for Israel.

But along with victories come defeats—even for the influential. Former President Gerald Ford, a board member of the Flying Tigers, an American air-cargo carrier, this year failed to dissuade the administration from giving a Japanese cargo line access to the U.S. market.

That example shows that lobbying extends well beyond Congress to key federal agencies. Currently, CBS, its local affiliates and such supporters as the United Church of Christ are besieging the Federal Communications Commission to block an attempted takeover of the network by Atlanta businessman Ted Turner.

## All-Star Cast

Washington's most-influential lobbyists come in a variety of guises, although most are lawyers, trade-association representatives or public-relations consultants. Some are full-time employes of corporations, labor unions or interest groups, while many are "hired guns" who may represent dozens of clients.

As always in the lobbying game, access is the key to success. For that reason, former government officials, with ready-made contacts in Washington's power circles, are among the most successful. The current roster includes more than 300 former lawmakers and others who once held high-level White House and cabinet posts.

Superlobbyist Gray, a millionaire many times over, was communications adviser to Reagan's 1980 campaign and

---

### When PAC's Give Money—

**Candidates for Senate who received the most money from political-action committees in 1983-84—**

| | |
|---|---|
| Phil Gramm (R-Texas) | $1,326,875 |
| Charles Percy (R-Ill.) | $1,084,988 |
| Rudy Boschwitz (R-Minn.) | $ 998,793 |
| Thad Cochran (R-Miss.) | $ 956,361 |
| Paul Simon (D-Ill.) | $ 897,395 |
| Roger Jepsen (R-Iowa) | $ 861,892 |
| Howell Heflin (D-Ala.) | $ 843,623 |
| Jesse Helms (R-N.C.) | $ 840,630 |
| James Hunt (D-N.C.) | $ 833,046 |
| Walter Huddleston (D-Ky.) | $ 805,979 |

**Candidates for House of Representatives receiving the most PAC money in 1983-84—**

| | |
|---|---|
| James Jones (D-Okla.) | $ 662,861 |
| Jerry Patterson (D-Calif.) | $ 419,438 |
| Les AuCoin (D-Oreg.) | $ 399,545 |
| Robert Michel (R-Ill.) | $ 388,896 |
| Gerry Sikorski (D-Minn.) | $ 388,627 |
| Bruce Morrison (D-Conn.) | $ 357,565 |
| Jack Fields (R-Texas) | $ 345,216 |
| Bob Carr (D-Mich.) | $ 329,666 |
| Joseph Addabbo (D-N.Y.) | $ 324,521 |
| Dan Rostenkowski (D-Ill.) | $ 321,231 |

USN&WR—Basic data: Federal Election Commission

---

cochairman of the President's first inaugural. His staff of 100 includes former government officials and congressional aides of all political stripes.

Two other major firms in Washington have multiplied their power by combining talents from both sides of the political fence. William Timmons, aide to two previous Republican presidents and allied with Reagan in the past, has hired both Democrats and Republicans as top legislative lobbyists. Members of his firm volunteer time to the Reagan administration to help shepherd appointments and legislation through Congress.

One of President Carter's highest White House aides, Anne Wexler, has joined forces with a friend of the Reagans', Nancy Reynolds, and their client list is rapidly expanding.

Another lobbying star with valuable ties is Charls Walker, a tax lawyer who chaired Reagan's 1980 tax-policy task force. Walker is assembling special interests to protect business-tax breaks he helped write into the 1981 tax-cut law.

Washington is in the blood of top lobbyist Thomas Hale Boggs, whose family has represented a New Orleans congressional district since 1947. And one of his firm's members, former Detroit congressman James O'Hara, draws on experience as former head of a higher-education subcommittee in repre-

senting the huge California state-university system. For him, the lobbying life—"being able to go sailing on weekends"—beats the congressional grind of flying back to his district every week.

Just getting started in the lobbying business is former White House counsel Michael Deaver, whose long, personal association with Reagan is almost certain to yield big dividends in lobbying influence.

## Tools of the Trade

Few of today's lobbyists fit the old caricature of a cigar-puffing backslapper. "The days when a case of wine or a trip to the Kentucky Derby took care of things are over," declares Frank Mankiewicz, a former aide to the late Robert Kennedy and now a successful lobbyist with Gray.

Today's methods are far more sophisticated as a result of the computer revolution, an explosion of complex issues and post-Watergate reforms.

Often, lawmakers take the initiative in seeking lobbyists' views. "If an interest group doesn't contact me or my staff when a new issue arises, we contact them," says Representative Ted Weiss (D-N.Y.).

The U.S. Chamber of Commerce uses computers to analyze the potential impact of proposed legislation on the economy and provides results to legislators and their staffs. The AFL-CIO, the National Association of Manufacturers and scores of other groups rely on computer networks to communicate with their members and to keep tabs on where lawmakers stand on crucial issues.

"Today, it's a technocrat's world, where the most effective lobbyists are those who can satisfy Congress's thirst for information," notes a Senate aide. Says Jerry Jasinowski, lobbyist for the NAM: "Everybody is pretty sophisticated today—you can't go in and give them a lot of baloney and get away with it."

At least in part, changes in lobbying reflect changes in Congress itself, especially the waning power of party leaders and committee heads. "After Watergate and Vietnam, they democratized the place," says Gary Hymel, a lobbyist with Gray & Company and a former top aide to House Speaker Thomas P. "Tip" O'Neill (D-Mass.). "That made the job a lot harder. Instead of dealing with one or two powerful chairmen, you now have to convince hundreds of members."

Moreover, some members of Congress are now less inclined to be swayed merely by the arguments of a high-powered lobbyist. "If you can't show you have grass-roots support behind you, it's easy for a member to deflect you," says the AFL-CIO's Denison.

As a result, many interest groups try to generate local pressure on lawmakers by communicating with the public through press releases, publicity gimmicks or paid advertisements. One recent issue of the *Washington Post*, for

## Biggest Spenders

**Political-action committees that reported the highest outlays during 1983-84—**

| | |
|---|---|
| National Conservative PAC | $19,332,000 |
| Fund for a Conservative Majority | $ 5,451,498 |
| National Congressional Club | $ 5,222,378 |
| Realtors Political Action Committee | $ 3,874,782 |
| National Rifle Assn. Political Victory Fund | $ 3,774,796 |
| Republican Majority Fund | $ 3,531,125 |
| American Medical Association | $ 3,513,763 |
| Ruff Political Action Committee | $ 3,499,272 |
| Fund for a Democratic Majority | $ 2,955,393 |
| Citizens for the Republic | $ 2,754,549 |
| National Committee to Preserve Social Security | $ 2,400,526 |
| National Committee for an Effective Congress | $ 2,381,384 |
| Campaign for Prosperity | $ 2,186,144 |
| National Education Association | $ 2,177,756 |
| National PAC | $ 2,154,447 |
| United Auto Workers | $ 2,131,847 |
| Associated Milk Producers, Inc. | $ 1,997,805 |
| United Food and Commercial Workers | $ 1,933,898 |
| Machinists Non-Partisan Political League | $ 1,865,697 |
| National Association of Home Builders | $ 1,846,987 |

*USN&WR—Basic data: Federal Election Commission*

example, carried major ads by a defense contractor, a pro-Arab lobby, a consortium of brokerage firms and a hospital group—all trumpeting viewpoints on matters before Congress.

**Gray groups.** Using an aggressive direct-mail campaign, the National Committee to Preserve Social Security and Medicare claims its 1.2 million members have sent more than 2.5 million petitions to Capitol Hill to protest proposed benefit cuts. Some lawmakers cite the highly organized groups representing the elderly as a key factor in cementing House opposition to President Reagan's plan to freeze Social Security cost-of-living allowances.

"That crowd may represent senior

## Reaching the People— High-Tech Style

Do you live in "Hard Scrabble," U.S.A., or perhaps in "Money & Brains," America?

No matter. The computer will track you down so a lobbyist can design a message especially for you—one he hopes will lure you into writing your representative in Washington.

Using polling data and sophisticated computer analysis of census tracts, special interests seeking to influence legislators are able to pinpoint neighborhoods sympathetic to their cause in every congressional district.

They blanket these neighborhoods with mailings espousing their cause, tailoring the messages to the concerns of people in those areas. Blue-collar neighborhoods receive one appeal, farming areas yet another and people in neighborhoods earmarked as affluent or educated still another.

"Typically, there are four to eight variations in mailings," explains Mi-

chael McAdams, a senior vice president of Matt Reese and Associates, a Rosslyn, Va., firm experienced in high-tech lobbying.

"In upper-scale clusters, we may put in charts and graphs," he explains. Elsewhere, the material might warn that government is about to act, because people in some areas believe that "whatever the federal government does it will screw up."

In each case, the goal is the same: To muster popular support for a lobbyist's pet cause. Natural-gas producers successfully used this selective method to locate about 500,000 people who opposed a bill that would have reimposed controls on prices at the wellhead. Many wrote or sent mailgrams to Congress, and the bill was defeated. "We can find a constituency for almost any issue," explains McAdams.

This pinpoint lobbying is made possible by a market-sampling system called PRIZM devised by statistical expert Jonathan Robbin, who has placed every neighborhood in the

nation in one of 40 categories based on income, education, lifestyle and other variables. Classifications carry such names as "Blue-Blood Estates," "Shotguns & Pickups," "Bohemian Mix" and "Coalburg & Corntown."

Robbin says the system works because people of like backgrounds and views tend to cluster in similar neighborhoods found in most parts of the nation.

Many analysts worry that high-tech lobbying manipulates public opinion and benefits special interests with lots of money to spend. But advocates contend that the new methods merely take lobbying out of the back rooms.

What's the reaction in Congress? Some members claim they ignore anything that resembles a form letter, but Representative Bill Richardson (D-N.M.) says that "when all of a sudden you see 200 people writing on an issue, even if it is a form letter, it makes an impact."

*By ALVIN P. SANOFF*

citizens, but there's nothing gentle about the threat of reprisals in their approach," observes one Capitol Hill veteran. "It's trench warfare."

Equally aggressive, say congressional aides, was the National Association of Realtors' recent campaign against new user fees on mortgages. The realtors won a five-year phase-in for the fees, giving them time to block the higher charges in future legislative sessions.

Amid all the computerized write-in campaigns, lobbyists have by no means forgotten the time-honored tool of socializing. Almost nightly, they make the rounds of cocktail parties and dinners staged to fatten campaign war chests of senators and representatives. Prices of tickets to such affairs may range from $100 to $5,000 or more.

At one recent congressional fund-raiser, lobbyists bragged that they could drop in on as many as eight events in one evening. On the June calendar: A fund-raiser for Senator Alan Cranston (D-Calif.) at the posh Georgetown home of Averell Harriman—an event organizers hoped would raise $75,000, much of it from high-roller lobbyists.

During 1983 and 1984, political-action committees, or PAC's, for special interests also pumped nearly 113 million dollars into campaigns of House, Senate and presidential candidates. Almost 75 million went to incumbents and nearly 17 million just to members of the tax-writing House Ways and Means and Senate Finance committees.

Such donations can make a difference in close races. PAC money is credited with playing a key role in the 1984 victories of Senators Jesse Helms (R-N.C.) and Paul Simon (D-Ill.).

Speaking fees, or honorariums, are another popular conduit for channeling money to lawmakers. Members of the House and Senate may accept up to $2,000 per speech, plus expenses, and up to $21,780 per year for speaking engagements. Last year, at least 50 lawmakers reached or exceeded the legal limit, giving the excess to charity.

Interest groups spending the most on speaking fees in 1984 included the tobacco industry, cable TV, outdoor advertisers, broadcasters, the food industry, stockbrokers and bankers.

Sometimes, taxpayers even pick up part of the tab for lobbying forays. In late May, dozens of lawmakers and their spouses flew at government expense to the Paris Air Show—a lavish social event where the aerospace industry shows off its latest hardware while lawmakers are wined and dined by industry lobbyists.

One influential Senate staffer, deeply involved in military matters, admits to regularly dining at fancy Washing-

## Shortcut to Success—Be a "Party Animal"?

It's not until the bureaucrats go home and the hotel reception tables fill up with shrimp cocktail and wine bottles that much of the real business of Washington begins.

Fund-raising dinners and parties on behalf of charities, cultural groups and congressional-campaign chests give lobbyists a chance to mingle with lawmakers and government officials and, if they're lucky, even press a point.

"The appearance of access is a large part of the exercise," says labor lobbyist Hall Sisson of the Communications Workers of America. "It's the ability to tell your corporate client, 'As I said to Congressman X the other evening . . .'"

Sometimes, a brief talk with a member of Congress will yield solid results. "In a social setting, a lobbyist can get past a cabinet secretary's staff and make his point face to face," comments one social organizer. "Two minutes spent that way can be worth a million dollars."

Lobbyist Pat Reuss of the Women's Equity Action League recalls that a conversation with House Minority Leader Bob Michel at a congressional fund-raiser helped save a women's program from 1981 budget cuts.

A small sampling from this spring's social calendar in Washington provides a glimpse of an important stomping grounds for lobbyists—

■ Ted Turner, now making a bid for CBS, invited some 100 legislators to a birthday party at Mount Vernon for diver Jacques Cousteau.

■ Business executives and lobbyists were quick to contribute $150 a plate for a dinner on behalf of the Second Genesis drug-rehabilitation program. The big draw: A chance to meet and talk with wives of top White House officials.

■ At the President's Dinner—a GOP prestige fund-raiser—lobbyists paid $1,500 a ticket to see the President, the First Lady and Vice President and Mrs. George Bush.

■ Corporate clients of lobbyists gave $10,000 a table to show the flag at the Democratic Congressional Dinner, that party's top fund-raising effort.

■ In May, lobbyists paid $200 a ticket at a reception that raised $100,000 for the campaign chest of Representative Timothy Wirth (D-Colo.). Another affair for Representative Jack Brooks (D-Tex.) raised about $60,000. On tap: A supper for Representative Lynn Martin (R-Ill.), sponsored by Vice President Bush, to raise $30,000. Martin played the role of vice-presidential nominee Geraldine Ferraro when Bush was rehearsing for his 1984 debate with the New York congresswoman.

One prominent lobbyist, J. D. Williams, who himself maintains a home on Capitol Hill for entertainment purposes, received 50 invitations to fund-raisers for members of Congress for the months of May and June alone.

**"Power speaks."** With so many functions to attend, some lobbyists end up working 90-hour weeks. Notes Vic Kamber, a lobbyist and public-relations executive: "New York is a town where money speaks, but Washington is a town where power speaks, and the wielding of it doesn't stop at 6 p.m."

*By PATRICIA A. AVERY*

ton restaurants with lobbyists for major defense contractors. "It's the only time available to meet with these people," he says. "I'm not going to be bought for the price of a dinner."

With so many tools and so much money, have Washington's lobbyists become too powerful? Political pollster Pat Caddell worries: "Lobbying is all about money achieving access in order to effect results. It's legal, but it holds the possibility of latent corruption."

Harboring similar fears, some on Capitol Hill want tighter restrictions on lobbyists and their financial dealings. Two bills are pending to restrict PAC contributions. Another, sponsored by Representative Charles Bennett (D-Fla.), would toughen lobbyist-registration rules and beef up enforcement. But with many lawmakers view-

ing lobbying as a free-speech right that should not be tampered with, such measures have little backing.

Instead, the feeling in Congress is that it is up to each lawmaker to make sure that Washington's paid persuaders do not violate the unwritten rules of the game. In a sharply competitive business with much at stake, an ethical slip can destroy a lobbyist's credibility and kill what he or she values most: Access.

Says Representative Weiss: "A dishonest lobbyist only misleads you once. The word gets around and the doors close.

*By JEFFERY L. SHELER with ROBERT BARR, PATRICIA A. AVERY and THOMAS J. FOLEY*

# A Lawmaker's View of Washington Arm-Twisting

Few legislators on Capitol Hill present a more inviting target for lobbyists than Representative Thomas Downey (D-N.Y.).

A member of both the House Ways and Means Committee and the Budget Committee, Downey, 36, is at the center of some of Washington's most intense battles, ranging from tax reform to Pentagon spending and domestic-budget cuts.

"It has gotten so bad that they wait for him in the halls," says Carolyn Blaydes, Downey's legislative assistant. "They know he takes certain doors, eats in certain places. They can find him if they want to."

Yet Downey says the best lobbyists know their limits. "They haven't lined up at the gymnasium yet," he says. "That would be a cardinal sin —just unforgivable."

Downey has appointments with an average of four lobbyists each day, usually to discuss tax issues. His staff handles many more lobbyists, both in person and on the phone.

"It has become unmanageable since tax reform started with the Treasury I proposal last November," says Blaydes. "I could see lobbyists 5 hours a day at 15-minute intervals. But you can't do meaningful interviews in that short a time. It's more like 20 to 30 minutes for each one, and sometimes a lot more."

**Shower of favors.** Representatives of interest groups often ply lawmakers with meals, tickets to social or sporting events and other treats. Downey's assessment: "A dinner or a ticket to a baseball game helps humanize a lobbyist—but I don't think it influences votes."

Adds the six-term congressman: "Good lobbyists never badger. If they do, members don't want to see them. A good lobbyist sees you only infrequently—and takes as little of your time as possible." Downey says skilled lobbyists not only present their own arguments but also summarize other views so a legislator is not caught unaware.

As with most members, Downey often finds lobbyists help him reach his own goals. For example, lobbyists are useful in his fight to save federal deductions of state and local taxes, which President Reagan seeks to abolish.

Such a provision would hit especially hard in high-tax states such as New York, and Downey plans to work closely with home-state lobbyists and a variety of state and local officials to defeat the proposal.

Like other lawmakers, he is bracing for an even bigger deluge of lobbyists later this year, as interest groups try to fine-tune the tax-reform proposals. Predicts Downey: "This period of time will be the golden age of lobbying. If you can walk and talk and type, you'll be employed by somebody."

*By KENNETH T. WALSH*

# Populism and Individualism

## Robert Bellah

ROBERT BELLAH is professor of sociology, University of California at Berkeley, and coauthor of Habits of the Heart.

There is a close and deep relationship between the notion of American individualism and American populism. This relationship poses opportunities as well as dangers for those who would espouse a new populist politics.

Individualism means many things and this is not the place to describe the varieties of those diverse definitions.[1] But whatever else it means, individualism implies a sense of respect for the integrity and dignity of the individual person and a belief in the efficacy of the individual's action. Thus, individualism implies the capacity of the person to act in the world, to make a difference, not only to join a movement but to start a movement. From Rosa Parks who refused to move back in the bus to the founder of MADD, we have many examples, even in our recent history, of individuals who have had a significant political impact on our society. Indeed, the model of the individual with a concern who then reaches out and finds other individuals who share that same concern, and who together can make some change in the world, is close to the heart of the politics of empowerment. And that empowerment is exemplified by the self-help and quality-of-life movements. The vigor of these movements serves to demonstrate that the long-standing American tradition of voluntarism is still very much alive.

The proclivity of Americans to join voluntary associations was first noted by Alexis de Tocqueville 150 years ago, and that proclivity continues, according to recent research. Even today it is stronger than in most other advanced industrial societies.[2] But the strength of our voluntarism, which is perhaps just another name for "populism," seems to be positively correlated with the concurrent weakness of our political parties. For example, in many other industrial societies with less involvement in voluntary associations than ours, there is a concomitantly higher participation in political parties on the part of ordinary citizens. We could interpret this fact as an indicator of flexibility and openness in American politics as compared to societies where established political parties actually dominate. But it might be more useful to take it as a basis for some self-critical reflections about the limitations of our individualistic, voluntarist, populist politics. Populist politics, in good part because of its individualistic component, tends to be discontinuous, oriented to single issues, opportunistic, and therefore easily coopted, local, and anti-institutional. As a result it is difficult to sustain pressure over time for the attainment of principled political ends.

Populist politics suffers from the general problem of American voluntarism, namely that it depends on the moment-to-moment feelings of individuals to make it work. As a New Mexico activist, expressing his political motivation, said to Robert Coles, "I am in the struggle because it means a lot to me. It's where I'm at."[3] Such personal motivation may bring excitement and vitality to politics but it is also fragile and volatile, A new enthusiasm may lead the activist to espouse an oriental religion, or even to decide that making money is really more exciting than politics. What is missing is commitment to principles in a social context, where one can count on others to be similarly commited so that together it will be possible to sustain long-term political engagement.

When an individual is propelled into political action on the basis of some immediate impulse it is likely that political concern will not extend beyond the single issue that has aroused the impulse. Often the impulse arises from some interest. The pursuit of interest is a legitimate aspect of democratic politics. But narrow interests must be tempered and balanced against the interests of others before the common good is served.

Tocqueville believed that the very process of participation in public life tended to educate people beyond their narrow interests. When citizens take part in public affairs, he said, they "must turn from the private interests and occasionally take a look at something other than themselves. . . . At first it is of necessity that men attend to the public interest, afterward by choice. What had been calculation becomes instinct. By dint of working for the good of his fellow citizens, he in the end acquires a habit and taste for

From Social Policy, Fall 1985, pp. 30-33. SOCIAL POLICY published by Social Policy Corporation, New York, New York 10036.

serving them."[4] But often this does not occur.

Where the reason for entering politics is too narrowly focussed, involvement may be quickly extinguished before the educational process has had a chance to begin, and this can be the result of success as much as of failure. The parents who are incensed because their child must cross a dangerous intersection on the way to school lose interest in civic politics when they and their neighbors succeed in pressuring the city to put in a traffic light. Or they lose interest because they do *not* succeed—"you can't fight city hall."

Sometimes the narrowness of single-interest politics is not due to self-interest at all. Rather, it may arise from the personalization of an issue about which an individual feels strongly. For example, sympathy with whales or with unborn fetuses may so dominate the political motivation of individuals that they simply do not see other issues or the place of the issue that most concerns them in some larger whole. Single-interest politics lends itself to opportunism and cooptation whether deriving from self-interest or sympathy. The person concerned with a single issue tends to give his or her support to the politician who does something actual, or perhaps only symbolic, in favor of the issue in question, even though the politician might not on some larger political view deserve support at all.

Where political involvement derives largely from an immediate impulse of interest or sympathy, it is likely to remain local in scope. It is a problem that is visible in one's neighborhood or locality that galvanizes us into action. Often this is seen as "getting involved" for the good of the community rather than as politics. One wants to "make a difference" in the life of one's community, and usually in a quite tangible way. So one works with the YMCA in helping them raise money to provide new recreational facilities for needy Mexican-American children. Or one helps the Kiwanis Club in its effort to provide a free optometry clinic for senior citizens. Or one joins the PTA in order to try to improve the local school.

Activities of this sort involve face-to-face cooperation with people one knows and understands. Conflicts may develop but they are seldom irreconcilable. But if "outside interests" are involved, local politics can become ran-

corous. Developers seek to preempt the last remaining open space in a community. The city proposes to locate a new housing project nearby that would bring in people whose social class or racial background are seen as posing a threat to the neighborhood. The state is planning to put a freeway right through the middle of a residential area. Under these circumstances, "concerned citizens" can become involved in bitter political battles. Yet they are likely to see themselves as resisting "politics" more than engaging in politics, for they see politics as the quasi-illegitimate things that professional politicians do in governmental bodies, often representing "special interests."

Localism is the strength of individualistic populist politics: people are

---

**The strength of our voluntarism seems to be positively correlated with the concurrent weakness of our political parties.**

---

participating in the processes that directly affect them. But localism also has serious weaknesses. Few significant problems in modern society can really be solved at the local level. Decisions of large corporations, national and international market forces, actions of federal and state governments can seldom be controlled at the local level. Yet it is very difficult for people who have "gotten involved" at the local level to see themselves as political actors in these larger arenas. Indeed they actively resist such involvement. Their suspicion of "politics" is one of the reasons they got involved. They tend to be resolutely anti-institutional; but it is large institutions that must be confronted and altered if political change is to be effected.

A degree of anti-institutionalism, in the sense of dissatisfaction with the way existing institutions are operating, may be effective in mobilizing people for political action. But where anti-institutionalism becomes a pervasive orientation, as it does in the ideology of American individualism, it hinders the development of the counter-institutions that are the only vehicles for substantive change. Indeed, no politics beyond the level of spontaneous pro-

tests can exist without some degree of institutionalization.

## POPULIST POLITICS AND INSTITUTIONS

It could be argued that the social movement is the form which Americans have characteristically used to reconcile their anti-institutionalism with only the necessary degree of institutionalization. The social movement is an ad hoc response to a social issue. It is flexible and spontaneous in its organization. It lasts as long as the issue that brought it about, and then it fades away. Sometimes its successes are major: for example the civil rights movement or the movement against the Vietnam War. One could argue that the very volatility of the social movement gives a spasmodic quality to reform politics. With each new issue we start almost from scratch and have to reinvent politics, as it were. Yet the point I would like to make is somewhat different. American politics, even the politics of the social movement, is never as anti-institutional as our ideology would lead us to believe. Indeed, for good sociological reasons, it could not be.

Let us take the civil rights movement as an example. It may have been the individual action of Rosa Parks that ignited the fire, but there would have been nothing to ignite if there had not been a long history of institutional preparation. Decades of careful legal work by the NAACP were an essential precondition. The existence of the Black church, the largest institutional complex under autonomous Black control, was even more indispensable. Out of these churches came a number of well-organized associations such as the Southern Christian Leadership Conference. White churches and synagogues provided the allies without whom the movement could not have succeeded. Other long-standing organizations such as the ACLU also made significant contributions. It is interesting to note that the movement against the Vietnam War was indebted to the civil right movement in that it drew not only from the enthusiasm and organization of that movement itself but also from its institutional basis, especially the churches.

These examples of recent populist movements show how they transcended the limitations of radically individualist populism. I would argue that it was

## Populist politics tends to be discontinuous, oriented to single issues, opportunistic, and therefore easily coopted, local, and anti-institutional.

their institutional basis that allowed them to overcome, to the degree that they did so, the volatility, opportunism, and localism that often plague populist politics. What the institutions provided were principles and the loyalty of others committed to those principles.

Principles make it possible to test the emotions that prompt individuals to engage in political action. In the white churches, for examples, there was a real struggle over whether segregation was in consonance with Christian belief. Many whites who had accepted segregation came to see that their views were mistaken. (We should not forget, of course, that some white churches provided support to those who opposed the civil rights movement.) Principles also help to overcome the single-issue myopia that has often characterized the social movement as well as local populist politics. Martin Luther King, Jr., because his Christian principles extended beyond his loyalty to his own racial group, could not speak out against injustice at home and at the same time keep silent about the horrors of a war in Vietnam, even though some of his political advisors thought the linkage unwise. Institutions, civic organizations, and especially churches provide the continuity that populist politics otherwise lacks. It is institutions that provide the principles that make for sensitivity to issues and the loyalty of ongoing membership that again and again are the indispensable resources for successful social movements.

It is interesting that in our discussion of the institutional basis of populist politics we have not mentioned political parties. In the examples cited, political parties were not absent but they were not central either, until late in the day. It is true that the Democratic party had a civil rights plank in its platform since its 1948 convention, but it neither led the movement nor, despite legislative majorities, did it make significant

changes in the laws until the movement itself had gained enormous popular success. Some Democratic politicians began to oppose the Vietnam War early on, but it was not until 1972 that the party in principle opposed the war, by which time public opinion was overwhelmingly against it.

Why do American political parties so often come in on the coat tails of successful popular movements rather than leading them? I think it is because they are primarily parties of sentiment rather than principle, and because they are not membership organizations that sustain the loyalty of their members. Aside from rather vague orientations of sentiment—the Republicans are the party of "things are alright as they are" and the Democrats are the party of "things could be better than they are"— our political parties are as volatile and opportunistic as our most individualistic local politics.

For the most part, our parties are local, the local followings of local office-holders or office-seekers, more concerned with election or re-election than any consistent principle. Our national parties are congeries of local leaders and their followers rather than organizations composed of active members dedicated to principles and loyal to each other as supporters of those principles. Party politics then suffers from the same individualism that populist politics does, though it takes somewhat different form. Party politics is particularly vulnerable to the cult of personality. This has always been important in America but has become even more so in the era of television.

When one thinks about third parties the situation is not much different. Most third parties have arisen from temporary emotional issues and have evaporated as fast as they have appeared. One would have to go back to the period before World War I to the Populist and Socialist parties to find significant American third parties that sustained continuity, devotion to principle, and the loyalty of active membership.

We have not had for many decades in America anything like a Labor party or a Social Democratic party or a Christian Democratic party, that could provide sustained leadership toward well-understood ends. Such parties are not without their difficulties in the world today but we are without their virtues.[5]

## The social movement is an ad hoc response to a social issue. It lasts as long as the issue that brought it about, and then it fades away.

It is because the political parties have not provided the institutional basis for a principled politics that the churches and their associated religious organizations have been so consistently central. Though the churches too have been seriously penetrated by our individualistic ideology,[6] they are among the few places where that ideology is effectively resisted.

Though individualism provides much of the vibrancy of populist politics, it can cause serious problems unless tempered by the resources that only on-going institutions can provide, particularly ethical principles and loyalty. In *Habits of the Heart*, there are examples of individuals whom we could call heros and heroines of everyday life, who are dedicated to the common good and joyful in their dedication. Most of them have found an institutional context that sustains them when things do not go well. Some of them had parents or grandparents who, through their religious or political dedication, serve as exemplars. Many of them have a sense of larger relationships and longer time spans than American politics usually encourages. They work in organizations like the Campaign for Economic Democracy, the Institute for the Study of Civic Values, or through committees of their local congregation or parish.

We found that people who had found a vital institutional context were stronger individuals not weaker ones. For example, Mary Taylor, a member of the California Coastal Commission with whom we talked, found in her family and the network of people concerned with environmental issues the strength to deal with sustained political commitment under sometimes trying conditions: "Of course I feel lonely. I would be lying if I said I didn't. People who are willing to love are always going to be lonely—that's what you are going to have to cope with. I'm lonely all the time. It goes with the territory."[7] But Mary Taylor has no interest in being a martyr. What keeps her going is the sense that she is contributing to making our society better for the long haul, and the loyalty and support of those who share her concerns.

Populist politics, then, if it is to resist the diffusion that radical individualism imposes on it, must find the principles and institutions that can sustain continuity and coherence. Only strong civic and religious organizations create the possibility for the emergence of social movements that will address the great questions before us.

## NOTES

[1] On some of the forms of American individualism, see chapters 2 and 6 of Robert N. Bellah, Richard Madsen, William M. Sullivan, Ann Swidler, and Steven M. Tipton, *Habits of the Heart: Individualism and Commitment in American Life* (Berkeley: University of California Press, 1985).

[2] See, among many studies, Sidney Verba, Norman H. Nie, and Jae-on Kim, *Participation and Political Equality: A Seven Nation Comparison* (New York: Cambridge University Press, 1978).

[3] Robert Coles, "Civility and Psychology," *Daedalus*, vol. 109 (Summer, 1980), p. 140.

[4] Alexis de Tocqueville, *Democracy in America*, trans. George Lawrence (New York: Doubleday, Anchor Books, 1969), pp. 510, 512.

[5] See, for example, Steven Lukes's analysis of the British Labor Party in "The Future of British Socialism?" *Dissent* (Spring, 1985).

[6] See chapter 9 of *Habits of the Heart*.

[7] *Habits of the Heart*, p. 194.

A generation raised with great expectations of the good
life has found that its reach exceeds its grasp. The American
dream—a house, a new car, a college education—is getting
harder to afford. The struggle is on for new ways to cope

# Middle-class squeeze

■ *"I have three college degrees, and I make less than a public-school teacher," says Kimberly Quintero, editor of a 6,600-circulation weekly newspaper in Gilbert, Ariz. She would rather be a stay-at-home mother, but she and her husband Joseph, a customer-service representative for Premier Industrial Corporation, need their joint income of about $35,000 to support their four children.*

*"My $225 car payment is more than my parents' mortgage payment," laments Barbara Stevens, 30, who earns $30,000 as a media buyer at a Los Angeles advertising agency. She owns a 1985 Volkswagen Jetta; her parents own a four-bedroom house with swimming pool in San Marino, an affluent Los Angeles suburb.*

*Desmond Moody, 24, was graduated from the University of Massachusetts with an economics degree two years ago. He'd like to work in banking or finance but can't break in. As an assistant manager in a Cambridge, Mass., photocopying store, he earns $260 a week. "College just wasn't the big ticket my parents and I expected it to be," he sighs. Most humiliating to him, he has had to move back home with his parents.*

America's middle class is in a fix. After decades of rising living standards, many in the middle now find they're clambering up a descending economic escalator. They are having a harder time than ever buying houses and cars. Despite the Reagan income-tax cuts, total taxes are taking a bigger chunk of family incomes than they once did. When all the bills are tallied and infla-

tion is accounted for, a typical middle-class family actually has *less* money to spend these days than it did more than a decade ago. Says social critic Alvin Toffler, author of *Future Shock*: "It has become clear that it's not all onward and upward."

**A receding economic tide**

Unlike earlier decades of expansion—when all it took to be upwardly mobile was to be lifted by the generally rising economic tide—members of today's middle class find they must work more to wind up with less. A generation raised with great material expectations has discovered there's a big gap between its reach for more satisfaction and what is within its grasp. Relief isn't in sight. Tax reform, which once held the promise of easing the burden, now seems likely to benefit middle-income individuals only slightly—if at all. Consumers also are burdened with a record amount of installment debt.

Some experts insist that Americans never had it so good but just don't realize it. More people attend college, start new businesses, own second cars and second homes and buy luxury items such as sailboats and snowmobiles. The problem, they suggest, lies not in people's wallets but in their minds. "The upper boundaries of desires have climbed, and that's changed the criteria for what it takes to stay in the middle class," argues author and political scientist Ben Wattenberg. "People are straining because they're buying more things than they used to—spending more for college educations for their children, videocassette

recorders, home computers, European vacations."

But if things are really so swell, why are so many feeling squeezed? In large part, it is because things have gone sour. The sputtering stop-and-go economy of the last 13 years has included several steep recessions and an extended bout of severe inflation that pushed up the cost of such basics as housing, food, transportation, medical care and college education. Interest rates climbed into the double digits. Inflation has recently subsided, easing family-budget pressures. But an equally ruinous deflation now is racking key industries such as farming, energy and mining.

The spotty nature of the present recovery—where some sectors and regions are thriving while others are in the throes of recession and even depression—contrasts sharply with the more homogeneous economic landscape of the 1950s and 1960s.

Although the nation is in the middle of a sustained economic recovery, by almost all statistical measures, keeping up is harder to do in the 1980s. Consider the standard symbol of achieving the American dream: Owning a home. Housing-price jumps now outpace wage gains, and even with the recent drop in interest rates, the mortgage bite is substantially bigger than it was in the 1960s and 1970s. A typical 30-year-old male who bought a median-priced house in 1984 would have to devote 44 percent of his gross monthly income to carrying charges, compared with 21 percent in 1973.

Putting aside enough for a down payment is an even greater impediment for would-be home buyers who might be willing to allocate the required portion of their monthly income to own a residence. Between 1970 and 1985, a 20 percent down payment on the average-priced new home has nearly quadrupled, rising from $5,320 to $20,160.

Other costs also strain middle-class-family budgets. Education at a private, four-year college consumed about 40 percent of the median family income last year, compared with 30 percent in 1970. Buying the average-priced car cost 23 weeks of pay, up from 18 weeks a decade ago.

While such expenditures might be considered discretionary, individuals over the last two decades have had no choice but to pay a lot more to Uncle Sam because of the federal government's growing reliance on individual-income and Social Security taxes as sources of revenue. The median-income, four-person family paid $4,570 in federal income and Social Security taxes in 1984. That's 542 percent more than in 1965, according to Joseph Minarik of the Urban Institute. During that same period, median family income grew by 280 percent, to $26,433, or about half the growth of the tax bite.

**Slim pickings from tax reform**

The effective tax rate for the same family rose from 10.2 percent in 1965 to 17.3 percent in 1984. That was somewhat below the 1980 rate of 18 percent, reflecting tax cuts under the Reagan administration. But it now looks as if middle-class taxpayers won't benefit very much from the sweeping proposal currently before Congress to overhaul the country's tax system.

Despite a lot of ballyhoo that reductions in individual tax rates will put significantly more money in consumer pockets, the gain in after-tax income in 1988 will amount only to about 1 percent for individuals earning between $20,000 and $100,000, according to estimates by the congressional Joint Committee on Taxation. "The average taxpayer would realize a cut of a few hundred dollars a year or from $5 to $10 a week," says Stephen Buschel, a tax partner with Seidman & Seidman. And the shift to only two individual tax brackets, as is proposed in the Senate's version of the tax-reform bill, will mean someone with $30,000 in taxable income will be paying the same marginal rate as someone earning $300,000 or $3 million.

As all these different expenses pile up, families have had less money available to meet them. Real family income has declined for most of the 25 million families that earn from $15,000 to $35,000 a year. From 1973 to 1984, families' median income, measured in constant dollars, fell 6 percent, compared with a 23 percent gain from 1965 to 1973. Helping to drag down median income has been a change in family

## Trying to make ends meet: What seven say

The American dream of a better life can still be achieved, but millions of people are finding that it isn't as easy as they'd hoped it would be. Some of what's making it tougher can be seen from the lives of individual Americans. They are taking cuts in pay at new jobs, trying to stretch income to buy what costs more, discovering that today's lifestyles create new family needs, paying higher taxes for Social Security, making do with older cars and living in apartments rather than their own homes. Here's how a handful of Americans from all parts of the country feel about getting by in the 1980s—

**Cindy Nagy, 25, of Livonia, Mich., lost a union job and now gets less as a word processor**

"Now you get a job and get laid off, get another job and get laid off again. Job security just isn't there any more. I'm single, and I don't know how people with families make it."

**New graduate Marc Fleischer, 30, of Houston must begin repaying college loans soon**

"I got my college degree, but doing it meant I had to go into the hole $5,000 in student loans—and I'm still sending out résumés. I don't think that's the ideal way to start out."

**Detroit psychologist Steven Baum, 32, finds it hard to make ends meet on $40,000 a year**

"One of the realizations I had is that I can't afford to live like my parents. I have a hard time saving. I just thought it wouldn't be as difficult as it is to be a success."

**San Francisco professor Alan Heineman, 42, needs two incomes to afford the good life**

"We make between us a sum I wouldn't have imagined in my wildest dreams 15 years ago, but it doesn't bring very much. After private school for our son, there isn't a whole lot left."

**James Corter and wife Lisa Church, both 32, of New York can't find a home they can afford**

"I'm outraged that two professional incomes can't afford more than a postage stamp for a home. It seems a false sense of well-being if you can't have a decent place to live," Church says.

**Bianca Miller, 33, of North Hollywood, Calif., pays $240 a month in Social Security taxes**

"I'm angry about the amount taken out of my paycheck because I'm not going to get any of it. People are led to believe it's going to be there when they retire, but I don't think it will be."

**Brenda Newton, 28, of Chicago can't buy a new car on what she earns at an animal shelter**

"I'd love to get a new car, but they're so expensive. Being a college graduate, I thought I'd definitely be in the bucks. It hasn't turned out that way."

structure. Soaring divorce rates, for example, have created many more family units with lower incomes. Among married couples, family income has dropped 3 percent after inflation in the last 11 years, compared with a 31 percent gain between 1964 and 1973.

Real wages have also been a downer. They haven't grown as fast since 1973 as they did in the previous two decades, when baby-boomers' expectations of future prosperity were shaped. From 1973 to

1985, real hourly wages sank an average of 0.9 percent a year, compared with an increase of 1.6 percent a year from 1965 to 1973.

More-optimistic analysts dismiss these gloomy statistics, claiming that the true measure of prosperity is per capita personal income, which registered a 21 percent gain between 1975 and 1985 after subtraction for inflation. But those individual gains aren't reflected in the median-family-income figures because of the addition of so many low-income households. Most people base their perceptions of well-being on what they can buy as a family unit, not as individuals.

The disheartening economic picture looks bleak enough, but career blockage makes matters worse. "There are so many of us that you get to a certain point on the career ladder and there's nowhere else to go," complains Detroit social worker Carol Campbell, 32. It's no wonder she feels crowded. The number of 25-to-34-year-old workers leaped 61 percent between 1965 to 1975 and an additional 47 percent from 1975 to 1985. An oversupply of people competing for a limited number of jobs, raises and promotions is the bane of the baby-boomers. Landon Jones, author of *Great Expectations: America and the Baby Boom Generation,* has dubbed them the generation "doomed to wait in line."

Many union workers, who usually hold some of the highest-paying blue-collar jobs, are finding their prospects dimming. U.S. companies, trying to keep up with foreign competitors, are holding the line on wage settlements. Pay hikes in the first year of new contracts haven't kept up with inflation during the 1980s. In 1986, these pay increases are averaging 1.2 percent, compared with an inflation rate of 2.4 percent. At the same time, union members are a declining portion of the work force. America's 18.3 million union members were 19.4 percent of nonfarm workers in 1984, down from 20.9 million, or 29.6 percent, in 1970. While the U.S. economy has added 10.6 million jobs since the start of the 1980s, these are overwhelmingly in service industries, which are not highly unionized. "We had job creation, but the new jobs have been disproportionately in the low-wage sector," says Boston College economist Barry Bluestone.

Robert Toboy, 34, earned $30,000 as a production supervisor until Stroh's Brewery closed its Detroit plant in 1985. Now, he works at a Heublein distillery for $6,000 less and tries to bridge the income gap by working more hours. "I'm probably putting in three times the overtime I worked at Stroh's," he says.

## Draconian decisions

With less money to go around and fewer high-paying jobs available, individuals have been making some dramatic choices to maintain their living standards. The most obvious—and the most dramatic—change is that more married women are working, even though some would prefer not to. In 54 percent of married couples, both spouses work, up from 33 percent two decades ago. The percentage of working mothers with children under age 6 has risen to 54 percent from 39 percent in 1975.

Valerie Straight, 30, of Medina, Ohio, left her $24,000-a-year nursing job last spring after having a baby. Her husband David earns about $50,000 as a marketing manager for a health-maintenance organization. The couple thought they could manage on one income, but they're starting to feel the pinch. "Two people have to work to have any luxuries or even just to meet the bills," says Valerie, who is planning to return to work soon.

Other couples, like the Stowerses of Elberton, Ga., say tight finances influence their family planning. "We waited nine years to have a child," says Ray Stowers, 34, a traffic manager for Martin Fireproofing, a local firm. Their daughter is 6 and probably will be an only child. The cost of child rearing and the potential loss of his wife's income as a hair stylist are powerful deterrents to having another child.

Jack Luthermann, 36, a computer analyst in Hingham, Mass., feels the same way. "It really shouldn't be that with two parents working, having one child should prevent you from owning a home or taking a vacation," he says. "But that's the way it is, unfortunately. We got angry about it more than once." Jack and his wife Peggy, who earn $75,000 between them, have a 6-year-old daughter and worry that a second child would stretch their financial resources too tightly.

Parents who thought their years of helping offspring were over were mistaken. More adult children are coming home to live. Last year, more than 19 million, or 28 percent, of young adults age 18 to 34 had come back or had yet to leave their parents' home. That's up from 13 million, or 27 percent, in 1970. The tight job market, the rise in the divorce rate and high housing costs are among the reasons, says Census Bureau analyst Arlene Saluter. In addition, people are getting married later. The median age for first marriages is 25.5 for men and 23.3 for women, compared with 22.8 for men and 20.6 for women in 1965.

These adaptations have their own costs. When both parents are away at work, someone else must care for the children, prepare meals and perform lots of other routine household tasks. These families may be pulling in more money, but more is also being spent. The net result is that saving isn't appreciably easier for many two-income families. "Things that never used to be bought have been turned into commodities," points out Toffler. "We're putting dollar signs on them. When you do that, you have to have more money to participate."

## Cash: No longer customary

Spending habits are changing along with family patterns. Paying cash for everything is a bygone custom. "I have something better than cash; I have credit," says Tom Popieski, 28, a bank manager in Oil City, Pa., who earns $15,500. "You need a refrigerator, you go out and buy one and pay $20 a month on it for a while." Rising interest rates didn't stem the credit binge. Not counting mortgages, the average household after inflation owed $6,166 to banks, retailers and other creditors last year, compared with $4,695 in 1975 and $4,070 in 1965. At the same time, average bank credit-card interest rates jumped to 18.69 percent, up from 17.31 percent in 1980. Consumer interest deductions will almost certainly be eliminated in the pending tax bill, making it more expensive to finance the purchase of automobiles and other big-ticket items.

However, many Americans aren't going into hock just to finance cars and appliances as they did in the old days. Millions of people, perhaps frustrated by their inability to buy two-bedroom condominiums, try to marginally improve the quality of their day-to-day lives with electric coffee grinders and compact-disc players. Grey Advertising recently identified the "ultraconsumers," who "want the best and want it right now. They expect and feel they deserve more." Although most ultras have annual household incomes of $25,000 to $40,000—only 1 in 20 of them earn more than $75,000—their purchases are based on a feeling of entitlement, not what they have in their bank accounts.

## Uneven distribution of wealth

The middle-class squeeze isn't uniform. The people at the top are getting richer and the poor are becoming poorer, according to a recent study by the Congressional Research Service. The richest 20 percent of the population has 43 percent of the income, up from a 40 percent share in 1967. The poorest 20 percent of the population has nearly 5 percent of the income, down from a 1969 peak of almost 6 percent. The middle 60 percent of Americans had 52 percent of the income, the same as in 1947, but down from its 54 percent peak in 1966.

The winners and losers within the middle class cross many regional, occupational and demographic lines. "Manufacturing is clearly going down the drain," says Harvard University sociologist Daniel Bell. "Farming is declining. The black community is split—one third of it does very well, two thirds of it, mainly households headed by females, does very badly. The Southwest is obviously hurting very badly because of oil and energy. The Northeast is doing very well.''

The elderly are faring well. And so are people who bought real estate before prices soared. "In the early '70s, you could still get 6 and 7 percent mortgages," says economist Richard Peach of the National Association of Realtors. "People bought a home for $30,000 and sold it for $200,000. Those who reaped the benefit of that inflation are set for life.''

Well, almost set. Those with children still have to worry about educating them. Average college costs will rise 6 percent this year, much faster than the inflation rate. Tuition, room and board and other expenses at public and private colleges almost doubled in the last five years, while federal aid to college students declined 10 percent. At Northwestern University in Illinois, tuition and room and board will set students and parents back $14,915 this year, compared with $6,166 in 1976. Millions of recent graduates have entered the working world laden with debt. Professional couples may rake in lots of money, but they pay a price. They barely have time to do anything else. "Time is the ultimate commodity," says psychiatrist Donald Bloch, director of the Ackerman Institute for Family Therapy. "When you try to combine career, family and social life, the butter is spread too thin on the bread.''

For many manufacturing workers, making do is a fact of life. More than 11 million of them lost jobs between 1979 and 1984, and half of the workers who found new jobs took pay cuts, says

the congressional Office of Technology Assessment.

Under two-tier union contracts, recently hired workers may never get a crack at the kind of wages being earned by employes who have more seniority. Kim Daily, 25, is a United Airlines stewardess earning the lower-tier wage. Her base salary is $1,000 a month, $400 to $500 less than an "A scale" stewardess. Daily flies extra flights to pick up cash. Her contract says she'll earn the higher rate after five years, but she's not so sure. "I was hired with about 1,000 brand-new people, and I'm afraid the company thinks that these young people will settle for a permanent B scale," she says.

**Bind for single mothers**

Of all the groups struggling to stay in the middle class, single mothers feel the most pressure. Families headed by women are three times more likely to live in poverty than are other families, says the Census Bureau. Maria Ramirez, 32, a separated mother of two, works as a secretary in New Bedford, Mass. Monthly rent of $550 for a one-bedroom apartment consumes much of her $308 weekly salary. After paying for child care, food, clothing and doctors' bills, "there's absolutely nothing left. I mean nothing. *Nada.*" She walks 35 minutes to work to reduce upkeep expenses on the 1979 Toyota she bought two years ago for $400. Her uniquely American dream of upward mobility: "I play the lottery every week, and then I say a prayer.''

A return to a healthier, faster-growing economy is probably the best pray-

er middle-class people have to climb out of this predicament. "If we make the heroic assumption that the turmoil we saw in the 1970s and early 1980s doesn't recur in the next 10 years—no shocks—then there's some reason to believe that we'll get back on a path of long-term growth," predicts economist John Hagens of Chase Econometrics. The bulk of the baby-boomers have already gone into the work force, promising relief from demographic pressures. One sign of things to come: Many firms that rely on teenage employes encountered a labor shortage this summer. Moreover, the baby-boomers are entering their prime working years, promising more gains in productivity and an expansion of real income.

Meanwhile, Americans are maintaining their resilience, even though the economy is beginning to stall. A recent *U.S.News*-CNN-Roper Organization poll of 1,003 people found that most Americans think there are more opportunities today than in the past. "You could pile up a hundred polls all showing the same thing. People are optimistic," insists Everett Ladd, executive director of the Roper Center for Public Opinion Research at the University of Connecticut.

Despite an abundance of immediate frustrations, Americans aren't giving up on the notion that tomorrow will be a better day.

by Beth Brophy with Maureen Walsh of the Economic Unit, Richard Alm, Nancy Linnon, Peggy Edersheim and bureau reports

# Can America Compete?

## STEPHEN S. COHEN and JOHN ZYSMAN

STEPHEN S. COHEN and JOHN ZYSMAN are professors at the University of California, Berkeley, and directors of the Berkeley Roundtable on the International Economy (BRIE). Major portions of this paper, which was delivered at the Symposium on the Fortieth Anniversary of the Joint Economic Committee of the Congress of the United States, will appear in Stephen Cohen and John Zysman, *Manufacturing Matters* (forthcoming). Research for the larger work from which this paper was drawn was supported by special grants from the Carnegie Forum on Education and the Economy, and the Office of Technology Assessment, U.S. Congress, to the Berkeley Roundtable on the International Economy.

*Adjusting to shifting markets and changing technologies depends on how we use knowledge. That means investing broadly in human resources and in our communities, not just narrowly in engineers and scientists.*

We contend that production is changing in such profound ways and at such rapid rates as to seriously threaten our nation's place—and the places of most other nations—in the international economic hierarchy. We are, in brief, in the midst of a major industrial transition.

Transition is a word that triggers a reaction—usually bored annoyance. After all, nothing is more permanent than transition, especially in economics. A healthy economy is always in a state of transition. Indeed, as that oldest of professorial remarks has it, it was Father Adam who turned to Eve on the way out of Eden and announced, "I guess we are entering a period of transition." Technology is always changing: think of the railway, the motorcar, the electric grid, saran wrap. And competitors are constantly struggling for a new product, a new process, and a new kind of efficiency. That's what makes the game so constructive; it keeps us on our toes and busy citing Schumpeter. We argue that the present industrial transition is real and colossally consequential.

## International competition

Two principal forces—(1) changes in international competition and (2) changes in production technology—are driving the changes in the world's economies. The first motor force is the relatively rapid and massive exposure of major segments of American manufacturing and services to international competition that is different in extent and in kind from anything we have previously experienced. Over the past generation America preached, to itself and to others, a doctrine of interdependence. But it was the other nations that were interdependent, on each other and on the United States. We were independent. As late as 1970 imports into the United States totaled only $40 billion; by 1980 they had climbed to $245 billion; by 1984, to almost $350 billion. Until only yesterday imports in manufacturing averaged around 4 to 5 percent of sales and were easily balanced by exports; now they are about 25 percent of sales, and some 70 percent of U.S. industries are subject to foreign competition.

From *Challenge*, May/June 1986, pp. 56-64. Reprinted by permission of the authors.

The abrupt change in scale was matched by a change in kind. Old competitors, located mostly in Western Europe, caught up from an unnatural lag in the kind of production that created the wealth and power of the United States—complex manufacturing in such industries as autos, chemicals, and aircraft. They accumulated, or dug up, capital. And they have never been behind in the fundamentals, education and the ability to create technology.

But more important, new competitors have come on line, most prominently across the Pacific. To speed their development, many of the most successful of these new competitors have shaped economic structures, institutions, and policies that are marginally, but crucially, different from ours. We call these economies *developmental states*. Japan is the most successful and the biggest, but it is not the only one. Japanese competition in all lines of production—ranging from the most advanced high-technology products such as very large scale integration (VLSI) semiconductors and optoelectronics through products of complex manufacturing such as automobiles and consumer electronics to such advanced services as banking and process engineering—has, more than any other factor, been responsible for the current debate on American competitiveness.

## The developmental state— Japan

Since we cannot review here a long series of country and sector stories, let us at least briefly consider some fundamentals of the Japanese case. The Japanese government exerted influence on the country's economy during its boom years of the 1950s and 1960s in two important ways. First, it was a gatekeeper controlling the links between the domestic and the international economy. The Japanese government was, in T. J. Pempel's terms, an "official doorman determining what and under what conditions capital, technology and manufacturing products enter and leave Japan." (See T. J. Pempel, *Policy and Politics in Japan: Creating Conservatism*, Temple University Press, 1982, p. 139.) The discretion to decide what to let in and, at the extreme, out of Japan permitted the doorman to break up the packages of technology, capital, and control that the multinational corporations represent. In almost all cases, neither money nor technology could in itself allow outsiders to buy or bull their way into a permanent position in the Japanese market. This closed market then gave Japanese firms a stable base of demand which permitted rapid expansion of production and innovation in manufacturing.

Second, government agencies—most notoriously, the Ministry of International Trade and Industry (MITI)—sought to orient the development of the domestic economy. Although government bureaucrats have not dictated to an administered market, they have consciously contributed to the development of particular sectors. MITI is not so much a strict director as a player with its own purposes and its own means of interfering in the market to reach its goals. Government industrial strategy assumes that the market pressures of competition can serve as an instrument of policy. It is not simply that the government makes use of competitive forces that arise naturally in the market, but rather that it often induces the very competition it directs. This intense, but controlled, domestic competition substituted for the pressures of the international market to force development. The competition is real, but the government and private sector work together to avoid "disruptive" or "evasive" competition. We do not need to select between cartoon images of Japan, Inc., or a land of unfettered competition. It is the particular interaction of state and market in Japan that is interesting.

Seen from the perspective of the firm, government policy helped provide cash for investment, tax breaks to sustain liquidity, research and development support, and aid to promote exports. These public policies—the web of policies rather than any individual elements of it—changed the options of companies. Without protected markets, the initial investment could not in many cases have been justified by private companies. Without external debt finance, the funds to expand production rapidly would not have been available to the firms. Within a protected market, the easy availability of capital and imported technology was bound to attract entrants to favored sectors.

However, MITI viewed the stampede for entry, which it had encouraged, and the resulting battle for market share, which limited profits, as excessive competition that had to be controlled. The intensive domestic competition was controlled by a variety of mechanisms that included expansion plans agreed to jointly by government and industry, debt financing of rapid expansion that made the bankruptcy of major firms a threat to the entire economy and hence unthinkable, and the oft-cited recession cartels. The dual facts of purposive government influence on economic outcomes and real market competition are reconciled by seeing the system as one of controlled or limited competition.

The very success of Japanese industrial development—combined with intensifying pressure from Japan's trading partners—has begun to loosen the network of relations that characterized the developmental state and on which the strategy of creating advantage in world markets rested. Many formal restrictions on entry to the Japanese market have been lifted. Serious trade problems still remain, however. As long as Japan had to borrow generic technologies on which to build its growth and possessed undeveloped potential markets that could be seized by domestic or foreign producers, formal closure of markets was essential to a system of orchestrated development. Now less formal obstacles to entry may matter as crucially to competition in advanced technology as formal restrictions did a generation earlier.

Japan's imports of manufactured goods remain dramatically below those of the other advanced countries, not having increased as a portion of the national economy since the early 1970s. Japan's unique trade characteristic is the tendency, relative to its trade partners, not to import manufactures in sectors in which it exports. The system of administrative guidance that affects government programs of finance and procurement, the Byzantine distribution systems, and the habits of private coordination amid competition all evolved slowly. Indeed, the Japanese state still exercises a leadership role and exerts substantial influence in high-technology industries, on the one hand, and in declining or mature industries faced with oversupply on the other.

There is a crucial interplay between these two sets of interventionist policies that is likely to continue to spark problems in international markets and enduring tensions between Japan and its trading partners. Promotional policies in which the risks of domestic oversupply are at least in part insured against or underwritten, depending on how one chooses to characterize the particulars of Japanese policies, encourage bursts of investment for domestic demand that translate directly into export drives. Now that Japanese producers tie domestic investment decisions directly to world market strategies, the relationship between strategies in the Japanese market and their impact in the American market is immediate. There is a pattern of aggressive promotion of advancing sectors and of determined insulation and cushioning of mature sectors. This pattern amounts to confining open international competition in the domestic market to sectors in which major Japanese firms are dominant worldwide (or at least able to withstand foreign entry into the home market) and to sectors from which Japanese firms are absent. It implies sustaining closure in those sectors that are under pressure from abroad.

The Japanese system may slowly open and become fully integrated with its advanced-country trading partners. But other would-be Japans stand in line. The challenge of the developmental state will not pass from the contemporary scene.

## Technological revolution

The second major force is a technological revolution in production that is spreading across major segments of manufacturing and services. It is built on the advent of mass application of microelectronics-based telecommunications and automatic control technologies. Its emblematics are the semiconductor, the computer, and the robot; potent combinations of these technologies are computer-aided design (CAD), computer-aided manufacturing (CAM), and computer-integrated manufacturing (CIM). Their buzzword translations into business strategy, economic policy debates, and social anxiety include computerization, flexible production, de-skilling, re-skilling, and dislocation—a second industrial revolution.

These two forces—technological change and the new scale and nature of international competition—interrelate and compound: competition drives the development of the technologies, the rates of their diffusion, and, just as important, the ways they are used. In turn, the use of these technologies is a major component of the new strategies throughout the economy for responding to foreign competition. Their combined effect is to propel America smack into the middle of an industrial transition we didn't ask for and may not be prepared to cope with terribly well.

## The eroding competitiveness of American industry

In this era of fundamental industrial transition, American producers are not doing very well. Precisely because the changes are basic and likely to prove enduring, the outcomes of industrial competition today will matter powerfully tomorrow. The trade conflicts that have pushed their way onto the front page are not ordinary trade frictions about cars or blouses or semiconductors. They involve serious, long-term conflicts about shifting national positions in the world economy. The wealth and power of nations are the stakes. Once American firms dominated world markets; now they must adjust to them. A mere twenty years ago Europeans wrote books about the American Challenge and the Secrets of the Giant American Firms while they fretted about technology gaps and undoubted American advantages in product, production process, marketing strategy, and management techniques. Now we read about the East Asian Edge, Japan as Number One, and flexible production in Italy, while we worry about innovations in production and management coming from abroad. Unfortunately, the evidence is substantial that the American position has eroded dramatically.

Measured each of seven different ways—by unprecedented trade deficits in manufactured goods; by declining shares of world markets for exports; by lagging rates of productivity increases, eroding profit margins, and declining real wages; by the increasing price elasticities of imports; and by its eroding position in world high-technology markets—American industry confronts a severe problem of competitiveness such as it has never known before. Each measure has its limitations and can, perhaps, be explained away, but, taken together, they defy easy dismissal and portray a serious, long-term problem.

It is misleading to conclude, as many do, that America's comparative advantage in high-technology goods translates into a secure position in international trade in high technology, let alone in manufactures in general. Comparative advantage means, in the end, the thing you do less worse than you do others—not the thing at which you are better than your foreign competitors. It is misleading to conclude that, since there is no rapid "deindustrialization," the path along which American manufacturing is evolving is healthy or secure. American adjustment to the new world economy is quite troubled. Not only do statistical indicators tell the story; there is something going on underneath. Japanese producers, for example, have established real competitive advantages in a range of complex manufactured products. These advantages rest on a wider diffusion of advanced technology, as in steel; on greater investment in automated production technologies, as in segments of the electronics industry; and on an approach to mass production which uses fewer labor hours per unit than American companies in a broad range of consumer durables from machine tools through automobiles.

Though symmetry is the organizing principle of economic theory, as many students learned practicing origami in Economics 101, it is not the organizing principle of international competition. Temporary disequilibria, brought about by superficial causes—as the overvaluation of the dollar is generally treated—can have profound and enduring consequences. Foreign companies that establish sales, distribution networks, and even brand recognition in the U.S. market will tend to hold them as the dollar declines. The superprofits garnered by foreign industries as a result of the dollar's high have in many cases been used for reinvestment in more efficient production that will generate a competitive edge in the years to come. It is

perhaps worth noting that, when the dollar rose by almost 50 percent between 1980 and 1984, the prices of imported goods declined by only 2 percent. That means—despite what we are regularly told—it is not so much the U.S. consumer who has benefited from the high dollar as much as foreign producers, middlemen, and retailers [*New York Times*, December 9, 1985].

Similarly, U.S. corporations that moved production to offshore factories during a period of a high dollar will not necessarily move their facilities home when the dollar falls. Indeed, as we argue below, the move abroad to find cheap labor may preclude a strategy of sustained production innovation at home. The moves made during the era of the superdollar may thus have more than long-term locational consequences. They adversely affect the strategic choices of firms as well. Such traditional notions as symmetrical effects and rubber-band responses, in which the system goes back to the predisturbance equilibrium, are inappropriate organizing principles. Strategic choices made in response to one set of factors—often relatively small factors—can have consequences that are not likely to be reversible and that are far greater in scale than what caused them.

## American adjustments to change

The key to American adjustment to a transforming world economy and an evolving technology may prove to be the capacity to remain, or, better still, become once again, competitive in manufacturing processes. This can be seen clearly by considering the international market pressures to which firms and industries must respond and the technologies to which they must adapt. First, the low-cost labor of the newly industrializing countries has permitted firms in those nations to penetrate the markets of the advanced countries. In labor-intensive goods that are sold on the basis of low cost, advanced-country producers cannot compete without protection or basic strategic shifts. They must either reorganize production, making labor-intensive production into a game of automation, or alter their mix of products and, with it, marketing and corporate strategies.

Second, in consumer-durables industries such as autos and televisions, competitive advantage rests on the mastery of complex manufacturing processes, as well as on distinct product and marketing strategies. Those processes are being revolutionized by microelectronics. Finally, in advanced-technology sectors, the ability to implement new engineering and scientific knowledge in products and production is critical. The basic science and much of the generic engineering concepts used in these industries are in the public domain. The ability to commercialize these ideas successfully and to produce the products competitively is the basis of advantage.

American producers over recent years have moved their production offshore, not simply to be closer to their foreign markets, but to find inexpensive labor and components to reduce the cost of products they sell in the United States. Offshore production has been spawned both by the pressure of imports and by competition among American firms. It has been sustained by policy both in the United States and in the countries where export platforms have been located. Recently, some American firms have found another reason to move production abroad. They have sought to escape some of the consequences of the high value of the U.S. dollar.

The move abroad is cumulative; that is, it builds on itself in two ways. First, an offshore production network that is a real alternative to a domestic net has been built up. When the first producers went abroad they had to supply many of the component parts and production services from an American base. Their suppliers often moved offshore with them, to be closer to the point of final production and to capture some of the same advantages of aid and low-cost labor. Foreign component makers also began to supply American offshore producers. For example, the American semiconductor industry has found that, when their clients move offshore, they begin to buy components from offshore sources as well. In some cases American firms have subcontracted their production abroad, transferring the product and production know-how. This has often speeded the emergence of their own competitors. In fact, once component sources are offshore there is often a temptation to move product assembly offshore; as product assembly moves, additional moves offshore of component suppliers are again encouraged. Once the bulk of production is offshore, there comes a moment when it is seriously tempting to move product engineering abroad. This is not fanciful. We have heard such discussions in American firms. Let us be clear, though—the move offshore gives a one time labor-cost advantage. Production innovation and investment in capital offshore is required to sustain that advantage.

Second, after years of moving abroad to find cheap labor to produce existing products at lower costs, American firms build up an expertise in the management of offshore production. They do not build up an expertise in managing the implementation of the most advanced production technologies or in designing or redesigning a product to facilitate automated production in the United States. Over time, the perception that foreign competition could be met by offshore production took form and force. Even a few years ago, when it was already evident that the Japanese had massively invested in production, some in the semiconductor industry were still calling for more offshore locations as an effective response. Some major corporations have built formal models to set a framework for these choices, but the models (in our view) are built on quite incorrect assumptions about exchange rates and learning curves that serve simply to justify their biases.

We do not intend to exaggerate. There are many goods or pieces of production processes which cannot be effectively automated, which absorb enormous amounts of labor, and which have limited transportation costs. Those are clear candidates for offshore production or assembly. But as programmable automation emerges, the mix of activities which can be carried out in the United States will expand. We suggest simply that earlier moves offshore were often taken without clear attention to the possibilities of traditional automation and that the earlier moves offshore may blind firms to the possibilities and needs of automating at home.

America cannot maintain its wealth or high-wage economy by playing only the role of laboratory for the world, producing the ideas and prototypes and handling distribution, advertising, and sales in our own market, while others make the products. If we can't make the products, our technology edge will erode. After several rounds of product innovation, the innovative initiative will pass to the firms that make the products. These firms end up understanding the market and the product in a way that permits them to become the technology leader. Experience in steel, consumer electronics, and autos alone ought to convince us of this.

The proposition is simple. Lose control of the manufacturing or production process of your product and you risk losing control of both the technology and the final markets. A firm's or a nation's industry cannot survive at a substantial production disadvantage to its major competitors.

Common to these three categories of competition is the importance of manufacturing processes in retaining industrial competitiveness. The revolution in manufacturing is as important as the more often noted acceleration in the pace of product innovation. When pressed by low-cost producers, American companies can sometimes transform a labor-intensive production process into one that is technology-intensive. This, of course, involves substantial displacement of labor, a reorganization of the labor which remains, and changes in corporate habits. Sharp dislocations of workers and communities have generally produced political trouble that disrupts the adjustment process. Competitive position over time, in a broad range of products such as consumer durables, rests squarely on the ability to master the most advanced manufacturing techniques. Even in the so-called haven of high technology, the long-run competitiveness of firms and the national economy rests on translating product advantage into an enduring market position through manufacturing expertise. Manufacturing expertise is critical in this period of fundamental change in production processes. The central capacity required to remain competitive will prove to be dynamic flexibility—the capacity to adjust rapidly to new market and production conditions. That flexibility will turn on corporate strategies and structures, the capacities of the people throughout the production system, and the national technological infrastructure that will develop and diffuse new production technologies and approaches.

## Static and dynamic flexibility

The distinction between *static* and *dynamic* flexibility is to us critical, not the differences in techniques used to promote flexibility. *Static flexibility* means the ability of a firm to adjust its operations at any moment to shifting conditions in the market, to the rise and fall of demand, or to the changes in the mix of products the market is asking for. It implies adjustment within a fixed product and production structure. Flexibility has come to mean a whole variety of ways of adjusting company operations to the shifting conditions of the market. The term is used to refer to the ability of a firm efficiently to vary its strategic direction, level of production, composition of goods, length of the workday or week, level of wages, organization of work, or any of a variety of other elements of operations.

The techniques needed to achieve flexibility can thus be technological or organizational. Firms may employ new programmable machine tools to increase the efficiency of batch production, or they may reach an agreement with unions to reduce the number of job categories. The reduction in the number of job categories in the New United Motors (the GM-Toyota venture in Fremont, California) permits easier changes on the shop floor. American Airlines announces it is reducing the number of full-time employees in many airports, by shifting to part-time personnel in order to increase its operational flexibility. A worker buy-out of a steel plant in Weirton, West Virginia, permits a wage

reduction, with the workers accepting "wage flexibility" because they have a stake in the company profits. In static terms—that is, at any given moment—increased flexibility means greater capacity to adjust to short-term market changes. Static flexibility consequently decreases risk that the firm won't be able to adapt to changes in the number and types of goods demanded in the market; it increases the ability to adapt quickly to changed conditions.

*Dynamic flexibility*, by contrast, means the ability to increase productivity steadily through improvements in production processes and innovation in product. Burton Klein presents the notion well. He argues that Japanese firms, and auto firms originally, "have evolved a practice that can be described as dynamic flexibility . . . ; contrasted with static flexibility, dynamic flexibility is not concerned with producing more than one product (e.g., cars and light trucks) on single production lines—although the Japanese do this too. [See For Further Reading, Burton Klein.] Rather it is concerned with designing production lines in a way that they can quickly evolve in response to changes in either the product or production technology. In other words, the central pre-occupation is to get ideas into action quickly . . . [In practice in Japan] the main purpose of dynamic flexibility is to make rapid changes in production technology for the purpose of lowering costs and thereby improving productivity." We agree with Klein that "continuing productivity gains presuppose advances in relevant technologies and a keen desire to make good use of this progress." All studies of postwar economic growth in the advanced countries highlight the fact that technological advance, not the simple increase in the number of machines or the amount of capital or labor employed, is at the core of sustained increases in productivity and economic development. Indeed, productivity advances have waned in the years after drops in research and development expenditures. Increased productivity permits lowered costs or, depending on the response of competitors, higher wages and profits.

Dynamic flexibility is the corporate capacity to develop and introduce these technological advances. A commitment to such flexibility in Japan is reflected in the structure of the market for computer-controlled manufacturing equipment. In Japan many firms internally develop their own production equipment. Almost every Japanese auto company has a large machine tool operation in which 200 to 400 people do nothing but create new tools, which are quickly introduced into the production process. When successful, these machines are often sold on the market. In Japan as a consequence the machine tool market is highly fragmented, that is, it is shared among many producers who are developing equipment for their own internal purposes and then selling it on the open market. In the United States, where less development of production equipment occurs internally, the market for programmable machine tools is highly concentrated, that is, shared among a few big producers. The result, which we return to, is that American firms tend to introduce production innovations periodically, moving from one plateau of best practice to another. The Japanese, studies suggest, move through continuous and iterative production innovation, steadily improving the production process. In fact, the Japanese system, with greater flexibility, has achieved greater productivity gains over the last years than the more rigid American one.

Technological advance inherently involves risk; new ideas may not work in practice or may not work as well as hoped. Consequently, dynamic flexibility involves a management of levels of risk sufficient to match what competitors are doing. Levels of risk, Klein argues, vary from industry to industry. A norm emerges within a given sector. In part, this is a product of the possibilities inherent in the technologies of the moment. If the potential returns are very high and the risk relatively low, one or another firm in a sector may take the risk of product development. In addition, the risk norm, the propensity to engage in risk, depends on the intensity of competition in the industry. In the United States, in our view, firms in many oligopolistic sectors had established a low norm of technological risk that was part of a competitive truce or at least a corporate Geneva convention about the terms of civilized combat that reduced the need to take risks. American firms in a variety of sectors suddenly confronted competitors from foreign sectors where the norms of risk—partly a reflection of the pace of development— were higher. American firms were caught off balance, and the results are evident.

Static and dynamic flexibility are inextricably linked. Static flexibility to short-term shifts in market conditions can be achieved in a variety of ways; how it is achieved will affect the long-term capacity of the firm to introduce the evolving technology on which its product and production position depend. A decision to move production offshore may be taken because it will allow lower wages and/or because it will make it easier to shut plants during downturns. The move offshore, it seems to us, makes it harder to improve steadily the production process itself. When managers decide to reduce skill levels in domestic plants, aimed at reducing skilled-worker resistance to technological development, they may eliminate the very skilled workers required to implement effectively new production

technologies. In a similar vein, firms may have to choose between short-term economies of scale, which involve large fixed costs in the form of investment in equipment, and the long-term necessity of responding to evolving technologies, which may involve smaller and less efficient plants. Japanese and American firms have made different choices. Japanese plants for producing cars are only about one-third as large as comparable American plants, ostensibly to permit greater dynamic flexibility.

A period of economic transition is a time when "dynamic flexibility" is of predominant importance. Our contention is that the crucial change now is the transformation of manufacturing, not the replacement of industry by service. The transformation of manufacturing does not simply mean that a few "sunrise" manufacturing sectors, such as personal computers, are assuming the importance once held by certain traditional manufacturing sectors, such as automobiles. Rather, as we shall see in a moment, computers have begun to alter the production process throughout industry. The transformation is occurring because the new high-technology sectors are agents of change, sources of innovation, within the traditional sectors. Much of "high technology" really consists of producer goods—goods used to make other products. As individuals we do not buy a bag of silicon chips—we buy the products that incorporate semiconductors, or we buy products that incorporate semiconductors that have been made by machines that also incorporate those omnipresent chips. We do not buy high-speed computers or mainframe computers—we buy products that are developed or processed on those machines. It is for aircraft design and now automobile design that supercomputers are purchased, while the insurance industry long ago became a dominant buyer of mainframe computers and even minicomputers. The proper object of our concern should be how the new technologies spread throughout the economy as a part of a national response to changing competition. We must have a national economy that can absorb and apply the new technologies.

## Policy choice for change

America has a choice. Our economic and indeed our technological future will be a product of political decisions. It is not simply a choice of whether we do well or badly, but of the kind of society that the economy we create can support.

The need for choice is urgent, for America is not adjusting well to the changing world economy. The evidence is overwhelming that our competitive position in international markets has eroded. We are displaying rigidity where flexibility is required. Even the credibility of the counterarguments that the problem is centrally one of exchange rates or that it can be managed by increasing service exports is crumbling. Furthermore, many of the debates are simply formulated poorly. It is not a matter of deindustrialization, of whether American industry disappears or not. It is a matter of the composition of the manufacturing base. For example, we have been happy exporting capital goods to developing nations and importing the finished product made with those machines on the grounds (correct, we believe) that America should position itself in the segments of industry that can sustain high wages. Should we be equally content with the fact that America now imports the high value-added textile and apparel machinery built in Europe and Japan with high-wage labor to produce low value-added textiles and apparel produced with low-wage labor? And how should we feel about imports now taking more than 50 percent of our market for advanced machine tools—far more than that if we omit protected sales to defense contractors.

The task is to assure a dynamic adjustment to shifting market and technological conditions that will sustain our high-wage economy. We must sustain the ability to generate and apply product and process innovation. It is not just a matter of innovation, but of the ability to exploit innovation in the market. Technology diffuses quickly, capturing few rents when sold to licensees. The lessons of the last few years make that very clear. Using technological innovation to create and hold market positions for entire industries requires a deep and broad effort. Technology spreads quickly, leaving few advantages through the simple creation of scientific or technological knowledge or investment in simple machines. Thus, all depends on how knowledge is used throughout the economy. And this use rests in the end on investment in people, or human capital, not narrowly, in engineers or scientists—though certainly they are needed—but broadly, in the community as a whole.

Our policy problem is not a matter of capturing gains from others, but of assuring our own abilities to participate fully in the possibilities of the new economy that is emerging. Policy can expand our capacity to make the multiplicity of adjustments that will be required. It can help to upgrade a nation's position in international competition in a substantial and enduring way. Like much in economic reality, but little in economic theory, the relationship is not symmetrical. Policy, all by itself, can hold back an economy that has almost everything going for it; Argentina is a recurring

reminder. But policy, however enlightened and astute, can (by itself) only contribute to the upgrading process. It can't do it alone. But the contribution can be very important.

The thing policy is least able to do is to have *no* impact on a nation's competitive position. And that, of course, is what conventional economics sternly prescribes for it. That policy cannot simply go away, or be "held-harmless" in its impacts on the economy, is true not only for America, but for any complex modern society. Like it or not, government affects the economy—both as a direct economic actor (taxing, spending, and, often, doing) and as a set of all-pervasive and ever-changing rules. That truth is compounded by the fact that economic reality today consists of several large and complex economies that are all heavily policy-impacted. One nation's policies affect another nation's position. Were it achievable, policy neutrality in all nations might well be the best rule for the system as a whole (though not necessarily for any one nation in that system). In the absence of such universality, policy neutrality loses any claim for being the best rule for any particular nation.

## What about comparative advantage?

These thoughts take us right into another core notion that has shaped our policy debate, the forbidding doctrine of comparative advantage, remembered by the millions who once took Economics 101, in rather the same way Latin declensions are remembered by their parents. Revealed comparative advantage, to give it its full name, is the economic doctrine that addresses foreign trade. It tells a nation what its economy will specialize in: the British (because they wrote the text) in manufacturing textiles; the Iberians (because they believed it and lost) in port wine. A nation should, and will, find itself specializing in those activities in which it is the most efficient (or least inefficient) compared to all the others. Having a comparative advantage in something (say, machinery, or, better yet, complex manufacturing) does not mean that you are a world-class winner at it, or even better than the other guy. It means that you are just less worse at it than you are at other things. Your wage level tells you how good you are.

The American policy debate on trade is formulated by the prevalent view of comparative advantage in American economics. Our policy choices are framed by the notion that comparative advantage is revealed, not created. A nation finds its comparative advantage by looking backward in the trade statistics. It does not choose it by looking forward in its policy councils. Policy should not try to create comparative advantage. We are constantly told that nations who subsidize exports are only deluding themselves and, at the same time, subsidizing their consumers. Pull away the subsidy and things will rubber-band back to "normal." Enduring comparative advantage cannot be created by policy.

It is of course true that in a strict, definitional sense comparative advantage cannot be created. But saying that is a little like saying, as the economists do, that foreign trade will always balance out. Prices simply need time and freedom to adjust. That is true, but nugatory. If, for example, we were to let the price of the dollar adjust to the point where one dollar equaled one yen, we could sell the entire economics building at the University of Chicago, brick by brick, to the Japanese to use as disco space. The trick is not to balance trade; it is to balance trade at a high wage level. Similarly, we always have a comparative advantage in something. That is the way the thing is defined. The interesting question is, in what? Can we keep our comparative advantage in activities that pay a high wage? Government policy, we argue, can to a significant degree move the list of favorable activities upward (or downward).

## The economic future

In brief, the outcome of America's passage through the industrial transition need not be exclusively the affair of impersonal and imperturbable technological and economic forces. There is room for choice and action. That is the good news. The bad news is contained in that same sentence: there is room—and need—for choice. Just because we have a choice about our future does not mean that we will take advantage of that opportunity, use it well, and even enjoy the freedom and responsibility choice provides. We have a political system we cherish, one that is artfully constructed to avoid clear choices. And we have an economic ideology, based on a notion of choice, that minimizes the opportunity and desirability of making important, strategic choices.

There is a spectrum of possible economic futures open to us. At one end lies an internationally competitive U.S. economy in which highly productive, educated workers use new technologies flexibly to produce a broad range of high value-added goods and services. They thereby earn the high wages necessary to sustain both the standard of living to which many Americans have grown accustomed and to which most aspire, and the open society that has been so closely linked with a strong and open economy. At the other end of the spectrum lies the real danger of a competitively weakened economy in which a small minority of high-skilled jobs coexists with a majority of low-skilled, low-wage jobs and massive unemployment. Living standards—perhaps along with social equality and political democracy—would deteriorate rapidly as, in order to compete, manufacturing and services move more and more value-added operations offshore and automation strips the labor content from the remaining U.S. facilities and processes.

The industrial and trade transition sets an agenda of certain change, but there is nothing inevitable about the outcome.

# WHY JOHNNY CAN'T THINK
## The politics of bad schooling

The following books are discussed in this essay:
*A Place Called School*, by John I. Goodlad. 396 pages. McGraw-Hill. $9.95.
*The Good High School*, by Sara Lawrence Lightfoot. 399 pages. Basic Books. $19.95.
*Horace's Compromise: The Dilemma of the American High School*, by Theodore R. Sizer. 241 pages. Houghton Mifflin. $16.95.
*High School: A Report on Secondary Education in America*, by Ernest L. Boyer and the Carnegie Foundation for the Advancement of Teaching. 363 pages. Harper & Row. $16.95.
*A Nation at Risk: The Imperative for Educational Reform*, by the National Commission on Excellence in Education. 65 pages. U.S. Government Printing Office. $4.50.
*The Great School Debate: Which Way for American Education?*, edited by Beatrice and Ronald Gross. 481 pages. Simon & Schuster. $17.45.
*The Challenge to American Schools*, edited by John Bunzel. 256 pages. Oxford University Press. $19.95.
*The Troubled Crusade: American Education 1945–1980*, by Diane Ravitch. 384 pages. Basic Books. $19.95.

## Walter Karp

*Walter Karp is a contributing editor of* Harper's *and the author of* The Politics of War. *He is at work on a book about the Korean War,* The Empire and the Mob.

Until very recently, remarkably little was known about what actually goes on in America's public schools. There were no reliable answers to even the most obvious questions. How many children are taught to read in overcrowded classrooms? How prevalent is rote learning and how common are classroom discussions? Do most schools set off gongs to mark the change of "periods"? Is it a common practice to bark commands over public address systems in the manner of army camps, prisons, and banana republics? Public schooling provides the only intense experience of a public realm that most Americans will ever know. Are school buildings designed with the dignity appropriate to a great republican institution, or are most of them as crummy looking as one's own?

The darkness enveloping America's public schools is truly extraordinary considering that 38.9 million students attend them, that we spend nearly $134 billion a year on them, and that foundations ladle out generous sums for the study of everything about schooling—except what really occurs in the schools. John I. Goodlad's eight-year investigation of a mere thirty-eight of America's 80,000 public schools—the result of which, *A Place Called School*, was published last year—is the most comprehensive such study ever undertaken. Hailed as a "landmark in American educational research," it was financed with great difficulty. The darkness, it seems, has its guardians.

Happily, the example of Goodlad, a former dean of UCLA's Graduate School of Education, has proven contagious. A flurry of new books sheds considerable light on the practice of public education in America. In *The Good High School*, Sara Lawrence Lightfoot offers vivid "portraits" of six distinctive American secondary schools. In *Horace's Compromise*, Theodore R. Sizer, a former dean of Harvard's Grad-

*Overcrowded classrooms inevitably debase instruction, yet they are the rule in America's public schools*

uate School of Education, reports on his two-year odyssey through public high schools around the country. Even *High School*, a white paper issued by Ernest L. Boyer and the Carnegie Foundation for the Advancement of Teaching, is supported by a close investigation of the institutional life of a number of schools. Of the books under review, only *A Nation at Risk*, the report of the Reagan Administration's National Commission on Excellence in Education, adheres to the established practice of crass special pleading in the dark.

Thanks to Goodlad et al., it is now clear what the great educational darkness has so long concealed: the depth and pervasiveness of political hypocrisy in the common schools of the country. The great ambition professed by public school managers is, of course, education for citizenship and self-government, which harks back to Jefferson's historic call for "general education to enable every man to judge for himself what will secure or endanger his freedom." What the public schools practice with remorseless proficiency, however, is the prevention of citizenship and the stifling of self-government. When 58 percent of the thirteen-year-olds tested by the National Assessment for Educational Progress think it is against the law to start a third party in America, we are dealing not with a sad educational failure but with a remarkably subtle success.

Consider how effectively America's future citizens are trained *not* to judge for themselves about anything. From the first grade to the twelfth, from one coast to the other, instruction in America's classrooms is almost entirely dogmatic. Answers are "right" and answers are "wrong," but mostly answers are short. "At all levels, [teacher-made] tests called almost exclusively for short answers and recall of information," reports Goodlad. In more than 1,000 classrooms visited by his researchers, "only *rarely*" was there "evidence to suggest instruction likely to go much beyond mere possession of information to a level of understanding its implications." Goodlad goes on to note that "the intellectual terrain is laid out by the teacher. The paths for walking through it are largely predetermined by the teacher." The give-and-take of genuine discussion is conspicuously absent. "Not even 1%" of instructional time, he found, was devoted to discussions that "required some kind of open response involving reasoning or perhaps an opinion from students.... The extraordinary degree of student passivity stands out."

Sizer's research substantiates Goodlad's. "No more important finding has emerged from the inquiries of our study than that the American high school student, *as student*, is all too often docile, compliant, and without initiative."

There is good reason for this. On the one hand, notes Sizer, "there are too few rewards for being inquisitive." On the other, the heavy emphasis on "the right answer... smothers the student's efforts to become an effective intuitive thinker."

Yet smothered minds are looked on with the utmost complacency by the educational establishment—by the Reagan Department of Education, state boards of regents, university education departments, local administrators, and even many so-called educational reformers. Teachers are neither urged to combat the tyranny of the short right answer nor trained to do so. "Most teachers simply do not know how to teach for higher levels of thinking," says Goodlad. Indeed, they are actively discouraged from trying to do so.

The discouragement can be quite subtle. In their orientation talks to new, inexperienced teachers, for example, school administrators often indicate that they do not much care what happens in class so long as no noise can be heard in the hallway. This thinly veiled threat virtually ensures the prevalence of short-answer drills, workbook exercises, and the copying of long extracts from the blackboard. These may smother young minds, but they keep the classroom quiet.

Discouragement even calls itself reform. Consider the current cry for greater use of standardized student tests to judge the "merit" of teachers and raise "academic standards." If this fake reform is foisted on the schools, dogma and docility will become even more prevalent. This point is well made by Linda Darling-Hammond of the Rand Corporation in an essay in *The Great School Debate*. Where "important decisions are based on test scores," she notes, "teachers are more likely to teach to the tests" and less likely to bother with "nontested activities, such as writing, speaking, problem-solving or real reading of real books." The most influential promoter of standardized tests is the "excellence" brigade in the Department of Education; so clearly one important meaning of "educational excellence" is greater proficiency in smothering students' efforts to think for themselves.

Probably the greatest single discouragement to better instruction is the overcrowded classroom. The Carnegie report points out that English teachers cannot teach their students how to write when they must read and criticize the papers of as many as 175 students. As Sizer observes, genuine discussion is possible only in small seminars. In crowded classrooms, teachers have difficulty imparting even the most basic intellectual skills, since they have no time to give students personal attention. The overcrowded classroom inevitably debases instruction, yet it is the rule in America's public schools. In the first three grades of elementary school, Goodlad notes, the average class has

*Public-address systems teach the huge student mass to respect the rule of remote and invisible agencies*

twenty-seven students. High school classes range from twenty-five to forty students, according to the Carnegie report.

What makes these conditions appalling is that they are quite unnecessary. The public schools are top-heavy with administrators and rife with sinecures. Large numbers of teachers scarcely ever set foot in a classroom, being occupied instead as grade advisers, career counselors, "coordinators," and supervisors. "Schools, if simply organized," Sizer writes, "can have well-paid faculty and fewer than eighty students per teacher [16 students per class] without increasing current per-pupil expenditure." Yet no serious effort is being made to reduce class size. As Sizer notes, "Reducing teacher load is, when all the negotiating is over, a low agenda item for the unions and school boards." Overcrowded classrooms virtually guarantee smothered minds, yet the subject is not even mentioned in *A Nation at Risk*, for all its well-publicized braying about a "rising tide of mediocrity."

Do the nation's educators really want to teach almost 40 million students how to "think critically," in the Carnegie report's phrase, and "how to judge for themselves," in Jefferson's? The answer is, if you can believe that you will believe anything. The educational establishment is not even content to produce passive minds. It seeks passive spirits as well. One effective agency for producing these is the overly populous school. The larger schools are, the more prison-like they tend to be. In such schools, guards man the stairwells and exits. ID cards and "passes" are examined at checkpoints. Bells set off spasms of anarchy and bells quell the student mob. PA systems interrupt regularly with trivial fiats and frivolous announcements. This "malevolent intruder," in Sizer's apt phrase, is truly ill willed, for the PA system is actually an educational tool. It teaches the huge student mass to respect the authority of disembodied voices and the rule of remote and invisible agencies. Sixty-three percent of all high school students in America attend schools with enrollments of 5,000 or more. The common excuse for these mobbed schools is economy, but in fact they cannot be shown to save taxpayers a penny. Large schools "tend to create passive and compliant students," notes Robert B. Hawkins Jr. in an essay in *The Challenge to American Schools*. That is their chief reason for being.

"How can the relatively passive and docile roles of students prepare them to participate as informed, active and questioning citizens?" asks the Carnegie report, in discussing the "hidden curriculum" of passivity in the schools. The answer is, they were not meant to. Public schools introduce future citizens to the public world, but no introduction could be more disheartening. Architecturally, public school buildings range

from drab to repellent. They are often disfigured by demoralizing neglect—"cracked sidewalks, a shabby lawn, and peeling paint on every window sash," to quote the Carnegie report. Many big-city elementary schools have numbers instead of names, making them as coldly dispiriting as possible.

Public schools stamp out republican sentiment by habituating their students to unfairness, inequality, and special privilege. These arise inevitably from the educational establishment's longstanding policy (well described by Diane Ravitch in *The Troubled Crusade*) of maintaining "the correlation between social class and educational achievement." In order to preserve that factitious "correlation," public schooling is rigged to favor middle-class students and to ensure that working-class students do poorly enough to convince them that they fully merit the lowly station that will one day be theirs. "Our goal is to get these kids to be like their parents," one teacher, more candid than most, remarked to a Carnegie researcher.

For more than three decades, elementary schools across the country practiced a "progressive," non-phonetic method of teaching reading that had nothing much to recommend it save its inherent social bias. According to Ravitch, this method favored "children who were already motivated and prepared to begin reading" before entering school, while making learning to read more difficult for precisely those children whose parents were ill read or ignorant. The advantages enjoyed by the well-bred were thus artificially multiplied tenfold, and 23 million adult Americans are today "functional illiterates." America's educators, notes Ravitch, have "never actually accepted full responsibility for making all children literate."

That describes a malicious intent a trifle too mildly. Reading is the key to everything else in school. Children who struggle with it in the first grade will be "grouped" with the slow readers in the second grade and will fall hopelessly behind in all subjects by the sixth. The schools hasten this process of falling behind, report Goodlad and others, by giving the best students the best teachers and struggling students the worst ones. "It is ironic," observes the Carnegie report, "that those who need the most help get the least." Such students are commonly diagnosed as "culturally deprived" and so are blamed for the failures inflicted on them. Thus, they are taught to despise themselves even as they are inured to their inferior station.

The whole system of unfairness, inequality, and privilege comes to fruition in high school. There, some 15.7 million youngsters are formally divided into the favored few and the ill-favored many by the practice of "tracking."

About 35 percent of America's public secondary-school students are enrolled in academic programs (often subdivided into "gifted" and "non-gifted" tracks); the rest are relegated to some variety of non-academic schooling. Thus the tracking system, as intended, reproduces the divisions of the class system. "The honors programs," notes Sizer, "serve the wealthier youngsters, and the general tracks (whatever their titles) serve the working class. Vocational programs are often a cruel social dumping ground." The bottom-dogs are trained for jobs as auto mechanics, cosmeticians, and institutional cooks, but they rarely get the jobs they are trained for. Pumping gasoline, according to the Carnegie report, is as close as an auto-mechanics major is likely to get to repairing a car. "Vocational education in the schools is virtually irrelevant to job fate," asserts Goodlad. It is merely the final hoax that the school bureaucracy plays on the neediest, one that the federal government has been promoting for seventy years.

The tracking system makes privilege and inequality blatantly visible to everyone. It creates under one roof "two worlds of schooling," to quote Goodlad. Students in academic programs read Shakespeare's plays. The commonality, notes the Carnegie report, are allowed virtually no contact with serious literature. In their English classes they practice filling out job applications. "Gifted" students alone are encouraged to think for themselves. The rest are subjected to sanctimonious wind, chiefly about "work habits" and "career opportunities."

"If you are the child of low-income parents," reports Sizer, "the chances are good that you will receive limited and often careless attention from adults in your high school. If you are the child of upper-middle-income parents, the chances are good that you will receive substantial and careful attention." In Brookline High School in Massachusetts, one of Lightfoot's "good" schools, a few fortunate students enjoy special treatment in their Advanced Placement classes. Meanwhile, students tracked into "career education" learn about "institutional cooking and clean-up" in a four-term Food Service course that requires them to mop up after their betters in the school cafeteria.

This wretched arrangement expresses the true spirit of public education in America and discloses the real aim of its hidden curriculum. A favored few, pampered and smiled upon, are taught to cherish privilege and despise the disfavored. The favorless many, who have majored in failure for years, are taught to think ill of themselves. Youthful spirits are broken to the world and every impulse of citizenship is effectively stifled. John Goodlad's judgment is severe but just: "There is in the gap between our highly idealistic goals for schooling in our society and the differentiated opportunities condoned and supported in schools a monstrous hypocrisy."

The public schools of America have not been corrupted for trivial reasons. Much would be different in a republic composed of citizens who could judge for themselves what secured or endangered their freedom. Every wielder of illicit or undemocratic power, every possessor of undue influence, every beneficiary of corrupt special privilege would find his position and tenure at hazard. Republican education is a menace to powerful, privileged, and influential people, and they in turn are a menace to republican education. That is why the generation that founded the public schools took care to place them under the suffrage of local communities, and that is why the corrupters of public education have virtually destroyed that suffrage. In 1932 there were 127,531 school districts in America. Today there are approximately 15,840 and they are virtually impotent, their proper role having been usurped by state and federal authorities. Curriculum and textbooks, methods of instruction, the procedures of the classroom, the organization of the school day, the cant, the pettifogging, and the corruption are almost uniform from coast to coast. To put down the menace of republican education its shield of local self-government had to be smashed, and smashed it was.

The public schools we have today are what the powerful and the considerable have made of them. They will not be redeemed by trifling reforms. Merit pay, a longer school year, more homework, special schools for "the gifted," and more standardized tests will not even begin to turn our public schools into nurseries of "informed, active and questioning citizens." They are not meant to. When the authors of A Nation at Risk call upon the schools to create an "educated work force," they are merely sanctioning the prevailing corruption, which consists precisely in the reduction of citizens to credulous workers. The education of a free people will not come from federal bureaucrats crying up "excellence" for "economic growth," any more than it came from their predecessors who cried up schooling as a means to "get a better job."

Only ordinary citizens can rescue the schools from their stifling corruption, for nobody else wants ordinary children to become questioning citizens at all. If we wait for the mighty to teach America's youth what secures or endangers their freedom, we will wait until the crack of doom.

*The education of a free people will not come from federal bureaucrats crying up 'excellence' for 'economic growth'*

# Between Pro-Life and Pro-Choice

Victoria A. Sackett

No subject is so certain as abortion to silence a room or incite verbal warfare. Because disagreements about it revolve around the most fundamental, hence the most volatile, issues—sex, religion, the meaning of life—the disputes rarely lend themselves to compromise. And adding to the furor is that the opposing sides, whose disagreements with one another are irreconcilable, can *both* insist that public opinion agrees with them. Until recently, abortion rights advocates have been more successful than their anti-abortion opponents at convincing us that they have public sentiment on their side. We have heard few challenges to the notion that most people are in favor of legalized abortion and have taken the 1973 *Roe* v. *Wade* decision in stride.

Lately, though, the pro-choice faction has noticed that—public opinion aside—certain things aren't going their way. They've watched the overwhelming election and even more overwhelming reelection of an anti-abortion president. They've seen that same president break precedent and address the annual pro-life march on Washington. They've seen anti-abortion legislation narrowly defeated. How can this be happening, they ask, when, as one of them put it, "public support and acceptance of abortion seem to be increasing?"

One answer to the question is that the pro-choice side has mistaken public acquiescence for public enthusiasm. They can claim some aspects of public opinion and be correct, but that ignores a large body of equally convincing evidence on the other side. It may not be that the anti-abortion forces have been successful in dimming abortion's appeal, but that it was never terribly appealing in the first place. If this is true, what led abortion's defenders to believe they had not only the legal but the popular position? A look at the twelve years that have passed since the Supreme Court tried to settle the matter may help explain what has confused things.

## Before the Court Decided

*Roe* v. *Wade* came as a great shock to those who disapproved of abortion. They were less than an organized group in 1973 when the Supreme Court handed down the twin rulings that sanctioned abortion on demand. It was these decisions, in fact, that moved many to band together to protest what seemed to them the court's outrageous and immoral act. ". . . [W]e felt as though the bottom had been pulled out from under us," recalled a woman in an interview with author Kristin Luker (*Abortion and the Politics of Motherhood*). "It was an incredible thing. I couldn't believe it. In fact, I didn't." Many shared this woman's sense of shock, unable to believe that a climate of opinion or a court could differ so radically with the views that were to them so obviously and indisputably correct.

But the climate of opinion *had* grown more receptive to abortion over the years, whether or not its opponents had noticed. The people who had noticed were those who had been pushing for the changes *Roe* v. *Wade* signalled. It was possible in 1973 for those who cheered the Supreme Court decision to believe that organized opposition to abortion was only "small and sectarian." It looked like everything was going the way the reformers wanted.

The most comprehensive collection of questions on abortion, posed by the National Opinion Research Center (NORC), showed that from 1965 to 1972, support for abortion had increased. NORC asked people whether they thought it should be possible for a pregnant woman to obtain a legal abortion for each of six reasons: "if the woman's health is seriously endangered by the pregnancy," "if she became pregnant as a result of rape," "if there is a strong chance of a serious defect in the baby," "if the family has a very low income and cannot afford any more children," "if she is not married and does not want to marry the man," and "if she is married and does not want any more children." The first three circumstances have been called the "hard" reasons and the last three the "soft" reasons for abortions. Between 1965 and 1972, support for abortion increased for all reasons. There was a greater willingness to approve it for the hard than for the soft reasons, though the gap in approval for the two sets of reasons had narrowed.

Other surveys offered the same kind of encouragement to the reformers. Whereas a Gallup inquiry in 1969 had found a minority of 44 percent of its sample in favor of a law that "would permit a woman to go to a doctor to end pregnancy at any time during the first three months," by 1972 that had climbed to 51 percent. And the belief that the decision to abort should be reached by a woman and her physician had climbed from 57 to 64 percent within five months in 1972. Louis Harris found 48 percent that same year in favor of "allowing legalized abortions to take place up to four months of pregnancy" (43 percent opposed it). Though this support slipped 6 percentage points two months later, most of it went to the undecided category and not to the opposition.

It is small wonder, then, that the pro-choice side congratulated the Supreme Court in 1973 for issuing a decision that paralleled public preferences as well as their own. Many thought the battle had been won.

### What Meets Public Approval

Certain aspects of favorable opinion about a liberalized abortion law continued to grow following the Supreme Court decision, so that by 1982, an overwhelming 80 percent agreed mildly or strongly that "the decision to have an abortion should be left to the woman and her physician." By 1983, 54 percent supported the Court when a Gallup question explained *Roe* v. *Wade* as allowing "a woman [to] go to a doctor to end pregnancy at any time during the first three months of pregnancy." (A similarly worded description in a 1969 Gallup question had elicited 56 percent *dis*approval of a hypothetical law.) And by 1984, 62 percent agreed (either strongly or somewhat) that "a woman should be able to get an abortion if she decides she wants one," (ABC/*Post*) up from 61 percent in a comparable NBC question two years earlier.

More than a decade of NORC questions, following the Court's action, 1973-1982, further reassured the pro-choice side. These polls were among those cited most frequently as demonstrations of public support for abortion. With few dramatic fluctuations, approval of abortion under six circumstances ranged from around 50 percent at the low end (the lowest was the 49 percent who believed in 1982 that it should be possible for a woman to obtain a legal abortion if "she is married and does not want any more children") to a high of 93 percent in a case where the woman's health is seriously endangered. (See p. 27 of Opinion Roundup.) Support for abortion in cases of rape or a strong chance of a serious defect in the baby hovered in the realm of 83 percent.

Not only did the support for abortion look strong, but the opposition also looked weak. Gallup had been asking a question since 1975 that probed some of the subtleties of approval or disapproval—"Do you think abortions should be legal under any circumstances, legal under only certain circumstances, or illegal in all circumstances?"—and since 1975, no more than 23 percent had ever insisted upon absolute illegality. In 1983, that number was down to an all-time low of 16 percent.

### The Muddle

So, in the eyes of those who wish to maintain the current abortion laws, their beliefs were and are right in line with the public mood. Neither the public nor pro-choice advocates wishes abortion to be made illegal; neither favors a constitutional amendment to ban it; neither wishes to make a woman bear a child who might be deformed, might threaten her health, or who was conceived in a rape. If this is true, and if these things the public wants are on the anti-abortion hit list, then it would be easy for the pro-choice side to believe that their opposition couldn't succeed. But, of course, the pro-choice forces have begun to fear that their opposites *are* succeeding, and they seem to have no clue why.

Selective readings of statistics can make it appear that the Supreme Court made its abortion decision in harmony with the sentiments of the general public, and they can make it look as if the abortion opposition was bucking the majority. It's no wonder, then, that abortion rights advocates have been able to see their opinions reflected by the populace. What the pro-choice side failed to notice was the *magnitude* of sentiment on the other side—it is indeed a minority on many questions, but a sizable one.

What the pro-choice side seems to underestimate, as does the anti-abortion side, is the degree to which Americans have mixed feelings about abortion. Most think of abortion as a necessary, though not very attractive, evil. They endorse it only reluctantly. The tale of this reluctance can be told with the public opinion numbers that are less often cited.

### Abortion's Troubling Aspects

One culprit in the misunderstanding of public opinion about abortion is polling itself. It's possible to believe people support the Supreme Court decision simply because questions about it fail to tell the whole story. Queries about the Supreme Court decision, for example, most often specify that abortion is legal in the first three months of pregnancy. The decision, though, actually allows abortion far beyond that time, and this makes a difference to the public. The Gallup poll used to ask a series of questions (1979) in order to determine how opinion on abortion under varied circumstances might be affected by specifying first, second, or third trimesters. Once past the first trimester, it was impossible to muster a majority for any situation other than danger to the mother's life. (The question was posed to those who believed that abortion should be legal under only certain circumstances, not those who felt it should be legal or illegal at all times.) Because such a question allows us to see how people qualify their support, it is a truer test of their approval for *Roe* v. *Wade*.

Most, in fact, did not fall in with the opinions of either extreme on the abortion question—they thought it should be neither legal nor illegal all the time. And most people did not believe that most circumstances justify abortion. The possibility of a deformed baby (44 percent approved of abortion), or impairment of the mother's mental health (42 percent) or family financial trouble (15 percent) were all considered insufficient grounds for abortion even in the first trimester in this Gallup poll. In the second and third trimester, these disapproved situations expanded to include the possibility of severe physical health damage to the mother and a pregnancy that resulted from rape or incest. Though we have no more recent data to track the effect of adding advancing trimesters to questions, there is ample evidence from other surveys to buttress what Gallup found for the first trimester.

The NORC questions mentioned earlier are asked of the general population. They help demonstrate that people are troubled by certain occasions for abortion. In the cases of most severe hardship (threat to mother's health or life, chance of defect in the baby, cases of rape) most people approve abortion in these polls. In past years, there usually has also been a bare majority who supported abortion for a woman whose family has a very low income and cannot afford any more children. This turned around in 1983, when a 56 percent majority opposed abortion for financial reasons, as did 54 percent in 1984. Opposition in all three cases is at or close to a twelve-year high.

Abortion on demand has never been popular in anything but theory. At the same time that people supported the idea of relegating decisions about abortion to a woman and her physician, they have balked at circumstances that suggest this might be undertaken too lightly—for what people consider insufficient reason. Most people do not want to outlaw abortion (80 percent opt for legality in at least some circumstances), but it is also true in approximately equal proportions that they do not support abortion under *all* circumstances (also about 80 percent). Twenty percent would like abortion to be legal always, and 20 percent would like it to be illegal always. The bulk of the public (usually more than 50 percent) falls in the middle, which is a decidedly different spot from where the Supreme Court landed.

### Where the Public Draws the Line

Seventy-nine percent of the abortions these days are performed on unmarried women, most of whom are in their early twenties. Most abortions take place in the first trimester (91 percent, according to the Guttmacher Institute, the statistical arm of Planned Parenthood). It's impossible to be certain why these women decided on abortion, but one can tell from other data that most were not the victims of rape, nor were they faced with threats to their lives or physical health, or to their babies' health. If all this is correct, then most abortions that take place do so for precisely the reasons most Americans disapprove: financial or psychological reasons or convenience.

Polling analyst William Schneider has explained that people draw the line between approving and disapproving abortion where "the pregnancy was, at least to some degree, a deliberate decision." The public believes that once the decision is made, abortion is an unacceptable "way of getting out of it." In other words, says Schneider, "the American public does not endorse abortion as a form of birth control."

To the extent that the right-to-life movement can emphasize these circumstances as the ground upon which they disagree with present law, they will have the public on their side. The most current information reinforces this. Two polls taken in January 1985 showed majorities in favor of abortion only in cases of rape, incest, or a threat to the mother's life. In Gallup's poll for *Newsweek*, 62 percent approved a ban on abortion in all but those cases, up from 53 percent a year earlier. A January CBS News/*New York Times* poll asked whether people thought abortion should be "legal as it is now; legal only in such cases as saving the life of the mother, rape, or incest; or should it not be permitted at all?" Forty-five percent believed abortion should be allowed only in the situations named; 38 percent wanted things as they are; and 13 percent wanted abortion outlawed.

People are extremely uncomfortable with the idea of abortion. They think it is wrong, but they seem reluctant to make moral decisions about it for others. Fifty-three percent in 1982 (the last NBC query) personally believed that abortion is wrong, though only a little more than half of *them* thought it should be illegal. At the same time, in the same poll, 80 percent agreed that the decision to have an abortion should be left to the woman and her physician, and 61 percent agreed that "every woman who wants to have an abortion should be able to have one."

There are reasons for this lack of willingness to endorse laws that reflect one's own opinions about abortion. Part of the explanation must be our national tradition of individualism, but more specific to the abortion issue is probably the fear of the consequences. People do not believe that outlawing abortion would eliminate abortions. Ninety-three percent said this year that women would get abortions anyway. But perhaps most telling is that 92 percent believe now (as did 83 percent in 1973) that outlawing abortion would be dangerous; women would be forced to seek unsafe procedures performed by incompetent people, and they would be harmed.

People are reluctant to impose their standards on others, especially if it may cause damage, and they hesitate to curtail others' freedom to choose. When asked for their views, they don't care much for abortion, but when asked what ought to be done about it, they often opt for the status quo. Public debates about the subject tend to take place at the extremes, where people are most certain of themselves and where things are simplest. It's important to remember that the public itself, unlike some of its spokesmen, is far less single-minded.

# American Religion
## IN THE 1980'S

*In the 1980's, Catholic bishops are giving leadership in public affairs and conservative Protestants are continuing to grow in size and influence.*

**Paul Bock**

*Dr. Bock, Associate Religion Editor of USA Today, is professor of religion, Doane College, Crete, Neb.*

SINCE World War II, it has been possible to characterize each decade in American religion. The 1950's was a time of religious revival, church growth, positive thinking, Billy Graham crusades, and religious patriotism. It was then that the phrase "under God" was inserted into the Pledge of Allegiance. To some extent, the revival reflected the sense of anxiety and insecurity associated with the Cold War.

The 1960's was a time of activism and social change in which all institutions—including religious ones—were under attack. It was also a time of ecumenical advance spurred by the Second Vatican Council. The growing pluralism in America was reflected in the election of John F. Kennedy, the first Roman Catholic to become president. It was the time of the civil rights struggle led by Martin Luther King, Jr., and of the Vietnam War—issues that divided churches and families. The more radical youth viewed religion as an ally of the military-industrial complex. The "my country right or wrong" patriotism received a sharp setback. Many young people developed a lifestyle that went counter to traditional values. Supreme Court decisions regarding church-state separation reduced the possibilities of devotional activity in public classrooms.

By contrast, the 1970's was for many people a time of turning inward. To some extent, this was a reaction to and disillusionment with the activism of the 1960's.

Conservative groups flourished even more than in the previous two decades, and cults such as the Unification Church or the Hare Krishnas came into prominence. The Jonestown tragedy produced deep concern about cults. A neo-pentecostal or charismatic movement penetrated main-line Protestant denominations such as the Episcopal, Lutheran, and Presbyterian Churches and developed a strong following even within Roman Catholicism. Social concerns continued; they shifted, however, into areas of world hunger, ecology, energy, and women's rights. There was a great increase in the number of women studying theology, and in some denominations there were battles over women's ordination. Catholics experienced inner conflict over a number of issues, including birth control. Main-line Protestants were faced with a decline in membership and financial support, partly as a result of the liberal stand they had taken in the previous decade on civil rights, the Vietnam War, and other issues. Liberation Theology became well-known under the names of Black Theology, Feminist Theology, and Latin American Liberation Theology.

Is it possible at this point to characterize religious developments in the 1980's? To some extent, it is. Some are clearly continuations of trends in the previous decade, others are new.

**The strength of the main-line Protestant denominations keeps declining.** Although the membership decline seems to have leveled of, there is a shortage of young adults in many of these churches. For example, 41% of Methodists and 43% of the United Church of Christ members are age 55 or older. By contrast, none of the conservative Protestant groups have as many as 40% of their membership in the "over-50" bracket. It appears that the main-line Protestant churches have suffered most from the youth rebellion of the 1960's. There is also a lower birth-rate among he main-line Protestants than among the conservative Protestants.

Another reason for the declining strength is the fact that some people reacted negatively against the liberal stands taken by their church leaders. Their reaction was abetted by attacks on the National and World Councils of Churches by the *Reader's Digest* or "60 Minutes." However, there were other factors that were quite likely more significant. Some observers feel that the main-line churches have been impersonal and bureaucratic, that they have failed to respond to the need for religious experience, for clear-cut guidance and authority, and for a warm religious community. Furthermore, they lacked in the evangelistic zeal of an earlier era and, while they showed great concern for public affairs, they neglected to show concern for private matters. They were adapting, to some degree, to the secularity of the times, whereby people order their daily activities by pragmatic and utilitarian considerations, not by overarching moral and religious principles. Religion has become a Sunday affair or maybe a family affair. The great theologians of the earlier era, such as Reinhold Niebuhr or Paul Tillich, who made a great impact, particularly on the intellectual community, have not been replaced by thinkers with a similar impact.

**The most significant religious influence on national affairs is now coming from the Catholic bishops.** They have taken a very courageous stand in their pastoral letter of 1983 entitled "The Challenge of Peace." Some government officials became so disturbed by it that they sought to secure a modification of it. Later, the bishops drafted an equally courageous letter on the economy. It, too, was widely criticized by the general public. Meanwhile, a group of Catholic laymen launched a strong attack against the bishops, charging that they were exceeding their competence as bishops by assuming expertise in political and economic matters. The bishops' action is significant in view of the fact that, in the past, especially prior to John F. Kennedy's election to the presidency in 1960, they were cautious in their public statements lest they be accused of bringing about papal influence on American life.

Within the Catholic Church, there continue to be controversies over ordination of women, birth control, and divorce. There are some indications of independent thinking and of disagreement with the Church's position concerning these issues. Generally speaking, the Catholics have been the strongest supporters of the pro-life movement in regard to abortion.

**Conservative Protestant churches continue to grow.** Smaller groups such as the Assemblies of God and Seventh Day Adventists are among the rapidly growing bodies. The Southern Baptist Church, now the largest Protestant denomination, is continuing to expand, though there is an inner conflict between the less conservative evangelicals and the more conservative fundamentalists. TV evangelists have developed a sizeable following. Rigid and demanding beliefs, traditional values, certainty, absolutist moral teachings, and an enthusiasm for evangelism seem to fill the need of our times, and these groups offer them all.

It has become almost fashionable to be "born again." Among the reborn Christians are rock stars, folk singers, movie stars, professional athletes, and U.S. senators. Pres. Reagan has allied himself with the conservative religious movement. Evangelical books and journals are selling well. The outreach of various evangelical organizations is great among college students and other youth.

A parallel movement can be seen in Judaism. Orthodox Judaism has been growing more rapidly than either the Reform or the Conservative branches. There is a return to a more traditional faith in search of a distinct religious identity and prescribed way of life.

**Conservative Protestants, especially fundamentalists, are more active politically than in the past.** In previous decades, social action has been associated largely with the liberal churches, and they have focused on issues such as racial justice, disarmament, hunger, and civil liberties. Conservatives were concentrating on evangelism and personal moral issues. Now, however, they have become convinced that political action is necessary to save America from the "secular humanism" which has infected schools, colleges, and the media.

Holding to traditional morality, they have seen clear threats in campaigns for homosexual rights, the Equal Rights Amendment, the legislation of abortion, sex education in public schools, and the absence of prayers in public schools. Conservatives are now active in public affairs, but the issues they have chosen to work on are different from those pursued by the liberal churches. While stressing legislation to protect personal morality, they side with "the right" on political issues and hence are called "the religious right." They support an increase of *"laissez-faire"* capitalism and a decline of Federal involvement in the economy. According to Jerry Falwell, the book of Proverbs in the Bible teaches capitalism. They also support a strong military policy and a flag-waving patriotism. In this respect, the actions of the religious right look like the religious patriotism of the 1950's and unlike the civil religion of the 1960's. At that time, Martin Luther King, Jr., in his addresses such as "I Have a Dream," was linking patriotism with a critique of America's failure to live up to its own human rights ideals as enshrined in the Constitution and the Bill of Rights.

**There has been a decline in the influence of the cults.** The Bhagwan Shree Rajneesh's return to India is one indication of this. The Unification Church (the Moonies), which received a lot of attention in previous years, has experienced a decline in membership in the U.S. The fears expressed in the 1970's by the anti-cult movement proved to have been exaggerated. The deviance of the cults from their surrounding culture made them unlikely to gain widespread acceptance.

Although some groups were declining in membership appeal, it was recognized that the proliferation of new groups would continue. This has happened throughout our history. Some groups, like the Mormons and the Jehovah's Witnesses, have survived, while others faded away once the original leadership was gone or new circumstances necessitated a change. With each century, America has become more pluralistic. Now, one can find in the U.S. both the Eastern as well as the Western religions. Missionaries leave this land for faraway places, but they also come to this land from faraway places.

## Addressing issues

**Religion continues to have an influence on the issues of peace and justice.** Not only the Catholic bishops, but other churchmen as well, are taking courageous stands. The willingness of church groups to provide sanctuaries for illegal refugees from Central America has been quite noteworthy. Religious groups have taken stronger and stronger stands on disinvestment in South Africa, responding to the challenges presented by Anglican bishop Desmond Tutu and Reformed minister Allen Boesak. Most churches have been deeply involved in various aspects of the peace issue, including the nuclear freeze movement. There has been a wide outpouring of aid to starving people in Africa, an issue that drew support from all segments of the religious community—liberal and conservative alike. Among the evangelicals, there has been a striking awakening of social concern as reflected in journals like *Sojourners* and *The Other Side*. All of this would indicate that, despite setbacks, religious groups are continuing to be a social conscience of the nation.

**Religion continues to play a vital role in American life.** In the 1960's, there were signs of a declining influence of religion and an expectation that America would become a secular society. However, religion seems to be very much alive. Harvey Cox, who wrote *The Secular City* in the 1960's, revised his views in *Religion in the Secular City,* written in the 1980's. Whereas, according to the Gallup Poll, 75% of the American people thought in 1970 that religion was losing influence, only 46% were of that opinion in 1980.

The 1984 presidential election manifested the continuing influence of religion. Rev. Jesse Jackson and the black churches exerted a noticeable influence. The conflicts between vice-presidential candidate Geraldine Ferraro and the Catholic bishops over abortion brought religion very much into public view. The signs of religious vitality in this country are matched by similar signs in other parts of the world—in Poland, Korea, Africa, and Latin America.

Martin Marty, author of many books and articles on American religion, sees a switch in trends in American history from religiosity to secularity and back to religiosity:

Religion, from Iran through India and Ireland to Israel and Washington, bids stridently for power. The religious rationales may be all wrong; indeed, being mutually contradictory, they cannot all be right. Yet they speak afresh to the passional sides of life, while the dispossessed keepers of the secular myth settle for relations chiefly with life's operative sides, by which I mean the practical running of things in spheres such as science, commerce, government, and daily affairs. Two two-century long trajections have begun to trade courses.*

_____

*Martin Marty, "Transpositions in the 1980's," *The Annals*, July, 1985, pp., 12-13.

# Stratification and Social Inequalities

People are ranked in many different ways: by physical strength, education, wealth, or other characteristics. Those who are rated highly usually enjoy special privileges and opportunities. They often have power over others, special status, and prestige. The differences among people constitute their life chances, or the probability that an individual or group will be able to obtain the valued and desired goods in a society. These differences are referred to as stratification, or the system of structured inequalities that pattern social relationships.

In most industrialized societies income is one of the most important divisions among people, whereas in agricultural societies kinship has a major influence on life chances. Karl Marx described stratification in different terms. He used the term social class to refer to two distinct groups: those who control the means of production and those who do not. These groups overlap extensively with the rich and poor. This section examines the life chances of the rich and the poor and of various disadvantaged groups because they best demonstrate the crucial features of the stratification system in the United States.

The article by Maurice Zeitlin on the excessive power of the rich is already a classic. It analyzes the income and power distribution in the United States before and during the Reagan administration. It attacks the image of America as the land of democracy, equality, and opportunity, and finds that America is unfair to the majority of its citizens.

While Zeitlin focuses on the ownership of the rich, Gregory Fossedal considers welfare for the rich, or at least for corporations. Government handouts to rich corporations dwarf aid to poor people. Unfortunately efforts to trim corporate welfare will meet with powerful opposition and probably will not succeed.

In the 1980s the homeless, or street people, are very much in the public eye. Street people were primarily alcoholics and inveterate drifters until the economy became so troubled and before mental institutions began releasing large numbers of people to reduce their patient load.

As a result, many who are mentally unstable and others who have been squeezed by hard times and deserted by the government make up a majority of the homeless today. Wickenden explains their plight and discusses how governments and other groups have responded.

A major issue today is whether welfare for the poor does more harm than good. Charles Murray and Jesse Jackson have a heated debate on this and other issues involving the poor. Both, agree however, that the poor must be given incentives to better themselves. Murray would remove most welfare programs because they give the message, "You can get along without holding a job. You can get along if you have a baby but have no husband and no income." Jackson focuses on a different set of disincentives: redlining, discrimination, and countless closed doors. He argues that many of the poor will do surprisingly well when they are given a chance and some encouragement.

The last three articles vividly and perceptively describe the situation of the black underclass. While the black middle class is advancing rapidly and many poor blacks are holding jobs and taking care of their families, the black underclass continues to suffer from joblessness, broken homes, welfare, drugs, and violence.

The seven articles in this section portray tremendous differences in wealth and life chances among Americans. Systems of inequality affect what a person does and when and how he or she does it. An important contribution of this section is to help you become more aware of how stratification operates in social life.

## Looking Ahead: Challenge Questions

Will technology reduce or increase social inequalities?

Why is stratification such an important theme in sociology?

What social groups are likely to rise in the stratification system in the next decade? Which groups will fall? Why?

# Who Owns America?
## The Same Old Gang

**MAURICE ZEITLIN**

*Maurice Zeitlin is a professor of sociology at the University of California, Los Angeles. Detailed references for the facts cited in this article are available from the author.*

Do you remember those full-page newspaper ads that showed a little old lady stroking *her* locomotive, supposedly owned by millions of ordinary Americans just like her? Or Standard Oil's gushing claim, "Yes, the people own the tools of production.... How odd to find that it is here, in the capitalism [Karl Marx] reviled, that the promise of the tool has been fulfilled." Well, it's happening again.

A current Texaco television commercial has Bob Hope asking us to "take a look at the owners of America's oil companies," and then leads us on a tour of a typical community made up of just plain folks like you and me. A recent book, received with much fanfare in the press, repeats the refrain. Its author, long-time management consultant and publicist Peter Drucker, tells us that an "unseen revolution" has wrought "a more radical shift in ownership than Soviet communism." Even more amazing, "the socialism of Marxist theory has been realized for the first time on American soil."

Not only are the means of production now in everyone's hands, but the U.S. Chamber of Commerce confides that the United States has become a "post-industrial society." College textbooks inform us that a "dramatic shift from blue collar to white collar, from brawn to brain [has] occurred," and the best-seller *Future Shock* rhapsodizes that "for the first time in human history," a society — *our* society — has "managed within a few short decades to throw off the yoke of manual labor." A book on "power in America" celebrates the passing of classes and suggests that we organize popular visits to "Newport, and bus tours through Grosse Pointe, for purely educational purposes — like seeing Carlsbad Caverns once." It is time, the author advises us, to shout, "The Working Class is dead. Long live the memory of the Working Class." And, summing it all up, a popular book on how to be a politician announces that "the economic class system is disappearing.... Redistribution of wealth and income... has ended economic inequality's political significance."

So, what has happened to classes? Who does own America, and how has it all been changing? Has the capitalist class really been "lopped off" at the top, as Harvard's Talcott Parsons once pithily put it? Has the ownership of American corporations become so dispersed that control has shifted to "professional managers" who are merely the "trustees" for all of us — "stockholders, employes, suppliers, consumers, and the public" — as Donald S. McNaughton, the chairman of Prudential Life, announced in a recent speech? Has the yoke of manual labor really been lifted? Is the working class now a mere memory? Or are the claims that prompt these questions really pseudofacts that are as plausible and persuasive as they are deceptive? The answer, I think, is clear: Economic inequality weighs as heavily and cuts as deeply as ever, and neither capitalists nor workers have vanished from American life.

Let's look first at who owns what. It's certainly hard enough to find out, even if, like Government economists, you have access to Internal Revenue Service (IRS) data. No law requires Americans to report their net worth, and besides, wealth is deliberately hidden, whether out of modesty or to avoid taxes. Still, an ingenious method of estimating wealth has been devised, to make the dead disclose what the living conceal. It is called the "estate multiplier technique," and it uses IRS data on estate tax returns. It treats those who die in any year as a "stratified sample" of the living on whose estates tax returns would have to be filed if they died during the year — that is, those with estates worth $60,000 or more. All told, only 4 per cent of the adults in this country have estates as large as $60,000, counting *everything* they own, including cash in hand or under the mattress, and the mattress itself. But within that group, a minute number of Americans make up the real owners of America.

The Rose Bowl's 104,696 seats would still be half empty if only every adult American who owns $1 million or more in corporate stock came to cheer, and it would be even emptier if only those who have $100,000 in state and local bonds got a seat. If you counted all state, local, and Federal bonds (except U.S. Savings Bonds), and added Treasury bills, certificates, notes, and mortgages — and even foreign bonds — held by Americans in amounts of at least $200,000, you would still find well over a quarter of the Rose Bowl seats not taken. Only 55,400 adults have $1 million or more in corporate stock. A mere 40,000 have $100,000 or more in state and local bonds (all Federal tax exempt), and 73,500 adults have $200,000 or more if we count all bonds and debtholdings.

This tiny owning class at the tip of the top, barely more than one-twentieth of 1 per cent of American adults, has a fifth of *all* the corporate stock, nearly two-thirds of the worth of *all* state and local bonds, and two-fifths of *all* bonds and notes. No wonder it took five years of trying by an outstanding economist, James D. Smith, to get the IRS to allow him to study its information — and by then some of the data had been destroyed.

Contrast what this propertied class owns to what the rest of us have. Nine out of ten adults in the United States could sell everything they own, pay off their debts, and have no more than $30,000 left. Worse, more than half of all Americans would have a total "net worth" of no more than $3,000. The bottom half of all American families combined have only three cents of every dollar's worth of all the wealth in the country.

Back at the top, if we count up what the richest 1 per cent of the population own, we find that they have a seventh of all the real estate in the country, more than half the corporate stock, and almost all the trust assets. They even had a seventh of all the *cash* in every checking and savings account and pocket and purse in America.

Summed up, that is a quarter of the net worth of the entire population held by the top 1 per cent. If we take a slice as large as the richest 4 per cent — everyone whose total net assets (i.e. subtracting debts) are worth at least $60,000 — their combined wealth is more than a trillion dollars — enough to buy the entire national product of the United States and have plenty left over to pick up the combined output of a few small European countries, including Switzerland, Norway, Denmark, and Sweden.

So it's clear who owns America — but has this propertied class been slipping in its hold on the nation's wealth? Maybe, but if it slipped at all, it was not because of any egalitarian tendencies in American capitalism. It took the country's worst crash, the Great Depression, when many fortunes (and even a few of the fortune-holders) took the plunge from the pinnacle, to make a dent on what they own. Even the modest shrinkage that supposedly took place then is probably more apparent than real, because just before the crash there was a phenomenal rise in the price of stock, the biggest asset in the portfolios of the rich.

But since the end of World War II, there has been no change in their share of the nation's wealth; it has been constant in every year studied, at roughly five-year intervals, since 1945. The richest 1 per cent own a quarter, and the top half of 1 per cent a fifth, of the combined market worth of everything owned by every American. Remarkably, economic historians who have culled manuscript census reports on the past century report that on the eve of the Civil War the rich had the same cut of the total: The top 1 per cent owned 24 per cent in 1860 and 24.9 per cent in 1969 (the latest year thoroughly studied). Through all the tumultuous changes since then — the Civil War and the emancipation of the slaves, the Populist and Progressive movements, the Great Depression, the New Deal, progressive taxation, the mass organization of industrial workers, and World Wars I and II — this class has held on to everything it had. They owned America then and they own it now.

Any notion that *income* has been redistributed, even though *property* is intact, is also illusory: The higher the income bracket, the higher the percentage in it that derives its income from the ownership of property. At the top, almost all income is in dividends, rents, royalties, and interest. Among all American families and unrelated individuals combined, not more than one in eight receives any stock dividends at all. Not one in a hundred receives even a dollar from any "trust or estate." But among those with incomes of $100,000 or more, 97 per cent receive stock dividends and more than half receive inherited income directly from a trust or estate.

The 5 per cent of Americans with the highest incomes take in almost half of all the income from property in the country. They receive sixty-four cents out of every dollar in dividends earned on publicly traded stock and ninety-three cents of the dividends on stock owned in "closely held corporations" (those having just a few owners). Furthermore, they take in thirty cents of every dollar earned in interest, thirty-seven cents in rents and royalties, and sixty-four cents of every dollar in America coming from trusts and estates.

If we divide Americans into five brackets from low to high, and count all known income, the top fifth gets about forty cents of every dollar of personal income. The bottom fifth gets just one nickel. That is a ratio of eight to one, and that ratio has remained almost exactly the same in every year since World War II ended. (Here, in the capitalism celebrated by the Advertising Council and Bob Hope, the gap between the top and bottom fifths is wider than in Britain, Holland, West Germany, or even Japan. Among industrial nations, only France has a wider gap.) And the *real income* gap between the top and bottom has been growing, though the ratio has stayed the same: The average real income difference between the top and bottom fifth, measured in constant 1969 dollars, rose from $11,000 to $19,000 in the twenty years between 1949 and 1969.

All those "redistributive efforts" and wars on poverty we have heard about have not made a dent in income distribution. The overall tax burden has probably become more *regressive* since World War II — taxes are taking an increasing bite of the incomes of people in the lower rather than in the higher brackets. One reason is that state and local taxes, which are typically more regressive than Federal taxes, have grown in comparison to Federal taxes — from forty-two cents to every dollar of Federal taxes collected in 1950 to fifty-one cents in 1961 and fifty-eight cents in 1970.

But even Federal taxes have become more regressive during the same years. Corporate taxes have gone down, from twenty-seven cents of every Federal tax dollar received in 1950 to only sixteen cents in 1970, and at the same time Social Security and payroll taxes have jumped from just nine cents to twenty-six cents of each tax dollar pumped into Washington. So, when the impact of all taxes and all Government spending is taken into account — even though there has been a sizable increase in Government "benefits" to low-income Americans — the level of income inequality ("post-fiscal") has not changed since 1950.

The notion that classes are withering away in America rests not only on the mistaken assumption that the propertied have been lopped off at the top, but on the equally unfounded notion that the working class itself has been vanishing and the "white collar" strata of the so-called middle class have been multiplying. So renowned a pundit as Harvard's John Kenneth Galbraith, among many others, believes the class struggle is a "dwindling phenomenon" because "the number of white-collar workers in the United States almost fifteen years ago overtook the number in the blue-collar working force and is, of course, now greater.''

Of course? The sort of counting done here misses and distorts what has really happened; it confuses occupational composition with class lines. Since the 1900s, especially during World War II, and in quickening pace in recent years, women — and increasingly married women — have been moving into the labor force. About four out of ten people in the labor force are now women, and almost half of all women now have paying jobs or are looking for them. It is this influx of women into paying jobs that accounts for the growing number of ''white-collar'' jobs — mainly in ''clerical or sales'' work — in the past few decades. Of all working women, not even one in ten was a ''clerical or sales'' worker in 1900. By 1940, on the eve of World War II, the figure jumped to almost three in ten, and it climbed until it reached more than four in ten in 1970.

At the same time, the proportion of women working in crafts or as operatives and laborers (except on the farm) dropped. It also dropped in so-called ''service'' occupations which, for women, are typically dirty and menial jobs as domestics or ''food service'' workers. Some ''white-collar'' jobs are now almost entirely filled by women — and ten occupations alone, among them waitress, typist, cashier, hairdresser and beautician, nurse and dietician, sales clerk, and teacher, account for more than two out of five employed women. Of all clerical and sales jobs, two out of three, and the same ratio in service jobs, are filled by women. In contrast, of all those working in crafts or as operatives and laborers (off the farm), only one in six is a woman.

Among men, meanwhile, the portion with clerical and sales jobs has not risen in three decades. Only seven in a hundred men at work had clerical or sales jobs in 1900, and it rose to just twelve in a hundred by 1940. In the three decades since, the ratio has not grown at all: It is still about twelve in a hundred. In the same years, though, there has been a significant rise in the proportion of men classified as ''professionals and technicians'' by the U.S. Census — from three, to six, to fourteen in a hundred. But many such ''professionals'' are vocational school products, and about four out of ten in the rapidly growing category of ''technicians'' are not college graduates. This, of course, is scarcely the image evoked by the terms ''professional'' or ''technician.'' Many are really highly skilled workers; advanced education or certification is not required to fill their jobs, nor does their work differ much in independence and control from the work done by those classified as ''craftsmen.''

The plain fact is that the category of ''manual workers'' has not shrunk at all in this century. Fewer than forty in a hundred men worked in 1900 as a ''craftsman, operative, or nonfarm laborer.'' In 1920, the figure rose to forty-five in a hundred, and it has barely changed since: In 1970, forty-seven out of every hundred men in the labor force were classified as manual workers. But to this figure we must add many if not most of the men who are called ''service workers'' — a U.S. Census category that hides a host of blue-collar jobs within its semantic recesses: janitors, porters, waiters, garage mechanics, dishwashers, and laundry workers. How many of the seven in a hundred

men in such service jobs in 1970 should be identified as ''real workers'' is anybody's guess — and mine is that it is most. We must also add an uncounted number of jobs that strangely get catalogued in the Census as ''white collar'' — among them stock clerks, baggagemen, newspaper carriers (''sales''), and even mailmen. Their work is certainly — and often heavily — ''manual labor.''

A safe estimate, then, is that more than five of every ten men who work in this country are manual workers, maybe as many as six in ten — and this does not count the three out of a hundred who work as agricultural laborers. Perhaps the only real difference in the working class today compared to past decades is that many working men now count on their wives' (or daughters') earnings to make the family's ends meet.

In fact, their wives are typically manual workers themselves, for among employed women, the division is sharp between those whose husbands are workers and those who are married to ''professionals'' or ''managers.'' Among the latter's working wives, only one in six is in manual (or service) jobs. But among the working wives of craftsmen, two in five have such jobs; among the working wives of operatives, almost one out of two; and among the wives of laborers, about two out of three. They certainly are not smuggling any middle-class values, loyalties, or way of life into the working class based on their own experience at work. For them, on the contrary, as for most men in America, the ''yoke of manual labor'' is yet to be lifted.

Besides, whatever the social images ''manual labor'' evokes or whatever pain it involves, in real class terms the distinction between it and ''nonmanual'' or ''white-collar'' employment is, at best, misleading. How does wearing a white collar lift you into another class? Perhaps there is more prestige attached, though even this is doubtful, particularly among workers themselves. For some ''white-collar'' workers there may be increased security, but how many cashiers, typists, or beauticians get ''salaries'' rather than hourly wages, or are less subject to layoffs than highly organized manual workers?

Since most ''white-collar'' employes are women, and don't wear collars, white or otherwise, anyway, the name itself surely fools us about what it represents. The vast majority of the clerical and sales workers of today are, in any event, not the respectable clerks of yesteryear. Their work is not only routinized and standardized, but they often work in offices that are larger than (and even as noisy as) small manufacturing shops — tending steno machines, typewriters, accounting machines, data processors, or keypunch equipment. They work in supermarkets and department stores with hundreds of others who punch in and punch out and wait to be relieved before they take a break. They are as bereft of control over their work and the products of their work as ''manual'' workers — in fact, they have *less* independence and control than such workers as crane operators and longshoremen. Beneath their nice clean collars (if they wear them at all), they are propertyless workers, entirely dependent for their livelihoods on the sale of their capacity to work. And this is the essence of working-class reality.

So, neither the working class nor the propertied class has yet departed our fair land. But do the propertied really make up a *capitalist* class? Haven't they, because ownership of the large corporations has become so dispersed, lost *control* of these decisive units of production in America? Of all the pseudofacts behind the notion that classes have withered away in America, none is as persistent as the doctrine of the "managerial revolution" or "unseen revolution" implied by these questions.

The claim is that there has been a "separation of ownership and control" in large corporations — that as the corporations have grown immense, as the original founders have died off or their fortunes supposedly dwindled, as their kids have taken to mere coupon-clipping and jet-setting, and as stock ownership has spread out widely, the capitalists have lost control of the means of production. The result, we are told, is that not capital but bureaucracy, not capitalists but "anonymous administrators," now control large corporations and hold decisive power in contemporary America. The "managers" have usurped their capitalist predecessors.

With the capitalists gone and the managers no longer their mere agents, the inherent conflict that used to exist between labor and capital also supposedly becomes a relic of the past. Instead, we now have not a system of class domination but an occupational order based on merit: "rewards" get distributed according to ability ("functional importance"). What's more, with capital dissolved and new managers motivated by other urges and the pride of professionalism in control, pumping out profit is no longer what drives the corporations in the new "post-capitalist society" we are alleged to be living in. Instead, they have become the "trustees," as Prudential's chairman said — and he was just paraphrasing Harvard economist Carl Kaysen's words of twenty years ago — for all of us in the "new industrial state."

The intent of such notions is clear: We are to believe that "labor" and "management" are just parts of the same team, doing different tasks. It is a theoretical shell game that hides the fact of class domination — of the ownership *and* control of the mines, mills, and factories by a class whose lives are certainly made easier if we don't know they're there, right behind the "anonymous bureaucrats." It hides the simple but profound fact that they live on what the rest of us produce.

One reason that the illusion of managerialism persists is that it is incredibly difficult to figure out who does control a large corporation. And the illusion is nurtured, as the late Senator Lee Metcalf put it bluntly and accurately, by a "massive cover-up" of the principal owners. There are several closely related ways that capital really controls the corporations. First, the real owners do not actually have to *manage* the corporation, or hang around the executive suite with its top officers or directors, or even be formally represented on the board, in order to have their objectives realized — that is, to exert *control*. And how much stock it takes to control a corporation is neither fixed nor standard.

The few recent studies that claim to find "management control" in most large corporations simply assume that it always takes at least 10 per cent of the stock in one pair of hands in order to assure control, but it does not work that way. If you own 10 per cent of the stock in a corporation, you are supposed to report it to the Securities and Ex-

change Commission (SEC), but if the same percentage is split among several of your close associates, without any formal ties between you, or with a few of your relatives, you don't have to report it — and even if you *are* required to report, who is to know if you don't? When Senator Metcalf died, he had been trying for years to get at such information, but his staff so far has had to rely on its own investigations and volunteered data.

How much stock is needed to control a corporation depends on how big the other stockowners are — and who they are, and how they are connected — and how dispersed the rest of the stock is; it also depends on how deeply the firm is indebted to the same few large banks or other creditors. What sorts of ties the corporation has to others, and especially to big banks and other "financial institutions" allied with it, is also crucial. The ability to exert control grows with the number of other major firms in which any family, individual, or group of associates has an interest or actual control.

What a particular large holding of stock implies for any attempt at control depends to an unknown extent on who holds it. If it is held, say, by a leading capitalist family like the Mellons — who control at least four firms in the top 500 nonfinancials (Gulf, Alcoa, Koppers Co., Carborundum Co.) as well as the First Boston Corp., the General Reinsurance Corp., and Mellon National Bank and Trust (the fifteenth largest bank in the country, measured by deposits), and perhaps also, through the Mellon Bank's 7 per cent shareholding, Jones and Laughlin Steel — the meaning is just not the same as if some otherwise unconnected shareowner held it.

Even in corporations that a family like Mellon does not control, the presence of its representative among the principal shareowners, or on the board, can be critical. So the late Richard King Mellon as one of the principal shareowners in General Motors carried a rather different clout in its corporate policy than, say, Billy Rose did in AT&T, though he was reputed to be one of its biggest shareowners. Precisely because the number of shareowners is so large and their holdings typically so minute compared to the few biggest shareowners in a large corporation, it may not take more than 1 or 2 per cent of a company's stock to control it.

The critical holdings and connections that make control possible are invisible to the uninformed eye, and often even to the seasoned investigator. Senator Metcalf's staff found, for instance, that Laurance S. Rockefeller owns a controlling block of almost 5 per cent of the voting stock in Eastern Airlines, though his name did not appear on the required listing of its thirty top stockholders for the Civil Aeronautics Board. Neither the SEC nor the CAB nor Eastern itself could find all the accounts in which his shares were held and aggregate them until they asked *him* to do it for them — in response to Metcalf's prodding.

This helps explain why even the "insiders" who work as financial analysts at *Fortune, Forbes,* or *Business Week,* with their immense research resources and excellent files, have to rely heavily on gossip to estimate the holdings of even the leading families in corporations they have long controlled. These holdings are hidden in a welter of accounts held by brokers, dealers, foundations, holding companies, other corporations, associates, intermediaries, and "street names" (as the fictitious firms that just hold stock for someone are called on Wall Street) or other "nominees."

The extent of a leading capitalist family's holdings is also concealed by a finely woven though tangled web of kinship relations. Apparently unrelated persons with entirely different surnames can be part of a single cohesive set of kindred united to control a corporation. In Dow Chemical Company, for instance, there are seventy-eight dependents (plus spouses) of H.W. Dow who own a total of 12.6 per cent of Dow's stock. So, without research aimed at penetrating the web of kinship, any effort to find out who really controls a large corporation is hobbled at the outset.

In an outstanding recent study, Philip Burch Jr. mined the "inside information" presented over the years in the financial press and found that at least 60 per cent of the 500 top industrial corporations are "probably" (236) or "possibly" (64) under the control of an identifiable family or group of associates. Even these estimates are probably short of the mark because, in Ralph Nader's words, "no one really knows who owns the giant corporations that dominate our economic life." My own guess is that behind the thick veil of nominees, there are real controlling owners in most if not all of the large corporations that now appear to be under so-called management control.

Even if some large corporations were not really controlled by *particular* owning interests, this would not mean power had passed to the "new princes" from the old economic royalists. The higher executives would still have only *relative* independence in their activities and would be bound by the *general* interests of capital. The heads of the large corporations are the main formal agents or functionaries of capital. Their personal careers, interests, and commitments are closely tied to the expansion of corporate capital. Some are among the principal shareholders of the companies they run, and most own stock that not only provides much of their income but ranks them among the population's largest stockowners — and puts them in the propertied few.

Typically, the managers also move in the same intimate circles as the very rich. You'll find them together at debutante balls, select clubs, summer resorts and winter retreats, and other assorted watering places; and their kids attend the same private schools and rush the same fraternities and sororities — and then marry each other. Scratch a top executive and the chances are he will prove to be related to a principal shareowner. Intimate social ties and entangling kinship relations, common interests and overriding commitments unify the families of the heads of the largest corporations and their principal owners into the same cohesive, dominant class in America.

Finally, even if "management" alone had full control of the corporations, it would still have to try to pump the highest possible profits out of their workers and make the most of their investments. The conduct of management is shaped above all by the imperatives of capital accumulation — the competitive struggle among the giants (now global rather than national), the types of investments they make and markets they penetrate, and the relations they have with their workers. High managerial income and status depend, directly and indirectly, on high corporate profits. "Stock options" and bonuses and other forms of executive "compensation" aside from salaries are closely tied to corporate profit rates. Whatever their so-called professional motivations or power urges, their technocratic teamwork and bureaucratic mentality, managers' decisions on how to organized production and sales have to be measured against the bottom line: They dare not imperil corporate profitability.

The recent spate of articles in the financial press on "how to fire a top executive" — you have them "take early retirement" — and the new placement services now catering to them, are rather pointed indicators of what happens to supposed "management control" in times of receding profit margins. In 1974, a year of severe economic crisis around the world, about half of all the chief executives in the nation's top 500 firms were expected to be replaced — in what a weekly newsletter to corporate heads called "a wave of executive ousters" that would "cause the greatest disruption in the business community since the 1929 depression."

Any obvious lowering in profit rates is also reflected in a drop in the price of the corporation's stock; this squeezes its capital base and makes it an attractive — and vulnerable — target for takeover. And this, in turn, leads to executive ousters. In addition, with the marked centralization of huge shareholdings in the trust departments of a few of the biggest banks that administer the investment portfolios of the very rich — typically, they will not take a trust of under $200,000 — the tremors would be deep and the impact rather painful for any managers who turned out a below-average rate of return. The banks must unflinchingly act as "trustees" only for the top investors and real owners who control the large corporations.

Any political strategy that ignores or distorts these realities or is blind to the deep class divisions in our country cannot meet the common needs of the majority of Americans. So long as the illusion persists that our economic life has been "democratized" or that a "silent revolution" has already interred capital, emancipated labor, and redistributed wealth and income, we can be sure that a real effort to achieve those aims will be slated for yet another postponement.

Handouts for the able-bodied man in the gray flannel suit.

# CORPORATE WELFARE OUT OF CONTROL

## GREGORY FOSSEDAL

Gregory Fossedal works for the editorial page of *The Wall Street Journal.*

RONALD REAGAN has elevated the anecdote to an art form—and an effective weapon against the welfare state. Whether relating the tale of a woman receiving $65,000 in undeserved benefits, or wondering aloud whether there are really many unemployed people in "South Succotash," Reagan has effectively portrayed a social welfare budget riddled with "waste, fraud, and abuse." Now it's time he turned to perhaps the largest, fastest growing, yet least discussed public relief program of the federal government: corporate welfare or, as the Congress Watch lobbying group has dubbed it, "Aid for Dependent Corporations."

Corporate welfare has emerged as a pet theme among many free-enterprise liberals and supply-side conservatives. Both Bill Bradley and Jack Kemp, when attacked about the revenue implications of their tax reform plans, propose trimming corporate welfare as a means of cutting the budget deficit. Yet the subject has received little comprehensive research or analysis. When an aide to Kemp was asked two years ago for specific corporate welfare cuts, he could only offer, "Synthetic fuels . . . the Chrysler and big bank bailouts . . ." before his voice trailed off. Nothing beyond those two? "Well, some others. There really isn't any long list. Jack would love to see one, but right now it doesn't exist."

What research has been done suggests that corporate welfare is more costly than even Kemp or Bradley realizes. Annual studies by Ralph Nader's Congress Watch place the figure at $80 billion to $100 billion. A 1984 paper by the Congressional Budget Office estimates $90 billion. But both studies omit the defense budget, possibly the largest single source of such spending, and most "indirect subsidies"—that is, the impact of programs and regulations that help large corporations and cost the taxpayer money, but do not show up in any well-defined line-item. Add in a conservative estimate for those types of subsidies and for

defense spending, and you arrive at the annual corporate welfare check: $140 billion.

The problem with the corporate welfare freeloaders is that, like the social welfare cheaters, they are hard to find. "Instead of being listed as line-items in the budget, like the Food Stamp program," explains Congress Watch, "corporate welfare resides between the lines—in tax revenue not collected and loans not repaid. . . . While the budget process involves open debate of social programs and military spending, corporate subsidy programs easily escape scrutiny." Even CBO's vast staff expressed frustration in its modest attempt to list the most direct forms of corporate welfare. "Many industrial support program costs are hidden and not voted on explicitly by the Congress," a CBO report says. "It would be beyond the scope of this paper" to identify such items line by line. What is needed is a few Reagan-like vignettes to make all the waste, fraud, and abuse understandable to the average citizen.

*The Corporate Welfare Cadillac:* Reagan touches a nerve when he tells stories about poor people who, at taxpayer expense, lead lives of moral dissipation. Remember the one about the guy who bought vodka with his food stamps? Reagan might take a look at the International Monetary Fund and at Continental Bank of Illinois. The IMF was bailed out with $8 billion in federal money in 1983. The money was intended, the IMF said, to help Third World countries "restructure" their debt, and to prevent the collapse of the entire world banking system. The money, however, was not used to promote any real reforms in economic policy. Its chief effect was to save the careers of loan officers at large banks, whose ill-advised orgy of foreign lending created the threat to the "system" in the first place. In fact, in 1983 and 1984 a record number of small and medium-sized banks went belly up, more than at any time since the Depression. Not to worry, though: when Continental Bank teetered near the brink, the Reagan administration and the Federal Reserve quickly put together a $4.5 billion rescue package. The banking "safety net" may not catch everyone, but it misses few of the biggies.

*Private Sector Public Assistance:* Worse than the sleazy recipients who exploit overly generous benefits, however, are the miscreants who go on the dole even though they are well off. Many of the country's largest corporations fit into this category. For example, Exxon and other big energy companies not only receive research grants from the government amounting to $1.9 billion. In 1983 they also enjoyed $4.75 billion in tax "incentives" to encourage oil exploration in 1984. Just as the Reagan administration has proposed tighter rules for those on the social welfare dole, it might raise "eligibility standards" for corporate welfare recipients. In 1983 Congress did cut off one of the wealthiest welfare mothers of them all, the Clinch River Breeder Reactor, thus saving $8.5 billion. But it left intact the energy research expenditures, 84 percent of which go to the nuclear power programs of the big utilities—even though not a single nuclear plant has been ordered in the United States since 1974.

Also intact is the $7.4 billion in loans to the nuclear industry made by the Export-Import Bank from 1981 to 1984, and the $13.5 billion which the Synthetic Fuels Corporation is authorized to hand out. Lest anyone think that the Synfuel Corporation will offer support to Gilderesque entrepreneurs developing a miracle formula for turning chicken feathers into gasoline, guess again. Of 52 important synthetic fuel patents, 49 are owned by the major oil companies.

OTHER ABUSERS can be found at the Small Business Administration and the Export-Import Bank. Both pose as friends of the little guy. Yet one popular SBA loan guarantee program devotes 65 percent of its assistance to firms worth $100,000 or more, mostly to finance large shopping centers, parking lots, and the like. The Ex-Im Bank, meanwhile, in 1982 directed $4 billion of its total $4.4 billion in lending authority to large corporations able to fill huge export orders. As Doug Bandow wrote in *The New York Times* last fall, the bank "is a classic example of corporate welfare: Roughly 70 percent of its loans enrich seven large corporations." Boeing, Westinghouse, General Electric, and McDonnell Douglas alone take up $17 billion of the bank's outstanding credit.

*Stretching the Dollars:* Conservatives often illustrate the excesses of a social program by noting that the dollars already spent for it would stretch from here to the moon and back. On the corporate welfare rolls, subsidies to agribusiness can be used to make the same point. They have ballooned from a modest $5 billion in the early 1970s to $20 billion or more today. Approximately 70 percent of the subsidies go to the 250,000 biggest farmers in the country. Laid end to end, 20 billion dollar bills would stretch to the moon and back four times.

*The Handout That Wouldn't Die:* Perhaps the greatest source of corporate welfare is the tangled web of provisions governing federal procurement. Reagan himself now likes to recount the horror stories of U.S. defense contracting—the $8,000 screwdriver and the $25,000 coffee pot. But even greater institutional waste is generated every year by Congress and the White House, as they extend the life of

endangered weapons to see if a little more research and development can fix what's wrong with the latest gun that won't shoot or plane that won't fly. The typical time needed to construct a major weapons system has grown from three to six years in the early 1960s to more than ten years today. If we accept the General Accounting Office's rule of thumb for the cost of delay—a 30 percent increase for each year tacked on to the weapons procurement cycle—then delays in weapons procurement may be the single greatest source of corporate welfare in the budget.

Other agencies and departments have not been rocked by as many recent procurement scandals. Yet they buy goods and services from the private sector in even larger amounts, among them Medicare ($61 billion in 1984), Medicaid ($21 billion), food programs ($17 billion), and housing assistance ($10 billion). More competitive procurement in these agencies, according to estimates from the GAO and the Grace Commission on waste in government, could save between $5 billion and $10 billion, most of it presently going to medium and large corporations, and all of it unjustified by the rigors of free-market price competition.

*Candy from Babies:* The maritime industry is the corporate equivalent of the bureaucrat who, earning a $60,000 annual salary, remodels his office with millions from the federal school lunch program. Not content with several hundred million dollars in direct subsidies, U.S. shippers have established a "cargo preference" law, under which all official government travel must be conducted in American vessels—even if foreign transport is more available and cheaper. Half of all shipments bought, furnished, or financed by the U.S. government must be shipped on American vessels, regardless of costs. The cargo preference law cost the Food for Peace program $100 million a year in 1981—money that could have gone to the starving in Ethiopia.

Last but not least on the corporate welfare ledger is the kind of abuse that the social welfare recipients never benefit from: special tax breaks. The largest, such as accelerated depreciation and investment tax credit, spread their benefits across broad classes of industries. Others—permitting the passing of exploration costs for fuel along to consumers, the exclusion of interest on state and local pollution control bonds, and so on—were quite consciously designed to benefit particular sectors.

The hodgepodge of special breaks and exemptions has gradually eroded the corporate income tax. In 1975 the government collected 32 cents in corporate income taxes for every dollar in personal income tax. This year, the figure will be closer to 23 cents on the dollar. The increased complexity of the corporate code has also created wide disparities in the taxes collected from various sectors, greatly distorting the decisions of private investors. A pair of 1983 studies by the Congressional Research Service found effective corporate tax rates as low as 13 percent in the construction industry and as high as 37 percent in the finance, insurance, and real estate businesses.

IT WOULD SEEM a simple matter to cut corporate welfare abuses from the budget and the tax code. Yet this apparently attractive fiscal target has drawn little criticism from journalists or the leaders of either party. The cost of entitlements, the military, and Social Security are regularly identified as candidates for cutbacks in articles on the deficit. Corporate welfare, by contrast, is rarely mentioned. Why?

First, several of the self-proclaimed oracles on the budget and federal spending are corporate welfare recipients themselves. The names of Lee Iacocca and J. Peter Grace come to mind. They have a vested interest in not calling attention to the corporate dole. The original draft of the Grace Commission report, for example, named numerous politicians who had been especially sycophantic toward corporations and other special interest groups. Among those singled out frequently were Senators James McClure, Robert Byrd, and Ted Stevens; and Representatives Tip O'Neill, Silvio Conte, and Marvin Leath. Grace and his colleagues decided to delete the names in the final version so as not to hurt the report's chance to win acclaim. At about this time, Grace appeared on the cover of *U.S. News & World Report* under the headline "Washington: City Without Guts."

Second, if corporate welfare is hidden, its powerful proponents are not. Business political action committees in 1984 gave as much money to political candidates as labor, liberal, and conservative PACs combined. The business PACs are bipartisan, giving mainly to incumbents and committee chairmen of both parties: $24 million to Republicans, $21 million to Democrats in 1984. Not surprisingly, the old guard in both parties is committed to protecting corporate handouts.

Of the top ten Senate recipients of business PAC money in 1984, five were Democrats, including Jim Hunt, Jay Rockefeller, and Lloyd Doggett; on the House side, six out of ten, including the top three: Jim Jones, Joseph Addabbo, and Bruce Morrison. House Majority leader Jim Wright has led the fight to preserve the synthetic fuel program. Democratic presidential candidates Walter Mondale and Alan Cranston joined the Chamber of Commerce (which is otherwise willing to criticize businessmen for feeding at the public trough) in fighting to save funding for the Export-Import Bank.

Among Democrats, then, the impetus for trimming back corporate welfare will have to come from the party's younger wing: Gary Hart, Bill Bradley, and Bruce Babbit. A similar generational split emerges among Republicans. Representatives Jack Kemp, Trent Lott, Jim Courter, Robert Walker, and other young turks who drafted the party's 1984 platform are keen to tackle corporate welfare—partly to deflect blame for the deficits from their supply-side tax cutting. Yet Republican leaders in the Senate seem determined to take the old-fashioned route, namely cutting social programs in exchange for defense cuts. The package being drawn up by Republican Senate chieftains Dole, Domenici, Simpson, and others is likely to include Social Security cuts, cost of living freezes for welfare mothers, surgical cuts in Medicare, you name it. The strategy is to get leading business groups and lobbyists behind closed doors and then barter among them to cut the deficit. The unneediest are not likely to suffer in the process.

Thus, any major assault on corporate welfare will probably have to be a joint effort by the young intellectual vanguard of the two parties—a political bridge over the Republican and Democratic establishments. Both sides have much to gain: to attack corporate welfare is to support smaller government, fairness, fiscal responsibility, and free enterprise all at once. But both sides also have to buck the corporations and the conventional wisdom that says corporate welfare is sacred. Can they pull it off anyway? That's the $140 billion question.

What Ronald Reagan could learn from Charles Dickens.

# ABANDONED AMERICANS

## DOROTHY WICKENDEN

ON SUNDAY, November 4, a few hours after he ended his 51-day hunger strike, Mitch Snyder appeared on "60 Minutes." Mike Wallace began by calling him "the shepherd of the homeless in Washington, the nation's capital," and, toward the end of the interview, asked in his most seductive manner: "Gandhi, Mother Theresa, Martin Luther King—Mitch Snyder?" "No," Snyder replied in a rare burst of modesty, "I wouldn't go that far." He had already gone pretty far: he had starved himself nearly to death in order to bludgeon the Reagan administration into supplying up to five million dollars to repair the moldering shelter for the homeless he runs at 425 Second Street NW, just north of the Capitol. The administration, faced with the prospect of a martyred Snyder on television's highest-rated news show two days before the election, capitulated.

Four months later, the repairs are still in the planning stage. In the meantime, the building remains, as Snyder pithily puts it, "a place fit for vermin and trash." Heavy metal screens have been affixed to all of the windows to keep out vandals. The cavernous concrete basement serves as a feeding and "drop-in" center for up to 1,000 men during the day and early evening. At 8 p.m. the upper-floor dormitories open. (A separate section of the building houses about 100 women at night. They are asked to leave at 8 a.m. There is as yet nowhere for them to go during the day.) The stairways reek of urine and many of the walls have been kicked in. Five or six live-in volunteers patrol the shelter's labyrinthine corridors and dormitory rooms with walkie-talkies in case of trouble. As I arrived one night this winter, a man was being ejected from the premises for attacking another "guest." Snyder matter-of-factly pointed out a pool of congealed blood near one stairwell: "A guy was stabbed here a few nights ago. No one's cleaned it up yet."

The First District police, who file the reports on assaults, disorderly conduct, and thefts at the shelter, refer to it as "the Second Street Hilton." Health and Human Services Secretary Margaret Heckler, who granted Snyder the ini-

tial temporary lease on the federally owned building last winter and was a guest speaker at its festive opening, billed it as "a sanctuary" and "a symbol of hope. . . . There is enough love here today to heat this building for many years. So that is no problem." Heckler's optimism proved to be premature. Snyder is well known for his imperious manner. He refuses to work with other shelter administrators in the city, and as a self-proclaimed anarchist he believes that "the federal and local governments have no right to exist." "We accept only neutral things from them," he told me, "like buildings." A few months after the opening lovefest, Snyder announced that if the lease was not extended, he and his group would set up tents in Lafayette Park across from the White House. The administration agreed to his demands, as it did when he began appearing, wraithlike, on "Nightline" and "60 Minutes."

What should we do about the homeless? Preventing people from starving to death or dying of exposure in the streets is the absolute minimal obligation of society. To his credit, Snyder has forced America to recollect that obligation. Yet the sprouting of emergency shelters like the one at Second Street are hardly "symbols of hope." These new "sanctuaries," chronically underfunded and poorly staffed, are often dangerous as well as squalid. They are the end product of a long chain of abysmal social failures. They started off as temporary havens. In the absence of any coherent policy, they have evolved into an alternate form of public housing and psychiatric care. The truth is that they resemble nothing so much as the poor houses and insane asylums of the past.

There is still considerable confusion about how many homeless people there are in America, who they are, why they are on the streets, and how they should be provided for. And it's not for lack of attention. Over the past several years, countless reports have been written, congressional hearings held, task forces formed, and lawsuits filed on behalf of a group of people that was once politically powerless and socially invisible. Politicians and the public, dismayed by accounts of rapidly growing numbers of people living in alleys, cars, and cardboard boxes, are beginning to address an issue that used to concern only Salvation Army workers and religious charities.

Yet the causes of homelessness are not a mystery. There is the massive release from large state hospitals of mental patients over the last 20 years, in a movement known as "deinstitutionalization"; the ever-dwindling supply of affordable housing for the poor; continuing high unemployment; and the shaving of welfare benefits and the tightening of eligibility requirements. Solutions are harder to come by.

The administration has been called to task in two congressional hearings. The first was for a report issued last May by the Department of Housing and Urban Development that, according to critics, whitewashed the crisis. The other, in November, focused on the administration's failure to fulfill its pledge to supply empty federal buildings and surplus food for the homeless. At the time of the hearing, only three buildings had been obtained, including Mitch Snyder's shelter. The food distributed through 190 military commissaries was found to be negligible. And $7.1 million of the eight million dollars Congress had appropriated to the Department of Defense to renovate empty military facilities had been spent on routine defense maintenance instead.

HUD's *Report on the Homeless and Emergency Shelters* became a cause célèbre for concluding, among other things, that there were "only" 250,000 to 350,000 homeless people nationwide seeking shelter on an average night in December 1983 and January 1984. "For most people who become homeless," the report says cheerily, "their condition is recent and likely to be temporary." Most studies judge the correct number to be two or three million. An enraged Mitch Snyder demanded that HUD retract its figures. For a time, this was one of the conditions for ending his fast. The congressional hearing showed fairly convincingly that the methodology of the report was indeed slipshod and that the numbers were too low.

But the HUD report, for all its inaccuracies and complacency, implicitly confirmed what other studies and newspaper stories have been saying. First, the problem is getting worse, and the rapid proliferation of shelters cannot keep pace. Even using HUD's figures, there are only about half as many beds in emergency shelters as there are people in need of them. And second, the widespread impression that most of the homeless are chronically alcoholic or mentally ill is wrong. The shelter population is actually getting younger; the average age is usually judged to be 34. HUD says that at least 35 percent to 40 percent of the total is recently unemployed. And this group is getting to look more like the typical poor: there are more minority people, particularly blacks, and more single-parent families.

MUCH HAS BEEN made of the failures of deinstitutionalization. A widely cited clinical study published last December in *The American Journal of Psychiatry* claimed that at one supposedly typical shelter in Boston at least 40 percent of the residents were psychotics, 29 per-

cent were chronic alcoholics, and 21 percent had severe personality disorders of one kind or another. The implication is that 90 percent of homeless people are drunks or lunatics. That's a big exaggeration. The Task Force Report of the American Psychiatric Association, *The Homeless Mentally Ill*, the most thorough and widely respected investigation of the subject, estimates that of about two million homeless people in the United States, perhaps "as many as half suffer from alcohol, drug abuse, or mental health problems." Most other nationwide studies confirm this conclusion.

Clearly a lot of homeless people got that way as casualties of a cruelly ineffective mental health system, and emergency shelters are a poor substitute for sustained psychiatric care. Many of the deinstitutionalized who had been living relatively independent lives lost their Social Security Disability Insurance and Supplemental Security Income—and subsequently their homes—in the Reagan administration's 1981 paring down of benefits and purging of the rolls. What's more, a new generation of "space cases," as they are known among other street people, is beginning to show up in city shelters. Many of them are schizophrenics; others are strung out on drugs like PCP. Apart from occasional trips to hospital emergency rooms, most have received no professional help of any kind.

Nevertheless, the composition of the homeless population is changing. The hundreds of thousands who crowd through the doors of city shelters, welfare hotels, churches, and synagogues each night for a meal and a mattress are not only the traditional social outcasts—the bag ladies, skid-row alcoholics, and muttering schizophrenics who are a familiar part of the urban landscape. In growing numbers they are being joined there by battered women, elderly poor and disabled, and—most significantly—unemployed people with their entire families.

IN THE MIDST of the recession a few years ago, the papers were filled with stories of lines at soup kitchens, Great Depression-style. Today, in the midst of the economic recovery, the stories are about unemployed workers in the industrial Midwest whose benefits have expired and who can no longer afford their rent; or about people living in cars; or about families seeking temporary shelter at city welfare offices. It is becoming apparent that many of the poor have not shared in the economic recovery. Indeed, many of them have suffered from it.

Every major recent study cites neighborhood gentrification and the decline in low-income housing (particularly single-room occupancy hotels, or SROs) as principal causes of homelessness. *The Making of America's Homeless*, the latest report by the nonpartisan research group, the Community Services Society, estimates that 2.5 million Americans every year lose their homes, and about 500,000 low-rent apartments vanish as a result of conversion, arson, abandonment, inflation, and demolition. In Denver, which is experiencing both rapid redevelopment and an influx of unemployed from the industrial belt, the problem is particularly severe. Boarding houses in the low-rent districts are being replaced by condominiums; the number of boarding-room beds decreased from about 1,300 to about 400 over the last eight years, according to the National Coalition on the Homeless. Numerous shelter administrators emphasized that most of their charges are the new poor.

In mid-February Ruth Marcus reported in *The Washington Post* that shelters in the suburbs are now being inundated by the working poor. "Often working at service jobs for the minimum wage of $3.50 an hour . . . they may be hit by a run of bad luck, or their housing situation may simply collapse under the strain of skyrocketing suburban rents." Even when the overall unemployment rate is going down, people still lose their jobs—and their homes. A report by the U.S. Conference of Mayors, *Homelessness in America's Cities*, concluded that although unemployment had dropped in the ten cities it studied, the population in need of emergency shelter had increased. Spokesmen in San Francisco said that 63 percent of those in shelters have "marketable skills." New York City's Human Resources Administration, which runs the city shelter system, says that about 30 percent of recent arrivals were there because they had recently lost their jobs. As the Community Services Society explains in *Hardship in the Heartland*, "Something happens—a job is lost, unemployment benefits run out, creditors and banks move in to foreclose, eviction proceedings begin—and quite suddenly the respectable poor find themselves among the disreputable homeless."

One especially vulnerable group is poor young families. They have suffered at the hands of the Reagan administration over the last four years: in slashes in housing assistance ($1.8 billion), Aid to Families with Dependent Children ($4.8 billion), child nutrition ($5.2 billion) food stamps ($6.8 billion), and low-income energy assistance ($700 million). For many years shortsighted local housing policies have fostered urban renewal but have given scant attention to those removed from condemned buildings. And families that lose their homes soon discover that social service bureaucracies are already overextended.

In New York City the number of homeless families housed by the city in hotels has more than doubled since January 1983, rising from 1,400 to 3,285 last December. On January 9 this year, New York's shelters and hotels took in an unprecedented 20,000 people; 63 percent of them were families. Tens of thousands of other poor families are believed to be "doubling up" with friends and relatives. Even more disturbing, according to Robert Hayes, counsel to the National Coalition for the Homeless, there are now more children under the age of 16 than there are single adults staying in the city's emergency shelter system. A wrenching story by Jane Gross in *The New York Times* in January chronicled the seven-month ordeal of a pregnant woman and her five children who spent countless days and nights being sent from local welfare offices to overcrowded shelters to an HRA Emergency Assistance Unit—none of which had so much as a bed to spare. "Often, those in the shelters yearn for a berth in a single-room occupancy hotel. But those who have braved the

hotels, where they say they are often robbed and molested, return gratefully to the shelters they once clamored to leave. Some say they prefer the streets to the degrading and debilitating process of finding a bed, but are chased indoors by fear, cold, illness, or terror that the Bureau of Child Welfare will separate them from their children."

Here in Washington, the city currently copes with family homelessness through what is known as the "open market" system. Homeless families must go each day to the aptly named Pitts Hotel at 14th and Belmont Streets NW, where they receive their meals and a room assignment for the night. If the Pitts is full, they are given bus fare and sent to one of two other dismal hotels on the outskirts of the city, or to the Greentree Shelter in Bethesda, Maryland. The next day they return to the Pitts, and begin the process again. Many families shuttle among the hotels for months as they search frantically for an apartment they can afford.

Some of the luckier open-market families wind up just down the road from the Pitts, at the Community of Hope,

housed in a renovated apartment building on Belmont Street. The organization, which is funded by the city, is run by Tom Nees, a minister in the Church of the Nazarene. Families pay a small rental fee to live temporarily in the building. The money is put into an escrow account and given to the family when it leaves, ideally within 90 days. Nees's group includes health and social services, legal aid, job assistance, emergency housing assistance, and counseling, and so on.

"Family homelessness," Nees says, "is primarily an economic problem. Street people are traumatized, and will be dependent regardless. That's not true with families, where homelessness produces the trauma." The families at the Community of Hope rarely include a husband or father. Five of the dozen women staying there at the time of my visit worked full-time, but didn't earn enough to rent apartments of their own. Others were welfare mothers who had parceled out their children to friends and relatives or foster care. Nees tries to get such families back together. Most of the women had been living in cramped quarters with friends or relatives. Their families broke up when overcrowding in a small apartment became intolerable, or when the landlord threatened to revoke the lease, or when they realized the impossibility of finding a place cheap and big enough for all of them. Washington's public housing office is still processing applications filed ten years ago; there are no federal funds to speak of.

Nees also tries to urge the women on to greater self-sufficiency. But he can help only the employable—"We don't know how to begin with the others." And for many of the women, a minimum-wage job would hardly help. "A woman with five or six kids could be getting $1,000 a month in food stamps and AFDC. She'd have to earn $12,000 a year to compare with that. It's a terrible dilemma. There is now a disincentive to enter the job market at the minimum wage—you can't raise yourself above the poverty line."

Cities are spending considerable sums on emergency measures like the Pitts that do little or nothing to solve these families' problems: no housing and no jobs. The D.C. government shells out between $80 and $250 a day for each open-market family. Nees's costs are $40-$45 a day. New York spends a minimum of $1,200 a month to put up a family of four in a city shelter. As the Task Force Report of the American Psychiatric Association describes it, "City policy toward the homeless is best described as one that lurches from court order to court order. . . . Harvests of waste rather than economies of scale are reaped when crisis management becomes the modus operandi of housing and social service agencies." Or, as Nees puts it, "They're just putting out fires and picking up the bodies."

THESE PIECEMEAL, insufficient, and expensive efforts are an accurate reflection of ambivalent policies and beliefs. Two decades ago, during the Kennedy administration, the wards of state mental hospitals were emptied out at the urging of progressive politicians and psychiatrists who justifiably denounced the mistreatment of inmates and the wretched conditions, and who believed that the mentally ill had the right—and, with proper medication and counseling, the ability—to live productive lives in the community.

Today the betrayal of that vision is well known. Patients were precipitously released regardless of whether local facilities could provide adequate follow-up care—indeed, regardless of whether those facilities even existed. Communities fought the establishment of halfway houses and clinics in residential neighborhoods, and local governments were reluctant to fund them. The mental health centers that were established were designed more for treatment of people with occasional problems than for chronic patients. Families often found themselves unable to cope with the strains of caring for a disturbed sibling or parent or child. And the new miracle drugs proved to be less of a cure-all than the psychiatrists had hoped. Though

untold numbers successfully made the transition from years of custodial care to independent lives outside, many thousands of the most needy did not.

One of the deeply held principles of the Reagan administration is that people not only have a right to self-determination, but a duty as well. Last winter when President Reagan was asked on "Good Morning America" about the widespread impression that his policies are causing misery among the poor, he replied: "What we have found in this country—and maybe we're more aware of it now—is one problem that we've had, even in the best of times, and that is the people who are sleeping on the grates, the homeless who are homeless, you might say, by choice." That is, if people choose not to get a job, and not to care for themselves responsibly, it must be a matter of life-style. In any case, it should not be a matter of pressing concern to the federal government.

The failures of deinstitutionalization, the sluggishness of city bureaucracies, and the Reagan administration's laissez-faire precepts have led to a contrary notion among those concerned about the homeless: the "right to shelter." The 1979 case of *Callahan* v. *Carey* in New York state's Supreme Court established that the city had a legal obligation to provide shelter for the homeless. A few weeks later, in one of the most ironic repercussions yet of the community mental health movement, New York City opened the Keener Shelter on Wards Island—an empty building in one of those large, isolated state psychiatric hospitals that had been shut down. But the city balked when it came to overseeing the shelter: two subsequent lawsuits were brought—and won—against the city for failing to maintain adequate health standards, and for allowing severe overcrowding. A facility designed to hold up to 180 men was taking in 600 each night.

Many citizens are ready to recognize the right to shelter, but not to welcome the homeless into their neighborhoods. This point was neatly made in Washington recently. On election day an initiative—conceived by Mitch Snyder's group, the Community for Creative Non-Violence—requiring the District to provide shelter to everyone who requests it was passed by a resounding 72 percent, despite the opposition of virtually every politician and activist in the city. A few weeks after the vote, during a town meeting in Georgetown to discuss the possible opening of a small shelter for women in the neighborhood, a woman serving on the Advisory Neighborhood Commission stood up and objected, "What do you mean support services? I voted for Initiative 17, but I thought I was just voting for mattresses on the floor."

PARTLY for this reason, some are now advocating a return to the days of asylum. On "Nightline" recently, George Will made the case bluntly. "We constantly in this country talk about every problem in terms of a clash of individual rights," he said. "The community has some rights here. If it is illegal, and it is, and ought to be illegal, to litter the streets, frankly it ought to be illegal for people who must survive in panhandling among other things to sleep on the streets. Therefore there is a simple matter of public order and hygiene in getting these people somewhere else. Not arrest them, but move them off to someplace where they are simply out of sight and no longer a visible, in some cases intrusive, in some cases even an aggressive, public nuisance." The trouble with Will's trash removal solution is that the problem is not a "simple matter of public order"—or a simple matter of anything else. For the vast majority of the homeless, reinstitutionalization is not a sensible solution.

The first, most obvious, step is to create respectable, affordable, permanent housing. The National Low Income Housing Coalition estimates that at least 750,000 new apartments a year are needed. City and state governments are now beginning to recognize the urgency of the situation. Since 1983 New York has renovated for the homeless 4,500 vacant apartments owned by the city. Mayor Koch—under relentless pressure from advocacy groups and City Council members Ruth Messinger and Carol Bellamy, his opponent in the mayoral race—has stopped awarding tax breaks to real estate developers eager to convert SROs into luxury condominiums. New York governor Mario Cuomo and Massachusetts governor Michael Dukakis have made specialized housing programs for the poor, disabled, and elderly—closely connected to mental health and social service programs—a top priority.

The Reagan administration, on the other hand, appears to have decided to renounce once and for all any meaningful federal support. HUD's budget authority for assistance to additional households was cut from $30 billion to $11 billion in Reagan's first term. In his fiscal 1986 budget, he proposes to chop that by an additional 95 percent, to $499 million. The impact of these cuts, which are spread over a period of 20 years, has hardly been felt yet. Most housing analysts agree that although cities and states and private organizations may be better suited to administer effective housing programs, they simply don't have enough money for the initial investment, especially in cities like New York, where the need for low-income housing has become desperate.

IN THE LONG RUN, emergency shelters will cost everyone a great deal more than permanent apartments, group homes, and a mental health system that values patients' well-being as much as their freedom. Public policy is being driven by defensiveness and a failure of nerve. There are efficient and even modestly successful organizations out there that have put to good use whatever truncated services are available, without placing undue strain on the public purse.

Doubtless a small percentage of the chronically mentally ill will need continuing supervised care in a structured setting. The St. Francis Residence on Manhattan's East Side and now the St. Francis Residence II on the West Side are repeatedly cited as examples of decent, long-term, inexpensive care for the mentally ill. Both were former SRO hotels that were renovated through donations to the St.

Francis of Assisi Friends of the Poor. "Our intention," says Father John Felice, who founded the homes, "is to make the social service system work." Unlike the huge armories and flophouses run by the city, St. Francis demands that the dignity and privacy of each resident be respected. Tenants are guaranteed a room of their own, for which they pay $145-$210 per month out of their welfare payments, Social Security, SSI, or—if they have a job—their paychecks. Occasionally one of the men or women will require a period of hospitalization, in which case his or her room is held open. It costs St. Francis a modest $15-$20 a day for each of its residents. Many men are afraid to spend a single night at the city shelters. The tenants at St. Francis consider it their home. There is very little turnover.

For those whose suffering is less existential than economic, there are any number of possibilities. In Washington the Community of Hope, which assists families, is only one of them. There is McKenna House, which takes in unemployed men, assists them in finding jobs, and helps them to become fully independent again. There is the Reverend John and Erna Steinbruck's "N Street Village" at Luther Place on Thomas Circle, which includes—in addition to an emergency shelter for homeless women inside the Luther Place Church—a health clinic for the neighborhood poor and three group homes for women, where they are helped to find jobs and permanent living arrangements.

THESE UNDERTAKINGS share several fundamental principles. Insofar as it is possible, they reduce the need for shelter rather than perpetuate it. They attack both institutional and welfare dependency with strong doses of old-fashioned practical self-help. They are small and admittedly selective, recognizing that homelessness can't be effectively treated as long as people are being housed in vast warehouses, or as long as it is considered a mere matter of "mattresses on the floor."

The Steinbrucks emphasize that the most fragile of their charges—the women, most of them mentally ill, who spend each night on the floor of their chapel—would be better served at St. Elizabeth's mental hospital, where at least they would be safe. One woman was assaulted on the steps of the Luther Place Church. Another, 80 years old, was beaten while she was out on the streets. Erna Steinbruck says, "Some of them can't make a decision for their own well-being. But St. E's doesn't want them; it wants to get them out." One night recently a schizophrenic woman was sent from The District of Columbia General Hospital to St. Elizabeth's to the streets because no psychiatrist had been willing to sign an involuntary committal form and she herself couldn't cope with the paperwork. She showed up at Luther Place the next morning.

Still, the Steinbrucks have shown an adroitness at coaxing casseroles and clothing from their parishioners and neighbors; at convincing students to staff their group homes and doctors to work in their clinic; and at negotiating the complex of city welfare offices, zoning ordinances, police emergency units, and the recalcitrant mental health system. They have had less success with the biggest proponent of voluntarism: Ronald Reagan. The most the Steinbrucks have received from the administration is a few consultations with Harvey Vieth, the chairman of the Federal Task Force on the Homeless, and a visit from some of the cabinet wives, who stopped by one day at Christmastime laden with toiletries for the women.

Some of the solutions for the homeless will not be cheap or politically popular. But the Community of Hope, the St. Francis Residences, and Luther Place have demonstrated that providing for the majority of the homeless need not entail hiding them away. Neither passive acceptance of places "fit for vermin and trash" nor calls for a return to custodial care are the only ways out of this quandary. They are simply the least imaginative.                    □

# WHAT DOES THE GOVERNMENT OWE THE POOR?

An American's distrust of welfare should come as no surprise. Public assistance threatens what is after all the central doctrine of capitalism: that the incentive to work is born of the burning desire to *have,* and then to have more. Why risk dulling the spur of poverty, and thereby dooming the supposed beneficiaries to perpetual dependence?

Critics of the Great Society voiced these concerns during the mid-1960s, but in the last three or four years much louder, more confident voices have raised them again. The new critics maintain that America's inner cities have become great wastelands of poverty, a poverty largely subsidized and thus encouraged by our own government. Far from "lifting Americans out of poverty," welfare has succeeded mainly in breaking up families, encouraging young girls to have babies out of wedlock, and generally denigrating the value of hard work. So why not dismantle it?

Charles Murray's *Losing Ground* is the most influential presentation of the radical view that government can best help the poor by leaving them to their own devices. Jesse Jackson is a longtime civil rights activist known for his eloquent and sympathetic advocacy of the interests of the poor. *Harper's* invited Murray and Jackson to discuss welfare, government, and the nature of American poverty.

*The following conversation took place at the Harvard Club in New York City.*

### CHARLES MURRAY

*is a senior research fellow at the Manhattan Institute for Policy Research. He is the author of* Losing Ground: American Social Policy, 1950–1980, *which criticizes the effects of social programs on the poor. He was formerly chief scientist at the American Institutes for Research, where he evaluated government programs involving urban education, welfare services, child nutrition, day care, adolescent pregnancy, juvenile delinquency, and criminal justice.*

### JESSE JACKSON

*is president of the National Rainbow Coalition and co-pastor of the Fellowship Missionary Baptist Church in Chicago. From 1967 to 1971 he served as national director of the Southern Christian Leadership Conference's Operation Breadbasket. In 1971 he founded Operation PUSH, which promotes excellence in inner-city public schools and negotiates with major corporations to increase the amount of business they do with minority-owned companies. Jackson sought the Democratic presidential nomination in 1984.*

CHARLES MURRAY: How can government help the poor? The problem is that, so far, we haven't been very good at it. During the late 1960s and early 1970s, we began a major effort to bring people out of poverty, to educate the uneducated, to employ the unemployable. We have to confront the fact that the effort to help the poor did not have the desired effect. In terms of education, crime, family stability, the lives of poor people have gotten worse since the 1960s, and we have to explain why.

During those years we, in effect, changed the rules of the game for poor people. Essentially we said, in a variety of ways: "It's not your fault. If you are not learning in school, it is because the educational system is biased; if you are committing crimes, it is because the environment is poor; if you have a baby that you can't care for, it's because your own upbringing was bad." Having absolved everybody of responsibility, we then said: "You can get along without holding a job. You can get along if you have a baby but have no husband and no income. You can survive without participating in society the way your parents had to." And lots of young people took the bait. So the question remains: What, if anything, does the government owe the poor?

JESSE JACKSON: I'm as unimpressed with boundless liberalism as I am with heartless conservatism. Creative thinking has to take place. But to begin to think creatively, we have to be realistic: about the role of government, for example.

We cannot be blindly anti-government. The government has made significant interventions in many, many areas for the common good. Without public schools, most Americans would not be educated. Without land-grant colleges, the United States would not have the number one agricultural system in the world. Without federal transit programs, we would not have an interstate highway system. Without subsidized hospitals, most Americans could not afford decent medical care. And the government has played a significant role in providing a base for many American industries. The defense industries, for example, may be considered private, part of the market, but many of them are almost wholly supported by government contracts.

Now, we consider spending the public's money toward these ends to be in our national interest. When we saw the devastation in Europe after World War II, we devised the Marshall Plan—a comprehensive, long-term' program. Had the Marshall Plan been a five-year investment program—as the War on Poverty essentially was—Europe would have collapsed. But we determined that the redevelopment of Europe was in our national interest. That's an instance where a vigorous government investment made something positive happen.

But when we shift from the notion of subsidy as something that serves our national interest, to that of welfare, the attitudes suddenly shift from positive to negative. In this country there is a negative predisposition toward the poor. We must learn to see the *development* of people who are poor as in our national interest, as cost-efficient, as an investment that can bring an enormous return to every American. The government definitely has a big role to play.

MURRAY: I agree it has a role. There are some things government *can* do, and one of them is to ensure that a whole range of opportunities is available to everyone. For example, in my ideal world, whether a child lived in the inner city or in the suburbs, everything from preschool to graduate school would be available to him—free. In this ideal world, if someone really looked for a job and just couldn't find one, per-

haps because of a downturn in the economy, some minimal unemployment insurance would be in place to help him.

Opportunity should be assured, but attempts at achieving equal outcome abandoned. What would happen if you took away all other government-supported welfare, if the system were dismantled? Well, believe it or not, a lot of good things would begin to happen.

JACKSON: The notion of "opportunity" is more complicated than it sounds. For example, some people are poor *because* of government. When a nation is 51 percent female yet can't get an equal rights amendment passed; when many women still cannot borrow money with the same freedom men can, cannot pursue their ideas and aspirations in the marketplace because they are not equally protected—that amounts to government interference, too, but on the side of the status quo. Many blacks and Hispanics cannot borrow money from banks, on subjective grounds—because some bank official doesn't like their color, or because whole neighborhoods are redlined so that money will not be loaned to anyone living there. Government must be committed to the vigorous enforcement of equal protection under the law and other basic principles; without that enforcement, it is not a government handout that's the issue as much as it is the government's shoving people into a hole and not *letting* them out. When Legal Aid is cut, and the poor no longer have access to the courts, that's an example of government playing a role in *perpetuating* poverty.

MURRAY: If you try to rent an inexpensive apartment in my hometown of Newton, Iowa, even if you're white, you may very well not be able to rent that apartment, on "subjective grounds." I mean, you come to the door, and because of the way you act or the way you look or whatever, the landlord says to himself: "My apartment's going to get trashed." These subjective grounds often have a basis in fact. And it's real tough for people renting out apartments—and maybe even for banks—to operate in ways that enable them to make money if they aren't permitted to make these kinds of subjective judgments.

JACKSON: Dr. Murray, the farmer wearing his bib overalls who walks up to that apartment door and is rejected for the way he looks is not a victim of racial prejudgment. That man could put on a suit and get the apartment. Blacks can't change color. The idea is that bankers choose not to make loans to blacks *institutionally*.

Now, I'm not just throwing around a charge here. John H. Johnson, the president of Johnson Publishing Company, which publishes *Ebony*, is perhaps the most established black businessman in the country. Yet several banks turned down his loan application to build in downtown Chicago. Maybe the most established black businessman in the country was turned down for a loan simply because of the institutional racism of banks. And so we need laws enforced, we need the government to protect people who are black or Hispanic or Asian or Indian or female, from the bankers' ability to do that.

A lot of people, to this day, are simply locked out. Until 1967, there had never been more than a couple of black car dealerships, because the automobile industry's policy was not to allow a black to invest in a car dealership or to learn to run one in any neighborhood, black or white. So blacks now have fewer than 240 dealerships out of the 22,050 in this country. Blacks always had the ability, but they were locked out by race, even if they had the money. Operation PUSH confronted Ford as late as July 1982, when there were fewer than 40 black automobile dealerships out of 5,600. Ford finally agreed to grant thirty new black dealerships in one year, which they had previously claimed was impossible. Well, those thirty dealerships are still operating, employing an average of more than fifty people each, and those jobs represent the alternative to welfare and despair.

MURRAY: If you say that in 1960 blacks as a people were locked out, well, I have no problem with that. But that is no longer accurate. Let's talk about black youth unemployment. Are you saying that America's black youth are marching resolutely from door to door, interviewing for jobs, and that they are getting turned down because they're black? If so, then a jobs program ought to do wonders. CETA ought to have done wonders. But it didn't.

JACKSON: The private economy, by being so closed for so long, has pushed many people into the public economy. There's just no reason why, in a population of 30 million blacks, there are only two black beverage-bottling franchises. You can't explain it by lack of ambition or an unwillingness to take risks, because for the past twenty years blacks have been the top salesmen in that industry. A lot of people got locked into poverty because of the government's failure to enforce equal protection under the law. Until the Civil Rights Act of 1964 and Lyndon Johnson's executive order of 1965, beverage companies could get lucrative government contracts to operate on U.S. military bases around the world, even though they locked out a significant body of Americans.

MURRAY: I'm not in a position to argue with you about wholesalers and franchises. But I don't think we can assume that if blacks gain more access to entrepreneurial business positions—which I'm all in favor of—it will have a fundamental effect on poverty and the underclass.

JACKSON: If there is an artificial ceiling limiting the growth of the so-called talented 10 percent—I use the term advisedly—then it compounds the problem of the disinherited 90 percent. If where we live, our money won't "spend" because of redlining, which becomes a de facto law; if where we live, our money cannot buy a car franchise or a beer franchise or a soft-drink franchise—which are some of the great American ways out of poverty—then blacks are effectively locked out of the private economy. And so, just as the political grandfather clause locked blacks out of the political system, economic grandfather clauses have effectively locked blacks out of the economic system. Blacks today can take over a town politically, because its population is mostly black. But the economic territory—the entrepreneurial opportunities, beyond mom-and-pop businesses, which allow a people to develop a leadership class in the private economy, which in turn begins to lift others as it hires them and trains them—is still closed. Blacks who worked as salesmen and saleswomen for the first generation of black entrepreneurs now have franchises of their own, because they have access to the franchise head. But that has not happened historically.

MURRAY: Why is it that the Koreans and Vietnamese and all sorts of other people who come here with very few resources do well, including West Indian blacks? They come here, start businesses, and manage to earn a median income which rivals or surpasses that of whites. I'm not trying to say racism doesn't exist. I'm saying it doesn't explain nearly as much as it ought to.

JACKSON: Do not underestimate the impact of 250 years of legal slavery followed by a hundred years of legal segregation. The damage it did to the minds of the oppressor and the oppressed must not be played down. When I grew up in South Carolina, I could caddy but I couldn't play golf. That's why I can't play golf now; I could have been arrested for hitting a golf ball at the Greenville Country Club. I could shag balls, but I couldn't play tennis. I could shine shoes, but I couldn't sit on the stand and couldn't own a stand at the train station. I could wait tables, but I couldn't sit at them; and I could not borrow money to build a competing establishment.

The other groups you mentioned have not known that level of degradation. The Cubans came to Miami as beneficiaries of a cold war between this country and Cuba; we used money and subsidies to induce them to come here, and those who came were in large measure from a class that had some history of business acumen. Many of the Vietnamese were beneficiaries of the same kind of cold war policy.

Now, shagging balls and not playing tennis, caddying and not playing golf, not voting and seeing others vote—all of this had the cumulative effect of lowering people's ambitions and limiting their horizons. Let me give an example. I saw a story in *USA Today* last summer headlined "More Blacks Graduating from High School, Fewer Going to College." A young lady from Chicago was quoted in the story, and I decided to meet with her and her mother. It turned out she had a B+ average, was a member of the National Honor Society—the whole business. I said to the girl, "Do you want to go to college?" She said she did. I said, "Well, have you taken the SAT tests?" She said she hadn't. "Why not?" "Well, the counselor told me that since I couldn't afford to go to college, that stuff was a waste of time." In other words, she was being programmed for failure, taught to be mediocre, programmed downward.

Once I discovered what was happening, I went on the radio and asked any high school student—black, white, brown—who had every college qualification except money to come to Operation PUSH. Seven hundred fifty young people came with their parents; we have placed 250 of them in colleges, including that young lady. But if that young lady hadn't gone to college, she would have been written off three or four years later: people would have said the family was subsidized, dependent; she didn't go to college; now she's pregnant; and the whole cycle begins again. She was programmed into lower ambition, programmed away from college. Yet many schools, especially the better ones like Harvard and Columbia, provide scholarship money. But so many students don't know this; it's a well-kept secret. Those who have, know; the circle remains essentially closed.

MURRAY: Getting that information out would serve as an *incentive*. I know how I'd spend money on educational programs. I'd put up a bunch of posters saying that anybody who gets such-and-such a score on the SATs will get a free ride through college. I'm willing to bet that I'd get more results from my program than the government would get by trying directly to improve the schools.

JACKSON: There's a role for that kind of motivation. There's also a role for increasing opportunity. Often it's not lack of ability or ambition that locks people out, but lack of information.

MURRAY: I'm worried, because I'm starting to agree with you too much!

JACKSON: Just give me time, you'll be all right.

MURRAY: Oh, I think we'll find some things to disagree on. I come from an all-white town. I went back to visit this Christmas, and I said to myself, "I wonder what poverty is like here in Newton, Iowa." So I got in touch with the human services people and spent some time riding around

with a caseworker. And as I listened to this caseworker describe what her problems were, I realized that if I closed my eyes, I could have been listening to a caseworker in the South Bronx. The problems were indistinguishable from what are usually considered "black problems."

JACKSON: Yes, we must whiten the face of poverty. It's an *American* problem, not a black problem. But the face of poverty in this country is portrayed as a black face, and that reinforces certain attitudes. I mean, John Kennedy holds up a sick black baby in his arms and people say, "Gee, he's a nice guy." He holds up a sick white baby in West Virginia and people say, "We've got to *do* something about this."

Of the 34 million people living in poverty in America, 23 million are white. The poor are mostly white and female and young. Most poor people work every day. They're not on welfare; they're changing beds in hospitals and hotels and mopping floors and driving cabs and raising other people's children. And there is no basis for taking a few people who cheat the system as examples, and using them to smear millions of people who by and large work very hard.

MURRAY: The welfare queen is not the problem. And the dynamics of dependency operate pretty much the same for both blacks and whites. For example, I did some checking on what the out-of-wedlock birthrate is among poor whites. Guess what? Middle-class blacks don't have much of a problem with out-of-wedlock births, just as middle-class whites don't; but poor blacks *and* poor whites alike have a big problem with it.

Now, when I visit a school in inner-city Washington, I see a couple of different kinds of kids. A lot of kids are sent out of their houses every morning by their moms and dads, who tell them, "Get that education. Study hard. Do what the teacher says." And these youngsters go off to school and study hard, do exactly what the teacher says, and still graduate a couple of years behind grade level—not because they're stupid, but because of what has happened to the school systems during the past twenty years. A great deal of energy and attention has been spent catering to the kind of kid who, for whatever reason, makes it real hard for the first set of kids to learn.

So I think we need to reintroduce a notion which has a disreputable recent history in America: the notion of class. A good part of our problem can be characterized as one of "lower-class behavior," which is distinct from the behavior of poor people.

JACKSON: In other words, the Watergate burglars, though white, male, and rich, were engaging in "lower-class behavior."

MURRAY: No, but if you talk about the danger posed

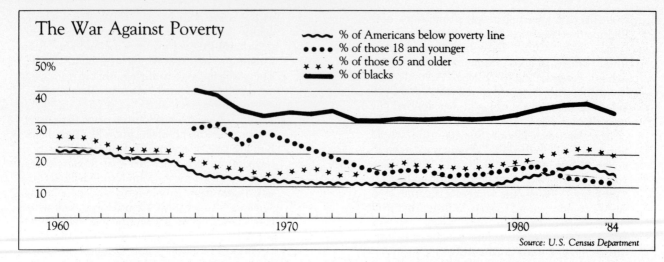

The War Against Poverty

~~~ % of Americans below poverty line
•••• % of those 18 and younger
*** % of those 65 and older
━━━ % of blacks

Source: U.S. Census Department

by the increase in crime, it so happens that it is not the rich white folks who are suffering.

JACKSON: Back up now, back up. You introduced a phenomenon there, Dr. Murray, about "lower-class behavior." I suppose that means low morals.

MURRAY: You added that.

JACKSON: Well, I *guessed* that's what it means. What does "lower-class behavior" mean?

MURRAY: The syndrome was identified long ago, although the term is more recent. People in the nineteenth and early twentieth centuries would simply talk about "trash," for example, and later there was the concept of the "undeserving poor." The sociologist who did the Elmstown study certainly recognized the syndrome, as did Edward Banfield. It is characterized by chronic unemployment due to people working for a while and then dropping out, unstable family life, and so on.

JACKSON: But you know, Dr. Murray, you made a distinction here on this "lower-class behavior," and I was trying to get a definition of it, but I did not get it. I'm sorry, I haven't read all those books you mentiond. But I suppose it means *immoral* behavior.

MURRAY: I'm not using words like "moral" and "immoral."

JACKSON: Well, I guess it means violence against people, unprovoked violence—lower-class behavior. Sex without love, making unwanted babies—lower-class behavior. Taking what belongs to other people—lower-class behavior. Filling your nose full of cocaine, driving drunk—lower-class behavior. That's not lower-class behavior, Dr. Murray, that's immoral.

It seems to me that whether it is stealing in the suites or stealing in the streets, whether it is

happening in ghetto, barrio, reservation, or suburb, we should condemn lower-class behavior. Cain killing Abel, brother killing brother, is lower-class behavior because it's low morals, it's unethical, it's not right. Whether they're welfarized or subsidized, people should not engage in lower-class behavior. Is it more moral for a business executive to sniff cocaine than a welfare recipient?

MURRAY: If you are saying that rich white people can be lousy, I agree. But my point is that if we continue to pretend that all poor people are victims, if we do not once again recognize in social policy the distinctions that have been recognized all along on the street, we will continue to victimize those poor people who most deserve our respect and our help.

Parents, black or white, who are working at lousy jobs but who are *working*, paying the rent, teaching their kids how to behave—yes, those people are behaving differently, and certainly in a more praiseworthy way, than parents who fail to do those things. Poor people fall into very different classes, distinguished by differences in work behavior, such as chronic unemployment whether there are jobs or not. And there are differences in child rearing. Working-class people pay a lot of attention to how their children are doing; they talk to them, ask how they're doing in school. But there are children who come to school at the age of five and do not know, for example, the words for the colors; nobody's talked to them, they've been utterly neglected. Finally, when there is divorce among the working class the man takes continued responsibility for supporting the children. Lower-class behavior, on the other hand, is characterized by serial monogamy or promiscuity and a failure of the man to take responsibility for his children.

JACKSON: Dr. Murray, the lady who lived across the street from us while I was growing up ran what they called a "bootleg house." She was a woman of high character: she was a seamstress, and all her children graduated from college. But on the weekend people came over to her house to drink and gamble, and so Mrs. X was considered an outcast. Now, another lady named Mrs. Y, who lived about three blocks from us, owned a liquor store; because she was white she could get a liquor license. Mrs. Y was an entrepreneur, Mrs. X was a moral outcast. But something told me early in the game that the only difference between Mrs. X and Mrs. Y was a license.

Men and women would come over to Mrs. X's house sometimes and have sex down in the basement: promiscuity, also a sign of lower-class behavior, and another reason why people looked down on her. Well, I began working at the hotel in town; I was paid to carry in the booze for the men who would meet women there, often other people's wives, sometimes even their friends' wives. They'd each leave at a different time and by a different door to maintain their respectability, but I knew where they lived because I used to cut their grass and rake their leaves. This is distinctly lower-class behavior—sleeping with other people's wives.

MURRAY: No, engaging in sexual behavior, even promiscuity, does not make you lower class. What makes you lower class is having kids you can't or don't take care of.

JACKSON: Now, Dr. Murray, are you saying that a lawyer who has sex with his partner's wife and uses a prophylactic is engaging in behavior that's higher class than that of someone who does the same thing but does not have the sense or ability to use a prophylactic?

MURRAY: Look, I'm not against sex. I'm not even necessarily against sex outside of marriage.

JACKSON: Now, don't get too swift on me here. The act of going to bed with another man's wife is adultery.

MURRAY: Fine.

JACKSON: It ain't fine. It's *immoral*. It's lower-class behavior, and whether it takes place in the White House, statehouse, courthouse, outhouse, your house, my house, that behavior is unethical.

MURRAY: But that has nothing to do with what I'm saying.

JACKSON: It shows a certain attitude: If you do something and it's subsidized, it's all right. If others do it and it's welfarized, it's not so good.

I was in inner-city Washington several months ago, talking to a gym full of high school kids. I challenged those who had taken drugs to come down front. About 300 came down. Next

day the *Washington Post* published three pictures and the headline "Jackson does phenomenal thing—kids admit drug usage." Editorial: "It's a great thing that Jackson did, but you know he has a special way with black kids." Next day I went to a school in Maryland—in one of the richest counties in America, about 97 percent white, single-family dwellings, upper middle class, and all that. The principal said to me, "Well, you can make your pitch, but of course it won't work here." So I made my pitch. I said, "Taking drugs is morally wrong, except in controlled medical situations; it's morally wrong and ungodly." Six hundred students were present. I said, "Those who have tried drugs, come forward." About 200 came forward. This was a junior high school; these kids were thirteen, fourteen years old. The principal was in a daze. Now *that's* lower-class behavior and upper-class economic status. Rich folks embezzle and poor folks steal; rich folks prevaricate and poor folks lie. But I think a lie is a lie is a lie.

MURRAY: If we agree that lying is lying and stealing is stealing, that doesn't help the little old lady who is trying to get from her apartment to the grocery store without getting her Social Security check ripped off. If we take the attitude that white-collar crime is just as bad as street crime, so let's not go after the street criminals when we let the embezzlers get away, the problem is that we ignore that little old lady, who is not in much immediate danger from embezzlers. Poor people, first of all, need safety. We'll take care of the white-collar criminals as best as we can, but first I want to make it safe in the neighborhoods. And if that requires putting a whole bunch of people behind bars, let's do it.

JACKSON: We should remember that four years at a state university in New York costs less than $25,000; four years at Attica costs $104,000. I am more inclined to take these young kids and lock them up in dormitories, give them years of mind expansion and trade development. It costs too much to leave them around for years without education, hope, or training.

The present welfare system should be replaced with a human development system. As presently constructed, the welfare system has built-in snares: there's no earn-incentive, no learn-incentive to get out. Assume you are locked into this box: a girl with a tenth-grade education and a baby. If she's making, say, $200 a month on welfare, why not provide some positive incentives? If she went back to school and got her junior college degree, she should get $240, $250. Why? Because that's making her employable, moving her closer to the market, where she can earn her own money. She can go back to junior college and study computer science, or learn cosmetology or business. The way it is now in most states, if she went out and found a job and made $200, they would take away $200 from welfare. So why earn the $200? Maybe if she earns $200 she should keep at least $100.

The point is that incentives to earn and learn must be built into the system. As it is now, if the young man who fathered the child doesn't have a job but comes back to live with the mother, she loses her check. So there's an incentive to keep the father away. And one of the few ways she can get any extra money is by engaging in an activity that may get her an extra child.

Now this young girl—white, black, Hispanic, Asian, Indian—is the victim of a system that is not oriented toward human development. We must take away the punishment and threats and disincentives and move toward a sense of optimism and increasing options.

MURRAY: One part of me endorses what you're saying in principle. But when I think of all the practical difficulties I get depressed. Most of all, it is extremely difficult to make much progress with youngsters who already have certain behavior patterns. If we go to a poor part of New York City, white or black, and pick a hundred kids who really have problems—drugs, illegitimate kids, the rest of it—and I say: "Here's a blank check; hire the best people, use the latest technologies, do whatever you can." At the end of three or four or even five years, if you start with seventeen- or eighteen-year-olds, *maybe* you will be able to point to ten or fifteen out of that hundred who show any major signs of getting somewhere.

Human beings aren't plastic. We don't know how to deal with certain kinds of problems after a certain age. The only route we have is prevention. So if you're hearing me say we're going to have to write off a generation, you can certainly back me into that corner.

JACKSON: Dr. Murray, I have seen these same kids, who you say can't do anything, volunteer for the Army, and in six to eight months they are building bridges, assuming responsibility. Why? Because it's an effective program that teaches, inspires, and sets clear goals.

So many young people step into sex and have babies because of ignorance, lack of discipline, and the like. If there was sex education before the fact, as well as the teaching of moral values, then there'd be less debate about abortion after the fact. Today, there is this whole group of people who *love* the fetus; they march across America to save a fetus and march right back to cut off aid for a baby.

Aid to women for prenatal care has a lot of value. The Head Start program saved and salvaged a whole generation. The drive to wipe out malnutrition by Senators McGovern and Hollings in the food stamp program actually worked; it brought about balanced diets where there had

been none. We should drop programs that aren't working, not those that are.

MURRAY: It is beginning to percolate into the consciousness of policymakers that we just don't know how to affect large numbers of people who are leading blighted lives. The only way we can deal with this is by prevention.

JACKSON: I agree that there are ways to change this situation without just paying another top-heavy layer of overseers and administrators who'd be sending paperwork back to Albany. I would take 500 young people and say, "How many of you would like this neighborhood to be cleaner?" Most hands would go up. "How many of you would like to have windows in your buildings in the wintertime?" Hands would go up. "How many of you would like to make $12 to $20 an hour?" Many hands. "Then here's what you must do if you want to make $12 to $20 an hour. We'll teach you how to be a mason. You can lay bricks and not throw them. You can learn how to be a glazier, how to be a plasterer. And at the end of this time we'll get you certified in a trade union. You will then have the skill to build where you live; if the floor's buckling in your gymnasium, you can fix it."

And so these young men and women would be empowered and enfranchised: they would much rather make $20 an hour than be on welfare. Just to do things *for* them while keeping them economically disenfranchised is no systemic change at all. And, Dr. Murray, people who can lay bricks and carpet and cut glass have no intention of going back on welfare.

MURRAY: I should point out that in my ideal world, by God, any black youngster who wants to can become a glazier, any poor youngster can learn a trade. And, Reverend Jackson, in my ideal world I would also clone *you*, because I've heard you speak to these kids.

JACKSON: But why do you think black kids everywhere are playing basketball so well? I submit to you that they're playing basketball and football and baseball so well and in such great numbers because there is a clear and obvious reward; there's a carrot. Do this and you'll be in the paper, on the radio, on television. And you'll get a college scholarship. And if you're real good, you'll get a professional contract. So these same kids that you say are unreachable and unteachable will gravitate to a carrot if they can see it. There must be a way out. And right now we must come up with ways out.

MURRAY: Yes, education and training opportunity—the carrots—are absolutely central. But once you have those, you have to have a support system, and this is where we've got a real problem. For example, let's say a youngster graduates from high school without many skills. He gets into a good job-training program, one that will really teach him a skill if he buckles down. But the youngster has never learned good work habits, so he flunks out of the training program. For that youngster to come out of high school ready to take advantage of a training program, there must be changes in the school he came from.

Now, what about the youngster who is offered an opportunity but who is below average in intelligence? I mean, half the country is below average in intelligence, and in industriousness.

JACKSON: Does that apply all the way through the government?

MURRAY: Let's just say this youngster is no great shakes, not much of anything. How is this youngster going to have a life that lets him look back when he's sixty and say, "Well, I did O.K., given what I had. At least I always supported myself and raised my kids and so on." The only way that eighteen-year-old kid is ever going to get to that position is by taking jobs that aren't much fun and don't pay much money. In order to reach the point where he feels good about supporting himself and his family, he's got to survive those years of eighteen, nineteen, twenty, when kids want to do things which make a whole lot of sense when you're that age but turn out to have been real stupid by the time you're thirty. Here is where, after you've provided the opportunities, which I am for in abundance, you've still got to worry.

JACKSON: But Dr. Murray, democracy must first guarantee opportunity. It doesn't guarantee success. Now, why do you think these ghetto and barrio youngsters are doing so well in athletics?

MURRAY: Because they see people just like them, who came out of those same streets, making a whole lot of money doing it.

JACKSON: So successful role models are a great motivator.

MURRAY: They make a huge difference. Now, how do we get the Jesse Jacksons of the world to be more visible role models?

JACKSON: Well, I've been working on that for a few years. But the point is that where the rules are clear, even though the work is hard, the locked-out tend to achieve. Ain't no low-class and high-class touchdowns. But there are no black baseball managers and no black professional football coaches. Why? Because in those areas where the decisions are made behind closed doors and where the rules are not so clear, those who are locked out don't do well.

That is basically true in the private economy:

the more subjective the rules, the less the penetration. When people go behind closed doors to, say, determine who the dean of the medical school will be, eight people who are doctors, all of them graduated from the same school, tend to come up with someone from the same lineage. Why are there so many blacks in government? Because if you do well on the test, you can get in, and the rules of seniority are established.

MURRAY: In 1983, the New York City Police Department gave a sergeant's exam, and 10.6 percent of the white candidates passed but only 1.6 percent of the blacks. So it was decided that even though the rules were clear, some blacks who had failed the test would be promoted in order to fill a quota. Now, either you assume that the test measured nothing relevant to being a sergeant and that skill is randomly distributed, so it didn't make any difference that a whole bunch of blacks were arbitrarily promoted despite the fact that they didn't pass the test, or you assume that the test did in fact measure abilities that are important to advancement. If that's true, a few years down the road very few of the black sergeants will become lieutenants. This ensures, in an almost diabolically clever way, that no matter how able blacks become, they will continue to be segmented, and whites will always be looking at black co-workers who aren't quite as good at their jobs as the whites are. You build in an appearance of inferiority where none need exist.

Now, your son went to St. Albans and my daughters go to National Cathedral. These are among the finest schools in Washington. Your son, when he applies for a job, doesn't need or want any special consideration. The fact that he's black is irrelevant.

JACKSON: You're making dangerous comparisons here, Doctor, which tend to inflame weak minds. My son is not a good example because, like his father, his achievements are above average. The fact is that all of America, in some sense, must be educated about its past and must face the corrective surgery that is needed.

When there's moral leadership from the White House and from the academy, people tend to adjust. When Lyndon Johnson said—with the moral authority of a converted Texan—that to make a great society we must make adjustments, people took the Voting Rights Act and affirmative action and said, "Let's go."

There are a lot of positive examples around the country where integrated schools have worked, where busing has worked, where affirmative action has worked, when that spirit of moral leadership was present. The same school where the National Guard had to take two blacks to school in 1961—the University of Georgia—is where Herschel Walker won the Heisman Trophy. Later he was able to marry a white woman without protest in rural Georgia. Why? Because people had been taught that it was all right.

MURRAY: You've got the cart before the horse. By the mid-1960s, white folks finally, after far too long, had had their consciousnesses raised. They said to themselves, "We've done wrong. We have violated a principle that's one of the taproots of America; we haven't given people a fair shot just because their skin's a different color." A chord was struck that triggered a strong desire not only to stop doing the bad things but also to help people make up for lost ground.

That additional response was, from the very beginning, sort of pushing it. The principle that had actually been violated was that of the fair shot; but the black civil rights movement isn't feeding off that important nutrient anymore. It's gone beyond that. Today, when white folks aren't making public pronouncements, I hear far too many of them saying things which are pretty damned racist. I see a convergence of the old racism, which is still out there, with a new racism, from people who are saying, "Well, gee, it's been twenty years now. You'd think they'd be catching up by now."

JACKSON: They're getting strong signals from the highest pulpit in the nation. When the White House and the Justice Department close their doors to the Afro-American leadership; when the Congressional Black Caucus cannot meet with the President of the United States; when the government closes its doors to the NAACP, the SCLC, the Urban League, Operation PUSH; when the White House will not meet with the Conference of Black Mayors; when those who work in the vineyards daily will not even engage in the dialogue you and I have engaged in today—that's reprehensible behavior. It sends out signals that hurt people. When leadership is present, people behave differently.

MURRAY: In addition to spending a lot of time talking to white people in general, I also spend a lot of time talking to conservatives. And I happen to know that their passion for a colorblind society is not just rhetoric.

JACKSON: Are you a consultant for an optometrist? Because the only people who would benefit from people going colorblind would be optometrists.

Nobody wants to be that way, man. We don't *need* to be colorblind; we need to affirm the beauty of colors and the diversity of people. I do not have to see you as some color other than what you are to affirm your person.

MURRAY: I mean that the ideal of giving everybody a fair shot—of not saying to anyone, "Because you're black I'm going to refuse to give you a chance"—is something which a lot of conserva-

tives feel more passionately about than a lot of your putative friends do.

JACKSON: But if two people are in a one-mile race and one starts off with a half-mile head start and one starts off at point zero—O.K., now let's take the chains off, every man for himself—well, such a race is not just. We are starting out behind. I mean, of the top 600 television executives, fewer than fifteen are black.

MURRAY: I had a talk with somebody from one of the networks a few weeks ago, as a matter of fact. He said to me: "Well, we figured we ought to have a black producer, so we went out and hired the best one we could find. But he really isn't very good, so we do most of his work for him." Now, insofar as people aren't allowed to be TV producers because they're black, that's bad. But insofar as white people go around saying, "We had to get our black TV producer, so we brought in someone who can't make it on his own," they are not doing blacks a service.

JACKSON: Man, for most of my life I have seen black people train white people to be their boss. Incompetent whites have stood on the shoulders of blacks for a long time. Do you know how impressed I am when a white rock singer who is selling millions of records explains how he got his inspiration from a black artist, who can't even afford to come to the white man's concert? A few months ago *Time* said in an article that Gary Hart was the only Democrat who has run a coast-to-coast campaign. I was on the cover of *Time* twice during the 1984 campaign. But Hart's the only one. Isn't that a strange phenomenon? It's like Ralph Ellison's invisible man: they look at you but they don't see you.

By and large, the black people the White House sees are those one or two exceptions who did something great. They take a Hispanic kid or a black person and try to impose that model on the nation. I could take the position, "Well, if I can make it from a poor community in South Carolina, explain to me how a white person can be in poverty," and it would be absurd. But I could argue it and get lots of applause.

MURRAY: I'm willing to grant that we shouldn't make so much of the exception if you grant me that just because folks may be against certain kinds of programs, it doesn't mean that they're mean-spirited, or don't care about problems.

JACKSON: If we can avoid the demagogy and turn debate into dialogue and stereotypes into creative thinking, we can begin to develop ideas. I mean, I agree that this welfare system hurts people fundamentally. Many of the things that come from this Administration, like the enterprise zone idea, have a lot of validity. If an enterprise zone creates a green line, instead of a red line, where if you live in that area you get certain incentives—that idea has merit. It may mean that a young man or a young woman teaching school will want to move to a district because of a tax incentive, or perhaps a doctor or a lawyer will want to move his office there. You establish an incentive for people to locate there, through the tax system or otherwise; you begin to shift capital, and the people who live there have first option on the new jobs. But the Administration has never really discussed this idea with those who would have to communicate with the masses about it.

So that idea has merit. Together we could make sense of such an idea. I'm anxious to open up the door of social policy, and I'm impressed with this opportunity today.

# A NATION APART

■ It has been a long time building, but only now is the country paying attention to it: The alarming emergence within black America of a nation apart—a lost nation in a land of comfort.

The great majority of blacks are working out better lives for themselves. Over the past two decades, the percentage of blacks in the middle class has doubled. A young black man with a college education now earns just about as much as his white counterpart. Six of the 10 largest cities have black mayors. In living rooms across the U.S., the "Bill Cosby Show" is the most popular fare on television.

But a second nation has grown up within black America, and life is desperately different there. It is a nation outside the economic mainstream—a separate culture of have-nots drifting further apart from the basic values of the haves. Its growth is now the central issue in the country's urban centers.

A charged atmosphere of fear permeates the cities, heightening racial tension between blacks and whites. Though segregation is outlawed, subtle barriers are being solidified between races. Last year, violent protests broke out in Philadelphia when blacks moved into a white neighborhood.

The emergence of the black underclass, as it is now popularly known, is clothed in uncertainty and controversy. For one thing, no one is sure just how large the underclass is. About a third of all blacks live in poverty, but most of them—like most poor whites—hold jobs or use welfare temporarily before shifting back to the mainstream. The underclass, in contrast, is the seemingly irreducible core of poor inner-city blacks, those trapped in an unending cycle of joblessness, broken homes, welfare and, often, drugs and violence. That core is estimated at about 2 million to 3.5 million, or about one third of all poor blacks.

Statistics that are more reliable—and also more startling—relate what it is like for a black youngster growing up today:
• One in 2 lives in poverty.
• One in 2 grows up without a father.
• Nearly 1 in 2 teenagers is out of work.
• One out of 4 births is to a teenager.
• And 1 in every 21 young black men winds up murdered.

Such conditions, of course, are not limited to black neighborhoods. Some 23 million whites are poor in the United States today, and many of them have become mired, too. But the growth of an underclass in black urban centers, less than 20 years after the death of Martin Luther King, Jr., is a special agony for America.

## Changing minds

The problems of the black underclass are baffling. Most immigrant groups in America—and indeed, many blacks—have moved up the economic ladder. As Prof. Glenn Loury of Harvard University puts it: "Every finding of a diminution in discrimination raises the terrifying question: Why then do blacks not succeed?"

Among civil-rights leaders, politicians and academics, a fierce debate is heating up about causes—and solutions, if any. Black leadership itself is fracturing. Those representing the Old Guard blame lingering racism and cramped economic opportunities. They see affirmative action, job training and expanded federal programs as the way out. Black intellectuals, such as William Julius Wilson of the University of Chicago, say that radical changes in the job market are swelling the underclass.

Disputing these views is a new breed of bootstrap conservatives, including some blacks, who say that race is no longer the critical factor. Political scientists Loury and James Q. Wilson of Harvard point to declining family values and ghetto culture as the central problems. They argue that far more self-help is needed among blacks themselves.

That view is gaining support among a growing number of blacks, too. *Washington Post* columnist William Raspberry wrote earlier this month about the rise of the black middle class and warned its members that a new message was needed for those left behind: "It would help enormously if the well-off would let the poor—especially the children—in on their vital secret: You can make it if you try."

Injecting even more emotion into the debate is the fact that within white America many influential minds are changing. Two decades ago, most white Americans readily supported federal assistance programs and new civil-rights laws. Some believe that such public support flowed from a guilty conscience about past injustices; others think it was part of a generous American spirit.

But clearly, the national mood has shifted. Popular political leaders from President Reagan to New York Mayor Ed Koch are publicly questioning how much good has come from hundreds of billions of federal funds spent on public assistance, education, income security and housing for the disadvantaged. Reagan asserts that federal assistance has only created a dependency on welfare and argues that employment-training programs of the past—such as the Comprehensive Employment and Training Act—were miserable flops. Implicit—and often explicit—in their argument is that the system is no longer to blame: Responsibility must rest more squarely on the poor themselves.

Perhaps as significant to the outcome of the national debate is that important black leaders also have shifted position. Two decades ago, when Senator Daniel Patrick Moynihan (D-N.Y.), working in the Johnson administration, produced his controversial report on the collapse of black family life, he was bitterly criticized by civil-rights leaders for even bringing the subject up.

That code of silence is now broken. Most civil-rights leaders are publicly discussing the problems of unwed mothers and fatherless families.

"There is a general cultural crisis where the basic moral standards of the society are dropping," says Jesse Jackson. "Somebody must say that babies making babies is morally wrong. . . . We shouldn't be equivocating and hee-hawing about that."

## Joblessness as a norm

Even the term *underclass* is controversial, as it connotes a special subculture beyond hope and suffering, a lack of values as well as income.

It is a world where men are without jobs and women are without husbands. Some are career criminals; others broker numbers and hustle stolen goods. Many are addicted to drugs and alcohol; in hospital emergency rooms, cocaine-related deaths tripled for blacks between 1982 and 1984.

Central to a swelling underclass is the

quiet transformation of the urban job market during the past two decades.

Today, almost half of the 8.8 million working-age black men lack jobs, says a report from the Center for the Study of Social Policy. "They are either unemployed, out of the labor force, in correction facilities or unaccounted for."

Unlike ethnic groups in the century's first half, unskilled blacks have been unable to shed poverty by taking manufacturing jobs that offer decent wages. By 1970, the door to these jobs was virtually shut. In the last 15 years, only 1 percent of the 23 million jobs created in the private sector were in manufacturing—while more than 90 percent were in the service sector.

Many new jobs required relatively high education levels and were in the suburbs. As a result, members of other ethnic groups or white women took a significant proportion. Young black men, for whatever reason, took only 1 out of every 1,000 new jobs created between 1970 and 1983.

In New York, Philadelphia and Baltimore, entry-level jobs in both service and manufacturing industries dropped by more than 600,000 in the central city during the 1970s.

For most inner-city blacks, new service jobs—janitor, messenger, busboy—have not come near to compensating for the loss of manufacturing jobs.

Some conservative social scientists, such as Charles Murray, a research fellow at the Manhattan Institute for Policy Research, argue that inner-city blacks do indeed have opportunities in low-level jobs but are turning them down—in part because the fast life of the street makes it more attractive not to work. Others strongly disagree, pointing out that when decent-paying openings occur, employers are sometimes overwhelmed. In Washington, D.C., Marriott received 11,000 job applications for 363 openings in its new downtown hotel.

"Cyclical unemployment was the problem for black men in the past," says Eleanor Holmes Norton, head of the Equal Employment Opportunity Commission under President Carter. "Permanent unemployment is at the core of the black underclass today."

### Flight of the middle class

Ironically, the collapse of inner-city communities has been accelerated by the success of middle-class blacks, who have been leaving the ghetto over the past decade. Gone with them are community role models: The doctor, the police officer, the straight-A student, the teacher. The vacuum they leave behind, says psychiatrist James Comer of Yale University, gets filled by "drug pushers, pimps and prostitutes. They're often the only successful people—the only ones with money—that the kids see."

As an alternative to working, many turn to the underground economy. A survey of 2,000 inner-city black teenage males found that about one fourth of their income was from crime.

Dominating underclass life is the continuous threat of violence. Homicide is the leading cause of death for young black men. High crime rates are accompanied by pervasive fear on the streets—between middle-class and poor blacks as well as between blacks and whites. To many community leaders, the underclass is increasingly outside the law.

"The issue is not poverty," says Harry Spence, former Boston Housing Authority administrator. "The real issue is social membership. People can live poor if they have some sense of participation and membership in the community."

### The rise of matriarchy

All of this has a major impact on women and children in the inner city.

With so many men dropping out of the labor market, the pool of eligible males shrinks. Sociologist Wilson has calculated that for every 100 black women between the ages of 20 and 24, there are only 45 employed black men.

"This disparity," contends Norton, "has a lot to do with the change in mores in the poor-black community. Women grow up where they not only do not see people marry, they in fact don't see eligible men."

The decline of two-parent families is striking. In 1965, only 1 of 4 black families was headed by a woman. Now, almost half are headed by females. In contrast, 80 percent of black middle-class families have two parents present.

The ghetto is also reeling from the recent rise of black families headed by women who have never married, especially among teenagers. "Marriage," warns one report from the Children's Defense Fund, "is now an almost forgotten institution among black teens."

The prevalence of matriarchal families in the underclass has hastened what economists call the feminization of poverty. If present trends continue, 70 percent of black families will be headed by single women by the turn of the century. Says John Jacob, president of the National Urban League: "The absence of black males as heads of households has had a devastating effect on black America."

### Economics and values

A large number of other minorities and whites also belong to an underclass culture of crumbling family structure, crime and poverty.

What's more, throughout U.S. history, different ethnic groups have experienced similar social disintegration and worked their way up from the slums. The Irish, for example, at the turn of the century, were among those plagued by domestic violence, broken families and alcohol problems.

Blacks, the largest and most visible minority, have met stiffer resistance compared with other immigrants.

Still, the collapse of the ghetto raises disturbing questions about the widening gap between poor blacks and those who have made it.

If part of the problem lies in the lack of opportunities for unskilled blacks, the upside-down value system of the underclass is also an obstacle. "We need to inculcate middle-class values," says the Rev. Charles Stith of Boston's Organization for a New Equality. "Children need to learn that hustling is very different from balancing a checkbook."

### Politics of poverty

As Republicans and Democrats argue over budget cuts that affect the urban poor, a key issue is the role of welfare payments in fueling the underclass.

Concern that incentives are misdirected were stirred by Murray, author of the controversial book *Losing Ground*.

Yet the welfare-underclass link is complicated. In fact, welfare does not seem to be the key factor in forming female-headed families—since the number of black single mothers who are *not* on Aid to Families With Dependent Children grew just as rapidly during the 1970s as those who were.

The Reagan administration is attempting to force those on welfare to work. Some officials are also calling for a national family policy to curb high rates of illegitimate births and fatherless families—trends also soaring among whites. "The only way we're going to deal with some of these problems is by preventing future generations from growing into them," says Murray.

But with the budget deficit dominating the legislative agenda, no new federal initiatives are expected soon. In many cities, local programs to help students finish school and prevent out-of-wedlock births are trying to meet the growing needs of the underclass.

Yet to many political leaders, the existence of an underclass is a burgeoning problem for the whole nation and time is running out. "We're building social nitroglycerin that is going to explode," says Representative William Gray (D-Pa.), "and the country is going to pay for it one way or another."

by David Whitman and Jeannye Thornton with Maureen Walsh of the Economic Unit and Ronald A. Taylor and the magazine's domestic bureaus

Unlike women, no welfare and no place in the home

# For men on the streets: Hustle without heroism

■ Lateef Carter says he knows what it's like to leave the camaraderie of ghetto streets to look for work.

"You go to see someone and you wait, for 20 hours, for 50 hours, for 60 hours, and they just chit-chat while you sit there wanting to work. They act like you're not there. They talk over you. They talk about their hair or where they're going for dinner or what they had for lunch. Nobody helps you, so you turn to the streets."

Frustration and anger drive many men like Carter, a Vietnam veteran, to the corner of Seventh and T Streets, N.W., in Washington, D.C., where regulars gather each day.

The streets. From Harlem to Watts, they are the bedrock of broken lives for males in the underclass. And when the culture of the ghetto comes under scrutiny of social scientists, often it's the men who bear the brunt of criticism despite disagreement about the causes of their plight.

While most black men are earning a living and paying taxes—and a small fraction are making their way into the power elites of America—men of the ghetto are blamed for abandoning their children and leading shiftless lives that may often involve crime. By comparison, underclass females, despite the controversy over welfare payments for which most men are ineligible, are portrayed semiheroically as they struggle to raise their families.

But there's some solace in the streets. Joe Louis, 48, stands near Lateef Carter and puts it this way: "You can always get something to eat. There are shelters. People come around with food in wagons."

Louis, who was laid off from a counseling job nine months ago, finds work for two or three days at a time but nothing permanent. "It's degrading. A man is supposed to take care of his family. . . . When things are really bad, I can get help from my mother. Look, you know, I should be helping *her*. I show up and make her think I'm her no-good son who isn't making it."

Most of the government's attention has been targeted on the plight of women in the underclass, but increasingly the black male is now seen as the center of the crisis. With no job—and few prospects of employment—the uneducated black man of the ghetto is witness to his own economic impotence.

Low-skilled manufacturing jobs have steadily declined—and so have the males' traditional roles as breadwinners and fathers.

**The welfare check,** moreover, can give a woman independence from a man she doesn't want to live with. "The average black woman is being

---

**BLACK CRIME**

## The myths and the realities

Among whites in urban America, fear of black crime is significant. The reality is that blacks—not whites—are more likely to be harmed by blacks.

Victims and offenders are of the same race in 3 out of 4 violent crimes, reports the Bureau of Justice Statistics. Government figures also show—
• Black men have a 1-in-21 chance of becoming victims of murder during their lifetimes, compared with a 1-in-131 chance faced by white men.

• Nearly 95 percent of black homicides were committed by blacks, sta-tistics show. Only 10 percent of white victims were killed by blacks.

• Blacks are more likely than whites to be murdered in arguments with relatives or acquaintances, rather than in robberies or street crimes.

While the rate of crimes committed by blacks against whites is low, whites have an exaggerated fear of blacks. "I can see it," says Dr. Alvin Poussaint, a black psychiatrist at Harvard Medical School. "It happens to me. Whites react to blacks as if they were potential thieves and criminals."

• Blacks, 12.1 percent of the population, were 46 percent of the 462,442 persons in federal or state prisons in 1984, the latest figures available.
• For all races, the lower a family's income, the greater the risk of becoming the victims of violent crime.

As Dr. Mark Rosenberg, a public-health expert in Atlanta, notes: "We need to understand patterns. The first step is to apply scientific methods to patterns. Poverty is a more important factor than race. If you control socio-economic status, the homicide rate is the same for blacks and whites."

told, 'You don't need that worthless, no-good so-and-so,' " says Horace Whitfield, a counselor with the Phoenix House drug-rehabilitation program in the nation's capital. "Her man has been replaced by a welfare check."

Because ghettos are usually economic wastelands, many of the jobs that emerge often are located beyond reach in better areas of the city. "It's terrible," says Richard Dixon, 30, laid off in 1976 from a Chrysler plant in Detroit. "People need jobs. Reagan says there are jobs out there. But most of the jobs in Detroit are out in the suburbs. A lot of poor people don't have transportation."

Some blacks have been out of work so long that they don't know how to get a job or cope with the details of filling out application forms and making a good impression on a prospective employer. Notes Clayton Singleton of the Armstrong Adult Education Center in Washington, D.C.: "We teach them not to go to a job interview with an open shirt, chewing gum or talking street talk. Some of them have grown up never thinking past tomorrow."

Rejected—or not even beckoned by the labor market—many black men turn to the business of the streets. Dropping out of school and into street life begins at an early age.

"The streets," says a 17-year-old 10th-grade dropout in Harlem, "took over for me. School ain't no fun after hanging out for a while.

"All of my friends talk about getting a job, but they don't do it," he says. "Other than look for work, I go and see my female friends. You know, I'm single and I like to mingle. I think about getting them pregnant sometimes and leaving something to show the world that I was here. But that ain't no big thing either."

The street economy thrives as hustlers make ends meet by peddling drugs, mugging a few passers-by, and even some "cattle rustling"—stealing meat from a grocery store. Everybody has a role, as the Phoenix House's Whitfield explains: "You get into a lot of juggling.

"Someone says, 'I've got a package [an ounce of cocaine]; I give the package to someone else to be my lieutenant.' To sell the drugs, he gets a sergeant. You put together a little organization and run it like a real business with everybody getting a salary for their role. You've got drive-in drugstores on the street so that you don't even have to get out of your car anymore."

Many working the streets find it exacts a heavy price while providing little long-term security. As one New York youth says: "I know that a hustle won't get me over. I'll take whatever comes. I know that I will be successful in something. A lot of people get lucky and get over without hard work. But I understand that you always pay for whatever you get. There's always a price."

But despite the glory of the hustlers, there are those who get broken by the streets. Often, they're the ones still trying to break into the job market, and they keep getting pushed back.

**That's when alcohol** and drugs start to take over. Joe Louis on Washington, D.C.'s Seventh Street explains it this way: "You come out in the morning. Your hopes are high. Your expectations are up. You're going to go out today and you're going to get a job. . . . And then the third day, you don't get a job and you say, 'To hell with it,' and you drink and come back here [to the street]. You need a little escape, know what I mean? So you drink."

Meanwhile, the neighborhoods suffer. "I've lived here and watched it all go down," says Herbert Hall, 64, a homeowner and disabled construction worker, surveying his neighborhood along Florida Avenue in the nation's capital. "The buildings, the people, the whole thing just kind of evaporated. Now, they just don't give a damn. They just don't care about anything, not about themselves, the places they live, about working, their kids. They've given up."

## AN ADDICT'S STORY

# The hardest trip is the one back

New York

He's a man of the ghetto, a recovering addict who's out of work and undergoing treatment at a rehabilitation center. Separated from his wife and five children, he has been in jail twice—an attempted-murder conviction and drug charges. Although he doesn't want to reveal his name, he tells a common story:

"I used to shoot up coke now and then. I also liked to speedball [shoot a mix of cocaine and heroin] because the coke would keep me going for hours.

"My last job was in a nursing home. My boss was always coming down on me. The cat stayed on my case until, one day, he pushed me and I floored him. They fired me after that. Now, I baby-sit, do odd jobs, and some sidewalk business [hustling drugs]. I haven't given up, though. I spend my time trying to make a dollar any way I can. No stickups. But a black man ain't going to be idle too long. If I can't do something productive, I stay home because I get into too much trouble.

"Nine years ago, at [an after-hours place], a guy pulled this large 007 killer knife on me, so I pulled my piece. Somebody hit my hand and a shot went off. The cops took me in. The other guy passed his knife to somebody; he got off.

"My kids never wanted for anything; I always brought my house money home to my wife. She never saw me shoot up, but she found the coke. She was not a street person. She was a square. Our sex life dropped off to nothing. After the coke would get me off, I'd pass out. So we split up after 14 years.

"Whites are scared of blacks; that's why they discriminate. If you have something in your past, they keep throwing it in your face. They never let you forget. First thing they do is say you can't do this or that if you have a record. I paid for my mistakes, but they won't let me forget."

Where the future is a mirror of past and present

# Mothers raising mothers

■ It's a world where women don't have husbands and children don't have fathers. In the rhythm of the neighborhood, the sexes lead separate lives: Mothers raise children alone; the fathers' whereabouts are often unknown.

Just as the underclass as a whole is isolated from mainstream America, men and women in the inner city are often isolated from each other. Although the fathers may come and go, half of all black children live in single-parent, female-headed homes. Eight out of 10 of these families in central cities live in poverty.

The struggle to make do—economically and spiritually—takes its toll, especially on the children.

Yet the matriarchal network of grandmothers, cousins, aunts, nieces, daughters and mothers is trying to pull together. Caring for the young, agonizing over their future and helping them fight off the traps and temptations of crime are what dominate the lives of women in the fatherless black urban family.

## The woman alone

The cycle of single motherhood and dependence on social services has become so entrenched that there is even a label for it—YGM—to identify a "young grandmother" who is receiving a welfare check for a household of children and grandchildren. Many such families are longtime welfare recipients. The standard 30-year generation has been compressed. Daughters are the same age as their nieces and nephews, with mothers in their 30s having babies and their children having children—all under the same roof.

*It's a large family in a small room in Harlem for Renee Elder, who lives with her five daughters and five grandchildren (see photo). Last April 8, fire destroyed the house they were living in along with all of their belongings. Renee had just remarried, but her pipefitter husband doesn't go with them to the city shelter. "He hates this place and us be-*ing here," says Renee. Her first marriage at 16 ended abruptly, leaving her to raise three children alone. In between marriages, she met a welder in New Jersey and had her fourth child by him. "I regret not finishing school," she says, but she's pleased with her family. "I did a good job raising them," she says. "They turned out all right. They don't use drugs, and I'm not sorry they had children. They're good mothers."*

## Teen moms

It used to be that the main reasons behind single motherhood were divorce and widowhood. Today, an increasing number of mothers never marry, and in some cities, 80 to 90 percent of births to black teenagers are out of wedlock.

In most cases, the first pregnancy is unplanned, and it triggers radical changes in a girl's life. Jill Latimore, 17, of Atlanta, first got pregnant four years ago and is now expecting her second set of twins. "I still kind of want to be a teenager, but I had all these children and now I have to be an adult."

The risks associated with teen pregnancies are significant. In addition to many health problems, there are long-term consequences. One national survey found that teenage mothers were half as likely to graduate from high school as those who had their children after age 20. As a result, they can expect to have low-paying jobs and are more likely to be on welfare.

Many cities have programs aimed at reducing illegitimate births by instructing youngsters on birth control. In Atlanta, Grady Memorial Hospital offers comprehensive services to teenagers, including a one-week course entitled "Postponing Sexual Involvement," which is taken by all eighth graders. Teenage mothers can usually enroll in alternative school programs to get the equivalent of a high-school diploma. For some of them, getting pregnant may change their lives for the better.

*Becoming pregnant was the last thing on the young girl's mind when she was a 10th grader at DeWitt Clinton High School in the Bronx. "I was 15. I was taking the pill, but I kept getting sick," she says. "School was kinda wild because of the boys. They were pretty rowdy. I was off with the wrong crowd, hanging out and cutting classes. People would go to Jerome Avenue to drink, get high.... A girl got shot in the head there last year. In a way, I'm glad I'm out of there."*

*Now she's finishing high school. "Being a mother is hard," she confesses, "especially when you're tired and the baby wants to play. She's a good baby. I have a lot of help from my mother, my sisters and my aunts. They give me a break when I need one." She wants someday to marry the father of her child. "I'd like to live somewhere upstate or in the suburbs. Things are changing for me now. I'm not going to mess up."*

## Fear in the streets

A common bond for inner-city women is fear—fear for themselves and for their children. In Washington, D.C., Rachel Dacoster, 33, the mother of six children, talks about the recent shooting in the laundry room of her building. "There are drugs sold on the corner," she says. "That gives me a lot to worry about. I wish to God I could move them out of here."

For many mothers, the fear is doubled. They are afraid that their children will be lured into the underground economy of the streets and look up to the pimps and pushers, with the gold chains and flashy cars, as their role models. There's also the constant fear that someday their children just won't make it home from school—that they will become crime statistics.

"A lot of kids just go to school to score drugs," says welfare mother Marsha Gibson, 38, of Philadelphia. "Of course I'm afraid for my children. School today is a battleground. I want to know what my children are wearing each day in case I have to make an identification at the end of it."

Sometimes, though, the crime and despair of the ghetto are too much, and families collapse.

*The daughter of Georgia sharecroppers, she's a Harlem grandmother now. Her husband left her and her children 30 years ago. "I tried to raise them the best I could with the money welfare gave me," she says. Her oldest son, 34, is on welfare. The oldest daughter, 32, has four children born out of wedlock and receives welfare. A son, 24, is in jail for robbery. Her 30-year-old son disappeared. "The last time I saw him, he was ironing a shirt. After that, he left. I ain't seen him since." She believes he got killed in a drug deal. "Sometimes people say they see him on the street. . . . Oh, God, it hurts me so bad." With the remaining daughter, 16, she's a lot stricter. "When I look at my children, I feel bad because it's not what I wanted for them," she says. "That's why I'm pushing the last one to finish school."*

## Impact on children

For many children of single mothers, the future is a mirror. Living in poverty—a virtual certainty for children of teenage mothers—is the major obstacle to climbing out of the underclass. With economic poverty comes emotional impoverishment. Teenage mothers, says a report by the National Urban League, do not have the education or maturity to address children's needs. The risks of child neglect and physical abuse increase. The stress of the mother's unemployment and the absence of a father figure help push a child further into the underclass. At the same time, sociologists find that in many instances the children in fatherless families can do just as well as those in two-parent homes.

The key seems to be the existence of a supportive network of extended family in the child's life. A survey of a black community in Chicago found that mothers who were raising children completely alone were under the most stress.

Ironically, the availability of welfare to teenage mothers encourages some of them to set up their own households at a time when they might be better off as part of a larger family.

And despite the obstacles, many children in the ghetto can and do persevere, keeping alive the dream of getting ahead.

*Richard Randolph, 11, lives with his mother, three sisters and brother in the Carver Homes Public Housing project in Atlanta and is in the program for gifted students at the Lena J. Campbell Elementary School. "I figured it out," he says. "The people who hang out on the corners don't have an education." "He's been smart since he was 2 years old," says his mother. Richard sings with the school chorus and is first baseman on the neighborhood team. "I want to be a lawyer when I grow up," he says. "I want to move into a big house. . . . I don't see myself as poor. I see myself as in between."*

---

## PROGRAMS IN SYRACUSE AND PHILADELPHIA OFFER HOPE TO BLACKS IN THE INNER CITY

# Social Change
# and the Future

- New Population Issues (Articles 40-42)
- New Technology Issues (Articles 43-45)
- Choices Ahead (Articles 46-47)

Fascination with the future is an enduring theme in literature, art, poetry, and religion. Human beings are anxious to know if tomorrow will be different from today and in what ways. Coping with change has become a top priority in the lives of many. One component of change is stress. When the future is uncertain and the individual appears to have little control over what happens, stress can be a serious problem. On the other hand, stress has positive effects on people's lives in many ways if the changes can be perceived as challenges and opportunities.

Any discussion of the future must begin with basic demographic trends and then consider how new technologies will affect these and other trends. This section begins with the demographic trends in the world and in the United States. Next, some of the problems produced by new technologies are discussed. Finally, two efforts to identify the crucial dangers and opportunities for the future of America are presented.

In 1984 the United Nations held the International Conference on Population in Mexico City. It was ten years after the Bucharest conference, and the concern about the population explosion in the Third World had increased substantially during the decade. The first selection is a *Time* magazine article which, at the time, reviewed the issues of the conference and assessed the world population situation.

The next two articles detail demographic issues in the United States. Richard Stengel reviews dozens of demographic statistics which indicate important ways that the country is changing geographically, in family structure and life-style, in employment and income, and in age and age-related activities. William Broyles, Jr. tells the glorious story of immigration symbolized by the Statute of Liberty. America was built by immigrants and Broyles sees much evidence that today's immigrants will contribute greatly to the continued building of America.

Technology is a dynamic force which influences the course of history and the shape of tomorrow. The following three articles discuss new technologies. The first one focuses on the dangerous side of technology. In a short period Chernobyl erupted and three spacecraft, including the Challenger, exploded. The chemical industry leaves a trail of death, and biological technology has the potential to accidently kill millions. The next article presents the beneficial side of technology. It describes a fully automated factory in Milwaukee which produces 500 different relays and contactors and is run by only 14 workers. Some new technologies may not cause physical illness or endanger lives but they do cause social problems. Fred Best explains how computers, robots, and other innovations will greatly affect the workplace. Workers will be displaced, but he predicts that new jobs will open up as a result. Only if America embraces these technologies, he argues, will the economy become strong, standards of living rise, and unemployment be kept relatively low.

America is entering a new era. The volume ends with two visions of the future. Scott Thomas Eastham sees the present generation making many decisions which greatly worsen the chances of future generations. Environmental deterioration, the proliferation of nuclear arms, and the wastes of a greedy civilization may be the inheritance of future generations. Newt Gingrich sees both dangers and opportunities in America's future. The main driving force is the communications revolution which will reshape both the economy and personal life-styles. An information explosion will require people to constantly adapt to changes and update their education and it will also restructure most of the institutions of society.

## Looking Ahead: Challenge Questions

What are the significant factors bringing about social change at the present time?

In what ways will social change accelerate? How can it slow down?

What are some ways to deal with social change?

# People, People, People

*Despite some progress, global population is still growing at an alarming rate*

Diplomats and demographers, economists and family planners, the elite brigades of global social science, will converge on Mexico City next week to tackle a formidable issue: the relentless growth of world population. They will hear some good news. In the ten years since the last United Nations–sponsored International Conference on Population, which was held in Bucharest, the annual growth rate of the world's population has declined from 2% to 1.7%.

But that positive statistic stands out amid an otherwise sobering array. During the past decade, the number of people on earth increased by 770 million, to 4.75 billion. The World Bank estimates that in 2025, a date within the foreseeable lifetime of most Americans under 30, global population could nearly double, to about 8.3 billion. Of that total, about 7 billion will be residents of the undercapitalized, undernourished Third World.

The consequences of a failure to bring the world's population growth under control are frightening. They could include widespread hunger and joblessness, accompanied by environmental devastation and cancerous urban growth. Politically, the outcome could be heightened global instability, violence and authoritarianism. Says Science Fiction Writer Isaac Asimov, the author of numerous essays on demography: "Population growth at current rates will create a world without hope, gripped by starvation and desperation. It will be worse than a jungle because we have weapons immensely more destructive and vicious than teeth and claws."

The U.N.'s decision to hold its population conference in Mexico City could hardly be more appropriate. In all its splendor and squalor, the Mexican capital is the archetype of Third World megacities that are climbing to the top of the list of the world's major urban centers *(see following story).* Says Allan Rosenfield, director of Columbia University's Center for Population and Family Health: "We in the West haven't done very well managing our big cities. How Indonesia, In-

dia, Mexico and other Third World countries can handle them is beyond my comprehension."

Among those who have tried to focus increased attention on the population issue is former World Bank President Robert McNamara. Writing in the latest issue of *Foreign Affairs,* he argues that the much heralded drop in the world's population growth rate during the '70s has led to overconfidence and the mistaken idea that "efforts to deal with [population] problems can therefore be relaxed." McNamara points out that the global figures for the past decade have been distorted by the experience of China, where a draconian birth control program that includes financial rewards and penalties to encourage one-child families has reduced the fertility rate by half.

There has been no such improvement in many other areas. In black Africa, some national fertility rates have actually increased in the past decade. The average number of children born to a woman in Kenya is now eight; when that is combined with a declining infant mortality rate, the country's population could balloon from 20 million today to 83 million in 2025. In Bangladesh, the fertility rate figure is 6.3, which means that 266 million people (nearly three times the present population) might be squeezed into an area the size of Wisconsin by 2025. With a fertility rate of 4.7, India will become the world's most populous country by about 2045, with 1.5 billion people. By comparison, Soviet women now have an average of 2.4 children, while American women have 1.8 children; the figure for Western Europe is even lower, 1.6.

Although in the past two decades Third World economies have had higher growth rates than those of the U.S. and Western Europe, in many countries that advance has been severely diluted by rapid population growth. Between 1955 and 1980, for example, per capita income in the U.S. grew from $7,000 to $11,500 (expressed in constant 1980 dollars), while in India it increased from $170 to $260, nearly doubling the disparity between the two countries. By the year 2000, some 630 million young adults will join the Third World's labor force, while industrialized

countries will add only 20 million young workers. As a result, Third World wages will probably remain at their low levels. That may encourage the flow of manufacturing jobs from industrialized countries to developing nations, but it could also provoke protectionist threats to the international free-trade system.

Some of the baleful effects of excessive population growth are already evident. In addition to unrestrained urban growth, McNamara notes the increasing inadequacy of Third World agriculture, owing in part to rural overpopulation and economic distortions caused by efforts to palliate the rising tide of urban consumers. In such countries as Tanzania and India, where people depend on firewood for fuel, deforestation is damaging flood control, speeding erosion and adding to the hardship of merely staying alive. Citing the example of China, McNamara warns that rapid population growth may also lead to greater and more coercive state intrusions into private life, ranging from forced sterilization to restrictions on freedom of movement.

Many population experts accept McNamara's facts, while objecting to the tone of his conclusions. According to Rafael Salas, executive director of the United Nations Fund for Population Activities (UNFPA) and chief organizer of the upcoming Mexico City conference, "There is room for concern, but not panic." He points out that countries in the Third World increasingly recognize the importance of population control. In its 1984 *Development Report,* the World Bank notes that 85 nations in the Third World, containing about 95% of its population, now provide some form of public support, however inadequate, to family-planning programs. An additional 27 countries do not. Almost half of these are in Africa, where incomes are the lowest and population growth rates the highest in the world.

While the conference delegates debate whether the world's Malthusian nightmare is lifting or drawing closer to reality, they will also face a challenge from the Reagan Administration. As part of its vocal antiabortion stance in a U.S.

presidential election year, the Administration has announced sharp new restrictions on family-planning assistance for any organization or country that sanctions abortion. The impact of the policy change may be substantial: it is estimated that U.S. contributions of $240 million represent nearly one-quarter of total worldwide aid spent on family planning. The Administration will also inject its free-market philosophy into the population debate. In Mexico City, the U.S. delegation, headed by Radio Free Europe Director James Buckley, will argue that government interference with economies is a major reason why world population growth has changed "from an asset in the development of economic potential to a peril."

The Administration's policy requires that family-planning aid be allotted in ways that prevent its use in population-control programs that include abortion. The real loss may fall upon private organizations that currently receive about $100 million of the $240 million annual U.S. allotment. Groups that promote abortion would be cut off entirely. Ironi-

cally, the policy is unlikely to accomplish the one thing that its right-to-life supporters might expect. An estimated 50 million abortions are now performed each year around the globe; perhaps half of those occur in Third World countries that have antiabortion laws.

One encouraging sign for the future, according to U.N. experts, is the substantial "unmet demand" for population control among Third World residents. In a survey of 17 slowly developing countries, the U.N. found that while the average number of children per family ranged from 3.8 to 8.3, the average number of children desired was 3.7 to 4.7. The difference between desire and reality is due to the lack of available family-planning education and services.

One of the most impressive examples of a Third World country that has made progress in curbing population growth is Thailand (pop. 49 million). In the past three decades, the Thai birth rate has declined by nearly 40%, from 46.6 per 1,000 people to 28.6. The population growth rate has dropped from about 3.4% to

1.95%. One reason for the change is a determined effort to extend health care and family planning to rural areas. Thailand has more than 4,000 village health centers staffed with 220,000 paramedics in addition to village doctors and local assistant midwives. One Thai private group offers farm production and marketing assistance to contraceptive users; as a result, rates of contraceptive use have risen as high as 80% in some villages.

Such efforts, however, require not only will but money. The World Bank estimates that $7.6 billion will be necessary if the Third World is to achieve a rapid decline in fertility by the year 2000. That figure pales against the estimated $600 billion a year that the world spends on armaments. Indeed, the funds spent on population control would probably turn out to be a bargain. Says Conference Organizer Salas: "There is a lack of understanding among policymakers of the links between population and global stability."

—*By George Russell.*
*Reported by Raji Samghabadi/New York and Barrett Seaman/Washington*

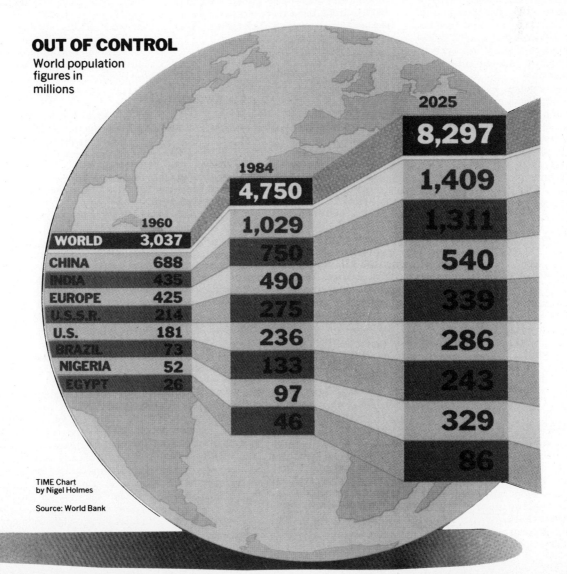

**OUT OF CONTROL**
World population figures in millions

|  | 1960 | 1984 | 2025 |
|---|---|---|---|
|  |  |  | 8,297 |
|  |  | 4,750 |  |
| WORLD | 3,037 | 1,029 | 1,409 |
| CHINA | 688 | 750 | 1,311 |
| INDIA | 435 | 490 | 540 |
| EUROPE | 425 | 275 | 339 |
| U.S.S.R. | 214 | 236 | 286 |
| U.S. | 181 | 133 | 243 |
| BRAZIL | 73 | 97 | 329 |
| NIGERIA | 52 | 46 | 86 |
| EGYPT | 26 |  |  |

TIME Chart
by Nigel Holmes

Source: World Bank

# Snapshot of a Changing America

## The U.S. population is growing older and thinking smaller

**"T**he United States themselves," wrote Walt Whitman, "are essentially the greatest poem." That epic is remade by every new generation, and today its rhythm, structure and content are unlike any that went before. The nation is growing middle-aged and more solitary. Men and women are delaying marriage, delaying childbirth, having few or no children at all. Real income, once expected to rise as naturally as a hot-air balloon, has leveled off. For many, home ownership, once thought of as practically a constitutional right, has become a dream denied. Demography is destiny, and Americans of today, in ways both obvious and subtle, are inventing the America of tomorrow.

Most of the changes have been triggered by the baby-boom generation. Born between 1946 and 1964, they are 75 million strong, one out of every three Americans, the largest generation in U.S. history. Next year the oldest of them will turn 40. The generation that could hum TV jingles before it could hum the national anthem, that made rock 'n' roll and protest into rites of passage, and swore never to trust anyone over 30, is becoming middle-aged.

In 1983 the median age of the population reached 30.9, the oldest ever, and is expected to exceed 36 by the year 2000. People who fox-trotted to Tommy Dorsey now outnumber those who hip-hop to Cyndi Lauper; for the first time in history, there are more Americans over 65 than there are teenagers. Notes Karl Zinsmeister, an economic demographer at the American Enterprise Institute: "By the late 1980s, one-half of our households will be headed by baby boomers. One-fourth of our population will be elderly. These two groups will define our society for a very long time."

**Single people now account for 23% of all U.S. households. As many as 8% of today's adults will never marry.**

Remember when unmarried men were called bachelors and unmarried women spinsters? Many of the 50 million "singles" in America are too young to recall. The Census Bureau reports that from 1970 to 1983 the proportion of never married singles ages 20 to 24 increased from 36% to 56% among women and from 55% to 73% among men. During that period, single-person households increased by 8.5 million. According to the Census Bureau, the increasing number of unmarried people in the pivotal 30-to-34 age bracket "suggests that an increasing proportion of persons may never marry."

**Families with single heads grew by 69% from 1970 to 1983. One out of every five children, and more than half of all black children, lives in a one-parent household.**

"Typical" is no longer an adjective that can describe the American household. Fifteen years ago, 40% of all households consisted of husband, wife and children; today that figure is 28.5%. The stereotypical nuclear family of mom, dad and two kids now accounts for only 11% of all households.

The number of female-headed households with one or more children under 18 doubled from 1970 to 1982, from 2.9 million to 5.9 million. During the 1970s the divorce rate shot up by half. Although it has dropped slightly, the U.S. rate remains the highest among all Western nations. Out-of-wedlock births jumped by 67% from 1970 to 1980.

**Since 1970, the number of first births to women age 25 and older has more than doubled, while first births to women under 25 have declined. As many as one-fourth of all women of childbearing age may remain childless. The lowest total fertility rate in American history, 1.7, occurred in 1976.**

Many working women of childbearing age have decided against having a child, while women with children are working in unprecedented numbers. In 1960 only 19% of women with children under six were in the work force; today half of them are. In general, women are waiting longer to have children and having fewer of them. From 1970 until 1982 the number of first births among women ages 30 to 34 tripled.

The total fertility rate declined from 3.7 births per woman in 1960 to 2.5 in 1970, and has wavered between 1.7 and 1.9 since 1976. The years from 1965 to 1976 are often called "the baby bust." While there was something of a "baby boomlet" in the late 1970s, it was due mainly to the enormous increase in women of childbearing age.

Immigration will keep the U.S. from shrinking. Without transplants, the population would crest at about 245 million in the year 2000 and then start declining. If the projected rates of immigration and fertility are realized, 100 years from now America will have a population of about 300 million, of whom 16% will be black, 16% Hispanic, 10% Asian and a diminishing majority of 58% non-Hispanic whites.

**One out of four Americans is over the age of 50. By the turn of the century, more than 100,000 Americans will be 100 years or older, about three times the number today.**

Demographers call them the new old. Healthy, vigorous and solvent, they confute the view that old age, as William Butler Yeats put it, is nothing but a tattered coat upon a stick. The 26% of the population over 50 controls three-quarters of the nation's financial assets and, with $130 billion in discretionary income, half of its spending power. "Today's elderly, especially the young elderly under 70, are a marketer's dream," says Alma Triner of Arthur D. Little Inc., a consulting firm based in Cambridge, Mass.

The over-65 set is doing almost as well. In 1965 one-third were classified below the poverty line; today only 14% are. But in 2025, when there will be some 64 million people over 65, the nation will have fewer than four working-age individuals for every retirement-age person. "This is the lowest ratio ever," says Gordon Green of the Census Bureau, "and has serious implications for the solvency of the Social Security system."

The "old old," or the "superelderly," as they are sometimes called, represent the fastest-growing segment of the U.S. population. The number of Americans over 85 could double by the year 2000.

Older people represent the fastest-growing segment of the U.S. population. By the year 2000, the number of Americans over 85 could double.

**In 1980, for the first time, the majority of Americans lived in the South and West. During the 1970s, California, Florida and Texas had 42% of the U.S.'s total growth.**

Imagine that every American had the same weight and was placed on a flat, rigid map of the entire country. The balancing point would be just west of De Soto in Jefferson County, Mo. The center of population has been inching west by about 40 miles a decade, from outside Baltimore in 1790 and finally crossing the Mississippi in the 1970s.

"During the 1970s," says Calvin Beale, chief of population research at the U.S. Department of Agriculture, "every Sunbelt state had a rate of population growth that was higher than the U.S. as a whole." Some of the Sunbelt, however, is now in the shade; in the 1980s, population

growth in Alabama, Mississippi, Arkansas, Tennessee and Kentucky has been lower than in the U.S. as a whole.

Migration drained the Frostbelt in the late 1970s. More than 1 million New Yorkers, for example, packed their suitcases and headed for the Sunbelt between 1975 and 1980, 375,000 of them bound for Florida. But in the past two years, states that were once synonyms for exhaustion have had small revivals: Ohio, Indiana, Illinois and Michigan have gained population.

For two centuries, cities were an irresistible magnet for internal American migration. In the 1970s, however, that path was reversed as nonmetropolitan areas grew by 14.4% and metropolitan areas by 10.5%. Since 1980, however, that "rural turnaround has again turned around, with metro areas. But one aspect of the 1970s trend endures. "People are moving to smaller, less crowded communities," says

Peter Morrison of the Rand Corp.'s population research center, "particularly those with a population under a quarter-million." Notes Bryant Robey, founder of *American Demographics:* "America's past has been one of steady centralization; its future is likely to be one of steady population deconcentration."

**The workers most in demand since the 1970s have been secretaries. In the next ten years, the economy will need 800,000 custodians and 425,000 truck drivers.**

Calvin Coolidge notwithstanding, the business of America today is service. Since World War II, the U.S. has made the transition from smokestacks and assembly lines to copiers and computers. Today, two-thirds of all people work in wholesale and retail trade, communications, government, health care and restaurants. The buzz word of the 1970s job market was high tech. In the next decade it will downshift to low tech. There will be tremendous expansion in such decidedly unglamorous occupations as cashier, registered nurse and office clerk.

**Average household income in constant dollars is dropping steadily: from $21,400 in 1980 to $20,600 today. In 1981 less than a third of all households headed by a person under 35 had any discretionary income.**

Baby boomers are having a hard time matching the living standards to which they were accustomed to as children. Demographers call it the promotion squeeze. There is not enough room at the top. Today the combined income of a young married couple, both of whom are working, is likely to be less than what either of their fathers earned at the same age. Baby boomers are not able to afford the houses they grew up in, and home-ownership rates have fallen for the first time since World War II.

The BMW-driving, Reebok-clad, madly acquisitive yuppies so beloved of Madison Avenue have proved to be something of a myth. They account for only about 6% of all baby boomers. The reality, says Ralph Whitehead Jr., an associate professor at the University of Massachusetts and an adviser to the Democratic Party, is the "new-collar" voter. The new collars are the college-educated sons and daughters of blue-collar parents; they earn between $20,000 and $40,000 and outnumber yuppies at least 5 to 1.

**Between 1985 and 1995, there will be a drop of 18% in college-age Americans. In 1982, there was a decrease of 3% in both violent and nonviolent crime.**

Colleges, the military and fast-food merchants depend on an endless supply of 18-year-old recruits. As Americans grow grayer, says Leon Bouvier of the Population Reference Bureau, "there could be real shortages in the labor force and the military." Baby boomers turned higher education into a multibillion-dollar business that employed more people than the automobile industry. Now universities will have to scale back.

Serious crime, traditionally a youthful failing, rose by 232% between 1960 and 1975, when baby boomers were in their teens and 20s. With fewer teenagers around, it should decline sharply by the end of the decade.

The skimpier the generation, the more room at the table. Demographer Richard Easterlin has a theory that economic well-being yields earlier marriages and higher fertility. Then fertility swings back and forth like a pendulum, from boom to bust, bust to boom. Members of the baby-bust generation will not face the teeming competition their parents did. They will struggle less and earn more. Rather like their grandparents. Sound familiar? Past being prologue, they could just produce another baby boom and start the cycle over again. —*By Richard Stengel. Reported by Joelle Attinger/Boston and Patricia Delaney/Washington*

# PROMISE

MICHAEL GEORGE—BRUCE COLEMAN INC.

# OF AMERICA

They come across the South China Sea in tiny boats and brave the Rio Grande in rafts made of automobile hoods welded together. Violence, repression, persecution and poverty may encircle their lives, but they dream of something better—of freedom. Almost 500 years old, the dream still works on the imagination like a magnet. The dream has a magic name: America.

For each new immigrant—as the ordinary and famous attest on the following pages—the dream is born again, fresh and powerful. "Come," it says, "no matter who you are, and be one of us. Come and be free."

"Who is the American, this new man?" asked essayist Michel Crèvecoeur in 1784. Two hundred years later, his question is still as provocative and the answer just as elusive. We are a nation without a nationality, a people without a race. We are an idea. We are Americans because we believe we are.

"Once I thought to write a history of

Essay by William Broyles, Jr.

the immigrants in America. Then I discovered that the immigrants *were* American history." So Oscar Handlin began *The Uprooted,* his masterly work on immigration, in words that could have been engraved on the Statue of Liberty. Walter Prescott Webb, no less a historian, wrote in *The Great Frontier* that the history of America "is the history of the frontier"—the vast continent stretching west behind the great statue's back.

It was not enough simply to come to America: Jamestown, the first English colony, perished from "unsufferable hunger." In the New World the old ways didn't work; the immigrants had to change. The parable of the first Thanksgiving is the parable of America. Starving and helpless, the Pilgrims learned from the Indians how to prosper in the wilderness. We are a nation in passage, learning and changing as we cross ocean and continent, bound always toward the setting sun.

Consider America as a play in three acts. First Act: The great immigration. Some 50 million people—the vast majority of them Europeans—abandon their traditional cultures and brave the Atlantic Ocean to begin a new life. Act Two: The great frontier. The vast continent they encounter transforms the immigrants into a new people—Americans. Both acts transpire in the same time frame—from the early 17th century to the beginning of the 20th. Act Three: The new people find their destiny—a tale as yet without end. And at the curtain other immigrants appear, from entirely new quarters, to begin the drama again.

It is tempting to romanticize the immigrant and the pioneer, and no doubt our celebrations of the 100th anniversary of the Statue of Liberty this Fourth of July will do so. Their triumph is all around us, their tragedies by and large distant memories. The great immigration and the great frontier are such powerful themes in our history precisely because they are grounded in tragedy.

Every man who turned his back on the Old World and went to America was, in a way, defeated: If he had been successful where he was, why leave? And every pioneer who left the settled life of the East and went west was recreating that original immigrant experience. The frontier was where a man could start over—implying that he needed to.

The American dreamed new dreams, yes—but because the old ones had failed. To make new traditions, old traditions had to be destroyed. Each new American is a small death of an old life, born again into a new one.

## SURGE OF NEW FACES

Today we are living in a reawakening of the immigrant experience; not since the first decade of the 20th century have so many new immigrants become Americans. Some 7 million legal immigrants are expected this decade, with perhaps millions more entering illegally. New ethnic neighborhoods are transforming our cities; new faces are turning up in our shops and factories; new languages buzz in our schools. This bubbling stew may seem strange to us, but until immigration was all but cut off in 1924 it was the normal condition of America.

In fact, even though the flow of immigrants this decade will be among the largest in history, the annual number of immigrants hovers around only 0.2 percent of the total population; before 1924 the figure was routinely more than 1 percent. The foreign-born population in 1980 was less than half what it was in 1910. In Boston in 1885 almost 70 percent of the population was foreign-born. Today even Los Angeles, where almost a third of

the population is foreign-born, does not begin to approach these figures.

For the first time in our history, however, the majority of immigrants do not come from Europe. The great westward movement that began with Columbus is over. Almost half the new immigrants today are from Asia, with South Korea alone sending more than England, West Germany, Ireland and Italy—the nations that for the past 350 years furnished the great majority of new Americans—put together. [See maps and graphs on pages 30 and 31.] The next-largest group is from Mexico, the Caribbean and Latin America.

New York City, the original ethnic metropolis, is being renewed yet again. The older immigrants—the Irish and the Italians—still hold their own in the police and sanitation departments, but coffee shops have long since passed to the Greeks and vegetable stands to the Koreans, who have brought a sense of aesthetics and quality—and a fierce devotion to hard work—back to neighborhoods around the city. Russians and Haitians are transforming Brooklyn and Queens, and the Chinese are overwhelming "Little Italy."

New York remains the classic laboratory of the three-generation immigrant story: The first generation works hard and sacrifices; their children go to college, and their grandchildren, who no longer speak the old language, move to the suburbs. And in come new immigrants to repeat the process.

For all its vibrant immigrant life, New York City is no longer the gateway to America. If the Statue of Liberty were being erected today, it would more likely shine its beacon from Los Angeles International Airport or the Rio Grande.

The melting pot of the new America is Los Angeles. One in 5 of the millions of immigrants since 1970 lives in Southern California. Away from its affluent pockets Los Angeles is like a booming Third World city: "Koreatown," "Little Saigon" and a host of little Philippines, Irans, El Salvadors, Cambodias, Taiwans and Israels stretches for miles. And, of course, everywhere is Mexico: Los Angeles is the third-largest Mexican city.

The downtown market teems with a bewildering variety of ethnic foods, goods and people. Grocery stores do a thriving business in books on how to

---

That immigrants work harder to get ahead is now a well-established American legend. Many of those who came here from humble foreign origins have risen to become paramount figures in the commerce and culture of this nation. These pages bring the voices of four for whom—through their sweat and perseverance and luck—the American dream has come true.

## KYUPIN PHILIP HWANG, 50, COMPUTER MAGNATE

"A few years ago [in 1983] *Forbes* magazine said I was the 28th richest man in the United States—worth 575 million dollars on paper. Can you believe it? An immigrant who came with $50 in his pocket?

"Lately my company has had its troubles. A lot of computer companies have gone bankrupt. We've reorganized and made a strong foundation. I am still a 100-million-dollar guy. I can still laugh.

"You can do that in America. Sometimes you're way up, sometimes down, but you still have the chance to go back up. Most Americans don't appreciate this opportunity.

"I sold pencils and shined shoes in Korea while in high school. I came to the U.S. in 1964 on a student visa, finished a bachelor's degree at Utah State and found a job with Ford Motor as an engineer. They paid the tuition and books for me to get a master's. Fantastic! After working for Ford and Burroughs, I answered an ad that said, 'Sunshine California company looking for engineer.' Two years later I had an opportunity to have my own business. Last year we did 100 million dollars in sales.

"It was not easy. During college summers I washed dishes during the day and cleaned bathrooms at night—16 hours a day, six days a week. The body was aching so much I took aspirin at night to sleep. But with strong determination you can do it.

"I started TeleVideo in 1975 with $9,000—all of our savings. The bank, an investment company, wouldn't give me any money. I put up my car, my furniture to get a loan. We had a hard time. I took out a second mortgage to pay our employes; there were about 15 then.

"We were within two weeks of running out of money again. Then the product started coming out of the factory. We could send out invoices and go to the bank for more credit. Soon we doubled in sales almost every year.

"This is what I call a wonderful country. In many countries you work so hard and have no opportunity. Here there is opportunity for everybody—especially in Silicon Valley. It is all up to you. I never believed I was more talented. I had a vision. I tried hard, and I did my best."

speak Spanish to the maid. Assembly workers at high-tech plants speak a babel of languages, and the $3-billion-a-year clothing industry survives on immigrant labor, legal and illegal. Beverly Hills High School has a distinctly Iranian look, and everywhere Oriental students are regularly claiming the highest scores in math and sciences and a share of admissions to the best universities far out of proportion to their numbers.

Along the Rio Grande, Texas is being reclaimed by Mexico. This is the most heavily crossed border in the world; the Texas border alone is as long as the line from the Baltic to the Mediterranean that divides the free world from the Communist empire, but it can be crossed casually by a boy on a mule ambling over the dry river bed above Terlingua.

Spanish is the language of the Texas border counties, but Texas is also being transformed by Asians and other new immigrants. The Vietnamese have taken over shrimping on the Gulf of Mexico and in Houston are reclaiming downtown neighborhoods and pushing blacks out of public housing. At times the ethnic mix becomes almost incomprehensible: Houston's best Cuban café is run by Koreans, the best Thai restaurant has a Mexican cook.

Although the sources of most new Americans have changed, the process is still much the same. Samuel Gompers, who created the American Federation of Labor, recalled how in the sweatshops of England in the 1860s the young workers sang a song called "To the West":

> To the West, to the West, to the land
> of the free,
> Where mighty Missouri rolls down
> to the sea,
> Where a man is a man if he's willing
> to toil
> And the humblest may gather the
> fruits of the soil.

A Norwegian immigrant remembered years later how he and his brother heard people in their village talk about a country called America: "This was the first time we had heard that name." Three months later they were on their way there. That story was repeated millions of times—from Sicily to Sichuan, from Galway to Guadalajara. As one Croatian wrote: "America. Suddenly somehow the name appeared in village minds."

First the name began to circulate; then the idea of it took hold, and the flood began. Tens of millions of people forsook the land where their ancestors had lived back into the mists of time— and crossed the ocean. The ones who left were the adventurous, the brave and often the maladjusted. And they were usually the poor. "I want to go to America," wrote a Polish peasant, "but have

no means, because I am poor and have nothing but the 10 fingers of my hands, a wife and nine children."

### RISKS OF PASSAGE

For most of those who come, the passage to America is the hardest ordeal. For centuries the ocean crossing—the trial by wind and wave, hunger and sickness—was each immigrant's lot. They were fair prey for the elements and unscrupulous captains; it was a voyage that marked them forever and that made the first vision of the Statue of Liberty in New York Harbor so intense an experience that few immigrants ever forgot it.

One example from the records of the New York State Commission of Emigration: The schooner *Leibnitz* left Hamburg on Nov. 2, 1867, and arrived in New York Harbor on Jan. 11, 1868. Its 544 passengers included 395 adults, 103 children and 46 infants. By the time the ship reached New York, 108 of its passengers had died. The commissioners report that they "spoke to some little boys and girls who, when asked where were their parents, pointed to the ocean with sobs and tears and cried, 'Down there!'"

Today the passage can be equally harrowing. Any waiter in a Vietnamese restaurant in Houston or Orange County has a tale of walking across Cambodia or fleeing Vietnam by boat, of attacks by ruthless Thai pirates and long months in a refugee camp. The Cambodians have their holocaust, the Haitians their small boats, the Mexicans their encounters with the feared *La Migra*—the border patrol.

But no danger seems too great, no obstacle too large to stop those who are determined to come. Listen to the Mexican song of the wetbacks, *"El Corrido de los Mojados"*:

> If they kick one out through Laredo,
> Ten will come through Mexicali.
> If another is kicked out of Tijuana,
> Six will come through Nogales.
> Long live all the wetbacks! . . .

Each wave of immigrants has had to brave not only the ordeal of uprooting and passage but the resentment of earlier arrivals and their descendants who, all too often, wanted to close the gate behind them. The refrain has always been the same: That "we will lose our 'old' values to the 'new' immigrants"; that the new immigrants won't become proper Americans. "They are the strangers in the land—come to take, not to give."

Anti-immigration sentiment fueled the Immigration Restriction League, the Know-Nothing political party and the Ku Klux Klan, which considered immigration "an attack upon Protestant religion . . . and a

menace to American liberties." The American Federation of Labor, although led by immigrants, backed restrictions to protect its hard-won wage-and-bargaining gains. In California the Native Sons of the Golden West became a powerful political force from the turn of the century until World War II. Their creed (ironic to consider today as California becomes a "minority" state) was that "California should remain what it has always been and God himself intended it shall always be—the white man's paradise."

### BARRING THE GATES

Restriction took two forms: Literacy tests and quotas. In 1882 the Chinese were excluded. Presidents Cleveland, Taft and Wilson all vetoed literacy tests, but in 1917 they were passed over Wilson's veto. In 1921 came the first quotas, which led to the Draconian law of 1924, whose permanent quotas and other provisions ended three centuries of immigration. The quotas were based on the population as of 1890—a blatant ploy to restrict immigrants from Asia and Central and Southern Europe. The quota for Italy was reduced in one year from 42,000 to fewer than 4,000; for Poland, from 31,000 to 6,000; for Turkey, from 2,700 to 100.

After 1930 there were years in which more people left America than came; for the first time the Statue of Liberty lit the way *out* of America. Between 1929 and 1947 we admitted only 1.2 million im-

---

## SARA BERMUDEZ, 36, TV PERSONALITY

"One thing I'll always remember about coming to America is how kind people were. When our neighbors saw we had nothing, they began to bring us things. One woman brought a chair; another brought an old television set. It made the first months livable.

"Today my husband and I both work for Channel 34 in Los Angeles. He is a producer; I am hostess on a Spanish-speaking show called 'Mundo Latino,' broadcasting to a potential audience of 30 million from Central America to Alaska. I give viewers in Mexico and Central America a glimpse of American life while giving Americans a look at the Latino world.

"I hope that by seeing me and what I do Hispanic Americans will realize they can be successful. I want to tell them it's time to move on. We have enough busboys and cabdrivers; now we need doctors and lawyers.

"Though my family has less money here than we did in Mexico, we are very happy. In this country, no matter how bad things are, there is always hope."

# THE GREAT MELTING POT

■ How numerous are America's roots? The government tried to find out during the last census when it asked this question: "What is this person's ancestry?" It got 134 different responses.

The largest number—nearly 50 million, or 22 percent of the population at the time—claimed English lineage. That's slightly more than the number of people now living in England.

Americans of German ancestry are almost as numerous. Just behind them are people with Irish ancestors. They outnumber Ireland's current residents by nearly 12 to 1.

The smallest ethnic group are the 1,756 Turkish Cypriots. Almost as few are the Greek Cypriots, Saudi Arabians, Romanian Gypsies, Ghanaians and Moroccans. There are 8,485 Ruthenians—from a region now in the Soviet Union—and 9,220 Manx, with ancestors on the Isle of Man in the Irish Sea.

One third of the people reported having more than one ancestral strain. Thus, those calling themselves English-German are counted in both the English and the German categories. ■

| Ancestry | Millions |
|---|---|
| ENGLISH | 49.6 mil. |
| GERMAN | 49.2 mil. |
| IRISH | 40.2 mil. |
| AFRO-AMERICAN | 21.0 mil. |
| FRENCH | 12.9 mil. |
| ITALIAN | 12.2 mil. |
| SCOTTISH | 10.0 mil. |
| POLISH | 8.2 mil. |
| MEXICAN | 7.7 mil. |
| AMERICAN INDIAN | 6.7 mil. |
| DUTCH | 6.3 mil. |
| SWEDISH | 4.3 mil. |
| NORWEGIAN | 3.5 mil. |
| RUSSIAN | 2.8 mil. |
| CZECH | 1.9 mil. |
| HUNGARIAN | 1.8 mil. |
| WELSH | 1.7 mil. |
| DANISH | 1.5 mil. |
| PUERTO RICAN | 1.4 mil. |
| PORTUGUESE | 1.0 mil. |

CULVER PICTURES

**WHERE WE CAME FROM**

The 20 largest ancestry groups as census respondents identified themselves in 1980

*USN&WR*—Basic data: Bureau of the Census

## FELIX ROHATYN, 58, INVESTMENT BANKER

"My family is Jewish and came from a village in Poland called Rogatyn. My father was a brewer, and his business took him to Vienna, where I was born. There was a wave of anti-Semitism in Austria, and we moved to France. The Nazis invaded France, but we were lucky and managed with false papers and all kinds of stratagems to go the classic escape route: Marseilles, Oran, Casablanca, Lisbon, Rio.

"I was 14 when we arrived here in 1942. We lived on our savings, and I got a job in a pharmacy. After attending Middlebury College, I got a summer job in 1949 as a clerk at Lazard Frères, the investment house. I used to work late, and André Meyer, who was the head of the firm, liked young people who worked late. I think I was making $37.50 a week. He raised me to $50 a week. I stayed with the firm, and I'm now a senior partner.

"I think once you've been a refugee, you're always a refugee. But I feel at home here. In fact, this country is the only place I've ever felt at home."

## ELIA KAZAN, 76, FILM DIRECTOR

"I was born in Constantinople. My father was Greek and a rug importer. Constantinople was an uncomfortable place for Greeks, and there wasn't much opportunity. America was something that was romantic to us all. I was 4 years old when we came to America, and I never saw the Statue of Liberty. We arrived on the New Jersey side of the river. That's where I made 'On the Waterfront.'

"My English was slow in developing, but I've always worked very hard—maybe out of desperation. I waited on tables for four years at Williams College and attended the Yale Drama School. Always I wanted to be a director. I don't say it's the best film I made, but 'America, America' is the film I'm fondest of. It was about my family and how it got here; it was also about immigrants—something I felt strongly about.

"I think America is the most exciting, marvelous, mixed-up, chaotic, romantic, unusual place. America is the place where anything can happen. It's corny as hell to say it's the land of opportunity, but it's true."

A majority of Americans are wary of new immigration even though many recognize that the nation's melting-pot culture is one of its great strengths.

That double-edged feeling is the key finding of a *U.S.News & World Report*–CNN poll of 1,000 adults conducted in mid-June by the Roper Organization with Everett Ladd of the Roper Center for Public Opinion Research. The survey has a 4-point margin of error.

Asked whether they wanted to see the number of legal immigrants, now about 500,000 a year, raised or reduced, respondents said it:

**Should be decreased ....51%**
**Should be increased .....8%**
**Is about right now .......35%**

On the other hand, 49 percent cited the nation's mix of people from all over the world as "a major reason for this country's greatness," and 28 percent in the poll gave that some credit.

The unease over legal immigration may reflect the national concern over illegal aliens, whose arrests total more than 1 million annually. For years, the public has been barraged with reports of overrun borders, and Congress has grappled since 1982—so far unsuccessfully—with measures to halt the surge of illegal immigrants.

# Foreign roots on native soil

## WHAT WE THINK

Those who believe that aliens take away good jobs from Americans are the strongest backers of closing the door to foreigners. But that is clearly a minority view. Respondents say that immigrants mostly:

**Take only jobs Americans**
**don't want anyway .....42%**
**Take away good jobs ....28%**
**Create new jobs .........17%**

Nothing in the poll suggests a virulence resembling the sentiments that gave rise to the nativist Know-Nothing movement of the 1850s and to the post-World War I antiforeign agitation that resulted in severe clamps on immigration, starting in the 1920s.

A plurality of the respondents, 44 percent, cite Europe as the area of the world from which they would like to see the bulk of future immigrants come. This finding may reflect the fact that four fifths of the nation's population is of European descent. Only small percentages want to see future immigration from the areas where it is most likely to originate: Latin America, Africa and Asia. On a related question, more than 4 in every 5 agree that "anyone who wants to stay in this country should have to learn English."

The poll also found:

● Individual freedom was cited by 88 percent as a major factor in America's strength, free enterprise by 72 percent, free public education by 68 percent.

● Fifty-four percent believe that the nation offers more opportunities today than in the past. Only 21 percent contend that they are more scarce, and 22 percent say they are about the same.

● Three of every 4 people want to stick with the "Star-Spangled Banner" as the national anthem and not switch to the popular "America the Beautiful."

● Favorite national symbols are the Statue of Liberty, named by 57 percent, and the flag, named by 46 percent.

● Most Americans no longer think of themselves in terms of their ancestral origins. Instead of claiming to be Irish American, Afro-American or Polish American, for instance, 86 percent say they are "just American."

by Susanna McBee

migrants—fewer than came in 1906 alone; deducting for those who left America during the same period, the net immigration was only 600,000—or about the number of legal immigrants in 1985. Even the Nazi horror in Europe couldn't reopen the doors. From 1933 to 1944 we let in fewer than 250,000 refugees from the killing fields of Europe, and only 40,000 displaced persons were admitted in 1947 and 1948.

Finally the Immigration Act of 1965 reversed the trend: It repealed the national quotas and opened the way for the great increase in immigrants from Asia, which now accounts for almost 50 percent of all immigrants. The policy on refugees has also changed: In the past 10 years we have admitted more than a million Vietnamese, Cambodians and Cubans, plus hundreds of thousands more from other countries.

Some anti-immigrant feeling still remains. [See poll results on page 31.] And immigration is still a powerful and divisive issue. Since 1981 the Congress has been deadlocked over passage of a new immigration bill designed to

control illegal immigration. The number of illegal aliens apprehended by the Immigration and Naturalization Service is up 50 percent so far this year and should exceed 1.8 million people by year's end.

Facts on how these illegal aliens affect the American economy are hard to come by. Certainly they are overwhelming the schools and hospitals in the poor counties along the Mexican border; El Paso recently sent the State Department a bill for $10 million to cover the hospital costs of treating illegal aliens. Rice University economist Donald Huddle estimates that for every 100 illegal workers, 65 Americans lose their jobs.

But other studies conclude that the illegal aliens pay more in taxes than they draw in services and that they help stimulate economic growth. The INS estimated that a recent pilot program in Houston would show anywhere from 30 to 90 percent of Texas applicants for unemployment benefits were illegal aliens; in fact, fewer than

one half of 1 percent were. Los Angeles has absorbed well over a million legal and illegal immigrants in the past 15 years—and during that period its unemployment rate declined to less than the national average. In 1985 the Rand Corporation concluded that "over all, Mexican immigration has probably been an economic asset to California."

And in spite of the common belief that floods of immigrants depress the level of wages, the evidence seems to point to the contrary. During the peak years of immigration into New York City at the turn of the century, average daily wages went up. The President's Council of Economic Advisers argued that immigrants have a net positive effect on the economy in general, but the poor whites and minorities who feel displaced by new immigrants don't think "in general": They see Vietnamese fishermen, Cambodian computer assemblers and Mexican carpenters taking their jobs.

Despite the costs—and even the pain—that may be caused by immigration, the benefits are incalculable. Our neighborhoods, our schools, our workplaces are being renewed and invigorated. Each immigrant re-creates the American dream.

For most of us, America is a gift long since given; for each new arrival, it is fresh and dynamic—and not to be squandered. "We came to America thinking the streets were made of gold," recalled Max Lerner, himself an immigrant. "But the gold wasn't here. The immigrants themselves—their talent and their potential—were the gold."

## WE ARE ALL IMMIGRANTS

A recent poll in Connecticut found that 83 percent of those surveyed believe that a person "who has just come to this country [can] be every bit as much an American as someone whose ancestors fought in the American Revolution." We now seem agreed on what President Franklin Delano Roosevelt once reminded the Daughters of the American Revolution: "We are all the children of immigrants."

When the Statue of Liberty is rededicated this Fourth of July we shall say similar words. At the end of June came a reminder of just what those words really mean. Several Cubans were found off the coast of Florida. They had made their way across a hundred miles of ocean—on inner tubes. The voyage of the Pilgrims could not have been more dangerous. Those Cubans crossed an ocean on inner tubes for the idea of freedom. They risked their lives to become Americans.

The story never ends.

# LIVING DANGEROUSLY

■ Technology was supposed to solve problems, not cause them. To free mankind, not hurt the innocent. But in the span of a few months, the dark side of technology has asserted itself.

Experts still don't know what went wrong at Chernobyl on April 26. More than two weeks later, as small amounts of radiation were settling over parts of the U.S., there was uncertainty over how much the reactor core had melted.

On the frontier of space, the worst series of rocket mishaps in U.S. history has shaken the country's confidence. Not only was the crew of Challenger lost, but in recent weeks, two other spacecraft have exploded and a research rocket misfired. Now a slew of scheduled flights have been grounded, and across America the question is being asked: Why so many disasters? What is happening to the technological fix?

According to a new *USN&WR*-Cable News Network poll, the vast majority of Americans still say that science and technology do more good than harm, but the margin has fallen from 83 percent three years ago to 72 percent today. What's more, nearly a quarter of those surveyed think that over the next 20 years, technology will cause more harm than good for the human race.

The chief source of high-tech anxiety today is nuclear power. In a kind of post-Chernobyl referendum, three Massachusetts towns voted on May 6 against opening the Seabrook, N.H., nuclear power plant, not far from the state line.

At the same time, there is little chance of the nation's turning its back on new technologies. "We have chosen a lifestyle dependent on high technology," says management consultant John Ketteringham of the Arthur D. Little firm in Cambridge, Mass. "To revert to low-tech solutions, we have to be prepared to die young of cold, disease and hunger."

## What's gone wrong

Often, major technological disasters occur after bureaucrats take over from scientific pioneers. Then, complacency sets in, or commercial needs are allowed to dominate.

Both these factors took hold of the National Aeronautics and Space Administration in the mid-1970s. Lulled by the exemplary safety record of the lunar flights and pared down by budget cuts, the agency tried to transform itself from a high-tech research operation into a commercial venture.

According to a recent congressional disclosure, a NASA budget squeeze over the last 15 years eliminated 70 percent of engineers who monitor the quality of equipment used for space flight. Al-

> When the dreams of scientific pioneers come down to earth, they can become nightmares. The most potent technologies tolerate the fewest mistakes

though a 1979 memo characterized the seals on the solid-fuel rocket boosters—the main culprit in the Challenger accident—as "completely unacceptable," the space agency stuck to its design.

Critics charge that NASA treated the shuttle as a "space bus" instead of an experimental test vehicle. Teacher Christa McAuliffe was included in the crew even though an Air Force report had recently rated the chances of a fatal accident on the shuttle at 1 in 35—compared with 1 in 10,000 for a nuclear disaster or a dam failure. And more ominous for the general public is the fact that the next shuttle was to carry deadly plutonium as fuel for two space probes—a potential source of lethal radioactivity should a crash occur.

More than space flight, nuclear power is a "mature" technology that has moved from the laboratory into the commercial arena. Yet in the past 15 years, 151 "significant" incidents have been reported in nuclear plants in 14 countries.

"When things become routine, we become very sloppy," explains physicist Frank von Hipple of Princeton University. "The first team of the Nuclear Age has moved on, and now we are trying to contain a technology that we can't handle on a routine basis."

**Another unique requirement** of managing complex technologies, such as nuclear power and space flight, is a tricky balance of power. According to Charles Perrow, a Yale professor and author of *Normal Accidents,* both managers and technicians must retain enough control to make split-second decisions at the first sign of trouble.

At Chernobyl and Three Mile Island, the combination of "several highly improbable and therefore unforeseen failures" as the Soviet Union's Deputy Prime Minister Boris Y. Shcherbina puts it, led operators to lose control of conditions in the plants. The problems were compounded by management's failure to respond quickly. At Chernobyl, hundreds of lives may eventually be lost because authorities failed to evacuate the nearby population for 36 hours.

In contrast, Perrow argues that the airline industry "became the best example of a near-error-free technology" when it successfully balanced the central control of air-traffic controllers with the local control of pilots.

## Technologies at risk

The proliferation of technologies has widened the scope of risk exponentially. With more people flying than ever before, for example, air-traffic safety—despite its former record—is a growing concern. A 33 percent drop in the number of qualified air-traffic controllers has led the independent Flight Safety Foundation to conclude that standards have slipped since 1981, when 11,400 controllers were fired after a strike. All this adds up to what retired airline captain Richard Ortman, director of airline

# 7. SOCIAL CHANGE AND THE FUTURE: New Technology Issues

## MILESTONES ON THE ROCKY ROAD OF PROGRESS

**1945** The Atomic Age opens with the mushroom explosion of the first test bomb over the desert skies near Alamogordo, N.M.

**1947** The transistor is invented at Bell Laboratories in New Jersey, paving the way for the computer revolution.

**1951** The first electric power from a nuclear reactor is produced at the National Reactor Testing Station in Arco, Idaho, heralding the era of nuclear energy.

**1953** The chemical structure of genes is revealed by James Watson and Francis Crick at Cambridge University, opening the way for today's biotechnology boom.

**1954** The Salk vaccine against polio is tested on nearly a million children, offering the first largely effective protection against the paralyzing disease.

**1957** The U.S.S.R. launches Sputnik 1, signaling the dawn of the Space Age.

**1958** An accident at a plutonium weapons facility near Sverdlovsk, in the Soviet Urals, contaminates 1,500 square kilometers with radioactive debris.

**1959** A patent for the first integrated circuit is filed by Jack Kilby of Texas Instruments, leading to the development of the revolutionary "computer on a chip."

**1960** The laser is invented by Theodore Maiman of Hughes Research Laboratories, in California,

leading to the creation of new tools for medicine, industry and the military.

**1961** Soviet cosmonaut Yuri Gagarin becomes the first human in space, orbiting the earth in his Vostok 1 satellite for 108 minutes.

■ Thalidomide is banned in West Germany and Britain after more than 2,500 deformed babies are born to European women who took the drug during pregnancy.

**1967** The three-man crew of what was to have been the first Apollo flight is killed by a fire that erupts during prelaunch tests.

**1969** American astronaut Neil Armstrong takes man's first step on the moon.

**1971** Soviet three-man crew aboard Soyuz 11 perishes when the spacecraft's cabin decompresses upon re-entry.

**1973** The first genetically engineered organism is created by California researchers Stanley Cohen and Herbert Boyer, opening a new age of made-to-order microbes and plants for medicine, agriculture, energy production and the chemical industry.

**1976** An explosion at a Swiss-owned chemical plant near Milan throws into the open air a cloud of the highly toxic gas dioxin. Tens of thousands of birds and animals perish, and more than 500 children develop skin rashes.

**1978** First test-tube baby, Louise Brown, is delivered

by Caesarean section in Oldham, England, by doctors Patrick Steptoe and Robert Edwards.

■ Residents of the Love Canal section of Niagara Falls learn that their neighborhood was a dumping ground for about 21,000 tons of toxic waste in the 1940s and 1950s. Alarmed by studies pointing to high rates of cancer and other illnesses in the community, more than 2,000 residents leave their homes in the next three years. In 1980, Love Canal is declared a federal emergency area.

**1979** A near-disastrous accident in the nuclear reactor at Three Mile Island, near Harrisburg, Pa., released a cloud of low-level radioactive gas into the environment.

**1981** U.S. space shuttle Columbia makes first orbital test flight, ushering in the era of the re-usable "space plane."

**1984** A chemical storage tank explodes at a Union Carbide Plant in Bhopal, India, releasing a cloud of lethal methyl-isocyanate gas. More than 2,000 people are killed, and the number of injured total tens of thousands.

**1986** U.S. space shuttle Challenger blows up only moments after takeoff, killing the crew of seven, including the first teacher in space. Within weeks, three more rockets misfire, effectively grounding the U.S. space program.

● Fire burns through the core of a Soviet nuclear reactor at Chernobyl, spewing lethal radioactive debris over the Ukraine, other parts of the U.S.S.R. and Europe.

---

training at Purdue University, calls a lot of "thrashing around up there."

More than 2,000 people were killed on scheduled and chartered flights worldwide last year. On large planes in the U.S. alone, the toll was 526 people, the worst since 1977, when 655 died.

In the past few years, the Federal Aviation Administration (FAA) has stepped up enforcement of airline-maintenance regulations. Last year, the agency slapped carriers with $2.8 million in fines, up from only $298,245 in 1984.

But the agency continually assures the public of aviation safety. "When you consider the numbers we deal with," says Anthony Broderick, the FAA's associate administrator for aviation standards, "the safety record is mind-boggling." Furthermore, a $12 billion modernization of the air-traffic-control system is also under way to increase the amount of traffic that controllers can safely handle.

The chemical industry is another area of worry. Only 18 months ago, a leak at a Union Carbide plant in Bhopal, India, killed more than 2,000 people and injured many thousands. Then, at Union Carbide's plant in Institute, W.Va., a leak last August of the same chemical released in the Bhopal accident—lethal methyl-isocyanate gas—sent six workers and 134 residents to

hospital emergency rooms. The Occupational Safety and Health Administration charged Union Carbide with 221 safety violations at the Institute plant—a penalty the company is appealing.

The dangers of a chemical accident are not confined to plants. Hundreds of mishaps occur annually in the storage and transport of hazardous chemicals. In a study made after the Bhopal disaster, the Environmental Protection Agency (EPA) found that between 1980 and 1985, 135 people died and 4,717 were injured in chemical accidents—with roughly a quarter of the accidents involving transport of lethal compounds. Barges that carry dangerous materials, including uranium, have a stunning accident rate worldwide of 1 per day.

Since the Bhopal incident, many companies have become more cautious. Monsanto, for example, has cut its inventory of hazardous chemicals by about 50 percent and increasingly uses ultrasound devices to detect ruptures in steel storage tanks.

Still, the skill of those handling dangerous chemicals is a vexing issue. "I'm not terribly confident about our ability to manage these facilities," says John Henningson, a water-pollution-control expert and vice president of Malcolm-Pirnie, Inc., in New Jersey. "I've always been comfortable with the technologies

but not the personnel running them."

**Nowhere is the worry** so deep as over the handling of the government's arsenal of nuclear weapons.

One concern is the nightmare scenario—dramatized in the 1983 movie "WarGames"—in which the U.S. receives a false warning of an attack by Soviet missiles and nearly sets off World War III with a counterattack. Occasional false alarms have gone off, but there have been no serious responses on the part of the U.S.

Recently, concern has shifted to the military's development of chemical and biological weapons. In 1968, some 6,400 sheep perished mysteriously after the Army secretly tested deadly chemical agents at the Dugway Proving Grounds in Utah. Eleven years later, 45 people near Richmond, Ky., were hospitalized after a toxic cloud formed over the Lexington-Bluegrass Army Depot when the Army tried to destroy some old canisters of nerve gas. Chemical weapons are stored in nine military facilities. The debate over safety is heating up because of Defense Department plans to develop new chemical weapons and destroy its World War II nerve-gas arsenal.

The newest technology with risks potentially as great as those of nuclear energy is genetic engineering. Late this month, the EPA is expected to allow a breakthrough experiment—the outdoor testing of bioengineered bacteria that prevent frost from forming on certain plants.

Biotechnology promises a range of miracle products from drugs for acquired-immune-deficiency syndrome to heartier plants. But critics charge that the risks associated with releasing genetically manipulated organisms into the atmosphere have not been clearly established. "These genetically engineered microbes are alive and are inherently unpredictable," charges leading biotech critic Jeremy Rifkin. "Unlike chemicals, they reproduce, migrate, grow. If something goes wrong, you can't recall them, seal them up, clean them up or do anything about them."

History shows that major accidents often lead to tighter regulations and improved safety standards. Roughly half of the safety standards for nuclear power plants were instituted after the Three Mile Island accident. In the space program, a fire in 1967 that swept through the Apollo spacecraft on a launching-pad ground test, killing three astronauts, led to a complete overhaul of NASA and redesign of the spacecraft—action that many engineers say ultimately guaranteed the lunar program's success.

To keep risks within acceptable bounds, some argue that new ways are needed to regulate the sophisticated technologies such as biotechnology, artificial intelligence, and "smart" satellites that will dominate the next 20 years. "I think there is serious concern these days about whether we're adequately set up to handle today's technology," says Marc Vaucher, program manager of the Center for Space Policy, Inc.

Government regulators are often caught between insuring public safety and promoting new technology. The National Institutes of Health, for example, funds genetic-engineering research and helps regulate it. The FAA, too, regulates air safety and promotes the industry. The Nuclear Regulatory Commission's predecessor, the Atomic Energy Commission, was often accused of being both advocate and arbiter of nuclear power—and some make the same charge against the NRC today.

**Critics say** that regulators inevitably experience a conflict of interest that leads to a dimmed vigilance. Contends consultant Joseph Coates, former member of the Congress's Office of Technology Assessment: "We've always gotten ourselves into trouble because administrative bodies have conflicting duties."

Technology advocates insist that overzealous regulation has held back important advances and weakened the nation's competitive position vis-à-vis rivals such as the Japanese. Robert

---

# Accidents waiting to happen?

In technology we have trusted, but unthinkable, unimaginable accidents do happen, be it in the deafening crash of two airplanes or in a silent chemical leak. The record suggests that the following, and worse, could occur again.

**False alert:** It looked as if the Soviets were attacking, but it was a computer malfunction at the North American Air Defense complex in Cheyenne Mountain, Colo., in 1979 and 1980. Forces went on low-level alert and bomber engines were fired up, but within minutes the errors were caught.

**Bombs away:** Crashes of B-52s carrying unarmed nuclear warheads over Spain and Greenland in the late 1960s caused radioactive emissions as well as conventional bomb explosions. Other accidental detonations are unlikely, the Air Force insists, because of improvements in warhead construction.

**Leaky landfills:** At Love Canal, it took years for poisonous materials dumped by nearby chemical plants in Niagara Falls, N.Y., to leach into back yards. Even state-of-the art disposal systems can fail. A site near Pittston, Pa., was blown apart by Hurricane Gloria last year, spilling 100,000 gallons of waste into the Susquehanna River.

**Too close for comfort:** Not only do planes have collisions and near-collisions in midair, but they have accidents on the runway. The worst runway collision involved KLM and Pan Am jets in the Canary Islands in 1977 when 583 died. Some accidents are due to pilot error, but others happen when air traffic controllers mix up directions.

**Shaky foundations:** Skyscrapers stand tall and bridges straddle rivers and railroads, but collapses do occur. In 1978, the roof of the Hartford Civic Center came tumbling down hours after a basketball game. Above a crowd of dancers at a Kansas City Hyatt Regency in 1981, two concrete skywalks collapsed, killing 114 and injuring more than 200. In 1940, the 5,979-foot Tacoma Narrows Bridge, known to weave in the wind over Puget Sound, fell with a roar.

**Looking for a home:** The spent fuel rods from 67 nuclear plants sit silently in water-filled storage tanks near reactors, awaiting a decision on potential reprocessing. Experts predict disaster should one of the storage tanks spring a leak, leaving the fuel exposed. Congress wants other nuclear wastes buried by 1998, but critics worry that nuclear leftovers will stay lethal thousands of years.

**Computer crashes:** The Bank of New York last November found itself taking a $23.6 billion overnight loan from the Federal Reserve Bank of New York to cover a foul-up in the handling of U.S. securities caused by a glitch in a computer program. Other computer problems can be avoided by duplicating data.

**Lights out:** Twenty-five million people were left in the dark in 1965 when a minor equipment failure in Canada triggered a blackout in the Northeast. Twelve years later, much of metropolitan New York was without power up to 25 hours.

by Cindy Skrzycki with the domestic staff

Gale, for example, who was called to the Soviet Union to perform lifesaving bone-marrow transplants on Chernobyl victims, was censured by the University of California at Los Angeles for conducting bone-marrow transplants in 1980 in violation of NIH guidelines.

To help bolster the spread of technology, the Reagan administration has just changed the rules governing the regulation of new technologies. On April 24, it abolished requirements that "worst case" scenarios be considered in the evaluation of potential hazards.

Warns Senator Albert Gore, Jr. (D-Tenn.): "There's a certain hubris in the Technological Age, tempting us to invest our hopes in dramatic new advances. We have to make choices along the way, instead of ducking tough decisions." Indeed, as Chernobyl, Challenger and Bhopal prove, disaster strikes when nations forget that worst-case scenarios can come true.

by Abigail Trafford and Andrea Gabor with Melissa Healy, Kathleen McAuliffe, Cindy Skrzycki and Ronald A. Taylor

## POLL RESULTS

# More than just a Soviet problem

The Soviet nuclear accident at Chernobyl has shaken Americans' faith in nuclear energy more deeply than the Three Mile Island accident of 1979, according to a poll for *U.S. News & World Report* and the Cable News Network by the Roper Organization.

The poll was conducted on May 7 and 8.

Fifty-two percent of adults oppose building new nuclear plants, up from 29 percent after the mishap in Pennsylvania. Approval of nuclear power has dropped from 53 percent to 45 percent.

Behind concern lies a belief that the Soviet meltdown illustrates the "inherent danger of nuclear power" rather than weaknesses in Soviet engineering. Four out of 5 now support 24-hour federal inspectors at nuclear plants. Twenty-eight percent favor a permanent shutdown of existing plants, up from 14 percent.

Almost 7 out of 10 people attributed the Chernobyl accident and setbacks in the U.S. space program to accidents that are part of the "price of progress." Yet when asked what risks were acceptable, Americans by better than a 2 to 1 ratio accepted risks in space rather than from nuclear energy. Said one: "With the space shuttle, you don't have the survival of the human race at risk."

Here are key results:

**Would you favor not permitting any more new nuclear power plants to be built?**
Favor: 52%
Oppose: 38%

**Do you think the Soviet nuclear-power-plant accident shows the inherent danger of nuclear power in all countries or only weaknesses in the Soviet Union?**
Inherent dangers: 52%
Only Soviet weaknesses: 34%
Both: 2%

Random telephone survey of 1,003 adults was conducted May 7 and May 8. Margin of error is 4 percent. Results do not add to 100 percent because of deletion of "don't knows."

# In Old Milwaukee: Tomorrow's Factory Today

The oak floor glistens through four coats of polyurethane, reflecting red, blue and yellow blinking lights. The machinery, tenderly adjusted and lubricated and looking like mobile sculpture, whirs and swivels competently behind transparent plastic enclosures. The employees are gung ho, and the most enthusiastic of all is their boss, John Rothwell, 41. "This is my life's dream," he says. "I love it." The atmosphere where they work is electric, suffused with a feeling that what is taking place here, in its boldness and sophistication, is happening nowhere else on earth.

And that could just be true. Because behind the doors on the eighth floor of Allen-Bradley's good gray corporate headquarters near downtown Milwaukee is an operation that may signal a renaissance in U.S. manufacturing. Department 260, as it is known, is the company's innovative and expensive ($15 million) attempt to make its popular lines of sturdy industrial-control devices better and cheaper than those of competing companies in the U.S., Western Europe and Japan.

In stark contrast to Allen-Bradley assembly operations elsewhere in the same building, where some 1,650 workers still put products together largely by hand, Department 260 is run by 14 people. Six of those are white-coated attendants who man the floor's 26 machine stations, clearing equipment jams and feeding the machines' voracious appetites for raw materials. Department 260 is what engineers call a CIM plant, for computer-integrated manufacturing. Computers, from programmable controllers on the floor to a large IBM 3090 Sierra mainframe across the hall, tell the machines how to fashion 600 different varieties of relays and contactors, essentially boxy switches that turn electric motors on and off. Only 14 months old, Department 260's assembly line is not yet running at full speed. But when it does, working at a rate of 600 devices an hour, it will be able to make 4,800 in a single eight-hour shift. If required, it could turn out this volume for orders received the same day.

And yet unlike the overwhelming machines of Charlie Chaplin's *Modern Times,* Department 260's equipment is mostly nonthreatening, with sometimes vexing personalities. *"Mamma mia, ti prego comincia a lavorare!* [Please, start working!]" implores Mechanic Bruno Lockner to one balky contraption. "This machine understands Italian," he jokes. Some machines have names. Clarabelle is a complex wonder that churns out 1,000 crossbar assemblies an hour. It was designed by Allen-Bradley engineers, and is tended by 18-year veteran Employee Cheryl Braddock. Says Braddock: "I talk to her every morning. I pat her on the side. I say, 'It's going to be a good day.' "

For the machines, the day begins just before dawn, when much of Milwaukee's human population is still asleep. All night, orders have been flowing to the IBM from Allen-Bradley distributors in London, Singapore, Hong Kong, Caracas, Melbourne and 400 locations in the U.S. From the IBM, they travel silently across hidden cables to Department 260's own network of 29 smaller computers.

At 6:30 a.m., the ceiling lights turn themselves on. At 7:30, on cue from electronic signals speeding through an overhead conduit, the factory goes through its morning calisthenics. The machines begin moving and stretching, flexing conveyor belts, cams, steel-armed grippers, hissing pneumatic tubes, spot welders, laser beams, grinding stones, power drills and screwdrivers. Warning lights, strung like Japanese lanterns across the ceiling, start blinking. Soon the assembly line is running, producing the day's orders.

On the largest scale, the 45,000-sq.-ft. facility is Allen-Bradley's bid to stop chasing cheap labor in distant locales. Since 1977 the company has moved manufacturing to Texas, North Carolina and Mexico, resulting in the loss of 1,300 Milwaukee jobs. Now, with Department 260, Allen-Bradley is putting a factory where its skilled work force is.

To Company Chairman C.R. ("Bud") Whitney, automation is possibly the only way to prevent the U.S. from becoming entirely a paper-shuffling service economy. The soft-spoken Whitney believes that the most important wealth of nations comes from manufacturing. "You get it out of mother earth," he says. "You mine it, farm it or fish it. Then you take that basic raw material and add value to it. That's what we call manufacturing. If we don't create wealth, we are going to become a third-class country."

Other Milwaukee manufacturers have cut back in recent years, lowering the city's blue-collar employment from a peak of 223,600 in late 1979 to about 171,300 now. Schlitz, "the beer that made Milwaukee famous," is no longer brewed there. Allis-Chalmers no longer makes tractors in its suburban Milwaukee plant, where employment has plunged from 4,900 in 1979 to just 750 today. After losses in the early '80s, Harley-Davidson has staged something of a comeback in its battle against big Japanese motorcycles, helped by some automation, Japanese-style management techniques and tariff protection.

Though Allen-Bradley was sold to Rockwell International for $1.67 billion in 1985, that is no reason, feels Whitney, to do what some other companies have done and halt manufacturing in Milwaukee. In Department 260, Allen-Bradley makes two lines of its unsung, unglamorous electrical-control devices. They click through their critical duties unseen by the typical consumer, yet they help run the motors that raise elevators in skyscrapers, drive the machine tools that power Detroit's auto-assembly plants, twist the huge drills that coax coal from West Virginia and oil from East Texas, and start rides rolling—and passengers squealing—at Disney World.

Founded in 1903, the company started with an idea for a rheostat dreamed up by Lynde Bradley. Building on that idea, the company was well positioned as American heavy industry, led by autos, began its lusty journey through the 20th century. Owned solely by the founders and their descendants until the sale to Rockwell, Allen-Bradley had 1985 sales of about $1.15 billion, making it far larger in its particular field than such competitors as Square D, Gould and Westinghouse.

By the late 1970s, though, Whitney and President J. Tracy O'Rourke realized that the marketplace was changing, and Allen-Bradley would have to evolve to survive. The company was too dependent on the machine-tool industry and its biggest customer, Detroit's automakers. Both were reeling under the attack of lower-cost foreign competitors. Although Allen-Bradley's domestic sales had not been severely hurt, the day when they would be seemed just around the corner.

What to do? A planning team assembled by Whitney came up with the answer: Allen-Bradley, since its founding a parochial company doing almost all its business in North America, would aggressively expand in Europe, but with a major new twist. Instead of making industrial controls almost exclusively to American standards, the company began designing them to the specifications of the International Electrotechnical Commission, the European arbiter. And instead of buying a foreign company to make the controls, which several competitors had done, it would make them in Milwaukee, in a new facility.

Thus was born the idea for Department 260. Says Whitney: "The light bulb came on." But an unprecedented degree of automation would be required to pull it off. Reason: a representative contactor that sold for $20 in the U.S. sold for just $8 in the highly competitive markets of West Germany and Australia. To make a profit at the lower price, Allen-Bradley had to get costs down. By using automated equipment, the company could produce contactors for 60% less than it could by relying on a manual assembly line. "Labor costs," says Whitney "obviously had to be a nonissue."

One big advantage was that since Allen-Bradley would be making entirely new products, it could design them in tandem with the new assembly process. Moreover, by labeling each product at the outset with a computer bar code, Allen-Bradley could program its assembly line to vary the specifications; as a result, contactors and electrical relays can be tailored without slowing down the line.

Most of the normal ways of looking at such an investment were ignored because adhering to them would discourage even starting the project. Department 260 was high in risk and cost, but if it worked it would yield far more than its price tag. O'Rourke, in persuading the company's directors to pump money into the project, was blunt: "I figured if we could produce $30 million to $50 million a year in sales, and it cost just $15 million to build, that was a good deal."

An air of excitement swept through the company. Even organized labor went along with the idea. Since the planned products had never been made before by Allen-Bradley, workers would not be displaced by the new operation. Mindful of past job cuts, the union's leaders were at least happy to see the operation take root in Milwaukee. Says Ted Krukowski, president of Local 1111 of the United Electrical, Radio and Machine Workers: "There's concern, but there's also a feeling of accomplishment that our folks played a role."

Still, Department 260's near total automation amounts to more than the old and familiar threat to the shrinking blue-collar work force. Says Krukowski: "Before, you always needed people out there to build the special items. It's the sophistication of the automation here that has to have people worried."

More change will certainly come as U.S. manufacturers try to compete with foreign producers. "This is an issue the whole country is going to have to deal with," says Whitney. Yet not even Allen-Bradley plans to automate existing product lines; the cost of redesigning traditional manufacturing processes would be too great. The totally automated, problem-free factory that can turn out complex consumer products like cars and dishwashers remains a science-fiction fantasy. What does exist, for now, is Allen-Bradley's Department 260, a step toward the future, with temperamental machines named Clarabelle that need patting. —*By John S. DeMott. Reported by J. Madeleine Nash/Milwaukee*

**IBM is not only the largest computer manufacturer but also the most profitable industrial corporation in the world.**

Its 1985 profit of $6.5 billion was nearly twice the gross national product of Bolivia.

# Technology and the Changing World of Work

### Fred Best

Fred Best, president of Pacific Management and Research Associates (1208 Seventh Avenue, Sacramento, California 95818), has written extensively on management and human resources, economic development, and the impacts of new technologies. His books include *The Future of Work, Flexible Life Scheduling,* and *Work Sharing.* This article is excerpted from his report *The Future of Work: A View from the United States,* prepared for the Swedish Secretariat for Future Studies.

Computers and other technological innovations are changing the nature of work and the balance between our jobs and our personal lives. Here, an expert on the impacts of new technologies offers some long-term speculations on the future of work.

The United States and other industrial nations are now experiencing wave after wave of innovations that bring profound changes in our personal and occupational lives. At the core of these changes is the computer. More than 3 million Americans purchased home and personal computers during 1982, with that figure doubling to 6 million in 1983. If the cost of purchased or rented computer time continues to decline at its historical rate of 50% every two and one-half years, and if the complexity of utilization is reduced by "user-friendly" software, computers and allied technologies will soon be assimilated into every aspect of our lives.

The impacts of such technological change on the economy, the world of work, and our personal lives will be phenomenal. These innovations are likely to alter the nature of work activities within all economic sectors, dramatically affect the growth and location of employment opportunities, and shift the relationships between our jobs and personal lives.

## Changing Skill Requirements

Up to 45% of existing U.S. jobs will be significantly altered by technological changes over the next 20 years, many through an upgrading of skills.

The historical trend toward mechanization is becoming increasingly sophisticated as robots and computer-coordinated operations take over routine and dangerous tasks now performed by workers. For example, the installation of robots in the United States has been growing by 30% per year, increasing from 200 in 1970 to 3,500 in 1980. Moderate estimates indicate that there will be 35,000 installed robots in America by 1990 and that applications will skyrocket during the last decade of the twentieth century.

Small computers, sophisticated sensors and servo-mechanisms, and design and control instruments that are easier to understand and use are moving us rapidly toward the "cybernetic promise" of highly integrated and flexible production systems. For example, the growing application of CAD/CAM systems (computer-assisted design/computer-assisted manufacturing) now allows industrial planners to design products on computer screens and then reformat machinery on the shop floor to produce products by centralized programming. The implications for increased productivity and product diversity are spellbinding.

Many workers will have to be reassigned to new tasks. While some of these new tasks might not require greater skill, many necessitate an understanding of new and more complex technologies. For example, General Motors Corporation predicts that 50% of its work force in the year 2000 will be categorized as skilled tradespersons (technicians, inspectors, monitors, etc.), compared with 16% in 1980. Thus, there will be a need for more highly trained personnel such as engineers, technicians, computer specialists, and managers with basic technical skills.

Technological innovations will also profoundly affect the nature of work in both office and service occupations. Just as we have moved from manual typewriters and carbon copies to memory typewriters and photocopy machines over the last few decades, newer technologies will vastly increase the efficiency and output of information processing.

Dramatic reductions in the cost of computers, the development of user-friendly software, and the availability of high-speed printers and telecommunication systems will create a fundamental shift from paper to electronics as the main medium of operation. Typewriters, file cabinets, and mail systems will increasingly be replaced by word processors, computerized data retrieval systems, and video transmissions between computer terminals.

As in the case of manufacturing

From *The Futurist*, April 1984, pp. 61-66, published by the World Future Society, 4916 St. Elmo Avenue, Bethesda, MD 20814. Reprinted by permission.

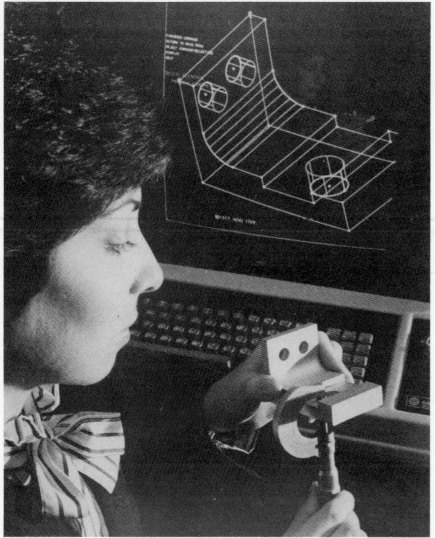

SPERRY CORPORATION

Applications analyst compares computer-generated drawing with finished bracket produced by computer-assisted design and manufacturing system. Innovations such as this CAD/CAM system are increasing demand in manufacturing sectors for computer specialists, engineers, technicians, and managers with basic technical skills.

isolated cases of worker dislocation, most experts believe that technological advances have generally fostered economic and job growth by increasing the quality and quantity of products while lowering the costs.

Because costs are lower, producers can afford to sell at lower prices, which in turn commonly causes consumers to buy more. As a result of increased demand, producers generally employ as many or more workers than before technological innovation began to increase output. When this process occurs throughout the economy, the result is economic growth, with higher real wages and an increase of employment.

Two historic examples illustrate this process. First, during the early stages of the Industrial Revolution, the introduction of the Hargreaves jenny in 1770 ultimately allowed one worker to produce as much as 200 spinners could without the jenny. Yet employment in Britain's textile industry increased from less than 100,000 in 1770 to about 350,000 in 1800 because productivity allowed major reductions in price, leading to even more dramatic increases in market demand for textiles.

A second example is the introduction of the assembly line by Henry Ford. As a result of this combination of machinery and industrial organization, it took 56% fewer hours to produce the average car in 1920 than it did in 1910, leading to a 62% reduction in the real dollar price of an automobile. Consumers who previously could not afford a car began to make purchases, sales increased tenfold, and Ford employment rose from 37,000 to 206,000 in just 10 years. Workers may have been shifted to new assignments, but there was no overall loss of jobs.

From the standpoint of preserving and creating jobs, there appear to be few alternatives to technological innovation. While these changes are likely to cause considerable displacement and reassignment of workers, failure to modernize will cause affected industries to lose pace with national and international competition and

and material processing, many jobs will become unnecessary. Demand will gradually disappear for mail deliverers, file clerks, stenographers, and other workers. Familiarity and skill with computers will become essential to all office workers, from manager to secretary.

## Displacement and Realignment

National Cash Register reduced its U.S. work force from 37,000 to 18,000 between 1970 and 1975 because of productivity gains from using microelectronic rather than mechanical parts. The General Motors plant in Lordstown, Ohio, reduced its work force by 10%

after increasing productivity 20% through the introduction of welding robots. In Providence, Rhode Island, the *Journal Bulletin* cut its printing staff from 242 workers in 1970 to 98 in 1978 as a result of new typesetting technology. These examples underscore the fact that workers have indeed been displaced by technology; however, the question remains as to how extensive such displacement will be in coming years.

Concern over job loss due to the higher productivity of machines has historical roots, beginning with Luddite resistance to industrial mechanization in early-nineteenth-century England. However, despite

# Work in a High-Tech Future

The proportion of American workers involved in agriculture and manufacturing declined from 83% to 30% between 1860 and 1980, while services expanded proportionately. Recent trends indicate that this historical transformation will continue, if not accelerate. In the medium-range future, this will not mean an *absolute* decline of jobs in agriculture and manufacturing sectors, but a *relative* decline as the size of the work force increases. However, as advanced technology is applied to heavy industry during the last decades of the twentieth century, some analysts speculate that the proportion of the work force employed in manufacturing will gradually decline to about 3% over the next 50 years.

The relative decline of employment in manufacturing and agriculture does not indicate that they will become less important to our economy; rather, these sectors will produce more with fewer workers. Just as the number of persons fed by the average American farmer increased from 9 to 25 between 1940 and 1962, advances in technology and management will allow workers in manufacturing and other sectors to produce far more per hour of labor.

California, a recognized center of technological innovation, exhibited shifts in the distribution of its work force that parallel national trends. Many forecasters speculate that the large and growing proportion of businesses involved in the development and production of high-technology products within California will foster a rate of change that is faster than that seen nationally. To provide an overview, the number of jobs within the United States is projected to increase 15.9%, from 103 million to 119 million, between 1981 and 1990; the number of jobs in California will increase some 24.9%, from 11 million to 14 million.

Projections to 1985 from the California Employment Development Department indicate considerable variation of job growth among different occupations. These forecasts, which roughly parallel those for the nation, indicate a greater than average growth rate for most technical occupations, as well as skilled craft and operative positions. However, many observers feel that these forecasts are conservative due to the growth of California's high-tech industries and the demand for highly skilled labor.

As in the past, shifts in the skills required for employment will be due primarily to technological change. The high-technology sectors will increasingly account for new jobs created in the coming decades and will change the skills required throughout the entire economy.

These high-technology industries include computers, communication equipment, instruments, electronic components, and computer services. The aerospace industry is occasionally included in the high-tech category, as are a variety of fledgling enterprises such as energy innovations, biotechnology, robotics, chemicals, new materials, selected medical products, and home entertainment equipment.

Although high technology now employs a relatively small proportion of the total work force, job growth within these sectors has been phenomenal. Between 1970 and 1980, job growth for the five core high-tech industries within California was 80.3%, compared with 38.8% for the state work force as a whole. During the 1980s, job growth for these same industries is projected to be 47.6%, compared with 24.9% for the entire state economy. Moderate projections indicate that the number of California jobs in these core high-tech industries will increase from 591,795 to 726,700 between 1980 and 1990.

The aerospace industry is expected to add at least 24,400 new jobs (possibly more due to defense contracts) to the California economy during the 1980s, and fledgling high-tech enterprises are likely to add another 10,000 jobs during the same period. Consolidation of all high-tech related industrial growth suggests that these sectors will account for approximately 268,900 new jobs during the next decade. To put these figures into historical perspective, these high-tech industries and enterprises directly created 6.9% of overall California job growth during the 1970s and are expected to account for 9.7% during the 1980s. Some studies have forecast even greater growth.

These high-tech sectors will require workers with more extensive and diverse training than the work force in general. Engineers, scientists, technicians, and computer specialists, representing 5.7% of the total California work force, will make up about 28.7% of the employees in the state's five core high-tech industries by 1990.

The growth of California's high-technology industries will foster an increasing demand for technical, scientific, and skilled workers. Demand for computer specialists will increase 106% among the five core high-tech industries between 1980 and 1990. The demand for technicians will increase by about 46% and for qualified assemblers and operatives by about 30% over the same period.

As a result, high-technology industries will probably need 19,000 additional technicians, 21,000 additional skilled craft persons, and 44,000 more qualified assemblers and operatives by 1990. Correspondingly, there will be increased demand for managers, clerical workers, and other support personnel who are familiar with basic technical issues.

—Fred Best

## The Evolution of Work

The social, institutional, and human roles associated with work have changed dramatically as human civilization has evolved. The work of antiquity was essentially direct physical toil, required for immediate survival. For primitive peoples, "work" and "leisure" were almost completely integrated. As civilization developed, work and nonwork activities continued to be integrated within families and tribes.

With the emergence of agriculture, economic surpluses, and culturally transferable knowledge, work became easier and more distinct as a social activity. Specialization and individual roles and responsibilities began to emerge as key elements of human existence.

As economic surplus, development of productive tools, and specialization continued to grow, the goals and conditions of work continued to change. Work became increasingly oriented toward the improvement of the human condition rather than bare survival. The resulting surpluses gave rise to increasingly productive tools, and ultimately machinery, which correspondingly allowed and re-quired further refinement of skills and increased specialization.

While work dominated life, the concept of "leisure" as distinct from "work" began to crystallize. Industrial society was a natural outgrowth of these trends. As machinery became increasingly important and sophisticated, work became progressively specialized and oriented toward the use of tools and capital within the context of complex human organizations.

Organizational interdependence and division of labor gave rise to the ultimate predominance of employment. While productive human activity continued to be performed outside the context of employment, work became commonly viewed as an activity performed by "holding a job."

These dramatic shifts have caused a near inversion of the concepts of "work" and "leisure." As defined by classical philosophers, leisure was restricted to reflection and the fine arts; it was commonly viewed as nonmanual activities within preindustrial societies. Commerce, science, politics, writing, and all arts came to be viewed as the freely chosen "leisurely" pursuits of the elites.

Today, as progressively larger proportions of the work forces in advanced industrial societies become employed in "white-collar" jobs doing "knowledge work," the work activities of today are increasingly like the "leisure" activities of the past. While contemporary work conditions are commonly far from utopian, today's jobs tend to require more autonomy, creativity, freedom of expression, and skill than that required during the pre-industrial and early industrial eras.

While the work of the foreseeable future is likely to resemble much of what we do today, historical perspective suggests the importance of keeping an open mind to the possibility of radical changes in the medium- and long-range future. Just as the all-encompassing struggle for physical survival that commonly epitomized primitive humanity has little resemblance to "jobholding" within the offices of today, the nature of work in the future may take on new dimensions that we can scarcely perceive.

—Fred Best

ultimately cause even greater loss of employment and economic growth.

### Technology and Non-Job Work

There are increasing signs that technological change may also alter the balance between job activities and our personal lives. If we define work as "productive human activity," it is clear that work has never been confined to "holding a job." There have always been people who are self-employed, who build their own houses, raise children, provide voluntary social services, and perform countless other productive actions outside the context of employment. The balance of productive activity inside and outside the workplace has undergone many changes in recent years and will probably change considerably in the future.

Just as the development of heavy machinery drew work out of the home and into factories and offices during the Industrial Revolution, new technologies may cause households and neighborhood groups to become more self-sustaining and to abandon institutional settings for many productive activities. Harbingers of such realignments are suggested by the emerging uses of many new technologies:

• **Home and personal computers.** The potential of home and personal computers, which didn't exist 10 years ago but now are an increasingly common new "home appliance," has scarcely been explored. This technology, which is greatly expanding in power and diminishing in price, is already being used for home entertainment centers, long-distance communication and mail systems, cookbooks, medical advisors, high-speed typewriters, portable offices, family business and tax filing systems, art and graphics devices, educational tutors, library reference services, financial planning, and control of other household appliances. Countless new uses, many of which are integrated with other new technologies, are being developed daily.

• **Video recorders.** Like home

and personal computers, video recorders and disc players have emerged from nowhere in the course of only a few years. As archives of television and motion picture entertainment are rapidly transferred to video tapes and discs, a progressively larger portion of entertainment is likely to be pulled back into the home. The use of video recorders as substitutes for home movie cameras also affects the entire film development and processing industry.

• **Decentralized energy production and conservation.** A variety of new, improved, and rediscovered technologies are being developed as alternatives to centralized energy sources. Photovoltaics, solar heating, windmill generation, a variety of conservation measures, and other energy-related technologies are replacing or reducing dependence on central energy sources. These devices are likely to become more attractive as prices decline and the costs of central energy increase.

• **Decentralized medical care.** A number of affordable devices and services are being developed that provide patient-utilized and home-based medical care. For example, new technologies make it both desirable and less expensive to undertake sophisticated "do-it-yourself" medical treatments such as kidney dialysis, cancer chemotherapy, and intravenous feeding.

• **Decentralized and interactive communication systems.** Home-linked and controlled communication technologies are being developed that greatly expand the choice of information and provide options for interaction and local control. Cable and satellite television greatly enhance viewer choice, provide the potential for two-way communication, and open the option of local and neighborhood stations. Teleconferencing expands the concept of conference calls on the telephone to include visual communication. Satellite and microwave transmission greatly reduce the cost and difficulty of long-distance communication. When these communication systems are used with other technologies such as personal computers, work tasks that formerly had to be located and coordinated

COURTESY OF DIGITAL EQUIPMENT CORPORATION

Computer terminal and telephone allow office work to be done at home. Individuals can move work activities out of formal organizations and create new balances between their jobs and personal lives.

at a central location can be decentralized.

While the ultimate impact of these and other technologies is uncertain, their utilization will dramatically change the activities and skill required for work. They might significantly alter the timing, location, and organizational context of work in the future. These same technologies will increase self-sufficiency, open new options for individual business ventures, and generally reduce the need for "holding a job."

### An Exploratory Scenario: Toward a Home-Based Economy?

Many novel developments are emerging that might make it desirable, efficient, and necessary to reduce traditional jobholding as the focus of "purposeful and pro-

ductive human activity." High unemployment and growing job instability suggest the need for individuals to find backup modes of activity that are economically and psychologically rewarding.

The emergence of relatively inexpensive and user-friendly technologies may make it economically efficient and personally rewarding to move both job and non-job work activities out of formal work organizations. Greater flexibility in work arrangements could allow many individuals and groups to meet personal and economic needs through a better balance of job-linked work and other productive efforts.

There are already countless jobholders with computer-based home businesses and flexible worktime and workplace arrangements that allow them to perform job responsibilities without having to be "at work" in the usual sense of the term.

If such conditions become more prevalent, the average worker of tomorrow might work "full time" for six or seven years within a traditional work environment. Then, in order to better handle family responsibilities, the worker might arrange to perform most job responsibilities at home using information technologies. He or she might then reduce worktime given to employment and develop an auxiliary business enterprise, perhaps to increase home-based self-sufficiency. Ultimately, the worker might return to work on a part-time or part-year basis while retraining for new skills.

Without doubt, such arrangements would pose some costs and dangers to individuals, employers, and the economy. For example, the worker might worry about being able to return to suitable employment after an extended period away from an organization. Organizations might have trouble de-emphasizing and re-emphasizing the roles of individual workers. There might also be concern with the loss of social-professional networks, problems of maintaining income during de-emphasis of employment, and discontinuance or reduction of fringe benefits.

Certainly such a system would entail individual responsibility, initiative, and accountability. However, more people might be willing to confront the costs and dangers if recurrent unemployment and job insecurity make it necessary, if individual preferences for more autonomy within work settings increase, and if institutional and social policies provide the necessary options and resources.

While new balances between household- and employment-

Couple tries out program on home computer. About 6 million Americans bought home and personal computers in 1983—twice as many as the year before. The impact of computers and other new technologies will be felt in every aspect of our personal and working lives, says author Best.

based economies may emerge primarily via individual initiative, they could be encouraged by a number of institutional and social policies. Policies that might support such developments include:

• Tax incentives to defer use of earnings for utilization during periods of de-emphasized employment.

• Guaranteed credit and loans.

• Individually vested retraining vouchers.

• Guidelines for job-return rights.

• Subsidies and tax incentives for the purchase and use of home-based technologies.

• Options for flexible worktime arrangements.

• Financial incentives to encourage use of homes as offices and to reduce job-related travel.

• Standardization of selected information technologies.

• Options for selecting and continuing fringe benefits during de-emphasized employment.

• Options for using income maintenance payments to start

small business enterprises.

The costs of such policies are not likely to be undertaken unless private and public expenditures for other policies such as income maintenance, retraining, public transportation, public service employment, and general social services are reduced. Clearly, the political consensus for such a tradeoff is not likely to emerge until a significant number of individuals have developed nontraditional home-job work patterns on their own.

Although jobholding will probably continue as the prevalent pattern of work for the immediate future, ongoing transitional instability, shifting human preferences toward work, and new technologies may foster continued growth of hybrid balances between job and household activities. We can only speculate on whether such patterns will develop into a major trend or prevalent pattern; however, private and public policy makers must begin now to think about the implications, costs, and benefits.

# Apology to the
# FUTURE

*This letter to an unborn grandchild
explains and apologizes for the state
of the world today that could trigger
disaster tomorrow.*

## Scott Thomas Eastham

*Dr. Eastham is assistant professor of
religion and religious education, The
Catholic University of America, Washington, D.C.*

My Dear Unborn Grandchild:

By the time you read this, I shall be dead—and probably not from old age. You have grown to maturity now, and by rights expect very little from your forebears. This is as it should be. Nevertheless, I feel I owe you at least two things—an apology and an explanation.

The apology takes precedence. I can guess that you are living on a devastated Earth, the ruin of a garden planet, an Earth rendered well-nigh uninhabitable by forces set in motion by my generation and those that preceded us. I apologize for all of us who may be responsible. I am especially sorry because all the portents foretelling the kind of world you will inhabit are already present today. I wish I could say we don't know any better, but we do.

We know that the chemical wastes we have been dumping heedlessly for decades have probably caused irreversible damage to the human gene pool. There is undoubtedly more congenital suffering in your time, more weakness of limb and of brain, more people born then than now who might prefer to be dead. We know further that there is no safe way to dispose of or isolate the mountains of nuclear waste we are accumulating; by your day, the damage will be done. We know also that our societal addiction to fossil fuels is releasing far too much carbon dioxide into the atmosphere. We have even predicted the catastrophic results of this "greenhouse effect": an inevitable warming and shift in the Earth's climatic regions, melting of the polar ice caps, and thus floods, mass migrations, famines, etc. Nevertheless, we scoff at alternatives to fossil fuels and nuclear energy. They are

costly and unrealistic, we say, and so we gouge ever more deeply into the flesh of the Earth to find and burn up more of the same.

In a single century, we have turned the Earth into a sick old lady. Species are going extinct at the incredible rate of one every other day. Some of that is natural selection, of course, but the lion's share of the damage is man's doing. The food chain is going to collapse out from under us one day, but that's a problem for the future to solve, or so we say. Oh yes,, we can see all around us the grim beginnings of your world.

It's not just what we're doing to the environment that speaks of the world we are creating for you, but just as evidently what human beings are doing to one another. At the latest estimate, some 50,000 people die of starvation every day—that's one death every other second. Instead of offering real help to these starving millions, the superpowers sell them weapons—meanwhile spending about a billion dollars a day on their own suicidal arms race. Most people are afraid of World War III, but don't realize that the "Third World War" is already well underway; more people have died in the approximately 160 wars since World War II than perished in that great conflagration. Even as I write you, there are about 40 shooting wars being fought in and between so-called Third World nations, most of them like quicksand pits—the more you struggle, the deeper you sink.

### The Thermonuclear Time Bomb

The human death toll is already enormous today, even if we never use the massive thermonuclear arsenals we've been building up for the Big Finale—which could come at any moment. Every city in the U.S. and the U.S.S.R. with a population of 25,000 or more is presently targeted with at least one nuclear bomb, and the computer controls are not only on hair triggers, but in

addition they are notoriously unreliable. Every time lightning strikes the municipal power grid in Colorado Springs, the North American Air Defense Command computers there register a Soviet missile strike and prepare to strike back. Perhaps this is all old news to you. For you and your contemporaries, it may well be too late. Perhaps you are already living in the radioactive rubble of our nightmares; perhaps you know first hand about genetic mutations, radiation damage, infant leukemia, shortened life-expectancy, and all the other horrors we've been saving up for you.

I fear there is an inevitability here, too. Humankind has never yet developed a weapon it did not eventually get around to using on itself. When Alfred Nobel invented dynamite in 1866, he supposed that, with such a terrible weapon in the world's arsenals, nobody would ever countenance waging war again. In the nuclear age, that kind of innocence is lost forever. Even if you have by some incredible stroke of providence been spared an atomic Armageddon, you will see our handiwork in all the other gruesome legacies we have left you and with which you must try to live—or should I say survive?

You probably wonder, if we could see all this coming, why in the name of sanity we didn't get together to do something about it. People struggling under totalitarian regimes have sufficient evil to cope with day by day. You might be able to excuse them for not worrying too much about tomorrow, but what about those of us living in relative comfort and security in stable democracies? We've been asserting our right to govern ourselves for a couple of centuries now, but our worst tendencies—paranoia, mistrust, deceit, and belligerency, for example—still subvert our best intentions.

Government is supposed to be the way we human beings handle our collective affairs, but we just can't seem to get the hang of it. You'd be appalled at what passed for government in this, our "enlightened" modern age. In the U.S., for instance, you'd think we don't really believe anybody knows how to run anything properly. We've gotten very cynical, and expect fraud, malfeasance, and liars in public places. Don't mistake my meaning; it's not one political party or the other that's at fault—it's the system, the bureaucratic megamachine. Our entire society has been politicized, polarized, and factionalized to the extent that everybody is, in the final analysis, at odds with everybody else.

In such a perverse state of affairs, affairs of state tend to undergo some rather bizarre reversals. We have a "Defense" Department that prepares for and covertly wages aggressive war. We have an "Interior" Department that sells off public lands for private profit, and uses wasteful "slash-and-burn" clearcut lumbering techniques on the lands it does retain. We have an Environmental "Protection" Agency which stymies enforcement of the meager environmental legislation we do have on the books. We have a "State" Department whose unstatesmanlike business is to meddle in the internal affairs of other states, and a "Commerce" Department which does everything in its considerable power to put up barriers to free trade between free nations. We have an "Energy" Department whose major utility is to serve as a front for nuclear weapons procurement. We have an "Education" Department whose main function appears to be to dismantle public education from the top down. We have representatives to the United Nations who not long ago invited the assembled delegates to depart our fair shores. The list goes on and on.

For all of this, our generation owes yours an apology—but not without explanation. The explanation, however, is going to be harder for you to comprehend. I can tell you what it is, by and large, but you will probably be unable to accept it. I'm alive now, witnessing the genesis of your terrible world, and I can scarcely believe it myself. It's all the old human follies, writ large. It's greed and stupidity and self-interest and all the banal and routine evils that go unnoticed as we singlemindedly conduct our "business-as-usual." The religions of humankind have been warning us for two or three thousand years that we'd

better shape up, or else, but we generally don't take free advice. It is no hideous horned monster that has arisen in the latter half of the 20th century. It's just the same old vices of the squabbling, petty, self-centered, bad-tempered, cantankerous human species, but the effects have been hugely magnified by our new technologies, magnified and projected directly to you. It is not a birthright we've left you, it's a "birthwrong." You have been grievously wronged long before the day of your birth, and I am ashamed to admit that you are going to have to judge our generation by its worst and most destructive elements.

## Lost Opportunities

You won't see the other side of it, of course, but there is another side. It must seem incomprehensible to you that we of the 1980's could foresee all these things, yet collectively and individually squander our last best moment to turn the world around and leave a habitable planet for our progeny. So let me tell you a little of what we might have done, had we given ourselves—and you—half a chance.

After Hiroshima, we knew very well that, if humankind was to survive, we would have to find alternatives to head-on conflict—creative, constructive, dialogical ways to deal with the irreducible diversity of the human family. Peace is not just an accident, a lull between wars; peace is a hard-won achievement, a creative act, a societal work of art. It is also an imperative. Nuclear weapons leave us no choice—either we human beings learn to live with people who disagree with us, or else we all go to hell in a handbasket. For human life in its entirety to endure, we are going to have to shed some of our deeply rooted cultural biases and pretensions. We are in the midst of discovering, for example, that Western technocracy is not the only way to live a human life, and that it is plain wrongheaded to try to solve global human dilemmas from within the structures and strictures of a single civilizational model—one, be it noted, which seems increasingly prone to flirt with its own total destruction.

We are also well aware that we've taken the Earth for granted far too long. Things have changed rapidly for the worse on our crowded planet; we've worn out our welcome in the old homestead. These are the signs of our

times. If the air is to be fit to breathe, if the grass and the trees are to continue to grow, if human life is to flourish along with its companion species, then we are going to have to learn—and learn damned quickly—to collaborate with the Earth, to become responsible partners with all the rhythms and dynamisms of the living Cosmos. This means that we are going to have to rely less on mechanisms of force and more on the vital connections we share with the entire Creation and with one another.

Along the same lines, we know also that human civilization, however high its technical or aesthetic attainments, is peculiarly vulnerable to its own garbage. Athens, medieval Europe, and Elizabethan England all succumbed to plague spawned in streets that ran with raw sewage, and our new techniques of biochemical interference are likely to be far more devastating than the occasional rat-infested ship. We rightly fear that we shall be poisoned, buried, and memorialized by our own garbage.

I think we do know, above all and despite all, that life is a gift, a miracle, really, that it is fitting to celebrate and pass on enhanced to our descendants. Slow as we are to acknowledge it, we know that this gift is in our hands now—for better or for worse.

So what can I tell you? That in my generation, *homo maniacus,* the crazy fellow, is busy writing the epitaph for *homo sapiens,* the supposedly wise fellow with 6,000 years of accumulated human experience to draw from? That all the beauty and wisdom and dignity that human life has painfully but steadily acquired over millennia will be squandered by a single, mindless generation in a wild frenzy of destruction? I don't know.

I certainly hope not, but it often seems like a hope against hope. I hope our generation can see the alternatives and make the responsible choices—livingry instead of weaponry, creation instead of destruction, life instead of death. I wish I knew the outcome, but only you can know that for sure. Only you, my unknown and nameless grandchild, can properly judge your parents and grandparents and the world they've handed over to you, the life they've passed on to you. As for me, I only wish I knew whether we are even going to allow you to exist.

Hollowly,

Your Grandfather

# *Window of Opportunity*

**Newt Gingrich**

Newt Gingrich, a U.S. congressman from Georgia, was first elected to the House of Representatives in 1978. His previous article for THE FUTURIST, "Post-Industrial Politics: The Leader As Learner" (co-written by his wife, Marianne Gingrich), appeared in December 1981. His address is U.S. House of Representatives, Washington, D.C. 20515.

There exists today a window of opportunity through which we can look and—with luck and hard work—reach to create a bright and optimistic future for our children and grandchildren.

At the moment, this window of opportunity is open and the optimistic future is reachable, but reaching it will require changes in our current behavior and institutions. This optimistic future will necessitate accepting the possibilities inherent in our emerging technologies and accelerating the transition to a high-technology, information-based society.

There is hope for a continuing revolution in biology that will allow us to feed the entire planet; hope for jobs, opportunities, and adventures in space; hope that computers and information science will allow us to work at home, to help everyone live fuller lives, to save energy and resources by expanding our potential while exchanging transportation for communication.

## The Communications Revolution

Distance will evaporate as a limiting social factor when communication replaces transportation as the primary mode of human interaction. We already see geographic neighbors being replaced by electronic neighbors: Your best friend is probably not the person next door but a person you talk to on the phone.

Our grandchildren, as we view them through our window of opportunity, will be using a complex information-set telephone as easily as we dial the directory-assistance operator or call our best friends. They will utilize the library by telephone, shop by telephone, send information to and from their workplaces by telephone. As satellites and computers keep bringing down long-distance rates, people will make calls to any spot on the globe—and perhaps to friends on

---

**Advances in space, communications, and biotechnology are creating a window of opportunity and hope for the future. A U.S. congressman identifies the major opportunities for the United States—and the challenges that first must be met.**

---

space habitats or on the moon—as routinely as we now call friends across town.

Many of our grandchildren will do much of their work from their homes by connecting keyboards to their telephones to write letters, books, and purchase orders. Hotels will routinely have full information-set connections in every room. Wherever you are in the world, you will be able to work, shop, and learn.

This decentralized work system will almost certainly mean a decline in 9-to-5 jobs and the re-emergence of piecework. People who love freedom will rapidly adapt to working on their own schedules and being paid for the product on delivery, creating an extremely fluid marketplace of skills and services.

Home occupations have always existed, to some extent, in America, but the new possibilities inherent in advanced technology will soon allow millions of people to work at home. People will contract to produce 10,000 words of material per day or to do a particular project over a week, month, or year, and the employer will not be concerned with how or when the work is done—while the baby is asleep or late at night—because the employer is buying the product, not the process.

Working people will find no single change more valuable in increasing their leisure time and real income than the development of workstations in the home. Consider, first, the hidden costs. Today, most working people pay for transportation to and from work, parking while they work, and a commercially prepared lunch. Deduct these hidden costs and take-home pay decreases drastically. If we further deduct the cost of dressing for work, there is an additional decline in real income.

Today, big companies deduct the costs of providing a work environment; tomorrow, when people work at home, they will be able to benefit personally from deduction for work rooms and work-related expenses that increase their after-tax income.

Our work force will, however, gain benefits in lifestyle that outshine those in income when workstations are common in American homes. Today, millions of people spend hours in their cars or on mass transit commuting to and from work. Because work is currently a process rather than a product, and because most people work the same hours, we endure seemingly inevitable traffic jams and surges of peak traffic unrelieved by our attempts to create freeways and augment mass transit to meet our growing needs.

People who work at home gain an average of an hour of travel time, each way, which amounts to the equivalent of 12 weeks per year. These extra hours of new free time gained by working from home can be devoted to earning more money or used for leisure.

Neighborhoods will be revitalized when more people are in their homes during the day; there will be fewer burglaries, less crime, and a significant increase in neighborhood businesses as well as a return to utilizing the neighborhood as a community center.

More importantly, the family unit will be strengthened by the shift to working at home: Once you control your own time, you are free to schedule that birthday party or Cub Scout meeting, which used to be so troublesome. Home workstations will allow both male and female partners to share in parenting and family chores and permit a far more flexible lifestyle in which self-directed work choices rather than the coercion of an inflexible employer-dictated routine dominate our lives.

The coming era of expanded machine-accounting may allow us to build a more free and open society in terms of work, pensions, and government. We might build personal pension accounts that will keep track of us all our lives: Credits toward retirement could be transferred when we move to a new job as easily as computers now convert currencies when we buy goods in one country and pay for them in another.

# "Home workstations will allow both male and female partners to share in parenting and family chores."

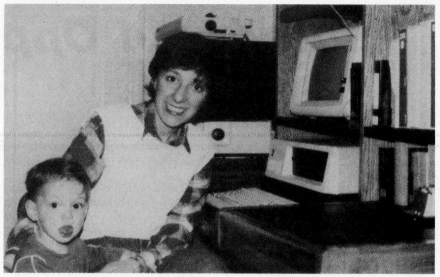

COURTESY OF KATHERINE ACKERMAN AND ASSOCIATES

Information broker Katherine Ackerman of East Lansing, Michigan, and her son, Bradley. Ackerman, a former librarian at the Chicago *Tribune*, began her home-based computer-research and information service in 1983, shortly after the boy's birth. The communications revolution will allow more people to work in their homes, resulting in strengthened family ties, says author Newt Gingrich.

## Opportunities in Space

Many of the opportunities we glimpse through our window have little to do with developments here on earth. One of the great revolutions in our lifetime has been man's leap beyond the planet. As astronomer Carl Sagan is fond of noting, for all the rest of human history there will have been only one magic moment when we first left the planet, braved the near-vacuum of space, and reached our nearest neighbor, the moon.

Since 1969 and the landing on the moon, we have been waiting for someone to give us a new vision of our purpose and role in space. We are *still* waiting for such a visionary, someone able and willing to translate technological capability into human opportunity.

If visionary thinking succeeds, by our grandchildren's time we will have factories in space producing medical goods, special alloys, vacuum-formed surfaces, and a host of other materials. In medicine alone, for example, we may find that the effect of weightlessness on certain manufacturing processes carried on in the relatively sterile and pure environment of space will result in a multi-billion-dollar industry.

If we will make an intensive effort to develop space, we will create millions of jobs on earth and thousands more in space, while ensuring a solid balance of payments in foreign trade by producing goods and services others want but cannot produce for themselves. The late futurist Herman Kahn once suggested that the biggest growth industry of the twenty-first century will be space tourism. As people grow wealthier and the cost of space transportation comes down, spending a week's vacation on a space station or a honeymoon on the moon may become commonplace. People aboard space shuttles—the DC-3s of the future—will fly out to the Hiltons and Marriotts of the solar system, and mankind will have permanently broken free of the planet.

## Breakthroughs in Biology

While space is an important area

228

of growth for the next generation, it may not be the most dramatic. The greatest changes ahead may come in the area of biology.

Biology is entering a period of intellectual flowering like that which transformed physics after the turn of the century. The discovery of the structure of DNA by Watson and Crick is symbolic of a new era in biology that may reveal the very secrets of life.

This biological revolution may enable us to feed a world with a population vastly greater than that of any current projection. The next two generations may see such significant breakthroughs in our understanding of the biological world that we will develop sustainable farming that will improve and enhance nature while producing nutrition for humans.

The biological revolution will transform far more than food production. Already there have been enormous advances in health care, and the lessons we are learning in microbiology may soon remove cancer from the list of life-threatening diseases.

The exercise boom is the first major step toward the form that preventive medicine may take in years to come. Our grandchildren may invest time and money in avoiding illness by staying in shape; they will recognize that the greatest enemies to our health are no longer

the viruses of the past but our own behavior and habits.

There is a growing market of future senior citizens who believe that their own habits can determine whether they spend their last years in a nursing home or in productive pursuits. As we discover that understanding and manipulating the biology of aging will allow us to

FLORIDA DEPARTMENT OF COMMERCE/DIVISION OF TOURISM

Space shuttles may become the "DC-3s of the future" as people begin traveling in space regularly, says author Gingrich.

remain young far longer, people will begin to develop a different outlook on the prospects for life in their 80s and 90s.

As life-spans of longer than 75 years become commonplace, our children must inevitably change their image of retirement. Most people have no wish to spend 25 years or longer in enforced inactivity. The desire to remain active will increase as jobs become more knowledge-oriented and less physical.

## Youth in the Information Age

I first came to realize how much the information age will change our vision of youth when I was teaching a federal executive seminar in Washington. One of the seminar's members owned a small software company in partnership with her husband. The couple got summer-job applications from 12- and 13-year-olds—young people with home computers who were adept enough in their use to be employable at a much higher wage than the average teenager could expect to earn from a menial summer job.

Recently I heard a story about an eighth-grader in Florida who built a successful business as a weather consultant serving large corporations by processing free information—information that the government had on its computers but that normally could not be processed for two or three months. This young man, who was doing the processing and sending out weekly reports via electronic mail to more than 40 national corporations each week, was making money by providing his clients with a valuable service for less than they could obtain it elsewhere.

It is conceivable that, by our grandchildren's time, adolescence will have become a thing of the past: Future historians may conclude that adolescence was an invention of nineteenth-century parents to protect their children from exploitation in textile and steel mills.

If young people enter the labor force earlier, there might be a revival of the concept of apprenticeship. Youngsters could be paid a modest wage to work and study under a

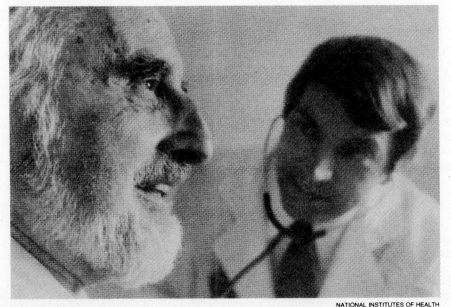

NATIONAL INSTITUTES OF HEALTH

Improvements in biomedicine will help people lead longer, healthier lives.

master of their chosen trade. Anyone familiar with Benjamin Franklin's autobiography or the pre-industrial lifestyle will recognize that there is much to be said for learning while working.

## Education for Change

Our children and grandchildren, having seen the costs of subsidizing those who will not change, may take the position that society owes its members only the *opportunity* to change, *not* the right to avoid change.

The retraining and reinvestment programs of the next century will be gigantic by today's standards. An information society requires as much investment in adult retraining and re-education as the industrial society required in public schooling. The greatest single problem we face in trying to manage the coming transition is that of making it relatively easy for people to adapt.

No society as wealthy as America's should allow people to suffer simply because they took the wrong job—or because the right job one year became the wrong job a decade later. Once a system for continuing self-education is developed, the able-bodied should be required to throw themselves into the game of life, instead of sitting on the sidelines with subsidies in their hands.

## Reforming the Great Bureaucracies

America today is in thrall to a number of monolithic bureaucratic structures, all of them expensive and personally burdensome to the public. These entrenched structures require real and innovative reform:

- The legal system.
- Health care.
- Education.
- Welfare.
- The Defense Department.
- Public bureaucracy.

These bureaucracies share certain characteristics. Each structure's insiders regard themselves as a professional elite serving society in a way that people outside their spe-

TIMBERTECH COMPUTER CAMP

Youngsters find computers fun and easy to use. The youth of the information age, adept at computer-based knowledge work, may start their work lives much sooner than preceding generations.

cialty can't really understand. In each area, the structure has now grown so large that most of the professionals spend their time talking only to other professionals. And any proposals for substantive reform by "outsiders" are derided as the views of amateurs who fail to grasp the sophisticated problems of these professionals.

In an age of change, such antiquated systems are expensive and inefficient, yet the inherent capacity of each structure to resist reform has prevented the growth of approaches that might benefit the public.

## A More Just Justice System

The United States is today the most lawyered and litigious society in the world. There are more lawyers in Georgia (population 5.7 million) than there are in Japan (population 119 million). Despite our wealth of attorneys, most Americans would agree that we have a dearth of justice: Criminal justice is too slow, too lenient, and too random; civil actions are too expensive and too protracted.

We must de-emphasize courtroom activity and expand the use of mediators and arbitrators who need not be lawyers. In most cases, law should be simple; only the more complex matters should require more legal sophistication.

A legal system that met the needs of ordinary citizens would differ markedly from the current model. For example, the criminal-justice system should make life easier for victims and witnesses. After reasonable notice, the burden of being prepared and being in court should be on the accused and the defense attorney.

We should also reduce the legal fees now built into the American business system that raise costs and make the United States less competitive overseas because of the overhead earmarked for possible litigation.

Finally, we must simplify the intricate processes of the legal profession that have resulted in additional paperwork, complicated formulas and procedures, and increasingly complicated systems for adjudicating claims.

## Better Health Care for All

Health care today is the most expensive single factor in American life, and its cost is increasing faster than any other element in the economy. The central problem with our approach to providing adequate health care at reasonable cost has been its focus on tactical, or operational, changes within the existing vision and strategies of health care. What is needed for the opportunity society, however, is a new vision.

**"People who know that another year without hospitalization might bring them a $1,000 bonus may watch their diet and exercise a little more carefully."**

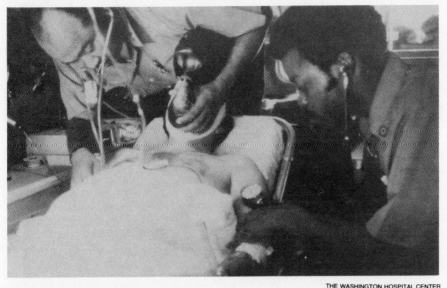

THE WASHINGTON HOSPITAL CENTER

Paramedics revive victim. Well-trained paramedics can provide many health-care services, relieving the burden on doctors and hospitals.

CHARLES BETHEL

Volunteer mediators help individuals settle disputes without costly lawyers and time-consuming court appearances. Expanding the use of arbitrators and mediators is one key to reforming the legal bureaucracy, says author Gingrich.

An example of a visionary change is the elimination of polio as a major threat. Inventing a better iron lung would have been a significant tactical breakthrough, but it would not have altered the world. The discovery of a polio vaccine, on the other hand, represented a paradigm shift—a response to a vision so great that it did indeed alter the world.

One new vision of health care in the opportunity society is to focus on preventive medicine and good health. We must convince people to watch their diets and habits. We may try rewarding people who do not need health care: In Mendocino, California, for example, the teachers' association gave people money at the end of the year for not using their health-care plan.

Changing our third-party payment system so that the individual is once again directly involved in the market costs might mean that insurance companies could find it worthwhile to offer bonuses to people who had not used their insurance for a period of time. People who know that another year without hospitalization might bring them a $1,000 bonus may watch their diet and exercise a little more carefully.

We should also increase research at the vision and strategy level to transform specific areas. There are a number of definable problems that are extremely expensive and that deserve major investments to solve.

Decision-making in health care should be decentralized so that we can move more rapidly to new technologies and procedures. We need to make it relatively easy for local doctors, hospitals, and communities to experiment, and new medical knowledge must be spread more widely and systematically so that people can adopt new methods without professional involvement. We must get new technology into the hands of the general public as rapidly as possible. Many of the procedures currently available could be used by laymen. New software for home computers will allow an individual to become proficient with relatively little training.

As in the legal profession, much health care can be done by "semi-professionals." It is in everyone's interest that individuals do for themselves as much as possible; when they cannot, a large, well-trained corps of paramedics should be available. For example, the return of midwifery is a good start toward decentralizing and de-bureaucratizing health care. There are many other procedures that, if encouraged, would lead to better-informed, more self-reliant citizens and to a more appropriate structure of health care.

The home health-care industry has been developing a number of systems and processes that allow people to take care of themselves or to be taken care of by their friends and relatives. It would be worthwhile to develop a system wherein your family could earn a tax credit, or even a direct payment from the government, for every day that the doctor certifies you would have been hospitalized, had not your family taken care of you instead.

### Rethinking Education

Ours is the first generation in American history to educate its children less well than itself. Of the major Western nations, the United States scores close to the bottom in math and science. What we are doing is not working.

The most important step in improving education today is not merit pay, tuition tax credits, or increased funds at any level, but rethinking the educational process and system. You would expect educators to be in favor of intellectually re-examining education; in reality, educators tend to be a special interest like any other.

We must shift the focus of education from teaching to learning. There are many strategies for successful learning—a reward system for learning, for instance, could change the speed with which individuals focus on achieving their next objective. One experiment worth trying would be to offer a $500 bonus for any child who enters the first grade reading at a fourth-grade level.

This shift would also recognize the need for lifetime learning. As our culture and society change with new technology, new medicine, and new government rules, people will have to keep learning until they die. The challenge to keep learning will be even larger in the future. Our grandchildren will have to plan multiple careers in a working lifetime.

The priorities for schools should be mastery of learning fundamentals and the development of academic discipline. We don't need to go back to the fundamentals of 1900. Instead, we need to move forward to the "triliteracy" that futurist Alvin Toffler prescribes for our schools—the traditional basics of reading, writing, and arithmetic alongside the new basics of computer literacy and information management. The truly autonomous citizen of the twenty-first century must be able to handle all five layers of competence to continue learning at the pace and in the systems that will dominate the information society.

## "No one must fall beneath a certain level of poverty, even if we must give away food and money."

WILLIAM SCHELL, JR./*NATIONAL GUARD* MAGAZINE

Army National Guardsmen receive briefing before live-fire exercises at Fort Carson, Colorado. Reforming the military bureaucracy may mean expanding the role of guardsmen and military reservists, who are paid only during training or when called into service.

There are a host of learning opportunities available in our society that the educational bureaucracy simply ignores: public libraries, newspapers, and educational television, to name just a few. An opportunity society would also develop apprenticeship programs as an alternative to high school, offering tax advantages and subsidies to both the apprenticer and the community. Many skills and trades are learned better through apprenticeship than in academia. There are young people who simply do not fit well into school but would love to learn a trade.

We have grossly neglected the potential educational resources of new technologies. The potential linkage between the home computer, the telephone, cable television, and the local newspaper is enormous. For a modest sum, we could build a software package that would make a large library available to home computers by telephone hookup.

### From Welfare to Workfare

We must compassionately reconsider poverty, unemployment, and the culture of being poor. Our present, inadequate solutions are no longer useful and must be re-formed.

Let me suggest just a few guidelines around which we might build an opportunity-society welfare system:

• Individuals, families, and poor communities should receive cash and credit-card vouchers directly in order to increase their choices and give them power over their own lives.

• Services going to the very neediest should be seen as state charity and should be generous rather than stingy. Our current system crimps those at the bottom of the welfare ladder. No one must fall beneath a certain level of poverty, even if we must give away food and money.

• Those who are able-bodied and under the age of retirement should work or study if they wish to receive aid—including unemployment compensation. Among other things, this principle could encourage the establishment of day-care centers where some welfare mothers care for the neighborhood children while others go out to work.

• The tax and welfare laws should be changed so that those trying to work their way out of the welfare system gain more than they lose at each step. Taxes, child care, and the cost of going to work should be set against gross pay in calculating welfare eligibility.

Our goal must be to help the helpless and the elderly so that they can lead full lives and to empower the poor to control their lives and rise from poverty. If we design the right programs now, then no members of the next generation will be able to say they live in poverty for lack of choice.

## Military Reform

While the Department of Health and Human Services may disburse more money in the form of transfer payments, there is no other system in the federal government remotely comparable to the Defense Department in size and complexity.

Everything that conservatives have said about bureaucracies in general applies in particular to the Pentagon: It is well protected by its allies on Capitol Hill and in the

TIMBERTECH COMPUTER CAMP

Tree-climbing boy reads his computer textbook. Computer literacy and the ability to use information media are the new "basics" of education, according to author Gingrich.

military-industrial complex; it is hidebound by traditions, some of them going back nearly 200 years; and it is a hive of internal political squabbles.

There are some weaknesses in the current military system that need to be dealt with directly. The most serious is the underuse of the national guard and the reserves. A regular-duty soldier is nine times as expensive as a reservist or a guardsman. Regular soldiers are paid every day, while the reserves and guard are paid only when they train. Further, the regulars retire after 20 years on half-pay pensions. Our military today is too small to meet all its potential commitments—and too expensive besides.

The time is ripe for a thorough overhaul of our military management system. There is no excuse for focusing on the smaller bureaucracies while ignoring this one.

## Deregulating the Federal Bureaucracy

Most federal civil servants want to do a good job and are as totally frustrated by irrational, obsolete bureaucratic systems as the people ill-served by them.

A free people may indicate public policy through their elected offi-

cials, but they can only implement those policies through a professional staff. In the information age, even a lean federal government is going to be an enormous structure to manage.

We have the capacity to revamp the federal government into an exciting, dynamic place to work. If we combine technology with a system of merit pay, idea bonuses, individual retirement accounts for those who desire them, and other steps toward a more flexible and desirable style of work, then I think that, in the twenty-first century, we can once again be proud of the quality of our civil service.

In each area of government there are great opportunities for an age of improvement. The time to start making those improvements is now.

Peering into the future through our window of opportunity, I am confident that our children and grandchildren *can* live in a positive, optimistic America—*if* we regain our morale and elan as a society. I am equally convinced that an America confident enough to take risks in space, computers, and biology can regain its capacity to lead the world economically, militarily, and politically.

# Glossary

*This glossary of 459 sociology terms is included to provide you with a convenient and ready reference as you encounter general terms in your study of sociology which are unfamiliar or require a review. It is not intended to be comprehensive but taken together with the many definitions included in the articles themselves it should prove to be quite useful.*

**Absolute Poverty** A condition in which one lacks the essentials of life such as food, clothing, or shelter. *See* Relative Poverty.

**Achieved Status** The position of an individual within a system of social stratification based on changeable factors such as occupations, high income, or marriage into hgiher social strata. *See* Ascriptive Status.

**Agents of Socialization** The people, groups, and organizations who socialize the individual. *See* Socialization.

**Alienation** A sense of separation from society. In the context of the bureacracy, one's feeling of not having control over or responsibility for one's own behavior at work. *See* Bureaucracy.

**Altruism** Behavior motivated by a desire to benefit another individual, or sacrifice by individuals for the benefit of the group as a whole.

**Androgyny** A combination of male and female characteristics. The term may be used in a strictly physical sense or it may apply to a wider, social ideal.

**Anomie** The loosening of social control over individual behavior that occurs when norms become ineffective.

**Ascriptive Status** The position of an individual within a system of social stratification based on factors such as sex, age, race, over which the individual has no control. *See* Achieved Status, Social Stratification, Status.

**Assimilation** The absorption of a subordinate group into the dominant culture.

**Authority** Power that people recognize as just, legitimate, and necessary; the basis for compliance with a government's laws.

**Authority Systems** Systems by which authority is legitimated. According to Max Weber, in a traditional system, positions of authority are obtained by heredity. In a charismatic system, leaders are followed because of some extraordinarily appealing personal quality. In a legal-rational system, the office is the source of authority, rather than the officeholder.

**Autocratic Leader** The type of group leader who is authoritarian and impersonal and who does not participate in group projects. *See* Democratic Leader, Laissez-Faire Leader.

**Awareness Context** The "total combination of what each interactant in a situation knows about the identity of the other and [about his or her] own identity in the eyes of the other."

**Belief System** Groups of basic assumptions about general concepts such as the existence and nature of God, the meaning of life, or the relationship of the individual and the state held by a culture.

**Bilineal Kinship** Kinship system in which descent is traced through both parents and all grandparents. *See* Kinship, Lineal Kinship.

**Biological Determinism** The view of behavior as a product of genetic makeup.

**Biological-Instinctual Theories** Theories of behavior that stress the importance of instinct. *See* Environmental Theories.

**Biosocial Interaction** The ways in which interrelationships with society influence and are influenced by biological factors. *See* Biosociologists.

**Biosocial Systems** Systems of social organization such as those among insects, which survive because behavior patterns are biologically controlled.

**Biosociologists** Sociologists who are concerned with the implications of biology in the study of society. They study the genotype-environment interactions in the production of behavior. *See* Genotype/Phenotype, Sociobiology.

**Birth Rate (Crude)** The number of people born in a single year per 1,000 persons in the population.

**Bourgeoisie** The class that owns the means of production. *See* Proletariat.

**Bureaucracy** An authority structure arranged hierarchically for the purpose of efficient operation.

**Case Study** A research method which involves intensive examination of a particular social group over time. *See* Sample Survey, Participant Observation, Research.

**Caste** A rigid form of social stratification, rooted in religious standards, in which individuals spend their lives in the stratum into which they were born. *See* Class, Estate, Social Stratification.

**Census** A periodic count and collection of demographic information about an entire population. *See* Demography.

**Central City** The core unit of a metropolitan area. The term is also used to mean "inner city" or "ghetto," with its urban problems of poverty, crime, racial discrimination, poor schools and housing, and so on.

**Centrality of the Leader** A concept of group interaction formulated by Sigmund Freud which considers the group leader's power and authority to be centrally important to the group.

**Charisma** Exceptional personal leadership qualities which command authority as contrasted to legal or formal authority. A driving, creative force that attaches both to individuals and to social movements.

**Clan** A lineal kinship group. *See* Kinship, Lineal Kinship.

**Class** A form of social stratification in which groups are divided primarily by economic positions. According to Weber, people with the same amount of property belong to the same class. *See* Caste, Estate, Social Stratification.

**Class Conflict** According to Marxist theory, the dynamics for change created by the conflict between ruling classes and subordinate classes in society.

**Class Consciousness** According to Marxist theory, the awareness of what it means to be a member of a certain class.

**Classless Society** According to Marxist theory, the goal of socialism and the state in which all social stratification on the basis of class is eliminated. *See* Class, Social Stratification.

**Cliques** Tight clusters of friends and acquaintances who share relatively intense feelings of belonging. Cliques are primary groups. *See* Primary Groups.

**Closed Community** A type of community in which families within tight kinship groups cooperate closely and are closed to non-relatives. *See* Open Community.

**Closed System** A social stratification system which offers an individual no way to rise to a higher position; based on ascriptive status. *See* Ascriptive Status, Open System.

**Coercion** The power to compel people to act against their will, by using force or the threat of force. The constraint of some people by others. According to conflict theorists, it is that glue that binds society together. *See* Conflict Model, Power.

**Coercive Organization** According to Amitai Etzioni, an organization in which force is the major means of control. Examples include prisons and custodial mental hospitals. *See* Normative and Utilitarian Organizations, Compliance Patterns.

**Cognitive Category** Category of knowledge and experience into which people organize their perceptions of the world.

**Cognitive Development** A theory of psychology which states that cognitive processes such as thinking, knowing, perceiving, develop in stages although they function and influence even newborns' behavior. *See* Behaviorist.

**Collective Behavior** The behavior of a loosely associated group which is responding to the same stimulus. The concept embraces a wide range of group phenomena, including riots, social movements, revolutions, fads, crazes, panics, public opinion, and rumors. All are responses to as well as causes of social change. Elementary forms of collective behavior (panics, rumors) are relatively spontaneous and unstructured, but longer-lasting activities (social movements) require more planning and coordination. *See* Social Aggregate.

**Communalism** The need for scientific discoveries to be made available to the whole community. *See* Universalism.

**Communism** A political-economic system in which wealth and power are shared harmoniously by the whole community. The concept today refers mainly to the revolutionary socialism of Karl Marx and to the political systems that adhere to his principles. *See* Socialism.

**Community** The spatial, or territorial, unit in social organization; also the psychological feeling of belonging associated with such units. *See* Metropolis.

**Competitive Social System** A social system in which the dominant group views the subordinate group as aggressive and dangerous and thereby in need of suppression. *See* Paternalistic Social System.

**Compliance Patterns** According to Amitai Etzioni, the (three) ways in which formal organizations exercise control over members. *See* Coercive, Normative, Utilitarian Organizations.

**Comte, Auguste (1798-1857)** French philosopher who coined the term "sociology" and is considered the founder of the modern discipline.

**Concentric Zone Theory** A proposal by the Chicago School founders, Park and Burgess, saying that cities grew from a central business district outward in a series of concentric circles. Each zone was inhabited by different social classes and different types of homes and businesses. *See* Multiple-Nuclei Theory, Sector Theory.

**Conflict Model** The view of society that sees social units a sources of competing values and norms. See Equilibrium Model.

**Conforming Behavior** Behavior that follows the accepted standards of conduct of a group or society. See Deviance.

**Conjugal Family** A family type in which major emphasis is placed on the husband-wife relationship. See Consanguine Family.

**Consanguine Family** The family type in which the major emphasis is on the blood relationships of parents and children or brothers and sisters.

**Contagion Theory** A theory of collective behavior, originated by Gustave LeBon, which states that the rapid spread of a common mood among a large number of people is what forms a crowd.

**Conventional Morality** According to Lawrence Kohlberg, the second level of moral development, at which most adults remain. This level involves conformity to cultural or family norms, maintenance of, and loyalty to, the social order. See Preconventional, Postconventional Morality.

**Convergence Theory** A theory of collective behavior which states that people with certain tendencies are most likely to come together in a crowd. This theory assumes that crowd behavior is uniform.

**Core of the Aggregate** People in a particularly visible location within a social aggregate who may induce action by the aggregate. See Social Aggregate.

**Crimes Without Victims** Violations of criminal law, such as homosexuality, drug addiction, prostitution, or abortion, which raise questions about the enforcement of morality by legal controls. See Crime, Sin.

**Criminality** Deviant behavior that is punishable through formal sanctions, or penalties, applied by political authorities. See Crime, Deviance.

**Criminalization** The labeling of individuals as criminals, especially by the criminal justice system. See Criminal Justice System, Stigmatization.

**Criminal Justice System** Authorities and institutions in a society concerned with labeling and punishing criminals according to formal social sanctions.

**Criminology** The social science that analyzes crime as a social occurrence; the study of crime, criminality, and the operation of the criminal justice system. See Crime.

**Crowd** A type of social aggregate in which all participants are in the same place at the same time, and they interact in a limited way. See Social Aggregate.

**Cults** Small groups whose teachings stress ritual, magic, or beliefs widely regarded as false by the dominant culture. See Religion.

**Cultural Adaptation** The flexibility of a culture that allows it to change as the environment changes.

**Cultural Diffusion** The adaptation of a culture as it encounters another and undergoes social change.

**Cultural Lag** The condition that exists when values or social institutions do not change as rapidly as social practices.

**Cultural Relativism** The principle of judging a culture on its own terms. See Ethnocentrism.

**Culture** The knowledge people need to function as members of the particular groups they belong to; our shared beliefs, customs, values, norms, language, and artifacts.

**Culture of Poverty** As defined by Oscar Lewis, "an effort to cope with the feelings of hopelessness and despair that arise [when the poor realize] the improbability of their achieving success in terms of the prevailing values and goals."

**Death** Traditionally defined as the end of all vital functions. Some states define the cessation of breathing and absence of heartbeat as death. Others say death occurs when brain activity stops.

**Death Rate (Crude)** The number of deaths in a single year per 1,000 persons in the population. See Demography.

**Democratic Leader** A type of group leader who encourages group decision-making rather than giving orders. See Autocratic and Laissez-Faire Leader.

**Democratization** The process of making something democratic. According to Max Weber, political democratization is related to the growth of the bureaucratic state.

**Demographic Transition** The pattern in which death rates fall with industrialization, causing a rise in population and ensuing drop in birth rate which returns the rate of population growth to nearly the same level as before industrialization.

**Demography** The study of human population, focusing on birth rate, death rate, and migration patterns.

**Dependent Variable** The factor that varies with changes in the independent variable. See Independent Variable.

**Desegregation** Elimination of racial segregation in a society. See Discrimination.

**Determinism** The view of social change proposing that an inevitable pattern of change occurs in societies because of a universal principle, or dynamic, of the historic process. See Deterministic.

**Deterministic** Any theory that sees natural, social, or psychological factors as determined by preceding causes.

**Deterrence Theory** A theory held by some criminologists that punishment will prevent as well as control crime.

**Deviance** The label for all forms of behavior that are considered unacceptable, threatening, harmful, or offensive in terms of the standards or expectations of a particular society or social group. See Conforming Behavior, Norm, Secondary Deviance.

**Dewey, John (1859-1952)** American philosopher and educator, a functionalist, whose ideas about education had a strong effect on schooling. He pressed for a science of education and believed in learning by doing. Individualized instruction and experimental learning can be traced to his theories.

**Dialectical Materialism** The philosophical method of Karl Marx, who considered knowledge and ideas as reflections of material conditions. Thus the flow of history, for example, can be understood as being moved forward by the conflict of opposing social classes. See Communism.

**Discrimination** Unfavorable treatment, based on prejudice, of groups to which one does not belong. See Prejudice.

**Disinterestedness** The quality of not allowing personal motives or commitments to distort scientific findings or evaluations of scientific work. See Communalism, Organized Skepticism.

**Division of Labor** The separation of tasks or work into distinct parts that are to be done by particular individuals or groups. Division of labor may be based on many factors, including sex, level of technology, and so on. See Task Segregation.

**Double Standard** A moral judgment by which sexual activity of men is considered appropriate or excused while that of women is considered immoral. See Sex Role.

**Doubling Time** The time it takes a population to double its size.

**Dramaturgical Perspective** The point of view, favored by Erving Goffman, that social interaction can be compared to a dramatic presentation.

**Durkheim, Emile (1858-1917)** French sociologist and one of the founders of modern sociology. Deeply influenced by the positivism of Auguste Comte, Durkheim's major concern was with social order, which he believed to be the product of a cohesion stemming from a common system of values and norms.

**Dying Trajectory** A graph that plots the time span from the terminally ill patient's hosptial admission until the moment of death, and the course of the patient's physical deterioration. See Thanatology.

**Ecological Determinism** The point of view stressing how environment affects behavior. See Urbanism.

**Economic Determinism** The doctrine, supported by Karl Marx, that economic factors are the only bases for social patterns.

**Economic Modernization** Shift from an agricultural-based economy to an industrial one.

**Education** The social institution by which a culture is transmitted from one generation to the next. See Institutions, Sociology of Education.

**Egalitarianism** Emphasis within a society on the concept of equality among members of social systems.

**Egocentricity** The characteristic quality of very young children, their awareness of only their own point of view.

**Elaborated Code** According to Basil Bernstein, the formal type of language available to the middle class only. See Restricted Code.

**Elements of Culture** Factors such as customs, language, symbols, and values shared by members of a cultural group.

**Elite** Those at the top of a hierarchy based on status and on economic, social, or political power. See Hierarchy.

**Elite Groups** Members of the top ranks of society in terms of power, prestige, and economic or intellectual resources. See Power Elite.

**Emergent Norm Theory** A theory of collective behavior stating that social aggregates form in response to specific problems that cannot be solved through institutionalized action. See Crowd, Social Aggregate.

**Encounter Groups** Groups of individuals who meet to change their personal lives by confronting each other, discussing personal problems, and talking more honestly and openly than in everyday life. See Group Therapy.

**Endogamy** Marriage within one's social group. See Exogamy.

**Environmental Theories** Theories of behavior that stress the influence of learning and environment. See Biological-Instinctual Theories.

**Equilibrium Model** A view of society as a system of interdependent parts which function together to maintain the equilibrium of the whole system. *See* Conflict Model, Functionalism.

**Erikson, Erik (1902-    )** Danish-born psychoanalytic theorist who lives in the United States. He supplemented Freud's theory of psychosexual development with a separate theory of psychosocial development. He theorized that individuals move through a series of psychosocial stages throughout life, with the integrity of the personality depending largely on the individual's success in making appropriate adaptations at previous stages.

**Estate** A form of social stratification based on laws, usually about one's relationship to land. *See* Social Stratification.

**Ethnic Group** A social group distinguished by various traits, including language, national or geographic origin, customs, religion, and race.

**Ethnicity** The act or process of becoming or being a religious, racial, national, cultural, or subcultural ethnic group. *See* Ethnic Group.

**Ethnocentrism** The tendency to judge other groups by the standards of one's own culture and to believe that one's own group values and norms are better than others'. *See* Cultural Relativism.

**Ethology** The comparative study of animal behavior patterns as they occur in nature.

**Eugenics** The science of controlling heredity.

**Evolution** A process of change by which living organisms develop, and each succeeding generation is connected with its preceding generation.

**Evolutionary Change** A gradual process of social change. *See* Revolutionary Change.

**Exchange Theory** The viewpoint that stresses that individuals judge the worth of particular interactions on the basis of costs and profits to themselves.

**Exogamy** Marriage outside one's social group. *See* Endogamy.

**Experiment** A research method in which only one factor is varied at a time and efforts are made to keep other variables constant in order to isolate the causal or independent variable. *See* Research, Independent Variable.

**Extended Family** A family type consisting of two or more nuclear families. Also characterized as three or more generations who usually live together. *See* Modified Extended Family System.

**Facilitating Conditions** In a model of suburban growth, those factors that make movement from city to suburb possible. Such factors include commuter transportation systems and communications technology. *See* Motivating Conditions.

**Family** A set of people related to each other by blood, marriage, or adoption. Family membership is determined by a combination of biological and cultural factors that vary among societies.

**Family Life Cycle** The process of characteristic changes that a family's task (such as child-rearing) undergo over time.

**Family Planning** The theory of population control that assumes that parents should be able to determine and produce the number of children they want, spaced at the intervals they think best. *See* Population Control.

**Fashioning Effect** The tendency for role categories to determine people's behavior and thus to help shape their self-concepts. *See* Role Selection.

**Feral Children** Children who are not socialized because they have been, according to unconfirmed reports, brought up by wild animals. *See* Social Isolates.

**Fertility Rate** The number of births in relation to the number of women of childbearing age in a population.

**Folk Taxonomy** Classification system used by a culture to organize its cognitive categories.

**Formal Organization** A large social unit purposely set up to meet specific, impersonal goals. *See* Informal Organization.

**Freud, Sigmund (1856-1939)** Viennese founder of modern psychology and originator of psychoanalysis. Basic to Freud's theories are the beliefs that much of human behavior is unconsciously motivated and that neuroses often have their origins in early childhood wishes or memories that have been repressed. He developed an account of psychosexual development in which he said that sexuality was present even in infants, although the nature of this sexuality changed as the individual progressed through a sequence of stages to mature adult sexuality.

Freud also proposed a division of the self into the *id* (instinctual desires), the *ego* (the conscious self), and the *superego* (conscience). The ego mediates between the pressures of the other two parts in an effort to adapt the individual to the demands of society, and personality formation is largely the result of this process. *See* Psychoanalytic Theory.

**Functionalism** A dominant school in modern sociology which assumes that each part of the social structure functions to maintain the society and which views social change according to the equilibrium model; also called structural-functionalism. *See* Equilibrium Model.

**Game Theory** The study of situations in which the outcome of interaction depends on the joint action of the partners.

**Gemeinschaft/Gesellschaft** Simple, close-knit communal form of social organization/impersonal bureaucratic form. Typology of social organization devised by Tönnies and used to understand variety and changes in societies' social structure. *See* Tönnies.

**Gender Identity** A child's awareness of being either male or female. *See* Sex Role.

**Gene Pool** The total of genes present in the population.

**Generalized Others** According to George Herbert Mead, the developmental stage in which children adopt the viewpoint of many other people or, in short, of society in general. *See* Significant Others.

**Genetic Engineering** Altering the reproductive process in order to alter the genetic structure of the new organism.

**Genetic Load** The presence of genes in a population that are capable of reducing fitness. *See* Adaptive.

**Genocide** Deliberate destruction of a racial or ethnic group.

**Genotype/Phenotype** Genotype is the entire structure of genes that are inherited by an organism from its parents. Phenotype is the observable result of interaction between the genotype and the environment.

**Gerontology** The study of the problems of aging and old age.

**Group** Two or more people who know each other, interact regularly or systematically, share ideas or goals, and think of themselves as a unit.

**Group Marriage** Marriage among two or more women and two or more men at the same time.

**Group Processes** The dynamics of group functioning and decision-making and of the interactions of group members.

**Group Space** A concept of Robert Bales, from his research on social groups. Bales correlated many factors and then constructed dimensions, such as dominance, likeability, task orientation, along which group members could be placed. When these dimensions are combined in three dimensions, they form the group space.

**Group Therapy** A form of psychotherapy in which interaction among group members is the main therapeutic mode. Group therapy takes many forms but essentially requires a sense of community, support, increased personal responsibility, and a professionally trained leader.

**Hierarchy** The relative positions of individuals or groups within a body or society and their relationship to power and control. *See* Social Sciences.

**Hobbesian Question** The term referring to the question of the 17th-century philosopher Thomas Hobbes, who asked how society could establish and maintain social order. Today, sociologists apply this question to the problem of conformity within the social order.

**Hobbes, Thomas (1588-1679)** British philosopher and writer who theorized about social order and social confict. He was the first social conflict theorist.

**Human Ecology** Term used by geographers to define the impact of changes in human populations in the broader environment; refers to the relationship between humans and their environment.

**Hypothesis** An "educated guess," a statement of a probable relationship between variables in a research design. *See* Research, Scientific Method, Theory.

**Ideal Type** A conceptual model or tool used to help analyze social occurrences. It is an abstraction based on reality, although it seldom, if ever, occurs in exactly that form.

**Identity** According to Erik Erikson, a person's sense of who and what he or she is.

**I/Me** According to George Herbert Mead, the I is the spontaneous, natural, self-interested aspect of the self. The me is the socialized part that has adopted the norms of the community.

**Imperialism** According to Lenin, a nation's policy of building empires by extending its power and domination.

**Independent Variable** The causal variable, or factor that changes. *See* Dependent Variable.

**Individuation** The development and recognition of the individual as a distinct being in the group.

**Industrialization** The systematic organization of production through the use of machinery and a specialized labor force.

**Industrial Society** Society characterized by mechanized means of production for its goods and services, a high degree of economic development, and a specialized labor force. *See* Postindustrial Society, Traditional Society.

**Infant Mortality Rate** The number of children per 1,000 dying in the first year of life.

**Influence** A subtle form of power involving the ability to sway people to do what they might not otherwise do. *See* Power.

**Informal Norms** The rules governing behavior generally set by an informal group instead of the formal requirements of an organization. *See* Informal Organization.

**Informal Organization** In contrast to and within a formal organization, those groups of people or roles they play that cut across the official bureaucratic pattern. *See* Formal Organization.

**Instinct** An unlearned fixed action pattern that occurs in response to specific stimuli as a result of complex hormonal and neurological processes.

**Institutions** Complex and well-accepted ways of behaving aimed at meeting broad social goals. The major social institutions are government, family, religion, education, and the economy. *See* Organization.

**Intelligence** A capacity for knowledge. There is not agreement on a precise definition, although intelligence has come to refer to higher-level abstract processes.

**Intelligence Quotient (IQ)** A measurement of intelligence, defined as a relation between chronological and mental ages. Measured IQ is a good indicator of school performance. Relative contributions of genetic inheritance and environment are not known.

**Interest Groups** Political factions made up of citizens who associate voluntarily and who aim to influence communal action. *See* Pluralism.

**Intergenerational Learning** Learning by one generation from another. It is found generally among nonhuman primates as well as among humans.

**Intergenerational Status Transmission** The passing of the parents' socioeconomic status onto their children.

**Internalization** In the process of socialization, the taking into oneself of attitudes, values, and norms so that they are part of one's personality. *See* Socialization.

**Interpersonal Space** The physical distance between people. Cultures vary in the amount of space people leave between themselves when they interact in various ways.

**Iron Law of Oligarchy** According to Robert Michels, the tendency of formal organizations to give their officers a near monopoly of power. *See* Formal Organization.

**Kin Selection** A process in which individuals cooperate, sacrifice themselves, or do not reproduce so that their kin can survive and reproduce.

**Kinship** A system of organizing and naming relationships that arise through marriage (affinal kinship) and through birth (consanguine kinship). *See* Lineal Kinship, Bilineal Kinship.

**Kinship Networks** Family systems.

**Labeling Theory** The school of thought that sees deviance or criminality as a status imposed by societal reaction. *See* Criminality, Opportunity Theory, Secondary Deviance, Status.

**Laissez-faire Leader** A type of group leader who makes few suggestions and allows the group great freedom to do what it wants. *See* Autocratic Leader, Democratic Leader.

**Language** A means of communication using vocal sounds that make up units of meaning (words) and arranged according to rules of usage and order (grammar and syntax).

**Leisure Class** The social stratum which exists on inherited wealth. *See* Social Stratification.

**Level of Interaction** The way in which people relate to one another. Interactions may be subtle and nearly undetectable, or they may be clear and obvious. People may relate on a number of different levels with each statement or gesture. *See* Group Processes.

**Lineal Kinship** Kinship traced through one parent only. *See* Clan, Kinship, Bilineal Kinship.

**Linguistic Relativity** The concept that different languages analyze and portray the universe in different ways.

**Locke, John (1632-1700)** British philosopher and political theorist who put forward a social contract theory of government, which saw people as rational and dignified and entitled to overthrow any government that grew tyrannical. *See* Social Contract.

**Macrosociology** The sociological study of relations between groups. Some sociologists consider it the study of the entire society or social system. *See* Microsociology.

**Malthusian Theory** Pessimistic pronouncements by Thomas Malthus (1766-1834) about population growth outstripping increases in food production, thus resulting in starvation. *See* Demography, Thomas Malthus.

**Malthus, Thomas (1766-1834)** British economic and demographic theorist who predicted that population increases would outrun increases in food production, with starvation as a result.

**Marriage** The social institution that sanctions, or gives approval to, the union of husband and wife and assumes some permanence and conformity to social custom. Marriage patterns differ among societies.

**Marx, Karl (1818-1883)** The German-born economic, political, and social thinker whose ideas provided the inspiration for modern communism. Marx's social theory is based on a determinist view of history: according to the "materialist method" that Marx elaborated, the mode of production in any particular society determines the character of the economy of the society and hence the society's cultural characteristics. The economic base constitutes the substructure of society, and all other social and cultural phenomena, such as law, religion, or art, form a superstructure that is ultimately conditioned by the economic base. Social change comes about through a dialectical process of conflict between opposing classes; all history is but the history of class conflict. In capitalist society, class conflict reaches its most antagonistic form; the struggle between the bourgeoisie and proletariat will result ultimatley in the creation of a classless society. In such a society people will finally realize their own potential, no longer feeling themselves alien in the social world they have created.

**Mass** A type of social aggregate in which separate individuals respond to a common stimulus, but with little or no communication or interaction. For example, all of the people who watch the same television program constitute a mass. *See* Mass Society, Social Aggregate.

**Mass Communications** Those forms of communication, including especially the mass media, which involve the transmission of ideas and attitudes from a communications center to a diverse mass of people. *See* Mass, Mass Media.

**Mass Media** The press (newspapers and magazines) and broadcasting (radio and television). The mass media are important agents of socialization. *See* Agent of Socialization.

**Mass Society** The complex, industrialized society that displays a basic uniformity of material goods, ideas, roles, and lifestyles. Also used in the sense of those at the bottom of the social scale who produce a nation's goods and perform its services. *See* Mass, Mass Media.

**Matrilineal Kinship** The tracing of one's descent through the mother and her side of the family. *See* Patrilineal Kinship.

**Matrilocal** A pattern of residence in which a married couple lives with or near the wife's family. *See* Patrilocal.

**Mead, George Herbert (1863-1931)** American social psychologist and philosopher whose theories of mind, self, and society had a major influence on sociological approaches such as role theory and symbolic interactionism. *See* I/Me, Significant Others.

**Measures of Central Tendency** Descriptive statistical techniques used to measure the central tendency of distribution of group scores or results.

**Mechanisms of Perpetuation** In a model of suburban growth, factors that assure that successive generations of target populations will exist and will be drawn to the suburbs. Such factors include movement of industry from city to suburbs and cheaper land, taxes, and facilities in the suburbs. *See* Target Population.

**Median Age** The age that divides the population in half. Half of the population is older and half younger than the median age.

**Megalopolis** Urban areas made up of more than one metropolis, "supercities." The area between New Hampshire and northern Virginia is one megalopolis. *See* Metropolis.

**Methodology** The logic of applying the scientific perspective and the set of rules for conducting research. *See* Scientific Method.

**Metropolis** Urban area made up of separate cities, towns, and unincorporated areas which are interrelated. *See* Standard Metropolitan Statistical Area.

**Microsociology** The sociological study of interaction between individuals. *See* Macrosociology.

**Migration** The movement of people, a variable affecting the size and composition of population. Migration may be internal, within a country, or international, between countries. *See* Demography.

**Milling** The physical moving about of people in a crowd who spread emotions as their contact increases. Milling is an important factor in the escalation of excitement in collective behavior. *See* Collective Behavior.

**Mills, C. Wright (1916-1962)** The leader of mid-20th-century American sociological thought, who attempted to develop a radical sociological critique of capitalist society. His social-interactionist position, derived from Max Weber and Herbert Spencer, also influenced his thinking.

**Miscegenation** Mingling of races, particularly marriage or cohabitation between whites and other races. See Race.

**Modernization** The process of gradual change in a society from traditional social, economic, and political institutions to those characteristic of modern urban, industrial societies. See Industrialization, Social Modernization.

**Modified Extended Family System** A middle-class urban family pattern of related nuclear families participating in a kinship structure based on ties of affection rather than ties demanded by tradition. See Extended Family.

**Monasticism** An organized system of withdrawal from everyday life and devotion to religous principles.

**Monogamy** Marriage of one woman and one man. See Polygamy.

**Moral Absolutism** The idea that one's own moral values are the only true ones and that they are the proper basis for judging all others. See Cultural Relativism.

**Moral Development** The growth of a child into an adult who is willing to make the sacrifices necessary for social living. Study of moral development has focused on how people come to adopt their culture's standards of right and wrong and how they resist the temptation to defy the rules of acceptable conduct.

**Mores** Folkways or customs to which group members attach social importance or necessity; standards of behavior that carry the force of right and wrong. See Socialization.

**Motivating Conditions** In a model of suburban growth, factors that stimulate the shift of population from city to suburb. Such factors include deteriorating conditions in the cities and rising economic productivity. See Facilitating Conditions.

**Multiple-Nuclei Theory** Theory of urban development stating that a city grows from a number of centers rather than from a single point. See Concentric Zone Theory, Sector Theory.

**Natural Increase** Births minus deaths per 1,000 population.

**Natural Selection** The evolutionary process by which those individuals of a species with the best-adapted genetic endowment tend to survive to become parents of the next generation. See Evolution.

**Negative Rites** According to Emile Durkheim, rites which maintain taboos or prohibitions. See Piacular Rites.

**Neoidealism** A philosophy that rejects the positivist approach to social phenomena as inadequate. Neoidealists believe that a full explanation must take into account the experience and subjective values of the social actors. See Positivism, *Verstehen*.

**Non-participant Observations** A research method used in case studies by social scientists who come into contact with others but do not interact and behave primarily as a trained observer. See Participant Observation.

**Nonperiodic Assemblies** Gatherings that occur sporadically and whose membership is rarely the same over a period of time. Parades, protest demonstrations, and rallies are examples. See Periodic Assemblies.

**Norm** A shared standard for judging the behavior of an individual. Norms are elements of culture.

**Normative Organization** According to Amitai Etzioni, a formal organization to which people belong because of personal interest or commitment to the organization's goals. Examples include religious, political, and professional organizations. See Coercive and Utilitarian Organizations.

**Nuclear Family** The smallest family type, consisting of parents and their children. In Western society, custom has broadened the basic definition to include childless couples and single parents.

**Open Community** A type of community in which families interact with relatives and friends and have selective attachments to a variety of associations and secondary social groups which offer relatively impersonal relationships. See Closed Community.

**Open System** A social stratification system which allows an individual to rise to a higher position; based on achieved status. See Achieved Status, Closed System.

**Opportunity Theory** The school of criminology that sees criminality as conduct. It is based on the writings of Robert Merton, who reasoned that deviance results from pressures within the social structure. See Criminology, Labeling Theory.

**Organization** A deliberately formed group of people who achieves the aims of a social institution. For example, the aims of the educational institution are carried out by organizations such as schools and colleges. See Institution.

**Organization Development** A field of endeavor that seeks to help organizations adapt to a difficult and changing environment by techniques such as sensitivity training, and which aims to humanize and democratize bureaucracies. See Formal Organization, Sensitivity Training.

**Organized Skepticism** The suspension of judgment until all relevant facts are at hand and the analysis of all such facts according to established scientific standards. See Communalism, Disinterestedness.

**Parsons, Talcott (1902-1979)** An American sociologist and one of the most controversial and influential of social theorists. Although clearly identified with the functionalist approach to social analysis, Parsons avoided becoming personally involved in the debates surrounding that concept. His career has passed through a number of phases, ranging from a substantive approach to social data involving a moderate level of abstraction to an analytic approach of almost metaphysical abstraction. See Functionalism.

**Participant Observation** A research method used in case studies by social scientists who interact with other people and record relatively informal observations. See case study, Non-Participant Observations.

**Party** According to Max Weber, made up of people who share political interests. Parties are goal-oriented, and they aim to acquire social power.

**Paternalistic Social System** A social system in which people or groups are treated in the manner in which a father controls his children. See Competitive Social System.

**Passive Euthanasia** The practice of letting a very ill person die naturally when there is no hope of recovery.

**Pathological Behavior** Conduct that results from some form of physical or mental illness or psychological problem. See Deviance.

**Patrilineal Kinship** The tracing of one's descent through the father and his side of the family. See Matrilineal Kinship.

**Patrilocal** A pattern of residence by which married couples reside with or near the husband's family. See Matrilocal.

**Pecking Order** A hierarchical relationship of dominance and submission within a flock, herd, or community.

**Peer Group** Group of people with whom one has equal standing.

**Periodic Assemblies** Gatherings that are scheduled in advance, have a preset time and place, and draw repeated attendance if they are part of a series. See Nonperiodic Assemblies.

**Personality** The individual's pattern of thoughts, motives, and self-concepts.

**Phenomenology** A scientific method that attempts to study an individual's awareness of experience without making assumptions, theories, or value judgments that would prejudice the study. See Relativism.

**Piacular Rites** According to Emile Durkheim, religious rites which comfort or console individuals, help the community in times of disaster, and ensure the piety of the individual. See Negative Rites.

**Piaget, Jean (1896-1980)** Swiss biologist and psychologist who has demonstrated the developmental nature of children's reasoning processes. He believes that humans pass through a universal, invariant development sequence of cognitive stages. Intelligence is at first a purely sensorimotor phenomenon. But it develops through a hierarchical process until it can finally be applied to formal, hypothetical thinking.

**Pluralism** A state of society in which a variety of groups and institutions retain political power and distinctive cultural characteristics.

**Pluralistic Society** A society in which power is distributed among a number of interest groups which are presumed to counterbalance each other.

**Political Modernization** The shift in loyalty or administrative structure from traditional authorities, such as tribal and religious leaders, to large-scale government organizations or from regional to national government. See Social Modernization.

**Political Socialization** The social process by which political values are acquired, particularly by young children. See Socialization.

**Political Sociology** The sociological study of politics, which, in turn, involves the regulation and control of citizens; closely related to political science. Traditionally, politcal scientists have been concerned with the abstract qualities of the political order and the formal behavior of citizens, especially in voting and political party participation. Sociologists generally claim that they are more inclined to focus on the actual power relations cloaked by the formal political structure. See Political Science.

**Polyandry** The marriage of one woman to several men. *See* Polygamy, Polygyny.

**Polygamy** The marriage of one woman to several men. *See* Monagamy.

**Polygyny** The marriage of one man to several women. *See* Polygamy, Polyandry.

**Population Control** Lowering the rate of natural increase of population. *See* Natural Increase.

**Population Explosion** A sudden, dramatic growth in the rate of natural increase of population. *See* Natural Increase.

**Positivism** A philosophy that rejects abstract ideas in favor of a factual, scientific orientation to reality. *See* Neoidealism.

**Postconventional Morality** According to Lawrence Kohlberg, the final level of moral development, which few people ever attain. This level is concerned with the moral values and individual rights apart from the group or society. *See* Conventional, Preconventional Morality.

**Postindustrial Society** A ''service'' economy of relatively recent development, in which the principal economic activity has advanced from industrial production to services that depend on significant inputs of knowledge. *See* Industrial Society.

**Power** The ability of people to realize their will, even against others' opposition. *See* Coercion, Influence.

**Power Elite** According to C. Wright Mills, the leaders in an organization or society who have a near monopoloy on policy making. *See* Elite Groups.

**Preconventional Morality** According to Lawrence Kohlberg, the first level of moral development. At this level, children know cultural labels of good and bad, although they judge behavior only in terms of consequences. *See* Conventional, Post Convention Morality.

**Prejudice** A biased prejudgment; an attitude in which one holds a negative belief about members of a group to which one does not belong. Prejudice is often directed at minority ethnic or racial groups. *See* Stereotype.

**Primary Groups** Groups such as the family, work group, gang, or neighborhood, which are characterized by face-to-face contact of members and which are thought to significantly affect members' personality development. *See* Secondary Group.

**Products of Culture** Religion, art, law, architecture, and all the many material objects used and produced by a given cultural group.

**Projection** According to Sigmund Freud, the tendency for people to attribute to others beliefs or motives that they have but cannot bring themselves to recognize or admit consciously. *See* Prejudice.

**Proletariat** According to Karl Marx, the working class. *See* Bourgeoisie.

**Protestant Ethic** According to Max Weber, the belief that hard work and frugal living would ensure future salvation.

**Psychoanalytic Theory** A theory of personality development, based on the work of Sigmund Freud, which maintains that the personality develops through a series of psychosexual stages as it experiences tension between demands of society and individual insticts for self-indulgence and independence. *See* Personality.

**Public** A loose, heterogenous social aggregate held together for a specific period by a shared interest in a public event or issue. Participants are not usually in the same physical location. *See* Social Aggregate.

**Public Opinion** Open verbal or nonverbal expressions by members of a social aggregate who are giving attention to a particular controversial point at a particular time. *See* Collective Behavior, Public, Social Aggregate.

**Race** Biologically, the classificiation of people by observed physical characteristics; culturally, the meaning we give to physical characteristics and behavior traits when identifying in- and outgroups.

**Race Relations** Social interactions among members of different groups that are based on, or affected by, an awareness of real or imagined racial or ethnic differences. *See* Race.

**Racial Group** As defined sociologically, any collection of people that other groups treat as a distinct race. *See* Race.

**Racism** A belief in racial superiority that leads to discrimination and prejudice toward those races considered inferior. *See* Discrimination, Prejudice, Race.

**Rationalization** According to Max Weber, the systematic application of impersonal and specific rules and procedures to obtain efficient coordination within modern organizations. *See* Formal Organization.

**Recidivism** The return to criminal behavior after punishment has been administered. *See* Deterrence Theory.

**Relative Poverty** Poverty of the lower strata of society as compared to the abundance enjoyed by members of higher strata. *See* Absolute Poverty.

**Relativsm** The idea that different people will have different experiences and interpretations of the same event. *See* Phenomenology.

**Reliability** A criterion for evaluating research results that refers to how well the study was done. A reliable study can be duplicated and its results found by other researchers. *See* Validity.

**Religion** A communally held system of beliefs and practices that are associated with some transcendent supernatural reality. *See* Sect.

**Replacement Level** The rate of population increase at which individuals merely replace themselves. *See* Zero Population Growth.

**Research** In the application of scientific method, the process by which an investigator seeks information to verify a theory. *See* Scientific Method, Theory.

**Resocialization** Major changes of attitudes or behavior, enforced by agents of socialization, that are likely to occur in institutions in which people are cut off from the outside world, spend all day with the same people, shed all possessions and identity, break with the past, and lose their freedom of action. *See* Socialization.

**Restricted Code** According to Basil Bernstein, the kind of ungrammatical, colloquial speech available to both middle-class and working-class people. *See* Elaborated Code.

**Revolutionary Change** Violent social change, most likely to occur when the gap between rising expectations and actual attainments becomes too frustrating for people to bear. *See* Evolutionary Change, Rising Expectations.

**Rising Expectations** The tendency of people to expect and demand improved social, economic, and political conditions as social change progresses within a society.

**Rite of Passage** A ceremony that dramatizes a change in an individual's status. Weddings and funerals are examples.

**Role** The behavior of an indivdiual in relations with others. Also, the behavior considered acceptable for an individual in a particular situation or in the performance of a necessary social function. *See* Role Allocation, Role Label, Role Performance.

**Role Allocation** Assignment of people to separate jobs, such as cook, table setter, and dishwasher. *See* Division of Labor.

**Role Convergence** A growing similarity in roles that were formerly segregated and distinct. As men and women come to share domestic tasks, for example, their roles converge. *See* Sex Role.

**Role Label** The name assigned to an individual who acts in a particular way. Role labels may be broad (''laborer'') or specific (''people who get colds easily'').

**Role Performance** The actual behavior of individuals in a particular role.

**Role Portrayal** The adapting of roles to fit one's style of interaction. *See* Fashioning Effect, Role Selection.

**Role Selection** The process of choosing a role that allows one to fulfill one's self-concept. *See* Fashioning Effect, Role Portrayal.

**Rumor** Unconfirmed stories and interpretations. They are the major form of communication during the milling process in collective behavior. *See* Collective Behavior, Milling.

**Rural Areas** Settlements of fewer than 2,500 residents or areas of low population density, such as farmlands. *See* Urban Areas.

**Salience** The degree of importance of a group to its members; its impact on members. Generally, the smaller the group, the more salient it can become. *See* Small Groups.

**Sample Survey** A research method in which a representative group of people is chosen from a particular population. Sample surveys may be conducted by interview or questionnaire. *See* Case Study, Experiment.

**Scapegoat** A person or community that is made the undeserving object of aggression by others. The aggression derives from the need to allocate blame for any misfortune experienced by the aggressors. *See* Prejudice.

**Scientific Method** The process used by scientists to analyze phenomena in a systematic and complete way. It is based on an agreement that criteria must be established for each set of observations referred to as fact and involves theory, research, and application. *See* Research, Theory.

**Secondary Group** A social group characterized by limited face-to-face interaction, relatively impersonal relationships, goal-oriented or task-oriented behavior, and possibly formal organization. *See* Primary Group.

**Sect** A relatively small religious movement that has broken away from a larger church. A sect generally is in opposition to the larger society's values and norms.

**Sectarianism** Having characteristics of sects, such as opposition to and withdrawal from, the larger society. *See* Sect.

**Sector Theory** Theory of urban development which states that urban growth tends to occur along major transportation routes and that new residential areas are created at the edges of older areas of the same class. These developments produce more or less homogeneous pie-shaped sectors. *See* Concentric Zone Theory, Multiple-Nuclei Theory.

**Secularization** The displacement of religious beliefs and influences by worldly beliefs and influences.

**Segmental Roles** Specialized duties by people in a bureaucratic society and over which they have little control. *See* Role, Specialization.

**Segregation** Involuntary separation of groups, on the basis of race, religion, sex, age, class, nationality, or culture.

**Sex Role** The culturally determined set of behavior and attitudes considered appropriate for males and females. *See* Gender Identity.

**Shaman** The individual in a tribal or nonliterate society who is priest, sorcerer, and healer all in one. The shaman treats diseases, exorcizes evil spirits, and is considered to have supernatural powers.

**Significant Others** According to George Herbert Mead, parents and other relatives or friends whose viewpoints children learn to adopt. *See* Generalized Others.

**Simmel, Georg (1858-1918)** German sociologist and conflict theorist who proposed that a small number of stable forms of interaction underlie the superficial diversity of manifest social occurrences. *See* Conflict Model.

**Small Group** An interaction system in which members have face-to-face contact and which tend to have important effects on members' behavior. *See* Primary Group.

**Social Aggregate** A relatively large number of people who do not know one another or who interact impersonally. Aggregates have loose structures and brief lives. There are basically three types of aggregates: the crowd, the mass, and the public. *See* Collective Behavior, Crowd, Mass, Public.

**Social Bonding** The quality of forming relatively permanent associations, found in both human and some animal and insect societies.

**Social Change** An alteration of stable patterns of social organization and interaction, preceded or followed by changes in related values and norms.

**Social Conflict** Disagreement over social values and competing interests. *See* Conflict Model.

**Social Constraints** Factors that produce conformity to the behavioral expectations of society, such as ridicule, expulsion from a group, or punishments. Knowledge of social constraints is taught during socialization. *See* Socialization.

**Social Contract** An agreement binding all parties that sets up rights, responsibilities, powers, and privileges and forms a basis for government.

**Social Control** Techniques and strategies for regulating human behavior.

**Social Darwinism** The view which sees society as an organism that grows more perfect through the natural selection of favored individuals. In this view, the wealthier and better-educated classes are more "fit" because they have competed their way to success. Social Darwinism applies Darwin's theory of biological evolution to social groups. *See* Evolution, Natural Selection.

**Social Disorganization** The breakdown of institutions and communities, which results in dislocation and breakdown of ordinary social controls over behavior.

**Social Distance** The relative positions of members or groups in a stratified social system; the degree of social acceptance that exists between certain social groups in a society.

**Social Dynamics** All the forces and processes involved in social change.

**Social Engineering** Systematic planning to solve social problems.

**Social Epidemiology** The study of illness rate in a population within a specific geographic area. *See* Sociology of Medicine.

**Social Group** A collection of interrelating human beings. A group may consist of two or more people. The interaction may involve performing a complex task—a surgical team—or simple proximity—all the drivers on a road during rush hour. Groups may be classified as primary or secondary. *See* Primary Group, Secondary Group, Small Groups.

**Social Interaction** The effect that two or more people have on each other's behavior, thoughts, and emotions through symbolic and nonsymbolic modes of expression.

**Socialism** An economic system in which means of production (land, equipment, materials) are collectively owned and controlled by the state rather than by private individuals. *See* Capitalism, Communism.

**Social Isolates** Children who have had minimal human contact because of abandonment or parental neglect. Also refers to people cut off from social contact voluntarily or involuntarily. *See* Feral Children.

**Socialization** The complex process by which individuals learn and adopt the behavior patterns and norms that enable them to function appropriately in their social environments. *See* Agents of Socialization, Personality.

**Social Mobility** The movement of people up or down a social hierarchy based on wealth, power, and education.

**Social Modernization** A process of change in social institutions, usually viewed as a movement from traditional or less-developed institutions to those characteristic of developed societies. *See* Economic Modernization.

**Social Movement** A long-term collective effort to resist or to promote social change. See collective behavior.

**Social Organization** A general term used in different ways in different contexts, but usually referring to organizational aspects of societies, communities, institutions, and groups. Perhaps the most basic aspect of social organization is a common understanding among members of the organization about the interpretation of social reality.

**Social Relations Perspectives** A view which emphasizes factors other than intelligence, such as family, in determining an individual's economic positions. *See* Technocratic Perspective.

**Social Sciences** Branches of learning concerned with the institutions of human societies and with human behavior and interrelationships. Social sciences draw their subject matter from the natural sciences.

**Social Stratification** A system of social inequality in which groups are ranked according to their attainment of socially valued rewards.

**Social System** The arrangement or pattern of organization of any social group. A system is a whole made up of interacting parts.

**Society** A social group that is relatively large, self-sufficient, and continues from generation to generation. Its members are generally recruited through the process of socialization. *See* Conflict Model, Functionalism, Socialization, Sociology.

**Sociobiology** A realtively new field which is a branch of behavioral biology that studies the biological bases of the social behavior and social organization of all animal species. *See* Biosociology.

**Sociocultural** Social organization in which patterns of behavior are largely governed by a network of learned values, norms, and beliefs. *See* Culture, Norm.

**Sociogram** A diagram showing the interaction among group members. A sociogram of a group might show, for example, who is most liked and who is least liked. *See* Group Processes.

**Sociological Perspective** The point of view of the sociologist. It aims at precision and objectivity through the scientific method. *See* Scientific Method.

**Sociology** The social science concerned with the systematic study of human society and human social interaction. *See* Society.

**Sociology of Death** The inquiry into the impact of dying on a patient's relationship to self, to others, and to the social structure as a whole. *See* Thanatology.

**Sociology of Education** The scientific analysis of both formal and informal learning in a society. *See* Education.

**Sociology of Medicine** The study of the definition, causes, and cure of disease in different societies and social groups. The sociology of medicine also studies the social organization of modern medical care and the social roles of staff and patients at various medical facilities.

**Sociology of Work** A study of the relations of production and consumption and the influence of work on social organization and social change. *See* Social Change.

**Specialization** A concentration of work in a specific area. According to Max Weber, specialization is a characteristic of an ideal type of bureaucratic organization. *See* Bureaucracy, Ideal Type.

**Spencer, Hebert (1820-1913)** British philosopher whose descriptive sociology was very influential and formed the basis for Social Darwinism. *See* Social Darwinism.

**Standard Metropolitan Statistical Area (SMSA)** A Census Bureau concept for counting population in core cities, their suburbs, satellite communities, and other closely related areas. SMSAs ignore usual political divisions, such as state boundaries. *See* Metropolis.

**State** The political-legal system that represents a whole country, its territory, and people. A state is a more formal legal and technical entity than the broader concept, "society." *See* Society.

**Statistics** A method for analyzing data gathered from samples of observations in order to: describe the amount of variation in each of the variables; describe hypothetical relationships among variables; to make inferences from the results to the larger population from which the sample was drawn.

**Status** The position of the individual (actor) in a system of social relationships. *See* Achieved Status, Ascribed Status.

**Status Group** According to Max Weber, people with similar lifestyles and social standing.

**Stereotype** An exaggerated belief associated with some particular category, particularly of a national, ethnic, or racial group. *See* Racial Group, Sex Role.

**Stigmatization** The labeling of individuals in such a way that they are disqualified from full social acceptance and participation. Criminalization is part of this process. *See* Criminalization, Deviance.

**Structural Differentiation** The specialization of institutions, social roles, and functions that accompanies social change.

**Structural-functionalism** *See* Functionalism.

**Structuralism** An intellectual approach which emphasizes studying the underlying structures of human behavior rather than obvious, surface events.

**Subcultures** Various groups within the society who share some elements of the basic culture but who also possess some distinctive folkways and mores. *See* Culture.

**Surrogate Religion** A belief system that substitutes for a traditional religion. Communism is an example.

**Symbol** Anything that stands for something else. For example, words may be symbols of objects, ideas, or emotions.

**Symbolic Interactionism** A theory in academic sociology founded by George Herbert Mead that says humans communicate through symbols—words and gestures—and develop self-images through others' responses.

**Symbolic Interactions** Interactions conducted through the use of symbols.

**Target Population** In a model of suburban growth, a group of people who are affected both by facilitating and motivating conditions. This population consisted of young to middle-age white married couples. *See* Facilitating and Motivating Conditions.

**Task Segregation** A division of labor based on a feature such as the sex or age of the participants. Task segregation is common in most societies. *See* Division of Labor.

**Taxonomy** A classification system of cognitive categories. *See* Folk Taxonomy.

**Technocracy** The domination of an industrial society by a technical elite. *See* Elite Groups, Technocratic Perspective.

**Technocratic Perspective** The view which sees the hierarchical division of labor as a result of the need to motivate the ablest individuals to undertake the most extensive training, which will allow them to perform the most difficult and important occupations in a society. *See* Technocracy.

**Thanatology** The study of theories, causes, and conditions of death.

**Theory** A set of generalized, often related, statements about some phenomenon. A theory is useful in generating hypotheses. Middle-range theories interrelate two or more empirical generalizations. Grand theory organizes all concepts, generalizations, and middle-range theories into an overall explanation. *See* Hypothesis, Research.

**Tönnies, Ferdinand (1855-1936)** Classical German sociologist who was the first to recognize the impact of the organic point of view on positivism. He identified the social organization concepts of *Gemeinschaft* and *Gesellschaft*. *See* Gemeinschaft/Gesellschaft.

**Totemism** Religious belief in which a totem—a representation of some natural object in the environment—figures prominently. Totems serve as symbols of clans and sacred representations. *See* Clan.

**Traditional Society** Rural, agricultural, homogeneous societies characterized by relatively simple means of production. *See* Industrial Society.

**Tylor, Sir Edward Burnett (1832-1917)** British pioneer anthropologist upon whose central ideas about culture all modern definitions are based.

**Typology** A classification system of characteristics. An example is *Gemeinschaft/Gesellschaft*, two types of social organization.

**Universalism** A rule for scientific innovation, according to Robert Merton. It refers to an objectivity which does not allow factors such as race, religion, or national origin to interfere with scientific inquiry. *See* Communalism, Disinterestedness, Organized Skepticism.

**Urban Area** According to Census Bureau definitions, a settlement of 2,500 or more persons. *See* Rural Area.

**Urbanism** The ways in which the city affects how people feel, think, and interact.

**Urbanization** The movement of people from country to city as well as the spread of urban influence and cultural patterns to rural areas. Also refers to the greater proportion of the population in urban areas than in rural areas. *See* Urban Society.

**Urban Society** A form of social organization in which: (1) economic exchange and markets are very important; (2) social roles are highly specialized; (3) centralized administrative and legal agencies provide political direction; and (4) interaction tends to be impersonal and functional. *See* Urbanization.

**Utilitarian Organization** According to Amitai Etzioni, a formal organization that people join for practical reasons, mainly jobs and salaries. Examples include blue-collar and white-collar industries. *See* Coercive and Normative Organizations.

**Validity** A criterion for evaluating research results that refers to how well the data actually reflect the real world. *See* Reliability, Research.

**Value-added Theory** Neil Smelser's theory which postulates five stages in the development of collective behavior. *Social conduciveness* describes situations that permit collective behaviors to occur. *Structural strain* refers to problems in the social environment. The growth of a *generalized belief* involves the interpretation of structural conduciveness and strain in a way that favors collective behavior. *Precipitating factors* are events that trigger collective behavior. *Mobilization for action* is the "organizational" component and usually involves explicit instruction and/or suggestions. *See* Collective Behavior.

**Values** Individual or collective conceptions of what is desirable. This conception usually has both emotional and symbolic components. *See* Norm.

**Variables** Factors that can change. Reserachers must state the specific variables they intend to measure. An independent variable is causal. A dependent variable changes according to the independent variable's behavior. *See* Research, Scientific Method.

**Verstehen** Subjective understanding which, according to Max Weber, must be employed in sociological investigation. *See* Neoidealism, Positivism.

**Weber, Max (1864-1920)** German sociologist whose work profoundly influenced Western sociological thought and method. The key to Weber's analysis of the modern world is his concept of *rationalization*—the substitution of explicit formal rules and procedures for earlier spontaneous, rule-of-thumb methods and attitudes. The result of this process was a profound "disenchantment of the world," which had been carried to its ultimate form in capitalist society, where older values were being subordinated to technical methods. The prime example of the rationalized insitution was bureaucracy.

Weber's writings on methodology have been singularly influential. He argued that the social sciences were inherently different from the natural sciences, for a full understanding of social action must involve *Verstehen* (empathetic understanding). He firmly believed that, although true objectivity was impossible, the sociologist should attempt to remain value-free. *See* Rationalization, *Verstehen*.

**Woman Suffrage** The right of women to vote. *See* Women's Movement.

**Women's Movement** A social movement by women to gain equal social, economic, and legal status with men. *See* Feminists, Social Movement.

**Zero Population Growth** The point at which population stops increasing. *See* Population Control, Replacement Level.

**Source for the Glossary:**
This glossary of 459 terms is reprinted from *The Study of Society, Second Edition.* ©The Dushkin Publishing Group, Inc. Guilford, CT 06437.

# Index

# Credits/ Acknowledgments

Cover design by Charles Vitelli

**1. The Discipline**
Facing overview—Dover *Pictorial Archives* Series.

**2. Culture**
Facing overview—UN photo. 23-26—Colin M. Turnbull. 39—United Nations.

**3. Socialization**
Facing overview—Colonial Penn Group, Inc. 62—Clemens Kalischer. 64-67—Courtesy of E. Richard Sorenson.

**4. Groups and Roles in Transition**
Facing overview—United Nations/John Robaton.

**5. Social Institutions in Crisis**
Facing overview—Vermont Development Agency.

**6. Stratification and Social Inequalities**
Facing overview—UN photo/P. Sudhakaran. 180—Illustration by Guy Billout.

**7. Social Change and the Future**
Facing overview—Ford Motor Company. 205—UN photo by Gaston Guarda.

# We Want Your Advice

## ANNUAL EDITIONS:
## SOCIOLOGY 87/88
### Article Rating Form

Here is an opportunity for you to have direct input into the next revision of this volume. We would like you to rate each of the 47 articles listed below, using the following scale:

1. **Excellent: should definitely be retained**
2. **Above average: should probably be retained**
3. **Below average: should probably be deleted**
4. **Poor: should definitely be deleted**

Your ratings will play a vital part in the next revision. So please mail this prepaid form to us just as soon as you complete it.
Thanks for your help!

Annual Editions revisions depend on two major opinion sources: one is our Advisory Board, listed in the front of this volume, which works with us in scanning the thousands of articles published in the public press each year; the other is you—the person actually using the book. Please help us and the users of the next edition by completing the prepaid article rating form on this page and returning it to us. Thank you.

| Rating | Article | Rating | Article |
|---|---|---|---|
| | 1. The Sociological Imagination | | 26. Lobbyists Go for It |
| | 2. Invitation to Sociology: A Humanistic Perspective | | 27. Populism and Individualism |
| | 3. Why I Love America | | 28. Middle-Class Squeeze |
| | 4. What Price Ethics? | | 29. Can America Compete? |
| | 5. The Mountain People | | 30. Why Johnny Can't Think |
| | 6. Social Time: The Heartbeat of Culture | | 31. Between Pro-Life and Pro-Choice |
| | 7. The New Lost Generation | | 32. American Religion in the 1980s |
| | 8. Brave New Wave of the '80s | | 33. Who Owns America? |
| | 9. Childhood Through the Ages | | 34. Corporate Welfare out of Control |
| | 10. Erik Erikson's Eight Ages of Man | | 35. Abandoned Americans |
| | 11. Growing Up as a Fore | | 36. What Does the Government Owe the Poor? |
| | 12. Sexism in the Schoolroom of the '80s | | 37. A Nation Apart |
| | 13. What Is TV Doing to America? | | 38. For Men on the Streets: Hustle Without Heroism |
| | 14. Alex Haley: The Secret of Strong Families | | 39. Mothers Raising Mothers |
| | 15. The American Family in the Year 2000 | | 40. People, People, People |
| | 16. Cities Won't Drive You Crazy | | 41. Snapshot of a Changing America |
| | 17. Work: The Right to Right Livelihood | | 42. Promise of America |
| | 18. The Politics of Motherhood | | 43. Living Dangerously |
| | 19. Working Women: How It's Working Out | | 44. In Old Milwaukee: Tomorrow's Factory Today |
| | 20. Strategies of Corporate Women | | 45. Technology and the Changing World of Work |
| | 21. Great Expectations | | 46. Apology to the Future |
| | 22. Another Stereotype: Old Age as a Second Childhood | | 47. Window of Opportunity |
| | 23. Conquering a New American Frontier: Changing Attitudes Toward the Disabled | | Glossary |
| | 24. Growing Up Gay | | |
| | 25. From Ouagadougou to Cape Canaveral: Why the Bad News Doesn't Travel Up | | |

(cont. on next page)

## ABOUT YOU

Name _____ Date _____

Are you a teacher? ☐   Or student? ☐

Your School Name _____

Department _____

Address _____

City _____ State _____ Zip _____

School Telephone # _____

## YOUR COMMENTS ARE IMPORTANT TO US!

Please fill in the following information:

For which course did you use this book? _____

Did you use a text with this Annual Edition?   ☐ yes   ☐ no

The title of the text: _____

What are your general reactions to the Annual Editions concept?


Have you read any particular articles recently that you think should be included in the next edition?


Are there any articles you feel should be replaced in the next edition? Why?


Are there other areas that you feel would utilize an Annual Edition?


May we contact you for editorial input?


May we quote you from above?

SOCIOLOGY 87/88

### BUSINESS REPLY MAIL

First Class      Permit No. 84      Guilford, CT

*Postage will be paid by addressee*

## The Dushkin Publishing Group, Inc.
## Sluice Dock
## Guilford, Connecticut 06437

No Postage
Necessary
if Mailed
in the
United States